Archaeologists have long been interested in the onset of political differentiation, and how this can be inferred from the archaeological record, and they have proposed a variety of different models to account for it. In this ambitious and innovative book, Christine Hastorf looks at the nature of power and political differentiation in the Andean region of central Peru over a thousand-year period, from AD 200 until the Inka conquest in the fifteenth century. Hastorf argues that no one model or theory can usefully explain all social change, and that archaeologists should instead focus on a particular region and seek to understand the context of change and why it occurred. She looks at political inequality from a number of different perspectives, collecting material from many sources, and suggests a series of "cultural" principles that shaped political developments. She also traces changes in agricultural production within the region, which she considers were fundamental to its social and political evolution.

Aside from its innovative theoretical approach to the nature and origin of political inequality, *Agriculture and the onset of political inequality* is a substantive study of prehistoric agricultural systems. Hastorf's comprehensive and sophisticated methodology for studying prehistorical agriculture – based on the analysis of modern and prehistoric plant remains – should be followed widely.

NEW STUDIES IN ARCHAEOLOGY

Agriculture and the onset of political inequality before the Inka

NEW STUDIES IN ARCHAEOLOGY

Series editors

Colin Renfrew, *University of Cambridge*
Jeremy Sabloff, *University of Pittsburgh*

Other titles in the series

Ian Hodder and Clive Orton: *Spatial analysis in archaeology*
Kenneth Hudson; *World industrial archaeology*
Keith Muckelroy: *Maritime archaeology*
R. Gould: *Living archaeology*
Graham Connah: *Three thousand years in Africa*
Richard E. Blanton, Stephen A. Kowalewski, Gary Feinman and Jill Appel: *Ancient Mesoamerica*
Stephen Plog: *Stylistic variation in prehistoric ceramics*
Peter Wells: *Culture contact and culture change*
Ian Hodder: *Symbols in action*
Patrick Vinton Kirch: *Evolution of the Polynesian chiefdoms*
Dean Arnold: *Ceramic theory and cultural process*
Geoffrey W. Conrad and Arthur A. Demarest: *Religion and empire: the dynamics of Aztec and Inca expansionism*
Graeme Barker: *Prehistoric farming in Europe*
Daniel Miller: *Artefacts as categories*
Rosalind Hunter-Anderson: *Prehistoric adaptation in the American southwest*
Robin Torrence: *Production and exchange of stone tools*
M. Shanks and C. Tilley: *Re-constructing archaeology*
Bo Gräslund: *The birth of prehistoric chronology*
Ian Morris: *Burial and ancient society: the rise of the Greek city state*
Joseph Tainter: *The collapse of complex societies*
John Fox: *Maya postclassic state formation*
Alasdair Whittle: *Problems in Neolithic archaeology*
Peter Bogucki: *Forest farmers and stock herders*
Olivier de Montmollin: *The archaeology of political structure: settlement analysis in a classic Maya polity*
Robert Chapman: *Emerging complexity: the later prehistory of south-east Spain, Iberia and the west Mediterranean*
Steven Mithen: *Thoughtful foragers: a study of prehistoric decision making*
Roger Cribb: *Nomads in archaeology*
James Whitley: *Style and society in Dark Age Greece: the changing face of a pre-literate society 1100–700 BC*
Philip Arnold: *Domestic ceramic production and spatial organisation*
Julian Thomas: *Rethinking the Neolithic*
E. N. Chernykh: *Ancient metallurgy in the USSR: the early metal age*
Lynne Sebastian: *The Chaco Anasazi: sociopolitical evolution in the prehistoric Southwest*
Anna Maria Bietti Sestieri: *The Iron Age community of Osteria dell'Osa: a study of socio-political development in central Tyrrhenian Italy*

CHRISTINE A. HASTORF

Agriculture and the onset of political inequality before the Inka

CAMBRIDGE
UNIVERSITY PRESS

Published by the Press Syndicate of the University of Cambridge
The Pitt Building, Trumpington Street, Cambridge CB2 1RP
40 West 20th Street, New York, NY 10011–4211, USA
10 Stamford Road, Oakleigh, Victoria 3166, Australia

First published 1993

Printed in Great Britain at the University Press, Cambridge

A catalogue record for this book is available from the British Library

Library of Congress cataloguing in publication data

Hastorf, Christine Ann, 1950–
Agriculture and the onset of political inequality before the Inka /
Christine A. Hastorf.
p. cm. – (New studies in archaeology)
Includes bibliographical references
ISBN 0 521 40272 7 (hardback)
1. Incas – Agriculture. 2. Incas – Politics and government.
3. Incas – Social conditions. 4. Plant remains (Archaeology) – Peru-
Jauja (Province). 5. Jauja (Peru: Province) – Antiquities.
6. Peru – Antiquities. I. Title. II. Series.
F3429.1.J37H37 1993
985'.24 – dc20 91–38265 CIP

ISBN 0 521 40272 7 hardback

WD

To my mother and father, Barbara and Al

Catherine Scott

and the people of the Jauja district

CONTENTS

FIGURES

TABLES

ACKNOWLEDGEMENTS

This project has taken many turns and stages to end where it is now. At each bend I have many people to thank for influencing and helping me. It has taken up the majority of my archaeological life and has traces of each act and process I have encountered. I hope that all of the people who have participated can find themselves somewhere. Foremost to thank are the members of the original UMARP team, Tim Earle, Cathy Scott, Terry D'Altroy, and Terry LeVine. I, as well as this book, have been formed out of our many years of work together and I cannot thank them enough for their attention, intelligence, guidance, patience, and for being there through all the stages of our work. UMARP has now reformed. I hope this book will provide some sense of our happy and engaging work together. After our initial years our family expanded to include some super people, including Elsie Sandefur, Glenn Russell, Cathy Costin, Lisa LeCount, and Heidi Lennstrom. They too have all become part of my archaeology of Jauja.

In Peru I was greatly assisted by the staff of the Instituto Nacional de la Cultura, who granted us permission to complete the field research and export the charred botanical remains. During my visits to Peru, both Ramiro Matos and Jorge Silva of the Universidad Nacional Mayor de San Marcos were my sponsors; they guided me through all aspects of permit procurement, Andean archaeology, and survival in Lima. The Paredes family's kind friendship helped during my months in Lima.

The assistance of Dra. Emma Cerrate de Ferreyra of the Museo Historia Natural de Javier Prado and the Universidad Nacional Mayor de San Marcos and of Dr. J. Soukup of the same university, in the identification of the modern botanical collections was invaluable. The researchers of the International Potato Center in Lima, especially Greg Scott, Doug Horton, and Robert Rhoades, gave me much information and help as well as a place to discuss agricultural research, crops, and farmers.

In addition to the stalwart assistance of the UMARP members I would like to thank the following people who also participated in the field work during the 1979–80 seasons when the bulk of the data was collected: Andy Christenson, Manuel Escobedo, and, from Ataura, Juan de la Cruz, José Moya Yachachin, and especially Andrés Moya Castro. Andrés was not only the field crew chief but was my fellow interviewer in the agricultural study and the person who, along with his whole family, made me feel at home in the Mantaro Valley.

Sr. Miguel Martinez and his Jauja family graciously opened up their home to me, making Jauja my home town. Over the years I have grown to love Jauja and have felt my own development of a connection with the land. And now with our forced exile, I often miss it and its people. The conflicts and war the region is experiencing make my heart sad for the Sausa and for all of the Peruvian population. My hope is that this time of *ch'axwa* will pass and everyone will be able to return again to the valleys.

Help with botanical research problems at UCLA came from Dan Walker, Michael DeNiro, Mildred Mathias, and Hank van der Werfe, who each worked with me to identify my archaeobotanical collections. Assistance in the laboratory analysis came from Lois Davis, Laura Kling, and Melinda Leach. Mel Widowski at UCLA and Heidi Lennstrom at the University of Minnesota have both helped me to sort out continuing computer problems, and I have much to be grateful for in their help. Sissel Johannessen has provided the Mac graphics and Rebne Kerchefsky drafted the base topographic maps and plotted the sites on them.

While my knowledge of Andean agricultural practices was gleaned mainly in the Andes with the farmers, the development of these theoretical ideas and writings occurred during my year as a fellow at the Center for the Advanced Study in the Behavioral Sciences in 1986–87. Besides the history reading group that brought me in contact with many new social and political theories, I am especially grateful to Jane Atkinson and Bob Netting. Together we explored each other's projects and ideas. I learned a tremendous amount from both of them. I would like also to thank Gardner Lindzey for making it possible for me to be there.

I have also had the good fortune to be able to interact with several Andean scholars whom I respect a great deal. While they are probably not aware of it, their thoughts on the Andes have had a major impact on my ideas. In particular, Denise Arnold, Olivia Harris, Florencia Mallon, and Enrique Mayer all helped expand my narrow archaeological horizons. My ideas have also been challenged and extended by the participants in my graduate seminars at the University of Minnesota with special engagement from Sissel Johannessen and Heidi Lennstrom.

Several people have read drafts of this book and given me helpful comments. Besides Bob Netting, who has been immeasurably helpful, Ben Orlove, Steve Brush, Jerry Sabloff, and Geoff Conrad provided insights and filled gaps in my knowledge.

Financial support for the field work came from a Fulbright-Hays Doctoral Dissertation Fellowship and an UCLA University Grant. Support for some of the analysis came from an UCLA Academic Senate Grant, and further analysis was supported by the National Science Foundation Grant BNS 84–51369. Support to write was funded in part by the National Science Foundation Grant BNS 84–11738.

While many people have helped in this process, great patience has come from my parents Al and Barbara Hastorf, who over the years experienced my long dedication to this project, in Jauja, California, and Minnesota. The greatest thanks, however, go to my husband Ian Hodder. During the writing and rewriting he has listened to ideas transform, while receiving a crash course in Andean agriculture and ideology. He has had to suffer hours of crop talk, French translations of *tinku* accounts, as well as consume experiments in Andean cuisine. Throughout, his support has been important, not just in household tasks but also emotionally. He has given me the strength to try to merge my two loves of the Andes; the people's relationships with their landscape and their wonderful organic world view.

NOTE ON THE TEXT

The decision to spell "Inka" with a "k" is based on recent linguistic Quechua research and a desire to use a more systematic spelling of the language. The reader may pursue this further by consulting the glossary index by Jorge I. Urioste in Guaman Poma de Ayala, 1980 1614, *El primer nueva coronica y buen gobierno*, J. Murra and Rolena Adorno, 3 vols, Mexico: Siglo Vientiuno.

Introduction: politics, agriculture, and inequality

In archaeology, political change has been one of the most central themes over the past thirty years. The origin of hereditary inequality is one of the "thorniest issues" in archaeology (Flannery 1972: 402). Because it is such an intriguing and complex question there have been many theories and counter-theories, allowing all who wish to join in this continued debate. There has been some progress in that we are gaining a fuller sense of the many aspects of change that transpired in the past. I join this discussion here. But rather than present an explanation of why these processes occurred via changes in the material record only, I include a series of nexes from which such change might be initiated, in order to look at political change through cultural realms, albeit through the dark glass of other times and peoples.

Most archaeologists studying such a change place the cause in the economic sphere, suggesting that polities centralized as differential control of production, finance, and access increased (Steward and Foran 1959; Service 1962; Fried 1967). These ideas were based primarily on the Marxist conception of class stratification, where controlling the means of production is the method by which individuals or groups gain power over other people (Marx 1904). The means of production, in turn, affect all other domains of society, leading to centralization of power and complexity wherever the conditions are sufficient. A more integrative use of this model is that centralized leadership solved economic problems that arose from increased population by organizing production and managing security and services for all (Service 1975). This holds a lot of satisfaction in that it is easy for us to quantify these elements in society.

Another hypothesis that has been put forward for the rise of political hierarchy has a more political orientation. This places the cause of hierarchical development in the changing political identities and boundaries of a group, the number of social positions within a society, its scale, and the intra- and inter-group relationships, including war or the threat of it (Blau 1977; Cancian 1972; Oberg 1955; Carneiro 1970; Weber 1947). But while this presents a more complex view of inequality and power, it restricts the locus of change to limited and specific political channels.

More recently a social perspective has added to this archaeological debate, placing the nexus of social change in internal competition and social domination, focusing on how changing social forms or structures allow individuals to gain economically and politically in new ways (Ekholm 1972; Friedman and Rowlands 1977; Bender 1978; Hayden 1990). While the causes of change are historically based and are generated out of local conditions and meanings, the mechanisms of social action are seen as universal.

Rather than political change emanating out of the structure of a group epigenetically, there is another orientation within the social perspective that gives power relations a more prominent role as the mechanism of social change (Giddens 1979). Here, change is initiated by human actions rather than solely out of structural or organizational forms. An aspect of this exists in the sociological concepts of agency and structuration, which state that people act, create, and alter social structures, and this then leads to recursive changes. In change, the culture is segmented, part of it remaining the same, while part of it is altered through structural transformations, and part of it is neglected. Which of these aspects of culture become central inform us about what was important in a particular culture. Perhaps the most important point to be gained in these latter perspectives is that change, including increased hierarchy or inequality, can be initiated out of any domain. It does not always develop out of economic relations.

While no one model provides us with a universal explanation for all political change, a focus on power negotiation as an active principle and the multiple nexes from which change can be initiated bring us closer to the basis of societal change. At least they provide us with a sense of action and change. These theoretical premises I build on and investigate in this book.

Authority and power can be gained and maintained in a number of different ways: out of tension and conflict (Coser 1956; Marx 1971), contestation and negotiation (Giddens 1979), consensus and competency (Durkheim 1965), agreement through naturalizing or legitimating the inequality (Jackman 1987), or from a balance between domination and moral leadership (Gramsci 1973). Within each of these basic strategies, change is generated in the practice of people's daily negotiations, which constantly provides the potential for stasis or change (either through contestation and reforming the rules or consensus and maintaining the status quo). Negotiations that lead to change may be premeditated and active, where parties try consciously to alter the system. Alternatively, change may occur accidentally, triggered by unintended events. When archaeologists sense a shift in the economics, politics, or social structures of a group, it indicates a change in power relations. And here we must go beyond the change to get at the underlying causes.

But how do we gain any sort of explanation from such broad generalizations as action, realignment, or power? How do such concepts reflect humans with culturally embedded goals? Changes in custom, action, and desire have to be linked to a combination of small shifts in material culture.

As archaeologists, we look at the trends in the material culture over time and investigate changes and developments that we assume link to decisive cultural change. But not every cultural example is appropriate for every theoretical question, not every material change suggests a political upheaval. Nor can one look at all parts of a society through archaeology. From this retrodictive perspective, however, we should be able to focus on certain arenas in order to study the transformations that best track changing social relations (Steward 1955). While I assume that change may be instigated from any domain in a society, it is on economics and agricultural production that I focus my attention. I use these as a window through which to track the onset of political inequality to other realms: these domains should be involved in and reflect political inequality, although not all change is initiated from agricultural production. Agricultural change ties in with political change but does not necessarily direct it.

It is a complex position to put oneself in: studying one aspect of a culture to explain a broader change and at the same time acknowledging that it is not necessarily the cause of that change. I think, however, that it may provide new insights to past strategies. While I begin with land-use, crops, and agricultural change, all important to farming communities, I am not assuming that agriculture is the basis of cultural change, but rather that it was ongoing throughout the onset of political inequality.

Archaeologists believe that it is possible to see change in the archaeological record. Most often, however, in our studies of long-term change, we have assumed that traits co-vary and transform together (White 1959). This assumption has developed out of the concepts of evolutionary stages derived from Morgan (1964) and Marx and was applied heavily in all of the earlier major models (Adams 1966; Childe 1951; Flannery 1972; Fried 1967; Service 1975; Wright 1969). Directional cultural change has meant increasing hierarchy, inequality, and heterogeneity all together. Archaeologists have charted this universal change in various cultures around the world. Underlying this orientation, the different domains of decision making in society are thought to change together in a unified way.

Over the last twenty years, as more detailed studies have been completed and better methodologies developed to interpret data trends, unified explanations for political change have been less satisfying and archaeologists have begun to break away from the strictly unilineal and materially based causes of change (Feinman and Neitzel 1984; Marcus 1989; Patterson and Gailey 1987; Paynter 1989; Renfrew and Cherry 1986; Upham 1990). Investigators have moved away from broad cross-cultural comparisons that looked for similar processes and traits throughout the world to closer examination of specific sequences and causes of societal change. With these projects have come more detailed descriptions but fewer regularities (Feinman and Neitzel 1984).

Even with this awareness, the debate over how to study inequality has not stopped (Johnson 1982; Brumfiel and Earle 1987; McGuire 1983; Patterson and Gailey 1987; Paynter 1989; Renfrew and Cherry 1986; Upham 1990; Wright 1969). The debate tends to define specific economic avenues in a culture as the key forces of inequality: population size and density, trade, control of production, management, or competition between elites. This research trajectory has blocked archaeologists from getting at explanations for such changes (McGuire 1983: 99; Paynter 1989). The subject is particularly difficult because inequality may exist, be dampened, or be accentuated within every domain just mentioned as well as in others not traditionally studied. Inequality may also take different shapes, with a group having few or many social–political categories, with different distributions of people in each category, and/or by authority and power being centralized into many or few positions. This fluidity leads us to the many definitions of inequality we use.

How can we proceed given such a complex situation? First, I want to define what I mean by inequality and what constitutes political change. With this, one may look more closely at cultures believed to have undergone political change and identify the major components of that culture that might have been involved in increasing inequality and difference. We must identify the economic, political, and social domains within a society and specify the relationships between them (Blau 1977; Flannery 1972). I will discuss how I define the extent of difference between the various social positions identified in a group (Tainter 1977) and what constitutes their difference, how different leadership positions participate (Johnson 1982), how fluid or rigid are these statuses, especially over time, how they were formed, and what maintains them if they continue.

One important point is that one must avoid automatically linking the different elements, such as political control and economic wealth, as if they expand or shrink together over time (Upham 1990). Identifying change in one domain does not mean that change occurred in other domains. For example, economic change might be identified, but social organization may not appear to alter. Or, as new political positions develop, for example, the family unit may continue to function as before. It is important to separate, "unpack", and follow the array of developments through time in order to determine how they each link into changes that are thought to have occurred.

Closer study of societal change is important in gaining an understanding of its causes, but it gives rise to multiple explanations. This multidimensionality has made archaeological inquiry more complex but also more exciting, for it opens up new dimensions and understandings of culture. It prompts us to recognize that humans are actors and decision makers within their cultural medium as they act on past conventions in new settings, and also to see that their decisions are based on a series of different simultaneous goals and views that are generated in an internal process. This makes the processes we see in the big picture, such as increased hierarchy, empires, settlement hierarchy, not as inevitable outcomes but as hard negotiated creations in a cultural world from which only fragments remain.

To study prehistoric political change, therefore, I discuss several cultural domains, how they change through time, and how they interact with each other. To do this I detail the political, the economic, and the cultural spheres of one ethnic group in the central Andes. After looking at these aspects separately and together, a more precise sequence of the events and processes that occurred in the past can be envisioned. I concentrate on economic change seen in agricultural production because the economics of a society has been one of several ingredients of political change (Wittfogel 1957 vs. Earle 1978), and I want to "unpack" and track the relationship between the politics of social control and economic production as they link to centralized decision making (Marx 1971; Weber 1968).

Although agriculture may not be the instigator of political change, nor an indicator of cultural change, it is an indicator of some forms of social change. There are real material constraints to economic production, since people have to produce enough food to eat. Annual environmental fluctuations greatly affect yields, and shortages of labor alter what can be planted, harvested, and traded. Yet, in any production system there are always alternative strategies of labor organization and land-use that may yield the same potential amount. The choice depends on different environmental and historical settings: social relations, political negotiation, and power structures enter into agricultural decision making.

In order to study such relations prehistorically, we need to consider where were the nexes of access to power in a particular group, who made the decisions about production, and whether these were made mainly in domestic settings or also in the public sphere. Are we viewing political change where power was only reallocated or did power actually expand or centralize?

I track agricultural change over time, but I also look closely at the habitations and artifact frequencies within and between communities. This allows me to define change, but it necessitates placing the artifacts in their cultural context. I will present arguments for the relationship between artifact patterning and inequality. In particular I will suggest why certain artifacts were used in certain ways to negotiate social positions. Thus I must ask what were the possible cultural meanings of the use of specific artifact forms in different social contexts or times. I explore these questions partly by detailed studies of artifact patterning and association and partly by the use of ethnohistoric information.

While focusing on the material basis of crops, land-use and labor, we know that, conceptually, these participated in and reflected only part of the negotiations of power. Many additional social actions were ongoing in each community, based on neighbor and kin relations and customs. No group operates in isolation either. Its changes are contingent in the larger political and cultural world, and so the historical settings (and their associated material) within which a group operates must be considered (Marcus 1989).

Towards this goal of unraveling and tracking increased and/or differential power, I have studied change at the onset of political inequality developing over a millennium for the ancestors of the Sausa (also spelled Xauxa, or Shawsha, although Sausa is the modern spelling of the region), who have lived in the central Andes of modern Peru. Such change spans from approximately a.d. 200 until the Sausa were conquered and incorporated into the Inka empire around AD 1460. I focus on the evidence for changes in decision making and access and define how these were transformed through social negotiation, seen in changing resource access, demographics, group interaction, pan-Andean politics, and expanding political boundaries.

While I deal with the material manifestations of this culture through the excavated, mapped, and analyzed data, the cultural principles that organize this material are equally important. A society, with all of its objects, territories, histories, and values is maintained or changed through the redefinition of each individual's relationships to others and to the objects and places they live among. These relationships exist equally in the non-physical as well as the physical sphere. One major assumption I invoke therefore is that the local cultural principles that framed the negotiations between people are the bases for change, and that they leave evidence in the material record, seen as the socio-political structures of agricultural production.

I have chosen to study the ancestors of the Sausa from approximately a.d. 200 to the Inka conquest because it is during this time that their economic base was clearly agricultural, with some herding, and there is evidence of indigenous political change (increased numbers of statuses and differentiation as well as increased sizes of political polities). I focus on the agricultural systems because they are the basis of their domestic economy.

Several models that have been put forward for the Andean domestic and political economy attempt to explain how the inhabitants, over thousands of years, maintained dense, stable populations and supported large polities. These include Murra's (1972) archipelago model of permanent occupation, with specialized satellites scattered across the diverse landscape forming dependencies between communities; Brush's (1976) variations on Murra's verticality model, which includes a vertical but compact resource setting; the model of dispersed autonomous settlements brought together by intensive camelid herding and pack trains that circulated goods between communities located in the different zones (Browman 1975); and Yamamoto's (1985) model of localized compact use of resources in the agro-pastoral (camelid–tuber) complex that allowed for local autonomy. These models all have an economic–environmental base as their impetus for political development. My goal is not to accept or reject any one of these competing economic models. Rather I hope to show, by illustrating the multiple transformations of the Sausa over time, how these different models offer partial views into a fuller dynamic system. Portions of each may have initiated or participated in changes in political–cultural systems but none gives us a complete picture.

Part I of this book provides the theoretical orientation, beginning in Chapter 1 where different perspectives on political hierarchy and inequality are examined. Chapter 2 outlines the major economic issues in the study of Andean agriculture. Despite economics and production having a central position in previous classic models of cultural evolution (Childe 1951; Service 1975), being readily visible archaeologically, and being a window through which to view the larger societal changes, economics do not always drive politics, but rather they correspond to political systems.

Agriculture is not just an economic system, it is also a social system. Food is produced by people who must work together, claim land rights, allocate water, exchange labor, and perhaps share harvests. All of these aspects of production are created by and mediated through social interaction and political organization. One may look at the economics of agriculture, therefore, to view cultural change. This entails studying the culturally meaningful principles of a population and how their social ecologies interact with and use resources in the environment. Agriculture is created by the people inhabiting the landscape based on what they consider good land, appropriate crops, effective production strategies, sufficient work teams, and so forth. There is always more than one way to produce a harvest. The history of a group's land-use therefore may help to understand political use of the land as well as the group's social view of it.

Part II presents the socio-political background to the Andean region. Chapter 3 discusses a series of Andean cultural principles based on ethnographic and historical sources. These principles were chosen, being potentially important as the structures or nexes for change. They are important today in political change, and no doubt participated in change throughout the pre-Hispanic central Andes. While internal epigenetic changes are important in the local politics in this valley, these people were also intermeshed into a wider regional and pan-Andean culture whose dynamics impinged on the power structures of local groups, evidenced in the changing role of warfare, feasting, trade, and rituals through time. For this reason the major political and cultural dynamics are also discussed. They serve to place the Sausa traits and actions in a wider context, and help to track hints of these cultural principles through time.

For a closer view of the Sausa cultural context, Chapter 4 describes the regional pre-Hispanic sequence, the settlement pattern through time, and the specific sites that were excavated to collect data that apply to these questions. Changes in the settlement pattern are important indicators of political shifts but they also signal possible changes in agriculture. The settlements are the local setting of Sausa political integration accompanied by increased contradictions and exercises of power, seen in new architectural plans. In Chapter 5 historic information on the pre-Inka Sausa is presented, outlining local dimensions of socio-political change during the time span investigated. This chapter is important for it presents non-agricultural data that tracks the social, political, and economic changes, providing independent evidence of these avenues of change. Based on the documents and the settlement-pattern data, a sequence of political changes begins to take shape.

Part III focuses on the agriculture of the study region. To discuss pre-Hispanic agricultural practices, an analysis of modern traditional crop geographies and land-use must be completed and then transformed to enable us to discuss crop production in the past. Important Andean agricultural practices are described as well as important constraints on those systems. Chapters 6 and 7 define the climate, topography, crops, and modern land-use zones of the study region. Chapter 7, in particular, discusses the importance of crop rotation in Andean agriculture and presents analyses that substantiate defined land-use zones, and proposes regional cropping patterns that reflect a steady-state production scheme. In Chapter 8 traditional methods of agricultural technology are outlined, including evidence for pre-Hispanic intensive strategies in every zone of the local landscape. Chapter 9 collects all of the relevant agricultural data and constructs a series of pre-Hispanic potential crop-production strategies in the different land-use zones.

The final chapter in Part III turns to the pre-Hispanic agricultural evidence and presents the paleoethnobotanical data from the five sites representing three time periods, the Early Intermediate/Middle Horizon (Huacrapukio II), the Wanka I, and the Wanka II Periods. This provides production data with which to discuss the economic changes, presenting material that suggests production intensification.

The fourth section brings all of this material together to illustrate the place and use of resources (agricultural) in the power shifts of political change. In Chapter 11 I present a detailed discussion of agricultural change through a comparison of proposed optimal agricultural crop-production ranges, an agricultural base-line, and the production outcomes – the paleoethnobotanical data – for each of the sites by phase. These discrete comparisons provide a view of production change over time that includes changes in the emphasis on specific land-use zones and agricultural intensification. The evidence from the Wanka II Period suggests that radical changes occurred in the agricultural systems as a result of political developments, that also brought about demographic and social restructurings of the Sausa in the form of multi-settlement alliances. It is during this phase that we see a concentration of people, and also hints of political centralization.

In the last chapter the issues of power negotiation and action are again taken up in light of the cultural, political, and agricultural information presented. There is a discussion of what constitutes political hierarchy in this archaeological setting and what manifestations of its increase can be seen in the Sausa data. A series of different causes for development of political inequality evidenced in the Sausa material are presented, including a critique of the traditional concepts for political development. These causes are shown not to be adequate explanations for the change evidenced. The true cause of change cannot be attributed to one event, process, or cultural dynamic, but is embedded in the social actions that led up to the visible changes in the archaeological record.

The likely factors contributing to change involved an interactive situation of contesting allegiances, shifting outside pressures, and transpositions of cultural principles into other cultural realms. These realignments created some of the changes seen in the archaeological record. That is, political change was generated out of changing internal social relations that, through manipulation, made increased demands on economic production, and therefore made agriculture one of several loci of power. The internal power struggles were influenced by local environmental capacities, social historic conventions, and also a vacuum left by the Wari influence that had permeated the central Andes both directly surrounding the Ayacucho Valley and less directly throughout a wider area. These nexes of interaction that were vacated caused local realignments in the social order that altered the decision-making powers, the control of knowledge, intergroup relations, and finally some forms of production including agriculture.

The study of political change can reveal examples of power negotiation and shifting cultural norms. As the data unfold, a picture emerges of the process of negotiation. There was no endpoint or goal in this development. Nor did the ancestors of the Sausa "completely" transform their society (in the traditional sense) from small-scale autonomous entities into centralized polities with multiple tiers and centralized control of production. A web of change may be suggested, however, where some dimensions of the culture became more elaborate and centralized, while others atrophied. Without relying on the old causes for political change, we can begin to see a more complex view of a pre-Hispanic society that includes the actors. Not only does this study illustrate how the old definitions of political stages or causes do not suffice, but it also demonstrates how archaeologists may study action, such as political negotiation, economic change, or the process of social transformation, using archaeological material, including paleoethnobotanical data.

I

POLITICAL INEQUALITY AND ECONOMICS

I

The onset of political inequality

One cannot discuss the causes for political inequality fairly without including the economics of change, political power, and the cultural domains in which it is created. The economic realm centers on production of goods and extraction of resources. Political power is the capacity of a person or persons to hold decision-making positions within a group, to accumulate goods and services for personal use, to control the means of production, to manage group activities, and to have access to a method of physical influence or domination over others if needed (Fried 1967; Weber 1968). The political aspect, therefore, means that power goes beyond the individual into public or civic domains. By domains of culture I mean the social relations where power or authority may reside, the jurisdictions or special knowledge that leaders have, and the principles or practices through which negotiations generate change that might lead to more inequality, more power asymmetry, differential decision making, differential access, ideological hegemony, or new forms of political control (Bourdieu 1977; Friedman and Rowlands 1977; Gramsci 1973). In other words, cultural domains are social (individual and group) nexes where power or authority are generated that have an effect in the public sphere (Foucault 1980). As a result, the following types of questions can be asked in any example of the development of political inequality: What social concepts were invoked in the political and economic change, what cultural goals and structures opposed the group, how the group's identity was maintained, realigned or expanded through the change, what areas of social life were being contested, what economic patterns changed, from what nexus or vacuum was change initiated, and how did the social–cultural changes affect the economics? By addressing and answering some of these questions, I hope to provide a view of cultural dynamics that includes people's actions and their changing social concepts, as well as the material constraints and consequences of those actions through time.

The difference between being and becoming

The investigation seeks to discover why people consent to or are forced to change their interpersonal, economic, and social relationships in such a way as to accentuate and legitimate political asymmetries or domination in favor of a minority of the population. What occurs when power becomes more centralized? While these are not new questions, most discussions focus on the maintenance of stratified society and economic difference rather than on the onset of this major political change. Such a theoretical focus tends to conflate the methods of elite material maintenance with the processes involved in the onset and the restructuring of a group's relations, practices, and views. I think these are two phases in societal structure and should each display different cultural dynamics. Although they are generated from the same cultural principles, social mechanisms, and actors, I expect that the discourse and interactions at the onset of such a political change are different from the negotiations that maintain a political hierarchy.

An important and difficult aspect in studying the "becoming" of political hierarchy is the potentially invisible and indeterminate nature of the process due to its epigenetic character. New forms of power relations are constructed out of previous social and cultural forms. And therefore, as Fallers (1972) points out, inequalities should be investigated and defined within their cultural context to understand their impact. They not only will be constituted in their own world but also built out of its components and meanings. In societies, different domains will dominate in the process of power realignment. Inequalities are constantly generated within any group both privately and publicly, but some transform the whole system. The question in the process of becoming is not when do unequal relations develop, but what unequal relations develop that transform the political structures (Sahlins 1985)? When does a group legitimize its consent to unequal claims to power and access to material goods? How do the material and spoken influences converge to empower certain people?

Political inequality

In a society that is becoming politically more unequal, change occurs in both the extent of and in the realms of political power. Political inequality includes the exercise of political power where it has not been before. Inequality means there is a difference in the amount of or access to this power. Political inequality will always have an aspect of differential authority, which includes public influence, control, and responsibility (Gramsci 1973; Weber 1968).

A formal political inequality exists when certain people have claims either to *power over* others' labor, social resources, access to products, influence, information, and special knowledge, or *power to* organize, empower, or manage in cooperation within varied segments (Miller and Tilley 1984). Managing and organizing a group's necessities are duties of leadership that may not have an overt aggrandizing nature yet may grant leaders access to new power which they can manipulate. Inequality is created within while reaffirming the legitimate social order based on traditional cultural principles, faith, local rational value, legal rules with voluntary agreement, or legal rules of imposed dominance (Weber 1968: 36).

The number of political positions is limited, so there is not necessarily a position of leadership or influence vacant for everyone who would like one (Fried 1967). These positions are contested over, voted on, or negotiated for amongst the qualified participants. It is rare to find just one qualified person for a specific position, even in cases where inheritance is the normal avenue to position. As a position becomes vacant individuals vie for it. And such negotiation itself can create political power.

Political inequality, however, is not the same as social inequality. It is not always linked to the fundamental social asymmetries, such as gender or age, though these are very often the nexes from which these inequalities develop (LaFontaine 1978; Moore

1988). Asymmetry – whether material or social, pervasive or specific – exists in all human societies. Anthropologists have been studying inequality in gender and differences within "egalitarian" small-scale societies (e.g. Begler 1978; Collier and Rosaldo 1981; Leacock 1978; Moore 1986). They discuss inequality emanating out of male power over female resources. Asymmetrical power exists between genders. The extent to which other power differences are generated out of gender differences depends on the culture's structure. More than a difference of scale is involved when moving from gender relations to political hierarchy, however.

Political inequality is different from wealth inequality. Wealth differences do not have to correlate with political power over group decisions, although they may be linked. Some societies with intensive agriculture and wealth differences (both real and perceived), such as the Ifugao of the Philippines, do not have formal political stratification (Conklin 1980). Differences in production, land, wealth mobility, and agricultural competence create clear inequalities but this does not necessarily transfer to the political sphere, as Netting has shown for the Kofyar of Nigeria (Netting 1990). By this I mean that wealthy people do not always dictate or even claim to dictate the group's political decisions concerning issues within or outside of the group.

Intensive agriculture has been treated much like wealth in studies of hierarchy. Traditionally, social stratification was said to arise as kin-based senior lineages took control over certain resources, tightening access to them when resources became scarce because of a degraded environment, encroaching neighbors, or increased population density (Eggan 1950; Carneiro 1970). This control led to intensification of agriculture (Wittfogel 1957; Boserup 1965), with the potential for surplus production financing elite activities (Brumfiel 1976; Earle 1978; 1987). Such a scheme linked intensive agriculture with political stratification. But examples in the archaeological record have shown that intensive exchange or production does not always lead to political rank. Much of the European Neolithic had intensive agricultural production (Sherratt 1981) without the onset of permanent political rank.

I propose then that wealth and intensive agriculture are not sufficient causes for systemic political transformations, although they can participate in them. Whether or not they create political centralization seems to hinge on the perceived needs and social constructs of the population, on the type of agricultural organization, and on whether there are channels by which certain individuals or groups can gain control (by restricting access) over more domains in society. This is not just an increased level of production but a differential access, use, and value of that produce.

Models of political inequality

Over the past century, two models have been proposed for the formation of hierarchy: (1) inequality is formed and perpetuated out of conflict, or (2) it is formed by consensus (Clastres 1977; Davis and Moore 1945; Haas 1982). Both orientations assume the existence or creation of discrete groups within a society which have different and often competing interests. Both also assume that the economics of a society provide the fundamental force determining the shape of the society, including political inequality. While one model generates change out of agreement, with conflict the result of social breakdown, the other model positions conflict as the status quo, with the lack of struggle a sign of the breakdown of the group's functioning.

The conflict model emanates out of Hegel's ideas, building on Marx's (1904; 1971) writings about class conflict and Weber's (1968) theories of economics and social action. It focuses on the tension and contradiction between groups where one dominant group has control over another's economic basis for survival (their means of production), maintaining this through control of the modes of production and products, in addition to creating an ideology that shapes every member's world view and dictates his social relations. This doctrine sees social relations between groups as based on the spheres of production upon which the inequality is constructed (Gregory 1982). Struggle is pervasive within all social interactions (Murphy 1971).

A series of ideas is associated with this conflict model. People are motivated to accumulate power out of self-interest, identifiable groups are overtly in conflict over resources, the economic base is the foundation upon which political and social structures are formed, the means of production directs all other domains of culture, social constructs are dictated by the economic structure, one dominant group tends to exist with an accompanying dominant ideology that all subordinate classes live within and react to. This dominant ideology tries to determine everyone's behavior, independent of their wills. With many critiques and reworkings of Marx's and Weber's theories of social change through conflict, social theorists and scientists still see conflict and coercion as essential ingredients in inequality, with some of these motivations involved.

Anthropologists interested in cultural evolution have incorporated this conflict model into their explanations. Carneiro (1970; 1981: 64) sees the giving up of autonomy as a result of coercion by one group over another, not as a voluntary act. For him, permanent inequalities have a political basis, resulting from villages joining together "under duress," perhaps not in the face of overt warfare, but under strong threat of warfare. Due to any number of circumstances, be they encroaching neighbors, change in climate, external changes in trade patterns or political pressures, resulting in social circumscription, groups become unable to maintain their autonomy. People are forced to give up their separateness, either by acceptance of a dominant group or by defeat in war. Here politics in the form of conflict, constraint, and force is the cause of change. Overt conflict does not have to take place: fear, threat of conflict, or persuasion are sufficient.

Alternatively, the second viewpoint stresses the role of integration, consensus, and mutual benefit in groups which are joined together, allowing one segment to make decisions for the whole (Durkheim 1963; 1964; Merriam 1934). This orientation is based on the concept that overt conflict is abnormal (Durkheim 1963) and that all institutions want to manage conflict before it breaks out, most often through the use of persuasion and tradition. In this way power is actually weakest when the dominant group must resort to violence (Merriam 1934: 180; Radcliffe-Brown 1941). A sense of benefit when power is forfeited is essential in this philosophy. For a society to function smoothly the public ideology must give something to all members of society, not just the elite subgroup, so that the dominant doctrine is transformed into the morality of the entire society (Jackman 1987: 47). Further, members of a society, even subordinate members, may readily accept the dominant ideology if they believe that it is serving their own interests (whether or not it actually benefits them). Political centralization may also be beneficial because individuals can belong to multiple groups with shifting and sometimes conflicting interests, creating a lack of total domination by any one group (Coser 1956).

In this orientation, dominant groups can exist in society, but they create and maintain their position through a communal ideology, persuasion, compliance, and benefits for the masses. As Jackman (1987: 36) points out, however, there is always a power difference between the groups because coupled with consensus is always the threat of violence.

The consensual model assumes inequality is an integrative mechanism in society, the social contract to which all members adhere for the social good. This was proposed by Durkheim (1963) and elaborated by Radcliffe-Brown (1941) and Service (1962). Further specialization of tasks allows an increased division of labor and lessening of the per capita labor input. This model is supported, for Durkheim, by harmony, consensus, and the general lack of conflict that exists in most social intercourse. Political service for the group benefits all, as leaders are altruistic managers of redistribution, reciprocity, and act as group spokespersons. The unequal access and control that accompanies leadership are epiphenomena of the integration, sometimes mishandled, but not at the onset of hierarchy. When there is increasing inequality, there is not always aggrandizement by the elite. The issue of aggrandizement enters into the social contract only after stratification has become well formed. A cultural system is not functioning well when things are out of balance and conflict erupts or when there is too much overt power over the subordinate group (hints of this are also in Gramsci's historical bloc [in Lawner's introduction of Gramsci 1973]).

Service (1962) saw this asymmetrical political development as an economic integrative trade off for a group's need to organize the redistribution of goods and services. He claimed that, as groups became large, daily activities became harder to complete and everyone agreed to specialize, lowering the per capita workload by having a leader who would manage the network of exchange in order to maintain the different specialities. This manager might also become a political leader. Political inequality in this model has an economic basis, a managerial purpose for the social good.

Gramsci (1973) proposed that a "successful" hegemony would occur when dominance based on power was balanced by a leadership based on responsibility, being aware of the group morals that exist in any society. A more pessimistic view of consensual inequality is seen in Jackman's work (1987), where consensual actions have been incorporated into a conflictual model through her focus on social persuasion as the successful masking of the domination and asymmetry in relationships. In her view of a permanently unequal society, there is no escape from a dominant authority and no claim by the subordinate group to voice its opinion or get fair access to critical resources. When consensus and agreement occur, it means that the dominant group has successfully created a social ideology that everyone has accepted. When a compromise is reached for the "common good," it is merely a minor concession to keep the necessary subordinates from breaking away or organizing open hostility. An effective domination might never have hostile interactions, but it always has inequality. Compliance is realizing one's unequal status and accepting it without further negotiation, through a naturalizing of different statuses. Managing projects for the social good is merely a path of least resistance to keep control by providing a symbolic gesture of beneficial service. Domination is completed through manipulated ideology that naturalizes difference, and paternalism. Therefore, the subordinate group(s) will be unconscious of its/their position, while the dominant group is aware of its strategy. This is the insidious underbelly of "consensual" inequality (Jackman 1987).

This version of the conflict model creates a picture of unilateral divisions within society that are virtually unchanging. It does not allow for multidimensional cause at the individual or group level. But people often have more than one opinion about any decision, whether political or personal. Different interest groups do become powerful over others but they too can be compromised. That is why, as I argue below, it is within the dynamics between consensus and conflict, in the inconsistent, conflicting, multiple readings of the same rule, event, or convention that change emerges (Clastres 1977; Murphy 1971; Sahlins 1958; 1985).

The anthropological consensus model places the impetus for change inside of the cultural system, while the conflict model imposes change from outside. The two basic models, while providing some explanation, seem to be incomplete. Each lacks what the other offers. Perhaps merging them will give us a more accurate view of why this happens. Change can come from inside and outside. Influence can work against or can amplify building on the already extant social relations.

While both of these mechanisms, conflict and consensus, are part of social change and power over others, archaeologists, perhaps because of their preference for major processes, tend to miss the action of change by stressing those cultural traits that maintain inequality over time, after the change has been established. In other words, they stress models and variables that describe "being". This orientation assumes implicitly that traits to maintain inequality are also the nexes for increased inequality or change. But is this always the case? With a closer look I would suggest not. For example, the giving of goods to a leader who hosts a feast or distributes food publicly may become the mechanism by which leadership is consolidated and maintained, but is not necessarily the process by which that leadership position was formed. The activities involved in both parts of political change should be investigated if possible.

Avenues leading to change

How are these changes initiated? One idea is that cultural principles, which in one setting create stability and persistence, can be transferred into another cultural domain that will activate change. In other words, the transference of a trait or a meaning into a different realm of society can begin to transform that society. An action can be reformed and applied to solve a new problem or an old social structure can be used to fill in a new social space.

The rise of cultural complexity and political development has received much discussion in archaeology (e.g. Carneiro 1970; Sanders and Price 1968; Flannery 1972; Earle 1978; Brumfiel and Earle 1987; Renfrew and Cherry 1986; Sanders and Webster 1978; Haas 1982; Patterson and Gailey 1987; etc.). Some of the more common causes offered for political development are stratified reorganization due to inadequate information exchange and organization (Wright 1978; Johnson 1973); management of intensive agriculture (Wittfogel 1957; Adams 1966); population size and density (Spooner 1972; Cohen 1977); specialized production leading to elite surplus to finance elite activities (Brumfiel 1976; Earle 1978; D'Altroy and Earle 1985); control of critical exchange networks (Drennan 1984a, 1984b; Helms 1979; Flannery 1968; Rathje 1972; Upham 1982; Zeitlin 1978), and the control of production and circulation of prestige goods (Gledhill 1978; Rowlands 1980). These models assume that the participants act with intentional direction and economic goals at all times.

With these causes, much of the archaeological discussion has centered on the being rather than on the becoming of political inequality. A further problem with these archaeological models is that, just like conflict and consensus, they are primarily embedded in the economics of control and tend to omit how the material transformations seen in the archaeological record were culturally directed or socially transformed; that a group often has a series of different options or paths, and the path chosen is in part based on the real needs of the group, but also in part on its social norms or traditions.

In their 1984 paper, Feinman and Neitzel demonstrated how the cultural traits listed above do not regularly link up with the onset of political rank in pre-state societies. Investigating the traditional prime movers that lead to political complexity across many societies, they found no universal causality between rank and kin structure, agriculture, population, trade, warfare, surplus production, or storage. Rather, they noted that in all sedentary societies asymmetrical social relations are continuously created, maintained, and destroyed. These constantly forming asymmetries do not always lead to a political hierarchy. The key for Feinman and Neitzel is a nexus of social relations that forge political and productive changes.

The onset of political hierarchy can be initiated in many ways. Likewise, the combination of traits that maintain inequality also can vary. Therefore, there are multiple paths to stratification. How are these avenues formed to allow for such political change? Traditions are reworked, new rationalizations are put forth, and new orders (codes of conduct) are created, with and without contestation. These new actions allow individuals to make claims to certain decisions that previously had not been considered. The "leadership" can organize or instigate (control of) new functions for the group. Other forms of initiation include new managerial organizations over community activities (e.g. organizing feasts, policing of village storage and resources, new building projects, new trade routes or partners, new links to other groups, new military organizations), group knowledge (new religious activities, new moral codes, new or elaborated festivals, new cures or spirits), technologies (organizing new agricultural systems, processing raw materials, new access to resources), or the leadership can claim to take over management of already existing activities. A convergence of control and increased power is built on the consolidation of individual decision making over social domains that other individuals previously had claim to (Blau 1977). There does not have to be new cultural knowledge entering into the system for this to occur, but the structure of a society will change as positions expand their power, are more clearly defined, and increase in difference (Tainter 1977).

A small-scale, non-ranked group, with all of its asymmetries, conflicts, open discussions, and contradictions, may have "special" people, such as elders, shamans, war or peace leaders. These individuals have jurisdiction over specific activities and tend not to have power when that activity is not occurring. These positions often require support and consensus to reach decisions, especially outside of their very bounded domain. This dispersed and segmented decision making does provide nexes for social position within a community, even while the claims to power are dampened by refusal and constraint. Much social effort may go into consolidating jurisdiction and creating position. Individuals may continually make claims to additional domains of authority, but if the members do not comply, the power evaporates (Atkinson 1990; Trigger 1990). In this way we see social differences within a group without political inequality.

A difference may occur when individuals begin to make decisions in new domains that affect more members. The members find themselves less able or willing to contradict and rally dissenting voices and compromise, as political difference is initiated. The possessor of this position makes claim to an increasing number of domains simultaneously and a kind of specialization ensues. New rationales are given for expanded control based on transforming old rules. Although negotiation occurs among all members of the participating group, everyone does not have the same capacity to override the decision making of a leader. Through these leaders' negotiations power over others is repeatedly stated and reaffirmed (Giddens 1979). This consolidation of power may occur through the auspices of relieving social, spiritual, economic, or political stress as well as building on new opportunities opened up for the leaders (Johnson 1982: 403). Often it does not look like an overt usurpation, nor does it have to be intentional, as long as the followers believe they are benefiting from the new organization.

Atkinson's (1990) ethnohistoric example of local leadership development in highland Sulawesi illustrates how this differentiation and confluence of power can occur. Normally the Wana people live in small dispersed, consensual groups as swidden farmers, without any political hierarchy. In the nineteenth century local spokesmen, *basals*, arose who created and orchestrated new farming rituals that included larger gifts to them of food for group feasts. At the same time these shamans became the negotiators with the coastal rajs who were interested in trade for highland products. The *basals* used rituals to make claims to their new positions by having special contacts with the spirits. Through these contacts the people were protected. As self-appointed spokesmen, the *basals* also managed new trading and political activities with the coastal polities, receiving and distributing goods from the coast as manifestations of their political claim. Although the ethnohistoric documents alluded to these new powers of the *basals*, there is no evidence for direct domination over subsistence production or other social domains. Power was limited to certain realms though it was differentiated (Blau 1977). While one can see that new outside pressures aided the generation of these new political positions, the local leaders are the ones who instigated the change via their power in shamanistic rituals. *Basals* used internal cultural principles of the Wana perceptions, values (ethos) about power, and special knowledge to gain new authority through claims to religious knowledge, protective power, and trade. These claims provided the avenue for maintaining a new, albeit somewhat restricted, political position that included economic gain for the *basals*: people worked in their fields. New relations created this new vacuum in which to enter and create power.

One can sense the continuous debate and contestation that limits the creation of social groups in such small-scale political organizations. Change, when it occurs, does not have to ripple throughout the whole system though. The shape and extent of change through time depends on what was there before and what principles are being called upon to alter the cultural situation. As one relationship is altered, it may remain only in that domain, or it may initiate further change. It is the specific sequences of new power avenues within a society that must be tracked in order to learn about the type of change that occurred.

The most common underlying explanation given in anthropology for the onset of political hierarchy is the increase in total population size of the group (Fried 1967; Polgar 1972; Service 1962; Steward 1955; Spooner 1972; Cohen 1977). This thesis states that, as population increases, at some point it is too large to stay together as before and new institutions are formed (Wright and G. Johnson 1975; A. Johnson and Earle 1987: 209). From recent research in population demography and political organization, anthropologists, historians, political scientists, and archaeologists realize that population size is not an explanation for political hierarchy, since population sizes range widely over both small-scale (egalitarian) and hierarchical groups (Carneiro 1967; Cowgill 1975; Polgar 1972). Small-scale groups can range anywhere between 2,000 to 30,000 people (Trigger 1963: 91; Feinman and Neitzel 1984: 69); stratified groups can be as small as 5,000. Population size itself does not correlate with most cultural criteria applied to political rank (Feinman and Neitzel 1984: 67).

Nevertheless, demographers have found that there are some size thresholds that limit effective operation of certain organizational systems and associate with different scales of political inequality (Carneiro 1970; Dumond 1972; Lee 1986). Once either the population or the technology of a group has exceeded a certain balance, a different organizational structure is likely to develop (Johnson 1973; 1982; Blau 1977; Lee 1986; Trigger pers. comm.). Johnson (1982) makes a case for levels of information flow and management that a given population can maintain. He claims that additional tiers of decision making will develop as population increases. Feinman and Neitzel (1984: 69) support this in their survey with a high correlation between population size and administrative levels or organizational differentiation. (In fact this is further supported by a strong correlation between the number of organizational units extant and social differentiation [1984: 72], although here social differentiation is defined as status items, such as residential patterns, dress, and mortuary patterns, rather than by social relations.) These correlations suggest a general relationship that assigns managerial limits and political structures to certain population densities, directing us towards smaller- or larger-scale societies based on population size and administration levels, similar to Ronald Lee's Boserupian space concept (1986: 119).

The range of population sizes that occurs within the political types discussed by these researchers may provide a general guide to the type of political form, but does *not* direct us toward the causes of systemic change that occurs within these populations, nor does it predict in any way the number and type of relationships that will occur.

More and more anthropologists realize that what initiates political change must be viewed as a constellation of interacting, competing, forming, and reforming conditions that are continually generated out of social actions, practice, perceptions, unconscious ethos, and social relationships (Bourdieu 1984; Giddens 1979). This position, while not strictly anti-materialistic, does place action or practice before the material basis for change.

The role of negotiation

Recent studies of social process stress the dynamics of interactions in society. Change does not occur in a unified way throughout society, it has different tempos from gradual to rapid. Social theorists such as Foucault (1984) and Giddens (1979) state that inequality forms out of tensions between interest groups, where contestation, negotiation, and multiple interpretations all participate. In this change, they focus on the mediation between groups, expressed as negotiation. Interaction includes both conflict and consensus, whether for an individual or at an intergroup level. Every interaction therefore has the potential to produce change. Through each act, claims to position, power, and right are reformed, accepted, or rejected. Socially constructed meanings and values about existence and about such things as agricultural systems, neighbors, rituals, beliefs, public feasts, kin networks, or marriage partners are discussed and transmitted in these acts. All of these individual actions are based on conscious and unconscious cultural beliefs retained through use (Bourdieu 1977).

Within each interaction a relationship exists between the participants. Depending on the power of persuasion, force, or strength of the positions involved, different outcomes are possible. There can be both agreement and resistance at the same time. Everyone is in fact following his own strategy. Asymmetries can be contested overtly or covertly. How then can we link one cause to one event or process?

Giddens (1979) points out that in asymmetrical relationships, conflicting interest groups try to find a balance through negotiation. Interests operate at many levels, including individual, family group, age, gender, neighborhood, and social groups. This means that all decisions, including those of the dominant ruling group, can be affected by the different goals of the different memberships. Each party, whether it is a household or a community, will consider what it will gain and what it will give up. In the case of strong differences between parties, the negotiation may be symbolic rather than substantive when power differences exist (like five-year-olds trying to negotiate a later bed time).

Social theorists, while providing a more realistic vision of how individuals and interest groups interact and negotiate their positions within society, cannot explicitly identify the causes for a cultural transformation. Political change and long-term change at the scale archaeologists study falls in between their approach and a broad explanatory level of the unilineal evolutionary theories of change such as population size. One can define this level of change at the onset of political inequality as a shift from a loose political system with inequalities operating at the individual level but with no centralized relationships or positions (roles) recognized above the family level, to a system with more stratified, group-level differentiations where inequalities affect the individual and family as well as the larger social unit. This transformation is indeterminate, but it is hoped that we might be able to better understand the process by tracking it.

An individual can belong to many interest groups. Multiplicity of simultaneous membership, such as belonging to an age-based group, a gender, a series of kin relationships, and a marriage, allows a person to align with different people over different issues, be they political, economic, religious, or social. Fluidity and multiplicity of membership is the basis of cultural change. We see this in our own lives. With sufficient fluidity, a polity can look homogeneous. As positions become more rigid or more differentiated, inequality is more evident.

This fluidity of position can be manipulated by people with varying degrees of success. In a small-scale society, skill is involved in justifying asymmetries while developing increased differences between people. For example, in highland New Guinea, a skilled orator can gain greater influence in certain group negotiations, or a well-organized farmer can become the group's communal land organizer (Strathern 1971; William Rowe, pers. comm.). But they do not have the physical or material conditions to negotiate power in other loci.

On the other hand, the more structured and hierarchical a society, the more well defined are the limits to group membership and positions of authority. Cultural rules try to structure who can join which group, and which groups can be involved in which debates. Factions may ally over mutual interests. But, even when there are groups whose opinions tend to dominate, there are always opposing views. Negotiation between differing cultural principles creates the tensions that pervade cultural life, but also the nexes for political change. Change may occur when new problems or constraints exist and one opinion becomes more persuasive.

How can we track such negotiation in archaeological material? How can we understand and explain the creation and perpetuation of asymmetrical relations with such diverse social actions? If we assume that change emanates out of these social interactions, they are the underpinnings to the more permanent inequalities and political stratification seen in chiefdoms and states. Under what conditions do people choose to give up their personal and political autonomy? What was compromised by the dominant and the subordinate participants? How broad-reaching are these changes? These are the issues in the onset of political inequality that direct the archaeological search for the causes of political change within specific societies.

Negotiation is the activity of change in political development, both ideologically and materially. This negotiation is not always easy to see in the archaeological record, as negotiators trade intangibles (social relations, position in society, status, and personal–individual autonomy over aspects of daily life, etc.) for group stability, security, or even loss of personal risk (Miller and Tilley 1984; Tilley 1985). Incipient leaders, while working for their own self-interests, may suggest (and probably believe) that the group will gain an advantage by organizing labor, managing resources, or uniting its forces with others. Members might gain stability, security, or at least survival from such new organizations. Throughout negotiation and dissent, increased asymmetrical jurisdictions may develop, with a loss of individual decision making. Political change shifts the boundaries of contestation and may even redefine who can contest.

Differences do not have to be in the economic sphere, but they may be. Economics, like wealth, can play a major part in the shape and the timing of political change, but it is not the cause. Intensive agriculture, for example, can create certain patterns of accumulation and ways of interacting between members. These accumulations may form inherent inequalities within a group that may or may not effect social or political differences.

Summary

In the process of defining political inequality, we must track a series of social and economic changes in role differentiation, negotiation, and types of control. This type of information is gained in the data from residences, burials, and artifact distributions. By studying the use and distribution of resources, for example, we can see how production is linked to control and power. But production is also linked to cultural and social principles. Daily activities portray the principles at work in society. Through time different parts of the cultural heritage are continued and maintained while others are transformed and others are sloughed off. These can be studied through data such as site plans, artifact assemblages, and documentary sources.

The archaeological record therefore can demonstrate how resources and principles link. By tracking something which can be viewed both materially and culturally, we can see how power moves through societies. In this way, agriculture, which is a major economic force in many societies, plays a role in the negotiation of positions in society, both in power to provide and in power over people.

Agricultural production is particularly important because it can be tracked in the archaeological record; however, it is not merely because of this visibility that I focus my analysis on it. In the Andean region, modern and historic documents inform us that agriculture embues the core of all social relations and political integration. Therefore, while agricultural change may not have created political change, it was a channel for the negotiation of change which we can pursue.

2

The economics of intensive Andean agriculture

Intensive agriculture has been part of human adaptation in the Andean mountains for thousands of years. Within this production system, both the herding of camelids (recently cattle and sheep), and agriculture based on a wide array of indigenous plants (now including European vegetables and grains) have been critical. Because the prehistoric time span investigated here begins when indigenous domesticates already dominated the food procurement system and ends before the European introduction of new plants and animals, I consider agriculture to be the basis of the Andean production system under study. Exchange and the production of goods and specialized crafts are part of the economic complex, but are not the most fundamental in Andean subsistence economy. They become more important with larger-scale supra-community political interaction such as the Inka or Tiawanaku.

Agricultural economics can be discussed from several perspectives, especially ecological–ecosystemic and social–cultural (Orlove and Godoy 1986). Although agricultural data are often presented in terms of one or the other of these perspectives, optimally both should be synthesized into one dynamic cultural presentation (Sheridan and Bailey [1981] attempted to do this in their edited volume, but it ultimately lacked integration). A possible approach to this problem is one theme of this book.

Agricultural energetics, despite its insensitivity to cultural dynamics and its potential to be reductionistic, still provides specific evidence about basic activities and minimal needs. Much can be gained by implementing an economic framework in the study of long-term intensive agriculture (Bailey 1981; Earle 1980; Earle and Christenson 1980; Turner and Doolittle 1978). Agriculture is based on work and yields. Like exploratory statistics, used very successfully to organize and view complex data, production models as organizational tools can help identify some of the major shifts in production in a straightforward manner.

One of the major principles used to describe agricultural systems is energetics: input–labor and/or output–yield. In a formal economic manner, this has been described as farmers attempting to maximize yield while maintaining costs, if agricultural yield is the major goal of the work effort. Yet few farmers simply attempt to maximize output in their production strategies. Nor do we find in agricultural studies that farmers always choose strategies that minimize costs (Conklin 1961; Cancian 1972; Gudeman 1978). A farmer's behavior is affected by physical risks, his amount of knowledge, the alternative options available, the social requirements, and the cultural codes. Despite the many options farmers have, agricultural researchers often find, when looking at production over the long run, that a farmer's goal is to meet subsistence needs, while minimizing risks and loss. That is why farmers tend to follow a satisfycing model (Cancian 1972; Gould 1961; Halstead and O'Shea 1989; Hurwicz 1951; Shows and Burton 1972; Waddell 1973).

Rarely interwoven with formalist ecological ideas are the cultural constructs which affect, guide, and generate the strategies of agricultural production (Gudeman 1978). Social constructions of agricultural systems are not separate from their economics. Regularities seen in the social domain interact with the economic constraints. Conflicting goals in the social domains have the potential to ignite conflict and tension and can lead to changes in production strategies, differential access to the goods, or new forms of decision making. For a fuller understanding of the economic system within a culture, both orientations should be discussed and merged.

For the Andes some of the major socio-cultural structures or values that guide economic decision making are concepts such as the bounded territory (Harris 1985), group identity through communal participation (Bastien 1978), and division of the whole into equal parts (balanced opposition and equality) (B. J. Isbell 1978; Johnsson 1986; Orlove and Godoy 1986; Skar 1981). Methods to minimize risk include reciprocity (sharing or exchange), storage, and use of a diverse resource base (Alberti and Mayer 1974; Brush 1977; Mayer 1985; Werge 1979).

Economic principles in agriculture

Political changes are often associated with changes in intensive subsistence production, relative densities of human populations, and perceived limits to expansion (Carneiro 1970; Gilman 1981; Renfrew and Shennan 1982). Intensive agriculture has been organizationally linked to unequal patterns of accumulation (D'Altroy and Earle 1985; Earle 1978; Johnson 1973; Strathern 1971), certain unequal economic relationships (Wittfogel 1957), certain demographic structures (Flannery 1976; Steponaitis 1981; Wright and Johnson 1975), and certain types of interaction between participants (Brumfiel 1976; Carneiro 1970). None of these discussions provides completely satisfying models for production for they leave out the social and cultural linking arguments that embed production in political negotiation (see Chapter 1).

Anthropologists and archaeologists interested in the economics of food production continue to be concerned about the different ways, both potential and real, in which populations harness energy (Barlett 1980; Brookfield 1972; Carneiro 1967; Clark and Haswell 1971; Harris 1969; Harris and Hillman 1989). Because of this, many have turned to ecological approaches, ecosystemic theories, and the variables associated with them (Brush 1976; Jochim 1976). These approaches are effective when data can be collected on production, consumption, and nutrition (e.g. Hipsley and Kirk 1965; Lee 1969). With a corpus of data, studies are initiated about the different economic strategies employed by cultures, both as formalistic economic discussions and as cultural views of production goals. Here I focus primarily on the first of the three components of the economics of crop-growing – production; although foods, food values, and dietary needs are also important to the complete food-production picture.

Energetics

Fundamental to all of life, especially the production of food, is the movement of energy and materials through living systems. While there are several layers of energy capture, originating at the primary level with the sun, human populations have the largest range of energy capture, due to their transformative and transportation capacities. Energy is a useful measurement in archaeological study for several reasons: the data are neutral and can be quantified, tracking energy expenditure can describe a production system, energy produced can be compared to energy consumed, and the energetics of a particular procurement activity can be related to other technically different production systems (Ellen 1982: 120; Lee 1969).

Inputs are the set of food-procurement costs that are necessary to maintain and reproduce a human population. Input has been described as work, effort, or energy expended to extract a given amount of food. It can be measured in labor-time, calories expended, calorific expenditure by task, calorific expenditure per unit time, or relative time of the different tasks. While each measurement has its empirical problems, each has been applied usefully in anthropological research. Inputs are often labeled as modes of subsistence, or are identified with certain procurement strategies, such as gathering, extensive root cultivation, intensive dry-farm cultivation, or irrigation agriculture. Each strategy can have a range of labor, calorie, time (length or scheduling), etc. input values, differing by procurement strategy. This allows the investigator, in a general way, to describe and compare between the different strategies.

Outputs are the yields from these activities. Output can include a great many items, from stones to firewood, to mates, to dances, to food. Using energetic food terms, however, yield is usually tabulated in calories, proteins, minerals, or vitamins, again in measurable as well as absolutely-necessary-to-survive units. In addition to these life-support goods, there are always non-consumable items, by-products, or secondary products that are important to maintenance (hides for clothing, chaff for fuel, etc.) (Sherratt 1981). These non-food requirements also affect the choice of food and non-food resources sought (Ellen 1982; Keene 1981; Winterhalder and Smith 1981). Like input, these yields or products can be quantified in terms of calories, or in terms of other necessities such as clothing, making them comparable. There are several ways to present input and output in the investigation of human energetics. The most useful has been to compare efficiencies in energy extraction, based on the ratio of output to input (Boserup 1965; Lee 1969; Netting 1968; Pimentel and Pimentel 1979).

The natural resources used by a group vary according to the perception of the land and what it yields. Resource choice is also dependent on soil fertility, solar energy, elevation, temperature, biota presence and distribution, and biomass. There is a range of different potential resources from which the members of the population must choose. Choice is based on a number of different criteria, recognized and unrecognized by the participants. Many models have been applied to modern groups with the hopes of determining the most important assumptions about the basic set of choices (Gould 1961; Quinn 1971; Winterhalder and Thomas 1978). Archaeologists have therefore often relied on the energetics of procurement strategies as a guide in proposing what might be the likely strategies and goals of a prehistoric group (Earle and Christenson 1980; Jochim 1976; Thomas 1973). We, as distant observers, make decisions about what we think the participants were interested in pursuing, but this narrows our view of what was occurring prehistorically. Isn't it more effective to try to understand what they might have been pursuing and then build models about resource goals based on that?

The role of risk and insurance in production

Some archaeologists and anthropologists try to temper strict energy values with more sensitive indicators of human action within an ecosystem (Braun and Plog 1982; Gudeman 1978; Halstead and O'Shea 1989; Harris 1985; Lees 1983; Moran 1990; Sheridan and Bailey 1981). One important concept to consider in subsistence decisions is the factor of risk. All goal oriented actions are risky, some more so than others, as every strategy has its own combination of risks (Dillon and Anderson 1971; Roumasset et al. 1979). Risk has been described as the possibility or likelihood of danger, injury, loss, or uncertainty, where uncertainty has specific probabilities of occurrence (von Neumann and Morgenstern 1944). Many discussions about economic decision making focus on the alternate risks associated with each possible strategy. In agriculture, some risks can be controlled for. For example, the risk of not having enough water to irrigate a field can be eliminated by building a reservoir, or the risk of crop robbery can be eliminated by posting a guard in the field. Many risks, such as bad weather, frosts, hail, or volcanoes, cannot be so directly controlled for.

Just as yields are affected by the introduction of more intensive agricultural practices, so many groups have adopted a series of insurance mechanisms in order to dampen or buffer the various risks affecting production. Three of the most important methods of reducing risk are (a) diversifying the locations of field production, and diversifying the number of strategies or resources available (Browman 1987; Guillet 1981); (b) storage of resources (Coombs 1980; Halstead and O'Shea 1982; 1989) and (c) exchange, reciprocity, or sharing of resources among other groups (Cashdan 1985; Hegmon 1986; 1987; Wiessner 1982; Winterhalder 1986). These strategies can also be implemented when coping with more predictable problems such as seasonal fluctuations (Pryor 1986).

Diversification in resource exploitation has been shown to be an effective risk-management mechanism in places such as the Andes where variable climatic factors and a very diverse environment allow for such possibilities (Harris 1982: 92). This strategy has also been adopted in homogenous environments such as the Amazon basin, however, making it not unique to diverse environments (Kimura 1985). Diversification can involve mixed subsistence strategies using many different plots dispersed across the landscape in different microzones (Browman 1987; Guillet 1981; Hack 1942), a multitude of technologies (irrigation, drained fields, terraces) (Farrington 1985), mixed staple crop production, planting many different taxa and varieties of taxa (Brush et al. 1981; Camino et al. 1981; Gade 1969, 1975; Guillet 1981: 11), having a mix of animals, crops, and agricultural techniques (long fallow rotation, swidden, intensive dry farming, irrigation farming) (Guillet 1978; 1981: 10), or producing crafts to exchange for necessary resources, labor or goods, or to maintain social relations (Harris 1985; Kimura 1985). These different options to alleviate risk are not mutually exclusive, all can be risk reducing as well as considered part of an effective production strategy, especially in the Andes. The risk-reducing strategies may not however always be cost effective; controlling for risk has a cost (Orlove and Godoy 1986: 181).

Storage has been shown to be a successful mechanism to buffer risks in all agricultural societies. Types of storage can be silos, special rooms, subterranean pits or cellars, in the ground (root crops), or on the hoof (live meat). Prehistoric models of the effect of risk minimization always include storage because of its inherent flexibility and importance, once a group is involved with agriculture (Coombs 1980; Halstead and O'Shea 1982; 1989). Storage systems should be considered essential, if for no other reason than because of the periodicity of the harvest.

Another flexible and very important cultural method for survival is sharing, exchange, or reciprocity. Exchange can reduce risk by cementing social relations (*Hxaro* or support insurance for the !Kung San [Cashdan 1985; Weissner 1977], or *compadrazgo* and exogamous kin networks in the Andean highlands [Bastien 1978; Burchard 1974; 1972 quoted in Guillet 1981]). Virtually all human societies participate in this type of buffering mechanism. While Sahlins's (1972) domestic mode of production ideally portrays a subsistence oriented group only producing what it needs to survive and no more, he admits what Donham (1981) has found, that peasants in fact will produce extra for sale and exchange. Anthropological researchers on this subject have found a range of yields that are extracted for exchange within agricultural subsistence-based economies (Gregory 1980; Josephides 1985). These amounts are never as great, however, as when groups become incorporated into a larger exchange network of neighbors, kin, and trading partners (Harris 1982).

For gatherers and hunters, Cashdan (1985) suggests that reciprocity is more cost effective against group risk, while storage may be more cost effective for the individual. Cashdan claims that by operating with balanced reciprocity hunters and gatherers are acting optimally at the group level, while not necessarily minimizing their individual costs. She believes that sharing costs less than storage over the long run for mobile people. In support of the usefulness of this cost-effective behavior and risk management, Winterhalder (1986: 372, 389) demonstrates with simulated data that foragers who are minimizing risks of an energy short-fall through group pooling and sharing are also maximizing the net rate of energy acquisition. This effectiveness of risk and cost minimization through suprahousehold sharing/exchange has been shown for agriculturalists in Hegmon's study of the Hopi (1987), Guillet's work in the Andes (1978), and prehistorically by Braun and Plog (1982).

A model for viewing agricultural production

Risk-mediating activities become cost-effective activities in agriculture when they become part of a long-term optimal strategy. We begin with energetics to get an understanding about the form and types of influences affecting agricultural production. This information helps to identify the social and cultural influences as they affect production. Operating within the concept of optimal production over the long run allows us to look at a base line of changing energetics and relative agricultural intensity as well as possible options to maintain effective yields. An optimal agricultural production scheme helps to illustrate a group's productive strategies, especially changes in the requirements and goals of a particular culture. From this vantage point, social and political negotiations can be more clearly seen as they participate in the production changes.

With this approach, a series of likely procurement strategies can be proposed for a given region and its population based on its ecology and possible technologies. A procurement strategy is a series of activities carried out to obtain a desired resource. Each strategy involves a set of tasks which make up the total production cost or input (e.g. collection, maintenance, transportation, processing, and storage). These tasks each can have general energetics assigned to them based on empirical ranges. Individual sites then can have proposed production mixes based on their access and location. Although there are many aspects that cannot be discussed in a long-term approach to agricultural production, such as scheduling conflicts and cost fluctuations, the procurement strategy mixes that can be outlined for a given region present an aggregate view of all the individuals' activities within that population. This mix takes in account all strategies in an annual cycle, assuming that scheduling problems and differential yields average out.

This orientation was chosen because it can address production at the community level, rather than an approach that focuses on the individual household, such as Chayanov's (1966) peasant economy model. Much research has shown that the traditional Andean economy, although producing at the household level, actually organizes the agricultural land at the community or *ayllu* level (C. Franquemount, pers. comm.; Smith 1989: 39). Autonomy was important at both levels. A group production model is an appropriate level of economic analysis for the Andes, therefore (Harris 1982: 80; see also next chapter).

Agricultural ecology in the Andes

The diverse topography, extreme altitudinal differences, and seasonal yet temperate fluctuations of the highland intermontane region create a dynamic setting for dense, settled prehistoric human populations. This environment gives Andean agriculture some specific constraints, but for the most part it is a highly adaptive and multidimensional production system. The agricultural strategies are closely tied to the environmental zones available to a population, the elevation, the population size, the technological traditions, the moisture regimes, and the social organization of the work force.

For at least fifty years, since Carl Troll (1935) began writing about the human–environment interaction in the Andes, the effects of the environment on the task of developing a stable and successful existence have been a rich field of study. The Andes are exceptionally well suited to human ecological investigations because there are so many distinct zones with particular conditions and broad regularities across the zones. These regularities are illustrated in the plant and animal geographies, and also in the general use of the landscape and in the production organization. One can find similar forms of crop production or camelid herding hundreds of kilometers apart. A further exciting result of these studies is that, despite centuries of political, economic, social upheaval and change, some land-use strategies provide evidence of strong continuities in the production system.

Important ecological features that affect Andean crop production are the proximity of the different ecological zones, the constraints of low soil fertility, the varying moisture and cold regimes in the different zones, and differing crop life cycles throughout the zones. One of the most important characteristics of adaptation has been the complementary use of multizonal resources by individual groups. This was first brought to researchers' attention in the verticality model of Murra (1968; 1972). In essence, the model states that groups have adapted to the diverse environment by developing social and economic structures to access vertically and spatially separated ecological zones. Based on historic research, Murra suggested that this system was uniquely Andean and has been an Andean adaptation for a long time. He also proposed that a widely dispersed set of zones was controlled by single ethnic groups.

Murra's model focused most on the last pre-Hispanic kingdoms and there is evidence that multizone use did exist during Inka times in various locations (Dillehay 1979; Harris 1985; LeVine 1985; Murra 1972; Salomon 1986). There have been many versions of this model proposed for the Andes and elsewhere (Brush 1974; 1976; Rhoades and Thompson 1975) and equally as many critiques and other models (Browman 1987; D'Altroy and Earle 1985; Masuda et al. 1985; Nuñez and Dillehay 1978). Some of the cultural examples such as Harris's (1985) work in Potosi, or Stanish's (1989) in Otora Valley are close to Murra's ideals, stressing long-distance separation between a community and its producing outliers. Others, such as Brush's (1977) work at Uchucmarca in the north-central Andes, describe continuous and close zonal use. While the extent and form of this archipelago model is debatable and will be addressed again in Chapter 11, it is safe to say that groups of communities, communities, and households in the Andes can maintain long-term production success through the use of several ecological zones.

Awareness of these mountain adaptations has spurred much research on high-elevation Andean agricultural systems (Brush 1977; Camino, et al. 1981; Gade 1975; Guillet 1987b; Mayer 1979; Mitchell 1976; Rhoades and Thompson 1975; Soldi 1982; Winterhalder n.d., to name a few), production energetics (Flores Ochoa 1968; Thomas 1973; Winterhalder and Thomas 1978), and social organization of production (Brush 1977; Golte 1980; Guillet 1978; Mayer 1985; Scott 1985; Smith 1989). These studies investigate variations in multi-zone use and how the agricultural systems unfold with the ecological, economic, and political principles. There are many ways a group can meet its needs effectively even with struggle operating within the group.

These modern ecological results are particularly engaging because we learn that Andean households seem to optimize output while minimizing effort and managing risk to maintain subsistence needs (Guillet 1978; Mayer 1985; Winterhalder and Thomas 1978). These studies provide new insights into the emphasis farmers place on the different economic, social, and political influences on their production decisions.

Recent agricultural research by Guillet (1981, 1987b), with additional documentation from the ethnohistoric work by Rostworowski (1962), has suggested that Andean farmers have operated in a needs based economic production system, defined here as the notion of meeting the subsistence requirements of the household. Given this production goal, farmers will set out to meet their needs through a series of economic opportunities via a mix of agriculture, herding, and exchange. Andean residents undertake a series of different activities to minimize risk while maintaining a necessary level of output. These strategies are seen in the use of landscape, people, and crops in such activities as terracing, irrigation, communal sectoral fallowing, labor exchange (*ayni* and *faena*), and short-term absence for seasonal work when yields and stores are low (Browman 1987; Brush and Guillet 1985; Guillet 1981; Skar 1982; Thomas 1973; Winterhalder and Thomas 1978).

The localized multi-zone, multi-strategy adaptation is ecologically effective in maintaining yields in diverse environments, especially when the zones are contiguous (Yamamoto 1985). Golte (1980) has argued that multi-zone use developed because the productivity of any one zone is low and too restricted, and that several production zones are necessary to gain a sufficient dietary mix. Because yields of the different crops vary with elevation this stands to reason. For example, as Gade (1975) shows effective crop yields graphically in his maps along the Vilcanota Valley elevation gradient, and as my crop geography study also demonstrates (Chapter 6), maize produces better at a lower elevation than quinoa. Potatoes, *tarwi*, oca, and ulluco overlap productive yields across the next elevation gradient higher, and finally mashua and maca will yield in the highest arable elevations. Animals tend to be herded in the higher elevations where there are fewer crops grown. In order to produce this mix, at least three microzones must be used. Today, although there can be regular trade between groups that do not have access to these different zones, households prefer to have access and produce their own food mix, and be self-sufficient.

Of importance to archaeological settlement location studies is Mayer's view (1985: 65–66) that the number of zones used intensively depends on several factors: the distance from the community, including the gradient and ease of movement; the location of the village and its position within the zones; the population size (the labor force); and also the social organization that provides access to the labor. He also notes that villages are located closer to production zones that require or receive the most intensive care. These geographical constraints support the energetic argument of minimizing labor and time input for output in the land-use strategies within the social constraints.

The sectoral fallow system

One very important agricultural practice that has received much agro-anthropological attention because of its economic and ecological optimizing qualities is the sectoral fallowing system (Matos Mar 1964; Mayer 1979; Orlove and Godoy 1986). This agricultural rotation scheme is a method of organizing production through communal land allocation and cropping that claims to optimize productivity over the long run, especially in the upper altitudes where land is less fertile. This system cycles fields for agricultural cropping and animal grazing as a unit by the whole community or *ayllu*, not on an individual basis. Individual households participating in the community system receive plots of land in the designated areas to be planted, while the fallow zone is left open for grazing. Each family work unit must contribute labor in the community tasks (*faena*) in exchange for their plot (Wachtel 1973). This reciprocity assures that all households which participate do so at the same level of intensity, based on their labor contributions. Just how maximizing or satisfying this system is has yet to be systematically studied with a long-term study in the field.

There are many versions of this system. In general the system works on a large plot of land that is community owned and managed. It is divided up into parcels or sectors, equivalent to the number of years in the rotation cycle (cropping and fallow years). Each year, one of these parcels is brought into production, while one is put into fallow-grazing. The cropped parcel is divided into individual household allotments that each participating family unit in the community plants, tends, and harvests. Today, sectoral fallow systems tend to occur in the tuber-producing areas, commonly producing potatoes, Andean tubers, occasionally quinoa, and some of the hardier European grains. To participate, a household must contribute labor to the communal work projects. Mayer (1985) notes that there are many social controls of the land in this system that are based on providing labor to gain access. The community officials dictate when the communal work days occur, when to plant, what to plant, when to harvest, and when to graze.

Today the system is mediated through certain village officials (see Chapter 3) and thus allows for community based production that operates simultaneously with individual plots. But, as Smith (1989) points out, shared community land is not always shared community value. There are always many debates about which households do in fact have access to what plots of land and how much labor is enough to gain access to the land. This family participation also defines the community as well as maintains its autonomy from other communities (Gramsci 1973).

In many ways, sectoral fallowing is considered to be an effective way of using the higher elevation land (maximizing yields while keeping labor costs down), by allowing large parcels of land to be grazed by animals without the need to build fences. At the same time the system allows land to be fertilized by animal excrement and for wild grasses to grow in the fallow years, bringing nutrients up from the deeper soils. It also allows farmers to maintain irrigation systems in specific locations instead of throughout the whole landscape, and it institutionalizes control and conservation of the land so that it is not overexploited.

The system has been considered optimal also to maintain soil fertility (Guillet 1981; Orlove and Godoy 1986; 1978), control crop pathogens (Brush and Guillet 1985: 26), and to maintain crop yields (Mayer 1979). This form of communal rotation controls the farmers' decisions about crop choice and production, which is a social and an economic constraint on the individual household. It also channels individual household contestation over land rights while making dominant and re-stating the code of the community as provider and keeping a larger political entity out of the debate (Smith 1989).

Godoy and Guillet (pers. comm.) believe that this fallow system is derived from medieval Spanish systems. There is, however, no evidence that versions of this system did not exist before the Spanish arrived, especially as it is embued with many Andean values and principles that seem to be long lived. It is found in areas where haciendas existed but also where they did not. The system is found in certain ecological settings, the central Andes, and did not function on the coast. So, it does seem to be more associated with certain ecological settings and human adaptations to those settings rather than only to direct Spanish impact, although what we see now could be a blend of local adaptation and a Spanish system.

Private land versus labor

In addition to the communal fields, we know that since historic times both men and women have inherited parcels of land in scattered locations throughout the zones. The scatter of parcels is propagated through bilateral inheritance. A patchwork of fields provides individual families access to land in different microzones, in addition to the communal sectoral fields. This diversity of plots has also been considered a risk minimization strategy (Browman 1987). The private plots, occurring at lower elevations than the sectoral fields (Orlove and Godoy 1986: 188–99), further allow a household to plant a variety of crops and to gain a mixed diet of their own choosing. This strategy may possibly have been Spanish manipulated, due to its focus on individual land ownership, foreign to aspects of Andean principles (Chapter 3).

To what extent the communal land-use system and the private-plot system were in operation in pre-Hispanic times is difficult to determine. Today, this style of communal land-use is dying out in the Andes, not because of new techniques replacing the old but because of state level and world-system politico-economic pressures. Some ethnohistorians think that private land tenure for the individual family is Hispanic (LaLone 1985). This surely has been the case in kitchen gardens, or patches near houses that are more intensively tended. We know that the Inka allocated land to the state and the Sun, leaving plots of land for the communities (Conrad and Demerest 1974; D'Altroy 1987; Rowstrowski 1977b). The impression is that only Inka royalty had private land. But Cobo (1956: 42, 121) wrote of Inka times that no one owned more land than was necessary to support his family. This of course could mean that no one had *access* to more land. While land could have been owned by families, the concept of ownership seems less strong for land than it does for labor. Documents state that leaders had people who would work on their land, suggesting some potential for differential access (Toledo 1940). Late Intermediate highland leaders had *yanakona* servants for life who worked for the leader's family on its land.

Both communal and private land-use systems could have been in operation throughout the Andes in the past. Both are effective methods of production, although communal land seems to be the more controllable strategy politically in the less fertile microzones (with its sequence of long fallow). A mix of land tenure, with communal lands in the less productive areas and individual plots in the more intensive, continuously productive areas, is characteristic of mountain adaptations, perhaps including Spanish mountains as well as Andean (Guillet 1978; pers. comm.; Rhoades and Thompson 1975).

From recent highland agricultural production studies it is clear that the more intensively a plot of land can be worked the more independence farmers want to have over the production decisions (Mayer 1985: 61). The two patterns of access support multiple social strategies, both communal and individual. If these two options existed pre-Hispanically there could have been a locus of contestation over individual control and aggrandizement, especially in relation to the lower, more fertile lands. For example, today at the lower elevations land is intensively cultivated, individually managed, sometimes privately owned, often near home, and often the locus of surplus production for exchange (Yamamoto 1981; Fuji and Tomoeda 1981, quoted in Mayer 1985: 61). Individuals who wish to expand production most often do so in these lower elevations. If only communal lands were the system in the past, intensification would have to be decided and coordinated by the group or a leader of the group. But even if it was *ayllu* oriented, expanding agricultural production still would have led ultimately to a focus on lower, more productive land with individuals wanting more decision-making capabilities (Smith 1989: 174–81).

Agriculture requires labor from suprahousehold organization for the group projects (*faena*) and interhousehold labor exchange for the individual plots (*ayni*). Many agricultural activities therefore are linked to the social organization at the community level, be it *barrios*, single, or several settlements. Different forms of community land-use organization should look different on the landscape and might be visible archaeologically in the agricultural production data and in the technological material on the sites or across the landscape. For example, as will be mentioned in Chapter 8, there was an intercommunity irrigation canal operating in the Wanka II phase.

Other options to alleviate risk

Besides different land-use strategies across the landscape, the planting of crop varieties in a mix of microzones is an effective form of risk reduction. In the sectoral fallow and private land system, a fairly complete range of crops can be produced by individual households over several years, using mixed cropping within fields as well as having a set of fields in different vertical and horizontal locations. This has been demonstrated in a series of studies. Brush et al. (1981) have collected data on potato varieties, where many varieties are planted by a family, often in the same plot. Camino et al. (1981) also demonstrate a series of different crop mixes, planted in individual plots, some for the mutual benefit of the crops. For example *tarwi*, a bitter legume, is planted surrounding maize as a deterrent to grazing animals. In other areas small plots are planted primarily with one crop, although one family will plant a range of these small plots contiguously. Following this, one household has crop diversity. Altogether these strategies maintain a stable and diverse genetic stock, allow for optimal and flexible use of the land, and maintain yields.

Another method of risk reduction is storage. Storage in the Andes is simple yet diverse. Traditionally, people store their crops against the walls in their houses, in the corners of their patios, in bins (under beds or against walls), in jars, bags, or in silos (Hastorf n.d.; Sikkink 1988; Werge 1977). Silos were the method of wealth accumulation and finance used by the Inka (D'Altroy 1981; Morris 1967). Some type of preparation treatment is performed on all crops before storage. Because the Andean climate is somewhat moist, there is a problem of food loss after harvest due to microbial action. Post-harvest losses have been estimated as up to 25–30 percent of the harvest (Knapp 1984: 215).

One very efficient method for prolonging the storability of tubers is by freeze-drying (Gade 1975; Yamamoto 1986; Sikkink 1988). This technique is restricted to the upper zones where climatic conditions are suitable for freezing and sun-drying the crops during a cycle of nights and days. Freezing nights and sunny days are necessary to alternately freeze and then squeeze the liquid out of the tubers. The process extends the storage life of the tubers up to two years. They also become lighter and are more easily transported for trade or consumption. Drying or parching is used to preserve maize kernels, quinoa and tarwi seeds, and camelid meat.

Another form of risk reduction is to have large herds. Herders with larger herds suffer less diet loss when there is a drought or a frost that depletes the fodder (Flannery et al. 1989; Flores Ochoa 1968). A fourth method is sharing and exchange. These methods are important and will be covered more fully in the next section.

A question archaeologists must ask is whether all of these risk strategies were always operating in past agricultural systems, and how might they have changed through time? Activities such as crop storage and multiple cropping must have been present from the start of regular agricultural production. Labor coordination strategies and forms of land-use and access could have varied more through time. This is what we must try to track.

A cultural approach to Andean agriculture

A complementary orientation to the discussion of agricultural economics involves the cultural principles existing in Andean communities that also participate in maintaining production. These can be thought of as structures that allow the agricultural systems to operate, and/or as principles that shape the organization of production. The most prominent social influences in the agricultural domain of a community are the systems of exchange, reciprocity, and sharing, the boundedness and division of territories, and the allocation of land for labor.

In addition to Murra's archipelago discussion, much has been written about Andean exchange of goods (Alberti and Mayer 1974; Harris 1985: Lehmann 1982), labor exchange (*ayni*) (Brush 1977), seasonal travelling for trade or work (Alberti and Mayer 1974; Browman 1987; Thomas 1973), and marriage alliances that allow access to different zones (Bastien 1978; Brush 1977). All of these strategies provide increased flexibility when there is a short-fall or certain critical resources are not available. But they also operate when there is no short-fall of food, suggesting that they are part of a wider social fabric of the community.

No community is an island, even if several zones are within its territory and the population is endogamous; there is always some porosity in its social boundaries.

Some goods, such as salt, coca, *chonta* palm wood, peppers, and seed potatoes, must enter both vertically and horizontally on a regular basis. There are networks for exchange between groups, for example, trading partners must be honored when the partner comes to visit. Within a community or a group of communities there are many mechanisms for exchange, neighbors who exchange labor and crops, kin who share ownership or exchange goods, *ayllus* who exchange wives, community feasts, rituals, and work parties. These types of exchange should be seen as part of the resource extraction system as well as of normal social relations. Different types of exchange will, however, mean different cultural interactions (Earle and Ericson 1977; Fry 1980; Hodder 1982; Wright and Zeder 1977). Some of these different trade networks will be visible in the archaeological record, and should point to changes in the dynamics of trade through time.

Laced through these exchange mechanisms is the cultural value of this interdependence via principles such as the division of a whole into its parts, complementary duality, complementary opposition, and boundedness (Harris 1978; Orlove and Godoy 1986). These concepts integrate communal, intergroup, and interfamilial relationships that, when practiced, keep reaffirming the group's relations. Orlove and Godoy discuss how these principles support the sectoral fallow system and divide the landscape into equal parts. They see these structures as ways to keep the rotation cycle running smoothly. Village space and official management are divided into two parts with rotating authority, as discussed in the next chapter (B. J. Isbell 1978). Sherbondy (1982) also writes of the organization of irrigation ditches that parallel social organizational principles. The irrigation networks are spread across the landscape, marking the division of groups as well as agricultural field ownership.

One dimension of the Andean agricultural system and the social organization that controls contestation and constrains the individual is the requirement of universal participation (Orlove and Godoy 1986). It is seen in the community *faena* work system, but also in the planting rituals (Bastien 1978). There are strong rules and sanctions to insure universal participation from every household, even if its total labor pool is not necessary. The communal work structure provides the mechanism to organize the community when group decisions are needed in other domains, be it agricultural or political, and can be a place where leadership and social change can arise. It also provides a locus of control in the group. Although these structures exist to maintain a communal ethic and integrate the social group, they can also be the locus of economic difference and tension, where individuals try to change their position socially or economically.

Agriculture is also defined by boundaries. Boundedness strongly contributes to the conception of the landscape as divided into distinct units: agricultural plots, village, puna, wild, cultural, as well as the various use zones (Guillet 1987b; B. J. Isbell 1978; Mayer 1985). These definitions relate to resource access. Those who work on community labor projects and participate in the rituals are considered part of the community and thus can receive parcels of land to plant (Bastien 1978; Duviols 1973; Mayer 1985; C. Franquemont pers. comm.).

The different production zones, e.g. the puna-herding, the potato-growing, and the maize-growing zone, are defined and bounded by their production constraints but are also associated with the people who use them. Those who live in the puna are "foreigners" or "immigrants" when they visit the agricultural community (Duviols 1973; B. J. Isbell 1978). Boundaries create variability between households' subsistence production. The multi-zone access not only affects the economic diversity, it also creates the modes of social interaction families live within. Today, this communal boundedness constrains an individual family's actions of aggrandizement. What it does not constrain, however, is a community's potential for increased production and aggrandizement if it can expand its own borders (Smith 1989).

There is tension between the communal production organization and the individual household's production goals. These opposing desires of group versus household can provide support and insurance for the household as well as frustration regarding economic and social constraints. This tension and negotiation are seen in several guises in many modern agricultural studies, highlighted in Mayer's (1985) cogent article. Like Cashdan's (1985) discussion of the different strategies in group versus individual risk minimization for the !Kung San, Mayer proposes that the tension between group control over land versus individual production can exist. This tension is especially evident when there are different settlements within one community *ayllu*, linking producers to the central community through exchange with their relations. Everyone participates in the exchange, establishing a group oriented production. These interdependent specialists, he goes on to point out, are in constant conflict, the smaller settlements feeling dominated by the larger, yet they are also symbiotically allied (Fonseca Martel 1972). Some of the families may gain control over more labor or land than others as these exchange relationships are manipulated (Hastorf 1990b; Mallon 1983).

In this communal system therefore there are mechanisms for exploitation of households and hamlets by a few. While the agricultural system is maintained by the cultural principles of community, such as balanced opposition and accommodation over the long term, it breeds tension and possible inequalities through differential exploitation.

Orlove and Godoy (1986) have been very influential and creative in highlighting these two anthropological perspectives in their study of Andean sectoral fallow agriculture; the cultural and the energetic. They present the different hypotheses and approaches of the two orientations, claiming that there are important regularities in the agricultural system supported by both orientations. They point out that both aspects should be considered to gain a better understanding of Andean agricultural practices today. They do not however weave these two aspects of agriculture together into one cultural perspective nor focus on the negotiation and social actions inherent in the agro-social system. There is the possibility for synthesizing these components into one orientation.

Communal production and complementary labor exchange are effective agricultural schemes, but there are alternatives that can work in the Andes, as is seen in private land, colonial, historic, and hacienda agricultural strategies (Chapter 7). The structure of communal land-use maintains reasonable yields over the long term (Flannery et al. 1989), but it also works to maintain a nonexpansionistic cultural view and desire for small autonomous groups. Further, the actions are linked to cultural structures, such as complementary opposition, that help dampen tensions in such a system as well as maintaining production. Thus the cultural principles of balance can be viewed in the communal Andean agriculture as well as part of daily life in other social realms (Bourdieu 1977). On the other hand, private land offers realms in which different models flourish. Energetics and cultural principles both participate in forming Andean agriculture today; they are not separate entities.

We might ask therefore if we can track the history of cultural principles archaeologically through changes in agriculture practices. Surely as agricultural production changed through time so did the cultural principles that channeled it. What does this say about the formation, use, and adoption of these cultural ideas?

II

SOCIO-POLITICAL CHANGE IN THE MANTARO REGION

3

The Sausa cultural setting

The Sausa

Today the Sausa are the northern population of the Wanka ethnic group. Their ancestors have been residing in the central Andean intermontane region, the Upper Mantaro Valley (*Wanka Wamani*) for at least three millennia, according to archaeological evidence. The people of the district of Jauja, located in the northern section of the wide Mantaro River Valley in the province of Junin, today call themselves the Sausa (or Waycha Wanka: Cerron-Palomino 1972). The Wanka live in the southern two-thirds of the Mantaro Valley. These two groups were joined together in a tripartite political unit by the Inka. Local archaeological continuity suggests that they have considered themselves Sausa and Wanka at least since Middle Horizon times. From historic and ethnographic evidence it seems that the Sausa were distinct from the Wanka. Palomino Flores (1971) notes that there is an Inkaic village in Ayacucho that was made up of both Sausa and Wanka. Linguists also see dialectical Quechua differences between the two groups (Cerron-Palomino 1972) (Figure 1).

Although there were states forming in the central Andes at various times throughout prehistory, statehood was a localized and regionally variable phenomenon. The archaeological evidence suggests that the ancestors of the Sausa did not form a state organization until they were joined to the Inka. Despite the seemingly un-unified situation of the local inhabitants during various expansions of the major pre-Hispanic polities, the Sausa were very much an Andean ethnic group, living by Andean organizing principles, probably interacting with distant polities while developing strong cultural identities within their territory and population.

There are hazy and conflicting myths that tell of Sausa–Wanka origins. What seems clear from the archaeology of the early occupations is that the ancestors of the Sausa and Wanka became settled agriculturalists and herders more recently than in other intermontane locations such as Guitarrero Cave (Lynch 1980; Lynch et al. 1985) in the Callejon de Huaylas and at Pikimachay in the Ayacucho basin (MacNeish et al. 1970; MacNeish 1981). In these two regions people have been using domesticated plants for at least 8,000 years. The archaeological research completed in the Mantaro region and in the puna-plateau zones to the north shows that the precursors of the Wanka were not puna herders who moved out into the arable intermontane valleys, but were local valley gathering and hunting inhabitants who adapted agriculture and herding while occupying hillside and valley settlements at least by Formative times (Tschopik 1946; Fung Pineda 1959; Rick 1980; pers. comm.).

Historically, boundaries existed on all sides of the Sausa, defining their territory and their resource access. They lived in what can be called a compact archipelago, where the major use zones are closely adjacent to each other. Before the Inka conquest the Sausa resided in the three highland zones; the *ceja de montaña* (the upper eastern slopes of the Andes), the intermontane valleys, and the high, cold puna-plateau. No zone is more than 50 km from the central valley.

At least by the Late Intermediate Period the Sausa had a well-defined boundary to the west with the puna-herding Yauyos, separating them from the western coastal valley groups of Huarochiri (Spalding 1984). Hastings, working in the puna and Tarma Valley region directly to the north of Jauja, demonstrates that there was a difference in ceramics and house architecture between the southern Tarama and the Sausa ethnic groups, evident on the Huaricolca puna and Ricran Valleys (1986; 1987: 150–53). Bird (1970) also suggests that the Sausa–Wanka have had a different cultural tradition from their northern neighbors, the Tarama, basing this on the different distributions of maize varieties, different Quechua dialects across the Andes, and weaving patterns. In fact, he claims the Sausa–Tarama Quechua boundary reflects one of the main dialect boundaries of the Andes today.

To the east over the Cordillera Oriental in the upper eastern slopes, Hastings (1986; 1987) has also found that Sausa–Wanka ceramics show up in the Monobamba and Uchubamba Rivers northeast of the Jauja region. From ethnohistoric sources, LeVine (1979) has evidence of Wanka settlements in the upper reaches of the eastern *ceja de montaña* valleys paralleling the full eastern extent of the Sausa and Wanka intermontane territory.

Wanka cultural traits, both modern and prehistoric, extend slightly south of the Mantaro Valley beyond where it narrows into the Mantaro gorge. The Wanka are most similar to these southern neighbors in Huancavelica and Ayacucho. Today the Wanka–Sausa Quechua dialect is the same one that extends south to the northern border of Cuzco province. This dialect is thought to have been the original Quechua, which expanded out from the central coast region prehistorically (Torerro de Cordova 1974). The extent of interaction and political control with the south has not been studied sufficiently for us to understand this central Andean linguistic sphere and its political relations. Anders (1986), from her work in the northern Ayacucho area near Huanta, suggested that some of the later Middle Horizon northern Ayacucho ceramics were similar to the Wanka and Sausa Base Clara that was developing during that period. We also know that Wari-style architecture and ceramics occur at Wari Willka, a ritual site just south of modern Huancayo in the Mantaro Valley (Flores Espinoza 1959; Matos 1968). The Wanka's relationship to the Wari polity is a complex and very interesting archaeological problem, as is the Wanka relationship with Pachacamac. More research on the Wari political interaction north is critical. But it seems that, whatever the exact structure of interaction was with the Sausa–Wanka, the Wari collapse rippled through the Mantaro Valley to cause gaps and realignments within the local political relations.

The Andean pre-Hispanic sequence in overview

The indigenous people experienced a series of pan-Andean cultural and political shifts before the coming of the Spanish. We tend to view this sequence from Rowe's (1960;

1962a) and Lanning's (1967) chronological framework for the Andes. This sequence entailed a series of cultural horizons that identified the widespread social and political developments: namely the Early Horizon (including the earlier Initial Period), the Middle Horizon, and the Late Horizon. Placed between these horizons were intermediate periods, which were seen to reflect dissolutions of these overarching influences allowing for more unique, regional development. While this construct helps the uninitiated, it also forces the viewer to think that all major cultural change occurred in the horizons, which is not true. Each ethnic group created its own history, sometimes incorporating traits from other groups, but always building on its own cultural ingredients, such that every ethnic group today has its own unique variation

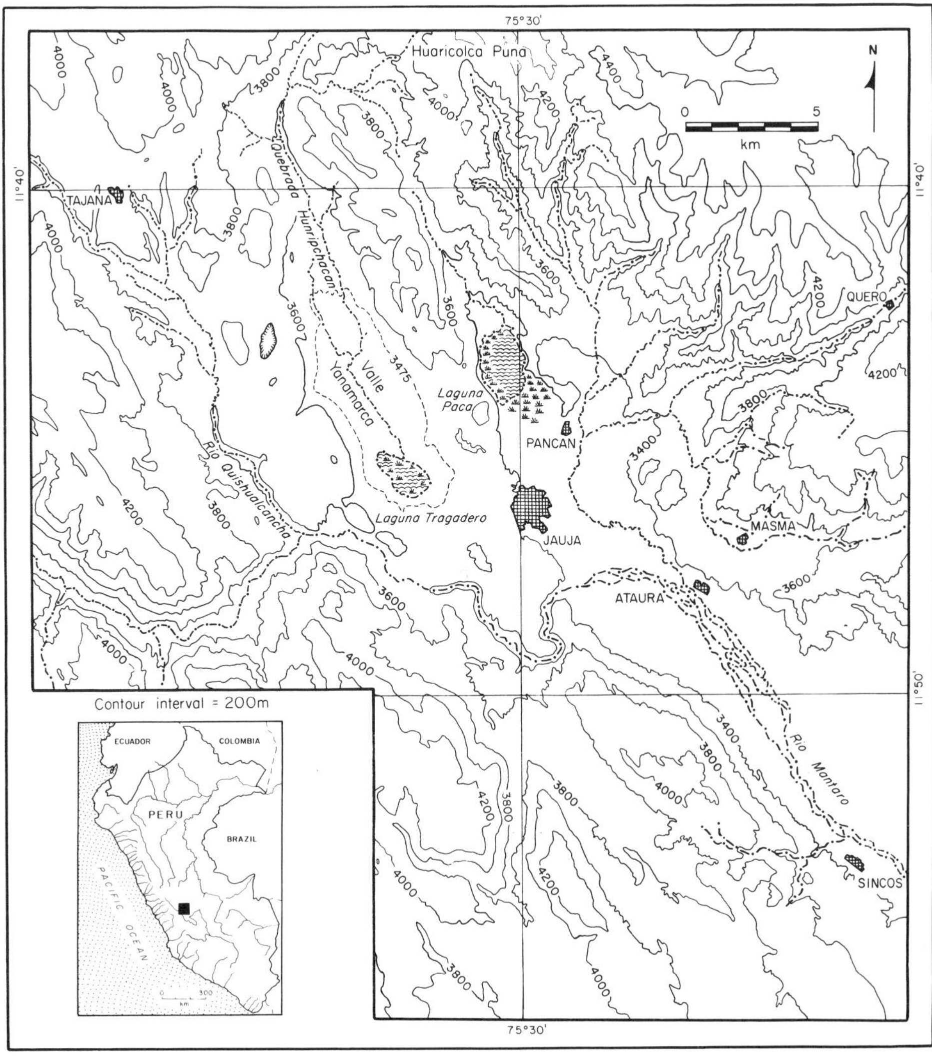

Fig. 1. Map of the Upper Mantaro study area in the central Andes of Peru

of the Andean theme. Every Andean archaeologist must redefine the sequence by the local cultural processes and absolute dates from their specific study area (e.g. Pozorski and Pozorski 1987).

Some scholars now believe that the original font of Andean people (and traits) is the eastern jungle, either down the west coast from Ecuador and into the Andes or westward directly from the jungle. The major symbols seen in the earliest settlements all have a jungle origin (Lathrap 1977). There is, however, also evidence for early coastal dwelling, creating a dynamic between two regions.

With absolute dating we are aware that complex social systems and regional distributions of styles developed on the coast and the eastern slopes of the Andes in the period between 1800 and 900 BC.

The Early Horizon, the Formative Period

Most often dated between 900 and 200 BC, this time is associated with increasing settlement size, the appearance of more elaborate ritual centers, and more distinct cultural differences throughout the region. Most discussions center on the site of Chavín de Huantar, due to its elaborate and large ritual nature and because of early research here (Lumbreras and Amat 1965–66; Rowe 1962b; Tello 1942, 1943), although earlier dates for this symbolic complex have been found at coastal sites: Huaca de los Reyes (Moseley and Watanabe 1974; Pozorski 1975), Sechin Bajo in the Casma coastal valley, Garagay in the Lima Valley (Ravines and Isbell 1975), and at Pacopampa, in the Ancash highlands (Rosas and Shady 1970). The data now suggest that Chavín was more of an amalgamation of previously developed motifs and concepts than an initiator (Burger 1984). It is as if this religious center focused on producing special ritual goods that were based on a series of additional influences through time. These traits spread across the central Andes in developing political leadership, supporting new ritual styles.

The most prominent artifact types and visible symbolic motifs to emanate out of Chavín at these Initial–Early Horizon sites are the jungle animal deities and front-facing human figures. The Amazonian animal figures can be divided into two general types, the harpey eagle, associated with heaven or sky, and the cayman, associated with the earth or underworld (Lathrap 1971). These animals perhaps were symbols of powers linked to rituals including food and drugs.

The second class of representation, the human figure, is often shown front-faced, holding something in each hand. This is thought to represent a deity holding items of symbolic power, or a leader with two lesser attendants, a primary one (larger on the right side) and a secondary one (smaller on the left side). Thus the first deities to be portrayed in the Andes are presented in oppositions, suggesting that the bilateral or dual concept could have been present perhaps as early as the Initial Period, but surely by the Early Horizon.

Human warrior figures can also be seen at these sites in association with captives, either tied up or cut up. They are sometimes portrayed as warriors holding trophy heads in their hands. This frontal human figure has been associated with another of the jungle animals, the feline, thought to represent the mountain deity, manifesting lightning, or more generally the creator deity (Demerest 1981: 50–52; Reinhard 1990).

The highland ritual sites are strategically located near the higher potato growing areas and the still higher puna hunting and herding zones, while also being near the lower eastern-slope valleys directly on a path to the jungle (Kotosh and the Chavín are two such examples). This suggests that there was importance in ecozone meeting places, transport routes, and river confluences (*tinkus*).

Although this "Chavín culture" has been thought to be a civilization expanding out from the site of Chavín, the data suggest more of a spread of ideas associated with exotic jungle goods, such as hallucinogenic plants, maize, textiles, symbolic images, and fertile deities. This ideology may have been used by interest groups throughout the Andes to negotiate positions of difference or consolidate power, as these traits are found in patches across the land during this time, even in Jauja at sites such as Ataura (Matos 1972).

The Early Intermediate Period

The next phase (200 BC to AD 600) demonstrates the lack of similarity across the Andean area. While people living at the time saw the abandonment of many earlier centers, there is also evidence of rapid localized political centralization, especially in three areas, the north coastal Moche Valley (Donnan 1978; Pozorski 1982), the south coastal Paracas culture (Tello and Xesspe 1979) with the Nazca and Ica Valleys (Silverman 1988), and in the Titicaca basin at the site of Pukara and later Tiawanaku (Kidder 1967; Kolata 1982; Mohr Chavez 1988; Mujica 1978). Although there is no major evidence for pan-Andean exchange, we can see evidence of local elaboration at the same magnitude as in the Early Horizon. Elsewhere the populations were, at a different pace, expanding production and exchange, and elaborating social structures that allowed them to form cultural identities and boundaries with their neighbors. Regional ceramic differences are visible in this period, though some of the Andean themes recur. This is the phase we begin with in the Jauja region, although the residents were sedentary farmers in the Early Horizon.

The Middle Horizon

This phase is associated with large interregional polities that expand across the south-central Andes, between the dates of AD 600 and 1000. The focus was in the south with the earlier development of the large ceremonial site of Tiawanaku, on the southern shore of Lake Titicaca (Kolata 1982; 1983; 1986; Ponce Sangines 1977; Posnansky 1945; 1958), and the slightly later Wari culture which is centered in the Ayacucho Valley (Isbell and Schreiber 1978; Isbell 1987; Schreiber 1978). The Lurin Valley on the central coast has evidence of a large ceremonial center, Pachacamac, and the Moche polity shifted into the Lambayeque Valley (Shimada 1978).

Both Tiawanaku and Wari were large urban centers. Tiawanaku had wide trade relations with eastern valley and western coastal valley outposts (Feldman pers. comm.), though not large occupations throughout all of the west coast (Owen pers. comm.). The deity found at both Tiawanaku and Wari is the front-faced human creator god. What the contact was between Wari and Tiawanaku is still much debated, but there was great stylistic affinity between the two polities.

Wari united the whole of the Ayacucho region with strong contacts down into the Nazca Valley (Isbell and Schreiber 1978; Schreiber 1987). Wari's impact on the coast and on up to the Cajamarca Valley is seen in artifacts and architecture found along the central and north coasts, especially the feline and the front-faced human holding a range of items, including potatoes and llamas.

The exact form of the Wari impact beyond the Ayacucho region in the central highlands and along the coast is still much debated. Wari sites are found at places such as Pikillacta in the Cuzco Valley (McEwen 1982; 1990), Wari Willka in the southern Mantaro Valley (Flores 1959), and Viracochapampa in northern Cajamarca (Topic and Topic 1983). Research suggests that these sites were either never occupied, as at Viracochapampa, or were occupied by local inhabitants, as at Wari Willka. Some think that the Wari conquered militarily and economically, reorganizing local production and transport (Isbell and Schreiber 1978; Schreiber 1978). Others think there was only an economic trading influence throughout the Andes (Shady and Ruiz 1979). What is clear from the data at this time is that the Wari impact was patchy across the central and northern Andean landscape, its greatest impact occurring in the modern province of Ayacucho, an impact which did not seem to be solely religious. Not enough research has been done for us to understand the mechanisms of core–periphery interaction at this time.

The evidence that the settlements and architectural traits of the Wari are not found with Wari artifacts supports the idea that local authorities were not interested in or forced to use Wari symbols, but did have some amount of exchange with them. In fact, what evidence we have of Wari presence suggests that the local groups did have trade wares, some stylistic motifs, and, very occasionally, a similarity in architecture. This pattern does not deny that each group, when possible, used the Wari power and economic network for itself politically and socially, but there is little evidence for a broad Wari takeover. This Middle Horizon interaction would have been something the Sausa surely were involved with at some level.

The Late Intermediate Period

This phase (AD 1000 to 1460) was the most stratified epoch for many local Andean polities. Although it is heralded by the arrival of the Chimu on the north coast, it is also labeled by the dissolution of the Wari influence. During these centuries most Andean polities were autonomous, with complex webs of internal alliances and feuds, competitively encroaching on neighbors' territories. This is seen in the defensive settlement locations found throughout the highlands at this time (Bonnier and Rosenberg 1978; Goland 1988; Hyslop 1976; Krzanowski 1977; LeBlanc 1981).

Every highland group had well-defined territories, local *huacas* and *wamanis* (ancestor-land deities), a strong sense of group (*ayllu*), and intensive crop and/or animal production. The impression is that there was a greater sense of local identity and of the differences between each local group than previously. There is no evidence, however, for a pan-Andean political or economic power directing trade or ideological doctrines (artifact styles) spanning the valleys and puna-plateau inhabitants. Throughout the highland areas, this post Wari–Tiawanaku situation fostered rising tensions within each polity, as the threat of encroachment on land or local autonomy from all sides is suggested in the historic documents (Guaman Poma 1944; Murra 1984). The archaeological evidence supports this also. The Middle Horizon symbols, such as the front-faced deity, disappeared.

Although the different groups had their individual artifact styles, exchange patterns, and mountain deities, in general the different Andean populations acted similarly in reaction to the downfall of the Middle Horizon polities, developing, sharing, and using many cultural principles that have continued through the Inka times up to today. One important question about each ethnic group's consolidation is whether this evidence for increasing ethnicity occurred because of the breakup of the Middle Horizon hegemonies, or if these cultural identities had been evolving during the Middle Horizon or before.

Picking up from the Middle Horizon dissolution, local polities consolidated by focusing on warfare. During the later part of the Late Intermediate Period some groups began to expand their local power and territory through attack and trading outposts, as illustrated by the Lupaqa in the Titicaca basin (Hyslop 1976; Julien 1978). It is out of these ever more widening circles of aggression and local hostility that the Inka arose.

The Late Horizon and the Inka empire

Historic documents tell us most about this era that began with the early conquests around AD 1460 and ended in 1532 when the Spanish killed Atawalpa at Cajamarca. Although interpretation of the ethnohistoric documents regarding the length and history of the Inka rulers is debated (Rowe 1946; Zuidema 1964), the archaeological data suggest that the Inka were similar to other highland polities in the Late Intermediate Period, except that they succeeded in expanding, dominating, and reorganizing their neighbors. Just as the Late Intermediate Period Chimu kingdom and the Lupaqa chiefs had alliances and enemies, so did the Cuzco Inka (D'Altroy 1987: 86, 94; Julien 1982; Rostworowski 1977b; Salomon 1986).

Andean cultural principles

When one studies Andean prehistory, an important aspect of the investigation should be the cultural principles that have formed and continue to form the inhabitants' societies. Their continuing existence reflects their active role in forming internal political relations, social and economic negotiations, and power asymmetries that developed at various points in the past. As well as dictating social organizational structures and interactions, these structural patterns organize the cosmology, the perception of and relations to the physical and conceptual landscapes. They give us insight into the likely strategies control enacted in the past.

These unifying principles are important because they may explain and provide meaning to the trajectories and developments seen in a prehistoric sequence, especially during changing social and political relationships. Cultural and symbolic structures shape viewpoints (Douglas 1985). These principles guide people's decisions and behavior. Another way of looking at the role of these principles is to think of them as cultural habits or "a way of doing things" on a group of cultural level (*habitus* as defined by Bourdieu 1977). All groups have options of what to do when faced with any decision, but often they choose one over another out of habit. The constraints on the options have to be borne in mind. The Andean region is a superb place to study such complexes in order to relate them to the prehistoric sequence.

Dual opposition and the "ayllu"

I begin with one extremely important general principle evident in many different aspects of Andean life. It is unifying yet oppositional, as stated in the principles of dual opposition, complementarity, reciprocity, hierarchical ordering, and the mountain metaphor (Bastien 1978; Harris 1978; B. J. Isbell 1978; Platt 1986; Silverblatt 1981, 1987; Spalding 1984; Zuidema 1964). This dual concept has both the sense of opposition in balance but also of bringing two different aspects together to maintain life. Olivia Harris speaks of this more complementary use as *chacawarmi* for the Bolivian Laymi, where the term literally means manwoman (Harris 1978). The marital pair represents the well-being of the entire community, linking the male and the female as a unit while placing focus on the household.

Reciprocity is also embedded in the relationship between land and people, involving the importance of optimizing resources as well as giving back to the land or recycling energy. This exchange is also expressed in the importance of productivity and fecundity of people, animals, and land (Bastien 1978; Skar 1979).

The second principle is more empirical, expressed physically by a sense of place in the world or bounded space, seen in the definition of community or group (*ayllu*). It can be represented by a group's population, territory, or a group's relationship with the ancestors via places in the landscape and through time. The family unit based on the household also can be seen like an *ayllu*, as a social and productive unit that is made up of individuals working together in a designated place.

The *ayllu* is a very Andean concept. Today it denotes any group of people that considers itself a group, from a family to the Peruvian state. In the past, the *ayllu* was a kin-based, neighborhood endogamous group that had control over a certain area of land. Today, it seems to be more specifically linked to a territory and the concept of sharing work. The residents of these neighborhoods not only share and distribute land amongst themselves, they also share *ayni*, work exchange that helps each family in turn. There can be a series of *ayllu* in one village. Skar (1979) uses the expression for a small group of kin who interact often. The *ayllu* can also form one half of a village moiety or *barrio* (B. J. Isbell 1978). The two barrios (moieties) are called upper (*hanan*) and lower (*hurin*) barrios. Both Platt (1986) and Bastien (1978) use *ayllu* for a multi-settlement group that shares in marriage, production, and ritual exchange based on earth shrines in common.

So even in *ayllu* there is this sense of dual balance that joins together two different and sometimes competing entities. These different cultural aspects continue to stress dualism in Andean culture, manifested as far back as the Early Horizon and used by groups since then in different ways for different purposes, not just in the Late Horizon deity of the Inka, Viracocha.

"Yanantin" and hierarchy

Both dual opposition and *ayllu* operate in the Andean concept of *yanantin*; equal but different parts, opposite entities working together but with a tension that can breed inequality (Platt 1986). This concept defines a person's position within society by his relationship to others, in ever larger opposing groups. Although dualities have been identified throughout the world to a greater or lesser extent (Lévi-Strauss 1963), the Andean version is coupled with a sense of balanced power opposition, and hierarchy (B. J. Isbell 1978; Palomino Flores 1971; Platt 1986; Silverblatt 1981; Skar 1979; 1981). This opposition operates at all levels of social, spatial, and religious life. Because of its dynamic qualities, it often seems that *yanantin* includes opposite meanings within the same definition. I prefer to see it more as an active principle that can maintain balance yet can also be the locus for inequality. It is interesting that Quechua has a word with this combination of meanings.

Scholars have noted that there are many divisions operating in the Andean world, twos, threes, fours, fives, and tens (Anders 1986; Bastien 1978; Palomino Flores 1971; Zuidema 1964). However, the fundamental division seems to be two (and four), creating a symmetrical, balanced tension. This duality is seen most clearly in the community division of two moieties, allowing for differences to be expressed within the community through competition, yet simultaneously providing a sense of wholeness or boundedness to the community. Duality is also expressed in marriage, as a male–female relationship represents difference, mutual respect, and competition (Harris 1978; Platt 1986; Skar 1979).

Today this opposing principle divides political, social, religious, and general maintenance activities of a settlement between the two halves of the population, the upper and the lower. This spatial dualism includes an ordering or ranking of the two groups, as the words imply. The barrios are often located higher and lower on a hillside, are larger and smaller, or have a slightly different rank and status. Zuidema (1964) and W. Isbell (1978) discuss how Inkaic Cuzco was divided into two barrios, the upper being uphill and above where the two rivers came together, while the lower was downslope. Four is expressed both in the Wari and the Inka state political divisions, *Tawantinsuyu* (Anders 1986; Zuidema 1964).

Opposition and ranking is also enacted in the traditional political village hierarchy (*varayoq*), that today (that is before the Sendero Luminoso military conflict) maintains social principles and traditions in some Andean communities (B. J. Isbell 1978; Silverblatt 1981; Skar 1979). Native leadership has many civic responsibilities: to organize community work, to judge and punish wrongdoers, to maintain peace in the village, to organize and perform religious ceremonies, to regulate communications with the supernatural, to allocate land and water, and to act as war leaders (*cinche*). Along these avenues, leaders have the responsibility to create and maintain the group yet also they have the potential to initiate inequality, claiming greater wealth and power, economically, politically, and socially.

In 1967 Billie Jean Isbell (1978) studied this type of political–religious organization in the village of Chuschi, Ayacucho. There she found a ranking of increasingly powerful positions within each of the two barrios. The two barrio hierarchies (*taksa*) are under, yet intertwined with, an overarching town leadership hierarchy (*hatun*), forming a power triad (1978: 85–86). In this system a person progresses through a series of positions, alternating between the barrio and the village leadership, finally becoming the village mayor (*hatun alcalde*). After this position is held, an individual retires out of the system as a prestigious person, an elder or "completed adult" (Bastien 1978: xvii). Prestige is gained through service to the community; the families that have worked their way through the cycle are considered wealthy. Even if they do not have many goods, their homes have evidence of dealing with more than average levels of activity. This is an excellent illustration of the importance of giving and receiving while occupying a leadership position (Chapter 1). These leadership positions are a place for negotiation of rights and privileges but also of obligations.

In this concept of power and hierarchy, power today is dispersed among a series of positions, always in opposition to another, and is never centralized in one position. This is accomplished in Chuschi not only through the two leadership systems that form a triad of positions (two barrios and one village leader), but, in addition, through other positions in the village. Most important are the guardians of the puna herds, the irrigation water, and the agricultural zones, each with their own power over resources, rituals, and people's activities.

This triad in community leadership is seen also in early historic documents in the Inka organization of conquered polities. As D'Altroy summarizes (1987: 92), the key local political positions were the paramount lord, the second lord, and the lesser elite head. The paramount lord headed the upper of the two paired divisions and spoke for both in external relations, the latter two headed each of the two lower divisions (Cock 1977; Rostworowski 1977a). Because the system seemed to be so well organized, it is thought that such political structures were operating in the Andes before the Inka conquest.

For Chuschi, this system expresses the principle of *yanantin*, as each position in the hierarchy has a counterpart. And this hierarchy is in the form of dispersed dynamic power, as no person can take over a position of power for more than one term of office but must move into the next position. It represents the reciprocity and circular exchange of *ayni*, as kinspeople and neighbors of leaders help in the religious ceremonies that the leaders officiate, gaining prestige by their association.

As the leaders work through their obligations, receiving help and gaining prestige, they are creating relationships which allow them to gather increased wealth not only in prestige but also materially. This structure also reinforces the closed territoriality or boundedness of the group by requiring leaders to reside in one of the two barrios. They are also required to uphold the traditional ways of life by completing their work obligations and work the land with proper respect for the spirits. They are the moral leaders.

Ancestors form the link between the living people and the land (Zuidema 1973). The dead return to the local mountain deity (*wamani*) and reside in the mountain inside the earth. Everyone is born out of the earth and returns to the earth. The ancestors in this way become almost the earth itself from which crops are grown, as they are the mediators between the living and the mountain spirits. They therefore must be remembered and considered in all important decisions. Ancestors are in fact still part of the process of life for they affect the living and are an important link in the recycling of energy between the spirits, the land, and the living. Therefore part of production and productivity in the annual harvest includes feeding the ancestors, the spirits, and the earth to recycle what the earth feeds the people (Bastien 1978: 193). The mountains, as homes of deities, are ranked by size. The larger peaks influence a larger number of villages, unifying the people by their common veneration (Reinhard 1990; Zuidema 1978).

Hierarchy and balanced opposition are seen in other relationships with the land. Chuschi landscape is divided into village = civilized, and outside the village = wild. The village and the agricultural fields surrounding the village are cultured, tame, controlled, and civilized by humans; the higher puna plateau is savage and wild (B. J. Isbell 1978). This difference condones different actions in the two zones; for example, more powerful yet risky religious rituals occur in the wild areas.

These spatial principles outlining differential power are also involved in the sources of water and the location of spirits. Water comes from springs and lakes in the puna and mountains. These water sources are the homes of spirits and deities. To use the water, especially for irrigation, rituals are undertaken to make and clean the ditches. Typically, two main irrigation ditches from the uplands are joined near the village in a unifying *tinku* (see below).

Jennette Sherbondy (1982), writing about pre-Hispanic Cuzco, B. J. Isbell (1978), writing about a modern village in Ayacucho, and William Mitchell (1976), writing about the modern village of Quinoa in Ayacucho, note how the social organization of a village is manifested in its local irrigation system. The concern is not simply to manage the ditches and their use. Ditches have symbolic and structuring implications. For the Cuzco Inka, irrigation ditches divide up the different social and political groups by the spatial distribution of the canals (Sherbondy 1982; Zuidema 1986). In Chuschi the two main irrigation canals are maintained by the two barrios, and their place of juncture represents their joining together in the worship of all the ancestors. The head alcaldes organize the cleaning of the canals for each barrio annually (*yarqa aspiy*) (B. J. Isbell 1978: 139). Participation in this *faena* labor by each household is obligatory, where one male from every household in the barrio must work. This labor force is larger than is required for the job, but it brings the households together, building on reciprocity and service to maintain the community, as well as reinforcing the concept of obligation and responsibility.

The household is the social and productive unit in Andean society. It can be composed of various members, but always includes a married couple with their unmarried children and perhaps one or more elder relatives. Individuals receive land and animals bilaterally, that is, either all children inherit alike from each parent or the males inherit equally from their father and the females inherit equally from their mother. This bilaterality allows for some degree of autonomy after marriage for each spouse. Marriage is the most important change of status in a person's life. It is the time when one begins a new household and becomes an adult in the community, both actually and symbolically. With adulthood begins responsibility for public works participation in exchange for receiving a portion of the communal land for household production. This household structure was important for Inka and earlier state labor taxation, which organized the labor taxes (*m'ita*) of the conquered populace by household, requiring so much labor from a household, no matter how large that household was (D'Altroy 1981; Rowe 1946; Smith 1989). These households were then grouped into sequentially larger groups (Julien 1982).

Modern social–religious examples express and play off the tensions to maintain balance within hierarchy through the use of reciprocity. These same principles can be seen in historic documents, as hinted at in the Inka use of ranked triads, households, and dual *ayllu* structures in settlements. Irene Silverblatt (1981, 1987), studying the position of women in Andean society, has found a variation in this hierarchy. She terms it *conquest hierarchy* (1981: 83), derived from Zuidema's work (1964: 40). This structure ranks two opposing groups, made up of the original inhabitants, the indigenous members of a community and the foreigners, the conquerers (in the past the Spanish, today the mestizos and school teachers). In this dichotomy, both groups have different types of power, but the foreigners have more. In this hierarchy, the relationship is unequal and ranked, not just opposed. Silverblatt (1981) finds this principle of the conquest hierarchy in many aspects of colonial life, including christian–indigenous rituals. Perhaps this was a method highland people had for explaining (naturalizing and legitimating) new positions in political life. Was this a new concept that came in with the Spanish conquest or did the people simply take a principle they had used amongst themselves, like the sequence of mountains and deities, and convert it to the Inka system and then to the Spanish system?

Rostoworowski (1987) notes that some words from the Muchik (the north coastal Moche Valley area, home of the Moche and Chimu) that connote superiority and subordination were brought into the Quechua language, probably by the Inka. The important Quechua word *yanantin* includes the word *yana* which means servant (Holguin 1952: 363). Another clue comes from Olivia Harris's (pers. comm.) Ayamara work, where she says that people in Potosi Bolivia associate the major break between their better past and the less good present condition with the time of the Inka conquest, the Spanish merely being more of the same. This suggests that at least by the Late Horizon, highland residents knew political hierarchy. These hints at pre-Inkaic hierarchy in politics, religion, and geographical perception suggest that it was probably diversely manifested well before the arrival of the Inka.

Rituals and feasting

Rituals reflect underlying social orders (Leach 1965: 16) and in the Andes the rituals connected with the ditches, the water, and the tilled land are clear examples of the land–deity reciprocity principle. In Chuschi, household heads direct rituals at the springs' and lakes' sources to appease the *wamanis* and water spirits for the future well-being and fertility of the group. The *wamanis* control water, and as all animals "belong" to the *wamanis*, they must be thanked and appeased for being able to tend the animals (Flannery et al. 1989). In this ritual the household head takes a cloth filled with a series of items to be offered at the spirits' source lake, with eating and drinking done afterwards at home. This food consumption always includes the symbolically charged maize beer (*chicha*) and coca chewing. The items used in this land and water blessing ritual mentioned by Isbell remind me of Bastien's field ritual where all of the different land zones including the jungle and the coast must be represented: small stone animal figurines (*illas*), maize meal, sea shells, a red mineral, a small knife, and crude gold (a local mineral), *chicha*, cane alcohol, tropical seeds including coca seeds (*Erythroxylum coca*), little red seeds from the jungle (*Cytharexylorherrerae*), and dark brown llama fat (B. J. Isbell 1978: 155-56). Larger rituals, relating to the various barrio and village shrines, are organized by the village leaders, giving them the responsibility to maintain the productive energy of the community. These entail food offerings but also feasting of the populace which often is organized by the leaders.

In the villages today, as in the past, agriculture, productivity, and fecundity are the focal points of most rituals. Many of the rituals, associated with the land, the irrigation canals, and the animals, point out the desire for regeneration, replacement, and optimizing (maintaining) the natural resources of the territory. Sherbondy (1982: 22) illustrated the integrative role of the irrigation canals in the social and political system. It is not simply a matter of ensuring fertility and yield in order to stay alive that underlies these rituals of regeneration, but it is also a sense of productivity and balance through the recycling of goods and energy; recycling through the ancestors, the earth, the water, the plants, the animals, and the humans. Rituals for the *wamani* are also hierarchical as larger mountains receive more people's worship and larger multi-valley and multiple *ayllu* festivals (Poole 1984). In some ways these modern rituals at the juncture of two zones are reminiscent of early centers like Kotosh and Chavín.

All of these rituals associated with the community and its resources, while integrative, also provide a locus for the development of inequalities in access and production. Leaders, while organizing and completing rituals, communal work events, and communal land division, can manipulate families' access to land, the extraction of goods to host community feasts, as well as the use of labor for different projects (*faena* or warfare). In some circumstances these structures help to maintain the balance of people to their land and to each other, yet at the same time they provide the loci for change as outcomes can be altered with each new enactment. Important to all of these rituals is not only the offering to the deities, but also the feasting of the participants.

Tinku

Silverblatt's (1987) colonial study also mentions another important Andean principle that links into both the dual opposition and the bounded group principles: the ritual war, *tinku* (or *ch'axwa*: Platt 1966). Above I presented some evidence of warfare, warriors, and conflict in the prehistoric sequence. With careful reading of historical documents, ethnographies, or a recent visit to Peru, one finds that the concept of war has been and is an active principle today in village life. It is based on the principle of conflict as a way of maintaining and challenging unequal power relationships. Silverblatt shows this in the act of conquest which itself creates a hierarchy, but there are other equally explicit examples.

Tinku in this setting is an actual confrontation between two groups, where words and blows are exchanged antagonistically yet in controlled ritual time and space (Platt 1986: 239; Zuidema 1964). *Tinku* can occur between all structurally opposed Andean groups: two sets of communities (Alencastre Gutiérrez and Dumézil 1953), two barrios within a village (Platt 1986), two groups within one *ayllu*, herders versus agriculturalists (Silverblatt 1987), and even males versus females within one *ayllu* (Bastien 1978; Platt 1986). These rituals may take place annually, biannually, or irregularly. Exactly what instigates them has not been explored sufficiently in the literature, but they are considered to be a legitimate form of resolving conflicts. The warfare itself has programmed social actions with rules of conduct for advancing, resting, and injuring opponents. *Tinku* expresses hostility on both sides, but the victors of the battle, that is, those who inflicted more damage, in some cases captured more women, or even killed more, gain a good prognosis for success in the coming year and sometimes even gain new land. They are often considered to be regular inter-group (inter-*ayllu*) tension relievers, settling differences about cumulative problems or encroachment (Arnold pers. comm.).

In a *tinku*, although eating, singing, and yelling may begin the ritual day, individuals use slings (*hondas*), wooden sticks, mits made of llama hide filled with sand, or maize stalks to attack the opposing group, often causing damage and even death (Alencastre Gutiérrez and Dumézil 1953: 28; Bastien 1978; Delgado pers. comm.). But even in the instances where death occurs, ethnographers report that there is no retaliation, or further reaction to the event after the day is over. Until the next *tinku* there is no resentment or aggression towards those specific opponents. In the one description where women were captured, they were not molested, but could be married in the proper way later if the capturers so desired (Alencastre Gutiérrez and Dumézil 1953: 27).

The fact that ritualized war exists in the Andes, using only pre-colonial weapons, supports the notion that overt conflict has continued to be a principle of Andean social action for a long time. An important point learned from the documentary and modern evidence about *tinku* is that it not only seems to allow for contestation over and gain of access to resources and political power but also it is a strategy for societal maintenance between and within groups that do not have an overarching centralized political authority. These *tinku* tie in well with pre-Hispanic Andean war motifs. In addition to the evidence of battles between settlements over land, ritual battles have been accepted as a legitimate way of interacting and dealing with tension within and between communities. As seen in the Inka's expansive use of warfare, they can be also a way to gain power and resources. These more aggressive battles, beyond the bounds of *tinku*, are called *ch'axwa*, or fierce warfare (Platt 1986). Such battles are in the style of the Inka; no attempt is made to maintain balance, and conquest is the goal.

Hierarchical principles in the Andes

The existence of hierarchy as a fundamental Andean principle is intriguing in the debate over whether Andean cosmological principles are based on hierarchy or on egalitarianism (Murra 1970; Schaedel 1988). This issue has many implications in the pre-Hispanic study of political change. Hierarchical structures are discussed in the ethnohistoric documents as part of the prehistoric religious practices (Avila 1939). Did the Inka build their hierarchy on an extant structure or did they have to create hierarchy out of a nonauthoritarian world? They certainly had a hierarchical system in place when the Spanish arrived.

Andean people have a pantheon of deities (*wamanis*) located in mountain peaks, stones, lightning, springs, and river confluences. The different mountain spirits are ranked according to their elevation. High peaks delegate duties to the subordinate mountain deities of lower elevations (B. J. Isbell 1978: 151; Zuidema 1978). These mountains are located in the landscape and their position and elevation dictate their relations to the local inhabitants (Salomon pers. comm.). The most important deity will be the highest mountain peak, visible throughout a region. It will be important for the many villages who can see it. The lower peaks will be important to fewer people, and finally, each *ayllu* has its own *wamani*.

Such an important spirit was Pariacaca, for example, the tallest glaciated peak in the central Cordillera Occidental. It was associated with and east of Pachacamac, a religious site on the central coast (Avila 1939; Bastien 1978; Demerest 1981; Spalding 1984; Zuidema 1964). The origin of this mountain deity is unknown, but we know that Pachacamac was a religious center from the Early Intermediate Period onwards. Pariacaca also occurs in myths associated with the Middle Horizon–Wari site Wari Willka in the southern Mantaro Valley. This mountain spirit has been associated with thunder, hail, and felines (evident before Chavín on the coast), as well as a series of passes, lakes, and rivers. The feline (*ccoa*) is thought to be a servant of thunder and lightning (Tello 1960) and therefore connected to the mountain deity itself (Mishkin 1946). It was such earth deities that were in opposition to the sun god Inti at various times during the Inka empire, placing local leadership below the sun (Demerest 1981).

For the Inka, an overarching state religion would have been essential to ideologically unify a very dispersed population, to reaffirm a hierarchy above the local deities, and to create a power that placed rulers at the top while justifying their position. It makes sense therefore that such a structure should be generated out of earlier cultural–religious traditions. We know that the Spanish looked for an overarching deity like that of their own religion. There is still discussion about the importance of the sun god and its existence before the Inka conquest, therefore. Documentary and archaeological evidence identify more than one Andean religious tradition and many different deities, but with few direct links to the sun image. Inti perhaps was a new creation of a myth perpetuated by the Inka to differentiate themselves from earlier ideologies, and perhaps remained only one deity of many.

Andean opposition goes further in Inka state religion. The main opposition to Inti in the Inka empire was Viracocha, a creator god (Demerest 1981; Zuidema 1974: 166).

While amorphous and ever present, Viracocha is associated with the coastal center of Pachacamac. Viracocha and the site Pachacamac represent the earth and water, while the sun, Inti, signifies the sky and fire (Zuidema 1964: 165). So, even in the Inkaic pantheon, there is dualism and confrontation between deities. This opposition could have initiated many dynamic political negotiations among the provincial Inka and the leaders of the "state" religion.

Different colonial writers have stated that one or the other of these two deities was the main Inkaic god (Avila 1939 [1598]; Pachacuti Yamqui 1950; Sarmiento 1947). The controversy exists because both deities (and their various manifestations) were important to the Inka, and were used for different political purposes, somehow both surviving within this tension. A further hint at the importance of this Andean duality was that Pachacamac was not destroyed by the Inka but continued to be an important oracle until the Spanish arrived (Demerest 1981; Patterson 1986). Why did the Inka allow the persistence of a Viracocha temple on the coast and actually help maintain its religious center, while clearly destroying many other religious centers and taking local *wamanis* to Cuzco? Probably political competition was involved. Perhaps this religious opposition expressed a political conflict that was ongoing throughout the empire.

Summary

We can see from the ethnographic examples and colonial documents that the organizing principles discussed here were operating in the Late Horizon. There is a sense from the archaeological sequence of even older uses of many of these principles: reciprocity with the ancestors, negotiation and tensions between oppositions both unequal and balanced, divisions of society linked to the divisions of the landscape, and finally and perhaps most important for social archaeology the concept of hierarchy, as seen in the triad of Chuschi's governing body or in the front-facing human figure who holds two attendants, seen at Chavín, Pukara, and Tiawanaku, or the Inka's local governing triad. Tilting balanced opposition towards hierarchy is likely to have been a major locus for power manipulation as this human image entered into the pantheon, at least since the Early Horizon Period. There are many manifestations of this motif in the Andes, which again suggests its long existence. Since this concept allows for and embues power, its recall could have legitimized stratification and even state formation. By following key principles and traits such as these through the archaeological record, we might begin to gain an understanding of how the local groups initiated and contested their claim to difference and hierarchy.

These oppositions, blatantly unequal in some instances, and balanced and regulating in others, can form an important nexus for social and political change within Andean society. I would propose that it is in situations where these oppositions are manifested in the archaeological record that we can look for active negotiation of power and political change.

While scholars discuss these principles differently, most agree that the interplay of concepts forms the culture of the farming/herding communities today and that this has been developing over millennia. It is because of these principles, in fact, that we can track the pre-Hispanic sequence and define Andean culture, not just because most people live in steep mountainous territory, but because of their relationship to and perception of the world around them (Bastien 1978; Zuidema 1964, 1986).

4

Upper Mantaro archaeological settlement and site data

Local settlement patterns

Settlement patterns are important data in the study of prehistoric social change and economic/political questions. In the broadest sense they display changes and continuities within a region's population. Although shifts in population do not always correlate with social hierarchies and the development of political change, settlement locations and demographics do express some basic changes in people's interests and orientations (Bintliff 1982; Flannery 1976; Green et al. 1978; Hodder and Orton 1976; Renfrew and Shennan 1982; Wright and Johnson 1975). Specific residence locations will be influenced by a combination of economic, exchange, religious, social, historical, and political factors.

Information on the Upper Mantaro settlement pattern is based on the previous archaeological work done in the valley (Browman 1970; Fung Pineda 1959; Kroeber 1944; Lavallée 1967; Lumbreras 1957, 1959; Matos 1959; 1966; 1972; 1978; Parsons 1976; Parsons and Hastings 1977; Parsons and Matos 1978; Rowe 1944: 54), on LeBlanc's 1977 and 1978 field work, refining Parsons and Matos's settlement and ceramic work (LeBlanc 1981), and also on more recent material collected by the Upper Mantaro Archaeological Research Project (UMARP) in 1982, 1983, and 1986 (Earle et al. 1987; Hastorf et al. 1989). As LeBlanc's study spanned the Wanka I (approximately a.d. 1000–1300), Wanka II (a.d. 1300–1460), and Wanka III (a.d. 1460–1532) phases, she used ceramic seriation and site architecture to discuss the onset of social hierarchy. A slightly earlier time frame will be studied here, including the two earlier phases, the Early Intermediate Period (EIP, approximately 200 b.c.–a.d. 600), and the Middle Horizon (MH, approximately a.d. 600–1000). These earlier phases are critical in the local cultural development, as noted in the previous chapter, for they include the cultural templates (Barthes 1973), and the cultural strategies that are elaborated on in later times.

The results of this recent settlement analysis are listed in Appendix A with the number of sites and their size by phase. Site location by time period can also be seen in the sequence of maps in this chapter. Parsons and Hastings site size estimates have been refined from UMARP's more recent analysis and these estimates are presented here (Borges 1988; Hastorf et al. 1989).

In the Early Horizon Period (Formative, 900–200 b.c.), we are now aware of at least twelve sites in the northern Mantaro region (Borges 1988; Hastorf et al. 1989). Both Matos (1971) and Browman (1970) mention sites from this time period in the southern Mantaro Valley. In general, the sites are just off the valley floors on the lower hillsides and knolls, ranging in size from 0.4 to 6.0 ha. Rectangular adobe structures approximately 4.5 meters wide with white plaster surfaces have been uncovered at the site of San Juan Pata (J223) (Garcia Soto 1987), while Browman found circular structures in the southern valley (1970). This long time span has been divided up into two phases named after ceramic types Pirwapukio and Cochachongos (Browman 1970). The Cochachongos ceramics, represented in the northern valley, suggest a similarity with the pan-Andean "Chavinoid" types, of thinly painted or engraved burnished wares (pebble polished light buff Cochachongos and plain brown Pirwapukio) (Browman 1970; LeCount 1987; Matos 1972). The ceramics consist of bowls (serving, not cooking), small jars, and bottles. Much work needs to be done in this time period before we can discuss it in the same detail as is possible for the later sequence.

Early Intermediate Period/Middle Horizon phase

The EIP/MH phase has the first substantial visible population in the northern Sausa area (Matos 1971; 1978; Parsons 1976). The long time span has been divided up into early EIP, called Huacrapukio I; late EIP, Huacrapukio II; and the Middle Horizon, also called Wanka Ia. Huacrapukio I phase is now dated to b.c. 200–a.d. 550; Huacrapukio II/MH to a.d. 550–900 (1420 ± 40 BP, QL-4204) calibrated to AD 637 (604–655); 1380 ± 210 BP, I-12-737, calibrated to AD 654 (430–880); 1280 ± 40 BP, QL-4203, calibrated to AD 689 (672–777); with the MH–Wanka Ia dating to 1707 ± 40 BP, QL-4204, calibrated to AD 980 (899–1008) (Stuiver and Reimer 1986). These locally derived cultural phases do not fit very neatly into the Andean sequence of Chapter 3, but I continue to use the common terminology, EIP and MH to identify the general time span of the sites. Because of the limited detailed excavation dating to this time and the not yet resolved dating and microseriation, I have grouped Huacrapukio II and the Middle Horizon into one phase, which I call the EIP/MH (AD 550–900).

Recent ceramic work on this time period by Borges (1988) suggests that Huacrapukio I is defined by the presence of pink paste bowls and Huacrapukio II by Wanka bowls (Borges 1988: 28). All of the sites from this time have a high percentage of Huacrapukio and/or San Juan Pata ceramics. Seriation finds that these two wares overlap geographically and temporally in the region, with San Juan Pata ceramics more common in the southern part of the study region, and Huacrapukio ceramics in the north, in the Yanamarca and Paca Valleys (Borges 1988). Until these pottery types can be more precisely located in time, we cannot unravel this period further.

There is evidence in the Huacrapukio I phase of approximately forty settlements being built on the hilltops and slopes that surround the small tributary valleys, especially concentrating in the Yanamarca Valley. Associated with Huacrapukio II ceramics, thirty-nine sites have been identified with a 40 percent abandonment of previous sites and a shift downslope as the new EIP settlements concentrate in the valleys and their edges. There continues to be a population concentration in the Yanamarca Valley with less in other tributary valleys. Twenty-two of the thirty-nine sites are in and around the Yanamarca Valley while the Paca, Masma, and western Mantaro Valley uplands each have only two or three settlements. In the MH, the population continues to be focused around the valleys but, because we can only define this period by an addition of Wari ceramics and subtle changes in the local ceramic frequencies, at this time we can only identify eighteen MH sites although we know there were many more sites occupied at that time (Borges 1988).

As seen in the settlement distribution in Figure 2, despite the collapsing of these subphases, the majority of the thirty-nine EIP/MH sites are located at the edge of the valleys near running water or springs that outcrop at the base of the limestone hills (Matos 1978). The sites are small hamlets and villages. Ranging between 0.4 and 18 ha, averaging 4.2 ha in size. The largest sites are found in the Yanamarca Valley, suggesting its early political importance. The sites occur between 3,400 and 3,700 meters in elevation, at the upper limits of modern maize production. This distribution implies that the population gradually dispersed along the ecotone between the two productive microzones: the long fallow tuber cropping-grazing hills and uplands (*sallqa* or *suni*) and the lower frost-free valley lands (*quichwa*).

We know from the ceramic analysis that settlement abandonment and relocation occurred during this period, while some sites were occupied continuously. Through time the settlements grew slightly in size, suggesting population aggregation, in addition to the creation of new settlements. In general, the sites are poorly preserved on the surface, which makes the study of their internal organization as well as size changes through time impossible without excavation.

At the beginning of the EIP several household traits change. The house structures are circular and measure up to 6 meters across (Hastorf et al. 1989; Woodburn 1987). They are made out of two types of adobe, small bricks and large *tapia*-like (mud-packed) slabs, stacked on top of large foundation stones. There is evidence of walled compounds enclosing work areas and small wall partitions. Structures bond and abut the outside walls as their doors open onto the central patio space. The basic lay-out is quite similar to that seen throughout the remaining sequence and is thought to represent a domestic unit (household, family), the basic production and consumption unit in Andean society (Figueroa 1982; Netting et al. 1984; Skar 1979; Spalding 1984: 25; Wilk 1989).

Domestic camelid and guinea pig bones are regularly found in the EIP/MH deposits, as are hunted animals: deer, vicuna, frogs, and fish (Sandefur 1988a; pers. comm.). The lithic tool assemblage is very simple, consisting of mainly unifacial flakes for cutting and chopping, hoe blades for digging, points for piercing and hunting, and mortars, pestles, rocker grinders, and batanes (slab grinders) for grinding soft substances, especially food (Russell 1988a). From the survey data, projectile points begin their steady decrease in frequency through time from the Huacrapukio II phase on, parallel with the wild hunted animal decline in the record.

The ceramic assemblage is dominated by small serving bowls, storage, and boiling jars. The jars often have lugs on them for aid in hanging and transport. Some pots in the assemblage suggest cooking over an open fire (LeCount 1987). The ceramic data suggest that while individual sites used local temper and paste for the production of serving bowls, Huacrapukio jar temper was more similar across the sites, and was probably widely exchanged between these northern Mantaro settlements. These Huacrapukio ceramics are well painted in general. The Early Intermediate assemblages include the Huacrapukio, pebble-polished cream wares, Andesite, San Juan Pata, Wanka, and pink paste wares (LeCount 1987). Through time the cream slips with painted camelid designs are replaced by other bowl types; coarse mica, painted Wanka wares, and the orange paste bowl associated with Middle Horizon (Borges 1988). The Huacrapukio jars gradually drop in frequency through this EIP/MH sequence. This ceramic tradition changes in the next cultural phase.

From the excavated deposits, there are front-facing human male figurines, often carrying knives and trophy heads, reminiscent of the pan-Andean creator/warrior image. By the end of the MH these human figurines drop out and camelid figurines become common, suggesting a shift in ritual focus to local fertility deities. The camelids are very fat or pregnant and often smiling, reminiscent of stone *illas* used

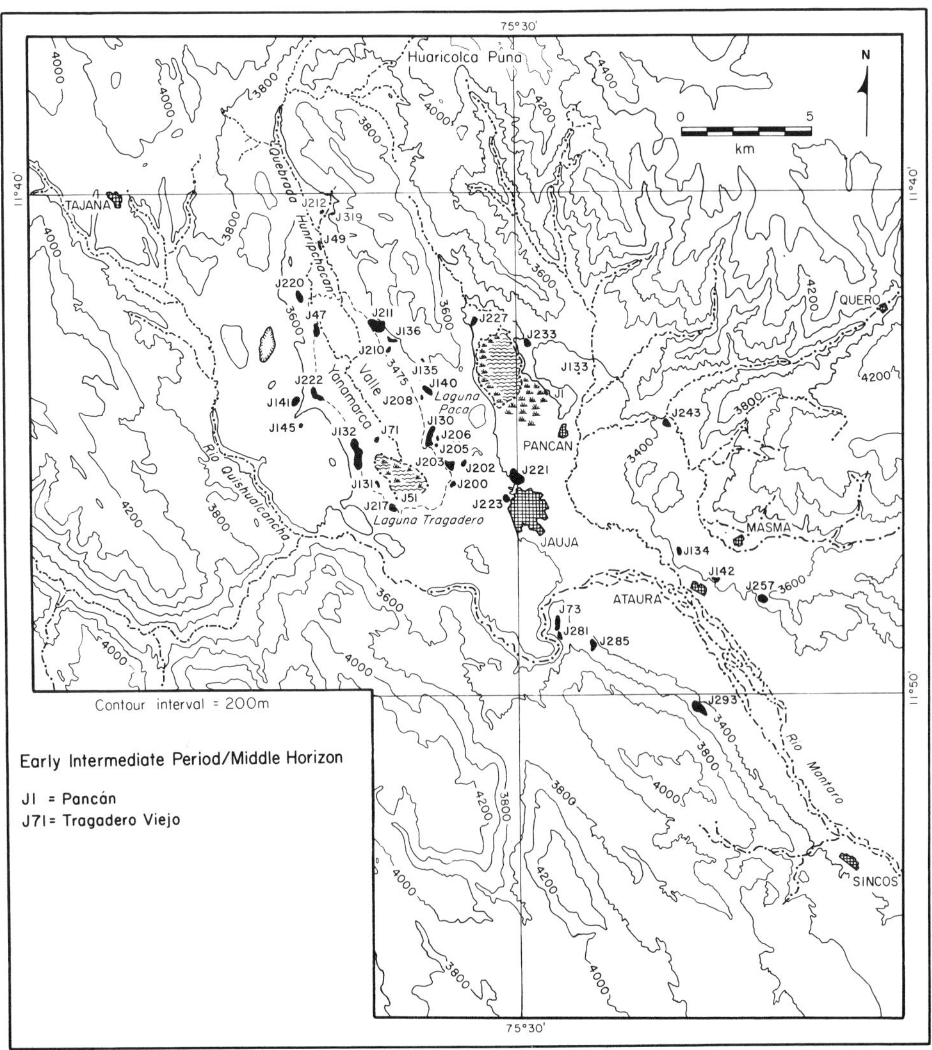

Fig. 2. The Early Intermediate Period/Middle Horizon settlement pattern

today in family-based fertility and planting rituals in the south central Andes (Allen 1988; Bastien 1978; B. J. Isbell 1978). The paint and surface treatment are purely local and the figurines are found in many contexts, but especially in the structure foundations. These figurines drop out of habitation deposits by the end of Wanka I.

There is no evidence for the direct incorporation of this region into the Wari state, although we know Wari was a dominant political force in the next highland area to the south (Isbell and Schreiber 1978; Schreiber 1987). What we can see in the local MH settlement pattern shows no evidence of major demographic or economic changes, with a continuing trend of the larger sites located in lower elevations. In this northern area, there is also no evidence of Wari architecture, most often used to identify Wari presence or major influence (Schreiber 1978; pers. comm.), nor is there much evidence of Wari ceramics. The effect the Wari political or economic force might have had on the residents was probably periodic trade with vague allegiance, perhaps for future consolidation. However much the Wari interacted with the Sausa, their eventual dissipation did affect their world as seen in the next cultural periods. The next phase shows the local reaction to this pan-Andean breakup.

Wanka I Period

The first phase in the Late Intermediate Period (a.d. 900–1300), locally called the Wanka I (or Wanka Ib) in the Jauja region, is identified by a series of new cultural traits in ceramic styles, in the lithic assemblage, in new densities of house structures, and in increasingly defended site locations (Borges 1988; Earle et al. 1980; Hastorf et al. 1989; LeBlanc 1981; Parsons 1976; Parsons and Hastings 1977; Russell 1988b). This phase is important because we see evidence of increasingly restricted interactions that suggest a process of political and economic constriction that prefigures the radical settlement reorganization of the next phase. This period is dated by two absolute dates: 1020 ± 80 BP, I-12-739 (calibrated to AD 1012 (range 960–1039) from Pancán (J1)) and 890 ± 90 BP, I-12-736 (calibrated to AD 1163 (range 1024–1245) from Ushnu (J49) (Stuiver and Reimer 1986)). In addition, the phase is bracketed by absolute dates from earlier and later phases.

Figure 3 displays this settlement pattern of 43 fairly dispersed sites located mainly on the low ridges and slopes above the valleys (e.g. J38). There is an even greater sense of valley clustering than before, many of the larger EIP/MH sites having been abandoned. Thirty percent of the earlier sites continue to be occupied. The new sites also continue to be located in the tributary valleys, increasing the number of sites in all valleys except the Yanamarca Valley. In the Yanamarca Valley, 14 sites are clustered in the north and the southeast, with the largest settlements in the north of the valley. There is still a group of 7 sites around Laguna Paca, 5 on the ridge near the Masma Valley, and 7 west of the Mantaro Valley. The movement out of the valley bottom proper into more defensive locations suggests an increased focus on separation and protection.

Wanka I settlements range in size from 0.4 to 15.1 ha. In general these sites are poorly preserved. From LeBlanc's 1978 survey, the visible architectural features are limited to the lower courses of circular structures, terrace retaining walls, and short sections of free-standing walls that could be outer patio walls. There are only a few more sites than the previous phase, with an average of 4.9 ha. The settlements are larger in the Yanamarca Valley, suggesting that there, especially, political consolidation was growing. But the size range in the Yanamarca Valley shows no strong hierarchy, the largest being 12 ha.

A new development in this time period is the decrease in size of the individual residential compounds and the increased density of the household compounds (Hastorf et al. 1989; Woodburn 1987). The circular structures within the walled patios are smaller, averaging 3 to 4 meters across. They are constructed as before of adobe on stone foundations on the valley floors, or stone double-faced *pirka* masonry on the

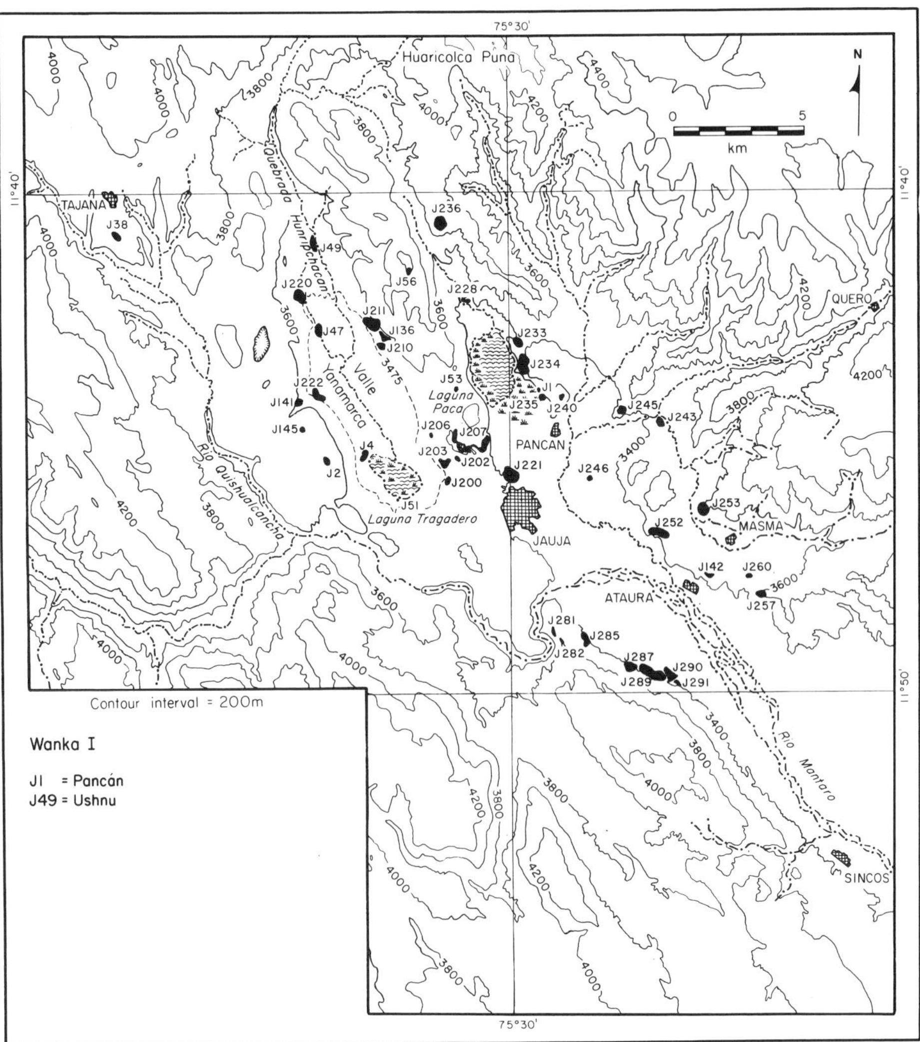

Fig. 3. The Wanka I settlement pattern

knolls. The patio compounds seem to be more contiguous within the settlements, suggesting a sense of clustering together.

Of particular note is the change seen in the Wanka I ceramics, morphologically, stylistically, and distributionally, though the range of types does not change (LeCount 1987). The new vessel styles are the precursors for the rest of the prehistoric ceramic sequence. In this phase we see a proliferation of new sizes of bowls, colors, and surface characteristics. Yet cross-cutting the types are much fewer pastes and tempers than in the previous phase. The new colors are purple on orange, purple on buff, with a new tan slip type Base Clara, described by Lumbreras (1959) and LeBlanc (1981). The painted designs become less complex and are more poorly executed. In particular deep straight bowls are larger, indicating an increase in size of food preparation (brewing) or short-term storage containers. There are more cooking jar shapes.

There is less distribution of ceramic types between the different valley site clusters than seen in the earlier phases, suggesting that production and/or exchange became more restricted in this period. These Sausa ceramic types tend to be limited to single tributary valley clusters. This, like the shift in the settlement pattern, suggests increased development of subregional alliances.

Chipped blades used for cutting increase markedly. These are often assumed to be sickles used to harvest plant matter for fuel, food (grains and legumes, not tubers), or fodder. Relating to food processing, the ground stone data show a marked increase in stone hoe blades, from 30 percent in the EIP (Huacrapukio II) to 80 percent in Wanka I (Russell 1988a). The increase in stone hoes suggests that the Sausa were adopting more labor intensive agricultural methods, using more hoes and digging sticks (Chapter 6). The most likely lands where they might have been used would be the deep, poorly drained soils that surround the lakes in the tributary valleys. Like modern drained field settings, spades would have been needed to empty the drainage canals and weed (recultivate, *chakma*) the fields. Besides the cooking jars that suggest an increase in boiled food, analyzed burned encrustations from within these pots support an increase of maize being boiled and not just toasted (Hastorf and DeNiro 1985). In addition, the mortars/pestles as well as the larger stone slab grinders remain common. These data begin to form a picture of increasing agricultural intensification with more emphasis on the valley lands, a trend that is suggested to have begun in the Huacrapukio II phase.

Wanka II Period

Sometime around a.d. 1300, major changes occurred in the region as the population abandoned many places and aggregated onto knoll-top walled settlements in the upland zone to the northwest of the Yanamarca Valley. The Wanka II period is defined by this demographic shift in the population and site hierarchy, and by a change in ceramic styles (LeBlanc 1981; Lumbreras 1959). As discussed more fully in the next chapter, these ceramic and other artifactual changes suggest that larger political and social alliances developed in conjunction with increased contestation and tension between these clusters. The site sizes and ceramic distributions in this northern Sausa area suggest evidence of four alliances, centered at four sites. This study focuses on two of these alliances above the Yanamarca Valley (with centers at J2 and J7). In addition, there is one alliance to the west over the Quishualcancha Quebrada centered at J109 (Llamap Shillon), and another to the south in the uplands west of the Mantaro River (J289). The latter two alliance clusters not only bind the two in question but they also suggest that this pattern continued down the Mantaro Valley throughout the Wanka ethic group.

The period's onset and duration is determined by fifteen absolute dates that have it begin around AD 1285 at Tunánmarca (670 ± BP, QL-4094) and run through 1474 (380 ± 30 BP) at Umpamalca (QL-4000) (calibrated using Stuiver and Remier 1986; Hastorf et al. 1989). We do not know the exact date of the Inkas' arrival but it must be close to 1460 (D'Altroy 1991).

When comparing the Wanka I settlement with the Wanka II (Figures 3 and 4), we see population aggregation, relocation, and site hierarchy. The Wanka II (Sausa) people abandoned many settlements and relocated into a total of twenty sites. There is a definite bimodal site size distribution in this phase, with two large sites of 25 and 74 ha. The remaining sites are around 15 ha or less (Appendix A). Certainly fusion of communities was occurring as the number of sites shrunk from forty-three to twenty over this hundred years. While these large centers were being built, the other settlements remained about the same size. The eighteen noncenter sites average 5.2 ha in size and range from 15 to 1.8 ha. One or two sites found in each of the subregions continue be occupied in the Paca and the Masma Valleys, and west of the Mantaro Valley. These isolated sites, however, are not large (2.0, 2.8 ha) and are difficult to interpret without further field research. There are also suggestions of a few field houses in the Yanamarca Valley, but these also must be confirmed. The new Wanka II sites are located above the rolling uplands at the edge of arable land in elevations ranging from 3,500 to 4,100 m. The valleys were abandoned as the population left the east and south, concentrating in the western uplands.

The settlement pattern suggests that this phase was a result of political upheaval, with the majority of people leaving their homes and joining others in new, densely packed settlements.

Increased focus on social control and security is seen in the stone masonry walls completely surrounding the new sites, except where rocky cliffs drop off sharply. These outer defensive walls were built at Hatúnmarca, Umpamalca, Tunánmarca, and Chawín. The outer walls vary in width from 1 to 2.5 m and they stand over 2 m in some places. Occasionally these outer walls also have trenches outside, further suggesting defense. While detailed studies of the walls have not been undertaken, they all have similar features. For example, at both Chawín (J40) and Hatúnmarca (J2), site entrances open out into semi-subterranean alleys which controlled entrance into the settlements. Tunánmarca (J7) also has a less elaborate form of this entrance. With few entrances to the sites, access was restricted. The purpose of these walls and entrances is difficult to specify. They could have been defensive fortification walls, but equally they could have been symbolic demarcations of the site, defining inclusion, membership, and restriction.

The two centers have surrounding walls that divide the living areas into two districts, the upper (*hanan*) and the lower (*hurin*) barrio (Figure 8). Walled rectangular plazas are at the center of Tunánmarca (J7), linking the two districts together. At Hatúnmarca, large Wanka II buildings in the central core area in each of the two residential zones could have served as public buildings. These core areas include large rectangular buildings, similar to the ones attached to Tunánmarca's central plaza.

The absence of comparable structures and plazas at the other sites along this upland spine supports the suggestion that these two large sites served as centers for their alliance population. Llamap Shillon (J109), the center to the west over the Rio Quishualcancha drainage and out of this study, is also divided into two districts. This subregion has the same pattern of site distribution that is seen in the Yanamarca uplands (D'Altroy 1987: 82). The distance between these three centers is approximately equal, suggesting that each did not control vast territories or numbers of satellite sites beyond those recorded on the maps.

The domestic compounds in these sites are tightly clustered within the inner walls. The sites are laced with narrow paths winding between the residences. All structures are built of double-faced chipped limestone masonry that can be quite well executed. Shape and format of the household compounds remain remarkably similar to the earlier forms, containing one or more round structures within each walled courtyard enclosure.

The local ceramic styles continue from the previous phase with a new slip, Wanka Red, and a new cooking vessel type, a deep hemispherical jar (LeCount 1987). There are several new shapes traded in from the south (Costin 1986). The Wanka I bowl shapes continue in this period, larger than before, and there are many more serving bowls in the assemblage (open necked, and no evidence of sooting). More serving bowls suggest that there are either new recipes being served or more people per household eating at a meal.

Lithic tool frequencies changed (Russell 1988b). Food production tool trends are mixed: blades, especially with sickle gloss, increase and stone hoes decrease, suggesting a shift in types of crops produced, agricultural strategies, or fields tended. All food processing tools are more common, especially the flat grinding stones used for quinoa, *chuño*, and maize. There is also evidence of specialized lithic quarrying and blade production at Umpamalca (J41), with their products distributed mainly to the northern cluster of sites (Russell 1985). The chert quarry source is about 7 km northwest of Umpamalca, across the Llamap Shillon cluster territory.

Faunal evidence shows that the meat component of the Wanka II diet was dominated by camelids (Earle et al. 1987: 85; Sandefur 1988b). The Wanka II deposits reflect an increased diet of meat in comparison with earlier periods, which could result from the move upslope closer to the herds, and away from other foods, or could simply be the product of a change in rubbish deposition. The latter change is seen in the calculation of kilograms of meat per cubic meter based on excavated bone densities, where the value doubled from the WI to the WII deposits (Sandefur 1988a, Figure 8). This is the largest increase in bone density for the whole pre-Hispanic period.

Agricultural production evidence, being the center of discussion in later chapters, will not be brought in here, except to note that, like the animal remains, the shift in settlement location is visible in the frequencies, with a decrease in maize and an increase in tubers in the house deposits.

The Wanka II phase came to an abrupt end when the invading Inka arrived, conquering and reorganizing the native alliances and settlements (D'Altroy 1987, 1991; D'Altroy and Hastorf n.d.). The Inka effect on the Sausa is not the focus of this investigation, but it is interesting that so many of the Wanka I sites are reoccupied during the Inka domination. It is as if the people were eagerly returning to their homes (Hastorf 1990a).

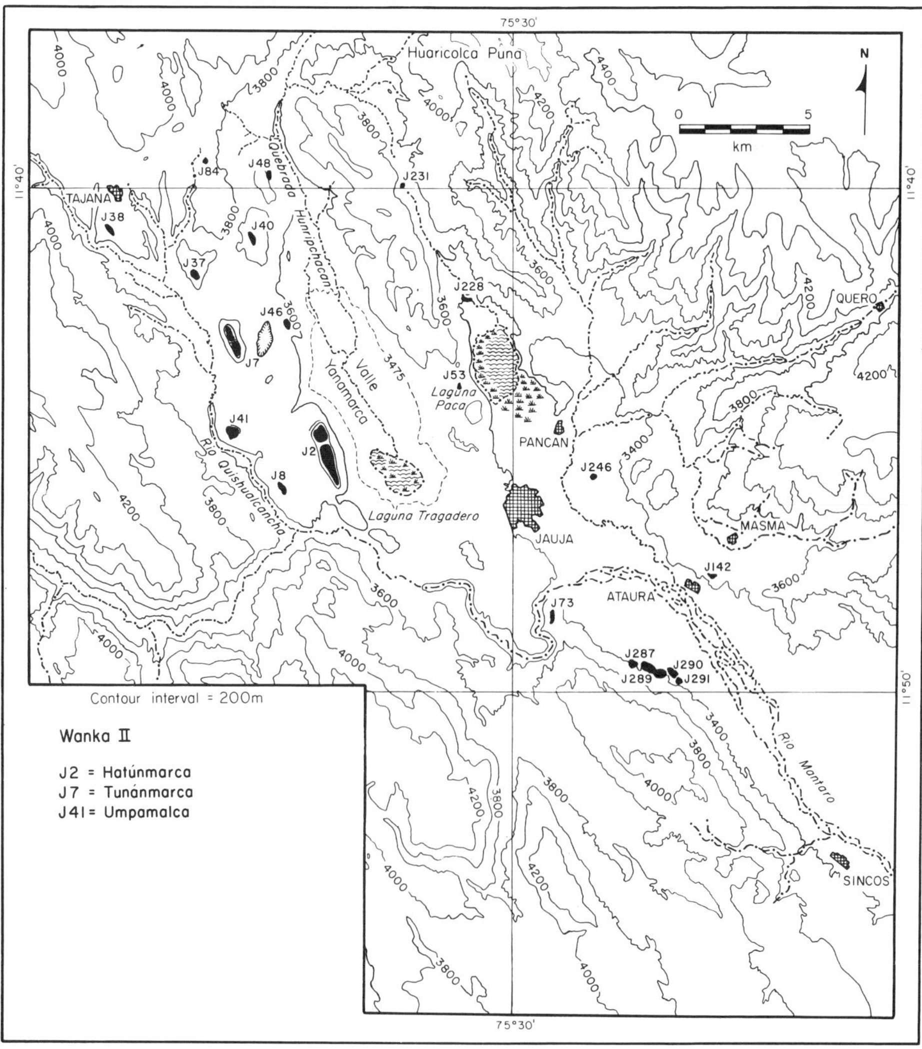

Fig. 4. The Wanka II settlement pattern

Pre-Hispanic population size estimates

The form of social and political life can be influenced by the size of the community, but there is no automatic link between specific political structures, economics, and population size (Feinman and Neitzel 1984). While interested in viewing past cultures in a more sensitive way and not automatically linking population size with social system, archaeologists such as Trigger (pers. comm.) make the point that there are in fact some population size thresholds that suggest different organizational requirements, as discussed in Chapter 1. I therefore present estimates of local populations to get a sense of the scale of change, not to conclude what organizations there were. In addition, these estimates will be used in Chapter 11 in the agricultural discussion to provide an idea of the relative intensity of land-use needed in these phases.

There are a number of difficulties in estimating the population size of settlements. Use of ethnographic data to interpret archaeological remains is based on the belief that regularities exist between behavior and observable physical remains (Sumner 1979). Thus, estimating use of space within prehistoric communities is dependent on continuities between the past and present in the way a domestic group and the larger community use space.

Despite the strong impact of the Spanish colonial society and the modern world economy on the traditional Andean world, there is much that links today's dwellers with pre-Hispanic times (Bastien 1978; Brush 1974; B. J. Isbell 1978; Silverblatt 1981; 1987; H. Skar 1982; S. Skar 1979; Webster 1973; Chapter 5). Because of the possibility of using both ethnographic information and ethnohistoric documents, we should be able to develop a fairly viable range of population sizes for the later pre-colonial periods. Important in this estimate is the number of households (I am using this term to mean a spatial entity that artifactually looks like a domestic unit). The household can vary in its number of occupants but its basic tasks of production, consumption, and community obligations have probably remained more or less the same. Lavallée's (1973) study in particular is especially appropriate here. In her excavation report on central Andean Late Intermediate sites in Asto, Huancavelica, she summarizes modern ethnographic information on structure use and population densities for traditional central Andean puna dwellers (1973: 112). She compares modern compound use life with Late Intermediate patio compounds, and makes a series of important observations and associations that will be applied here, as will D'Altroy's ethnohistoric study of population distributions (D'Altroy n.d.; Earle et al. 1987: 11).

A population range for sites with identifiable households can be estimated by multiplying the mean number of people in a residential household by the number of households present during that phase of occupation, tempered by the rate of abandonment. I will briefly present the method of estimation and then discuss in turn how each variable is calculated.

The Wanka I and II sites with standing architecture have been mapped by plotting the location of structures and adjoining walls on the ground with the aid of aerial photographs. The patios have then been counted (Earle et al. 1987; Hastorf field notes; LeBlanc 1981). The data needed to estimate the population of a settlement are:

residential area (A), density of structures in area (D), average number of structures per patio group (S), average number of individuals occupying a patio (I), and rate of occupancy (or abandonment) or the patio groups (K). With the exception of the area of the site, each of the variables must be estimated from sampled data. For ease of presentation I will begin with the Wanka II material, which is the most accurate.

The residential area (A) has been calculated for each site by measuring the area of structures or dense artifactual material plotted onto aerial photographs (digitizing UTM coordinates), or by measuring the area on the ground in the case of smaller sites. The procedures involve estimation when the sites have more than one occupation. Estimations are completed from detailed surface artifactual collections to identify the different zones that were occupied in the different periods. The settlement size estimates are listed in Appendix A, calculated from site survey mapping (Earle in Hastorf et al. 1989).

Density of structures in the residential area (D) has been calculated from on-site mapping and structure counting where architecture exists. For the Wanka II sites, the two densest sites are Tunánmarca with 174 structures/ha and Umpamalca with 146 structures/ha. The information for Wanka II non-centers is based on estimates from the small, well-preserved site of Chawín (J40). This site has 50 structures/ha. Estimation at Hatúnmarca is more difficult for the Wanka II occupation because part of the site was reoccupied in WIII and part of it was cleaned off for agriculture. In the relatively untouched Wanka II areas it is clear that the occupation was not as dense as at Tunánmarca. Its potentially habitable territory also was much larger, allowing the population to spread out. This site was completely mapped and systematic surface collections made (Earle, D'Altroy, and LeBlanc 1978). Because of this less dense habitation, an estimate of 50 structures/ha is used for it. At the two large sites (J2, J7), the central open areas between residential zones were not included in this population calculation.

At one Wanka I site, J38, LeBlanc calculated a density of one structure every 132 square meters, or 76 structures/ha. J56 has an average of 50 structures/ha as does the upland Wanka II site J40. For the Wanka I structure density estimates I will use 50 structures/ha. For the EIP/MH phase we have even less information, yet the compounds seem to be spaced farther apart. At Pancán (J1) we saw that the patio compounds tended to be more spread out in the earlier phases. I have chosen an estimate of 35 structures/ha for this phase.

The number of structures per patio compound (S) was calculated from an architectural survey (LeBlanc 1981). We counted structures within a number of patio compounds, which yielded an average of 1.9 structures at Tunánmarca. Umpamalca and Hatúnmarca yielded 2.3 structures per patio. We therefore use an average of the two at 2.0 structures/patio group (the same as at Pancán for EIP/MH).

Lavallée (1973: 112) estimated the average size of a nuclear family living in a patio compound today in Huancavelica as six (I). D'Altroy (n.d.) also arrived at this figure from a series of documentary sources on pre-Hispanic and early colonial household compositions. An important assumption here is that a compound is a domestic unit, and from ethnohistoric sources this included a married man and woman, their children, unmarried or widowed kin. What the household composition was farther back in time is impossible to say. I use 6 per patio as an average.

The rate of occupancy (K) is always difficult to estimate. Because the Wanka II settlements were only used for about a hundred years, the rapid shift into these settlements, and high labor expenditure to build the new houses, especially considering the lack of suitable building material like wooden beams for the roofs, suggest that the occupation rate was quite high. In addition, from our excavations we found little evidence of remodeling during the Wanka II times, and with the rapid and forced abandonment this seems reasonable.

In her own population estimation of Late Intermediate knoll sites, Lavallée (1973: 114) used a rate of structure abandonment, derived from her ethnographic puna material, of 80 percent below actual roofed area. Therefore for the short Wanka II Period I used an 80 percent (60–100 percent) rate of occupancy. For the Wanka I times, the occupation phase is much longer, about 400 years, and we do not know what events were affecting the use life of structures or sites. To be conservative, the rate should be lowered, to 60–80 percent, assuming that families could use their houses for over a hundred years. (From recent absolute dates through two rebuildings of a Pancán compound we have a date of approximately 200 years per rebuilding: Hastorf et al. 1989). The EIP/MH time is approximately 350 years, but with evidence of new sites being continuously built during these subphases I am lowering the occupation rate to 40-60 percent.

The formula to estimate the population by site and time period is:

$$P = \frac{A \times D \times I \times K}{S}$$

where P = population size, A = residential area, D = structure density, I = average number of individuals occupying an area, K = rate of occupancy, and S = number of structures per patio compound. The results of these calculations are seen in Table 1.

For individual site population estimates, the site's residential area is multiplied by the appropriate values (Table 1). Each time period has one or two large population aggregations that are as great as 1,300 for EIP/MH, 1,800 for Wanka I, and 11,000 for Wanka II. The magnitude of increase is so great between Wanka I and Wanka II that it is a significant population difference even if our calculations are inaccurate. A remarkable result shows the two Wanka II centers each having a population of around 10,000 people, while the Wanka I settlement population average is 490. The Wanka II centers therefore have a twenty-fold increase over the earlier settlements, as well as over their own non-center sites. The average Wanka I sites are similar to the small Wanka II sites in size, suggesting that not every Wanka II satellite was composed of aggregate populations even though most changed location. The average EIP/MH sites are smaller than the Wanka I sites.

From these estimates, we can see that the settlement data suggest a continual increase in population size, with the study region population having grown roughly from 8,600 to 22,000, to 32,000 inhabitants. Yet the people are not evenly distributed

Table 1. *Estimation of population sizes at Sausa sites*

Site	Residential area (ha)	Structure density str/ha	Occup. rate % (K)	Std.[1]	Pop. est. (P)
EIP/MH					
average site	4.1	35	40–80	1.2–1.8	172–258
J71	1.9	35	40–80	1.2–1.8	80–120
J1	1.4	35	40–80	1.2–1.8	60–88
Wanka I examples					
J38	4.2	76	60–80	1.8–2.4	575–700
J56	2.5	50	60–80	1.8–2.4	225–300
average site	4.9	50	60–80	1.8–2.4	441–590
J49	4.3	50	60–80	1.8–2.4	387–516
J1	1.4	50	60–80	1.8–2.4	126–68
Wanka II examples					
J7	25.0	174	60–100	1.8–3.0	7,830–13,050
J2	74.0	50	60–100	1.8–3.0	6,660–11,100
J41	15.0	146	60–100	1.8–3.0	2,940–6,570
J40	5.6	50	60–100	1.8–3.0	500–840
average Wanka II noncenter settlement	4.5	50	60–100	1.8–3.0	405–675

[1] Standard $= \frac{I \times K}{S}$, where I = average no. of individuals occupying an area, K = rate of occupancy, and S = no. of structures per patio compound

minimum EIP/MH $\frac{6 \times 0.4}{2} = 1.2$, WI and WII $\frac{6 \times 0.6}{2} = 1.8$

maximum EIP/MH $\frac{6 \times 0.6}{2} = 1.8$, WI $\frac{6 \times 0.8}{2} = 2.4$, WII $\frac{6 \times 1}{2} = 3.0$

throughout the landscape. At the beginning of this sequence the population is concentrated in the Yanamarca region, with other subregions lightly inhabited. After the Middle Horizon, all subregions, except the Yanamarca Valley, have more settlements, with larger and denser sites. The population seems to be consolidating in a series of different clusters. Consolidation continues in Wanka II but is even more focused, in that the vast majority of people surround the Yanamarca Valley. While the new upland sites are large and dense, other sites remain small, continuing the same tradition seen in Wanka I. Some of these small eastern and southern sites were field stations, special activity sites, or ritual locations. The stratified Wanka II settlement pattern suggests political hierarchy, with an emphasis on defense and population aggregation. A small cluster to the south and west of the Mantaro River Valley seems to have developed separately from the Yanamarca alliances. The dynamics of these socio-political developments will be discussed in the next chapter.

Calorific estimation for the Andes

To be able to use the population estimates in Table 1 to help gain an understanding of the relative intensity of pre-Hispanic production and socio-political changes, they should be transformed into a potential annual calorie requirement.

The calorie intake of Andean people has been studied by a number of researchers (Food and Agriculture Organization [FAO] 1957; Gursky 1970; Thomas 1973). The 1957 FAO report on native Andean calorific requirements determined 2,323 kcal per person per day as the average minimum for a population. Thomas (1973: 68), in his detailed study of energy inputs and outputs of Nuñoa, a southern highland community, calculated an average intake of 1,530 kcal per person per day. Although his estimate for the 7,750 individuals falls below the FAO mean daily requirement, he believes that the minimum Andean calorie need is in fact less than the FAO standard. He supports his calorie figure by noting an annual cycle of weight gain after harvest time and a consequent weight loss before the harvest. For the pre-Hispanic populations, I have chosen to use Thomas's value of 1,530 kcal, which when multiplied by 365 days becomes 558,450 kcal/person/year. This figure can be multiplied by the estimated settlement population range, providing an approximate lower limit of agricultural production for a group.

1979 excavations

Information about the excavations provides an understanding of the deposits, the contexts, and the internal site organization from where the artifacts in the study came and upon which the conclusions are based. Excavations were carried out from August through November 1979 at five archaeological sites in the Jauja region from three cultural phases: the Early Intermediate Period/Middle Horizon phase, the Wanka I Period, the Wanka II Period. Specific sites representing these periods were selected from the intensive regional survey data compiled by Parsons (1976; Parsons and Hastings 1977) and the more detailed survey and ceramic work of LeBlanc (1981).

The method used to choose the investigated sites was a combination of purposeful and stratified random sampling. A necessary characteristic was good preservation, either architecturally, as in the case of the Wanka I and Wanka II sites, or artifactually, as in the case of earlier phases. Two sites from each of the three phases were sampled. Since Pancán had both EIP/MH and Wanka I deposits, it was only necessary to work on four other sites. To get early material, Tragedero Viejo, J71, was randomly selected from the EIP/MH sites. Most Wanka I sites have large components of Late Horizon material on top of the Wanka I component. Ushnu, J49, was chosen from the Wanka I sites based on its predominantly Wanka I material and traces of standing architecture.

For the Wanka II phase, a central site and a satellite site were required. From the two central sites in the survey region, Tunánmarca (J7) was chosen because Hatúnmarca (J2) has a substantial Late Horizon occupation covering the central Wanka II remains. Umpamalca (J41) was selected as the smaller Wanka II site because of its association with the northern center, its good architectural preservation, and its accessibility.

A major excavation goal was to recover a representative sample of agricultural production remains from identifiable domestic contexts. My excavations focused on household trash deposits. Towards this end, many small excavation units were more effective than fewer larger ones. At each site from four to twelve units were excavated, averaging about 1.5 by 1.0 m in size. On the sites with no standing architecture, excavation units were located randomly. A combination of random and purposeful selection was applied whenever architectural evidence existed; domestic structures were excavated if visible. The standing architecture allowed me to define two excavation units, one inside the chosen structure and the other just outside in the courtyard area. In the inside of the structure a trapezoidal-shaped wedge was excavated, gaining a portion of the area near the wall and also part of the center of the structure. The orientation of the wedge was chosen randomly. Outside of the structure a rectangular-shaped unit was placed spanning the front of the doorway of the structure (Figure 10). These two locations were determined from the previous work by Lavallée. She and her team excavated similar structures in the Asto region of Huancavelica, to the south of the UMARP study area (Lavallée 1973; Lavallée and Julien 1973). Lavallée had found the main organic midden and ash concentrations against the walls within the structures and just outside the structures' entrances within the courtyard area, directing me in my choice of excavation location.

All artifacts were collected using a ¼-inch screen; each cultural provenience was excavated and catalogued in cultural levels based on soil type and cultural context. Continuing cultural levels were divided if they were thicker than 15 cm.

The EIP/MH is represented by J71 (Tragadero Viejo) and J1 (Pancán); J71 (Figure 5) is a single component EIP site located on a gently sloping limestone rise just to the north of Laguna Tragadero in the Yanamarca Valley. From ceramic analysis it seems to have been inhabited during the Huacrapukio phases. The site is approximately 1.9 ha in size and is poorly preserved due to shallowness and intensive modern agriculture. Because there was no surface architecture, the locations of the six trenches were chosen randomly. From the center point of the site, a random number between 1 and 360 was chosen for an angle. After measuring the distance to the edge of the site on the chosen angle a random distance within that was selected. This point was augered to determine the depth of cultural deposit. It was assumed that deeper deposits might yield more productive cultural material due to better preservation. When the auger discovered cultural material of a depth greater than 50 cm below the surface, this point became the northwest corner of a trench. Five of the six trenches were 2 by 2 m in size, the sixth was 1.5 by 1.5 m; while some structure walls were uncovered, it was very difficult to label cultural contexts for the J71 proveniences due to a lack of identifiable features and so most were called general midden deposit.

Pancán (J1) was the second site representing the EIP/MH (Figure 6). From surface and test excavations made in 1977 (Earle et al. 1978), we determined that it was a multicomponent site with Huacrapukio II, Middle Horizon, Wanka I deposits, and a small area of Wanka III (Late Horizon) material. This site is a 1.4 ha rounded mound surrounded by marshy water on the southeastern shore of Laguna Paca in the Paca Valley. Pancán is actually an artificial peninsula as it is surrounded by water on three sides. From geological studies of the site stratigraphy the cultural deposit is almost 4 m deep, sitting directly on hillside alluvium that washed down onto the lake shore (Hastorf et al. 1989). It has a twin site just to the south (J235 on Figure 3). This twin site seems to have been occupied only in Wanka I times. These two Wanka I sites could perhaps represent an early version of the dual divisions seen in the larger Wanka II sites. Only Pancán was reoccupied during Inka times.

Like Tragadero Viejo (J71), Pancán's surface shows poor preservation with only the rubble remains of one Inkaic rectangular building. The rest of the site's surface is under cultivation. Only two 2.5 by 2.5 trenches were excavated because three trenches has been completed in the 1977 field season and each one yielded a great deal of data. The two new locations were chosen randomly (see locations on the site map). Within these two trenches one wall from a circular structure was uncovered, as well as shadows of several adobe walls. The cultural contexts that determined were: occupation zone within a structure, subfloor-construction fill, and general midden. The artifactual evidence suggests that the site was a residential site involved in agriculture, herding, as well as in exploiting the lake's animal resources (Sandefur 1988a). Since

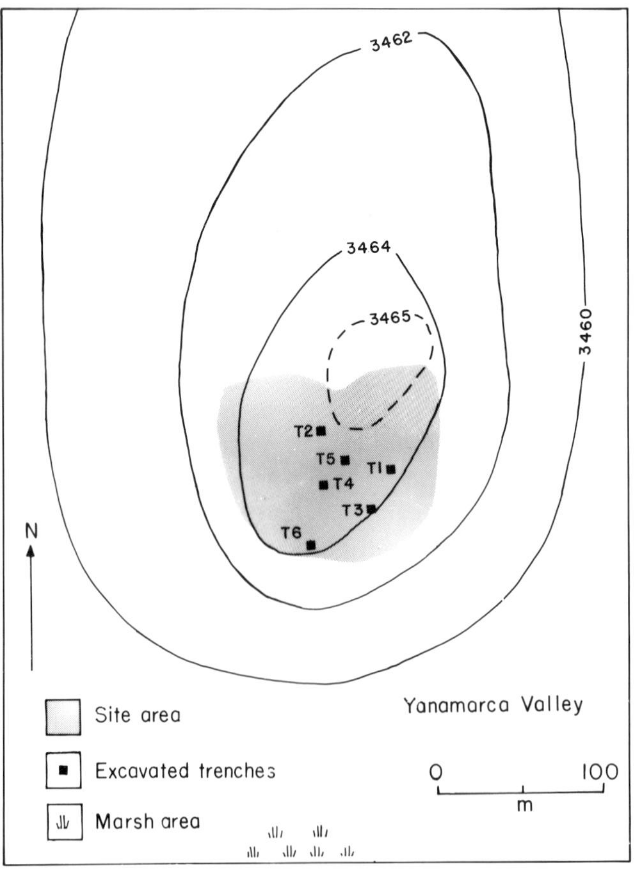

Fig. 5. Site plan of Tragadero Viejo (J71), with the excavation trenches located by number

these excavations, we have returned to open up a wide area and collect material in well-identified contexts (Hastorf et al. 1989). Although these new data are not reported on here, when appropriate the recent results will be used to illustrate points.

For the next period, the Wanka I phase, the upper levels of Pancán (J1) were sampled along with Ushnu (J49). In the Wanka I levels of the Pancán trenches, one circular structure was uncovered with an associated hearth, while the remaining contexts were labeled as general midden deposits.

Ushnu (Figure 7) is located on a low ridge, 100 m above the valley floor overlooking the Yanamarca Valley on its northern edge. The gentle terrain to the north provides easy access. The site has been cultivated for many years, consequently little standing architecture is left. Fragments of walls run perpendicular to the ridge crest creating patio compounds. In a couple of cases these walls were incorporated into a terrace retaining wall, indicating a prehistoric date for the household terrace construction.

Although contoured terraces on Ushnu exist, well-preserved circular structures are sparse across the 4.3 ha of the pre-Inka component. The structures that remained

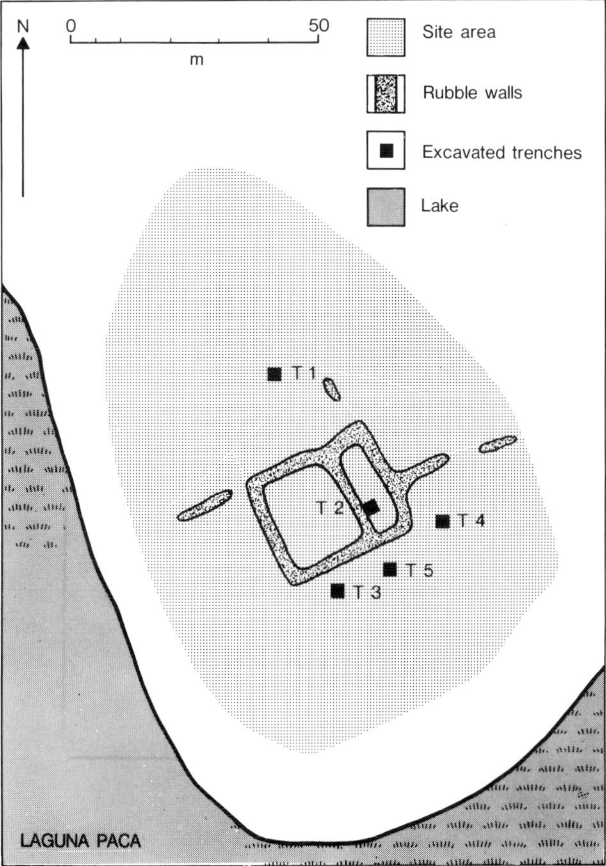

Fig. 6. Site plan of Pancán (J1), with the excavation trenches located by number; T1, T2, T3 were excavated in 1977, T4 and T5 in 1979

usually had only one course of rocks. Five surface collections were taken in 1978 (LeBlanc 1981). These indicated that the first occupation was during the Middle Horizon. The site was occupied through the Wanka I phase, abandoned and then reoccupied during the Late Horizon but only in the northern sector.

The selection of the sampled structures was purposeful, based on the existence of complete circular structure foundations under loose rubble piles from field clearing. The structure excavations at Ushnu were designed to sample Wanka I floors but some of the proveniences were of other phases. Five structures were sampled at Ushnu, although only three had single component Wanka I occupations. Three of the structures sampled are in the northern portion of the site, the other two are in the south.

Once a structure had been cleared of rubble and the walls had been identified, trapezoidal-shaped units were excavated to sterile. The identified cultural contexts at Ushnu are: structure wall fall (post occupation deposition), occupation zone, and subfloor (preoccupation construction material).

The two Wanka II sites chosen are both single component sites. Tunánmarca (J7) is located on a high ridge on the west side of the Yanamarca Valley. This site is over

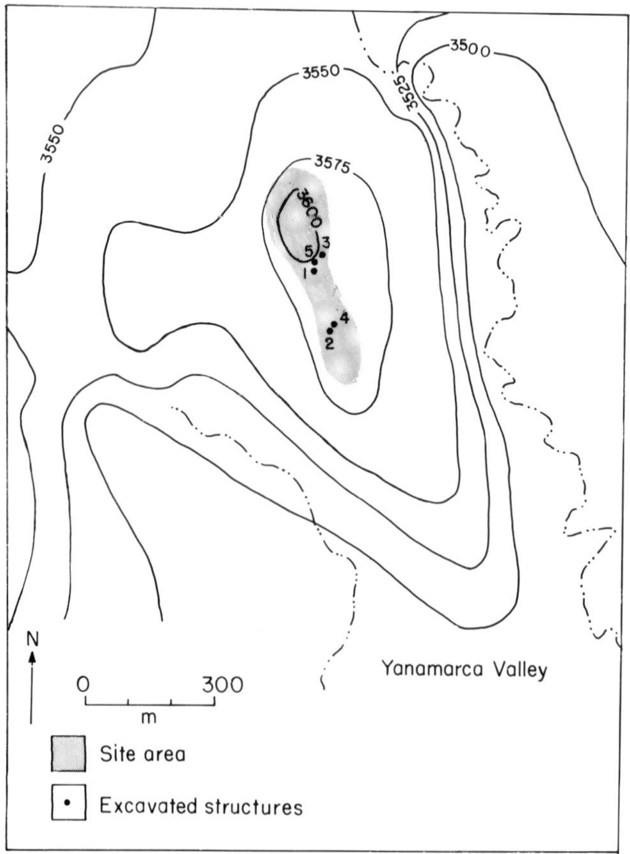

Fig. 7. Site plan of Ushnu (J49), with the excavation units located by number

200 m above the surrounding upland terrain and is defensively situated (Guttierez 1937). Within the outermost walls that enclose over 35 ha are two walled residential districts that together cover approximately 22 ha (the shaded area on Figure 8). In addition to a single wall that encompasses the residences, a second wall was built about 50 m downslope on the southwestern side, the most accessible side of the site.

The architectural preservation is good enough to study the internal organization of the site. Like the patio compounds excavated at Pancán, within these residential zones circular structures are grouped around small courtyards or patios with doorways facing onto the patio area. These domestic clusters include from one to six structures and may have one or more small stone burial chambers. The group of structures

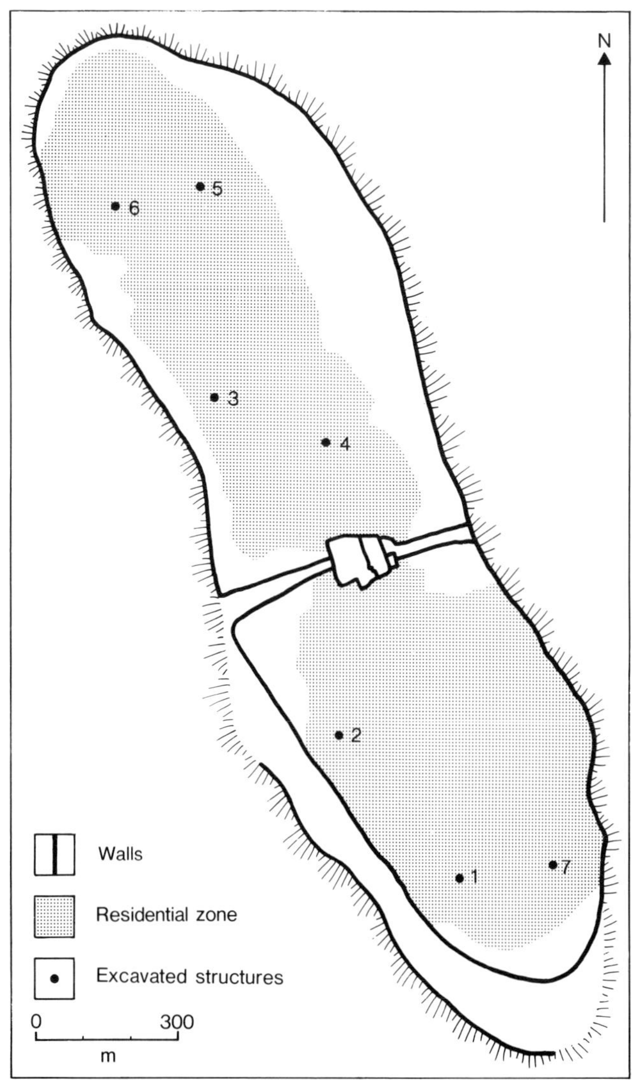

Fig. 8. Site plan of Tunánmarca (J7), with the excavation units located by number

opening onto a courtyard is surrounded by a stone wall (Figure 9). Patio compounds are separated from adjacent patio groups by terrace walls and free-standing walls that create winding pathways 1.5 to 2 m wide throughout the site.

The seven circular structures sampled at Tunánmarca ranged from 3.7 to 5.3 m in diameter. Sampling these structures involved probabilistic and purposeful methods. The site was divided into seven zones of approximately equal size, one division for each structure sampled. The same sampling procedure used at Tragadero Viejo (J71) was used here to choose a structure; that is, I randomly chose directions and distances out from a central point. At each randomly determined location, the best architecturally preserved circular structure within 10 m was excavated.

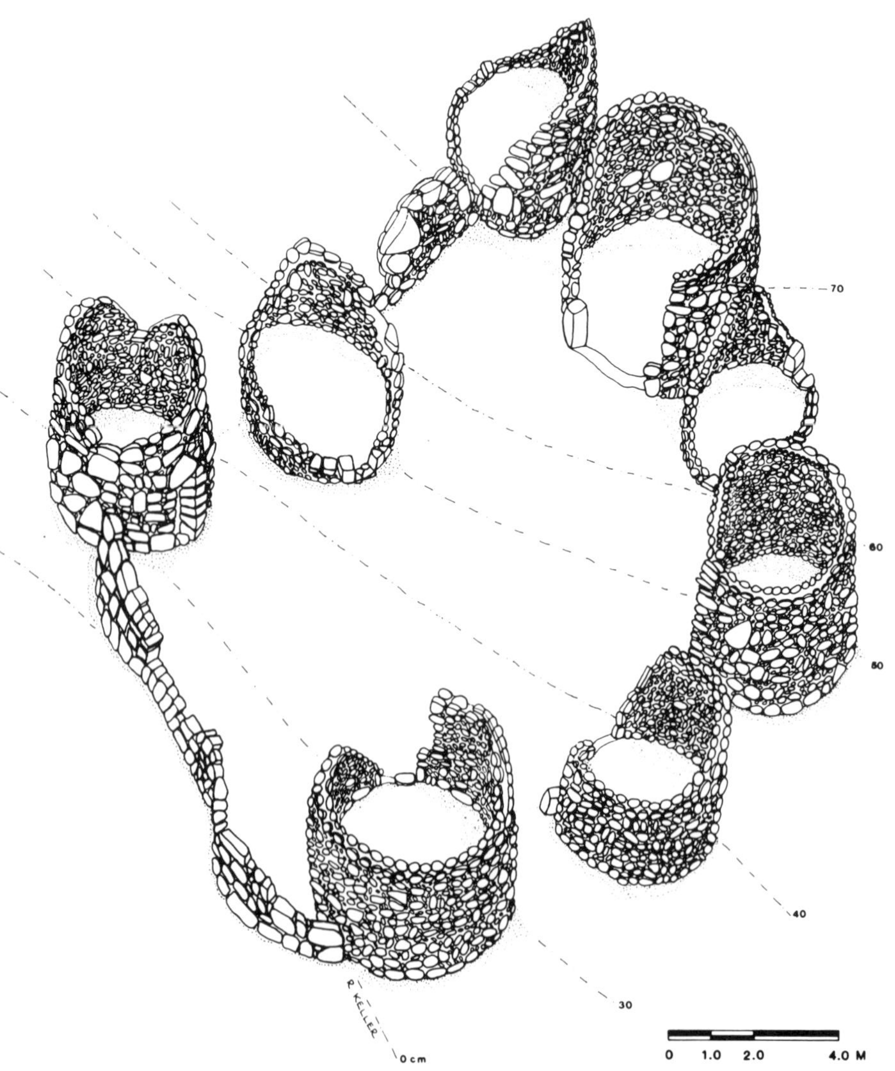

Fig. 9. Plan of a patio compound, J7-2, on Tunánmarca, drawn by Robert Keller

Six of the seven excavation units in the structures were trapezoidal in shape. Because of very sparse botanical recovery from these six excavations, the excavation strategy was expanded for the last structure; to excavate one half of the structure. For this, the chosen structure was divided in half, bisecting the doorway. At each structure a small 0.5–2.75 by 0.51–1.75 m unit was also dug directly to one side of the doorway within the patio area. All units were excavated in cultural levels, defined on the basis of soil texture and color. Figure 10 portrays one excavated structure at Tunánmarca as an example of the excavation unit placement.

Tunánmarca had very shallow deposits, 30 to 60 m deep. Because of this and the

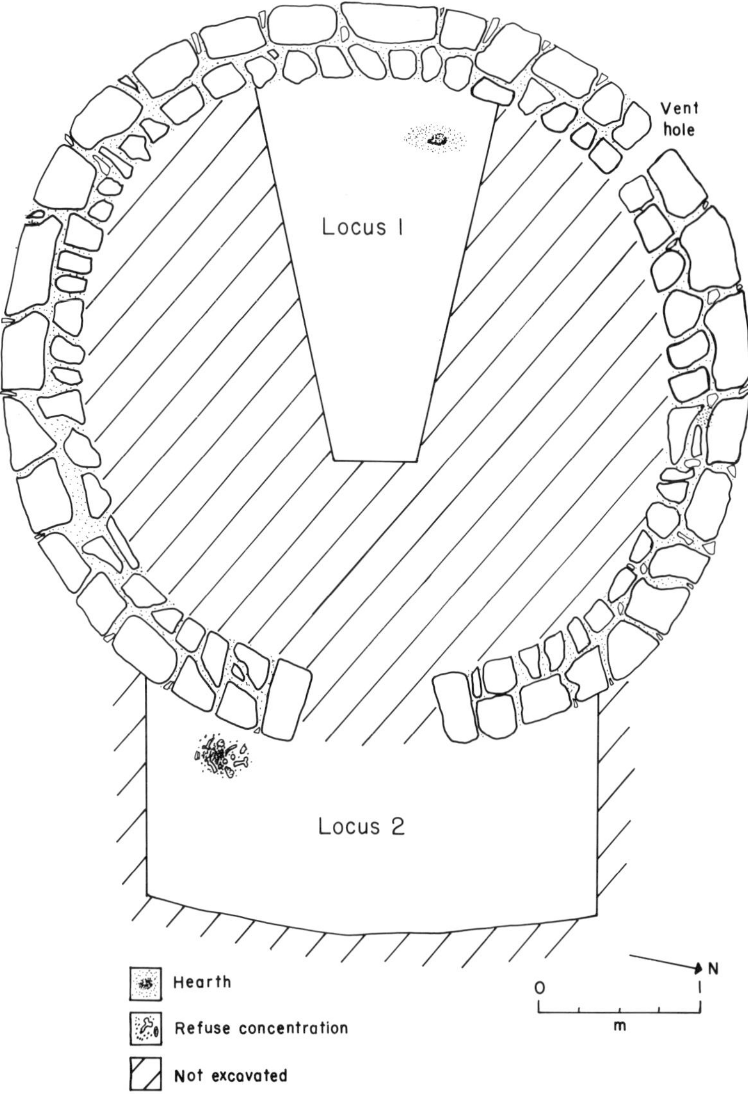

Fig. 10. Plan of structure 6 at J7 on Tunánmarca

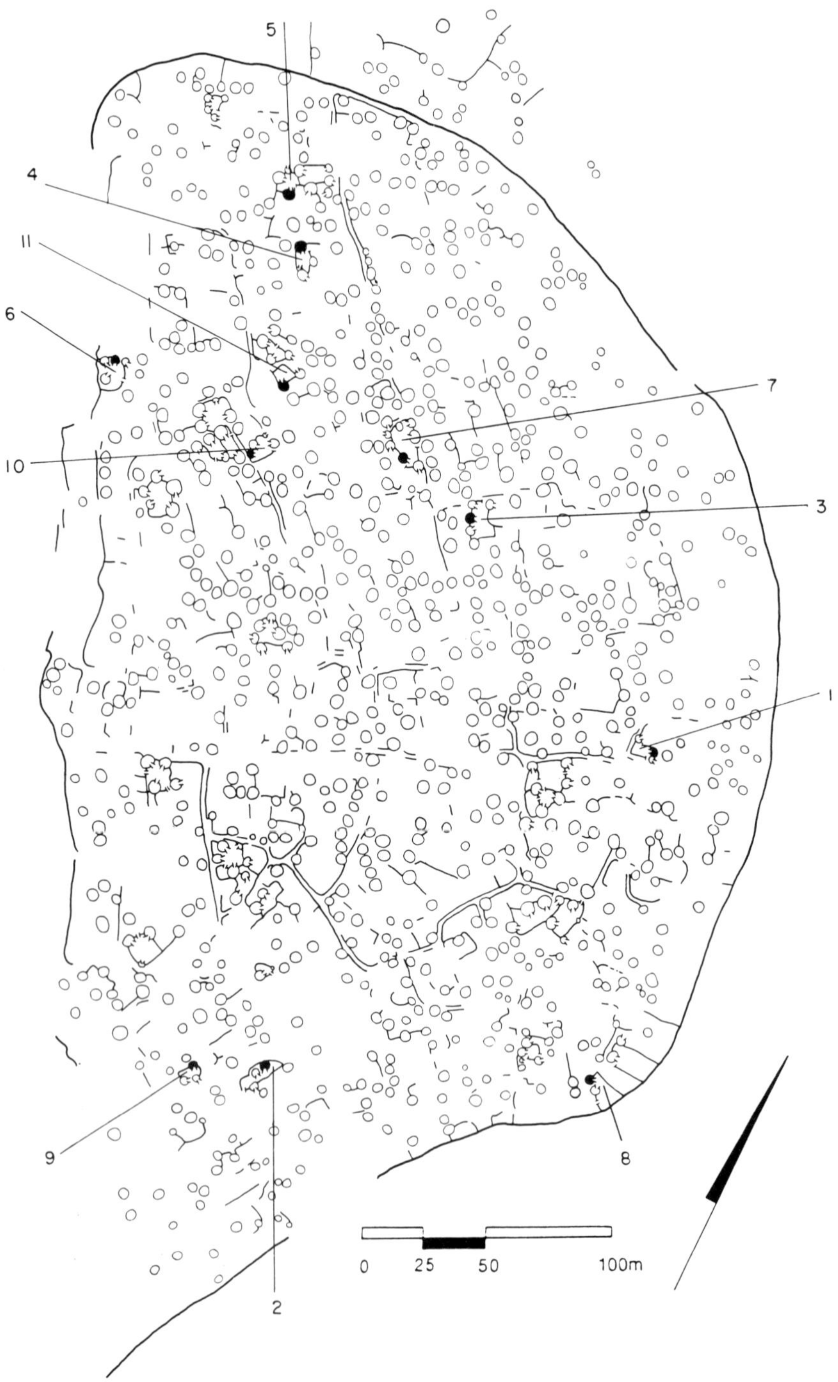

Fig. 11. Site plan of Umpamalca (J41), with the excavation units located by number, drawn by Glenn Russell

exposed nature of the site, the botanical preservation was sparse. Similar to Ushnu's situation, the identifiable cultural contexts were: wallfall, occupation zone, hearth, midden, and subfloor fill.

Umpamalca (J41), also on the western side of the Yanamarca Valley, is positioned on a knoll that overlooks the deeply dissected Quishualcancha Quebrada to the west (Figure 11). Umpamalca, like Tunánmarca and other Wanka II sites, is surrounded by a fortification wall. The site is just under 12 ha in size; within the walls the structures and patio groups are densely packed. From a map made in 1979, approximately 1,380 structures are still preserved.

Because Umpamalca is very dense and it is difficult to locate one's position on a photograph or map, a slightly different form of random sampling was used to select the structures. I divided the site map into 73 quadrats of equal size. Eleven of these quadrats were chosen randomly, and within each a well-preserved structure was chosen for excavation. As at Tunánmarca, the first six structures sampled had trapezoidal excavation units. Because these six units did not yield much botanical material, the excavation strategy was changed to expand each unit to half of the structure for three of the structures and, ultimately, two complete structures were

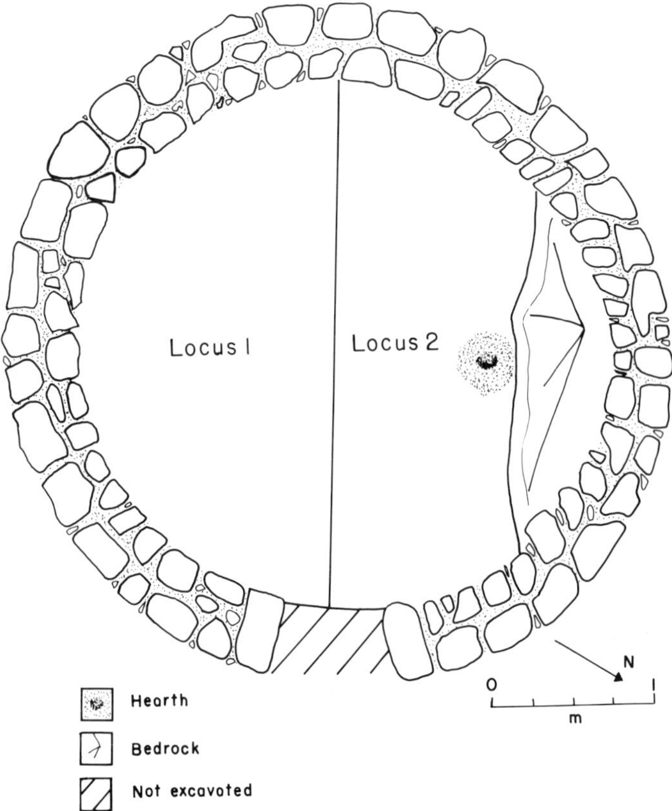

Fig. 12. Plan of structure 8 at J41-4 on Umpamalca

excavated. All units were excavated in cultural levels. In one of the completely excavated structures an intact hearth was uncovered (Figure 12). Small trenches were also excavated just outside of each structure's doorway. As at Tunánmarca, the identified cultural contexts were: post-occupational wallfall, occupation zone (this includes the structure and patio areas), pit, hearth, midden, and subfloor fill.

While the sampling goal was the same in all excavations – good contexts, unbiased collections, and systematic botanical collections – different sampling strategies were used at the different sites. These differences must affect the artifactual collections, but in the sites where there is the greatest problem of bias (the architecture of the Wanka II sites), I used more random methods.

From the artifactual, population, and settlement changes over time we know that a series of events transpired in the Sausa region. To gain another dimension on these events, I now turn to the documentary evidence for further hints about the social and political changes that transpired over the same millennium.

5

Regional socio-political structures: Wanka II hierarchical developments

Chapter 4 demonstrated a Sausa population movement that resulted in aggregation out of the valleys, escalating around 1300–50. These types of settlement shifts were common throughout the Andes in Late Intermediate times (the fourth age), as discussed by Guaman Poma de Ayala (1944: 64), where:

> fearing war, they had to leave the good places . . . They were forced to move from their towns of mud to the higher places and now lived on peaks and precipices of the high mountains and built fortresses with walls . . . There was much fighting and there was death . . . there were captains and war leaders . . . they took captives, even women and children. They took each other's lands and irrigation canals, and pastures . . . and many goods, even grinding stones.

This was a time of regional interests, local political escalation, aggression towards neighbors, movement into defended settlements, and warfare (Hyslop 1979; Krzanowski 1977; Murra 1984: 72; Spalding 1984; Thompson 1971). We know that the large Andean polities had collapsed by AD 1000, leaving power vacuums of different sorts throughout the Andes. The effect this had on each ethnic group varied, but the evidence at this time suggests that many regions were focusing on their own political/administrative strength. For many, this was a time of political change and increased hostilities. How did this affect the Sausa of the northern Mantaro Valley? What forms of political organization were initiated, what Andean principles were called upon to promote social change? By focusing on the Sausa, we may better understand these political and social events of the Late Intermediate throughout the Andes and even gain some enlightenment about other prehistoric group political change.

Wanka II site hierarchies

When aggregation is identified in the archaeological record, archaeologists often assume that new political interactions and pressures were operating among the settlements (Green et al. 1978; de Montmollin 1987; Renfrew and Cherry 1986). Increased social or economic pressures, interactions, and new ceremonial activities have been associated with the rise of centers (as suggested by Mesoamerican data: see de Montmollin 1987). Site hierarchy has been considered a feature of political hierarchy (Earle 1976; Haselgrove 1982; Johnson 1973: 15; Spriggs 1981; Steponaitis 1981; Wright and Johnson 1975) and of economic hierarchy (Brumfiel 1976; Hodder and Orton 1976). The reasoning is that formal political integration beyond a single community must be accompanied by distinctly larger and centralized management to integrate the larger population and the accompanying increase in interaction and conflict. Larger central communities are often the center of the promoted and centralized power structure, having new activities tied to new political, administrative, and religious production. If this settlement pattern shift seen in the Wanka II reflects at least some type of political change, then we would expect to see evidence for political hierarchy developing before the Wanka II.

The archaeological evidence presented in the previous chapter does suggest political hierarchy and economic realignments. This is seen in the increasing evidence of local exchange alliances in the Wanka I and Wanka II ceramics and the settlement aggregation and defensiveness in the Wanka II sites. As discussed in Chapter 1, different cultural domains can shift at different times for slightly different reasons. What does the political and/or economic evidence for difference look like in the Sausa settlement, artifactual, and documentary data?

The EIP/MH settlement pattern has a fairly even population distribution throughout the hills and valleys, with large and small settlements interspersed. Before the Wanka II Period the settlements and ceramic distributions form a picture of a series of three or four clusters of communities. Wanka I sites display a size range between 100 and 2,000 people. All site sizes are dispersed throughout the different clusters. In contrast, the Wanka II is a two-tiered hierarchy of centers and satellites (Appendix A). In addition, the Wanka II population differences between sites also suggest this more marked settlement difference, where the satellite sites range from 500 to 4,000 inhabitants and the central site populations are 10,000 or more. The absolute sizes of the largest communities, with these large populations, imply political ranking simply because of a need for management of local resources.

These values are even more significant when compared to the Wanka I estimates, where the average settlement housed around 500 people and the largest 2,000. Clearly new levels of organization and interaction were required in the Wanka II to create and maintain these large new communities, as well as generate the ten-fold magnitude of difference existing between the site sizes. The aggregation and associated movement up onto the knolls suggest new socio-political activities within as well as between these communities. The absolute number of patios alone suggests a need for new forms of policing, new rules of access, as well as providing new ways to unite villages or *ayllus* into one population, both symbolically and socially. New social mechanisms that joined at least three or four settlements together into each district (barrio or *ayllu*) at each large site, will have had to be initiated.

These settlement shifts require new social relations within the population, new concepts of community, new forms of settlement peacekeeping, as well as new levels of intercommunity warfare. The settlement hierarchy in the Wanka II can be compared to the nested religious hierarchy of lesser to greater deities as well as to the tiered hierarchy of community leaders or even to the Inka governing structure (B. J. Isbell 1978; Spalding 1984). But, as the discussion in Chapter 3 suggests, traditional Andean adaptation has not been geared to central places which control or distribute basic subsistence items *à la* Sanders and Price (1968). Rather, settlements are connected as part of a tiered system of political oppositions with a political prestige hierarchy securing and managing each subdivision's communal land-use, appeasing the earth/ancestors, and organizing warfare. These strategies of coordination and policing function today to maintain community relations, and we know variations on this theme were the bases for the Inka empire (D'Altroy 1991; Rowe 1946), as they built on indigenous ideologies of hierarchy and dualism to incorporate conquered groups (Platt 1987; Zuidema 1967).

Changes in community relocation and growth would also affect the organization of group labor projects needed to build the settlement, its walls, and the nearby intensive land-use strategies (Chapter 8), providing access to local resources such as water, lithic sources, clay sources, or space in the large enclosed spaces in the walled settlements. The larger projects would need some sort of *faena* or labor tax on a much larger scale than the ethnographic examples of Chapter 3.

Wanka II intercommunity political alliances

Above I suggested that the Wanka II site hierarchy probably reflects increasing political inequalities; certainly the settlement-pattern data suggest some new decision-making power. But what else can we see that accompanied this evidence? Let us pursue the possible shape of the Sausa political hierarchy that culminated in Wanka II by looking at some additional evidence of the dynamics in the intersite alliances in the Wanka II data, researched initially by LeBlanc (1981). The Wanka II settlement pattern data I focus on have two intercommunity groups or alliances, centered at the two large sites Tunánmarca and Hatúnmarca. Architecture, the distribution of public space, artifact variability among the communities, and historic documents provide evidence for the multi-community political entities around these two central sites.

Architecture

Coordination of large groups in the construction of monumental architecture has often been considered a sign of stratification (McEwan 1990; Moseley 1975: 102; T. Pozorski 1982). The construction of platforms, pyramids, and plaza complexes found elsewhere in the Andes clearly required much larger efforts than the Wanka II fortification walls or the irrigation ditches. Nevertheless, the coordination of the dividing walls and the layout of communities as large as Tunánmarca and Hatúnmarca could have also necessitated positions of central authority. Large construction projects can be accomplished by small groups requiring little management if the effort is spread over a long time. However, the construction of fortifications would most likely need to be rapid, thus requiring as large a work force as possible. The absolute dates of these Wanka II sites suggest rapid construction of the domestic areas as well (Earle et al. 1987: Figure 61). Further, we know that modern traditional Andean communities have leaders who bring together members of each household in a community to complete tasks such as the annual cleaning of the irrigation system. It is possible that this was elaborated on with the move up hill. Individuals that had the authority to lead a number of communities onto the knolls may also have directed the construction of the defensive features and associated needs such as camelid corrals.

Hatúnmarca and Tunánmarca are the two communities that have non-domestic/

public precincts and architecture. Although the sites each have a division of two residential areas, the dual plaza complex between the two districts at Tunánmarca is different from the two central plazas at Hatúnmarca, although both are on the highest point within each district. The central plazas at Tunánmarca are the most clear evidence of a concern for a sense of community at the site level. Bothering to build a central space defined by walls that could potentially hold the whole populace suggests that the leadership had group gatherings in mind in the planning of the central sector. At Hatúnmarca, only the plaza in each sector could gather a crowd. All these areas provide a defined space for social or political gatherings that is accessible to all people in the settlement, unifying the newly created group while maintaining the division between the two districts. This dual division in the central plaza at Tunánmarca is identical to the spatial divisions described by B. J. Isbell in the modern town of Chuschi, and it is also like the Inkaic Cuzco with its two districts, meeting in a central plaza (Zuidema 1967).

There is other public architecture found only on these central sites. Rectangular structures are found in association with the open areas at Hatúnmarca (Earle et al. 1987: Figure 28), similar to those along the edge of the two large central plazas at Tunánmarca (Figure 10; Earle et al. 1987: Figure 4). These rectangular structures up to 100 sq. m in size are unique in Wanka II architecture. Domestic buildings are round and much smaller. The absence of comparable rectangular structures and plazas at other sites indicates their central position as civic and ceremonial centers for a group of satellite sites.

In addition, these knoll-top sites clearly have restricted access with very few entrances which are defended by overlooking ramparts and entry corridors. Near these entrances are also unique architectural features such as unusually large circular structures.

Artifacts

The ceramic assemblages from the Wanka II communities lend support to the existence of two alliances dividing these communities. Although the sites' assemblages share many types, there are noticeable differences between the two alliances (Costin 1986; LeBlanc 1981). These differences are especially clear if we compare the ceramic collections from Hatúnmarca and Tunánmarca.

Among the important differences are higher frequencies of the local Wanka Red and Cream slip at Tunánmarca, with higher frequencies of the local slipped and unslipped Base Clara, micaceous self-slip, and Wanka Plainware at Hatúnmarca (Costin 1986; Earle et al. 1987: Table 9). Other Wanka II sites, Umpamalca, Chawín, and J37 have ceramic assemblages very similar to that found at Tunánmarca. These sites are west and north of Tunánmarca, creating the northern alliance. The ceramic collections from southern J8 and J42 are more similar to those of Hatúnmarca. Thus the ceramic frequencies divide the Wanka II sites into two clusters, reinforcing the idea of two alliances with similar ceramic exchange or distribution networks. Clearly these ceramic exchange networks are not merely economically based, but reflect political trade barriers, since both alliances have more or less the same pottery types.

The chipped stone material also suggests two intercommunity alliances. From chipped debitage frequencies, Russell (1988b) has found that the residents of Umpamalca extracted raw material from the Pomacancha red chert quarry located to the northwest, and then processed the chert into prismatic blade cores for exchange. No prismatic blade cores have been found at Hatúnmarca, suggesting exchange of these lithics only among the northern group (Earle et al. 1976: Table 13).

The presence of two competitive groups is also supported by the Inka action towards them. Those sites with the same ceramic assemblages were similarly affected by the Inka expansion. Tunánmarca, Chawín, Umpamalca, and J37 were all abandoned in the Wanka III times. In contrast, Hatúnmarca, J8 and J42 continued to be occupied through the Late Horizon. These Inka relations support the likelihood of intercommunity political relationships beyond a shared ceramic and lithic tradition. How loosely these sites were affiliated is not yet well defined, although the distribution of public buildings favors a fairly tightly integrated political entity.

The continued occupation of Hatúnmarca, J8, and J42 into the Late Horizon suggests that these communities were among the first to surrender to the Inka, while Tunánmarca and its affiliated settlements may have continued to resist. Unpublished historical documents cited by Espinoza Soriano (1971: 31) state that Tunánmarca was one of the last Sausa communities to surrender to the Inka. Because of this, the rebellious group was broken up and resettled elsewhere around the Inka empire, such as the Chachapoyas area (Cieza de Leon 1959: 99; LeVine 1979; Vazquez de Espinoza 1969) or in the Ayacucho province at Sarhua (Palomino Flores 1971).

Documents

Historic documents provide supporting evidence of intersite political alliances. This information is found in the native interviews conducted by Francisco de Toledo, the fifth viceroy (1940 [1570]) and Andrés de Vega (1965 [1582]), the corregidor of Jauja (the Junin province). These two documents (*visitas*) contain the only information which specifically pertains to the period prior to the Inka invasion in the Wanka region. The following discussion is based on document analysis completed by LeVine (1979; 1985); LeBlanc (1981), and D'Altroy (1987).

The five individuals interviewed by Toledo all claimed to be native leaders (*curacas*) between 83 and 94 years of age. The interviews were undertaken specifically to investigate the situation prior to the expansion of the Inka and the conditions surrounding their incorporation into Tawantinsuyu. The Spanish objective was to show that throughout the highlands the native populations had been independent of the Inka until recently and that they had submitted to the Inka under duress (Hemming 1970: 412). The report should therefore be viewed with some caution in the light of this political agenda.

Vega's inquiry was undertaken to report on the impact of the *reducción* of the previous decade. The *reducción* was the policy of resettling the natives into fewer towns in easily accessible locations, to increase Spanish control and facilitate conversion to Catholicism. His report is less precise than Toldeo's, for it synthesized the Sausa and Wanka responses. These informants were probably discussing the time of their great-grandfathers. Whether this lends doubt to the accuracy of the information depends on the type of material handed down from generation to generation, their consistency of responses, and on the importance that the group placed on remembering these types of events (O. Harris pers. comm.). While we know that the Wanka rebelled against the Inka by aiding the Spanish in order to regain their own autonomy, at the time of the interviews they were again conquered people. This suggests that they might find the pre-Inka times an important history to remember as a time of autonomous rule. In addition, there is consistency in the answers given by the five Toledo informants interviewed on different days.

From the interviews we gain a picture of a society that focuses on warfare and competition between groups. This competition forms the basis of intercommunity political interaction, something we have seen continuing in modern Andean settings through the use of *tinku* and *ch'axwa* fighting as part of intra- and intercommunity structure (Chapter 3). The leaders recognized by the Wanka were called *cinchekona*, translated as war leaders, *valientes*, valiant men, *capitanes*, captains, and in some cases *señores*, translated as lords: "cinchekonas los quales por hazerse señores . . . ", "*cinchekona* whom by being made lords . . . " (Toledo 1940: 22). Both documents state that each community and each individual was independent and did not recognize the authority of any one lord, yet many responses mention leaders in each community, and also that leaders formed groups of several communities. In response to questions about the pre-Inka government, they state:

> in the time of their heathenism, before the time of the Inka, they were never under the control of anyone, except that in each one of these districts they had as their lords the bravest natives there were . . .
> (Vega 1965: 169)

> before the Inkas there was no lord in this land other than that each town and the natives of it were lords of what they had and of their lands . . .
> (Toledo 1940: 22)

Given such emphasis on war and war leaders, there is a possibility that these "lords" were leaders only temporarily in time of attack. However, these references suggest a more multifaceted authority.

Several questions focused on the leaders' authority within one or more settlements. There was some variability in the responses, although all implied that no lord had control over the whole province. Most of the informants said or inferred that each *pueblo* (community) had a *cinchekona* that governed itself. There is one response which associates a *cinchekona* with several settlements, suggesting that one leader and his/her followers had control over more than one community, and another stating that one leader protected up to half of the southern Wanka province of Ananhuancas. One informant also noted that communities close to each other would more likely have amicable relations, suggesting that alliances did exist in spatial clusters. The interviews also provide evidence that settlements aggregated together at times under the power of one leadership.

> since there were wars among natives and towns, when there was a valiant man chosen from among them called *cinchekona* meaning "now here is this valiant man," those who could not [defend themselves] took shelter with him and with the town that had wars with the other and said, "this is the valiant man who defends us from our enemies, let us obey him" and thus they obeyed him and had no other manner of government.
> (Toledo 1940: 18)

It is possible that both governing circumstances are correct, that some settlements did govern and control their own actions and resources, while others banded together into larger polities under a more centralized authority, at least for a time.

In support of multiple community alliances, we see the existence of multiple site clusters, artifactual distributions, and settlement sizes for the two northwestern alliances, augmented by the historic documents' suggestions of intergroup relations and multiple village aggregation. In the next section, where a description of leadership and community relations is described, we will learn about what they claim they were fighting over.

Wealth differences within communities

With evidence suggesting that some of the later Wanka were in alliances that had political leaders while others may have had only their own village leaders, let us turn to more specific data about the political and economic relationships between the leadership and the populace. In the political sector leaders are called *cinchekona*, in the economic we have labeled richer people "elites." After reconstructing the economic domain from the archaeological and documentary evidence, we will see if two classes exist within the Sausa.

Architecture

The dual organization, architecturally visible within the two central sites of Hatúnmarca and Tunánmarca, suggests a level of village political integration that also might indicate economic differences. As already noted (Chapter 3), political leaders in Andean communities today, the *varayoq*, do not have a radically different life style from the other members of the community, though they more intensively accumulate and recycle material objects, do more work, have more people helping them at various times, and have higher status within the community, including wearing certain emblems of prestige (Bastien 1978; B. J. Isbell 1978). They tend to be both the political leaders and the goods accumulators. Using this as a guide, we can look at the Wanka II economic and the documentary data on the pre-Inka Wanka wealth distribution.

Within the intra-site districts and satellites we can examine archaeological evidence for economic stratification in the domestic context. Variation in the quantity and quality of resources found between different households and the variability of architectural features has been used by New World archaeologists to indicate unequal access to goods, with the possibility of reflecting different status (Whalen 1976; Winter and Pires-Ferreira 1976). It is assumed that domestic groups having more better-quality or higher-valued items in association with higher labor input in their houses will have had more access to goods and labor and will be of a higher economic status than other groups that do not have these characteristics.

In 1978 LeBlanc completed a small study of domestic architecture at Hatúnmarca to look for the range of different house types (1981). The objective was to identify structures which exhibited unusual features, higher-quality construction, or a larger size; characteristics that show a greater labor input into house construction. In all, 155 structures were investigated. The quality in execution of wall construction was quite uniform, although some walls clearly received more care with more chinking stones and better dressed stones. Local limestone rocks of about the same size were laid to form two courses with mortar and chinking stones. Similarly, there was only rare evidence of special architectural features such as ventilation holes and niches. There was, however, a real variation in structure size. The smallest architectural type was used for interment, being about 2.5–3 m in diameter. The remaining circular structures varied considerably, ranging from 3 to 6.5 m across, with a floor area between 6 and 30 sq. m. Some of these larger structures tended to occur together in larger patio compound groups, where there were more structures per domestic unit, and more patio space among the structures. From this architectural information and the spatial distributions of these larger patios, LeBlanc suggested that there were central residential zones within each Hatúnmarca district that may have been neighborhoods housing wealthier or "elite" families (1981: 303).

This architectural study was then extended in the 1982–83 field seasons, when seventeen of these Wanka II patio compounds were excavated to substantiate LeBlanc's identification of wealthy-elite households from "commoner" households. Using patio size, number of structures per patio compound, quality of masonry, and location within the site, patios were identified and excavated as being elite (large) or commoner (small) residences. We also returned to the 1979 excavations and labeled them as to their status based on these architectural criteria (DeMarrais n.d.).

Artifacts

These status definitions were borne out by the excavated artifactual data of ceramics, chipped and grinding stone, metals, spinning whorl evidence, shell, and faunal data (Costin 1986; Costin and Earle 1989; Earle et al. 1987; Russell 1988b; Sandefur 1988b). Almost uniformly, the artifactual data reflected our original status assessment of each patio compound (Earle et al. 1987; D'Altroy and Hastorf n.d.; Hastorf 1990a; Figure 13). That is, the large patios had more higher-quality goods, trade wares, and denser evidence of production. Because of these results, we feel comfortable using two different status designations concerning the Wanka II sites, especially to investigate economic differences.

In this analysis I also assume that denser artifacts reflect more activity within a patio compound (Costin 1986; Russell 1988b). It has been put forward that the denser deposits indicate different trash disposal practices or longer occupation rather than activity differences. I do not accept these criticisms, first, because the denser material correlates with higher-status goods and larger patios; second, these sites were all occupied for a short time (100 years) and there is evidence for only slight rebuilding; and third, there is no evidence of trash deposits outside of the residential area, suggesting that most trash was deposited within the living compounds. The larger compounds could have housed more people who produced more trash.

In general, all patio compounds had the full spectrum of goods, with only the frequencies changing. Thus each patio contained evidence of the typical range of domestic tasks, further suggesting families did not have servants or workers who completed basic activities elsewhere, and brought them into the elites' homes for consumption. Nor is there evidence for control over others' skilled labor in the form of attached specialists. There were no homes where only very special activities occurred as has been documented on the coast (Shimada 1978; Topic 1982). There are, however, a series of artifactual frequencies that support and illustrate economic differences between the statuses and show specialization and exchange between the communities.

Large compounds had higher densities of almost all artifacts, suggesting that the occupants were more productive, stored more goods, or perhaps had more residents or workers (kin, slaves, or servants). This is particularly well illustrated by the lithic frequencies. The red chert cores harvested by the Umpamalca residents and distributed as blades are more dense in elite patios, 3.51/cu. m. versus 2.21/cu. m in the commoners' (Figure 13; Russell 1988b). Increased activity is also seen in the higher densities of agricultural hoes in the large patios: 0.54/cu. m versus 0.13/cu. m (Earle et al. 1987: 95). These chipped and ground stone items are parts of tool kits used for processing plant and animal matter and preparing food. They suggest that all patios were involved in all of these activities. Based on shape and outer charring presence, the pottery has been divided into four functions: individual serving bowls, large serving basins, storage jars (for liquid or food), and open necked jars for cooking. The elite patio compounds had more storage jars (864 gm/cu. m for elites versus 164 gm/cu. m for commoners) and large serving basins (530 gm/cu. m for elites versus 110 gm/cu. m for commoners: Costin and Earle 1989; Figure 13). These higher densities suggest elites stored more food or liquids (water or maize beer) and feasted more with their large serving basins (Costin 1986; Costin and Earle 1989).

In addition to the status differences seen in the type frequencies, elite patio compounds had more labor-intensive pottery styles across the board. Elites had more locally made decorated ceramics. Wanka Red (elite 1,249 gm/cu. m versus commoner 408 gm/cu. m) and Base Clara (elite 3,056 gm/cu. m versus commoner 171 gm/cu. m), more regionally exchanged Andesite wares (elite 2,670 gm/cu. m versus commoner 666 gm/cu. m), as well as more exotic types from outside the Mantaro region (Costin 1986; Earle et al. 1987: Table 10). Perhaps the most radical difference between these two household groups occurs in the exotic ceramics, with many more (166 gm/cu. m) in the elite trash (versus 30 gm/cu. m). This suggests that the elite families had more networks within and beyond the local Sausa alliances to gain the southern Mantaro Valley Andesite wares as well as other items from beyond. In these data we see some of the domains in which the richer elites gained access and power.

Accompanying this evidence of greater food processing and serving in the elite patios, however, is the evidence of meat-bearing animals (guinea pigs and camelids), represented by the minimum number of individuals converted to kg of meat/cu. m (Figure 13). They do not show a status difference. The guinea pig bones are even more dense in the smaller patio compounds, with 0.28 kg/cu. m than the larger, with 0.24 kg/cu. m (Sandefur 1988b). The camelids are close with 137 kg/cu. m from elite versus 118 kg/cu. m from commoner patios. Interestingly, there is no more evidence for hunted deer in the elites than in the commoners (Sandefur 1988b).

Greater access to high-valued items by the elites is also seen in the metal distribution. Metal artifacts are often not industrial, as most of the objects uncovered from the Wanka II proveniences were decorative tumi pins and disks. One can see a real difference in access to these visible and valued items from the ubiquities of the different metal types, especially silver and copper (arsenical bronze), both utilitarian and decorative. Less than 4 percent of the elite proveniences had silver, while only 0.7 percent of the commoners did (Figure 13). While there is less copper present overall, it is still differentially distributed between the two compound statuses, though the commoners seemed to decorate themselves with copper almost as much as the elites. Lead, a derivative of the silver extraction process and much more commonly used for utilitarian items like needles, accounts for 0.8 percent in elite and 0.5 percent in commoner compounds (Owen n.d.: Table 6). The likelihood is that these metals were locally produced in the puna around the Sausa region, although a search did not locate any pre-Inka mines (Owen pers. comm.).

Also purely decorative or ritually important is the marine shell, which shows the elites having more access to these long-distance items (Figure 13; Earle et al. 1987). This trend of high-value goods being produced and used in elite patio compounds is also seen in the spindle whorl frequencies which represent wool processing and cloth weaving. These whorls are twice as dense per cubic meter in the elite than in the commoner patios (Costin 1984).

The artifact frequencies reflect better access to high-valued goods as well as more activity in the elite patios. In these compounds there is more production, more accumulation, and more consumption of goods. The elites, however, did not seem to control the production of goods or raw materials, as there is evidence of production throughout all sites and statuses. Nor did they have total control over the commoners' access, as all artifact classes and styles were also found in the smaller patio compounds. Many farming items are made in the smaller patios. But the larger patio compounds also had agricultural tools, suggesting that they too farmed fields, produced domestic pottery, and chipped stone for domestic use.

A likely scenario is that the elites had more people working for them either because of larger families or by having servants or slaves, and therefore they had more access to trade goods. Elite patio compounds did have more intensive production of certain highly valued products: silver, spinning tools, marine shell, and as we will see in the chapters to come they received and stored more maize. They also had more production and processing tools, such as stone hoes, storage jars, cooking jars, and utilitarian copper.

These data quite strongly corroborate economic status differences in the Wanka II times, with some very provocative insights into the activities of the more wealthy families. From the artifactual data we also learn that the Wanka II elites were like entrepreneurs, having more intensive exchange networks, producing for themselves and for exchange while focusing on certain objects to produce, to store, and to consume that were more visible and of higher value. There is also evidence that they perhaps more often hosted their allies, both from the settlement and from the alliance, in feasting and drink.

We do not yet know that these economic elites are the same people as the political *cinchekona* and their followers. By pursuing information on the political leadership we

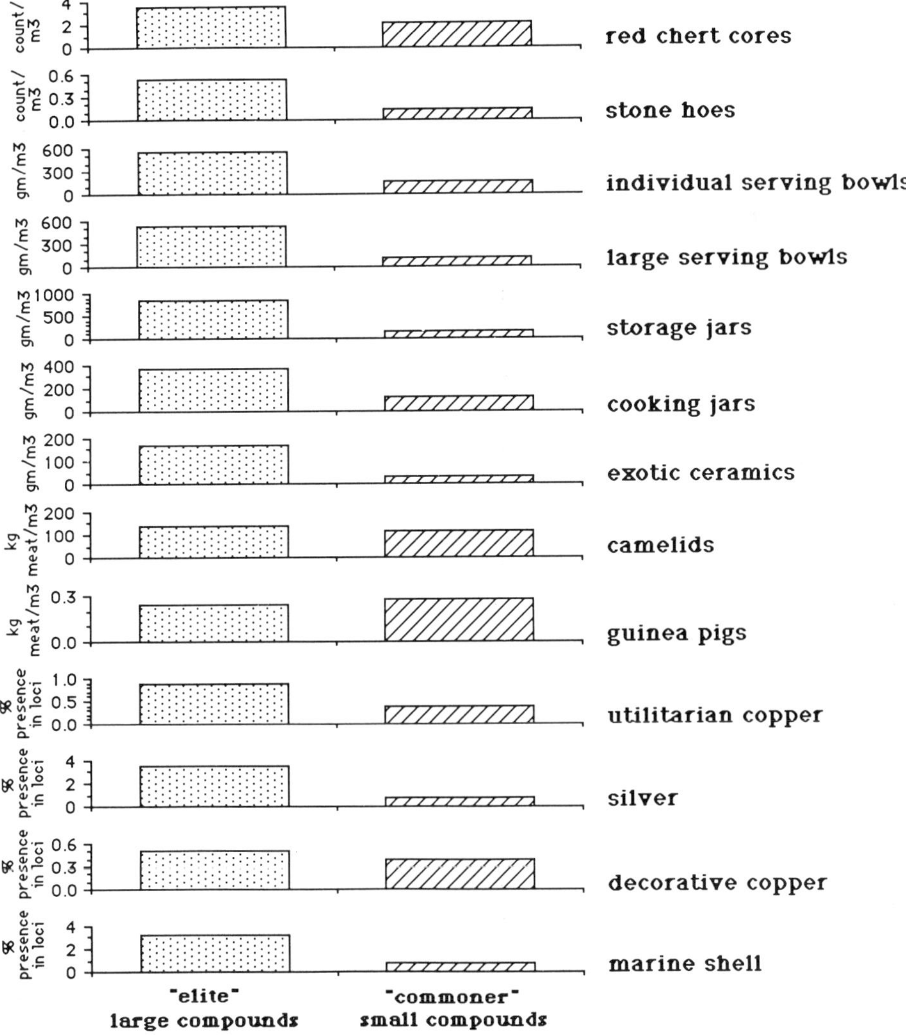

Fig. 13. Bar chart comparing Wanka II artifact presence for "elites" and "commoners". The first two rows are from Russell 1988b, rows 2–7 from Costin 1986, rows 8 and 9 from Sandefur 1988b, and rows 10–13 from Costin and Earle 1989.

can look for evidence of the *cinchekona*'s economic domains, determining if the two status systems were intertwined or separate.

Documents

The picture of Wanka II community life seen in the artifacts can be augmented with information from the two *visitas* of the sixteenth century. The economics and its relationship to politics can be studied by looking in the documents for information on the leaders' methods of gaining position, material goods, and their amount of control over resources.

We have learned that the leaders spoken of most often are the war leaders or *cinchekona*. We know that they were important in time of war, organizing attacks and protection. We also assume that some of them had protective power over several communities and even brought communities together. Of their power within their communities, we still must uncover evidence. One way may be to learn how they were chosen, for we might assume that the way people talk about succession can inform us about the form of the power structure. When asked how the *cinchekona* were selected, the informants interviewed by Toledo stressed that the leaders were individuals who were brave and who would defend the community from their enemies, often noting their authority in war.

> that they weren't afraid, that they defended and protected them and that thus they went before them and if the said *cinchekona* conquered and they saw that they were brave they chose them for their captains . . .
> (Toledo 1940: 34)

Being successful was necessary but risky; yet gaining these positions was actively contested over with some degree of coercion and even force. Holding onto these leadership positions was not done just through group consensus:

> the settlements selected them because they know them to be brave and so that they would defend them and that sometimes some *cinchekona* became their bosses by force of arms . . .
> (Toledo 1940: 27)

That leadership positions were desirable is hinted at when the informants discussed how leaders gained power, including usurpation of other leaders.

Asked specifically about the transferal of the position upon the death of a leader, several informants indicated that a son or other relative of the *cinchekona* could gain the position but would not automatically inherit unless he was able to do the job.

> when such a *cinchekona* whom they had selected for their captain died the said office died with him and his sons were not his successors and the natives turned to select another *cinchekona* of those whom they know would help them in the wars and who had a good understanding and that when the said *cinchekona* left a son who was brave they chose him . . .
> (Toledo 1940: 35)

> that during the lifetime of the *cinchekona* it happened that a *cinchekona* had sons and sent some to war with the people and that when he showed himself to be brave the natives said that he was good for the office of *cinchekona* and he was it after the death of his father and that[*cinchekona*] protected and defended them and that if a *cinchekona* had two or three capable and brave sons they chose all of them to be *cinchekona* and that when they were not they selected others and that when the sons of the *cinchekona* were young they named others until they were older . . .
> (Toledo 1940: 23–24)

If we go along with these statements, we learn how the leaders must be accepted by the group but must also perform successfully in the designated tasks of war. This position does not seem to be associated with a particular family or lineage, although when sons were aggressive and successful they may have been accepted as the next leader. This is not surprising for we would assume that the sons living in the household of a leader would experience the activities involved and know the network of people associated with the position. It is possible that a more politically powerful leader could ensure that his sons succeeded to the position on his death as well as help him run the communities during life.

From this evidence it can be suggested that the Late Intermediate Period populace had leaders at all times, and that the positions could have been in the process of becoming more codified, especially after the move up onto the knolls. The method of choosing leaders, however, seems more flexible. Basically, there was always a group of followers/warriors that could compete for the top position, given a death or a series of losses in battle. In fact, it is very possible that intercommunity alliances were created through rivalries for a *cinchekona* position.

Although the informants repeatedly stress war as the main sphere of authority, there are aspects hinted at of fierce warfare (*ch'axwa*), and of plunder and defense, indicating that war leaders had other roles and activities within the community. These could have allowed them to gain economically in the war leader position. Such a position probably entailed a broad set of responsibilities including hosting allies and troops at feasts, organizing community work groups, and even organizing agriculture and land divisions. The interviews mention defense as the important *raison d'être* for having a leader, but, in turn, the leaders could have used warfare to promote and transfer power to other domains like group cohesion: a feedback system that kept the leadership alive and the group aggregated. Again, what was the benefit for the leadership, besides securing prestige and safety?

> that these *cinchekona* always wanted there to be war among them because they [*cinchekona*] would hold fiestas for them [the community] and they [the community] would respect them [*cinchekona*] better . . .
> (Toledo 1940: 31)

> that these native *cinchekona* very much wished there to be war between some settlements and others for the purpose of becoming one of those who was

> well respected and esteemed and to have a greater position as lord (more power) . . .
> (Toledo 1940: 34)

Thus it would seem that a leader's ability to maintain his authority was through warfare, but with this he could also gain respect and power to act in other areas. In the above we see how feasts are linked to this position, to which the artifactual data already have alluded.

The extension of power into other realms is expressed most explicitly when the informant talked not of war but of peace and other dimensions of leadership. Three of the five informants speaking to Toledo said that the lords governed in peace as well as in war (1940: 23, 24). It is very likely that these war leaders were instrumental in settling disputes within the community, especially in large sites such as Hatúnmarca and Tunánmarca, where several previously separate communities were brought together within the same walls.

There are also statements in the documents about the economic functions of the *cinchekona*. Responses about compensation to the leaders state that *cinchekona* were respected but did not receive taxes in kind. Surely there was compensation in labor (Smith 1989; Wachtel 1973). The statements suggest this, that the *cinchekona* did gain resources from their position. For example, people may have worked in the leaders' fields, or maybe, when a battle was won, the successful lords received lands, women, goods, other material, and people to work the land (Vega 1965: 169; Toledo 1940: 23, 31).

> when some towns did not wish to submit peacefully the *cinchekona* made war on the opposing natives and killed them and took their lands and other times took control of the towns where the [opposing] *cinchekona* were from and to those who submitted peacefully they left them their lands because they wanted to be their vassals . . .
> (Toledo 1940: 24)

This form of warfare (*ch'axwa*), in which the defeated group becomes affiliated with and subservient to the conquering group, suggests that expansionistic control might have been part of daily life before the Inka. Leaders would have had means to increase the economic standing of their households through the acquisition of fields, plunder, women, vassals, and labor. All the while, the authority of a leader and the associated economic privileges were directly related to this success in defending the community and its resources. And this would have been linked together through the concept of balanced reciprocity.

If private ownership of land was not the norm, then this newly acquired land would be for the leader's *ayllu*, barrio, or kin group. It is also very likely that the incorporated inhabitants worked part of the land for the leader, as was done so commonly in the Inka empire on state lands (Wachtel 1973: 67).

The material payment of more wives, more people working, and the right to distribute plunder could lead to unequal distributions of wealth among the victor's community, creating an economic difference between the *cinchekona* and their close followers versus the remainder of the population. Different material frequencies would exist if the *cinchekona*'s household had a larger labor force with a large family and servants. More labor could also lead to larger allocations of communal land (*tupus*). Traditionally, land was allocated according to the amount contributed to the community labor force. Thus a family with more access to labor was considered rich and well placed to provide a leader, linking the economic aspect to a political position (Wachtel 1973: 64). Suggested by the artifactual data, the increased quantities of valuables produced, received, and exchanged in some houses were probably displayed or given away at the feasting activities held in the leader's compounds, to solidify his followers and keep his allies.

Feinman and Neitzel (1984) note that there is no constellation of tasks that associate with non-state leadership, but there are many that can be associated with the onset of stratification; organizing village meetings, ceremonies, warfare, distribution of goods, etc. This analysis suggests that the Sausa leaders were most probably involved in these same activities, using the cultural principles of reciprocity, communal participation, balanced equality through labor and feast exchanges, and war to gain and maintain power.

We can see from these diverse data sources that, for the Wanka II Sausa population, there was a promotion of leaders who gained power, prestige, and material wealth. Therefore it seems probable that the wealthier elite were at one time *cinchekona* or their followers. As time passed various families or groups could have gained a larger network over other *ayllus*, which meant handling larger amounts of goods, circulating through and consumed in their compounds. From this we have a mixed picture of economic control in the Wanka II times. The elites did not control craft production or access to goods, yet they did have more of everything.

One of the *cinchekona*'s mechanisms to maintain this higher level of activity would have been to keep hostilities and combat alive. It was through war, prowess, political negotiation, and increasing allies that the *cinchekona* retained their rights to their position. This allowed unequal political positions to flourish, using Andean constructs of duality, hierarchy, *ayllu* community work, and feasts.

At the height of Wanka II, leaders probably had domain over several *ayllus* and more than one settlement. Allies were brought in either through "volunteering" (relinquishing independence and joining for protection) or through force. Both of these paths to inequality and loss of autonomy were proposed in Chapter 1, and surely both were operating within the Sausa population as individual families and communities negotiated their security, autonomy, and survival within times of war. Yet no one leader became the dominant force in the region, for we do not see one center taking over all the others. Power was not regionally centralized.

The role of warfare in political power

What is the archaeological evidence that will clarify the types of warfare the Sausa were involved in and help us to situate the role of warfare in Sausa society?

We know that the Wanka II settlements express defense and hostility in their locations, architecture, and spatial organization. The forbidding walls reminded everyone that they lived in a state of war. The *visitas* mention the weapons used in Wanka warfare. These included hunting equipment as well as slings made of wool (*hondas*), spears (sharpened sticks), *bolas* (leather and small round stones), and maces (*sacmana*, stone mace heads and sticks) (Vega 1965: 169; and Delgado pers. comm. for modern *tinku* weapons). Only the round *bola* stones and the mace heads would be evident in the archaeological record. These stones exist in the Wanka II excavations but have not been analyzed for evidence of warfare. The mace heads are round like doughnuts or spiked like a star, with a hole in the middle that attaches the stone to a long stick. Their frequencies show that they were most common in Wanka II times (Hastorf et al. 1989; Russell 1988a). In the Wanka II the elites had more of these mace heads, with a standardized count of 0.20/cu. m as opposed to commoner densities of 0.09/cu. m (Earle et al. 1987: Table 14). There were probably many perishable weapons. We get only a hint about the Wanka II elites being more active in war from the artifactual data.

It is again the interviews that clarify the role of warfare for us. When asked about warfare, the informants noted that it was a normal state of affairs. Warfare was considered a part of daily life to the pre-Inka natives. Toledo did not specifically ask about the events which led up to conflict, but one of the informants proposed that an increase in the size of a community led to offensive actions by that community in order to acquire fields, stored food, and women (Toledo 1940: 24, 28). Most of the informants commented that they went to war to acquire land. In fact, mention was made several times that the objective of war was to take possession of land, kill the previous owners, and divide up the land among the victors, or take the inhabitants as working servants/slaves (Toledo 1940: 28).

The documents suggest that successful *cinchekona* took land and were responsible for organizing its apportionment, or took control over defeated communities, requiring tribute from them. Hierarchical relationships among communities and among their leaders would thus have been created for management and protection of these lands, in peace and in war.

Bastien (1978) mentions a type of aggressive war occurring in Bolivia earlier this century where several settlements banded together to defend their fields. Comments such as this suggest that communities could have been fighting in order to gain more land and more people to work it. Need for more land during Wanka II is discussed below, after the agricultural data have been presented, but the aggregated Wanka II settlement conditions must have escalated the focus on land with the move away from milder valley lands.

Platt (1986: 401; 1987) discusses a similar type of land acquisition with regard to modern *ch'axwa* warfare in Bolivia. These statements clearly link agriculture with war, as labor and land are prime targets in these "fierce wars". With war so important in the Late Intermediate, culminating in the Late Horizon conquests, it is curious that the documents do not mention *tinku*. Perhaps it did not fit into the Spanish vision of the Andean political order. Alternatively, *tinku* is a ritual while conquest warfare is not, being more similar to what they were seeking.

We have learned from the documents that warfare was an axis on which political power increased in Wanka II times. We also know that there are two types of warfare in Andean culture, *tinku* and *ch'axwa*. Both of these forms of war could have been extant in Wanka II times from the documentary interviews, the architecture, and the settlement patterns. Although warfare is not a universal cause of political or economic stratification, the documents dwell on its importance for the Sausa, and probably in many other pre-modern Andean cases as well (Haas 1982; Wilson 1988). War was one of the nexes from which individuals could transform the cultural principles to gain power.

The anthropological literature suggests intergroup conflict as an important mechanism for social stratification. Models by Fried (1967) and Carneiro (1970) are based on Marxist materialist views that suggest that the cause of the conflict is the control or expansion of the means of production and resources. I suggest that there are sufficient examples to show that this is only part of the path to inequality for the Sausa. Other factors are also relevant, such as labor exchange. Ethnographic literature reveals that the role of conflict varies considerably from society to society (Divale 1971), and so too the outcomes of warfare. Routing and plunder can be important for individuals to gain prestige and social position but they have no permanent domination over the raided (Ford 1972; Rappaport 1968; Spencer 1965). Such activities are suggested in the Wanka historic documents. Subjugation of the conquered requires more elaborate bureaucracies and organization to maintain. This aspect of power consolidation is seen of course in the Inka case (Rowe 1946), as it is in the pre-Iron Age tribes of Europe (Nash 1978). In this second outcome of warfare, greater political centralization must operate to manage and maintain these stratified relations. There is support for this in the Wanka documents.

To answer the question why warfare escalated in the Wanka era, we must remember a series of political and structural aspects of the Sausa situation. The broader political climate at the time must be considered. We know that the larger polities of the Middle Horizon had collapsed and whatever political or economic integration that had been achieved dissolved. Sometime during the Late Intermediate there began a series of skirmishes between the inhabitants of the Cuzco region (the Inka) and the Ayacucho region (the Chanka). This eventually spread up into Huancavelica, which borders the Wanka territory to the south (Palomino Flores 1971; Rowe 1946). This breakup of pan-Andean interactions, as well as the growing threat from the south, could have had repercussions that encouraged an escalation in local tensions and conflict.

Also relevant is the concept of war. Conflict in the form of *tinku* is a social structure within Andean society that today helps solve conflicts between communities, *ayllus*, and sexes. *Ch'axwa* is the fiercer form of war outside of ritual time, where aggrandizement can occur (Platt 1987). Given that we have evidence of war in the valley as well as in the rest of the Andes before the Inka expansion, it could have escalated in the post-Wari climate, at first to neutralize social tensions and affirm political boundaries but later in some cases it could have become a nexus for rapid power centralization.

Warfare surely played an important role in defining political and economic structures in the Jauja region, at times escalatory and hierarchical, at other times moderating and balancing. It seems to have been the way to gain prestige and wealth but it was always tempered by intense social mediation.

Summary

When we look at individual Wanka II domestic compounds we see a range of frequencies in the different artifact classes. These, like the range in settlement sizes, suggest that within the Sausa there were differences in political and economic involvement, even in the incorporation into the larger multiple community alliances. If, as proposed in this chapter, there is sufficient evidence for political stratification in the Wanka II phase, we might expect that some leaders became involved in generating more wealth in order to maintain their position of control. The wealth differences, however, do not suggest control over all resources or production but do show some differential access. In this way war was embedded in many domains of Sausa life, including political, social, and economic. In fact it could be said that war linked the political actions of the groups to the economics of agricultural production, especially for the Wanka II inhabitants.

We can further assume that these political dynamics were active during pre-Wanka times, for we have evidence of the impact of warfare in the pre-Wanka data, in the trophy-head figures. Up until the Wanka I Period we do not see much visible manifestation of discrete community alliances or conflict in the archaeological record. By the Wanka II Period, there is evidence of an increased inclusion of the economic sphere within the political. We can now look more closely at how agricultural production contributed to this process of political hegemony. Agriculture is the backbone of Sausa society and also intimately intertwined with warfare and politics.

III

AGRICULTURAL PRODUCTION IN THE MANTARO REGION

6

The regional environment and its crops

Andean agriculture is complex because of the rugged topography, intricate landscape, and many microclimates often found close to each other. Thus, when studying agricultural production, one cannot discuss a region as if it were one agricultural zone: the different possible uses and potentials must be elucidated. This diverse landscape forms the base of Andean life, both symbolically and economically (Chapter 3). As noted in Chapter 5, land and harvests were two of the targets in the endemic warfare encouraged by the pre-colonial Sausa war leaders (Toledo 1940). In the link between economics and politics, agricultural production and access are central. Agriculture generates sustenance as it ties people to their land, to their past through land inheritance, ancestors, resource maintenance, and to each other through exchange labor (Chapters 2 and 3).

The Mantaro River Valley lies in the central highlands of Peru, surrounded by small valleys, dissected foothills, and subalpine plateaus that step up to the two towering Cordillera ranges of the Andean mountain chain. The Mantaro, a major intermontane river, issues from the northwest side of Lake Junín (Chinchaycocha), flowing south across a high plateau, then through the Cordillera Occidental into a rugged gorge, where it enters the western side of the study region. Near the modern town of Jauja, the river flows out onto a large alluvial plain, 4 to 24 km wide, which extends 60 km southeast, beyond the city of Huancayo. From the valley plain, the river heads southeast through Huancavelica to Acobamba, turning east and dropping towards the Amazon basin, where it joins the Apurimac River. As in much of the Andes, the topography of the Jauja study region has been formed by a series of diverse sedimentary, glacial, and tectonic actions. The Mantaro Valley was formed by an uplift disconformity sometime between the Late Pliocene and Early Pleistocene (Harrison 1956). The eastern and western sides of the Mantaro Valley have very different geological histories, topographies, and soils (Harrison 1943; Megard 1968; SCIPA 1956).

The study region (Figure 1), approximately 25 by 43 km in size (11°37'70"–11°53'30"S, 72°22'20"–75°37'20"W), is bordered by high puna plateau on three sides and the widening Mantaro Valley to the south. It contains a series of small tributary valleys, the Masma, the Paca, and the Yanamarca, whose valley floors range in elevation from 3380 to 3550 m.

These valleys are watered by small streams flowing from the surrounding slopes and springs. The valley basins are filled with Quaternary sediments, deposited by retreating glacial outwash. The soils range from fine loamy silts to false bedded coarse gravels (SCIPA 1956). Today each of these valleys contains a small lake in the process of desiccation as the valleys fill with hillside colluvial erosion. Only Laguna Paca can still be considered a year-round lake. Originally these valleys drained into the Mantaro River. All three lakes, however, have been cut off from the Mantaro drainage catchment by interglacial fill, alluvial, eolian sedimentation, and perhaps some tectonics (G. Seltzer and H. E. Wright Jr. pers. comm.).

To the west of the Yanamarca Valley, an upland limestone ridge that rises gradually to the puna has been sharply divided by the steep-sided Rio Quishualcancha (Figure 1). To the south, this upland was cut by the Rio Mantaro as it flows through a gorge. In the interglacial phases of the Quaternary period, the southeastern side of the Yanamarca Valley was sealed off from the Mantaro River by unconsolidated glacial gravels, forcing Laguna Tragadero to drain subterraneously into a limestone sinkhole.

To the east, a limestone ridge separates the Yanamarca Valley from the Paca Valley. The Paca Valley has been cut off and is today filled with a lake approximately 5000 years old (Wright in Hastorf et al. 1989). Today there is a modern canal connecting the lake to the Mantaro River so that the lake's water level can be regulated. The Masma Valley to the southeast of Paca also has a silted-in lake draining north to join the Rio Quero, and finally into the Mantaro River.

The Mantaro basin, compared to other Sierran regions, has a relatively large expanse of flat arable land. It is known for its agricultural richness and its large harvests of maize, Andean tubers, European cereals, and garden vegetables (Mayer 1979; Salera et al. 1954; Toledo 1940). The Jauja end of the valley is the highest and narrowest, therefore the study region cannot produce on the same scale as the southern Mantaro Valley.

Climate

In this intermontane area the two climatic seasons are rainy and dry. The drastic topographic relief of the Andean mountains creates diverse, localized climatic conditions. This in turn has a major effect on agricultural production. From the west, the Pacific Ocean anticyclone pushes cool, dry air up into the western mountains; from the east, the Atlantic anticyclone carries moist, warm tropical air over the Amazon basin up the eastern slopes of the Andes. Therefore, rainstorms in the Jauja region generally move in from the northeast, and the eastern side of the region receives more rainfall than the west. In the austral summer (September–March), thunderstorms arrive in the afternoons and early evenings (Schwerdtfeger 1976: 193). The remaining half of the year is distinctly drier with clear, warm days and freezing nights.

The Andean moisture regime varies tremendously. In the Mantaro region, consecutive drought years are rare, although critical rainfall at the onset of the rainy season can vary significantly. Precipitation from September through November is a major determinant of agricultural success, for only after the onset of steady continual rains can seeds be sown. A late onset of the steady rains can shift the time of crop maturation into the colder season. During the height of the rainy season (November–March), the recorded monthly average of rain in Jauja is 17 mm, adequate for most nonirrigated agriculture. At the Jauja station of the Oficina Nacional de

Evaluacion de Recursos Naturales (ONERN), during fifteen years of recorded climatological data (1958–1972), September rainfall varied between a critically low 11 mm and a soggy 52.5 mm, with an average of 28.7 mm; November had a minimum of 22.8 mm and a maximum of 141.3 mm, averaging 62 mm, which is sufficient to ensure the germination of the seedlings. Within the altitude of the study area (3380–4100 m) hailstorms, although localized, can occur at any time during the rainy season, and can cause slight to extensive crop damage, depending on when they arrive in the crop's life cycle.

Unlike moisture, which varies with weather patterns and topography, temperature varies with altitude (Drewes and Drewes 1957; Seltzer 1987; 1990; Wright 1980). In Figure 14, the mean average temperature between 3,000 and 4,500 m has been charted for the higher Andes (Drewes and Drewes 1957; Johnson 1966; ONERN 1976; Papadakis 1961; United States Department of Commerce 1966).

Seasonal temperature variation is not pronounced. In fact, mean daily dry season temperatures can be nearly the same as those in the rainy season (Schwedtfeger 1976); it is the diurnal fluctuations that are seasonally different (Troll 1968: 19). In Huancayo the average daily temperature variation is approximately 17°C in the dry season and 13°C in the rainy season. Because of this diurnal effect, minimum temperatures are the most informative indicators of agricultural limitations; the mean daily minimum temperatures are lower in the dry season (US Department of Commerce 1966).

Despite the moderating effect of the rainy season's cloud cover, crop-damaging frosty nights may occur on the northern Mantaro Valley floor at any time of the year. Rainy season frost tends to hit in localized patches as cold air funnels down the water

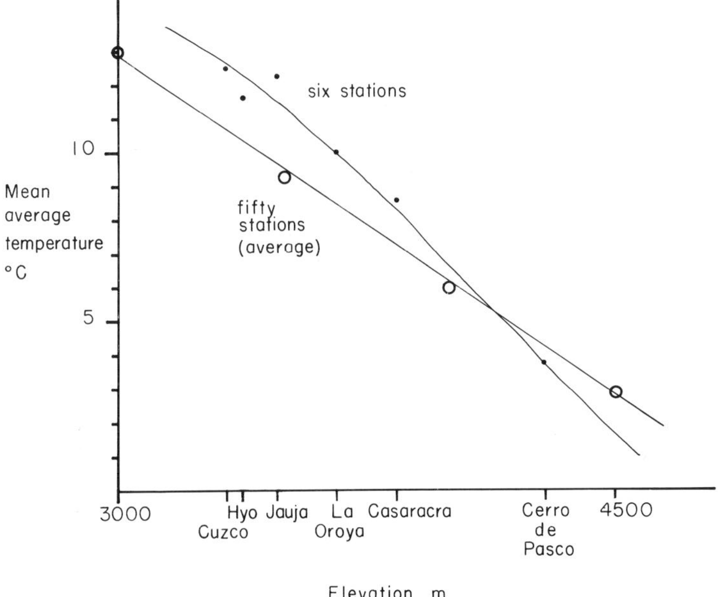

Fig. 14. Plot of mean average temperature from six field stations

drainages from the mountain sides and empties into the valleys. This localized frost is called *helada blanca* (Mayer 1979: 24). Frost damage increases with elevation, making serious crop damage rare below 3450 m. It is the settling property of cold air that leads farmers above 3500 m to prefer cultivating on slopes rather than flat land. Mayer (1979: 24) reports another type of frost, *helada negra*, which is much less frequent but potentially more damaging. It is caused by the movement of very cold, dry maritime air that can settle in large areas.

The frost free and frost prone zones of the study region are illustrated in Figure 15. The lower limit of frosts roughly coincides with the upper edge of maize production, especially in the hills and protected areas. In my modern agricultural study (Chapter 7), farmers in the small valleys of Paca, Masma, and Yanamarca all noted that they occasionally had to stay out all night burning shrubs to blanket their crops with warm smokey air when a *helada blanca* frost occurred on the valley floors.

In a xerophytic environment such as the Mantaro Valley, the rate of evapotranspiration is as important as is precipitation for the success of crops. The evapotranspiration rate, influenced by temperature, cloud cover, and humidity, is the amount of water lost out of the ground into the atmosphere as a result of solar radiation. If the evapotranspiration rate is low, meaning not much moisture is lost to the atmosphere, a low rainfall area can be as arable as a higher rainfall area with a higher rate of evapotranspiration (Kirkby 1973). In other words, an R/ET value of 1.0 or greater indicates that there is sufficient moisture in the soil for crop survival (R = rainfall, ET = evapotranspiration). A Jauja climate station recorded fourteen years of R/ET during the 1960s and 1970s. From this information we learn that December, January, February, and March all have R/ET values that lie above 1.0 and therefore have enough moisture for maturing crops. The critical months, October, November, and April, are at the beginning and end of the growing seasons. Their maximum and minimum R/ET ranges suggest that occasionally, but not always, these months provide adequate moisture. In the fourteen years of recorded data, seven years had R/ET values of less than 1.0 in both October and November, indicating drought conditions during the critical germination months. In this situation, the farmers can either irrigate at the onset of the agricultural cycle until the rains begin regularly, or they can sow later, making their crops vulnerable to the frosts that are more frequent at the end of the rainy season in May and June.

The paleoclimatic work that has been conducted in the central Andes has mapped and dated glacial advances, retreats, and maximal extensions (Hansen et al. 1984; Seltzer 1987; Seltzer and Hastorf 1990; Wright 1980; 1984). Wright's (1980) first study was of the glacial movements to the west of the Lake Junín basin. More recently, Wright and Seltzer worked in the eastern Cordillera at the southern edge of the Mantaro Valley. At both places they have tracked the glacial movements by dating the basal soils of terminal moraines and lake sediments that reflect the onset of glacial retreats. Each advance was less extensive than the previous one. The earliest and largest advance ended by c. 10,000 b.c. (SI-1490, SI-1489) and would have created an environment 2.1°C colder than today's average at Jauja. During the time span of this study, the ice advanced at least two more times, the first at approximately a.d. 250

(SI-6995A, WIS 1032). At this time the temperature in the Jauja region would have been approximately 0.6°C cooler than today's average. Although we do not know the exact timing of this onset we do feel confident with the sequence. After this advance there was a period of interglacial warming beginning at approximately a.d. 600, with temperatures much like today until the latest glacial advance, at approximately a.d. 1290 (WIS-1970, Wright 1988; Seltzer 1987; Seltzer and Hastorf 1990: 409). During this advance, roughly between a.d. 1200 and 1550, the average temperature was 0.6°C cooler than today's average. This 0.6°C average downward shift in temperature is comparable to an altitude shift of 70 m. In other words, around a.d. 1300 the central

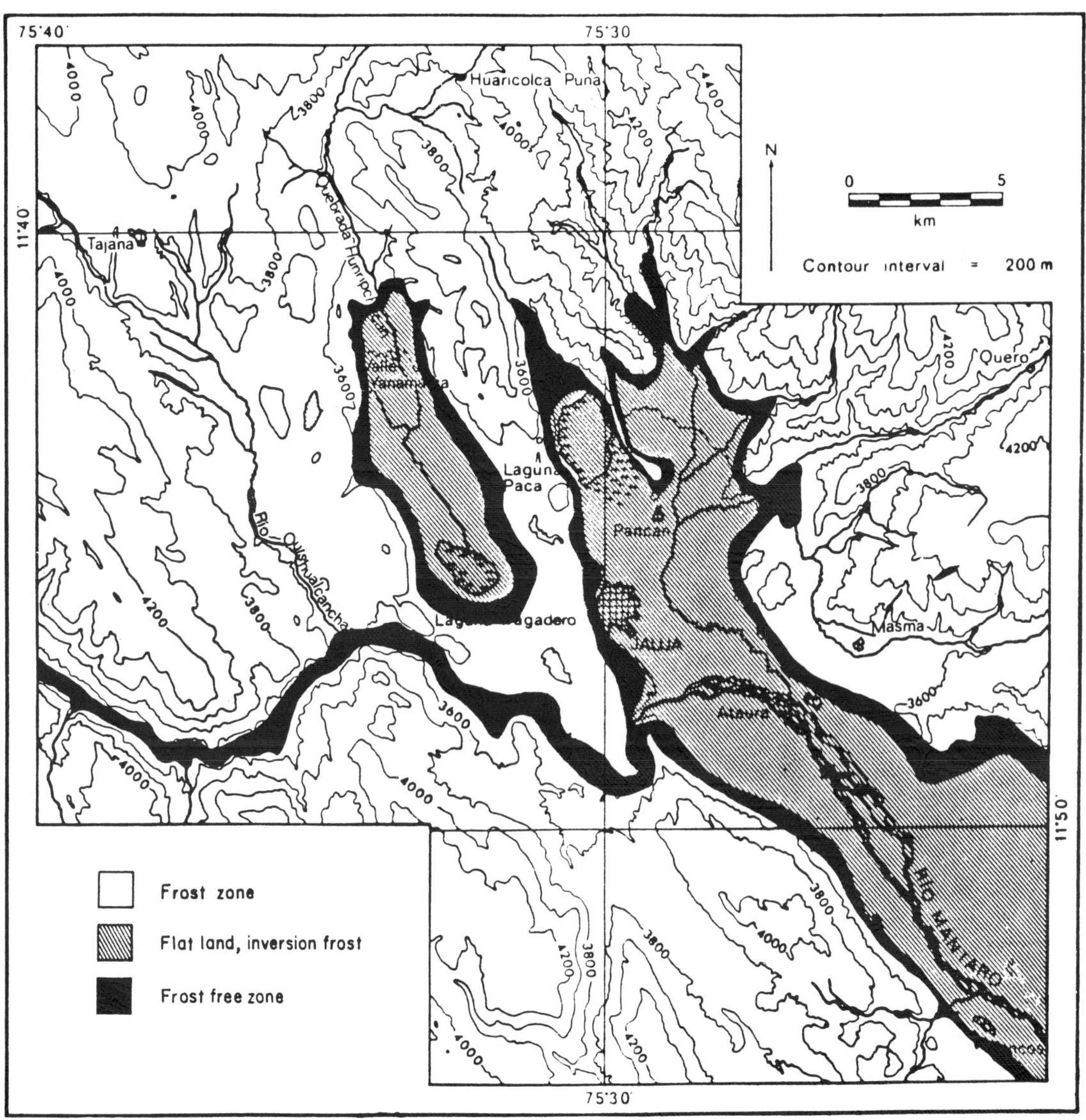

Fig. 15. Regional frost-free zone

Andean climate and vegetation we experience in the Mantaro Valley region today would have been shifted 70 m lower (Seltzer and Hastorf 1990).

The time depth of this archaeological project is from approximately a.d. 400 to 1460. Over this span of time the region moved into a warm interglacial phase and then, beginning around 1300, it became slightly cooler. In this cooler phase, the production zones would have retreated downslope some 70 m. During the Wanka II phase then, the frost free hillsides and protected areas would have been less extensive than at present, and the upper limits of production would have been restricted.

Regional biotic zones

Throughout the twentieth century a series of geographers and biologists have defined and described various microzones in the Andean region: they include Weberhauer (1945), Holdridge (1947), Drewes and Drewes (1957), Troll (1968), Tosi (1960), and Pulgar Vidal (1967).

The portion of the Mantaro Valley (3150–3400 m) in the study area consists of alluvial benches along the river and alluvial fans where the tributary streams enter the valley basins. This valley zone can be classified in Tosi's terms (1960: 11) as dry, lower montane savanna forest (*sebana o bosque seco montano bajo*), and by Pulgar Vidal (1967: 73), the *quichwa* zone. The subxerophytic vegetation in the Mantaro Valley zone is described by Weberbauer (1945: 421) as grassy steppe with scattered shrubs. The density of these "shrubs" varies with agricultural intensity and tree cropping. Patches of shrubs are now found scattered around irrigation canals and in side valleys; they are most frequently composed of *Schinus molle*, *Caesalpinia spinosa*, *C. tinctoria*, *Rhamnus pubescens*, *Tillandsia tictoreum*, *Anona cherimola*, *Acacia macracantha*, *Prosopis cassia*, and *Mentzelia* sp. *Alnus jorullensis* is found along the moister riparian areas (Tosi 1960; Weberbauer 1945). Field wind breaks are now mainly composed of eucalyptus (*Eucalyptus globulus*), introduced a century ago, replacing indigenous shrub and tree cropping, initiated perhaps in Wanka II times (Hastorf and Johannessen 1991).

Dry farming (water provided by rainfall only) is common, with irrigation primarily at planting times. In the southern reaches of the valley, somewhat warmer temperatures and higher evapotranspiration rates make irrigation more important. Intensive farming now produces a wide range of crops, including the frost intolerant crops maize (*Zea mays*), beans (*Phaseolus vulgaris*), and various garden vegetables. European cultigens such as wheat (*Triticum* spp.) have been successfully incorporated with the Andean crops of potato (*Solanum tuberosum* L. subsp. *andigena* Hawkes) and quinoa (*Chenopodium quinoa* Willd.).

The small valleys that surround the Mantaro Valley are somewhat higher, ranging in altitude from 3200 m near Huancayo to 3500 m in the northwestern Yanamarca Valley and near Yauli in the northeast. The climate is therefore slightly moister and cooler. Gorges (*quebradas*) in this zone offer protection against frost.

The surrounding hill slopes (3370–3850 m) consist of shallow rocky podzols created by weathering of the limestone in the west and the igneous and metamorphic bedrock to the east (Brady 1974: 342). The terrain is sloped and deeply dissected, with erosion thinning the soil. This zone is subsumed under Tosi's (1960: 19) humid mountain prairie-forest (*pradero o bosque humedo montano*) category. As is typical of the tropical zone to the east of the study region in protected *quebradas*, on the slopes above the valley floors the shrubby forest extends upward almost into contact with the puna, and the rocky exposed ridges are covered only with prairie grasses (Troll 1968: 29). These slopes lie within Pulgar Vidal's (1967: 89) *suni* or *sallqa* zone of extensive tuberous agriculture. Sparse shrubs and trees are found in the rocky grasslands, including the cold-adapted trees *Polylepis racemosa* (quinhual), *Buddleia* spp. (quishwar), and *Barnardesia* sp. (Tosi 1960: 117; Bird 1970: 94). Occurring in both the protected *quebradas* and the open grasslands are the smaller shrubs and succulents *Agave americana*, *Berberis*, *Senecio*, *Ribes*, *Monnina*, *Lupinus*, and *Solanum* (Tosi 1960; Weberbauer 1945: 426). Traditional agricultural practices concentrate on extensive farming of Andean tubers, potato as well as oca (*Oxalis tuberosa*), olluco (*Ullucus tuberosus*), and mashua (*Tropaeolum tuberosum*), quinoa, the indigenous lupine, tarwi (*Lupinus mutabilis*), and the hardier European crops such as wheat, fava beans, barley (*Hordeum*) and oats (*Avena*).

Above the hill slopes to the north and west of the valleys are the rolling uplands (3600–3900 m). These are still within Tosi's humid montane forest (*bosque humedo montano*) and Pulgar Vidal's *suni* or *sallqa* zone. The major difference between this zone and the hill slopes is that many of the wild plants are different, and the soil is deeper and more fertile.

Because of the area's fertility, it is farmed extensively today, and its indigenous vegetation has been virtually relegated to the borders of fields, roads, around villages, and in fallow fields. The most common grasses and herbs are: *Stipa ichu*, *Festuca horridula*, *Bromus unioloides*, *Paronychia rigida*, *Lepidium abrotanifolium*, *Trifolium peruvianum*, *Lupinus fieldii*, *Oenothera multicaulis*, *Oxalis ptychoclada*, *Plantago linearis*, *Valeriana thalictroides*, *Verbena villifolia*, *Solanum* sp., and the succulents *Opuntia* and *Echinocactus* (Weberbauer 1945: 421). Many of these genera are seen in the pre-Hispanic record of this area.

Although geographers refer to this type of zone as forested or covered with dispersed shrubs, the shrubs have been depleted by firewood collection and land clearing and are now found only in *quebradas* (Johannessen and Hastorf 1990). This zone is quite exposed to the elements, and frost can be a recurrent problem on the more gentle slopes, particularly in the swales. Tubers are the focus of rolling upland agriculture today.

At its upper edge the high upland zone (3800–4100m) intersects with a non-arable puna grassland zone. The soil is generally much more shallow than in the lower rolling upland elevations. Landslides, which wipe out agricultural areas altogether, are common on the steeper slopes. This zone, the low puna of Pulgar Vidal (1967), is equivalent to Tosi's wet subalpine puna (*paramo muy humedo subalpino*). Bunch grasses dominate the terrain with genera such as *Festuca*, *Bromus*, *Calamagrostis*, *Agrostis*, *Poa*, and *Stipa ichu* (Tosi 1960: 133). Even in the protected valleys, shrub growth is rarely found. When discussing the lower portions of the Huaricolca puna, Tosi mentions that it is more humid than most Andean puna lands. Despite its bleak appearance, this zone is highly valuable because of its forage capacity. The more frost resistant tubers

– the bitter potatoes (*Solanum juzepczukii* Buk. and *S. curtilobum* Juz. et Buk.) (Carney 1980: 3; Hawkes 1990: 177), mashua, and olluco – and the root crop maca (*Lepidium meyenii*) (Leon 1964) are the indigenous crops grown in this area. Forage crops are barley and oats, which are harvested or eaten in the fields by herded animals.

The puna zone is above agricultural limits (4000–4100 m in protected areas), and can extend up to 4650 m, where it borders on the frigid Cordillera, a climate suitable only to lichens and micro-organisms. The puna zone is found in the hills surrounding the study region to the east and the west and also to the north, where it extends up into the Lake Junín area. Most commonly found are grasses, mosses, ferns, polster rosettes, and stem-forming herbs (Pearsall 1980: 191–93). This is the zone where animals are herded, both camelids and sheep.

The final ecological zone that is involved in the pre-Hispanic inhabitants' resources is the *ceja de montaña* (1200–2000 m), located up and over the Cordillera Blanca to the east of the Mantaro basin. This is called *rupa* by Pulgar Vidal (1967). From the crest of the snow-peaked mountains, rivers plunge steeply towards the Amazon basin. The moist warm air moving upslope over this landscape creates a climate that maintains a dense tropical forest on the slopes. Genera of the families Bromeliaceae (bromeliads), Arecaceae (palms), Musaceae (bananas), Ericaceae, Orchidaceae, and Lauraceae, as well as bryophytes, are prevalent in this forest. Many more species are present here than in the upper zones west of the Cordillera (for a fuller list of the plants found in the *ceja de montaña* see Weberbauer 1945: 52). The soil is shallow, highly leached, and held in place on the hills by the dense plant cover.

Andean staple crops

Potato or "papa"

The most economically important crop of the Andes is the potato. Potatoes are classified in the family Solanaceae section Tuberarium and genus *Solanum*. Seven potato species are cultivated in the Andes today, ranging from diploid to pentaploid varieties (Hawkes 1963; 1990). The most widespread species are *Solanum tuberosum* L. subsp. *andigena* Hawkes and *Solanum tuberosum* L. subsp. *tuberosum*. The former is the major central Andean variety and is considered to be descended from the original domesticate, *Solanum stenotomum* Juz. et Buk. (Hawkes 1990). Many of these native variety potatoes have never been scientifically hybridized. It is thought that this *S. stenotomum* species was first domesticated in northern Bolivia, perhaps on the shores of Lake Titicaca out of the wild *S. leptophyes* and then, perhaps before 5000 b.c., it spread north throughout the high Andean region as it evolved into subspecies *andigena* (Hawkes 1990: 58). We still do not have the information to track this process. The latter subspecies includes the majority of potato varieties grown around the world and comes from southwestern Chile. This second subspecies was brought over to Europe after the earlier *andigena* was involved in the Irish potato blight.

The later triploid domesticate species *S. juzepczukii* Buk. and the pentaploid *S. curtilobum* Juz. et Buk. (Hawkes 1963; 1990; Werge 1979) are called bitter potatoes because they are high in glycoalkaloids, which make them inedible until they have been subjected to a water process technique. Their bitterness accompanies their selection to grow at very high elevations. Added desirable qualities of these bitter freeze-dried *chuño* and fermented *tongush* are their frost resistance during maturation and their storability after processing. These two species therefore are produced today in the higher zones (3900 to 4200 m), such as the low puna of the study region.

Hundreds of potato varieties are found in the Andes today (Brush 1990; Carney 1980; Hawkes 1990; Montaldo 1977; Ochoa 1975; 1976; Werge 1979). Both farmers and researchers consider the great potato diversity a method for preventing tuber pathogens and frosts from destroying harvests as well as for providing dietary diversity (Gade 1975; Ugent 1968). When Werge (1979) investigated potato varieties, he found that certain varieties had little resistance to blight and frost, but were planted because of their excellent flavor. The many varieties are biologically maintained today by mutation and crossbreeding within fields. Tubers are planted from seed potato clones that were harvested the year before. Cultural patterns that maintain genotypic diversity are seed networks among neighbors and villages and farmer selection based on taste, frost and pest resistance, and crop rotation.

In the Mantaro area, the most common indigenous potato names are *huayro*, *tarmeña*, *color*, *regalo*, and *comun*. Within each of these categories the people use many additional descriptive tuber names; a field of *papa color* may contain twenty or thirty varieties (Camino et al. 1981; Carney 1980: 11).

Potatoes are one of the world's staple carbohydrate sources. One hundred grams of a floury potato yields 32 calories (Appendix B; INCAP 1961: 36). Potatoes are high in carbohydrate and phosphorus but fairly low in protein (6.4 gm/100 gm). The freeze-dried *chuño* yields more calories and also more calcium than the floury potato. In the Andes, the production potential of potatoes varies greatly. According to studies by Salera et al. (1954) and Mayer (1979), the upper microzones in the Jauja study region are considered very productive for tubers. From my agricultural work, I have calculated an average yield of 329 kg/ha for *S. tuberosum* L. subsp. *andigena* without chemical fertilizer.

Although potatoes are the most important crop in the Andes today, archaeobotanists and archaeologists believe that the potato was domesticated as a staple well after the region was inhabited. This opinion is based on the scarcity of early pre-Hispanic tuberous remains in the archaeological record and also the terrible problem of not being able to tell a domesticate from a wild potato with the morphology. Engel (1970) claims to have domesticated tubers from the Tres Ventanas cave strata in the Chilca Valley (Yen 1974). While their age, run by the Oxford Accelerator Lab, is now approximately 500 BC (Hawkes 1990: 18), there has never been a report of the stratigraphy from which they came, thus making this potato find less useful. The earliest *in situ* tuber remains are on the coast from the Ancon area, dating to 2500 BC (Martins-Farias 1976; Moseley 1975), and at Huaynuma in the Casma Valley dating to about 2000 BC (Ugent et al. 1982). In the intermontane valleys, the earliest potatoes were uncovered at the site of Chiripa on the east side of Lake Titicaca. Carbonized tuber fragments resembling freeze-dried *chuño* (Erickson 1977: 6) were found in the fill dating to 800–500 b.c. Kidder (1967), who first excavated at Chiripa, found carbonized tubers dated to 400 b.c.–a.d. 50 (Towle 1961). It is in this region where we should find the earliest domesticates if the wild tuber genetics are any indication. At other early highland sites that have been excavated, such as Pachamachay (Rick 1980), Pikimachay (MacNeish et al. 1970), and Guitarrero Cave (Lynch 1980), potatoes have not been identified.

Much of the reason for their absence from excavated material may be the collection and analytical techniques used in excavating these early caves, as well as their preservation problems. Whole tubers are rarely encountered in archaeological contexts (Erickson 1977: 6). While detailed cellular analysis is a successful method for identifying Andean tubers, recent systematic and rigorous anatomical work has proved successful (Hathar 1988). Although I have identified tubers in later pre-Hispanic contexts, more analysis on Andean botanical collections must be included in archaeological studies before we can determine when *Solanum* became a major component of the Andean diet.

Although potatoes and other Andean tubers (oca, olluco, mashua) have similar production cycles today, the potato, requiring more nutrients, is most often planted just after a fallow phase. When the ground is wet, one year before planting, the plot is turned over (*chacmay*) once or twice. Opening the soil is repeated at planting time, when the seed potatoes are placed one pace apart (50–60 cm) in rows. If available, some fertilizer is added on top of the tuber; the most commonly used fertilizer for the native varieties is domestic compost (*guano de corral*). After 1.5 to 2 months, the fields are weeded and soil is added around the plants. These tasks are repeated three to four months after planting. When the plants are five to six months old, depending on tuber variety, microzone, and weather conditions, the tubers are dug up by loosening the soil with either oxen and plow, foot plow (*chakitaklla*), or hoe (*raukuna*). The tubers are then separated by size.

Tubers are stored in piles either by mounding them on a bed of wild mint branches (*Minthostaychis*) against a structure's interior wall or by piling them up on the roof's inner support beams. To discourage fungus growth, early sprouting, or greening, tubers need a cool dark place (Werge 1977; Hastorf n.d.). Seed potato tubers are often left in the ground unharvested for an additional month to increase their frost resistance. Tubers are most often boiled and peeled for consumption; sometimes they are roasted in the fire. *Chuño* must be soaked and then boiled to rehydrate them, or they may be ground and made into cakes or soups (Xesspe 1978: 217).

Mashua, "añu", or "isaño"

Tropaeolum tuberosum Ruiz et Pavon. (Tropaeolaceae) is another of the locally domesticated Andean tubers that grows in the cooler microzones of the study region. The tubers are cone-shaped and approximately 5–10 cm in length (Towle 1961: 57). Five varieties have been reported for the region (MacBride 1949 vol. 13, pt. 3 no. 2: 619; Espinoza and Mantari 1954; Leon 1964), distinguished by the tubers and above-ground plant morphology. Mashua is grown from southern Venezuela to northern Argentina not only as a food crop but also for medicine (Montaldo 1977). Johns and

Towers (1981) report significant levels of p-methoxybenzyl glucosinolates, which may have medicinal properties aiding adaptation to high elevations. Although mashua, like oca and olluco, is a tuber, it is used in the diet more like a green vegetable. Mashua is quite high in ascorbic acid and phosphorus and has little protein or calories (Appendix B, INCAP 1961: 28).

Mashua tends to produce best in the low puna zone, from 3500 to 4000 m. The farmers consider it to be the hardiest and the highest yielding of the minor tubers, because it grows on their more exposed plots. It yields up to four times more than olluco or oca in the same field. It also matures more quickly than either oca or olluco, requiring a 190–200-day growing season (Espinoza and Mantari 1954). Farmers consider mashua more resistant than other tubers to worms and blights, although this quality has not been documented scientifically. The agricultural experimental station in Puno reported an average yield of 5500 kg/ha (Espinoza and Mantari 1954); in the Jauja study region, the average mashua yield is 6525 kg/ha. We have almost no pre-Hispanic botanical data on mashua. Erickson (1977) found a "tuber" fragment along with his *Solanum* fragment at Chiripa. I have identified mashua in the excavated Jauja collection, and also in Middle Horizon era excavations at the site of Putaca in the Tarma area (Hastings 1986).

Olluco or ullucu

Ullucus tuberosus Loz. (Baselaceae), an Andean domesticate, is still produced on a small scale in the study region today. It contains only 51 cal/100 gm, and is quite low in the major minerals except for ascorbic acid and phosphorus (Appendix B; INCAP 1961: 34). Eight named varieties are reported by Soukup (1970: 358), with the names based on tuber color, although dozens of varieties exist throughout the Andes. The tubers also vary in shape, ranging from small and round to elongated and curved. Although not as frost resistant as mashua, today olluco is planted between 3450 and 4000 m. Agricultural studies in the Jauja area have shown that olluco is most productive in the loose, well-drained soil of the hill slopes. Its yield averages 629 kg/ha, substantially less than mashua's.

Harms (1922: 16) reported the first pre-Hispanic evidence of olluco at Chuquitanta, presumably from the pre-ceramic middens. No other pre-Hispanic olluco has been found and identified except at the Jauja excavations.

Oca or oka

Oxalis tuberosa Mol. (Oxalaceae) tubers are long and thin, varying in length from 7 to 13 cm, and have deep-set parallel eyes. Oca contains more iron and ascorbic acid per gram than the potato, and has the same mineral content as olluco, but many fewer calories than the potato (Appendix B; INCAP 1961: 35).

The crop is cultivated from Colombia to Bolivia in moist Andean zones. Oca grows optimally at lower elevations than the other two minor tubers, from the coast up to 3850 m. It produces best in humid soil, and unlike the other two it does not need well-drained soil, so it can be grown on the valley floors. Local farmers consider it "weaker" than the other tubers because of this quality. It needs 200-215 days for maturation.

Four varieties have been recognized, based on tuber color and size (Yacovleff and Herrera 1934: 39; Soukup 1970: 243).

Because the *Oxalis* tuber contains calcium oxalate crystals, it must be cured in the sun before it is consumed (Towle 1961: 57). Several of the varieties are also freeze-dried and are called *kalla*.

At the Puno Agricultural Station, oca produced 4500 kg/ha on average (Espinoza and Mantari 1954). In the study region, at altitudes from 3430 to 3850 m, the average yield was 2485 kg/ha. Towle (1961: 57) identified oca in the Late Horizon strata of Pachacamac; it has been found in the Jauja remains and in the Tarma drainage Putaca excavations (Hastings 1986); and in both instances it has been identified by morphological and cellular characteristics.

Quinoa or "kinuwa"

Chenopodium quinoa Willd. is a nutritious, productive grain. In the family Chenopodiaceae, it is one of several annual herbaceous genera that were selected and cultivated by early Andean inhabitants as well as in Mesoamerica (Wilson et al. 1979). Varieties of quinoa grow from 30 to 160 cm in height (Gandanillas 1968). The domestic seeds, which average 2 mm in size, mature in dense erect heads that extend above the main stalk (Tapia Vargas 1976: 18). Quinoa is produced in the sierra from 3000 to 4000 m where the humidity is adequate for seed germination. A descendant of hardy herbs that grow on disturbed soil, quinoa can survive in relatively poor soil.

It is believed that *Chenopodium* went through a selection process in the Andes beginning in the Archaic periods. This type of selection is suggested by the increasing seed size noted by Pearsall at Pachamachay (1980: 197), from 0.5 to 1.8 mm. Based on a more detailed analysis where she photographed the seeds using a scanning electron microscope, the testa thickness from both the Lake Junín and the Jauja region, Nordstrom (1990) suggests that seed domestication occurred before 2500 b.c. Small seeds identified by Erickson (1977: 4) at Formative Chiripa range from 0.4 to 1.3 mm. I have identified a size range, 0.6 to 2.1 m, in the late pre-Hispanic periods. Simmonds' (1965: 224) measurement of 2 mm is an average diameter for modern domestic quinoa. However, the seed coat thickness will probably be the determiner of domestication in future studies.

The frequent occurrence of *Chenopodium* spp. in most highland archaeobotanical collections implies its importance in the pre-Hispanic diet. This is further suggested by the many quinoa varieties found throughout the sierra. Local varieties can be found in every valley basin in the Andes.

The most frost-resistant quinoa varieties today come from the Bolivian altiplano area (S. Herquinio pers. comm.). In the study region, quinoa is densely planted on the valley floors. Because of its shallow roots, it can withstand the occasional poor drainage there.

The other domesticated *Chenopodium*, *C. pallidicaule*, is grown today only in the southern Andes and has a much lower average yield (600 kg/ha) than quinoa (S. Herquinio pers. comm.). *C. pallidicaule*, *kañawa*, grows in drier and higher climates (Winterhalder and Thomas 1978: 66). *Kañawa* still retains the shattering inflorescence that has been bred out of quinoa. Because of its propensity to shatter, *kañawa* must be harvested before full maturation (Simmonds 1965: 229; Gade 1970: 1975: 59).

Both *Chenopodium* species are not only high in calories and protein, they are also high in fat, phosphorus, calcium, iron, riboflavin, and Vitamin C (Tapia Vargas 1976: 4). Southern highland production averages 2000 kg/ha (Mintzer 1933: 66) and the common local Jauja type yields 1975 kg/ha. Intensive agronomic work has produced improved varieties with higher yields averaging up to 4000 kg/ha (Tapia Vargas 1976: 29). Quinoa is sown in rows 4 cm apart, or the seed is scattered over the field. The crop must receive adequate moisture the first fifteen days to insure germination. After two to three months, soil is piled around the plants, and sometimes greens are harvested at this time to be eaten. After five to six months, the quinoa plant has matured and dried and the seeds are ready for harvesting. The stalks are cut 1 cm above the ground. A blanket is laid on a flat area, and the branches are rubbed or beaten, loosening the seeds. Winnowing can also be done to aid the removal of the bitter perianth. The seeds are stored in sacks or ceramic jars. Quinoa is prepared by boiling in soup, by grinding for cakes and flat bread (Xesspe 1978: 213), or by brewing into a beer (Gade 1975: 155).

Tarwi, "tarhui," "talwi," or lupine

Lupinus mutabilis Sweet (Fabaceae), produced on a small scale today in the region, is the only legume domesticated from a local wild, high-zone Andean species. It was surely important as a protein and mineral source in the predominantly tuberous diet. Agronomists estimate that up to ninety-five types are extant throughout the Andes, growing between 2800 and 4000 m (S. Herquinio pers. comm.). As with quinoa and potatoes, local varieties have been developed for different micro-conditions. Farmers believe that production is lowered when the seeds are brought in from other regions, so local varieties do not move around much (Torres pers. comm.).

Tarwi pods nestle within the leaves and are considered more frost resistant than quinoa. In the higher elevations, however, these plants are vulnerable to hailstorms, which sometimes knock the maturing flowers or young pods off the plant. The individual seeds are 8 to 10 mm in length and oval in shape. The lupine seeds are inedible upon harvesting. Like the bitter potato, they must be leached to remove alkaloids.

Like other leguminous plants, lupine has the ability to fix nitrogen, allowing it to produce in nutrient-poor and acidic soil. Therefore, it is often planted at the end of a crop rotation cycle. It is more insect resistant than maize or the introduced European legumes (Gade 1969: 49; Towle 1961: 48).

Agricultural experiment stations show tarwi yields at 2200 kg/ha on hillsides and 1500 kg/ha on valley floors (S. Herquinio pers. comm.). Local yield studies average only 280 kg/ha. Such low yields are in part explained by the fact that tarwi has become a very minor crop in the region, replaced by European legumes and is now planted on the fringe of fields.

Furrows are made 4 to 5 cm apart and one seed is placed every 1 cm down the row. Tarwi requires no weeding or cultivating. After six or seven months the stalks are cut off 1 cm above the ground. The plants are beaten against a flat surface to release the seeds which are then winnowed from their pods. The stalks are used for firewood and the seeds are dried in the sun and stored in sacks or ceramic jars. The seeds must be leached in cold running water for approximately ten days before they can be consumed raw, roasted or boiled. They can also be ground and made into cakes (Gade 1969). *Lupinus* contains 17.3 gm of protein/100 gm, and was probably an important complementary source of protein in the pre-Hispanic diet. Towle (1961: 49) identified a possible lupine at Ancon. Pearsall (1980: 26) found *Lupinus* spp. in puna caves but believes them to be wild.

Maize, "sara," or "sala"

Zea mays L. (Poaceae) is the most important mild-environment grain crop in the region. Although maize was domesticated in the dry mountains of Mexico, literally hundreds of maize varieties in Peru have been described by investigators due to its very flexible genetics (Grobman et al. 1961; see Bird 1970: 18 for Peruvian maize literature). Maize is like the other Andean staples in that varieties have been tailored to the many different microzones. Maize varieties are distinguished by cob morphology, taste, color, use, and pathogen resistance. The different uses require different kernel characteristics and thus create a range of maize types grown within each microzone.

The upper elevation for producing an effective yield in the Mantaro region is 3550 m. Maize is a major crop only in the lower Mantaro Valley, below 3250 m (Salera et al. 1954: 21), where the frost cycle does not affect its maturation. There are, however, maize harvests in the Yanamarca, Paca, and Masma Valleys. Like the potato, maize is an important crop in modern Peru and therefore it has attracted many agronomic studies. In the greater Mantaro Valley, an earlier study found maize to average 1400 kg/ha with the Jauja area producing an average of 1800 kg/ha (Salera et al. 1954: 23). More recently I have found maize yields to average 740 kg/ha, ranging from 180 to 1600 kg/ha; this figure is closer to what might be expected for a marginal production area. As pointed out in various studies (Bird 1970; Hastorf and Johannessen 1992; Murra 1960, 1964; Rowe 1946; Skar 1979), maize is considered a very important crop symbolically, and if a farmer has land that will yield maize he or she will usually plant it. This is still evident throughout the Jauja study region, where farmers constantly plant experimental fields in the different microzones, pushing maize production up the *quebradas* and hillsides.

When maize is planted in a crop rotation cycle, the soil need not be prepared before planting. Furrows are made, two or three seeds are spaced 1 cm apart and covered with 1 cm of dirt and fertilizer. The field must be weeded after one or two months and recultivated again two months later. After six or seven months the whole plant is cut near the ground and brought home. The cobs are removed and dried in the sun, and the stalks are used for forage and fuel. The cobs are braided together in a *wayunka* and hung from the house rafters. The seeds for next year's planting are removed from the center of the chosen cobs and stored in a sack. Depending on the maize variety, the corn is prepared by toasting (*kancha*), by boiling in a stew (*mote*), by sprouting to brew a fermented drink (*chicha*), or by grinding and preparing in various ways (ground and toasted, *machka*, bread, *tanta*, or flour *mazamorra* [Cobo 1956 vl: 161]). Maize is high in calories 340/100 gm) as noted in Appendix B, although its protein level (6.5/100 gm) is more like that of the starchy tubers.

Maize has been grown on the Pacific coast of South America since at least 2500 BC, when it was added to the diet as a minor crop (Pickersgill 1969: 57; Bonavia 1982). Pearsall (1978: 20) dates coastal Ecuador maize to 2450 BC. Although Smith (1980: 115) reports maize in Complex III of Guitarrero Cave dated to 5780 BC, soil disturbance problems make this date questionable. Galinat (MacNeish et al. 1970) has identified maize in the Chihua Phase of the Ayacucho project (4300–2800 BC), but these levels also have stratigraphic problems. Although maize could have been raised as early in the Andes as on the coast, the excellent conditions for botanical preservation found on the Peruvian coast suggest that the earliest evidence should be found there. I have identified maize-cob fragments and kernels in all cultural phases in the Jauja area.

Minor crops

The minor crops of the region, such as *Phaseolus vulgaris*, common bean, *Capsicum pubescens*, chili pepper, *Polymnia sonchifolis*, aracacha, and *Lepidium meyenii*, maca, will not be discussed here in detail because they are not local staples today and would have constituted only a marginal part of pre-Hispanic agricultural production. The first three crops grow in the lower elevations of the study region. The fourth crop, maca, will grow only at the upper agricultural limit in the lower puna zone. Although it is not presently being produced in the study region, it is still grown on the Junín puna.

Introduced staples

European cool-weather cereals and legumes have been incorporated into the modern agriculture and diet of Andean peoples. In order to understand what pre-Hispanic crops they have replaced and what position in the rotation cycles they have assumed, we must look at the plant geographical information. Table 2 lists these introduced crop replacements, based on evidence about their cropping and production requirements.

Wheat Wheat species of *Triticum* L. (Poaceae) have been cultivated in the middle east since at least 7500 BC (Renfrew 1973), providing a carbohydrate cereal grain with tremendous variety. A staple food crop of Europe for thousands of years, viable wheat was brought to Mexico in 1529 with the Spanish (Feldman 1976: 125), and it is reported to have been in Peru before the end of the sixteenth century (Garcilaso de la Vega 1943; Soukup 1970: 352).

Today, in central Peru, wheat has been adapted to grow at altitudes up to 3800 m and in south Peru up to 4100 m (Winterhalder and Thomas 1978). In the study region the majority of wheat fields are between 3300 and 3600 m. In the Andes, wheat takes eight or nine months to mature. It is vulnerable to the persistent frosts of the dry months. Masson Mais (pers. comm.) of ONERN notes that European grains are more frost resistant than Andean tubers, though they can be ruined by hail or snow because of their thin supporting stalks (Winterhalder and Thomas 1978: 66). On the valley floors wheat is in the same cropping cycle as quinoa; on the western hillsides and uplands its cropping cycle is equivalent to that of all the tubers, especially olluco (Salera et al. 1954: 40). Its modern regional yield ranges from 800 to 1600 kg/ha (Salera et al. 1954: 23); yields reported in my interviews averaged 900 kg/ha.

Production is similar for all three of the European cereals: wheat, barley, and oats. The ground is turned over at the time of planting and seeds are scattered across the field. In areas where oxen and plows are used, the ground is lightly plowed to cover the seeds with dirt. In the higher areas, the ground is covered with soil by hand. This planting technique is similar to that of quinoa. Three months after planting, the fields are weeded. Upon maturation, the stalks are cut. Harvesting is often done during the night hours when there is no wind to dislodge the grain. Optimally, the cut stalks are taken to a flat open area where animals are driven over them, releasing the grains. The large stalks are removed and the remainder are winnowed in the afternoon when the wind comes up. Wheat kernels most frequently are consumed whole in soups but sometimes are ground for bread.

Barley *Hordeum vulgare* L. (Poaceae) was domesticated in mid eastern Asia in the seventh millennium BC (Harlan and Zohary 1966). It became an important crop because it has a short maturation cycle and high salt tolerance and because it is a cool-season crop, so it can mature where other crops cannot. Harlan (1976: 96) reports that barley was brought to Mexico by Columbus on his second voyage. Soukup (1970: 155) notes its presence during Pizarro's time, suggesting its immediate introduction in Peru by the Spanish. Its success is seen in its productivity up to 4000 m. In the study region, barley is found growing in the cooler zones, similar to the tubers, lupines, and quinoa. As in the Old World, barley is mainly used for animal fodder, although bread and beer are also produced from it. It has a yield of 1000–1600 kg/ha in the Mantaro region, about the same as wheat (Salera et al. 1954: 23).

Oats *Avena sativa* L. (Poaceae), another cereal grain from Europe, is much less important to the Andean farmer than wheat or barley. Its high percentage of husk reflects a lower caloric yield per hectare, and thus a low economic value. Oats are less sensitive to cold than the other grains and can yield in poorer soil (Renfrew 1973: 98). They can be grown up to 4200 m in the central Andes, and are most often grown in the bitter potato rotation cycle, where they are harvested as forage. Oats tolerate wetness and are more frost resistant than all other crops except bitter potatoes.

Beans and peas The legumes *Vicia faba* L., the fava bean, and *Pisum sativum* L., the pea (Fabaceae), were brought to Peru in the early days of the Spanish conquest (Renfrew 1973: 107, 110; Soukup 1970: 266, 365). With a long history in the Mediterranean, legumes have been important because of their nitrogen-fixing capability. The beans of the genus *Phaseolus*, which were important throughout most of the New World, cannot grow above 3450 m in the central Andes; thus their importance in the Sausa diet was minimal. The common bean can be grown only in

Table 2. *European crop equivalents of indigenous crops*

Crop	Valleys	Uplands
Wheat	quinoa, potatoes, Andean tubers	potatoes, lupine, Andean tubers
Barley, oats	quinoa, fallow	lupine, fallow
Beans, peas	maize, *Phaseolus vulgaris*	lupine, vegetables (Andean tubers)
vegetables (onions, carrots)	Andean tubers, *Ph. vulgaris*	Andean tubers

the lower valleys of the study area today, and it was possibly grown in this lowest zone pre-Hispanically as well. When the hardy European beans and peas arrived in Peru and were adapted to the Andean climate, they yielded more per unit area than lupine and *Phaseolus vulgaris*. Today, fava beans can grow at altitudes up to 3650 m and peas up to 3700 m. Although tarwi can grow higher than this, peas and beans have essentially replaced lupine up to 3650 m and the common bean down to 3200 m, relegating tarwi to production in the low puna zone of the study region.

Both beans and peas take seven or eight months to mature in the study region. They tend to be planted up to one month before potatoes and quinoa (Salera et al. 1954: 44). Today bean and pea yields average 315 kg/ha for beans and 442 kg/ha for peas, slightly higher than tarwi, which averages 280 kg/ha.

There is also a host of Old World and North American vegetables that have been introduced into the highlands, such as onions and carrots. These are most often grown in the valleys, and replace the indigenous vegetables: Andean tubers, and beans.

Equivalents

A prerequisite for a discussion of pre-Hispanic land-use is a workable reconstruction of the crop possibilities for each zone. A knowledge of climate, soil, and topographic conditions is essential to determine what crops can be grown in which zones and what range of production intensification can be expected. So that the modern land-use information discussed in Chapter 7 can be interpreted within pre-Hispanic parameters, I propose some indigenous equivalents for each of the European staples, as suggestions for the crops that have been replaced with these introductions.

Of course the European crops do not have an exact Andean equivalent. Nevertheless, European crops can be assigned roles within the cropping cycles based on similarity of life cycle, position in the rotation cycle, moisture and frost tolerance, and periods of vulnerability (Table 2).

Wheat, which is the most important introduced crop, is most similar to potatoes in the modern scheme. Both crops are major food sources. In the valleys wheat has the same production cycle as potatoes, oca, mashua, and quinoa – all of which mature in eight months. Like potatoes, wheat tends to be planted at the beginning of a rotation cycle. On the hills and uplands, wheat needs a month more than the tubers to mature. In the rotation cycle of the hills and low uplands, wheat is planted at any time in the cycle, making it more like quinoa. Therefore, in the upper zones, wheat has probably not replaced any one crop, but several indigenous cultigens.

Barley and oats today are primarily planted for fodder, and do not have a pre-Hispanic counterpart, other than the wild grasses and herbs grown in the fallow years. These cultigens therefore reflect modern intensification of land-use, as well as the importance of cows, sheep, and cuys in the modern regional production. These crops do show similarities to certain food crops. Barley and oats seem to be treated most like quinoa on the valley floors but like tarwi on the hill slopes and uplands. Today they are planted more frequently than either tarwi or quinoa, suggesting a new emphasis on domesticated animal fodder, rather than simply aiding wild grasses to grow.

Fava beans and peas are more complicated than the fodder crops. Because they contribute substantially to the modern Andean diet, determining their pre-Hispanic counterparts is important. In general beans and peas both need eight months to mature on the valley floors and in the uplands. In the valleys their production cycle is most similar to maize and tarwi. On the hill slopes the legumes are most equivalent to tarwi, oca, and mashua. In the lower elevations the legumes are found midway in the rotation cycle, similar to maize and oca. The European legumes are not directly equivalent to any one crop. On the valley floors and lower hillsides they have replaced a spectrum of minor crops: *Phaseolus vulgaris*, tarwi, mashua, and oca. In the middle elevations, they replace tarwi (Gade 1969). The legumes could have also assumed the vegetable role of mashua and oca in these same elevations.

7

Defining modern land-use zones

Six zones have been identified from an environmental survey conducted in 1979 and a regional agricultural survey in 1980. The goal of the agricultural interviews was to amass information on crops planted, yields, labor input, and crop rotations. From this, relative productivity, ratio of yield to labor input, and crop rotation patterns can be defined for each zone. The six zones are identified by soil type and fertility, cultivation intensity, elevation, slope, and location in the region.

In addition, before my own field interviews began, several weeks were spent analyzing a series of very detailed agricultural interviews made by the International Potato Center in Lima (CIP) (Franco et al. 1979 and their field notes). While these interviews focused on different aspects of production than I was interested in, they demonstrated how intensively cultivated the Mantaro Valley is today. One reason is the proximity to mining areas and Lima, providing food and labor since colonial times (Long and Roberts 1984; Smith 1989). Agriculturally, this outside contact is illustrated today by the large amount of European grains and seed potatoes grown in the region (Mayer 1979). Further, the local history of political and economic control suggests that first hacienda padrons and, since 1969, local ethnic leaders have acted entrepreneurially in production as they contested against each other to gain large tracks of land and laborers (Mallon 1983; Smith 1989). One trend, especially in the southern Mantaro Valley, has been an increased division between larger land holders and barely self-sufficient farmers (Long and Roberts 1984: 169).

Environmentally the valley is large and mild, making it very productive, especially the southern valley. With the average yields for the Mantaro Valley being high for the Peruvian Andes, as studied by the CIP, the northern part of the Mantaro region is slightly more marginal in production yields. While there have been many agricultural studies in the Mantaro Valley, which I have taken into account, I use my own results in this analysis, since my interviews were tailored to answer specific pre-Hispanic questions. The agricultural study may have slightly different regional conclusions than the broader reports, as I focused on a small region, the location of the archaeological sites under study.

Agricultural interviews

To be able to understand the local agricultural potential, I conducted interviews with 168 local farmers from January to June 1980. Trying to maximize the number of fields sampled in the area, as well as to gather local comparative information, I designed a sampling strategy to collect many brief interviews with farmers in their fields. In all, I gained information on 665 fields. Each hamlet and town in the study region was systematically visited, covering all environmental zones (Chapter 6). Interviewing each farmer I encountered in the area designated for the day, I gathered information about all land holdings farmed by that family, including the exact location of each plot. Thus the information covered the full spectrum of arable zones and farming goals, from barely self-sufficient subsistence production to cash-crop, surplus-oriented production.

Today, in the Jauja district, household land holdings are inherited parcels that usually cross-cut at least some of the local zones. Modern inheritance ideally splits parental holdings evenly among all siblings. Farmers also can rent additional parcels or gain them through the communal land holdings. The result is that individual families usually work small plots scattered throughout the community. These farmers rarely plant fields outside their hamlet territories, some 4–5 km in radius. The majority of the farmers I interviewed use 75 percent of their harvest for subsistence and 25 percent for cash (a cash crop is that portion of the harvest that is sold or traded for other goods).

Individual field histories covering field size, amount, and type of seed planted, crop type, yield harvested, water source, soil type, production technology, relative labor input, hindrances to yield, and crop rotation cycles, were gathered for each field over the three-year period from 1978 through 1980. I inquired about three years of cropping to learn about variations in crop frequencies, yields, and cropping sequences. Comparing these three years to the last twenty-five years of weather, it is fair to say they were reasonably average. Because many farmers worked fields in more than one zone, I was able to gather information about relative yields of the same crop within and between zones.

In this study, the mean field size was 0.50 ha (s.d. = 0.5 ha) and the mean farm holding was 2 ha (ranging from 0.05 to 40 ha). Most informants used the local term *yugada* or *yuntada* to describe a field area. These terms have been defined as one-third of a hectare or, historically, the area one team of oxen (*yunta*) can plow in one day. All field areas have been standardized to hectares for comparative discussion. Yields were described frequently by the local term *arroba* or *saco*. Because these measures could vary in size, I asked each farmer to define his or her *arroba* or *saco* in terms of kilograms, the measure used today in market sales. All seed and yield measurements have been converted to kg/ha.

Land-use zones

Land-use sub-areas that are used in the same general way and produce the same crops in the same elevation range and topographic setting were combined. This consolidation created six zones, as listed in Table 3. Note that the sixth is not used for agriculture, and so it will not be involved in this discussion. I plotted all fields onto a topographic map, assigning each field to one of the six land-use zones, which were further divided if irrigation was used (hence the "a" designation). From the 168 interviews, I found irrigation to occur mainly in the low valleys and on the low hillsides.

Table 3. *Jauja region land-use zone definitions*

1	First bench valley land: flat, less than 3500 m in elevation, dry agriculture on well drained first bench, sometimes gravelly soils
1a	Valley irrigation: less than 3480 m in elevation; flat land on the first bench
2	Fertile lowland valley: less than 3500 m in elevation; fine, deep valley soils; often poor drainage; surrounding lakes
3	Low hillside (intensive hillside): hillsides off the valley floors up to 3580 m in elevation; gently sloped; deep, fairly fertile soil
3a	Hillside irrigation: often good soil in protected sloping areas or upland swales; irrigated by puna springs, small streams, or local seeps
4	Extensive hillside: between 3370 and 4000 m in elevation; sloping land, rocky, shallow, thin soil on bedrock, often eroding
5	High elevation: between 3650 and 4200 m in elevation; undulating in generally high yielding, deep, fairly rich soils
6	Non-arable rock or puna: between 3800–4400 m in elevation, rocky, exposed, used for grazing and fuel gathering

Modern production

Land-use was the basic criterion used to define the crop production zones. Before proceeding to use the zones in analysis it is important to demonstrate what the cropping differences are in these zones. To do so, I began summarizing the cropping patterns within each zone. Table 4 presents the number of fields, the proportion of land in each zone by crop, and the area under cultivation. You can see immediately the relative intensity of use in the different zones from the fallow percentages listed in column 3.

To expand our understanding of these figures, I produced two-way frequency tables of the crops in their rotation patterns (1978–79, 1979–80) (Dixon 1981: 143). The observed frequency tables for each zone by crop were produced for two cycles. The different crop sequences are presented in six frequency tables, five arable zones and valley irrigation for the zones in Appendix B. There were not enough fields from the hillside irrigation for them to be included in this analysis.

Crop production decisions take into account social factors, resource availability, and risk minimization. Many diverse concerns are involved, including a crop's productivity and its possibility for failure, its marketability, the microzone's production potential, the household's food requirements (including the need for an adequate range of food types in the diet), its labor availability, scheduling of planting and harvesting, and the amount of land available to the household unit in each of the different land-use zones (Barlett 1980; Brush 1977; Golte 1980; Guillet 1981). To understand crop production variability in the Jauja region, I calculated crop yield by zone, productivity (efficiency), relative land-use intensity, and average crop rotation cycles for the different zones. I determined the relative productivity of each crop in each zone from calculated labor inputs and yield outputs. To get at land-use intensity, I incorporated field locations, field sizes, yields and frequency of cropping over time. Average crop rotation cycles were generated out of the frequency table in Appendix B and a Markov chain analysis.

Cropping efficiency

Crop efficiency is defined here as a ratio of each crop's yield to the labor necessary to produce it. The yields are from 893 fields, including the 1978 and 1979 harvests. Appendix C presents the mean yields calculated for each crop throughout the five arable zones, along with the two irrigation subzones. The greater the number of fields in a calculation, the more confidence I have in the modern average. It should be pointed out that some of these yield averages are low for the higher elevation potatoes when compared to the averages of the greater Mantaro Valley studies (Franco et al. 1979; Mayer 1979).

Because yield by weight is not comparable between crops and does not reflect their nutritional importance, they should be standardized to some comparable measure. Although people have other dietary needs (such as protein or vitamins), calories can be considered the most important requirement overall (Vayda and McCay 1975). While this is not the only goal by any means, it does give us a general guide when discussing long-term yields, and therefore I use calorific production to compare crop yields. Appendix D provides the basic food values for all crops involved in this study (kcal equals 1000 calories of food energy). Based on Appendices C and D, Table 5 summarizes the crop yields in kcal/ha for the Jauja region. Onions have not been included in this table, and the Andean tubers have been consolidated as have the various potato, maize, and quinoa varieties. The last two columns present a further summary of the valleys and uplands; the uplands including the hillsides and high elevations. To see the yield differences more easily, yields per hectare are presented in Figure 16 for potatoes, quinoa, maize, lupines, and barley/oats.

It can be seen both in Table 5 and Figure 16 that crop yields can vary considerably from zone to zone. Lupine yields best in the high zones, maize does not produce well above the valleys. Quinoa yields best in the irrigated valley floors and the hillsides and potatoes in the higher fields. Potatoes produce well in all zones except poor soil but do especially well in the high elevations with irrigation.

The denominator of a relative efficiency calculation is the labor input necessary to produce the crops. It was not possible to complete a comprehensive study of labor expenditure invested in the various crops within the different zones. Therefore I defined these values using three types of information: farmer rankings, in-depth interviews, and observations.

During the interviews, farmers were asked to rank the crops produced in each field by their relative labor expenditure. A compilation of these rankings by land-use zone is seen in the first section of Table 6. Labor input for the region is summarized in the lower portion of the table. This regional ranking, ordered from greatest to least mean expenditure, is *chuño*, potatoes, onions, Andean tubers, quinoa, maize, beans/peas, lupine, wheat, and barley/oats. Since these data reflect *relative* labor input, it is

Table 4. *Modern land-use distribution by crop (percentages)*

Zone	No. of fields	Fallow	Potatoes	Maize	Quinoa	Lupine	Wheat	Barley/ oats	Andean tubers	Beans	Veg- etables	Total ha	Mean field size in ha
First bench	107	5	30	22	5	0	16	5	0	13	4	40	0.37
Valley irrig.	58	3	27	46	0	0	5	1	1	10	87	25	0.43
Fertile lowland	38	5	44	35	13	0	12	5	1	12	5	38	0.54
Inten. hillsides	142	6	41	10	5	2	15	4	1	12	4	59	0.42
Exten. hillsides	143	11	30	8	1	1	19	10	4	15	1	43	0.30
Hill irrig.	16	6	31	0	4	0	18	10	0	23	8	6	0.38
High elevation	99	17	57	0	2	1	4	9	8	2	0	94	0.95
Uplands	400	13	39	4	3	1	12	8	3	13	4	196	0.50
Valleys	203	4	34	23	6	0	11	4	1	11	6	103	0.47

difficult to use them to compare with the quantifiable agricultural output data. To gain information about labor input the rankings of agricultural activities using actual time allocations were converted. To do so I completed in-depth interviews with two farmers who discussed time expenditures in various farming activities. I also observed and timed a series of agricultural activities myself, over the course of field research.

From this information, each activity in the cultivation of each crop could be defined in an equivalent of person/days per hectare. To make these labor input calculations comparable with pre-Hispanic technology, I assumed the use of traditional technology for field preparation, planting, and cultivating, the main tools being: the small pick/hoe (*raukana*) for weeding and cultivation, the foot plow (*chakitaklla*) for preparing and planting, and the pick (*asada*) and the sickle (*kuusha*) for harvesting. The production steps are: ground preparing (*chacmay*), planting, weeding, cultivating, recultivating, harvesting, special processing for storage, and transportation costs. Cooking was not included.

Transportation costs vary in the Jauja region, and often they can alter the total cost of production significantly (Chisholm 1962). The most distant field tended by an interviewed smallholder (holdings of 3 ha or less) is 2.75 km from his dwelling, but the few large farm holdings (greater than 30 ha) have fields only as far away as 4.25 km distance. In my calculations, transport costs were based on an average distance of 1.4 km from the field to the homestead.

Despite the very small sample size of the detailed labor interviews, the two data sets

Table 5. *Crop yields by zone, expressed in kcal/ha (number of fields in brackets)*

Crop	First bench	Valley irrigation	Fertile lowland	Intensive hillside	Extensive hillside	Hill irrigation	High elevation	Valleys	Uplands
Potatoes[4]	1211860 (56)	2825690 (21)	807380 (39)	481900 (64)	290720 (61)	8681310 (21)	2158280 (43)	188×10^4 (116)	139×10^4 (189)
Andean[3] tubers	151250 (2)	447159 (1)	7562500 (1)	1164350 (5)	693000 (21)	—	2438150 (9)	25×10^4 (4)	109×10^4 (35)
Quinoa	539030 (10)	2502630 (4)	670410 (10)	1467180 (8)	719550 (6)	1123200 (1)	881010 (11)	98×10^4 (24)	106×10^4 (26)
Maize	4726000 (35)	1574200 (35)	3219800 (8)	343400 (38)	622200 (17)	—	—	180×10^4 (78)	48×10^4 (55)
Lupine	328440 (2)	—	—	999120 (2)	797540 (5)	—	1418640 (3)	33×10^4 (2)	95×10^4 (10)
Chuño	—	—	—	—	—	—	3333800[2] (2)	—	725×10^4 (2)
Wheat	626340 (26)	1790360 (6)	1015300 (16)	197340 (41)	120120 (39)	3898180 (12)	337480 (2)	note 1	
Barley/ oats	621070 (10)	753900 (3)	3744370 (14)	412850 (15)	47290 (21)	2405300 (16)	5438850 (10)	note 1	
Beans/ peas	678590 (25)	1902780 (17)	1960750 (14)	419430 (32)	433070 (34)	167098 (14)	1087790 (4)	note 1	

[1] The European crops were not summarized for the valleys and uplands.

[2] Using *chuño* dry weight.

[3] The calorie value used for the Andean tuber calculations is an average of the three calorie values (Appendix D).

[4] The potato calculations were adjusted differentially in each zone by averaging the different potato variety data and by deleting the unusually high yields of the seed potato farmers.

produced compatible results, which I use for the dry agriculture labor costs. The increased cost of irrigation agriculture, due to canal maintenance, weeding, and regulating the water flow, is estimated at 10 extra person/days per ha, an average reported by farmers of irrigated fields. The results of these person/day per hectare labor estimates are presented in the last section of Table 6, below the ranked average labor inputs as determined from these procedures.

Table 7 presents a summary of the crop efficiencies (based on Tables 5 and 6) for the zones, including irrigation, with the two regional strategies on the far right. The results show varying productivities across the zones. Potatoes, quinoa, and wheat respond efficiently to irrigation. Quinoa is productive throughout the region. The Andean tubers (olluco, oca, and mashua), lupine and barley/oats are most productive in the region's upland zones, and the tubers increase in efficiency with increased elevation. Maize is productive in the valley floor soils, with efficiency dropping off as elevation increases. These differing productivities show why a farmer should desire to

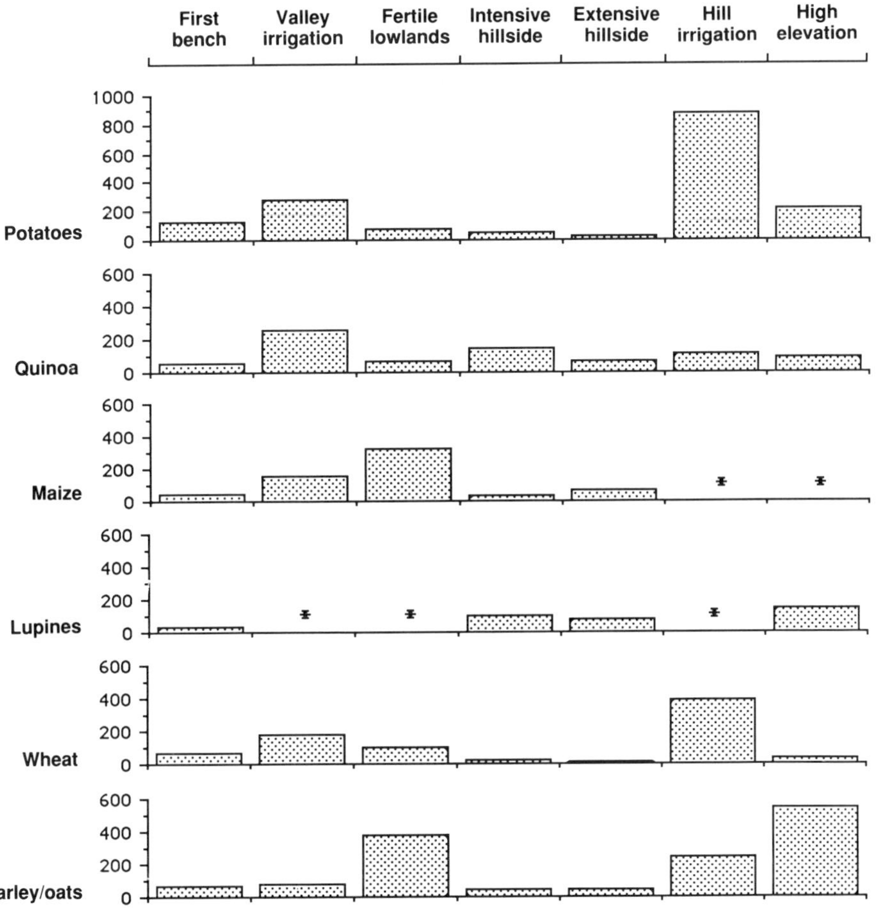

Fig. 16. Crop yields in kg/ha by zone of potatoes, quinoa, maize, wheat and barley/oats. Scale is in kcal/ha/10,000. * = not planted in these zones.

Table 6. *Ranking from greatest to least labour input by land-use zone*

First bench (27 cases)	potatoes, Andean tubers, beans/peas, maize, quinoa, lupine, wheat, barley/oats
Valley irrigation (19 cases)	potatoes, onions, maize, Andean tubers, beans/peas, quinoa, wheat, barley/oats
Fertile lowland (15 cases)	potatoes, onions, quinoa, wheat, maize, barley/oats, beans/peas
Low hillside (24 cases)	potatoes, onions, Andean tubers, quinoa, maize, beans/peas, lupine, wheat, barley/oats
Hill irrigation (7 cases)	potatoes, beans/peas, lupine, Andean tubers, quinoa, wheat, barley/oats
Extensive hillside (30 cases)	potatoes, maize, quinoa, beans/peas, wheat, Andean tubers, lupine, barley/oats
High elevation (30 cases)	*chuño*, potatoes, beans/peas, quinoa, lupine, Andean tubers, wheat, barley/oats

Regional mean	*chuño*	potatoes	onions	Andean tubers	quinoa
Person/ha (traditional labor)	240	120	120	120	108
Regional mean	**maize**	**beans/peas**	**lupine**	**wheat**	**barley/oats**
Person/ha (traditional labor)	105	90	90	69	60

have fields under production in each zone. Not only it is an optimization of yield potential, it is also a risk minimization strategy.

These efficiency values in part reflect the yield distributions of today. For example the Andean tubers are quite "effective" crops and therefore people continue to plant them. To gain an understanding of the influences on modern agricultural production decisions, I compared the actual percentage of crops in cultivation to the calculated efficiency values seen in Table 7. To do so, I tabulated crop frequencies by zone. Using the interview data, I calculated the percentage of land under each crop by land-use zones, summarized in Table 4. Included in this table are the total areas and mean field size of the 603 fields used in these calculations. These percentages reflect average crop production decisions, but also demonstrate relative land-use intensity (see next section).

Viewing the differences between potential production and energetic efficiency, Table 8 presents the percentage of land under each crop from Table 4, adjusted to exclude fallow, and the calculated crop efficiencies from Table 7 standardized to percentage.

On the whole, many crop frequencies track their efficiencies. Can we say anything about why there are differences between crop production efficiencies and land-use? Farmers in the valleys focus their production on the relatively efficient potatoes and maize, while in the uplands farmers emphasize wheat, beans, and peas. By far,

Table 7. *Crop efficiency estimates by zone (output/input) × 100*

Crop	First bench	Valley irrigation[1]	Fertile lowland	Low hillside	Extensive hillside	Hill irrigation[1]	High elevations	Valleys	Uplands
Potatoes	101	140	67	40	24	668 (168)[2]	180	95	165
Andean tubers	13	34	34	97	58	—	203	27	119
Quinoa	50	212	62	136	67	95	82	87	95
Maize	45	137	307	33	59	—	—	168	46
Lupine	48	—	—	145	116	—	206	48	156
Chuño	—	—	—	—	—	—	139	—	139
Wheat	91	179	113	22	13	390	37	109	76
Barley/oats	103	107	624	69	78	343	906	312	350
Beans/peas	75	190	217	46	48	16	121	155	64
Onions	168	—	341	—	—	—	—	255	—

[1] Because there are few cases, these technologies have less influence on the subregion mean efficiencies
[2] This figure excludes high-yielding fields

potatoes have the largest discrepancy between production and efficiency, followed by barley and oats, and maize (but remember that these potato yield and efficiency estimates are low for the region). Farmers living in the Jauja region today plant European crops not just to conserve labor, but also because of their marketability, giving the growers more security and flexibility in the form of options to vend, trade, or consume the products. The European food crops are more productive in the lower zones, but, because indigenous crops, like potatoes, are more productive cash crops when planted in the lowlands, farmers find themselves planting these in the lowlands, and European crops in the uplands (Gade 1975).

Potatoes and maize are cultivated more frequently than might be assumed in the valleys. This may be because a household's valley land holdings are closer to most homes, allowing for more tending. Potatoes have always been a dietary staple (Murra 1960). Today maize is produced in greater quantities than predicted in Table 8, supporting the earlier discussion about the inhabitants' desire to produce and consume maize for trade and for symbolic reasons (Hastorf and Johannessen 1992). Further south, maize is the major crop of the lower Mantaro Valley and is grown on 46 percent of the irrigated lower valley lands studied (Franco et al. 1979; Mayer 1979).

The under-produced crops, such as Andean tubers and lupine, are not very valuable in today's market. Since the ratios interrelate all crops within each zone, the lack of modern-day production of nonmarketable crops escalates the percentages of the marketable maize, wheat, potatoes, and beans/peas. Wheat, beans/peas, and onions all have calorific and protein yields comparable to the crops they replace, i.e. quinoa, lupine, and Andean tubers (Appendix D); therefore, it seems reasonable that their increased importance in the agricultural system is due to their marketability (Scott 1985).

Although productivity and marketability are both major influences on today's cropping in each zone, farmers plant less productive crops for many reasons, including the desire to enhance harvest reliability, to avoid risks, to insure variety in their diets, to prevent all their crops from ripening at the same time, to maximize scarce labor, and to use the different zones (Golte 1980; Thomas 1973: 44). Modern crop mixes may not produce the highest possible yields of any one year, but in the long-term production context they are balanced. There are major concerns for the farmer besides efficient cropping. All but that of market pressures are the same influences that would impinge on the pre-Hispanic farming community. This production efficiency comparison is useful in our pursuit of pre-Hispanic agriculture as well because we can further learn where European crops fit in.

Agricultural intensity

Another aspect of regional production that aids our understanding of the agricultural system is agricultural intensity throughout the different zones. Two common definitions of agricultural intensity are Boserup's (1965) notion that increasing intensity is based on increased frequency of cultivation, and Brookfield's (1972) concept that increased labor and capital input relative to a constant land area reflects intensity.

We can view Boserup's measure of intensification as the frequency of cultivation by looking at the rates of fallow. In the third column of Table 4, the percentages of land in fallow are calculated for the five land-use zones and the irrigated lands. The two bottom rows of the table provide a regional overview comparing uplands with valley lands. The valleys are more intensively cropped than the uplands.

Approximately 10 percent of the hillside and upland fields are unproductive during any one growing season, more than three times the percentage of fallow land found in the valleys. The amount of fallow increases with elevation, roughly paralleling the temperature gradient with increasing elevation seen in Figure 14. The positive correlation between increasing fallow and elevation is partly due to the greater pressure of pests and nematodes in the wetter soils – pests will destroy crops if they are not allowed to die out during fallow years (Goodey 1933; Thomas 1973). In addition, the soil is slower to rejuvenate with a lack of mineral accessibility in the higher elevations. Soils tend to be rockier, and frost problems increase with elevation.

The arable land under cultivation in any one year ranges from 82 to 96 percent. The average regional figure of 6.75 percent in fallow is similar to Salera's Mantaro Valley agricultural research results from 1954, in which he calculated that small farms (3 ha or less) had 8 percent of their land in fallow. This amount of fallow, and therefore land-use intensity, has not changed over the past twenty-five years. The same result is also reported by Long and Roberts for the greater Mantaro Valley (1984: 169). Despite this stability in the region, it is higher than the typical Andean cropping average (Brush pers. comm.). The region is therefore intensively farmed.

Brookfield's (1972) version of intensity emphasizes the addition of capital and labor in the form of new skills and technologies. In the study region, we see the technological intensification of irrigation on the valley floors and the hillsides. If we look at Table 4 again and compare the irrigated valley lands to the non-irrigated first bench and the

Table 8. *Comparative summary of crop efficiency and land-use in the two agricultural zone clusters*

	Valleys		Uplands	
	% efficiency	% land-use	% efficiency	% land use
Potatoes	8	35	13	4
Andean tubers	2	1	15	3
Quinoa	7	7	7	3
Maize	13	24	4	5
Lupine	4	—	12	—
Chuño	—	—	11	—
Wheat	8	11	6	14
Barley/oats	25	4	27	9
Beans/peas	12	12	5	15
Onions	20	6	—	5

fertile valley zones, we notice that there is less fallow in the irrigated fields, reflecting more intensification with technological input.

Comparing crop yields from irrigated and nonirrigated strategies of Appendix C we see that all crops produce higher yields, except some in the unirrigated fertile valley zone. Why might irrigation occur? More clues to this much more labor intensive strategy come from the planting and labor schedules (Golte 1980). In general, with irrigation, the planting time can be shifted one to two months earlier, making the sensitive flowering period occur before the onset of the severe frosts and hail in October (Salera et al. 1954: 40–42). This early planting increases the probability of an adequate harvest and puts food on the table before last year's stored produce is exhausted. In addition, today, these early crops bring a higher price in the market before the major harvest. So, throughout the region we see a mix of intensities and efficiencies that suggest a picture of diversity and balanced but optimal production, useful to apply to pre-Hispanic agriculture.

Crop rotations

Essential to highland Andean culture is the rotation of different crops on the same plot of land. Where farmers practice crop rotation, the decision to plant particular crops in a particular field is based on a series of criteria, including the crop previously produced in the field. Although the crop rotation concept is ubiquitous in Andean agriculture (Farrington 1978; Gade 1975; Golte 1980; Mayer 1979; Salera et al. 1954; Thomas 1973), specific crop rotations vary depending on political and environmental conditions. Since it is likely that crop rotations would have been important in the past, it is worthwhile trying to assess what types of rotations might have been possible, at least environmentally.

In order to determine potential pre-Hispanic crop rotations for each of the region's microzones, we must determine first, whether crop rotations exist today, secondly, what crops they include and thirdly, whether the rotation patterns are in a steady state.

This is done in order to assume that the rotation proposed represents viable agricultural production. If the land-use patterns determined from the interview data are steady, they can be used with more confidence as templates for a viable pre-Hispanic regional reconstruction.

Are there crop rotations in the Mantaro Valley today?

The existence of rotation cycles means that planting decisions are affected by what was planted the previous year or two. Because only three years of cropping data were collected in this study, this test can address only three possible effects: year 1 on year 2, year 2 on year 3, and year 1 on year 3. To test these crop-year interactions, I produced three-way frequency tables of 1978 crops by 1979 crops by 1980 crops (Dixon 1981). To create a significant sample size for this analysis, I had to collapse the zonal interview data into the two zone areas: valley fields and upland fields. I assume that if certain rotations are working in these two zone clusters, they should be applicable to all the microzones included in the area. For this analysis the crops were also consolidated into fallow, tubers (potatoes, oca, olluco, and mashua), indigenous grains (quinoa and maize), legumes (lupine, fava beans, and peas), and European grains (wheat, barley, and oats).

To learn about the amount of influence the planting of one crop has on the following year's crop I completed a log-likelihood analysis on the year by year interactions (Read 1974; cf. Feinberg 1970; Dixon 1981: 144). While the details of the analysis are presented in Hastorf (1983), the results suggest that there is no strong crop rotation sequence operating in the valley zones. By this I do not mean that crops were not planted in some cycle, but rather that the decision to plant particular crops is not influenced by what was planted the previous year. This could be linked to the increased intensification and technology in the valleys. In the uplands, however, the results are different, demonstrating that farmers plan their rotation cycles in upland fields based on what was previously grown, and plant in a definable rotation cycle. These rotation cycles will be discussed below.

Land-use stability

The optimality of the production scheme today is suggested by the stability in production over at least the last twenty-five years, despite much change in the national and world markets (Salera et al. 1954). To establish that the agriculture has been stable, I completed a Markov chain analysis on the cropping sequence by zone. Markov chain analysis is a mathematical model that assesses whether there are trends and changes over time (Kemeny and Snell 1960; McFarland 1981; 1982). The analysis can determine if a situation is in the process of change or is in a steady state. The Markov model generates transition matrices from observed frequency tables that can be used to make statements about the probability that certain events will occur through time. It predicts what *will* occur, not what *should* occur.

When a stable condition is reached quickly in the interaction matrices, the original condition is considered to be a stable system in equilibrium. If the condition changes over the iterations, then the observed data are in a state of change. The full analysis

Table 9. *Observed and stable-state percentages of land in each crop*

Zone	Fallow	Potatoes	Maize	Quinoa	Lupine	Wheat	Barley/ oats	Andean tubers	Beans/ peas	Veg- etables
First bench:										
Observed	10	26	21	5	0	13	5	1	13	5
Stable year 4	5	21	28	6	0	17	5	1	12	5
Valley irrigation:										
Observed	5	28	29	3	0	5	3	1	14	11
Stable year 5	2	28	45	1	0	4	0	1	14	6
Fertile lowlands:										
Observed	7	34	10	4	0	12	14	2	13	4
Stable year 4	7	33	9	15	0	12	9	4	13	5
Low hillside:										
Observed	6	26	18	6	1	14	7	2	16	5
Stable year 4	5	23	21	6	1	16	6	3	17	4
Extensive hillside:										
Observed	10	26	8	2	2	15	12	9	16	1
Stable year 4	8	23	8	1	3	18	12	9	18	1
High elevation:										
Observed	35	23	0	5	2	8	11	7	9	1
Stable year 4	22	34	0	8	3	12	10	4	9	0

and data are presented elsewhere and only the conclusions will be outlined here (Hastorf 1983, Chapter 5). Table 9 presents the observed data generated from the interview data (Appendix B data standardized to 100 percent) and the stable-state frequencies of crops planted by zone, generated from the Markov chain analysis. The year that the data reached a stable state is also listed for each zone.

The Markov analysis reached an unchanging stable state quickly (in five years) in all of the five zones and the one technology analyzed. These findings suggest that the cropping pattern recorded in the interview data reflects a steady trajectory throughout the region. Both Salera's (1954) agricultural cropping information and this Markov chain analysis suggest that Jauja area production has been stable for at least forty years. This picture of steady farming is significant, given that many different political and economic events have affected the production during that time, not the least being the agrarian reform of 1969 and the twentieth-century mining boom in the central Andes (Caballero 1980; Long and Roberts 1984; Mallon 1983; Smith 1989).

The steadiness is important because it means that the interview data reflect long-term intensive land-use patterns in each of the five zones. This gives me increased confidence in using the current rotation cycles of the region to create probable pre-Hispanic cropping patterns under dense population, as existed in the Late

Table 10. *Modern crop rotation possibilities by zone*

Zone	No.	Rotation
Valleys:		
First bench	1	fallow – potatoes – maize – maize – beans/peas – maize – wheat – barley/oats
	2	fallow – potatoes – maize – wheat – wheat – maize – quinoa – maize – beans/peas – quinoa
	3	fallow – potatoes – maize – maize – beans/peas – maize – wheat – Andean tubers – maize – maize – *Ph. vulgaris* – quinoa – barley/oats
Valley irrigation	4	fallow – potatoes – maize – maize – maize – onions – maize – beans/peas – maize – quinoa – maize – maize – maize – wheat
	5	fallow – potatoes – maize – maize – onions – wheat – maize – maize – Andean tubers – quinoa – maize – maize – peas/beans – wheat
Fertile lowland	6	fallow – potatoes – barley/oats – peas/beans – maize – potatoes – quinoa – peas/beans – wheat – maize – potatoes – wheat – potatoes – barley/oats – maize
Uplands:		
Low hillside	7	fallow – potatoes – maize – potatoes – peas/beans – wheat – barley/oats
	8	fallow – potatoes – wheat – peas/beans – maize – maize – quinoa – peas/beans – barley/oats
	9	fallow – potatoes – potatoes – wheat – barley/oats
Hill irrigation	10	potatoes – wheat – potatoes – peas/beans – wheat
Extensive hillside	11	fallow – potatoes –peas/beans – maize – wheat – lupine
	12	fallow – potatoes – wheat – peas/beans – barley/oats
High elevation	13	fallow – fallow – potatoes – barley/oats
	14	fallow – fallow – potatoes – wheat – peas/beans
	15	fallow – potatoes – potatoes – peas/beans – wheat – barley/oats

pre-Hispanic times. The results from the data and my analysis about modern agriculture make two main points about the region. First, the Jauja area is the scene of intensive but sustainable agricultural production today. Second, most of the region is fairly fertile, as demonstrated by the high yields in almost all microzones.

Crop rotation formulation

We can assume that the rotation cycles created in the Markov matrices and tested in the likelihood analysis reflect one stable system of land-use in the region, and that they are sustainable. The observed yearly crop frequencies cycles from the interview data (Appendix B) can now be used to generate average crop rotations in each zone. To do so, I constructed potential crop rotation cycles by beginning with the most frequently produced crop in year 1. Then I looked for the most frequently planted crop that followed each of those in year 2, etc. Table 10 gives a summary of these proposed crop cycles by zone. When a range of production intensities and rotation cycles were noted, I listed the variety within each zone.

To standardize the cycles, I begin each rotation cycle with fallow. After fallow, all fields first produce potatoes. The valley sequences are longer than those in the upland fields, reflecting a more continuous cropping pattern in the lower fields. These are not a rotation cycle *per se*. On the first bench and in the irrigated valley zones, the farmers plant maize after potatoes; in the low fertile fields, some grow a quinoa crop in the second production year. In the lower elevation fields the crop sequence after this grain crop is less rigid; any crop except lupine and tubers may be planted in no specific order. This more flexible valley rotation cycle reflects the lack of effect by the previous year's crop pattern indicated by the multi-way frequency analysis for the valley lands: a crop planted one year does not influence the crop decision for the next year.

The upland zones show more variability in the length of their rotation cycle. The upland cycles show a distinct crop rotation, where one year's decisions affect the next two years of the production cycle. All upland zones have at least one year of fallow followed by one year of potatoes and then one to four additional years of crop production. The lower upland zones have more intensive cropping. The higher, less fertile hillsides have two years of fallow and one to two years of production after the potato crop. Lupine and barley/oats tend to be planted at the end of the cycle, preceding fallow, when the soil's nutrients have been exhausted.

From a series of computations presented in the tables, we can see that this area has the potential for a highly productive region, which gives us a clue as to why the Sausa could have large populations, why the Inka were so interested in controlling the area early on in their campaigns, and why too the Spanish focused on its potential. Before this production cycle and crop mix information can be made relevant for pre-Hispanic time periods in the next chapter, the evidence for pre-Hispanic intensive land-use must be investigated.

8

Pre-Hispanic agricultural methods and cropping patterns

During the archaeological land-use survey in 1980, evidence for five pre-Hispanic agricultural technologies was discovered in the study region. The tangible remains of each strategy (in various states of disrepair) suggest intensive labor input leading to increased crop output. What is particularly intriguing about the technological data is that these pre-Hispanic capital improvements in water and soil conditions are located in each of the five arable land-use zones. They include drained fields, two types of hillside terrace, irrigation canals, and ridged fields. This evidence corroborates that there was pre-Hispanic agricultural intensification in each zone in the region, along with suggestions of communal work and symbolic connections with the landscape. The five systems will be summarized here very briefly since they have been described fully elsewhere (Hastorf and Earle 1985; Parsons 1978).

Stream irrigation

Although there are no clues to the pre-Hispanic age of the small, stone-lined irrigation systems emanating from the tributary streams flowing into the main Mantaro Valley, this agricultural strategy must have been implemented at the edge of the valley floors, as it is today. No datable material, however, is associated with them.

Raised fields in the tributary valleys

Each of the tributary valley floors has evidence of artificial drainage where natural drainage is poor. In the Jauja area, raised or drained field systems have been identified in the Yanamarca, Paca, and Masma Valleys next to the shallow lakes, and in the swampy sections of the Masma Valley. I also found small patches of such fields on aerial photographs in additional low spots around the region. Evidence from the aerial photographs suggests that parallel ditches were dug approximately 0.5 m into the fine, dense, clay alluvium, with the excavated soil piled onto ridges in between in all flat, poorly drained patches.

There are two types of raised fields in the region, an open checkerboard type and a linear pattern. The fields in the Yanamarca and Paca Valleys are similar to the open checkerboard pattern described for the western Lake Titicaca region (Denevan 1966; Lennon 1982; Parsons and Denevan 1967; Smith et al. 1968) and for the Colombian pampa (Broadbent 1963; Parsons and Bowen 1966). The most clearly demarcated field system comprises about 14 ha along the northern edge of Laguna Tragadero in the Yanamarca Valley. Trenches were dug to create broad ridges between 2 and 4 m across, grouped into parallel rows of two to eight ridges. These groups were aligned either perpendicular or parallel to neighboring groups. Each group appears to be an individual, separate plot organized along a main drainage ditch, between 50 and 100 sq. m in size.

The Masma Valley raised fields were constructed in a linear arrangement. This field pattern is similar to the linear pattern described for the southern Titicaca basin (Erickson 1985; 1988; Kolata 1986; Smith et al. 1968: 358–59). Most drainage canals of several hundred meters run parallel to the natural stream, as the individual downslope ditches that create the 1–2 m ridges emanate perpendicularly up from these canals.

In these three valleys, 195 ha of drained fields have been mapped. The distribution of the fields suggests that pre-Hispanic farmers reclaimed drainable soils in both large and small plots. At present, dating these fields is problematic because no associated artifacts were recovered in the test excavations. The field systems could have been built, expanded, and deserted at any time through the pre-Hispanic sequences, and no mention of their use is made in any historic document about the region. Within 0.5 km from any field, numerous pre-Hispanic sites have been located, dating from the Early Intermediate Period through the Late Horizon; therefore settlements are not associated directly with the drained fields as they are elsewhere in the Andes (Kolata 1986). In Chapter 11 the crop mixes will provide some insight into their use. Although I excavated trenches in every field system to view the deposition history, more extensive excavations for artifacts will have to be completed to date individual fields (as was done in Belize by Turner and Harrison [1983]). These fields are extremely productive and would have been valuable, even though they require considerable labor to maintain, as the fields in the Titicaca basin show (Erickson 1985; 1988). While the fields could be built and operated by individual families, a larger group from a community or *ayllu* had to keep the main drainage ditches open, with regular communal work parties.

Terraces on the hill slopes

On the slopes rimming the Mantaro Valley and the surrounding tributary valleys and *quebradas*, two distinct types of terrace are found: lynchet step-slope terraces, or *andenes rusticos*, and stone-wall terraces (*andenes*).

A lynchet is an earth-banked field, constructed by levelling soil and removing rock to make a gentler slope while retaining soil. Lynchets represent a land reclamation strategy. Terraces of this type step down many of the moderately severe slopes in the region. Lynchet clusters are evident on all hillsides surrounding the valleys; a block of them ranges in size from 3 to 135 ha. Lynchets tend to cluster around the EIP (Huacrapukio) sites. In the Yanamarca Valley, there is a much greater density of lynchets in the northeast than on the western slopes, where they are thin along the base of the hill below the Wanka II sites. Over 1487 ha of lynchets have been mapped on the region's limestone, generally in the western portion of the study area. In contrast, only 181 ha are extant on the eastern metamorphic rock. There are many more settlements in the west.

Constructing this kind of step-slope terrace does not require group organization. Individual families with labor-exchange help can construct and maintain the circumscribed fields independent of neighboring farmers. But because the fields always occur in large clusters with communal water diversions and erosion barriers, some form of coordination probably existed to maintain them. Most probably they were planted by individual families, but rotated as a group organized by the community.

The stone-wall terraces are located on steep hill slopes, usually on slopes greater than 15 degrees. They consist of a series of shored up, solid, vertical cobble walls, built along the contour of the hillside, stepping down the slope. The walled-in area was filled in with dirt to make a level but narrow planting surface, a pattern similar to Guillet's description of Colca Valley terrace construction (1987a: 411). These terraced areas apparently were not stable due to constant water erosion, and considerable annual upkeep would have been necessary for continued use. As Donkin (1979: 33) points out, the construction and maintenance of a series of stone-wall terraces would have required cooperative organization. Building and maintaining a series of terraces as a unit is necessary to secure the entire group against collapse. Although in some areas of the Andes these terraces are expressly associated with irrigation systems (in the Colca, Urubamba, and Tarma Valleys for example), in other locations, such as Cuyo Cuyo and the Upper Mantaro Valley, the terrace canals are used for drainage (Camino 1982).

The Jauja region terrace complexes range in size from 0.6 to 62 ha and are distributed sparsely throughout the region. They represent considerable capital investment, and their uneven distribution must reflect different economic decisions as well as settlement location. No ceramics have been found on the terraces, so their dates have been determined by their proximity to settlements. A single terrace area of 27 ha is located within the defensive walls of Hatúnmarca, and a second concentration is found on the south side of the Mantaro gorge, near the opening to the valley. The remaining stone-wall terraces are scattered throughout the higher elevations.

Irrigation canals in the high elevation uplands

In the upland zone, topography and elevation affect agricultural productivity. The sloping lands are the most dependable for annual production, because downward movement of cold air decreases the chance of frost. The cold air settles in the depressions, where frost lowers yields and destroys crops. As discussed in Chapter 6, the likelihood of frost increases through the rainy season. Therefore, modern farmers try to plant as early as possible, hoping their crops will flower before the killing frosts begin. It is reasonable to assume that pre-Hispanic farmers might have done the same. Irrigation in the upland zone can increase productivity and crop security (lowering risk), because it makes earlier planting possible, as well as requiring less fallow years (Chapter 7; Table 4).

The upland zone shows evidence of two pre-Hispanic stone-lined canal systems, built with simple technologies (Parsons 1978). They were capable of carrying water to five upland destinations (Figure 4). The more extensive, northern canal system tapped a high puna spring and carried water through four branches over a total of 21 km. Each branch ended in fields associated with one of the Tunánmarca alliance sites, the southernmost branch taking water to the base of Tunánmarca. There is no evidence of feeder canals along the branches, as each segment appears to have been constructed to a specific settlement. The average slope of the canals is 1.6 degrees. Three aqueducts across small depressions or valleys were part of this northern system. A smaller canal to the south emptied into the same basin as the longer canal, under Tunánmarca. This canal is only 2.6 km long and could have watered the same location as the southern branch of the larger system.

The confluence of the final branch of the northern canal is noteworthy, for it could have joined the canal head of the short southern canal. Perhaps the shorter canal was built first and was later in need of expansion; or its spring was too small for Tunánmarca's purposes; or perhaps there was a symbolic desire to converge two water sources at the new center, Tunánmarca. This type of stream convergence (*tinku*) is significant as a locus of power in Andean tradition, as seen in ethnohistoric and modern Andean perceptions of water (Bastien 1978; W. Isbell 1978; B. J. Isbell 1978; Salomon pers. comm.). Along with the fields south of Tunánmarca, these two canals could have watered a pond-like area. Like a similar valley depression upstream along the trunk canal route, this area could have been a *qocha*, an area that impounds water for camelid watering and alpaca fodder growth (Browman 1987; Mayer pers. comm.); or the water could have supplied domestic water for the more than 10,000 people of the settlement.

The canals' narrow size suggests that they would have had to be cleaned regularly. The relatively long distance from source to target area and the necessity for allocating water among the settlements imply intercommunity managerial requirements. Modern agricultural information suggests that this water might have increased crop yields, increased the security of crop production, and minimized fallow years in the cropping cycle. The canals could have also supplied domestic water. And finally, as discussed in Chapter 3, building and maintaining a canal system that links the northern alliance suggests that this too might have had a symbolic aspect through the participation in annual cleaning rituals (*yarqa aspiy*) with group *faena* labor.

Extensive hillside ridged fields

In the lower puna between 3750 and 3950 m, an area of deep ridged fields represents a fifth type of agricultural intensification. Frosts here are common throughout the dry season and often occur during the rainy season as well. In order to cultivate in this zone, farmers constructed ridges and deep troughs running downhill. The troughs served as runoff channels for rainwater and may have redirected cold air as well (Riley and Freimuth 1977; Waddell 1973).

Today, only one small puna valley in the Jauja region still shows evidence of ridged fields, although they could have been quite extensive in the past before tractors obliterated their traces (Matos 1975). This valley is located in the northwestern section of the study region, with evidence of only 4.7 ha of fields. The ridges are on average 2–3 m apart, alternating with troughs that are now 20–60 cm deep. Like the lynchets, ridged fields could have been individually constructed and maintained with some need for coordination of the drainage above and below.

These fields are impossible to date except by proximity to settlements, but since they are located within 2 km from two Wanka II sites and much farther from all other sites it is possible to propose that they were built during that phase. Alternatively, all villages might have had communal land up near the puna.

Land-use through time

Settlement distribution can affect agricultural production in several ways. To insure success in farming, subsistence farmers disperse into settlements that are located near the best agricultural land. For other economic, cultural, historical, and political reasons, however, settlement distributions often deviate from this pattern.

Characteristically, land-use practices that involve high labor costs are found close to settlements, and more extensive strategies, which require less labor, are located at greater distances (Chisholm 1962; for the Andes see Mayer 1972). If the population size is dense and aggregated people are confronted with commuting regularly a long way, dispersing into colonies and new villages, and/or intensifying agricultural practices near the settlements. If settlements increase in size and there is no fissioning, local intensification must occur.

In Chapter 4 we learned that during the EIP/MH phase settlements were located mainly in the Yanamarca Valley (Figure 2). Some sites were near the valley soils, but many settlements were just above, on the surrounding hill slopes. These sites are surrounded by tracks of lynchets, suggesting that the terraces were constructed when these sites were inhabited. After the focus on the Yanamarca Valley, the Wanka I settlement pattern is more dispersed throughout the region (Figure 3). The population could have continued to use the valley and hillside fields but there was also an increase in other valley agriculture, around the Mantaro and Paca Valleys. Additional labor intensification at this time is adduced by an increase in stone hoes, most likely used for cultivation (Russell 1988a). It is quite likely that the movement across the landscape to other discrete valley agricultural zones reflects increasingly separate political entities in the area (Chapters 4 and 5).

During the Wanka II phase, fortified communities are found at high elevations in the west, above the valleys (Figure 4). The Wanka II centers incorporated stone-walled terraces, were linked by upland irrigation systems, and were close to the puna ridged fields. This population aggregation suggests that there was agricultural intensification in the nearby upland and hillside zones but perhaps not in the valleys. Pastoral activities could have intensified as well.

The evidence supports continual use of intensive agricultural strategies throughout this archaeological sequence, though the actual strategies in use could have changed. Based on spatial location, site association, and artifacts, intensive agriculture could possibly have begun with a focus on vast lynchets and perhaps drained fields in the EIP/MH. The residents in Wanka I times could have used or expanded any or all of these strategies. There is evidence for Wanka I agricultural intensity, but this might have had a different focus from that of earlier agriculture, with more emphasis on the valley lands in need of hoes. The drained fields (fertile lowlands) may have become very important to the Wanka I population, who could have gained excellent yields but at a cost of more labor and labor organization (Figure 16; Hastorf 1990b).

Finally, in Wanka II, some terraces, the upland irrigation canals, the ridged fields, and at least some of the higher lynchets could have been built. The Wanka II agricultural strategies seem to be at least as intensive as those of Wanka I, but of a different sort. The evidence suggests that some of the intensive strategies in use earlier, like the drained fields, might have been abandoned. This abandonment could have been due to population aggregation and settlement relocation, which required local agricultural production in the uplands. The raised field abandonment also might have been due to tensions over the raised valley systems themselves.

What we still must learn is how crop production changed, given these suggestions of broad land-use shifts over time from the intensive agricultural evidence and the settlement patterns. To do this I return to the agricultural data to construct a base-line model to track crop production evidence in the paleoethnobotanical data.

Construction of cropping patterns

The first step to make modern agricultural data comparable with the pre-Hispanic material is to convert crop productivities (shown in Table 7) so they can provide a sense of the pre-Hispanic potential. In other words, I need to replace the introduced crops with indigenous counterparts. This conversion is based on the regional crop geography data, traditional production techniques, the crop's characteristics and their equivalents (Table 2).

Table 11 presents this conversion to indigenous crop efficiencies for each of the five arable zones and two irrigation strategies. The bottom two rows in the table average the productivity for valley lands and uplands. In the valleys, maize is the most efficient crop, followed by potatoes and quinoa. In the uplands, potatoes and lupine are most productive, with Andean tubers a close third.

Land-use by crop

The next step in computing potential pre-Hispanic production is to estimate the percentage of each zone that might have been devoted to the five pre-Hispanic crop groups in a steady-state production system. By applying the crop equivalents (Table 2) to today's cropping frequencies (Table 4), a hypothetical optimal plant strategy can be proposed that defines plausible pre-Hispanic crop frequencies, assuming the region was producing at a steady-state level (discussed in Chapter 7) (Table 12). These conversions result in determining that, in general, valley lands mainly produced maize and quinoa and that potatoes dominated upland production. As today, this prediction should reflect the effect of the individual farmer attempting to yield a mix of crops, so that the most productive crops are not the only taxa present in this prediction.

Indigenous crop rotations

While general cropping frequency predictions for the region help give a sense of the agricultural production, they do not provide a picture of its intensity. In order to have

Table 11. *Indigenous crop efficiencies × 100, taken from Table 7*

Zone	Maize	Potatoes	Quinoa	Lupine	Beans[2]	A. tubers
First bench	45	101	—	48	48[4]	13
Valley irrigation[3]	137	140	212	—	48[4]	34
Fertile lowland	307	67	62	—	75[4]	34
Low hillside	33[1]	40	136	145	—	97
Extensive hillside	59[1]	24	67	116	—	58
Hill irrigation[3]	—	668	95	206[5]	—	97[6]
High elevation	—	180	82	206	—	203
Valleys	168	95	87	48	48[4]	27
Uplands	46	165	95	156	—	119

[1] Maize is viable only in the valleys; this figure is from fields just off the valley floor
[2] Beans, *Phaseolus vulgaris*, are produced only in the lowest valley fields
[3] Because there are so few cases, these technologies have less influence on the subregion mean efficiencies
[4] These averages are for bean fields only, not bean and pea as in Table 7
[5] Because there were no modern lupine fields in the hill irrigation survey, the average from high elevation was used
[6] Because there were no modern A. tuber fields in the hill irrigation survey, the average from low hillside was used

a more precise view of pre-Hispanic land-use potential, it is more realistic to construct potential rotation cycles with pre-Hispanic crops. Using the fifteen crop rotations listed in Table 10, with the crop conversions from Table 2 as a guide, I have outlined indigenous crop rotation cycles. These rotation cycles are assumed to represent land-use at an intense but sustainable level, especially as there is archaeological evidence for intensive strategies through these phases.

I assume that pre-Hispanic farmers in the Wanka I and Wanka II eras did not crop the land more intensively than is done today, although the population today is close to what it was. By mechanizing and relying on chemical fertilizers and pesticides, some modern farmers have been able to eliminate fallow years, especially to increase yields for cash sales outside of the valley. However, today in the Mantaro Valley there are farmers who do not use chemical fertilizer but *guano de corral*, a compost generated in their household compounds. This would have been the main fertilizer in the past. Without this, prehistorically, the equivalent cropping patterns would have been less intensive, with more fallow years. This use of fertilizer is taken into account in constructing some of the proposed pre-Hispanic crop rotations, in other words, the cycles include different levels of production intensity.

Table 12. *Hypothetical optimal percentage of land in each indigenous crop by zone (percent within zone)*

Zone	Maize	Potatoes	Quinoa	Beans[1]	A. tubers
First bench	36	11	32	11	7
Valley irrigation	57	8	23	8	4
Fertile lowland	21	21	35	21	0
Low hillside	22	22	17	22	17
Extensive hillside	11	22	22	22	22
Hill irrigation	0	40	20	20	20
High elevation	0	33	22	11	33

[1] Beans represent *Phaseolus vulgaris* in valley fields and lupin in uplands

Table 13. *Indigenous crop rotation possibilities by zone*

Valleys:		
First bench	1	fallow – potatoes – maize – maize – beans[1] – maize – quinoa – quinoa
	2	fallow – potatoes – maize – A. tubers – quinoa – maize – quinoa – maize – beans – quinoa
	3	fallow – potatoes – maize – maize – A. tubers – maize – quinoa – quinoa – maize – maize – beans – quinoa – quinoa
Valley irrigation	4	fallow – potatoes – maize – maize – maize – quinoa – maize – maize – maize – quinoa – maize – maize – maize – quinoa
	5	fallow – potatoes – maize – maize – A. tubers – quinoa – maize – maize – beans – quinoa – maize – maize – beans – quinoa
Fertile lowland	6	fallow – potatoes – quinoa – beans – maize – potatoes – quinoa – beans – quinoa – maize – potatoes – quinoa – beans – quinoa – maize
Uplands:		
Low hillside	7	fallow – potatoes – maize – potatoes – maize – quinoa – lupine
	8	fallow – potatoes – A. tubers – A. tubers – maize – maize – quinoa – lupine – lupine
	9	fallow – potatoes – A. tubers – quinoa – lupine
Hill irrigation	10	potatoes – A. tubers – potatoes – lupine – quinoa
Extensive hillside	11	fallow – potatoes –A. tubers – maize – quinoa – lupine
	12	fallow – potatoes – A. tubers – quinoa – lupine
High elevation	13	fallow – fallow – potatoes – A. tubers
	14	fallow – fallow – potatoes – A. tubers – quinoa
	15	fallow – fallow – potatoes – quinoa – lupine – A. tubers

[1] Beans represent *Phaseolus vulgaris*

Generated out of the modern rotation cycles of Table 10, the proposed indigenous cropping cycles are seen in Table 13 as fifteen generalized but plausible rotations. The crop rotations and percentages of land planted to individual crops are correlated with soil fertility, climatic conditions, elevation, and the probable pressure on labor and

Table 14. *Proposed pre-Hispanic crop rotation cycles with crop efficiency estimates, expressed as output/input × 100, years in the rotation cycle, average crop efficiency of each cycle and its standard deviation, taken from Tables 11 and 13*

			Rotation cycle (years)	Average rotation cycle efficiency	s.d.
Valleys:					
First bench	1	fallow – potatoes – maize – maize –beans – maize – quinoa – quinoa 101 45 45 48 45 50 50	8	48	20
	2	fallow – potatoes – maize – A. tubers – quinoa – maize – quinoa – maize – beans – quinoa 101 45 13 50 45 50 45 48 50	10	45	22
	3	fallow – potatoes – maize – maize – A. tubers – maize – quinoa – quinoa – maize – maize – beans – quinoa – quinoa 101 45 45 13 45 50 50 45 45 48 50 50	13	45	19
Valley irrigation	4	fallow – potatoes – maize – maize – maize – quinoa – maize – maize – maize – quinoa – maize – maize – maize – quinoa 140 137 137 137 212 137 137 137 212 137 137 137 212	14	144	67
	5	fallow – potatoes – maize – maize – A. tubers – quinoa – maize – maize – beans – quinoa – maize – maize – beans – quinoa 140 137 137 34 212 137 137 48 212 137 137 48 212	14	123	60
Fertile lowland	6	fallow – potatoes – quinoa – beans – maize – potatoes – quinoa – beans – quinoa – maize – potatoes – quinoa – beans – quinoa – maize 67 62 75 307 67 62 75 62 307 67 62 75 62 307	15	110	102
Uplands:					
Low hillside	7	fallow – potatoes – maize – potatoes – maize – quinoa – lupine 40 33 40 33 136 145	7	61	54
	8	fallow – potatoes – A. tubers – A. tubers maize – maize – quinoa – lupine – lupine 40 97 97 33 33 136 145 145	9	81	50
	9	fallow – potatoes –A. tubers – quinoa – lupine 40 97 136 145	5	84	47
Hill irrigation	10	potatoes – A. tubers – potatoes – lupine – quinoa 668 97 668 206 95	5	347	296
Extensive hillside	11	fallow – potatoes – A. tubers – maize – quinoa – lupine 24 58 59 67 116	6	54	33
	12	fallow – potatoes – A. tubers – quinoa – lupine 24 58 67 116	5	53	38
High elevation	13	fallow – fallow – potatoes – A. tubers 180 203	4	96	16
	14	fallow – fallow – potatoes – A. tubers – quinoa 180 203 82	5	93	64
	15	fallow – fallow – potatoes – quinoa – lupine – A. tubers 180 82 206 203	6	112	58

materials necessary for cultivation. It should be noted that these cropping predictions are averages and are not to be considered individual field models.*

As pointed out previously, in the valley, first bench, and irrigated zones, maize would be the most likely crop to plant after potatoes, with quinoa planted in the final year before fallow. In the fertile, but poorly drained valley soils (fertile lowlands), quinoa was most likely planted after potatoes, followed by a cycle of alternating beans, maize, potatoes, and quinoa. The valley zone was probably cropped most intensively because of its sustainable fertility, mild temperatures, and good soil moisture. The length of the cropping cycle before another fallow year would have varied, depending on the amount of labor input and the soil fertility (either natural or fertilized).

In most upland zone rotation cycles, the first three years are fallow – potatoes – Andean tubers, followed by the possibility of maize, lupine, and tubers, depending on the zone. Usually in the fourth year maize, quinoa, or lupine is planted in the lower elevations and quinoa or lupine in the upper fields. These upland rotations can be described generally as a short cycle of fallow – tubers – tubers – grains – legumes (except in irrigated areas).

Conversions to pre-Hispanic land-use patterns

Current methods of agricultural intensification include the use of chemical fertilizer, pesticides, hybrid seeds, mechanized equipment, and large valley irrigation schemes. Many of these are modern counterparts to less mechanized extant or semi-abandoned pre-Hispanic intensification systems (*guaño de corral*, more labor, tributary irrigation systems, etc.). The pre-Hispanic land-reclamation technologies still in use are lynchets, a portion of the upland irrigation system, and small sections of drained fields. The stone-walled terraces, many of the lynchets, and the ridged fields are not planted. Although the modern intensification systems are not directly equivalent to the pre-Hispanic systems, I assume that there is enough similarity in land-use, traditional technology, and crop continuity to support using some modern crop rotations and relative land-use results as a base to view local pre-Hispanic agricultural practices.

A list of the potential pre-Hispanic crop rotation cycles incorporates all of the available data presented in the previous discussions of Jauja agriculture. Table 14 includes fifteen likely crop rotation patterns and their average crop production efficiencies. The average efficiency for each rotation cycle is noted on the right, presenting a view over the long run. These were calculated by tallying the individual crop efficiencies and dividing by the total number of years in the cycle.

Table 14 includes extensive rotation cycles likely to have existed pre-Hispanically. These are listed by zone in cycles 1, 2, 3, 7, 9, 13, and 14. The table also includes intensive pre-Hispanic strategies, lynchets in cycles 8, 11, and 12, stone-walled terraces in cycles 11 and 12, ridged fields in cycle 15, drained fields in cycle 6, upland irrigation in cycle 10, and valley floor irrigation in cycles 4 and 5. The results and the extent of these strategies imply that the most productive land (in terms of output in the

* Occasionally one field in the Andes will contain multiple crops (Chapter 2). The extent of this occurring in the past is impossible to determine but I accommodate for this by using these crop rotation tables as averages for a zone over the long term, not for an individual field.

long run) is also the land that requires more labor input. The costly fields are the irrigated valley lands (cycles 4 and 5), parts of the soggy, fertile land, which must be drained (cycle 6), and the upland soils that are irrigated by a canal system (cycle 10). Less labor-intensive strategies that yield well are found in the low hillsides (cycle 9) and the high elevation rolling uplands (cycle 15). These estimates suggest that there is and was a range of extensive and intensive strategies that have varying yields, once more supporting the notion that over-the-long-run an optimal yield is not the same as a maximum efficiency yield. While some of the more efficient strategies are the intensive ones, hill and valley irrigation, they also have higher start-up and maintenance costs, making them more expensive but highly productive. The least expensive strategies tend also to be the least efficient.

Summary

Based on settlement locations and artifacts, it is likely that lower-cost extensive strategies were more common in the earlier phases. But by Wanka I times, it looks as if several forms of intensification could have been undertaken. And, too, in the Wanka II phase, there is a quantum increase in evidence for land and labor intensification. It is possible that access to certain types of land might have been limited during Wanka II. Access to labor, as many ethnographies and historians mention, is linked directly to politics, as labor is exchanged for community land-use (Smith 1989) as well as help in one's own fields. Surely these factors would have dictated whether a plot of land was more or less intensively farmed. In fact, as presented in Chapter 5, when we have hints of reports about the local versions over which the Wanka II population was so competitive, land and labor are both mentioned. Increased labor in the fields not only meant more constraints on people, it also meant higher yields.

The question still remains as to how the changing agriculture practices participated in the changing social relations and political control; and did they help to create and maintain the burgeoning leadership that is evident in Sausa houses?

9

Pre-Hispanic production potentials

The organization of the data based on spatial energetics is only one of several possible methods for studying Jauja agriculture. I have chosen this geographic–energetics form to present the local pre-Hispanic agricultural production potential because I need a way to organize and make comparable the basic production costs and yields that are important considerations in Andean farmers' decisions and are physical realities (Chapter 2). There are of course other ways this could have been presented. Andean communities often are located such that they can take advantage of several zones within their diverse environment, even though there will still be some amount of walking to further zones, especially to grazing lands (Brush 1976; Thomas 1973; Skar 1979; Winterhalder pers. comm.; Chapter 3). In the Jauja area agricultural zones are all close to each other in a U formation, and people can live near several land-use zones. Today, most Sausa agricultural production takes place close to the settlement where the farmers reside.

The Andes also have another important production pattern, that of archipelago production stations, dispersed among different critical zones, often separated from each other by less useful territory. This production strategy has been important in many areas of Peru and Bolivia (Murra 1972; 1980; Harris 1985), but it is and was not universal, especially for the bulk of the subsistence diet in the central Andes of Peru (Brush 1976; Salomon 1986; Skar 1979). Distant land was and is often used for special crops that could not be produced locally but were necessary or desired, such as maize, chili peppers, coca, fruit, and certain woods. Historic documents mention the Sausa having eastern jungle communities during the Late Intermediate and Inka times (LeVine 1979; 1985), but the artifactual evidence suggests little inter-regional movement of goods into the Jauja region's homes until the LIP (no chili peppers, only three samples of coca in the Wanka II, and a few pieces of jungle wood: Hastorf 1987; Hastorf and Johannessen 1991). There is no documentary evidence for the Wanka having western outposts, and very little coastal material was found on the sites. These products may have been needed or desired but they do not form the bulk of the diet for this central Andean people. And so the artifactual evidence supports a focus on local production.

In building this comparison, I begin by defining agricultural territories for the excavated sites. The extent and productivity of the land-use zones (as defined in Chapter 8) are also tabulated. The sampled settlements can then be examined systematically for territory and land-use changes through time. From these land-use zone apportionments and their assigned productivities, we can get a sense of agricultural production trends.

Site catchment analysis

Catchment analysis was developed to study major local resources available to a community's inhabitants. First the site's territory is determined, then the land and resources within these confines are classified in use categories (Vita-Finzi and Higgs 1970). Many archaeological projects have used and refined this basic spatial technique in order to systematically learn about the environment and resources of a study area. Although there are many problems and drawbacks to such a simple technique, it can be effective in organizing information associated with specific sites.

A basic assumption of catchment analysis is that production costs will increase as the distance increases between the place of extraction or production and the place of consumption or storage. In fact, Chisholm (1962) found that the net output of subsistence farmers dropped 15 to 20 percent with each additional kilometer between their fields and their dwellings. He also noted that the most labor-intensive activities were generally found near residences and less intensive farming methods were used farther away. This spatial principle affects agricultural settlement location and site distribution, as well as resource use within each site's territory. These same principles have been noted in the Andes by Mayer (1972).

Productive land therefore can be in part defined by the effect distance has on production costs – both transport costs and costs of protecting the harvest. A second criterion that defines a settlement's territory is the presence of neighboring settlements that create competition and restrict access to immovable resources such as fields, water, or grazing land. Catchment territories can be quite restricted if settlements are dense enough.

When societies become larger, denser, or multifaceted, certain resources are increasingly outside a settlement's nearby territory, and new strategies of procurement must be implemented, as in the archipelago model (Murra 1972), or in the case of village specialization with intervillage trade (Hagstrum 1989; Harris 1985). Even so, as long as a community's local landscape can provide its basic dietary needs, I assume that its residents will extract food most intensively near their homes.

When intensive agricultural production strategies are employed, a site's resource territory can be defined with some assurance based on the effective distance between neighbors. The late pre-Hispanic ancestors of the Sausa were a settled and agriculturally oriented group. They also herded and hunted, but wild game and camelids were not major dietary contributors, as the nitrogen stable isotopes illustrates for the Wanka II population (Hastorf 1991).

We can be fairly sure of the agricultural territories for the Sausa, because most land of more than 5 km distance is often nonarable puna. The puna grasslands extend out on three sides of the region, and groups of settlements probably had access to these more distant lands for herding, hunting, gathering, and religious uses. Topography and elevation limit the amount of productive land in the Andes. The Jauja region inhabitants surely had herds in the surrounding puna, but whether there were

Table 15. *Regional and site hypothetical territories (in ha)*

Total regional area	40,385
EIP/MH sites	
J1 Pancán	686
J71 Tragadero Viejo	609
Wanka I sites:	
J1 Pancán	310
J49 Ushnu	1961
Wanka II sites:	
J41 Umpamalca	838
J7 Tunánmarca	907
J2 Hatúnmarca	3541

hamlet outposts or permanent villages in the puna is not known. The herding aspect of production is not the focus of this agricultural discussion.

Based on the two constraints defined above, the intensive agricultural territories are determined here mainly by contemporaneous settlement distributions, and a 5-km boundary (Table 15, Figures 18, 19, and 20 show the settlements and their territories). The study region's area is defined by the area within the site survey, that is, east of the Rio Quishualcancha, south Tajana, west of Masma, and north of the 11°50' latitude (Figure 17). The boundary lines for each settlement are demarcated first, by the contemporaneous sites (Chapter 4) and evenly dividing the distance between these sites, and second, observing a 5-km limit when necessary. As discussed above, I chose the distance of 5 km because the overall expense of intensive agriculture beyond this limit increases dramatically, and also because I found no modern plots more than 5 km from the dwellings of today's farmers. While these borders are almost surely not the actual territories of these settlements, they provide a concrete example of the nearby local field potential for the settlements with which to consider other production strategies.

The chosen settlements have a site packing such that their territories are often bounded by neighbors on all sides. The sites tend to be smaller than the phase average, except the center Tunánmarca, but their locations are typical. In the first two phases we see the development of a site clustering in the Yanamarca and Paca Valleys. In the EIP/MH both sites are typically bounded by neighbors and are on the valley edges. In the Wanka I, both sites have direct access up out of the arable lands. With relocation and aggregation in the Wanka II period, neighbor restriction is still evident, even with most settlements clustered in the western uplands. This clustering of large sites suggests that the inhabitants had to produce very intensively nearby. But also, due to the virtual abandonment of the eastern valleys, Wanka II residents may have commuted back to these zones for farming far away from their settlements. Only the botanical data will be able to determine the type of land-use change that accompanied such a radical settlement change. All zones except the lake area are included in the calculations.

Table 16. *Regional land-use zone areas*

Zone	Area (ha)	Regional % of land	Regional % of arable land
Valley:		22	32
First bench	7875	20	29
Fertile lowland	735	2	3
Uplands:		78	68
Low hillside	3720	9	14
Extensive hillside	6410	16	24
High elevation	8135	20	30
Non-arable	13,510	33	—
Total	40,385	100	
Total arable:	26,875	66	100

Several land-use trends are visible in Table 15. Valley sites have less available land than hillside and upland sites. The Wanka II sites, including J7 (Tunánmarca) and J41 (Umpamalca) have smaller territories than the comparative central settlement of the southern alliance site J2 (Hatúnmarca). The southern sites perhaps were settled by a slightly different process than the northern group, as the population distribution across this group of allied sites is different than the northern alliance.

Land-use territories

In Chapter 8, hypothetical crop rotations and production frequencies were constructed for the designated land-use zones. These zones, determined from the land-use and agricultural surveys, are plotted on the topographic map of Figure 17. The calculated area of each zone and its percentage in the region are presented in Table 16.

Although all zones are represented in the region they are not evenly distributed across the landscape. Non-arable puna covers the largest part of the study region, with 33 percent. Conversely, the fertile lowland, which has the greatest productive potential, is the smallest zone with only 2 percent. Regardless of the site distributions in the region, between the fertile lowland and the potential irrigation in the first bench lands, it is likely that the populace would have wanted access to these more restricted but productive valley lands.

The land-use areas for the two EIP/MH site territories are presented in Table 17. These are calculated by measuring the area of each zone within the catchment territories drawn in Figure 18. Valley lands dominate both of these settlements' catchments. These EIP/MH land-use distributions are not similar to the regional mix of Table 16, where fertile lowlands cover only 2 percent of the total land area. Here, the fertile lowland is a dominant zone. The proposed territory for Pancán (J1) has 76 percent valley land with 19 percent in the fertile lowland. If the area had been drained and maintained, it would have been a very productive agricultural territory. I have found vestiges of raised fields along the edge of the marshy zone to the south of Laguna Paca, suggesting that pre-Hispanic inhabitants did drain the area, though they might not have used all of the area in the early stages or in any one year. Tragadero Viejo (J71), located in the middle of the Yanamarca Valley, also has a large proportion of fertile lowland soil in its proposed territory (93 percent). It is hard to believe that much of this was not transformed into arable land by drainage canals, as evidence of drained fields

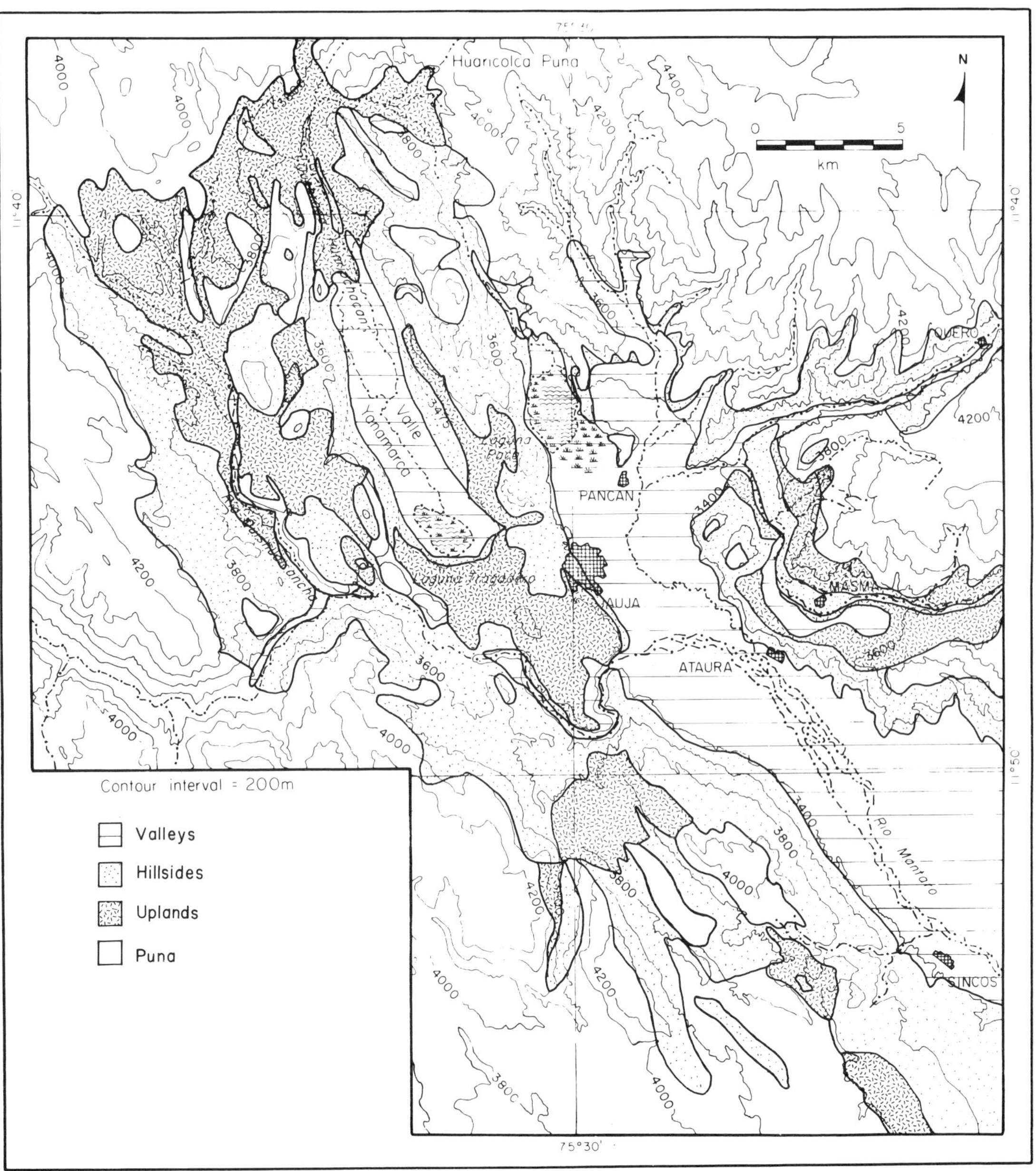

Fig. 17. Regional land-use zones in the study area

Table 17. *EIP/MH site territories and land-use zones*

Zone	Area (ha)	% of territory
Pancán (J1):		
First bench	390	57
Fertile lowland	127	19
Low hillside	47	7
Non-arable	122	17
Total	686	100
Tragadero Viejo (J71):		
First bench	40	7
Fertile lowland	569	93
Total	609	100

surrounds the site. Tragadero Viejo is hemmed in by neighbors who restrict its valley lands.

Both of these EIP/MH settlements had immediate access to valley floor and hillside land. Pancán has some non-arable land, nearby on the rocky hill. As the site distributions in Figure 18 suggest, the majority of these earlier territories focused on the lower land-use zones.

Figure 19 presents the two sampled Wanka I site territories and their land-use zones. These mapped land-use zones are tabulated in Table 18. Both sites are much smaller than the average site for the period, though not by much. At Pancán, the relative land-use zone frequencies have become greatly restricted, as well as shifting from the earlier distributions with more hillside land. Pancán's territory continued to include the fertile lowland area, but is diminished to 10 percent of the Wanka I land area. It was restricted by its southern neighbor (J235).

The second site, Ushnu (J49), represents a different catchment mix yet with the same shift; its territory comprises considerably more upland and less valley land (the first bench is only 6 percent of the total). It is located on a low ridge at the northern edge of the Yanamarca Valley and represents a common settlement location during this phase, as some settlements are off the valley floors. Ushnu has much more territory than Pancan as well as clear sets of lynchets.

The estimated Wanka I territories of Ushnu and Pancán contain less valley lands than their EIP/MH counterparts. Because many Wanka I inhabitants moved back to the sides of the valleys, the valley resources might have received more agricultural focus and been the subject of tensions and boundary disputes. Some of the Wanka I population may have moved uphill as a result of growing tension between settlements and increasing concern about defensive security. In addition, there may have been an increased interest in intensifying herding as seen in increased bone densities at Pancán (Hastorf et al. 1989: 105). If herding and farming were both intensified, settlements might have been placed between the valley maize-growing lands and the puna grazing land.

Figure 20 presents the catchment territories of the two sampled Wanka II sites as well as the southern alliance center, Hatúnmarca. The land-use areas within these catchments are presented in Table 19. The drastic shift in the Wanka II settlement pattern is seen in the maps and zonal percentages. Umpamalca does not have Yanamarca Valley lands in its territory. Tunánmarca probably received access to the valley lands through its satellites, especially J46, as is drawn on this map. J46 was a controversial site throughout our field work, as we could not easily determine its purpose, although it looked as if it was an agricultural center during the Wanka II. Tunánmarca's territory barely includes any puna lands, but as the major center of the northern cluster it might have had access to the northern Huaricolca puna. Tunánmarca splits its territory

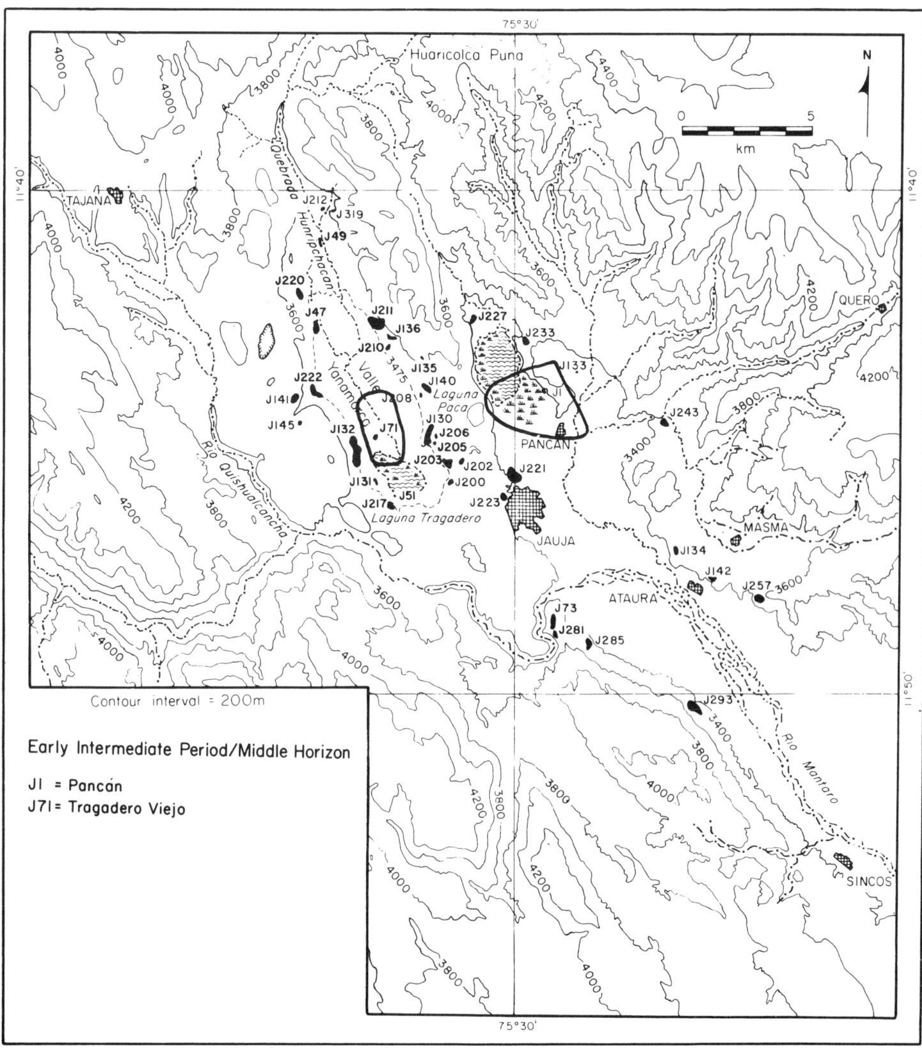

Fig. 18. Early Intermediate Period/Middle Horizon settlements with hypothetical territories for the sites studied

Table 18. *Wanka I site territories and land-use zones*

Zone	Area (ha)	% of territory
Pancán (J1):		
First bench	130	42
Fertile lowland	31	10
Low hillside	65	21
Non-arable	84	27
Total	310	100
Ushnu (J49):		
First bench	131	6
Low and extensive hillside	565	29
High elevation	915	47
Non-arable puna	350	18
Total	1961	100

between high elevation and hillside land. In some ways it is also worthwhile to consider that a center like Tunánmarca would have access to all of the northern alliance lands, perhaps including Umpamalca's.

While Umpamalca has no access to Yanamarca Valley land, there is the *quebrada* directly west with a thin track of protected flat land along the river banks that yields maize today. To the west, across the Quishualcancha Quebrada, there is a cluster of settlements in a different alliance. This group of settlements could have cut off the lands to the west of the *quebrada* from the Umpamalca residents and perhaps also made the mild *quebrada* lands constantly disputed. Umpamalca's territory is mainly high elevation long fallow uplands, with no direct access to herding land, though the occupants could have moved through the northern alliance lands.

The two Wanka II alliances studied here had different population distributions. The northern population was larger, with more satellite sites, while the southern population had fewer settlements and people. These different demographics affected the catchment territories of the northern and southern sites seen in Table 19, where the central site territories can be compared.

In this situation, Hatúnmarca (J2) had almost four times the area of Tunánmarca (J7), although, as discussed in Chapter 4, Tunánmarca's estimated population is larger. If this was the population distribution even including one satellite each, Tunánmarca's need for nearby land-use intensification strategies would be greater than Hatúnmarca's. Intensification strategies that may have operated within the northern catchment territories are irrigation canals, ridged fields, lynchets, and drained fields for Tunánmarca, compared to a large area of drained fields, hillside irrigation, terraces, and lynchets for Hatúnmarca. Tunánmarca would be under much more agricultural production pressure than Hatúnmarca if the territories were even approximately distributed the way suggested here.

The trend from the EIP/MH to the Wanka I suggests population dispersion throughout the small valleys and associated hillsides. Wanka I settlements hint at some agricultural intensification in several zones, especially the valleys and lower hills. The abrupt change in the Wanka II phase to clustered, upland dwellings (high elevation land-use) makes the valley fields less accessible and suggests that agricultural production had to be radically reoriented. We do not know yet if the Wanka I settlements were under production pressure. Looking at the settlement pattern along with the evidence of agricultural intensification and social tensions, it seems that there was pressure on the less available tributary valley lands. In addition, we know that around the time of the move up, about 1300, the Andean highland climate was cooling, making all zones less productive (Seltzer 1987; Seltzer and Hastorf 1990).

The demographic data imply that population aggregation made agricultural

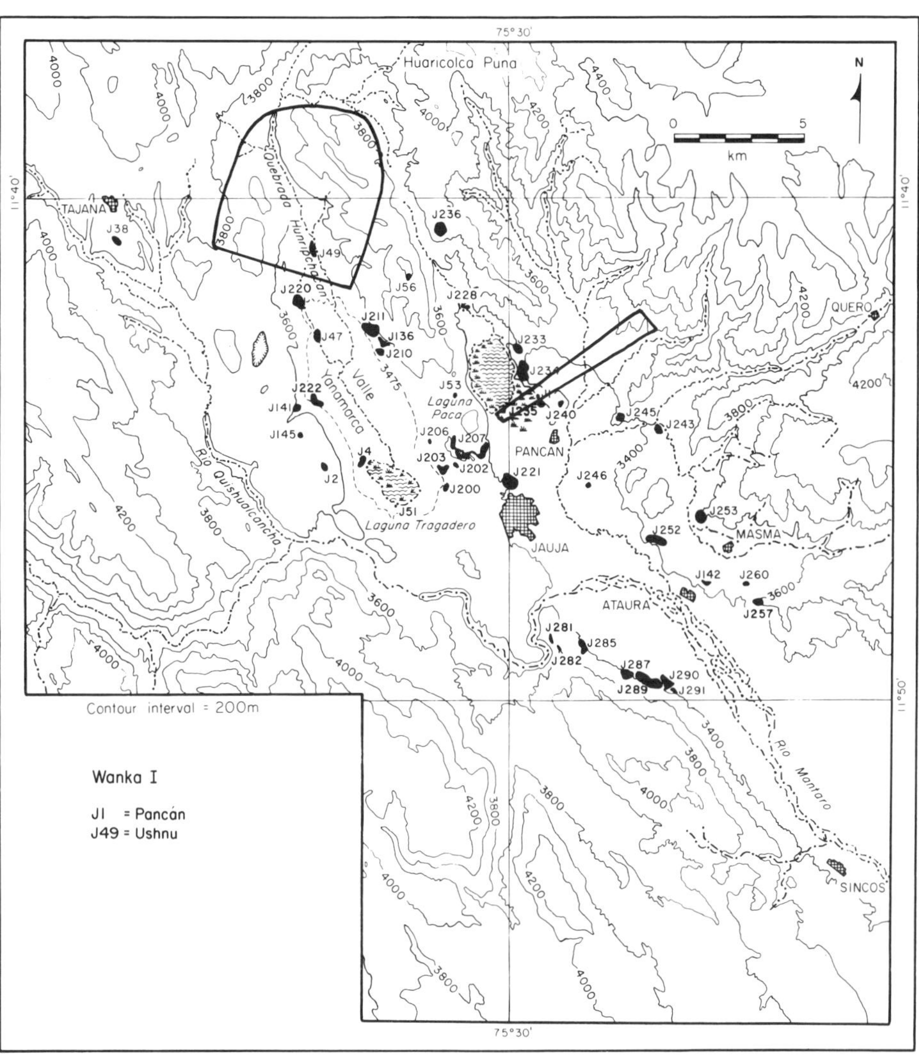

Fig. 19. Wanka I Period settlements with hypothetical territories for the sites studied

Table 19. *Wanka II site territories and land-use zones*

Zone	Area (ha)	% of territory
Umpamalca (J41):		
First bench	20	2
Extensive hillside	50	6
High elevation	618	74
Non-arable puna	150	18
Total	838	100
Tunánmarca (J7):		
First bench	30	3
Extensive hillside	347	38
High elevation	450	50
Non-arable puna	80	9
Total	907	100
Northern alliance		
Hatúnmarca (J2):		
First bench	308	8
Fertile lowland	600	15
Low hillside	1180	33
High elevation	1283	37
Non-arable puna	270	7
Total	3631	100

production more costly, suggesting that relocation would have made agriculture much more expensive than if settlements had remained dispersed in the valleys. The new costs include transportation plus the capital and labor investment in the upland intensification. While upland production is high yielding, it is also more expensive per unit output and at this time the climate made it more vulnerable than before. Therefore, the move up does not seem to be for economic (agricultural yield) reasons. Given the complex causes of agricultural change we need more information about the actual pre-Hispanic land-use and the intensity of production to better discuss the realities of the socio-political factors that were involved in the move and shift in production.

Calculating agricultural potentials

The next step in organizing the information on the possible agricultural production for these three periods is to calculate a potential crop mix for each site, based on data presented in Chapter 8 and the previous section. This crop mix will allow me to view the evidence for the production regimes through time. We can then take these predicted crop mixes and compare them to the paleoethnobotanical data from the sites. These comparisons of likely agricultural production to local landscape will provide a sense of shifts in decision making, agricultural strategy, and political pressures on the population.

In addition, if we calculate population estimate ranges for each site and compare these to a hypothetical calorific production associated with the territories, another picture of relative production intensities through time will emerge. Formulas exist to calculate the approximate amount of food necessary to sustain a population. This calorific need should be met largely by production within an agricultural group's catchment territory if the settlements are politically independent and under intensive production.

To gain a general view of the level of production possible and necessary at the time, I compare the potential territory productivities (yields) to population size estimates at each site. The differences between these values will give a rough indication of the relative intensity of production in the territory. This is based on the assumption that

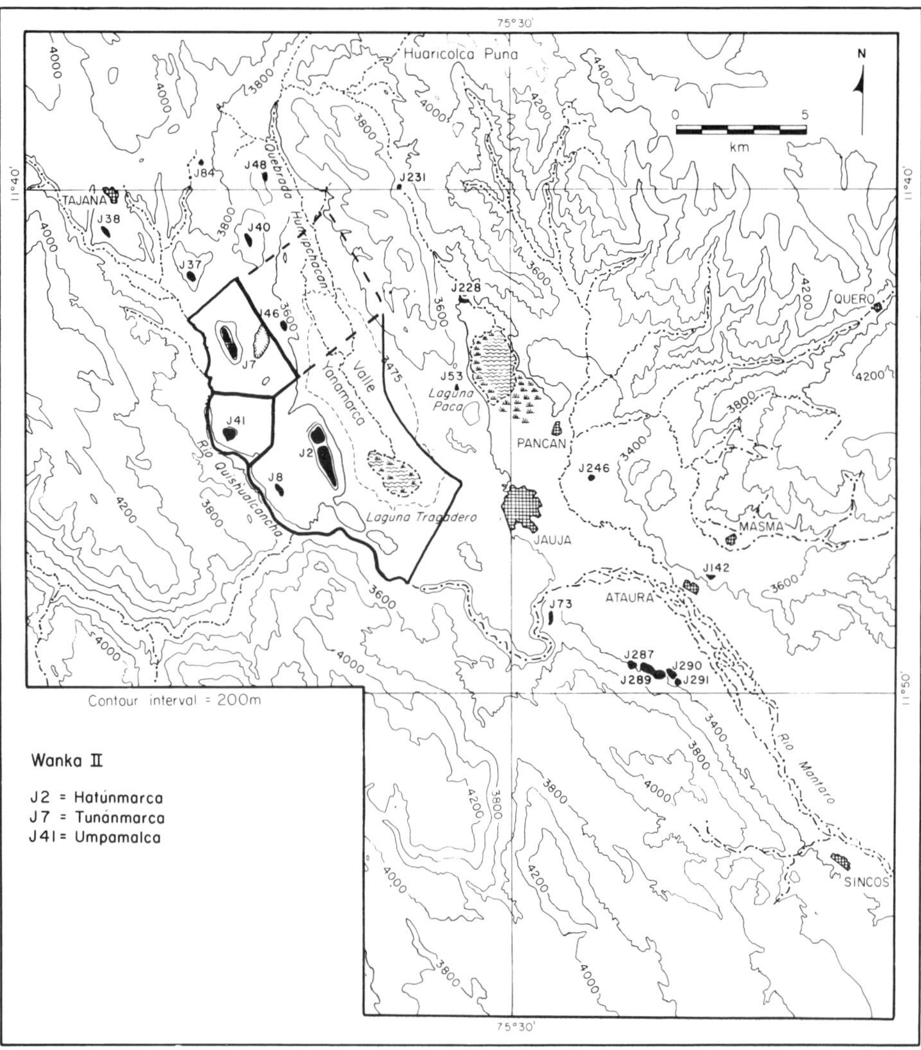

Fig. 20. Wanka II Period settlements with hypothetical territories for the sites studied

Table 20. *Initial production costs, optimal calorific yields, and efficient production by zone*

Zone	Initial production costs person/days/ha	Optimal potential yield kcal/ha	Effic. kcal/person/day
1 First bench	50	482,744	9655
1a Valley irrigation	109	1,557,915	14,293
2 Fertile lowland	100	1,603,618	16,036
3 Low hillside	69	984,373	14,266
3a Hillside irrigation	110	5,190,885	47,190
4 Extensive hillside	69	984,373	14,266
5 High elevation	72	1,131,314	15,713
5a Upland irrigation	150	3,161,100	21,074

the goal of food production in a subsistence economy is to meet the dietary needs of the population at a reasonable cost while managing scarce resources and minimizing risk.

On average, the annual output should be approximately the same as the food requirements of the population. It is important to note that this also holds if both producers and non-producers (local specialists, managers, war leaders, work organizers, peacekeepers, etc.) inhabit the same village and there is not a great deal of exchange in foodstuffs. If the political structure is larger or more unequal, with consumers who are not producers, and/or a group of settlements are politically linked, central settlements could have a different production ratio, as increased political factors alter the relationships of a population to its production.

In the following section productivity ranges for each of the settlements under study are calculated. The potential range of agricultural intensification strategies and estimated productivities for these sites can be presented.

Estimating agricultural productivity potentials

The optimal annual production mix is the sum of the output values determined by multiplying the area by the average yield per hectare. While in reality crop production in a region ranges from extensive, small-scale production to intensive, expansive production, I am including ranges of production through the different crop rotations possible in each of the different zones. A finer detail than that would not be appropriate, as the pre-Hispanic data are themselves not that fine grained. The averages of these potentials represent a composite of years, activities, and preservation problems, and cannot reflect the subtleties of minor production changes. We can therefore only make broad comparisons. To get a sense of a range of strategies, however, I present the initial production cost estimates as well as the estimated optimal yields.

To begin, Table 20 provides the initial production cost estimates, and the optimal potential yield for one hectare in each strategy, averaged over the long term. These optimal yields per hectare are calculated using the crop yield averages from Table 5 multiplied by the frequency of each crop within each zone, listed in Table 12.

The optimal yield for each zone is the total output that the group of crop rotation

Table 21. *Optimal yields for the six sites*

Zones	Arable territory (ha)	Optimal yield kcal $\times 10^6 \times$ ha
Early Intermediate/Middle Horizon:		
Pancán (J1)		
First bench	390 (0)[1]	188 (0)
Valley irrigation	390	608
Fertile lowland	127	204
Low hillside	47	46
Total	564	858
Tragadero Viejo (J71)		
First bench	40	19
Fertile lowland	569	912
Total	609	931
Wanka I:		
Pancán (J1)		
First bench	130 (0)	63 (0)
Valley irrigation	130	205
Fertile lowland	31	50
Low hillside	65	64
Total	226	319
Ushnu (J49)		
First bench	131 (71)	63 (34)
Valley irrigation	60	93
Low and extensive hillside	565	556
High elevation	915 (815)	1034 (927)
Upland irrigation	100	316
Total	1611	1926
Wanka II:		
Umpamalca (J41)		
Valley irrigation	20	31
Extensive hillside	50	49
High elevation	618 (418)	734 (473)
Upland irrigation	200	632
Total	688	1185
Tunánmarca (J7)		
First bench	30 (0)	15 (0)
Valley irrigation	30	47
Extensive hillside	347	341
High elevation	450 (350)	509 (396)
Upland irrigation (canals)	100	316
Total	827	1100

[1] The areas in parentheses are the areas or yields remaining after the more intensive production land has been subtracted.

cycles could produce within that zone. For the sites themselves, I combine the sites' territory areas (Tables 17, 18, and 19), the extensive and intensive strategies possible for each zone within the area (Table 13), and the optimal yields per hectare for each of these zones (Table 20). With these calculations, I can propose an agricultural production potential for each sampled site. The total yield calculated for each strategy (or zone) is figured by multiplying the zone and strategy areas within each territory by the average calorific yield per hectare. These annual yields can vary due to differences in rotation cycle length, total calorific productivity, and size of the zones in each settlement's territory. Fallow years are included in the average yield; when there are four years of production and one fallow, four years of yield are divided by five to get an average annual yield over the long run. These computations create a limit on the total yield possible for each strategy. While this is not actually possible, it does provide a relative average yield for a site's territory. When these figures are compared to the hypothetical needs of the population, we will see that the output is not always sufficient to support the estimated population.

Table 21 presents these optimal yields for each site's territory, including the contribution of each arable zone to the overall production. The total output represents the theoretical steady-state production in each given territory. When two strategies are possible on the same land, such as dry and irrigated valley lands, the maximum output is calculated by subtracting the area that can be irrigated from the dry farming area and calculating each separately. These adjusted results are seen in parentheses.

From the values presented in Table 21 we can see a few key aspects in the territorial trends. Both EIP/MH sites seem to be well balanced between the different land-use types with a great deal of land available to the populace. Pancán land becomes much more restricted in the Wanka I era while Ushnu has vast tracts of high elevation land. Most startling of all are the two Wanka II settlements, which do not have much greater potential yields than the earlier sites, yet we know that their populations were many times greater. Obviously local Wanka II agriculture was radically different than in previous times.

Despite the crudeness of these calculations, they can be used to compare differences in agricultural production between sites and phases. They help to present a picture of agricultural production change. These optimal output estimations for the six sites are hypothetical base-line production estimates and will be compared to the botanical data in Chapter 11. Before doing so the botanical data must be analyzed and made comparable with these estimates.

10

Paleoethnobotanical data, agricultural production, and food

Paleoethnobotanical data can be applied to many different archaeological questions. One of the main applications is the study of food procurement and agriculture. Botanical analysis was initiated out of an interest in human diet at the onset of agriculture (Harlan and Zohary 1966; Hillman 1973; Zohary 1969). Although much successful analysis has been completed in the study of origins, botanical data are equally useful in other economic and political pursuits, such as detecting changes in production. To ask such questions with this type of data, it is rewarding to study relative production changes and the changing contexts of plant use.

Cultural interpretation is the most crucial use of paleoethnobotanical analysis, but it is constrained and biased by a series of natural and cultural effects that must be kept in mind. Because paleoethnobotanical data have many interpretive problems, not the least being differential preservation and unstandardized collection procedures, researchers have been critical about the interpretation of botanical data used in archaeological research. The main reason for the infrequent recognition of prehistoric botanical data as part of the cultural data set has been the lack of a methodological formulation appropriate for anthropological questions. This methodological problem is being remedied with concerted efforts by paleoethnobotanists (Asch 1975; Hastorf and Popper 1988; Pearsall 1989; Van Zeist et al. 1991). While some hurdles can never be overcome, systematic work is showing that much more can be gleaned from these data than has been assumed. It is now clear that botanical remains can be applied to research questions like any other artifact. As part of this trend, I present a set of paleoethnobotanical data in the hopes of studying changing agricultural systems. These in turn will become part of the political discussion.

Collection of archaeobotanical data

In order to maximize the botanical information, as many samples as possible should be systematically collected and analyzed from each defined context and phase under study (Dennell 1976: 233; Lennstrom and Hastorf 1992). Sampling the same contexts many times statistically increases the interpretive value of each sample (Asch 1975). In other words, to interpret a cultural setting, many small samples are better than fewer larger ones. During excavation, I therefore increased the number of samples per context by collecting bulk samples from three distinct locations within every excavation provenience (smallest culturally meaningful excavation unit). I chose this method of collection rather than a pinch or scatter sample to try to identify specific activity areas or concentrations (Hally 1981; Popper and Hastorf 1988; Lennstrom and Hastorf 1992; Tiffany 1974). Because I had approximately three samples per unique cultural provenience, I did not use the data in a "one soil sample, one vote" type of analysis. In such a situation, the proveniences that happen to have more soil samples would have more influence on the resulting calculations. To control for different numbers of samples per provenience, I first averaged all counts per sample by provenience (hence Appendix G states that all proveniences are weighted equally).

The size of the soil sample collected affects the results of the analysis. I chose to standardize the sample size to 6 kg (5 liters). This size was based on the frequency and range of plant taxa occurring in the 5-liter samples collected in the study area during earlier experiments, the necessity of manually carrying the soil samples quite a distance from the excavation site to the flotation system, and the emphasis in the research design on many small samples rather than fewer large ones.

Biases in the data

Archaeological remains are not a random reflection of activities because human behavior is patterned. Yet, organic deposits are biased by natural characteristics, such as the sturdiness of the plant structure and the soil composition that plant remains are deposited in, as well as by cultural influences, such as their depositional history from the carbonization process to the method of sample recovery (Dennell 1976; Pearsall 1988).

Differential preservation is a function of the ability of a plant to withstand microbial and erosional activities (Munson et al. 1971). Plants can be preserved by desiccation, anaerobic conditions (water-logging), or carbonization. In the Mantaro region, for example, it is too wet for non-carbonized remains to survive microbial consumption from prehistoric times and not dry enough for desiccation. Anatomy, physical, and chemical make-up is important. Hard-surfaced seeds such as *Chenopodium* or maize will char and preserve better than soft tissue with a high water content, such as tubers or corms. Optimally we should create probability equations for differential preservation over time and add these to each taxon's counts to get a more accurate reconstruction of what was there at the time of deposition (Kadane and Hastorf 1988). Tackling the problem of preservation is difficult and in its initial stages of research, and so differential preservation will be discussed only qualitatively in the data interpretation stage.

Plant frequencies are also affected by use, disposal, and their potential to be charred, in other words, how the remains got into the archaeological record. Plants are deposited in archaeological contexts because they were used as fuel, food, fodder, for industrial purposes, rituals, or because they incidentally enter a settlement. When interpreting crop remains from an excavation, the paleoethnobotanist should keep in mind the life histories of the different plant foods, taking into account such matters as crop processing activities, storage methods, preparation techniques and their spatial correlates. For plant parts that are meant to be consumed, their remains represent accidents in storage, preparation, or refuse, and may not always be common in burned midden contexts (Sikkink 1988). The inedible parts, such as maize cobs, reflect direct production, processing and other uses.

For these reasons, therefore, botanical remains are not considered to portray consumption patterns as well as they do production patterns (Dennell pers. comm.). With detailed analyses, a specimen found in one context may not have the same meaning as the same specimen when found in another context. By identifying the context of the plant, interpretation can be enhanced. For example, domestic plant remains found in a hearth can be associated with food preparation, which can be discussed in terms of consumption, whereas the same taxa found in a burial may suggest a different symbolic meaning. The level of impact these depositional and contextual issues have on analysis depends on what question is being addressed with the data.

In circumstances such as this research area, with charred remains making up the archaeobotanical universe, it is important to consider the cause and effect of carbonization. Different plant foods have different chances of becoming burned (Hillman 1984; Jones 1984). There are three major processes by which organic material is carbonized: it is burned intentionally as fuel or in refuse dumps, it is burned accidentally as food in preparation, forgotten or lost in hearths, as part of an industrial process, or it is accidentally burned in outbreaks of fire (Hubbard 1976: 262; Hastorf and Popper 1988).

Sikkink's (1988) study of modern charred and uncharred plant distributions within Andean households shows that charred and uncharred remains have very different patterns of deposition. In general, charred remains are more dense in the special activity areas of domestic space, where burning regularly occurs. These include kitchen areas, ash dump areas, and inside work spaces. In areas where many different activities occur with only irregular burning, there will be fewer charred remains, although in these areas there is more uncharred material. Being aware of these patterns and their behavioral correlates aids in dealing with the biases.

Recovery techniques

Another bias arises from the recovery and the processing of botanical samples (Wagner 1982; 1988; Watson 1976). This is the problem of extracting the plant matter from the soil, while controlling for contamination of foreign botanical material, minimizing breakage, and loss. There is an array of water flotation systems that have been developed since the seminal article by Struever (1968). Each one has different qualifications and abilities to recover botanical remains (Jarman et al. 1972; Pearsall 1989: 19; Wagner 1982; Watson 1976, etc.). There are several aspects of recovery that are important to consider and control for. Because the fragile charred specimens must be extracted from the soil matrix while preserving their morphology, there is concern about too much alteration through wetting and drying and about the amount of agitation they receive. Loss of plant matter is very common in a water flow system, and must be tested and controlled for. The problem of contamination too is especially critical in macrobotanical procedures. Although modern carbonized specimens can find their way into the macrobotanical samples, more important is the problem of mixing between the prehistoric soil samples in a flotation system.

In addition, one must consider what one can afford to build and maintain during the project (what is the water source and how much is available), and how much time each sample takes to process. For this study, I determined that a 5-liter sample size was appropriate for the flotation system I constructed in Peru, bearing approximately 400 items per sample. I used a manual system designed to minimize water expenditure in the arid lands of the American southwestern (Minnis and LeBlanc 1976). This system and my procedures are described in Appendix E. During excavation, large botanical remains were encountered in the ⅛-inch screen used to extract artifacts from all the excavated soil. These specimens were catalogued as botanical collections, distinct from the flotation remains. From the 179 excavated proveniences with good cultural contexts, 543 flotation samples were analyzed, averaging three per provenience.

Laboratory procedures

Laboratory procedures can also affect plant assemblages (Pearsall 1989). In this study refloating and subsampling were not carried out on flotation samples in order to minimize further damage and differential treatment. All of the light (floated) and heavy (sunk onto the screen) fractions were sorted for charred plant remains in the same manner. The sorting procedure is outlined in Appendix E.

The domesticated crops have been described in Chapter 6. For most of the analyses, I have combined the three Andean tubers, oca, olluco, and mashua, into one category because they are all consumed like vegetables, tend to grow in the same environment, are extremely hard to distinguish, and seem to be rare. I have also combined the two domestic legume taxa, lupine (*Lupinus mutabilis*), and the common bean (*Phaseolus vulgaris*). The wild taxa that were identified in the analysis are described in Yacovleff and Herrera (1934; 1935), Weberbauer (1945), Soukup (1970), Pearsall (1980), and Hastorf (1981).

All raw counts in the flotation and screen samples are listed in Appendix F. To summarize the wild taxa, they are grouped into five categories by use. The uses were determined from ethnographic information, interviews, and field observations as medicine, construction, fodder, storage, and wild food (Table 22). These categories are crude but useful. All wild plants that could be identified in the archaeological material are still present in the local plant communities today. More species identification and detailed ethnobotanical studies must be done in order to use these data more fully when discussing their relationships to prehistoric agricultural production. For example, field collections of weed seeds associated with each crop type in each zone and each technology would aid in linking seeds to crops and production patterns (cf. Jones 1984). Sikkink began collecting some of this material for the Jauja region.

Given the many potential biases affecting the data, as many aspects as possible were controlled for in the collection and processing procedure. The same methods and procedures were implemented throughout the excavation season and laboratory analysis, and checks were made to insure that a systematic coverage was maintained. The soil samples were collected blindly, meaning that all soil and artifacts were placed in the bag without any sorting of material in an attempt to control for collection bias. I processed all soil samples using the same system and procedures in Peru, and I sorted every flotation sample myself, unaware of its provenience or site. I assume therefore

Table 22. *Pre-Hispanic wild plant taxa by use categories*

1	Medicine: Asteraceae, *Nicotiana* sp., *Plantago* sp., *Salvia* sp., *Verbena* sp. seeds
2	Construction: Cyperaceae, *Scirpus* spp. seeds, grass stalks, wood
3	Fodder: *Amaranthus* sp., Cruciferaceae, Fabaceae, *Malvastrum* sp., *Oxalis* sp., Poaceae, *Portulaca* sp., *Verbena* sp. seeds, wood
4	Storage: Cyperaceae, *Minthostaychis* sp. seeds, grass stalks
5	Wild food: *Berberis* sp., *Bixa orellana*, *Opuntia* sp., *Rubus* sp. seeds

that the plant frequencies from the different sites are comparable and can be applied to a study of crop production.

Paleoethnobotanical analysis

Quantification

Analysis must transform raw counts quantitatively or qualitatively so that they are interpretable. No one method is suitable for all analyses as each type of quantification procedure presents a different view of the material. Because of the biases inherent in the data, most paleoethnobotanists choose to use some form of relative presentation, maintaining an internal comparison, to control for preservation differences and other post-depositional effects. Some methods are more informative than others, however. Each of the common forms of quantification: ubiquity (percentage presence), relative percentage, standardization densities, standardized counts, and ratios, emphasize some aspect of the data while lessening or masking others (see Lennstrom and Hastorf 1992; Miller 1988; Popper 1988; Scarry 1986 for detailed discussions of these quantification schemes). I have found that no one technique gives a complete picture of what the data have to offer archaeologists. On the other hand every analysis provides a different picture of the material, and, presented together, gives a larger view of the evidence.

Therefore, I try here to gain a fuller vista by presenting the data in three forms: ubiquity, standardized density, and relative percentage. While ubiquity presents general trends in plant distribution, it loses any view of plant abundance (Asch and Asch 1975: 116). Standardized density presents actual counts of each taxon, adjusting them to a standardized volume. This format provides comparable densities and abundance between locations but must be used only as a relative indicator. It is helpful to learn about the actual deposition differences between proveniences. Relative percentage internally relates the amount of each taxon to the other taxa within a sample. While keeping the comparisons within an analytical unit, and therefore interdependent, it controls for biases when comparing different locations, and is good for tracking change across space or through time. I propose that variations in the percentages of plant presence, abundance, and standardized density, especially compared through time, will indicate changes in production patterns.

Once the data are compiled, we can look for meaningful patterns. Statistical tests of significance, used to make comparisons between samples, really only tell us how large the samples are, which is not what we, or statisticians, are concerned with (Kadane and Moses pers. comm.). Recently, statisticians have been searching for new ways to look at patterns in data and have begun proposing graphic pattern recognition as a more appropriate tool. Exploratory data analysis (EDA) is the approach that searches for patterns in data, allowing the viewer to see the data more clearly, not just in tables or complex multivariate models (Tufte 1983; Tukey 1977; Vellman and Hoaglin 1981). EDA has been applied to paleoethnobotanical evidence by Scarry (1986) with some success, especially in her box plots. Besides using graphs to illustrate this analysis as well as the data, I will use star diagrams to display variability and change over time while keeping the independence of ubiquities. My application of this orientation is very rudimentary, yet I hope that others will realize its potential and begin to apply these diverse procedures to their data (see Hastorf 1991; Jones et al. 1986; Lennstrom and Hastorf 1992).

Ubiquity or presence analysis is perhaps the most common approach used in paleoethnobotanical work (Dennell 1976; Hubbard 1975; Monk and Fasham 1980; Pearsall 1989; Popper 1988; Willcox 1974). Simply stated, regardless of the abundance of any one taxon within any sample, the analysis uses only the presence or absence of each taxon. The presence of each taxon is summed within a group of samples, producing independent frequencies for each taxon. In other words, one tallies the number of samples in which a taxon is present within a defined group of samples. That ratio becomes the ubiquity value for that plant. Using this approach, taxa that normally are over-represented, for example by tougher, more hardy seeds, are not counted more than the less well-preserved taxa. Here I tabulate the taxa frequencies by cultural context, site, and phase.

Standardized density analysis presents data in a ratio form (Miller 1988). It expresses the counts of each taxon adjusted to a given volume of soil. By using the soil volume as the normalizing variable, one can study different deposition patterns, differential preservation, and intensity of occupation (Asch and Asch 1975; Miller 1982; Pearsall 1983; 1988). It is best used to help visualize taxa clustering and abundance distributions. One should not use such a comparison if the data are from radically different environments. Because my samples have fairly similar preservation situations, come from the same region, and are processed in the same manner, I feel comfortable comparing them. Taxa counts are adjusted so that they are equivalent to 6 kg of soil through all proveniences.

Relative percentage, first applied by J. Renfrew (1973), allows us to track the replacement of one taxon with another, by following relative taxa increases and decreases between assemblages. This ratio presents the percentage within an assemblage that a plant comprises. Taxa are interdependent within each sample so one cannot assume that an increase in relative percentage means an actual increase in the abundance of a plant. The percentages are based on counts, which assumes that preservation is the same for all taxa. This situation is almost never true. Relative percentage is an analysis that should be applied in fairly well-controlled circumstances. I use it here because I want to compare the relative change through time of specific taxa, especially maize and potatoes, in the same types of contexts.

Table 23. *Taxa by phase and site, presented by ubiquity, standardized density, and relative percentage*

Phase	No. provs.	Maize	Legumes	Potatoes	Quinoa	A. tubers
Ubiquity (percentage presence)						
EIP/MH J71	28	18	11	32	79	—
EIP/MH J1	23	78	83	48	100	—
Wanka I J49	27	70	59	59	89	4
Wanka I J1	22	82	77	45	86	—
Wanka II J41	59	20	41	46	88	5
Wanka II J7	27	22	22	63	67	7
Standardized density (to 6 kg of soil)						
EIP/MH J71	28	0.1	0.1	0.9	24.3	—
EIP/MH J1	23	4.7	2.7	1.6	21.5	—
Wanka II J49	27	1.1	1.4	2.9	18.7	0.03
Wanka I J1	22	3.4	4.4	0.7	14.8	—
Wanka II J41	59	3.3	1.5	9.7	2773.0 (1.8)[1]	0.02
Wanka II J7	27	0.3	0.3	4.8	1.8	0.7
Relative percentage						
EIP/MH J71	28	3.0	1.0	20.0	76.0	— = 100
EIP/MH J1	23	23.0	23.0	12.0	42.0	— = 100
Wanka I J49	27	9.0	15.5	16.7	58.4	0.3 = 100
Wanka I J1	22	23.0	31.0	6.0	40.0	— = 100
Wanka II J41	59	2.0	3.7	8.4	85.6	0.3 = 100
Wanka II J7	27	6.4	5.1	42.2	42.2	4.0 = 100

[1] densities without the caches

Agricultural data computation

In Appendix G, the excavated botanical data have been summarized by phase, site, and cultural context using each of the above three data manipulations. In these tables, wild taxa groups are included along with the domesticates, although in the tables and figures in this text only the domesticates are presented. A summary of the data used here is in Table 23, which presents the taxa frequencies by phase and site of the major crops. Trends exist in the domestic and wild plant frequencies through time, space and context, although in this tabular form of presentation they are difficult to see. To comprehend the trends, plant comparisons should be viewed selectively, and so within this section we take a look at some of the more important trends using a portion of the data in the three formats to discover patterns and co-variances. This presentation will proceed from the general to the specific. The results will be compared with the theoretical agricultural production computations from Chapter 9 in the next chapter.

Temporal production patterns

Table 24 presents the domestic data by phase. The quinoa value in parentheses is the density measure without the two very dense pit caches in structures J41 = 8 and J41 = 11. To begin with a broad view of the trends, three star diagrams (Figure 21) have

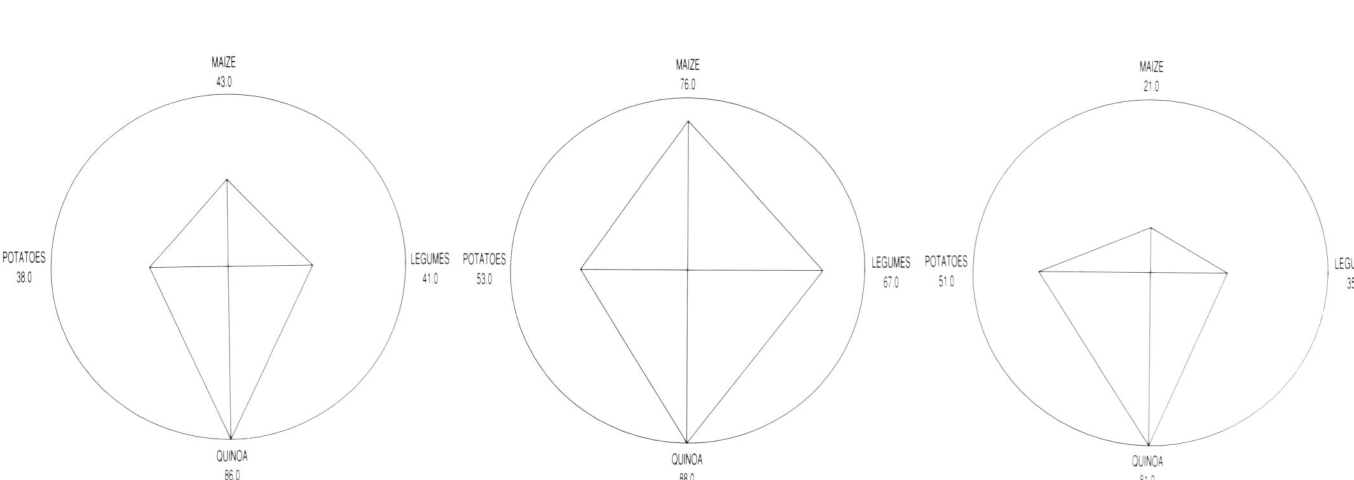

Fig. 21. Star diagrams of domestic taxa presence by phase

Table 24. *Domestic taxa by phase*

Phase	No. provs.	Maize	Legumes	Potatoes	Quinoa	A. tubers
Ubiquity (percentage presence)						
EIP/MH	56	43	41	38	86	—
Wanka I	49	76	67	53	88	2
Wanka II	86	21	35	51	81	6
Standardized density (to 6 kg of soil)						
EIP/MH	56	2.0	1.2	1.1	21.2	—
Wanka I	49	2.1	2.8	1.9	16.9	0.02
Wanka II	86	2.4	1.1	8.1	1903.0 (1.8)[1]	0.2
Relative percentage						
EIP/MH	56	11.4	10.1	15.2	63.3	0.0 = 100
Wanka I	49	15.3	22.8	11.4	49.8	0.7 = 100
Wanka II	86	3.0	3.9	16.4	75.4	1.2 = 100

[1] densities without the caches

been produced from the ubiquity data to show crop frequency changes through time (Helwig and Council 1979; Tufte 1983). Each taxon is independently calculated. The outer circles are set by the largest frequency values, in this case quinoa. The stars present a picture of general similarity over time, although quinoa dominates. All the crops increase in presence in Wanka I, especially maize, legumes, and potatoes, and decrease in Wanka II, again most prominently maize. Tubers, potatoes but especially the Andean tubers, increase through time.

A more comparative temporal view of the ubiquity data is graphed in Figure 22, along with the standardized densities and relative percentages. This overview shows a major change in the plant frequencies in Wanka II times. Comparing these three data configurations, we can see that in all analytical dimensions crop presence increases very slightly from the EIP/MH to Wanka I while maintaining the same overall density and relative proportions. Accompanying relocation in the Wanka II there is a shift in the trajectory with a significant drop in ubiquity of all taxa except the tubers and quinoa. In Wanka II the densities of quinoa and legumes drop while all tubers remain steady or increase. The relative percentage shows an increase in quinoa and potatoes (*Solanum*), while legumes decrease. For maize, only the density increases over time, although its presence drops radically in Wanka II.

Four intriguing results from these figures require comment. One is that, above all others, quinoa dominates in presence, counts, and proportion. This great amount of quinoa is clearly due to the additive effects of good preservation, seed size, crop processing location, and ease of deposition. These are small sturdy seeds that were probably parched in fires before storing or cooking and could have burned frequently and been lost easily. There are thousands of seeds on a plant, many more than on the other crop plants, making them easier to scatter into all contexts when carried or winnowed. The values for quinoa are inflated, but nevertheless it remains a staple. Maize, however, is also very common in Wanka I.

The second point is illustrated in the standard density graph of Figure 22. For all but quinoa the densities are fairly constant, showing that the rate of deposition and effect of preservation are very similar across the phases. To me this suggests that the style of deposition did not change substantially, nor did the impact of preservation vary much between the early and late phases. In other words, the general way the crops were handled and deposited in the houses remained the same over time.

Third, these data illustrate the similar tracking of maize and legumes. On all three graphs these two taxa change together, suggesting that they were produced in the same proportions, or at least processed and deposited in the same manner. In some ways this is not surprising from what we know about this duo with their complementary nutritive capacity and their co-occurrence in fields throughout Mesoamerica. It is possible that they were intercropped together, possibly in the raised fields.

Fourth, all tubers, despite their low presence due to their poor preservation capacities, track together while increasing. Tubers are a special case because of their extremely fragile nature, yet their density increases in Wanka II. What is preserved is not a tough seed coat but the soft tissue of a storage body. These large soft objects preserve in fewer conditions than seeds and often break into unrecognizable fragments. Despite this we can identify some of them, and thus know that they were present in the past, though at a much smaller percentage than all of the other crops discussed here. When present, one should amplify their presence, perhaps two or three times.

In sum, the prominent trends over time are that maize and legumes increase in Wanka I but drop again in Wanka II both relatively and actually. Tubers, while increasing their presence and densities over time, have a lower relative presence in the Wanka I. Quinoa, while remaining the dominant crop in all tabulations does decrease in Wanka II as the tubers become more important. While it looks like a mix of crops in the earlier phase, the new focus of the Wanka I times is on maize and legumes, with the focus shifting to tubers in the Wanka II.

Synchronic production comparisons

Given these trends through time, what can we see when we look at the sites in each phase? Throughout all three phases the botanical data suggest locally focused agricultural production, with little evidence of trade in foodstuffs that might have equilibrated the crop mixes across the region. Using data from Table 23, Figure 23 plots the crop ubiquities by phase and site. The bars show us that each contemporaneous pair of sites has different crop distributions. Pancán (J1) has more crop presence in the early phase than Tragadero Viejo (J71), especially maize and legumes. Pancán probably has much better preservation, as its early levels are deeply buried, while Tragadero Viejo's occupation levels are closer to the surface. The Paca Valley, tempered by Laguna Paca, today is a good maize growing region, and seeing that all crops are numerically and distributionally higher at Pancán this is not surprising. Despite this, Tragadero Viejo, in the center of the Yanamarca Valley, has very high quinoa production, not just in frequency but also in density with 24 seeds per 6 kg as opposed to Pancán's 21 seeds per 6 kg (Table 23). From the modern agricultural study

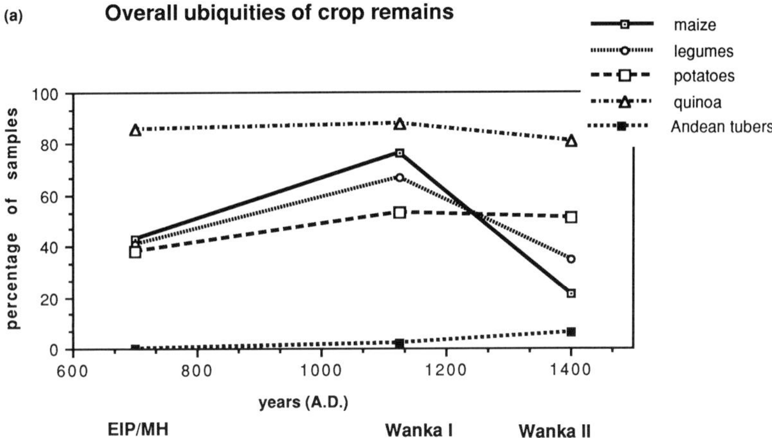

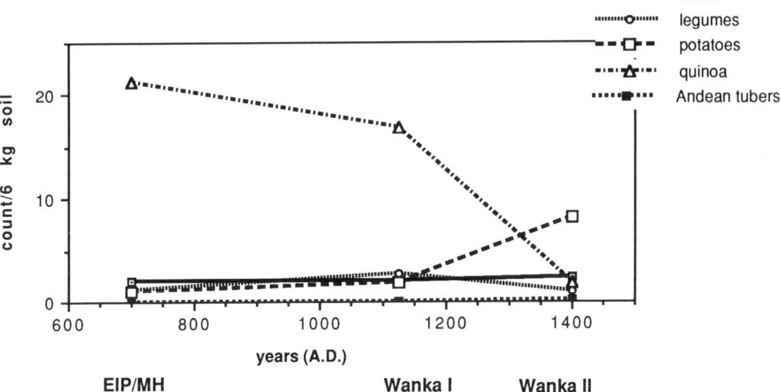

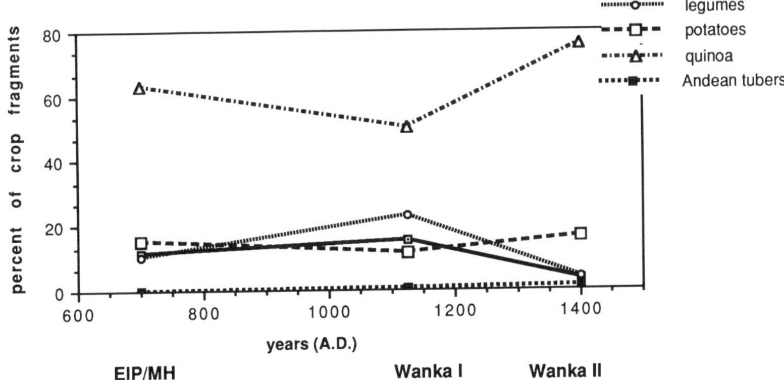

Fig. 22. Domestic taxa by phase: ubiquity, standard density, and relative percentage. Each phase is located at the median date of its time span

I learned that the Yanamarca Valley today is prime land for quinoa production, and here we see the same trend operating over one thousand years ago, as 76 percent of the domestic assemblage is quinoa (as opposed to 42 percent at Pancán).

The picture changes in Wanka I times, with Ushnu (J49) at the edge of the Yanamarca Valley having more and denser potatoes and quinoa than lower elevation Pancán (Figure 23, Table 23). The high quinoa presence continues the trajectory of Yanamarca Valley quinoa production (Tragadero Viejo and Ushnu). The high tuber counts at Ushnu are interesting because the site, like many Wanka I sites, is located up off the valley floor, in the hillside agricultural land where today there is an emphasis on tuber production. This is seen very clearly here in these Wanka I bars. Additionally, the maize and legume values, while still higher at Pancán, are more similar at both the Wanka I sites than in the earlier site comparisons. This suggests that maize and legumes become much more common for the Yanamarca Valley residents during Wanka I (also supporting the ideas of increasing raised field land-use at this time).

A model of site variability continues to be supported when we look at the next phase. While both sites are located up on knolls in the same microzone, their crop mixes are not the same. The analyses show that Umpamalca (J41) has more of all domesticates except maize and tubers, having particularly high frequencies and densities of quinoa (Table 23). This could mean that the Umpamalca inhabitants had access to more valley and hillside lands than the Tunánmarca residents. (Hatúnmarca [J2] has even greater densities of quinoa than Umpamalca, suggesting that these two sites both had access to milder valley or hillside land: Appendix G.) Another interpretation could be that the uplands produced a lot of quinoa at that time.

Overall, Tunánmarca has less dense deposits than Umpamalca, except in Andean tubers. Although it is complex to explain why this might be, one can speculate that it may reflect different depositional records, length of occupation, or represent different abandonment patterns. If we ignore the densities and only look at the ubiquities, both sites have a strong presence of tubers and quinoa, reflecting a focus on their extensive hillside and upland locations. Maize is radically lower than earlier, with both sites having about the same, which is more than might be expected, given the catchment territories.

Tributary valley trends through time

We can learn still more about agricultural production by focusing on the intra-regional spatial distributions over time. Chapters 4 and 9 present maps with the site locations. Basically we have botanical data from two subregions, the Paca Valley where the site Pancán is and the Yanamarca Valley with Tragadero Viejo, Ushnu, and Tunánmarca. Viewing these two areas separately can show us what, if any, subregional production differences existed beyond the different mixes of the catchment territories. The sites have been dated, and I assume that they were roughly contemporaneous, based on absolute dates and ceramic assemblages. The botanical results from Table 23 are graphically depicted for the two subregions in two sets of three graphs in Figure 24, illustrating ubiquity, standardized densities, and relative percentages. For comparative reasons, Tunánmarca (J7) has been included in the Yanamarca Valley group, since it sits just above the valley. Umpamalca (J41) is not included in these graphs because it is farther away from the valley, reflecting the radical relocation of the Sausa people around a.d. 1350.

Crop trends at Pancán are illustrated in the Paca Valley graphs of Figure 24. The ubiquity and relative percentage lines both show very little change, the main one being quinoa density, which decreases over time. This means that at Pancán, quinoa was present regularly throughout the site in both phases, but in the Wanka I phase there were fewer seeds when quinoa was deposited. The same could be said less strongly for potatoes and maize. Only legumes are more dense when they are found in the Wanka I deposits.

In the Yanamarca Valley set of graphs we see that all ubiquities and standard densities increase during the first two phases, except quinoa, when all but the tubers are less common and less dense. The relative percentage of each crop over time changes a lot, with everything dropping out as the tubers and quinoa gain ascendency in Wanka II. These crop distributions could be heightened by the diverse catchment territories of the settlements studied in the Yanamarca valley as well as the changing political scene.

Looking at just the first two phases in the two subregions we see a range of different density changes. The major difference between the two subregions is seen most clearly in the ubiquity data. Maize, legumes, and quinoa dominate the Pancán production scheme, while in the Yanamarca Valley potatoes and quinoa are more important than maize. The quinoa data especially in the Yanamarca catchment suggest that crop production was very local, mainly surrounding the individual settlements. Perhaps more important are the different relative percentages between the two valleys. Paca stresses quinoa, legumes and maize, while Yanamarca focuses on quinoa and

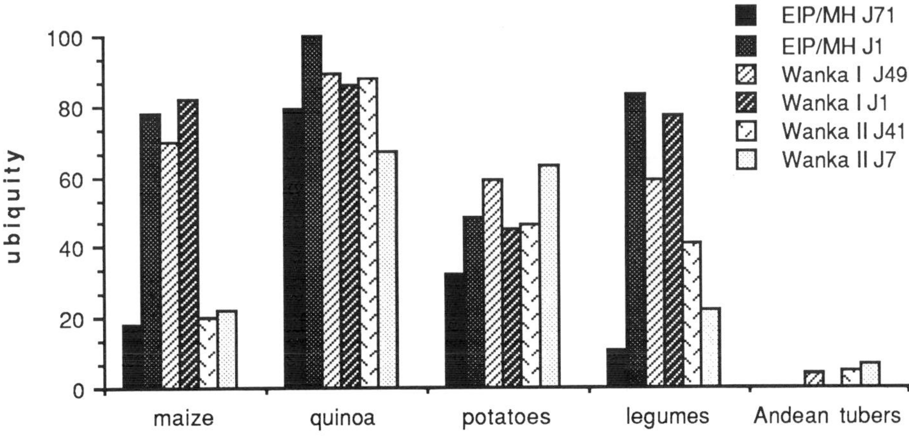

Fig. 23. Bar chart of taxa ubiquity by phase and site

potatoes. In the Wanka II, quinoa drops in density, ubiquity, and percentage, as potatoes increase markedly.

While the Pancán ubiquity values are steady, the Yanamarca sites show a major increase of 20 percent or more between the EIP/MH and Wanka I phases in all crops but the Andean tubers. The ubiquity changes between Wanka I and II sites in that valley show a drop in presence of all crops except the tubers throughout the proveniences (Figure 24). Therefore crop mix change is mainly increased tubers (relative percentage). Along with a more restricted deposition (ubiquity) in the Wanka II times, is also a decrease in crop density where it is found in the settlement (standardized densities). Most crops except tubers are found in fewer locations than they were in the Wanka I proveniences. This trend in restricted deposition is hard to speculate about. It could be simply that there is less to go around and so it was found less often. Or it could be that the residents were more constrained in their activities, scattering their refuse less freely. Again, from the more detailed Pancán excavations and the work on Wanka II architecture, we know that residential area per household compound diminished over time (Hastorf et al. 1989). Pancán shows some real shifts in internal deposition through time (Lennstrom 1992). Just as site access in the Wanka II was much more restricted, so the use of domestic space could have changed as well. Detailed intracompound spatial analysis must be done to understand this problem more fully.

The evidence from these data suggests that there were agricultural land-use differences between the two subregions before the large political and population aggregation in Wanka II times. The crop production information further supports the concept developed in Chapters 2 and 9 that, in this Andean region, crop production can be quite localized.

In Chapter 4, I discussed how, during the Middle Horizon phase (part of Huacrapukio II), population began to aggregate and settlements began to cluster in the tributary valleys, especially in the Yanamarca Valley. There is evidence of occupation at Ushnu during this earlier time (Appendix C). While only five proveniences were sampled from this MH period, when compared to the next period the comparison shows that maize, legumes, and potatoes all increased over time. The major change in Ushnu's territory is increased hillside lands; the valleyside neighbors did not change. We see the appropriate increase in tubers in the Wanka I, but with an unexpected rise in maize, given their predicted territories. In Wanka I times, settlement clustering is pronounced in three parts of the Yanamarca Valley, including the northeast, where Ushnu is located (Figure 3). Based on the settlement data, I suggested in Chapter 4 that there might have been a political alliance developing in the Yanamarca during Wanka I, after the Wari collapse. This new alliance might have been accompanied by more intensive valley production of maize, perhaps to supply increased numbers of feasts or work parties with the ritual *chicha* (maize beer)

Fig. 24 (*opposite*). Domestic taxa by the subregion Paca and Yanamarca Valleys: ubiquity, standard density, and relative percentage. Each phase is located at the median date of its time span

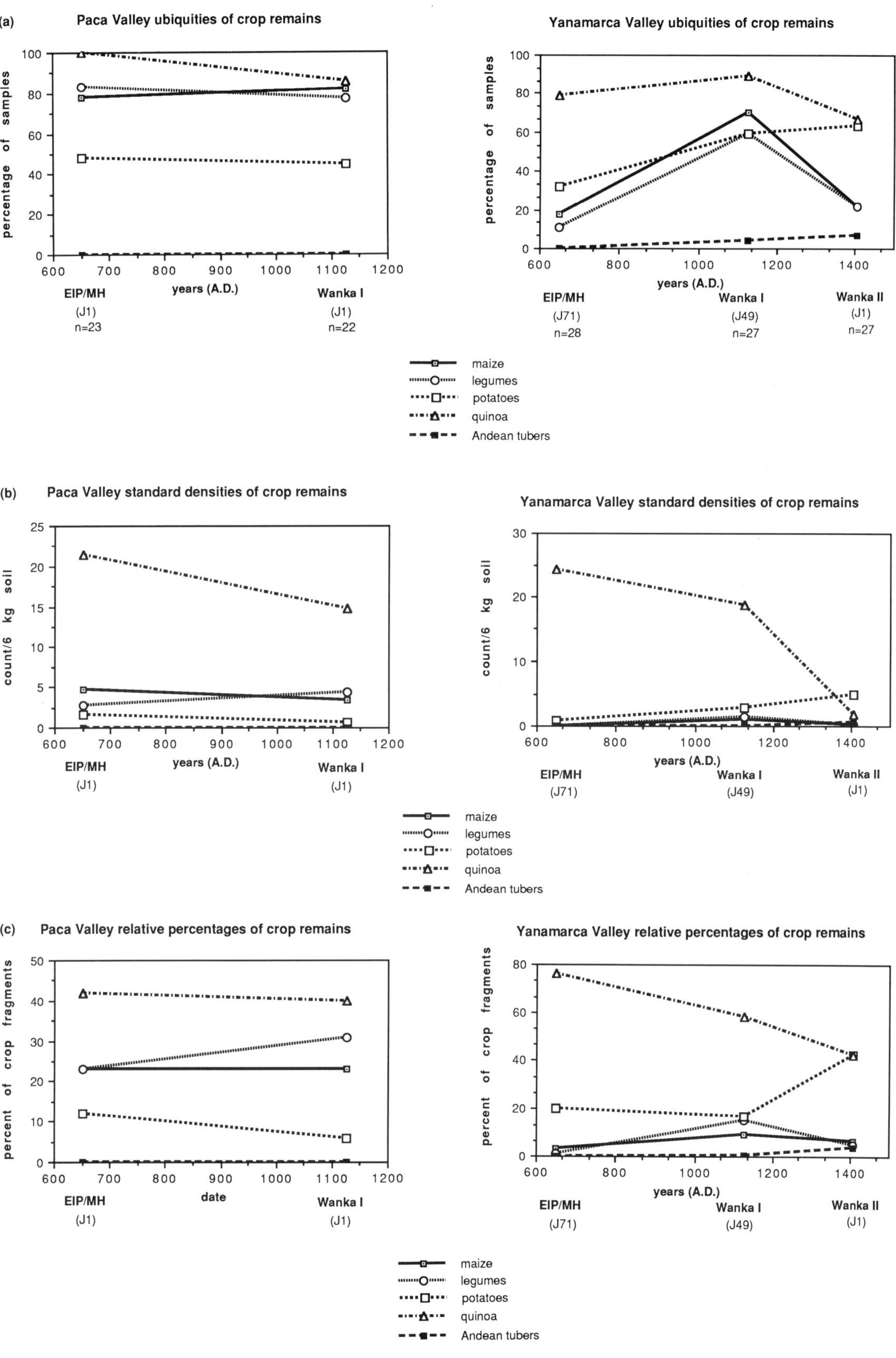
(a)
Paca Valley ubiquities of crop remains
percentage of samples
years (A.D.)
EIP/MH
(J1)
n=23
Wanka I
(J1)
n=22
Yanamarca Valley ubiquities of crop remains
percentage of samples
years (A.D.)
EIP/MH
(J71)
n=28
Wanka I
(J49)
n=27
Wanka II
(J1)
n=27
maize
legumes
potatoes
quinoa
Andean tubers
(b)
Paca Valley standard densities of crop remains
count/6 kg soil
years (A.D.)
EIP/MH
(J1)
Wanka I
(J1)
Yanamarca Valley standard densities of crop remains
count/6 kg soil
years (A.D.)
EIP/MH
(J71)
Wanka I
(J49)
Wanka II
(J1)
maize
legumes
potatoes
quinoa
Andean tubers
(c)
Paca Valley relative percentages of crop remains
percent of crop fragments
date
EIP/MH
(J1)
Wanka I
(J1)
Yanamarca Valley relative percentages of crop remains
percent of crop fragments
years (A.D.)
EIP/MH
(J71)
Wanka I
(J49)
Wanka II
(J1)
maize
legumes
potatoes
quinoa
Andean tubers

(Chapters 3 and 4; Hastorf and Johannessen 1992). Maize ubiquity at Wanka I Ushnu is 70 percent while in the EIP/MH it is 20 percent.

Looking at the Wanka II plots again in Figures 22, 23, and 24, accompanying the increase in upland tubers, the valley crops (maize and legumes) tend to become less common, though still present and dense. The presence of these valley crops suggests some sort of access to valley lands. Despite the difference in site location the plant frequencies imply that Wanka II agricultural land was more widely used than at the earlier settlements, or the territories were much larger than the settlement pattern suggests. Perhaps people were commuting back to their previous lands to plant. Something different was going on with the agricultural production at these Wanka II sites beyond just the relocation of the population. And there are suggestions that this production difference is politically based, with the central site having less of every crop, infering perhaps that the satellite settlements produced more than the center. These political links will be discussed more fully in the next chapter.

Food

Contextual patterns

Even though it is not central to the question of agricultural production, I want briefly to present the botanical distributions from the floor contexts to gain a better sense of the meaning of changes in crop-use over time. I focus on a data subset of structure floor contexts only to learn if they have discrete deposition patterns, for they are the contexts where household activities, such as crop processing, food preparation, and storage, most likely would be recorded. The paleoethnobotanical data from floor contexts are plotted in Figure 25 (data in Appendix G). A major constraint on this data set is that the number of proveniences is quite small (n = 37). In general, the trends are the same as the site-wide data for ubiquities, relative percentages, and densities. There are a few comparisons worth noting, however.

First, the overall relative crop mixes tend to parallel the site level data: quinoa is the most common, followed by maize and legumes in the early phases and tubers and legumes in Wanka II (Figure 25a, d, and g). Second, on the floors of Pancán in the Paca Valley, over time there is an increase in the frequency and density of crops (Figure 25b, e, and h). This is opposite to Pancán's site-wide trend, which was steady or decreased in presence and density, and also opposite to the patio areas that were steady in crop presence. This suggests that, over time, crop deposition continued within the house areas, rather than moving outside, although Lennstrom's (1992) more in-depth analysis shows a trend of tubers being moved outside into the patios as the maize and quinoa remain in the structures.

Third, looking at the sequence in the Yanamarca Valley site floors, another divergence from the site-wide data is seen, as maize is not at all abundant on the EIP/MH floors (Figure 25c, f, and i), whereas it is present at the site level. In the Wanka I phase at Ushnu (J49) we see a temporal difference, with potatoes and maize being more dense on the floors than across all contexts. This implies that potato storage, preparation, cooking, or discard increased or occurred more often inside the structures than before. The Wanka I data suggest that there was an increased concentration of deposits on the floors.

This is a provocative pattern that reflects changes in household activities over time. Linking this information up with other artifact distributions illuminates internal social changes in the Wanka I times, such as increasing physical constraints on individual households or more discrete activity areas (Hastorf et al. 1989; Lennstrom 1992; Muyskens 1989). The Wanka II botanical samples from the floors are more ubiquitous though less dense than in the total site data, suggesting continued use of structures as well as patios.

When the floor botanicals were analyzed in conjunction with metals, ceramics, and lithics at Wanka II sites, Muyskens (1989) found that there were discrete activity areas in the Wanka II houses. This discrete activity is an escalation of specific compound use that Lennstrom (1992) also finds in the later Pancán compounds. These spatial distributions suggest that, in general through time, there was a growing trend to demarcate and constrain household tasks, especially food processing, storing, and use. The question outstanding from this analysis is what, if any, links are there between increasing household constraints on daily life tasks, shifting politics, and types of agricultural intensification?

Processing evidence

Carbonized botanical remains from the excavations cannot inform us directly about patterns of consumption (Dennell 1976); the diverse behavior that leads to plant deposition, from preservation and differential processing to the accidental nature of some deposition, involves the control of too many influences. Fortunately, there are methods to get at more direct consumption evidence. Traditionally, coprolites have been used but only in extremely dry study locations (Bryant 1974; Callen 1963). More recently, stable isotopes, analyzed in prehistoric human bone, have been shown to demonstrate changes in consumption patterns through time (van der Merwe and Vogel 1978; DeNiro 1987; see Hastorf 1991 for Sausa isotopes).

Although still in the preliminary stages of research, a series of carbonized food deposits that were scraped off the insides of cooking vessels have been analyzed for isotopic values of carbon and nitrogen. It is assumed that these encrusted deposits are the remains of mistakes in food preparation and for some reason the vessels were discarded in their dirty state. As with the unknown plant fragments isotopically analyzed, these results are only a small experimental application to test this analytical approach (see Hastorf and DeNiro [1985] for this work). But in this analysis we can see shifts in cooking patterns.

Fifty sherd encrustations have been analyzed from these sites. All of the EIP/MH and Wanka II carbon and nitrogen values lie in the tuber or *Chenopodium* category (C_3 non-leguminous plants). Due to the agglutinated morphology of the carbon on the sherds, when compared to experimental cooking of the crops, the encrustations are more likely to be a result of burning tubers than quinoa, although we cannot separate these at this time. In the twelve Wanka I sherd encrustations from both sites, half of the samples trend towards the maize values (C_4 plants). This increased maize suggests

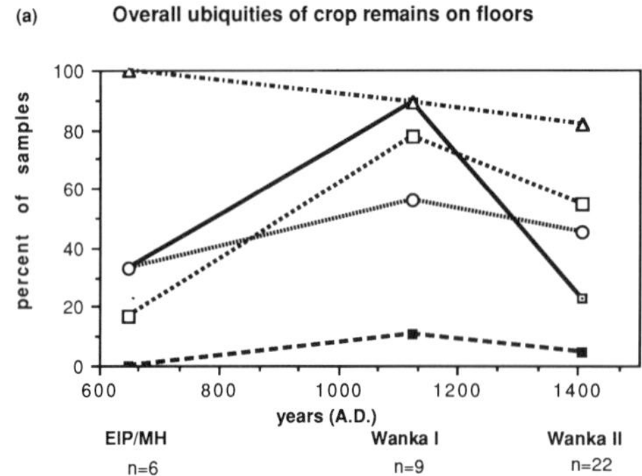
(a) Overall ubiquities of crop remains on floors
percent of samples
100
80
60
40
20
0
600
800
1000
1200
1400
years (A.D.)
EIP/MH
n=6
Wanka I
n=9
Wanka II
n=22

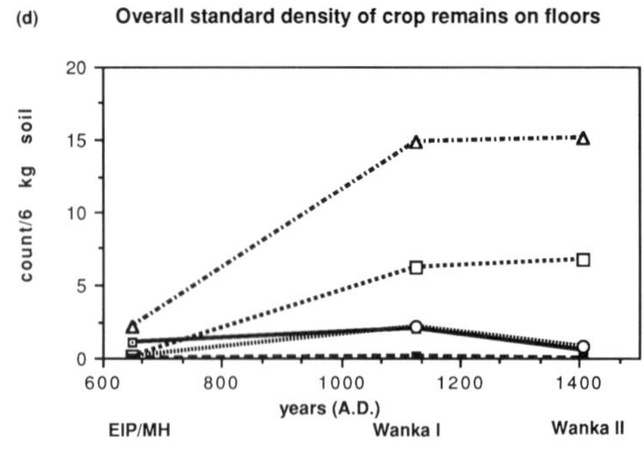
(d) Overall standard density of crop remains on floors
count/6 kg soil
20
15
10
5
0
600
800
1000
1200
1400
years (A.D.)
EIP/MH
Wanka I
Wanka II

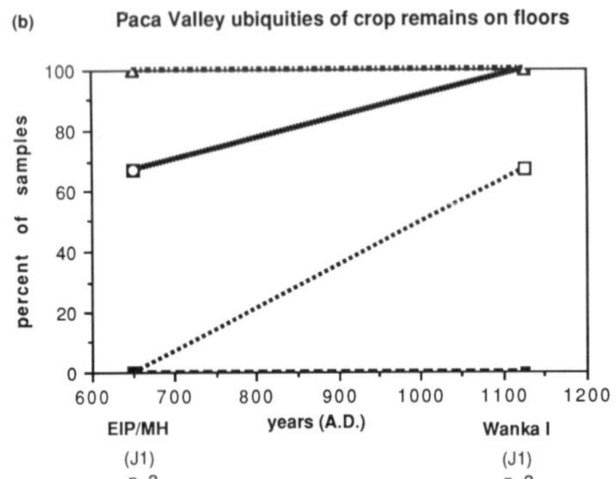
(b) Paca Valley ubiquities of crop remains on floors
percent of samples
100
80
60
40
20
0
600
700
800
900
1000
1100
1200
years (A.D.)
EIP/MH
(J1)
n=3
Wanka I
(J1)
n=3

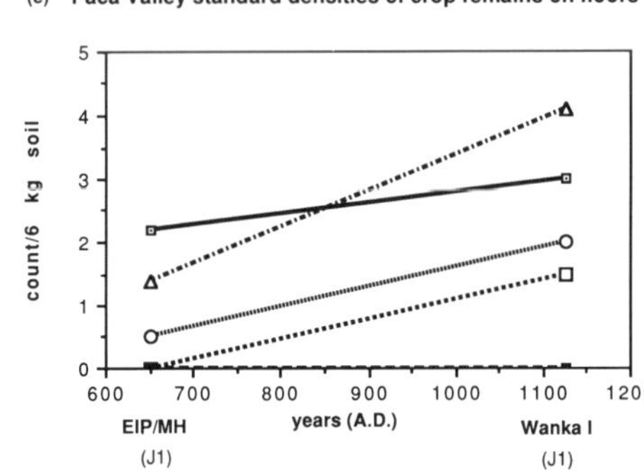
(e) Paca Valley standard densities of crop remains on floors
count/6 kg soil
5
4
3
2
1
0
600
700
800
900
1000
1100
1200
years (A.D.)
EIP/MH
(J1)
Wanka I
(J1)

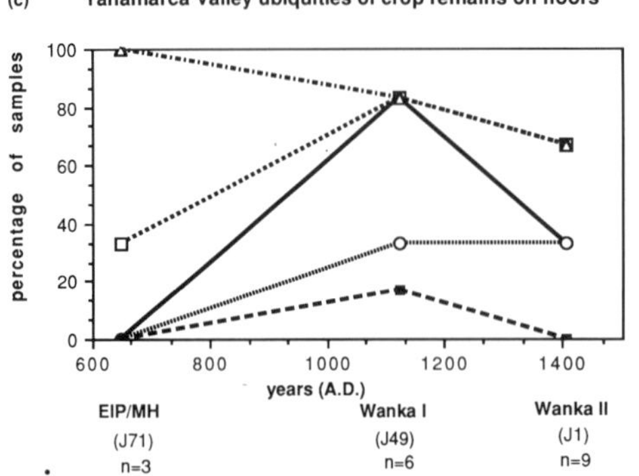
(c) Yanamarca Valley ubiquities of crop remains on floors
percentage of samples
100
80
60
40
20
0
600
800
1000
1200
1400
years (A.D.)
EIP/MH
(J71)
n=3
Wanka I
(J49)
n=6
Wanka II
(J1)
n=9

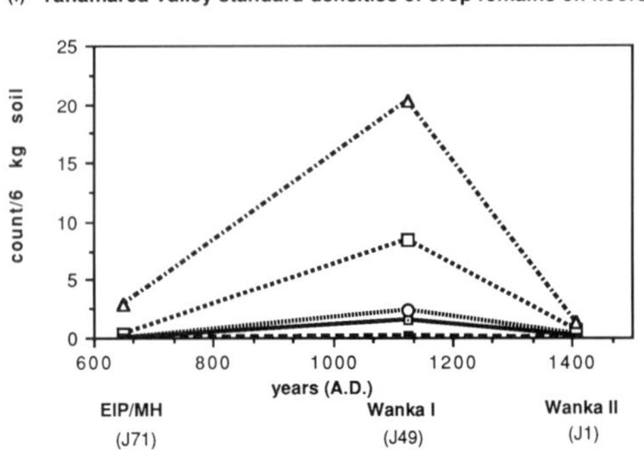
(f) Yanamarca Valley standard densities of crop remains on floors
count/6 kg soil
25
20
15
10
5
0
600
800
1000
1200
1400
years (A.D.)
EIP/MH
(J71)
Wanka I
(J49)
Wanka II
(J1)

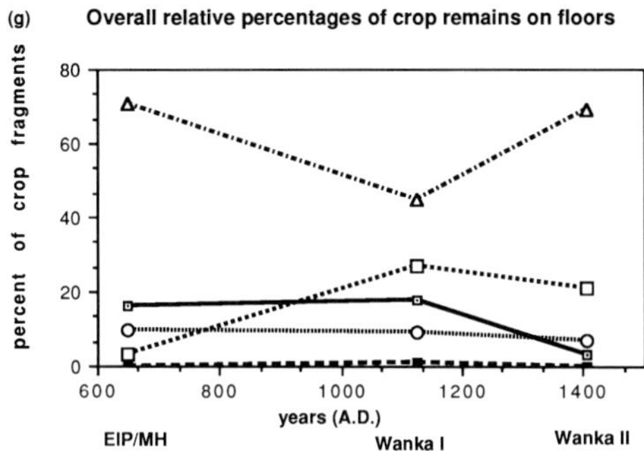

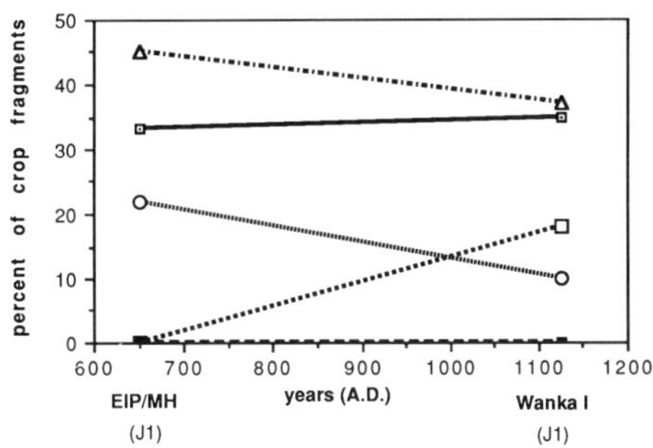

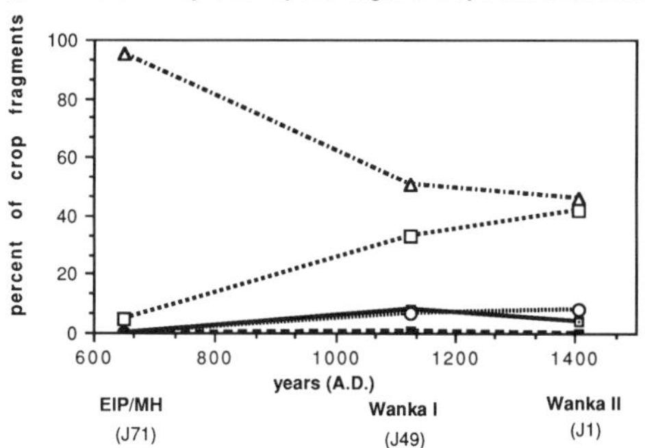

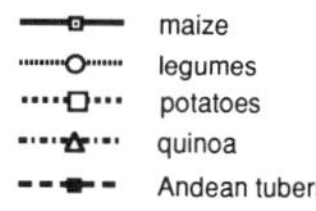

Fig. 25. Taxa by phase from floor contexts: ubiquity, standard density, and relative percentage. Each phase is located at the median date of its time span

that cooking patterns changed in Wanka I times, as did the production patterns, placing more maize in the diet. The sherd encrustations suggest that in Wanka I times maize was incorporated into the diet more regularly, boiled in soups or made into *chicha* beer, rather than used just as a condiment or extra dish, which was probably toasted or baked.

The importance of domestic animals in the diet

Faunal analysis of the excavated bone was completed by Elsie Sandefur and is reported in Hastorf et al. (1989) and Sandefur (1988a; 1988b). Her analysis shows a picture of regular animal presence in the deposits. The camelids (*Lama glama* and *Lama pacos*) are by far the most prevalent; they occur in 68 to 86 percent of the samples, while *Cavia* (guinea pig) range from 6 to 22 percent. Cervideae (deer) become less important in the Wanka II phase, suggesting a decrease in hunting. The percentage of camelid bone, which dominates all deposits, does not change significantly from the EIP/MH through the Wanka II, implying that there was no major shift, despite the move up closer to the puna lands. Guinea pig presence decreases in the Wanka II assemblages, as do the plant fodder densities and ubiquities. This decrease suggests that there might have been less guinea pig in the diet than previously. Camelids were used not only for meat, however, but also for transportation and wool, and were probably eaten when no longer of use. Preliminary stable isotope data on the human skeletons suggest that meat was never a major part of the Sausa diet.

There are shifts in food preparation and consumption throughout this sequence that provide a complex picture of change. These shed some light on the political changes, but in general parallel what we have sensed for the agricultural data.

Wild plant patterns

Wild plants present a wide vista of many activities, including food consumption and land-use. In Appendix G, where wild plant taxa are grouped into five functional categories, we see that the main trend is a drop in wild taxa frequencies in Wanka II contexts, paralleling the crop distributions. The Wanka II wild plant taxa suggest that fewer plants were brought back to the sites, as if the sites were more protected from accidental entry. We know these compounds and the sites were totally walled and that they were occupied for a shorter length of time than in the two earlier phases. And we are not sure that the earlier compounds were totally enclosed within high walls as the Wanka II compounds were.

Seed-types of plants used for fodder and construction are most commonly present throughout all phases, followed by medicinal plants. One of the more common taxa groups contains the Cyperaceae and *Scirpus* wetland sedges that are associated with storage and construction. These wetland taxa increased in the Wanka I times but dropped again in Wanka II: from 96 in Wanka I, to 74 in Wanka II. The Wanka II drop is not surprising, since the settlements move away from lake shores, home of the sedges used in construction. More significantly, these wild seeds provide another source of support for the hypothesis that the earlier people were focused on the wet drained/raised fields in the valleys; even Wanka I Ushnu had 96 percent presence of these plants and wood. In the Wanka II, this trajectory reversed, with a 59 percent and an 81 percent presence. Both storage and wild food taxa are rare in all three phases. It is unclear if these wild taxa were purposefully brought into the sites, but their distributions suggest that they were not important in the diet of the Sausa.

In terms of how these plants co-vary with the crops, a Boolean Factor Analysis was run to look for associations between all plants. This factor analysis is adapted for bimodal presence/absence data and was run on the ubiquity data (Dixon 1981: 538). A full description of how this was constructed is outlined elsewhere (Hastorf 1983). Three factors were generated. The first was maize, legumes, *Amaranthus*, *Verbena*, *Portulaca*, Fabaceae (fodder, especially for guinea pigs), the wet-land plants *Scirpus*, *Eleocharis*, *Plantago*, Cyperaceae, wood, and grasses. This links disturbed land and wetland environments (raised fields) to the milder crops, maize and beans. The second factor was *Chenopodium*, wood, and grasses, and the third, potatoes, wood, and grasses. None of the other wild plant taxa co-varied with anything. Again, we see the differences in association between the valley and the upland taxa, and how the wild taxa seemed to be utilized locally rather than being carried into other sub-zone sites. It seems likely that most seeds accompanied people arriving back from spending time in these associated zones.

Summary

While trends in the crop data are discussed further in the next chapter, some results can be mentioned now. Crop frequencies change across space and through time in this region. The evidence supports the assumption made in the catchment analysis discussion that the inhabitants in these settlements focused their production on local land-use zones, at least until Wanka II. Further, the people were not obliged to trade food to the extent that everyone had the same food mix across the region. Such variations in crop production across space also suggest differential land-use through time, with sites having independent access to different agricultural territories and intensive systems in their local catchment.

Through time we see that at first maize, legumes, and tubers increase in production absolutely, but then maize and legumes drop in abundance as potatoes become the focus of production (Figure 21). This suggests that Wanka I agricultural production was intensifying in valley lands, especially in the Yanamarca Valley, but then, as a result of political changes and population aggregation, agricultural production shifts to higher elevation crops, focusing on tubers and quinoa. Could this Wanka I change partly be intensification related to the raised fields? This seems likely. Is the radical change seen in the Wanka II botanical data a reflection of the settlement pattern change and population aggregation which required an accompanying increased production just to maintain the population? This too is most likely true.

Why then did the people move up onto knolls and shift their agricultural strategies? It certainly was not to pursue the agricultural intensification scheme that we see evolving in the earlier periods. Was it a shift to focus on crops in the higher reaches? I doubt it, especially as the climate was cooling at that time. The demographic move came first, then the agricultural adaptation to the higher land. The production shift was most likely a result of the move instigated for other social and political reasons. How much agricultural change did this entail? What additional strategies had to be undertaken? What do these crop production changes mean culturally? These questions are discussed in the next section.

IV

THE NEGOTIATION OF ANDEAN AGRICULTURE IN POLITICAL CHANGE

11

Analysis of change in agricultural production

All parts of the story have been presented: the environment, the agricultural production, the political setting, the Andean cultural world, and the people. These now must be woven together. In these final chapters, I bring together these parts of the Sausa past to try to understand their political change. Rather than choosing one explanation as the most likely cause of change I propose that multiple causes were involved in the onset of political inequality. I continue to move back and forth between the concrete archaeological data and the abstraction of political forces and cultural difference, examining the conflict and consensus the Sausa dealt with in their social and their physical constraints. In essence this is a history of the development of new boundaries, both physically of access to land and labor, and also of new cultural groups and meanings.

To begin, I assume that the optimal solution for agricultural production occurs when production needs are being met nearby, without undue pressure on labor or land. In this assumption, the optimal production does not have to be the "best" system of agriculture, but it is a strategy with known parameters that can be used as a base line from which to view the botanical data. In this way, whether or not the observed production fits the optimizing predictions, we have something specific about agricultural production to discuss. This comparison helps direct our attention towards likely causes for production difference and change. If there are variations from the local optimal production, one can suggest more confidently that the inhabitants tended towards either surplus, satisfying needs, or they were selecting for specific crops; they produced not only in their "territory" but also in fields farther away. Or they exchanged for food, received gifts or tribute of food, or were restricted in some other political way in their access to food production. The botanical frequencies may suggest what farming areas or techniques were emphasized or restricted. In addition, changing emphasis on individual crops can imply shifts in social views and values.

With a dense population that has limited arable land, inhabitants may not always be able to relocate while maintaining the same production mix. This can result in more costly production due to increased transport costs or new technologies. If social or political constraints also restrict access to certain lands, costs can increase and crop production will not reflect local territory use. Thus political influence should be reflected in the crop production data. Therefore I suggest that we should be able to see different political scenarios in different shifting crop data. What might these look like?

Distances between the different zones in the Jauja area are short. This permitted the Sausa to act within what Brush (1976) called the "compact verticality" model.

Contiguous microzones rather than spatially separated areas are farmed. Murra's (1972) Andean land-use model, on the other hand, proposes that an Andean farming community exploits a series of dispersed microzones. This scattered land-use occurs because no one zone is resourceful enough to provide the proper dietary mix and use of labor (Golte 1980). Murra maintains that sometimes laborers must travel many hours or days in order to reach these vertically dispersed zones. Both strategies were probably operating throughout the Andes in the past. The microzones in this study area are close enough, however, to allow most settlements access within one hour's walk to several different zones.

For the Sausa, therefore, I suspect that the compact verticality model was in operation, where residents could utilize their localized resources for basic subsistence (including calorific) needs. I assume then that it was possible for the major portion of the agricultural diet to come from the zones within 5 km. This would mean that optimally, individual farmers working together in small communities controlled access to different nearby microzones, cropping their parcels while exchanging labor when needed at a family level and participating in a few community-wide endeavors.

We know from historic and ethnographic material that arable land was fought over in the Andes. Up to and including Wanka I times the Jauja settlement pattern data imply a focus and interest on the lower valley lands within the Mantaro and tributary valleys. We also have indications that political alliances were developing more strongly during Wanka I and escalating in Wanka II. If political networks incorporated settlements into larger and possibly hierarchical orders, there may have been a shift away from local autonomous production to a system in which either satellite producers contributed crops to *curacas* in tribute or trade or in which families had to donate labor to leaders' fields (Smith 1989: 40). By gaining control over labor, Andean leaders might begin to control access to goods which could make them more wealthy and to decision-making positions which could make them more powerful.

A second agricultural possibility, therefore, would be that people in such a political system altered their household production either to produce for leadership or to provide labor to the leadership, in exchange for community rights (access to land, feasts, protection, and participation in the community). In this case agricultural production might not coincide with local crop potentials. There should be some evidence of altered decision-making, such as different agricultural production results or access to more Andean symbols of power. In this case leaders would have more high-quality crops, crops of value, in addition to many other items of status as the non-*curacas* would have production evidence closer to the local mix. This might also include additional production strategies organized by the leadership. They would, however, still participate in the production as part of the Andean reciprocity. Support for such a hypothesis should be found in the relationship between local territory, population size, and production, as well as shifts in access to specific crops and goods. As a result of such a political change, plant remains will not reflect optimal local production.

A third possible agricultural scenario for the Andean setting could be varying access to goods and labor between strata within the society, differentiating leaders from

Table 25. *Optimal regional crop frequency estimates*

Crop	Crop frequency (%)
Maize	17
Quinoa	25
Potatoes	22
Legumes	15
Andean tubers	20

producers (as with the Inka). That is, producers feed themselves from their own nearby fields and labor, and participate in the local community works. But they also work for the leaders, perhaps under the auspices of community labor, or even in the leaders' own fields. In this case the leaders have taken a position in society such that they no longer produce for themselves. They are managers, or war leaders, or religious leaders, who reciprocate not by exchanging labor but by other negotiated acts, whether symbolic or real. In this situation, producers' households might yield data similar to the local crop mix whereas the consumers' houses reflect a different mix of material, having no evidence of agricultural production.

While these are only thumbnail sketches of possible agricultural–political scenarios, they demonstrate how we can use the botanical data to guide us beyond demographics as the only cause of agricultural production change. Then we can bring social and political influences into the reasons for the change.

Agricultural production and the paleoethnobotanical data

To provide background for the individual site data, I have calculated a regional optimal production mix, using the regional arable zone distribution data from Chapter 9 in conjunction with the crop frequency summaries (Table 12). Table 25 presents this hypothetical regional optimal mix of crops. For the region, we see that the crops would be fairly evenly produced, with quinoa and potatoes dominating only slightly.

Early Intermediate Period/Middle Horizon

To calculate the crop mix prediction for this phase at Pancán, the areas of each arable zone listed in Table 17 are multiplied by the crop frequencies within each rotation cycle in each zone (Tables 12 and 14). These are standardized and presented in the first column of Table 26. The result of this calculation is a mix of 32 percent maize, 33 percent quinoa, 15 percent potatoes, 13 percent legumes, and 6 percent Andean tubers. With no valley irrigation, this territory includes first bench farming, fertile, moist lowlands, and extensive hillside zones. Differing from the regional mix, having less potatoes and Andean tubers and more maize, this site's territory emphasizes valley lands and its crops. The next three columns in the table provide the paleoethnobotanical data in three forms: ubiquity, standardized density, and relative percentage (described in Chapter 10). To visualize these results, Figure 26 presents bar charts comparing the optimal mix estimate (theoretical percentage) with the relative

Table 26. *Pancán (J1) EIP/MH crop production mix by percentage*

Crop	Theoretical production	Ubiquity presence	Std. density to 6 kg	Rel. % of sample
Maize	32	78	4.7	23
Quinoa	33	100	21.5	42
Potatoes	15	48	1.6	12
Legumes	13	83	2.7	23
Andean tubers	6	0	0	0
Total	99			100

percentages of the crops for the EIP/MH at Pancán. It should be remembered that quinoa is over-represented in the botanical data, while all tubers, including potatoes, are under-represented.

In general, the relative percentages are not far from the predictions. The bar pairs trend together. Because of its very high presence in all sites, quinoa is difficult to discuss. Remembering the biases of preservation and the differential deposition of quinoa, which scatters easily and is often parched for storage and therefore often burned, it is over-represented in the archaeological record. Even with its high density and ubiquity, the values tend to support the optimal prediction.

At Pancán potatoes seem to be more common than the optimal prediction, given that they are always under-represented. While maize is moderately ubiquitous and present throughout the site in many locations, it is not very dense in any one location. This medium presence of maize, in addition to its lower than predicted relative percentage, suggests that it was not grown as much as the theoretical optimal production model would predict. The isotope studies of ceramic cooking vessel encrustations also showed that maize was not a staple food product at this time (Hastorf and DeNiro 1985); while a study of Pancán prehistoric maize shows that EIP/MH varieties were small kerneled popping types (Johannessen and Hastorf 1989). Legumes are more common than predicted and have a high ubiquity. Perhaps due to different methods of storing or cooking, oca, olluco, and mashua are very rare in the floated soil samples. Andean tubers are poorly preserved and difficult to identify as they are throughout the whole data set. Adding both of these problems together, at Pancán the Andean tubers do not seem to be very common, although they could have had a 6 percent presence as predicted.

Taking into account the different representativeness of the crops, the paleoethnobotanical data present a picture of higher than predicted potatoes and legumes, with quinoa and maize slightly under-represented. These results might suggest that the Pancán residents in this period were not focusing so much on intensive valley strategies that produced more quinoa and maize, but were using the low hillside fields in addition to their first bench dry-farming valley fields to the north.

From this picture of extensive agriculture and the settlement pattern evidence in Chapter 4, I think that the Sausa population during this period was not under pressure in its agricultural production. In Table 1, Pancán had an estimated population of 60–80 people. Given this, the range of calories needed annually would be approximately 33 to 40 × 10^6 kcal. The calorific production estimates for the territory were 858 × 10^6 kcal (Table 21), twenty-one times higher than the calorie estimate required. This is a small amount of food when compared to the potential of the defined territory, suggesting that the farmers did not have to use the "optimal" (fairly intensive) scheme, but could have employed a more extensive strategy, such as no irrigation or drainage and longer fallow cycles. The botanical results suggest that the population seemed to be minimizing labor by focusing on the low input microzones, more of a satisfycing strategy.

It seems that the Pancán inhabitants were producing their crops locally and were not under land stress. The differences between the predictions and the data could mean that more potatoes and legumes were grown in the valleys or perhaps that the residents were using more hillside land than was predicted. In addition there is a sense of agricultural autonomy for individual families.

As with the EIP/MH at Pancán, the optimal prediction for Tragadero Viejo is valley oriented, including first bench, fertile lowland, and intensive low hillside zones, as in column 1 of Table 27. The second column presents the crop ubiquities from the paleoethnobotanical data, the third column the standardized density counts, and the fourth the relative percentages of the crops within the flotation samples.

The theoretical predictions suggest that maize, potatoes, and legumes were evenly produced, with quinoa dominating and almost no Andean tubers. This crop mix is not paralleled by the botanical data as graphed in the comparative bar chart of Figure 26. The most striking aspect of the paleoethnobotanical data is that the densities are much lower here than at Pancán, except for quinoa. Compared to the other sites analyzed, the botanical remains are very sparse at Tragadero Viejo. Low frequencies in the taxa presence accentuate trends that might not be present in more rich samples. Poor

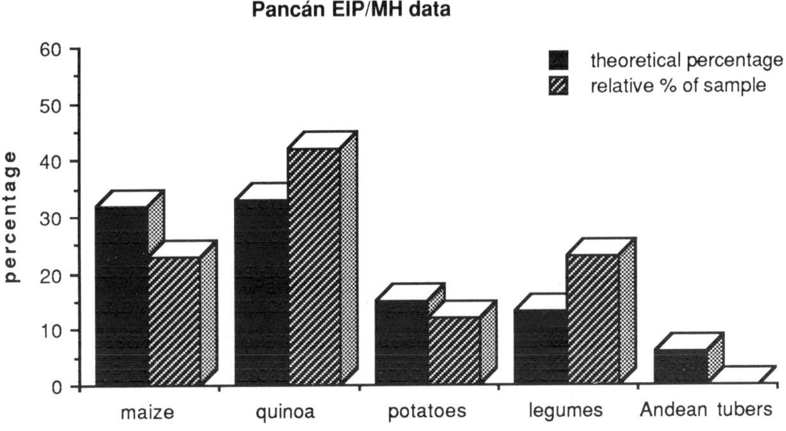

Fig. 26. Pancán (J1) Early Intermediate Period/Middle Horizon agricultural production predictions and botanical data

Table 27. *Tragadero Viejo (J71) EIP/MH crop production mix by percentage*

Crop	Theoretical production	Ubiquity presence	Std. density to 6 kg	Rel. % of sample
Maize	21	18	0.1	3
Quinoa	33	79	24.3	76
Potatoes	23	32	0.9	20
Legumes	21	11	0.1	1
Andean tubers	2	0	0	0
Total	100			100

preservation might be an explanation for this lack of fit between predictions and data, but other events may have affected this settlement's depositional behavior as well. There are two post-occupational facts that help account for this discrepancy. The first is that the site is very shallow (no more than 70 cm below the ground surface), open, and has been exposed to weathering and decomposition for over one thousand years. The second is that the site and the surrounding area are considered prime agricultural lands which have probably been cultivated for a long time.

The residents of Tragadero Viejo seemed to be meeting their dietary needs mainly with quinoa and potatoes. The relative percentage of quinoa is three times the optimal prediction, suggesting that, despite its over-representation in the archaeological record, quinoa was also very common in the settlement. This is supported too by the very high quinoa density, similar to the Pancán quinoa data.

The relative percentage of potatoes is similar to the predictions, suggesting a higher than predicted occurrence given their fragile nature. Especially when compared to the Pancán data, maize and legumes are both sparse. Maize represents 3 percent of the domesticates, and has a low presence. The legumes are even lower with only a 1 percent relative presence. This production evidence implies a lack of production of these two crops. The data do not reflect the "optimal" intensive predicted mix at Tragadero Viejo. There is more quinoa and potatoes than predicted and much less maize and legumes, suggesting that the producers were focusing on the nearby hillsides and well drained valley lands, as the residents do today.

I want to return to the agricultural interview data to try to understand the high quinoa and low maize at this site and the high maize and legumes at Pancán. I noted that today the Yanamarca Valley is known for its high-yielding quinoa, more so than any other area in the Jauja region, including the shores of Laguna Paca. On the other hand, the Paca area is one of the better areas for maize production today while maize yields irregularly in the Yanamarca Valley. If these ecological differences existed in the past, this would help explain the crop frequencies at the two sites.

Abandoned earlier than Pancán and nestling among many neighboring sites, it is likely that Tragadero Viejo housed families who were able to produce their subsistence locally without becoming involved in trade, expensive strategies, or transport. This site is 1.9 ha in size, and is estimated to have had between 80 and 120 people. To subsist, they had to produce between 45 and 67 × 10^6 kcal annually. Because of its location near Laguna Tragadero and away slightly from the hills, its territory includes mainly fertile lowland with some first bench and hillside land. The territory is estimated to be able to produce 931 × 10^6 kcal annually, fourteen times the estimated requirement. Therefore the residents would have been able to manage on the less costly strategies and long fallow cycles, perhaps only using the first bench and the hillsides. This ratio between production needs and potential yield also suggests that, despite neighbors in the Yanamarca Valley, there was no great pressure on arable land at this time.

From these EIP/MH period comparisons, one can propose that both populations were able to produce their staple food within small territories. Both settlements emphasized potatoes, planted on the hillsides or in the valleys. A contrast between the two sites is the higher maize at Pancán and the higher quinoa at Tragadero Viejo, suggesting that the two valley basins had different production cropping schemes then as they do now. This material supports the settlement and artifactual results (Chapter 4) that suggest that in the EIP/MH phase extensive farming villages lived on a diet of potatoes, quinoa, and legumes. The people seem to have lived in small, loose alliances with social relations and labor exchanges mainly operating at the neighbor and village level, and with family centered rituals.

Wanka I

Pancán was continuously occupied in this phase but within a different settlement relationship to its neighbors, now being restricted by more settlements. The same land-use zones exist in the territory: first bench, fertile lowland, and intensive hillsides, but the area has shrunk by half. The "optimal" crop predictions, calculated from

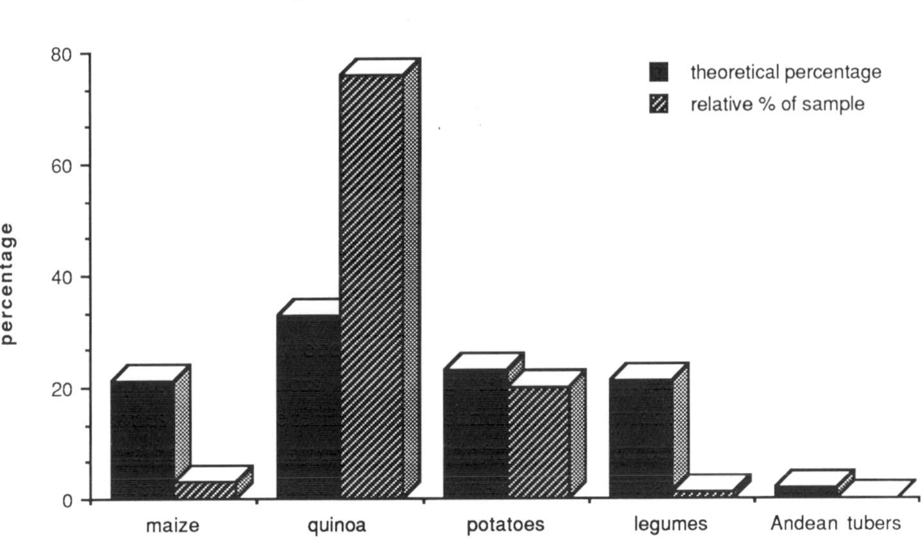

Fig. 27. Tragadero Viejo (J71) Early Intermediate Period/Middle Horizon agricultural production predictions and botanical data

Table 28. *Pancán (J1) Wanka I crop production mix by percentage*

Crop	Theoretical production	Ubiquity presence	Std. density to 6 kg	Rel. % of sample
Maize	44	82	3.4	23
Quinoa	24	86	14.8	40
Potatoes	13	45	0.7	6
Legumes	13	77	4.4	31
Andean tubers	6	0	0	0
Total	100			100

Tables 14 and 21, are presented in the first column of Table 28. The territorial predictions are similar to the EIP/MH distribution as are the crop ubiquities. Comparisons of the predictions and the relative percentages are shown in Figure 28.

The theoretical percentage predicts a dominance of maize above all other crops, followed by quinoa, then potatoes and legumes. Andean tubers would be rare. Looking at the paleoethnobotanical data, we see that in fact maize is common, comprising almost one quarter of the domesticates and present in 82 percent of the samples. Yet its density (how many pieces of maize present in any one sample) is lower than in the previous phase and lower than the predictions. This means that it is sparsely spread throughout the deposits. As in the EIP/MH, we see more quinoa than we expected, its ubiquity being three times higher than the prediction, and the relative percentage being almost double. Yet quinoa's density is much less than in the EIP/MH. Because quinoa is over-represented in the archaeological record, I assume that it was probably not much more common than predicted here. Potatoes, being under-represented, are low in density and ubiquity but no more so than at any other site. The legume data deviate from the predictions. Legumes are much more common than expected, with frequencies and a relative percentage well over double the optimal prediction. Andean tubers are not well represented in the data, reflecting their rare occurrence.

The Wanka I data suggest that crop production was not the same as predicted, but instead had more emphasis on legumes. The crops hint at a focus on valley land production more than in the previous period, as indicated especially by the decrease in the potato frequency. From other research on Pancán maize, we know that several new maize varieties entered the region during this time (Johannessen and Hastorf 1989). These were probably higher yielding types, and associated with more maize boiling (as seen in the cooking vessel encrustation isotope data), either in soups or in maize beer production (Hastorf and DeNiro 1985).

Over time the residences at Pancán are more densely packed (Hastorf et al. 1989). During this period we know that there were many sites in and around Laguna Paca, forming an aggregated population, with more intervillage exchange (ceramic evidence) and identity. The population size is estimated to range between 126 and 168 people, needing an estimate between 70 and 93 $\times 10^6$ kcal every year. These new demographics might have increased the land pressure so that some might have been farming the valley land using more intensive strategies, such as irrigation. The total optimal production of this territory is 319×10^6 kcal per year, three times the required yield. However, with no valley irrigation the maximum optimal estimate is 177×10^6 kcal, not even twice the population's requirements.

One can surmise from the population size estimates and the crops that Pancán's residents were probably using all of their available zones to produce enough food: the first bench, the fertile lowland, and the extensive hillsides. In addition, the residents could have been draining parts of the fertile lowland soils and irrigating the first bench to increase yields. These data suggest that the populace may have concentrated on certain types of land within their territory, with the possibility of encroachment, expansion, or skirmishes with neighbors. While the evidence supports the notion that people at Pancán were able to extract what they needed from their local territory, they would have focused on valley lands and the labor-intensive systems of raised fields or irrigation to increase their yields. The botanical data and settlement pattern suggest intensive agriculture, perhaps accompanied by new levels of social tensions at Pancán, instigated by readjustments to the post-Wari political vacuum with an increased sense of the larger group. This may have then led to tensions about local land availability and allocation.

Ushnu (J49) is a good example of the shift in settlement location that began in the Middle Horizon and continued into the Wanka I times. Because it is located on a knoll at the edge of the Yanamarca Valley, and the valley still has many sites in and around it, Ushnu's territory comprises a substantial amount of hillside and upland. Table 29 displays the predictions that are generated from the territory boundaries in Figure 19, where one can now see its orientation to the uplands in the increase in potato prediction. The land-use crop frequencies are multiplied by the zone areas. The crop frequencies calculated from Table 14 can be compared to the paleoethnobotanical data from Table 23 in Table 29. These are visually plotted in Figure 29.

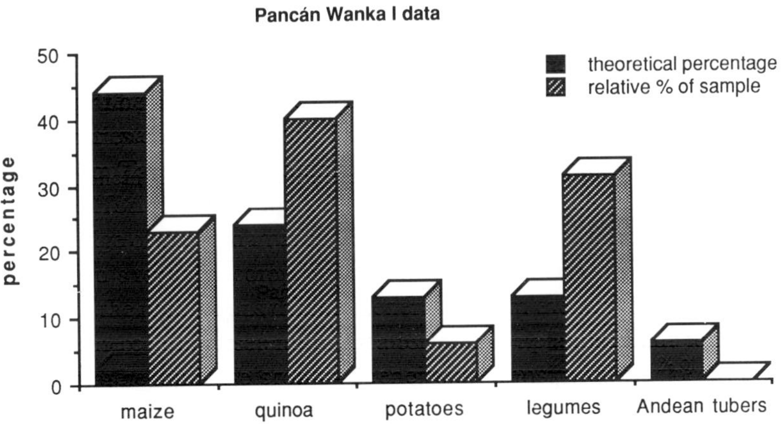

Fig. 28. Pancán (J1) Wanka I agricultural production predictions and botanical data

Table 29. *Ushnu (J49) Wanka I crop production mix by percentage*

Crop	Theoretical production	Ubiquity presence	Std. density to 6 kg	Rel. % of sample
Maize	11	70	1.1	9.0
Quinoa	20	89	18.7	58.4
Potatoes	29	59	2.9	16.7
Legumes	16	59	1.4	15.6
Andean tubers	24	4	0.03	0.3
Total	100			100

This bar chart shows how very similar the predicted crop mix is to the botanical data except for quinoa, remembering the differential preservation of the crops. The predictions are also similar to the regional average. Immediately one can see how different the Ushnu predictions and data are from the previously discussed sites, especially Wanka I Pancán. Assuming that the residents' production was for agricultural products (e.g. they were not getting the bulk of their diet from herding in the uplands), almost 50 percent of the predicted produce comprises tubers. The next most common crops would be quinoa and legumes, with maize being the least common. The ubiquity frequencies do not follow the predictions but have regular maize, quinoa, and tubers. While potatoes are predicted to be the most common and their ubiquity is high, their relative percentage is lower than expected. Keeping preservation in mind, I assume that they are approximately the same as their prediction. This is counter-balanced by the Andean tubers that continue to be rare in all samples. Quinoa is four times more frequent than predicted. It also dominates the relative percentages.

The bar chart shows how both legumes and maize are as common as they are predicted. Yet, when comparing their ubiquities to those at Pancán, we see that both of these crops are much less frequent and dense at Ushnu. The maize data are especially curious at Ushnu. While maize is well dispersed throughout the site with a 70 percent ubiquity, its density is low, and the relative presence is 9 percent. Overall, maize is not spatially clustered but is evenly dispersed across the site, meaning that every household sampled (6) had maize, which was mainly scattered across the floors. There seems to be no differential access to maize in the Ushnu households sampled. Today maize can be grown at the base of the hill Ushnu is situated on. These data suggest that this was also done in the past.

The botanical data at Ushnu, when compared to the predictions, suggest that quinoa and potatoes were the dominant crops, with legumes third in importance. As at Tragadero Viejo, there is less maize than at Pancán. But, like the Wanka I Pancán data, Ushnu has more maize than earlier. We have a picture then of an orientation to hillside production of quinoa, potatoes, and legumes with valley production of maize and quinoa. In fact the data suggest that the Ushnu residents may have been using many of their valley fields but only a portion of the hypothetical upland territory.

From the architectural structure densities calculated in Chapter 4, Ushnu is estimated to have had a population between 387 and 516 people. This produces a basic calorific requirement of 216 to 228 × 10^6 kcal per year. The higher estimated population would consume only one-seventh of the optimal production (Table 21), implying that the residents could have used their large upland area very extensively. Yet, the ratio of people to land is greater than it was for Tragadero Viejo. As people aggregated in the Yanamarca Valley settlements, there should have been an increase in people using both the valley and the uplands.

The land-use data for these two phases suggest that the Sausa populace, although having less and less valley land per capita through time, increasingly concentrated on that microzone, especially with the entrance of new maize varieties (Johannessen and Hastorf 1989). From this evidence, we get a complicated picture of increasing production accompanying an overall lack of pressure on arable land, yet a selective focus on the valley lands. This is similar to the scenario in the Oaxaca Valley sequence (Blanton et al. 1981). While some shifts in the selective use of land accompany heightened local political activity, Wanka I people still seemed to be using land compactly in an autonomous way with little or no intervillage or intravillage hierarchy or asymmetry.

Wanka II

The Wanka II sites occur on high knolls within upland areas, removed from the valleys (Figure 4). The Wanka I evidence suggests that the production capacities of the sites' territories were not at the upper potential limits and could have easily fed the population. The botanical data, however, suggest that some intensive strategies such as

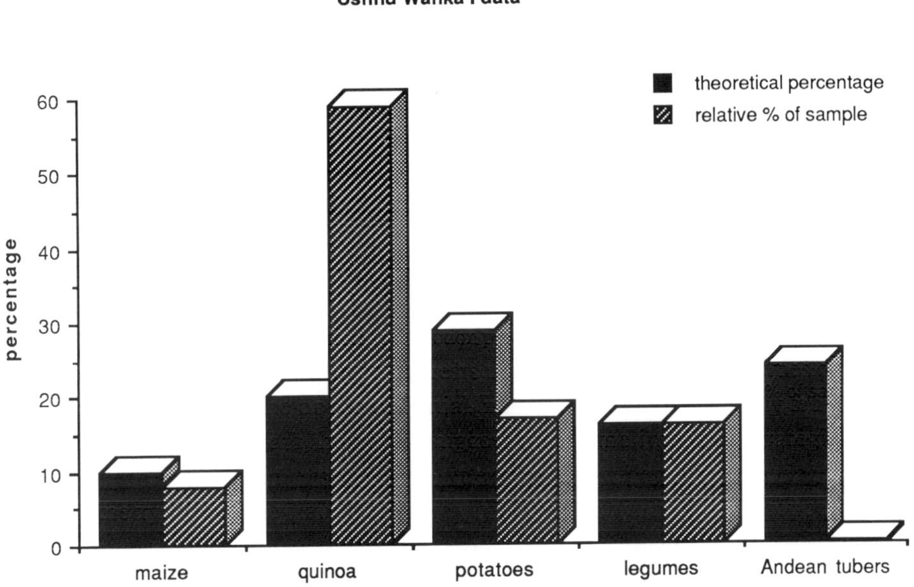

Fig. 29. Ushnu (J49) Wanka I agricultural production predictions and botanical data

Table 30. *Umpamalca (J41) Wanka II crop production mix by percentage*

Crop	Theoretical production	Ubiquity presence	Std. density to 6 kg	Rel. % of sample[1]
Maize	2	20	3.3	10
Quinoa	22	88	1.8[1]	56
Potatoes	32	46	9.7	19
Legumes	12	41	1.5	14
Andean tubers	32	5	0.02	1
Total	100			100

[1]These values are tabulated with the two quinoa caches removed

raised/drained fields and valley irrigation may have been adopted at both Pancán and Ushnu. The Wanka II settlements are away from these lands. As a result of the move, most of the settlement territories no longer include valley lands and certainly they are not near the valleys. Also due to the shift, upland agricultural intensification strategies can be expected due to the settlement locations and distributions. The residents might have been exploiting the farther away valley lands.

Umpamalca's theoretically drawn territory includes extensive hillsides, high elevation land, and a small section of irrigable land in the Quishualcancha Quebrada. The valley land makes up 3 percent of the arable 688 ha, the hills 7 percent, and the uplands 90 percent. Table 30 presents the predicted crop mix for the territory, bounded tightly by neighbors (Figure 20). These results are compared to the relative percentages of the crop data in Figure 30. I present the relative crop percentages with the two quinoa caches removed, since they swamp the presence of all the other crops.

If the Umpamalca residents were optimizing production in their surrounding fields they would plant potatoes, Andean tubers, and quinoa, with less emphasis on legumes. Maize would be a very rare item and probably would not be present, especially given the cooler environment suggested by the paleoclimate data for that time (Seltzer 1987; Seltzer and Hastorf 1990). In addition, the higher-elevation fields would produce less per unit area, due to a longer fallow cycle than that of lower fields, and so a larger area would have to be under annual cultivation. Potatoes, tubers, quinoa, and (less so) legumes could be grown in the uplands in long fallow cycles. The maize would grow exclusively in the protected *quebrada* valley, where cropping would be more intensive.

Turning to the archaeological material, we see that quinoa again dominates, being four times more frequent than that predicted while also having the highest relative presence. These quinoa frequencies suggest that it was perhaps produced above the predicted level. Potatoes are common in the archaeobotanical data, as seen in their high density and ubiquity, especially considering their fragile nature and less common recovery from the sites. They are probably about what is predicted given these constraints. Legumes are about what is predicted. While the Andean tubers are very scarce and the evidence extremely hard to interpret, they probably were more common than the data suggest. Compared to these high-elevation predictions, maize is much more frequent than expected.

Overall, the Umpamalca crop data suggest that quinoa and potatoes are the dominant crops with legumes close behind, followed by maize. The place of maize and potatoes in the crop mix has changed significantly from earlier times. While the ubiquity of maize in the Wanka I sites is quite high (82 percent and 70 percent), it has dropped substantially here to 20 percent. When these maize values are compared to the Umpamalca territorial predictions, however, they are much higher than expected. Potato ubiquity and relative presence too are regular, as is its density. Potatoes are more dense at Umpamalca than at any other tested site. The densities of all crops, except quinoa, average around 4 per 6 kg of soil. Potatoes are 9.7 per 6 kg making its density particularly high. This means that, while potatoes are not found in every context, when they are present there are a lot of them. Quinoa and potatoes can be produced easily in the zones encircling the Umpamalca residents, and so the data do support local production within the territory, with the addition of maize. This suggests at least upland intensification if not distant exploitation and even exchange.

There are complications to the production scenario when we think of the implications of such a large population residing at this site. Umpamalca is well preserved, densely packed architecturally, and is estimated to have had anywhere from 2940 to 6570 residents. The minimum annual dietary requirement for such a population ranges from 1641 to 3669 $\times$ 10^6 kcal. The assigned catchment territory is estimated to produce 1926 $\times$ 10^6 kcal annually, an "optimal" production value which lies within the minimum requirement necessary. Umpamalca's nearby lands could barely produce enough food for even the smaller population estimate. And the maximum production prediction assumes that 200 ha of high elevation soil was put into irrigation, which is

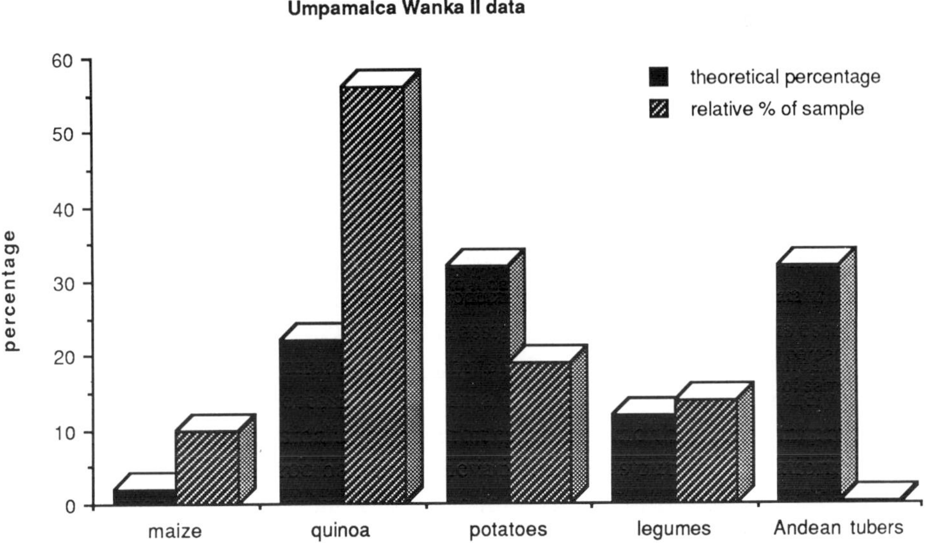

Fig. 30. Umpamalca (J41) Wanka II agricultural production predictions and botanical data

a very expensive (high labor input) practice. Even remembering that the estimates are rough, these comparisons suggest that the residents of Umpamalca would not comfortably be able to meet their annual calorie needs in the territory available to them. Other means of gaining foodstuffs would have been required. While the catchment territories are hypothetical, this exercise illustrates that Umpamalca farmers almost certainly had to farm beyond their nearby fields.

In addition to planting their land very intensively, perhaps even more so than the optimal rotation cycles predicted, the populace would have used additional fields farther away. These fields could have been up towards the puna, in the Yanamarca Valley, the Mantaro gorge, or even as far away as the *ceja de montaña*. The populace would have needed to gain more potatoes and quinoa, but also especially maize. To farm in these areas they would have had to claim the land in direct competition with other nearby residents, even if they were reclaiming the old lands where they had resided in Wanka I times, for example in the Yanamarca Valley. This might be where tree planting helped to indicate and validate land ownership based on the ancestral connections (Hastorf and Johannessen 1991).

Besides being more susceptible to losing crops from attack or theft, farming farther away is more expensive, as the farmers would have to transport seed, manure, and the harvest over greater distances. In addition, or alternatively, the residents of Umpamalca might have traded for food with people further south in the Mantaro Valley, perhaps exchanging the chert they harvested and processed (Russell 1988b) for andesite jars filled with maize from the south (Costin 1986), or perhaps they had more herds from which to extract meat or wool for exchange. These strategies would be more expensive, suggesting that the Wanka II populace expended much more energy to gain their food than did earlier residents. Life was more costly, but also on a larger scale politically as wider networks were more active.

These competitive and costly options led directly to the issues discussed in Chapter 5: historic sources state that Wanka war leaders were organizing people to defend and gain arable land. Here at Umpamalca, as at Tunánmarca, we have an example of a population that very likely had been involved in competition over more land, and most likely for prime agricultural land, such as in the Yanamarca Valley. This competition and leadership could bring about differential access to goods, especially crops and land, since the documents mention that the leaders handed out the captured land, goods, and labor. The amount and type of difference can give us an idea of the types of inequalities developing in this region. Were the warriors capturing labor and land for the whole community, or did the war leaders gain differential access to land, labor, and goods for themselves? Did these leaders farm themselves or only receive tribute? Is there any evidence for access differences in the Umpamalca paleoethnobotanical data?

From more recent excavations at Umpamalca, where several complete patio compounds were excavated, we have evidence for two economic statuses (D'Altroy 1992; Earle et al. 1987; Hastorf 1990a). "Elite" and "commoner" residential compounds are defined by compound size, quality of construction, and frequencies of artifacts within them. Overall the elites had more high-quality artifacts and trade items (see Chapter

5). The paleoethnobotanical data as well show that elites had more of all crops than the commoner patios at Umpamalca (Hastorf 1990a). Maize in particular differed, with a 51 percent ubiquity in the larger elite patios versus 31 percent in the smaller ones of the commoners. That is, the elite patio compounds had a maize ubiquity more like the Wanka I Pancán frequency. Maize is a prized food commodity, not only as part of the diet but also for symbolic uses in ceremonies, political gatherings, and alliance building (Hastorf and Johannessen 1992; Murra 1960; Rowe 1946). These differential densities are also seen in the higher elite potato data, suggesting that there were some families at Umpamalca who had different access to goods, including foodstuffs such as maize and potatoes (Hastorf 1990a).

Unlike the earlier valley dwelling sites where maize was ubiquitous throughout the samples, at Umpamalca it was a restricted commodity. It was brought onto the site by those families who could have been involved in trade, had differential access to more distant maize producing land, or had more access to the labor needed to work the distant fields. However many different strategies to gain access to maize were involved, its distribution reflects a new, more complex system of farming and food access compared to earlier phases, thus linking these new economic events to the political changes evident in the other data sets. But the elites are also producing their own crops; evidence of tools and processing tasks are present in their compounds. While they gained preferential access to certain labor or goods, the data suggest that they were most like modern *curacas* of the second agricultural production model stated above, in that they also had to produce and process their own daily needs. They were not specialized consumers. Wanka II family production was tied to the larger political setting as reciprocity was manipulated symbolically and materially.

In this study, Tunánmarca (J7) is an example of a large Wanka II settlement. From its size of 25 ha (as discussed in Chapter 4), it is assumed to be a Sausa center during these times. Because of its location, on a knoll surrounded by contemporaneous sites, Tunánmarca's territory is small unless it is united with its small neighbor J46. When it is not joined to this settlement we see that Tunánmarca has no Yanamarca Valley land in its own hypothetical territory. Fifty-four percent of its estimated territory is high elevation land, 42 percent is extensive hillside, and only 4 percent is valley land in the Quishualcancha Quebrada to the west (Table 21). Tabulating the crop frequencies from these zones, based on Tables 12 and 14, provides a crop mix prediction from this small territory of 6 percent maize, 21 percent quinoa, 31 percent potatoes, 17 percent legumes, and 25 percent Andean tubers, listed in column 1 of Table 31. The comparative paleoethnobotanical data are found in columns 2, 3, and 4. The relative percentages are plotted in Figure 31.

Potatoes and Andean tubers dominate the predictions, followed by quinoa, legumes, and finally maize with 6 percent. As predicted, potatoes are actually more dense than quinoa at Tunánmarca! The predicted maize frequency is, like that of Umpamalca, small. In the relative percentage view of the data, potatoes and quinoa dominate with the same frequencies. Given their preservation differences, these results translate into potatoes being extremely common in the archaeological assemblage, overwhelming all other crops. While Andean tubers are rare in the record,

Table 31. *Tunánmarca (J7) Wanka II crop production mix by percentage*

Crop	Theoretical production	Ubiquity presence	Std. density to 6 kg	Rel. % of sample
Maize	6	22	0.3	6.4
Quinoa	21	67	1.8	42.2
Potatoes	31	63	4.8	42.3
Legumes	17	22	0.3	5.1
Andean tubers	25	7	0.7	4.0
Total	100			100

they are more common at this site than at any other (with 7 percent presence), and, together with the potatoes, tubers are as common as they are in the predictions, comprising about 50 percent of the production. Legumes are less common than predicted by half in relative presence, suggesting that they are rare in the assemblage and have been replaced by potatoes in production.

We see that relative presence of quinoa is greater than the predictions, but the ubiquity value is not even double, suggesting that it probably was lower than predicted. This is also supported by the low quinoa density of 1.8. Given that the densities of all crops except tubers at Tunánmarca are less than at the other sites, this high potato density is even more impressive. Maize is low but is equivalent to the predictions, though its standardized density is very low and its ubiquity is only 22 percent. This means that it follows the Yanamarca trend in low maize but that, while it is very sparse, there is more than at Umpamalca. The people of Tunánmarca did not have much land nearby for the maize production reflected in these figures, yet they were getting it somehow.

The botanical data present a crop production mix that is not the same as the theoretical predictions, though they do trend together. Potatoes dominate over all other crops, suggesting that the inhabitants were focusing their production on one starchy staple, with less of an even mix. These frequencies imply that the diet was worse than before, with less protein and less variety.

With this tendency towards potato specialization one can speculate that there might have been a new preference for yield maximization nearby (rather than labor minimization), perhaps even dictated and organized by the leadership. In addition, the residents might have had their main access to more high-elevation fields where potatoes were productive.

A further sense of pressure on food production and access is evident when comparing the data to that of other sites. Tunánmarca has lower ubiquities overall. Accompanying lower site-wide densities, there are crop frequency differences between the two house compound types. Like Umpamalca there are two different statuses that were sampled in eight compounds in 1982 and 1983 (D'Altroy and Hastorf n.d.; Earle et al. 1987). Comparing these two statuses, defined architecturally and economically in the same way as at Umpamalca, there are higher frequencies of all crops in the elite contexts, including maize, 8 percent in commoners and 18 percent in elites (Hastorf 1990a: 277).

There is, however, about the same amount of maize at Tunánmarca as at Umpamalca; it is slightly more ubiquitous though less dense where it is present. This suggests that the residents at Tunánmarca and Umpamalca had about the same access to maize-growing areas outside the nearby territories, did not have much interregional trade, or that we did not excavate some of the truly elite compounds where traded or tribute maize was amassed. This difference in maize presence between Umpamalca and Tunánmarca suggests that Umpamalca's increased maize densities were tied perhaps to their access to the Mantaro Valley gorge lands or to trade, since we know that Umpamalca produced both pottery and chert blades that could be traded south, whereas Tunánmarca did not have such commodities and their alliance network was to the north.

The Tunánmarca elites, however, did have differential access to many goods, especially goods of value, metals, pottery, and labor. Like Umpamalca they seem to fit the second social–agricultural model, where leaders organized projects and gained access but did not in any way have total power over certain activities or have attached specialists who completed their daily tasks. The elite compounds have evidence of all activities.

The predictions of insufficient agricultural yields are more extreme for the local territory of Tunánmarca than for Umpamalca. The structures at Tunánmarca are more densely packed than at other sites, which tallies with an estimated population of between 6600 and 11,100 people (Table 1). Applying the per capita calorific requirement, a range of 3719 and 6199 × 10^6 kcal per annum would have been needed to maintain such a population. This is almost a two-fold increase over Umpamalca's needs, although Tunánmarca's territorial production is approximately the same. Its territorial optimal production is only 1100 × 10^6 kcal (Table 21), meaning that the local territory could have fed between one-third and one-sixth of Tunánmarca's

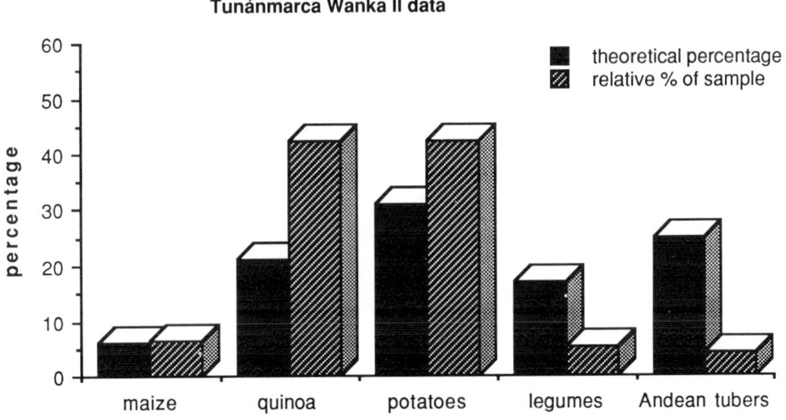

Fig. 31. Tunánmarca (J7) Wanka II agricultural production predictions and botanical data

population. Obviously much food would have had to be brought onto the site to maintain even half of the population. It is likely therefore that the Tunánmarca inhabitants intensified their local agricultural production more than the predicted "optimal" rotation cycles. This intensification would have entailed increased effort, escalated social interactions, and increased political negotiation over subsistence production in addition to aggressive actions over land rights.

With such pressure to garner food resources, the same strategies that were proposed for Umpamalca would have been undertaken by the Tunánmarca residents as well. There would surely have been an intensification in local agricultural production and perhaps camelid-herding during this time (though the data do not suggest that). All zones within the site's territory would probably have been under intensive agricultural strategies as well as leaning on their surrounding allies for land and labor.

As local intensification occurred, the uplands would have been the nearest focus. Additionally, the Tunánmarca populace, through political means, could have gained land or produce from their allied satellites, especially small sites like J46, just to the east of Tunánmarca (Figure 20). Such an agriculturally based centralization is seen in the canal that carries water to most of the northern alliance sites, augmenting yields near many of them (Figure 4). If Tunánmarca controlled part of these settlements' production either in labor or land, this political centralization would have designed specific production schemes. The labor intensive, intervalley canal system associated with Tunánmarca and its northern satellites, ridged fields, lynchets, and terraces, were all probably part of this project. In the Andes today, a canal is not just something that carries water to fields, it also links communities and *ayllus* together (Sherbondy 1982). This means that people must work together to maintain the canals and officials must regulate the water distribution; but canals also bring people together symbolically, as the water source is tied to the ancestors, weaving together tiers of ever larger kin groups (B. J. Isbell 1978). The northern alliance territory is dominated by high-elevation land which would have concentrated on tubers and quinoa, paralleling the average production mix seen at Tunánmarca.

Another plausible production strategy for Tunánmarca could have been to expand production beyond the satellite territories, traveling farther, perhaps to the east where many sites had been abandoned. The crop mix recovered at Tunánmarca, however, does not suggest much of a valley orientation.

For both Umpamalca and Tunánmarca, expanding land-use, whether near or far, would have incurred large transportation and security costs and required battles or aggressive threats to claim and defend access to this land. Today, this type of land capture and defense is associated with ritual battles, *tinku*, between settlements. This has been described as a way to demarcate and maintain territory throughout the Andes (Alencastre and Dumézil 1953; Bastien 1978; Platt 1987; Chapter 3). In addition, war leaders were surely involved in organizing the battles and distributing the captured goods (Chapter 5).

Other supporting evidence, such as the defensive position of these walled upland sites, suggests this type of warfare was going on. It is conceivable that large sites such as Tunánmarca or Umpamalca, with large warrior populations, might have continuously been aggressive towards other settlements, especially the Hatúnmarca group, the alliance west of Quishualcancha Quebrada, or north into the Huaricolca puna.

The botanical data indicate that potatoes and quinoa were commonly produced. The dominant potatoes and quinoa do not reflect a far-reaching expansion out of the Tunánmarca alliance area. If exchange occurred to the south, we would expect to see a different mix with much more maize. In fact, given that sites such as Umpamalca would have been hard pressed to give much tribute, the Tunánmarca elite would probably have had to continually press for tribute or extra labor, making it a volatile era with much negotiation over access to land, labor, and trade (Smith 1989: 41; Wachtel 1973).

This local and continuous use of land and labor resources suggests that most valley fields, predicted to be within the territory of Hatúnmarca, would have been farmed primarily by its residents. From the 1982–83 excavations at Hatúnmarca, we know that this center had very high ubiquities of quinoa (75 percent) and maize (57 percent), supporting not only a local land-use hypothesis but also the idea that Hatúnmarca controlled much of the Yanamarca Valley lands (Hastorf 1990a) or valley lands elsewhere. This substantiates the idea that, despite aggressive actions between settlements, each was actually held in check from completely expanding into one another's territory. While Hatúnmarca might have had agricultural hegemony over the Yanamarca Valley, the residents did not have political control over Tunánmarca.

While this contestation is obvious between Hatúnmarca and Tunánmarca, it also can be seen in the relationship between Umpamalca and Tunánmarca. Although the ceramics and lithics suggest regular exchange, the botanical evidence infers a different mode of interaction. The plant data, with more maize at Umpamalca, present a complex view of Umpamalca in fact not being completely dominated economically or politically by Tunánmarca, amplifying the sense of constant political negotiation between many local leaders or would-be leaders (*curacas*, *cinchekona*) and their populace (Smith 1989). While in some domains leaders would have successfully gained or maintained new management status, they did so only in certain realms, within the structures of reciprocity, kinship, and religion, the accepted domains of hierarchy. They never became economically differentiated enough to become consumers only. Therefore, at Tunánmarca, as at Umpamalca, the second possibility proposed above obtained: every household still produced crops at least for themselves, but some, the elites, also received extra labor and goods.

Concluding the Wanka II evidence for agricultural production, Tunánmarca seems to have been producing intensively as well as receiving food from nearby northern sites, managed through some form of multi-site political structure. Umpamalca was probably intensively farming to meet its population's requirements, and seems also to have traded for and/or obtained crops competitively from outside its territory. The elites were involved in more options than the non-elites at both sites. What alliances were evident in the Wanka I era were transformed into a more centralized network in the Wanka II. Yet the Sausa were not consolidated within one political entity; the leaders at neither Hatúnmarca nor Tunánmarca dominated all the sites. Even if ceramic, metal, and lithic goods demonstrate a sense of elite control, Wanka II agricultural production was only selectively controlled, even if it was greatly intensified.

Discussion

One conclusion to be gained from these comparisons is that pre-Hispanic farmers, like modern ones, do not always produce for the maximum yield possible, yet there is a case for them attempting to produce effectively on the land they have available while minimizing labor. Further, I suggest that the paleoethnobotanical data illustrate evidence for different agricultural strategies in use through time. EIP/MH people, for example, seemed to be farming near to their settlements with a mix of valley and hill-side crops, focusing on the land that yielded well for the smallest amount of labor, with no evidence for pressure on land. The settlement pattern and the botanical data suggest that the residents preferred to farm on the low hillsides, avoiding periodic valley frosts and inundations. They lived at the edge of a grassy shrubland–marshland.

In the Wanka I Period, production strategies continued to be a mix of valley land and hillsides with more sites having more land in the uplands. When the population grew, sites clustered into spatially discrete groups, increasing the focus on the valley lands. This is not a case of land-use pressure per se, but suggests an interest in certain valley fields and/or crops, especially maize. This is supported by the new maize varieties entering the region or locally developed at this time as well as the new ways to process them. More effort would have gone into valley fields, as farmers cleared off the grasslands and drained the marshes.

In LeBlanc's (1981) discussion of the social setting in the Wanka II, she suggests that a desire for settlement defense played a critical role in the move to the hilltop sites. Increased pressure to aggregate was surely at work even in the Wanka I and is seen in several aspects of society. Associated with these cultural transformations is evidence for a new degree of unequal status within the population. Based on this supporting evidence, I propose that the Wanka II move reflects political and social coercion rather than an empirical need for increased production.

The latter evidence suggests that the Sausa might have been fighting over access to certain lands, and these were most likely the valley lands, as they tried to build their developing political alliances. Given that there was a cooling trend beginning by at least AD 1300, dampening all yields, it is not hard to imagine even more pressure on warm valley lands participating in the political escalation. This scenario gives us a view of increased pressure on certain lands while at the same time no pressure on arable land resources at the regional level. Economic pressure is not a sufficient explanation for the growing tensions between the clusters of settlements.

Somewhat poignantly for the Sausa inhabitant, the settlement relocation was double-edged. While there was enough arable land for produce, this was not the picture painted by the burgeoning elite. First, pressure for certain lands could have been heightened by the increased need for certain symbols of power, such as maize. These lands could have been fought over in order for the leadership to have more maize to give as beer in "reciprocal exchange" to allies and warriors to maintain their allegiance. The desire for increased social identity and alliances to "protect" would have created a spiral of pressure on the valley lands and labor for cloth making, metal work, or agriculture. The normal family would end up giving much more labor than previously to participate in this cycle of political escalation.

This dialectic between socio-politics, and economy was heightened with the move upslope, making the pressure on agricultural production more intense. With the radical settlement reorientation in the Wanka II, we see the social–political clusters altered, such that previously separate villages came together within one settlement. This and the relocation into defensive positions created a new dynamic also between the people and their landscape. This reorientation brought new levels of labor intensity in agricultural production.

If the valley lands had been important to the Sausa, it is ironic that the prime valley lands of the past became virtually inaccessible to the northern Wanka II alliance. Larger groups were linked in production and were dependent on centralized decisions and managers. While overall pressure on agriculture did not seem to force the change seen in the Wanka II, the settlement change and associated politics activated the initiation of a very different agriculture production system for the Sausa.

Political effects are visible in Wanka II agricultural production, especially if tribute and long-distance exploitation was intensified, as Murra (1972) has suggested for the Lupaqa at the same time. Given that the crop-production evidence shows markedly different crop frequencies from the territory yield predictions, it can be proposed that the communities or perhaps the leadership altered the production strategies substantially. Accompanying the local intensive production was aggressive war and tribute extraction, exploiting and defending fields or farmers in more distant territories, or perhaps even dictating what crops should be produced. In other words, while positions of control might have been created through social means, these positions were based on power over resources.

The data suggest that the Sausa did not need to move into the uplands because of pressure on local resources. Rather, the real pressure for land transpired after the move. In other words, what selective pressure on land had been occurring was exacerbated by the move. I conclude therefore that the move up occurred because of political decisions. In this case, it is not environmental resources, population density, or lack of food that escalated cultural change but a series of other events that reformed the populations' politics. These new political expectations, along with agricultural tensions, contributed to the development of the sorts of inequality that existed as community leaders expanded their spheres of coordination, decision making and coercion.

12

Defending the heights

In the process of investigating the history of the Sausa peoples I have discussed a series of current issues in archaeological thought. I approach interpretation in a new way by including cultural principles and the role of power negotiation in political change. To complete an in-depth analysis of change, I have concentrated on the role of agricultural production and its relationship to the political, social, and economic dynamics within society. The idea behind discussing Sausa agriculture was not to present just another example of hierarchical development and its economics but to provide a closer look at the daily life pressures, desires, and negotiations of people undergoing a type of political centralization. The Sausa example cannot tell us everything about political hierarchy but I hope that it makes clear how we can explain cultural trends more meaningfully than by predicting the effects of "prime movers" or disassociating structures from their on-going culture.

Presenting archaeological data, historical evidence, and ethnographically derived cultural principles, I have illustrated different interests operating within society through the tasks that were undertaken. While every data set does not represent a different interest group, by developing the cultural implications of each set of data and weaving these together through the sequence, small changes and dynamics are visible. Social relations begin to be evident as daily practices are linked to the data and then brought together to form a larger picture. One can get a sense of changes in autonomy and control from answering questions such as who produced what, who had access to what, where did people live, what type of communal labor projects did they initiate, how different were the family sizes, how intensive were the agricultural systems and what types of equality and inequality existed in the society.

Archaeologists are beginning to be aware that they should try to include more than one group's perspective to gain a better sense of the different pressures that were present. The more orientations that are brought into the argument the more robust will be the picture of change. Traditionally, archaeologists tend to describe societies from the elite point of view, focusing most research on the increasing controls over resources and labor. I too have discussed elites' increasing control and manipulation of the cultural system and how they might have used the principles of balance and hierarchy to gain power. However, this is a partial view.

In an increasingly unequal situation, while non-elites may at times go along with the dominant ideology and participate in the elite system, they may at other times try not to participate at every ritual or in every battle; they may trade in their own networks, or even try to initiate activities separately from the leaders. In times of change the non-elite may resist new and different activities put forward by the elite; they may have different views as to what should be done and different opinions about constraints and restructurings. They will act in their own best interests to enhance their position. Both consensus and conflict will occur as the groups vie to enhance their own self-interest.

I have tried to note alternative goals and constraints when evident in the data but this is a hard task. I have identified and discussed the activities where contesting groups might be visible in the archaeological record, such as organized agricultural projects, access to goods of value as well as basics, access to exchange, access to labor, and feasting. When these activities can be indicated in the record, evidence of differential participation is noted. For example, in the Wanka II times households contained different amounts of exotic goods. This difference suggests that some people traded more outside the *ayllu*, traveled more, or desired more of these items.

Power

The main mechanism of change is seen as power. At the same time that power is fluid and can be non-material, it is ever-present. Channels for increasing power will be formed in the particular social principles of a society. As elites, big men, chiefs, shamans, and other people who perform special tasks for a group come into existence, their powers must be socially constituted and legitimated through these principles. Some ideologies and associated social actions therefore will be more acceptable than others. And given the world view of a group, some paths to power will not be possible: despite the vast population conquered by the Inka of Cuzco, they never abandoned a political organization based on kinship and *ayllus* for the purely bureaucratic structure that we associate with state powers.

Social power can be directed in many different ways, leading to recursive change in both the capacity to control and its accompanying responsibilities (Gramsci 1971). When civic positions are growing in power, there is conflict and negotiation inherent in the relationship. But this is only the first hurdle. The holders of power must also maintain their positions. Remaining in power does not require the same strategy as becoming a leader. Hence, in the power creation I associate with the Wanka I, we see hints of specialization, increased risk/protection, and a focus on certain crops. After the resettlement we see a heightened focus on warfare, labor intensive activities, special architecture, and allegiance building that did not exist in Wanka I. These new activities suggest an extra effort to solidify the newly formed positions.

The study of power increases the importance of the cultural setting in understanding the past, not only of what went before but what was important or of value in that culture. Because different cultural settings and principles (structures) direct the choices and actions people have, they shape the forms of power relations that can occur through time. These cultural principles will inform us about why some political or social developments arise and others do not. While there is a group of "cultures" in any one society, some cultural trajectories will not occur due to the styles of behavior in the past. These cultural principles are important not only because they channel behavior, but they are continually recreated through people's actions and relations.

That is, the past is in a dialectic relation with the living people, creating change and continuities while hampering and directing potentials for development.

Great shifts in political organizations that have been called evolutionary stages or cultural transformations (Service 1962, 1975) can be understood in new ways if we focus on the actions and the practices of daily life in both the domestic and the civic/ritual arena. Power dynamics can be studied in both small and large changes within societies by focusing on increasing differences. One major transformation discussed here is the fairly rapid but not uniform change seen in the archaeological record during the Late Intermediate Period. I called this manifestation a power vacuum. I think this type of social change is quite common in human society and deserves a closer look in archaeology.

This type of rapid cultural change can come about in different ways, but it tends to occur sometime after a breakup or readjustment of distant but influential political hegemonies and their alliances. These external powers did not necessarily have any direct control on the local residents, that is, they did not rule or politically dictate local actions. Nevertheless, when their associated large loose networks, relationships, and even ideologies are destroyed or reformulated, there is a ripple of realignment throughout a wide area (Wallerstein 1974). After such a collapse, local–outside relations become "empty," so that new people or interest groups may enter and reform them (Foucault 1980). Every local population must react in some way if only to shore up its relations with its neighbors. This realignment of local power and ideology will happen relatively quickly and will be internally generated as new alliances are formed (Marcus 1989). These changes often occur in small-scale societies that, after the collapse of external powers, at least for a time become more centralized, encompass a larger population, have a stronger ethnic identity (and/or more interest groups), are more aggressive, or produce more intensively. A rush to fill the empty positions is made and in this, as Foucault notes, new powers can then be created and interpreted. Depending on the use of this new, accessible power created from and channeled through the cultural principles, we might see increased power in various cultural domains.

In the past, archaeologists have claimed that this type of change is due primarily to population increase. But there is enough evidence now to show that production intensification and political change do not always track with population change, nor is population growth innate, as illustrated in the Neolithic or the Bronze Age of Europe (Cowgill 1975; Sheratt 1981; Thomas 1988). The type of action initiated by a power vacuum is a combination of regional and internal adjustments. For example, pan-regional alterations can trigger rivalries between two age classes or moieties, such that younger rebels gain a voice and call up new versions of a principle to support new claims to power (Mallon pers. comm.). This means that large internal power alignments can be instigated by small external changes if residents act on them and tap into the local cultural principles. In this way, pressure on land and labor may increase not because of population growth, conquest, or even competition, but because new nodes of power and demand are legitimated within certain cultural frameworks that reorient land-use.

As I have demonstrated here, Andean cultural principles contained elements that could be used to gain power through the concepts of hierarchy, opposition, and reciprocity, given situations where the principles could be called upon. From the Andean archaeological sequence we know that this increase in power occurred many times within the different cultural groups, such as Wari, Nazca, and Moche. But each time it was manifested in different ways as the local populations used their indigenous principles to reform crucial relations into new powerful positions. By close scrutiny, we can see the variations in each political theme, although all of them used the mechanism of power to change their social relations.

Finally, I have connected these social relations of power to the material arenas of society. The social cannot be defined without reference to the material world. It is not enough simply to say that groups wanted more exchange or leaders wanted more food and so political hierarchies were formed (Bender 1978; Hayden 1990). Nor can one say that the innate population increase in a diverse, productive environment caused agricultural intensification and surplus production (Sanders and Price 1968). Neither position is sufficient. Social values alone do not transform a social order, they must be acted upon by humans. Social acts based on desire use labor to transform the world. And in so doing they create the domains and capacities of their environment. While climate and technology may influence what can be produced from an environment, as important is the value and perception of the environment by the people. Many studies show how different cultures use and extract different resources and yields out of the same environment based on their views of the world. The example in this book does not just involve different technologies or a changing environment but includes the different relationships humans have within their environment in politically different settings. We should try to see how the material world participated in change through the cultural principles that shaped the use of the landscape. In the case of the Sausa, we see the major political change linked to changes in certain labor projects, the glue between the landscape and the social world.

Based on the range of data presented in the previous chapters, emerging political inequalities are suggested in pre-Inkaic times. They are reflected in settlement demography, agricultural land-use, artifact production and distribution, trade, and the use of the principles of hierarchy and balance. The social alliances that were developing in Wanka I, seen in the site clusters within the tributary valleys, escalated to more consolidated and visible power in Wanka II. Yet in Wanka II there is still evidence of a balance or check in the diverse powers. In this example we have a population becoming more unequal as the jurisdictions of power expand and become more visible in the archaeological record.

Notions of power within archaeological inquiry focus on its fluidity and relational qualities. As Foucault (1980) states, power must have a base and from that base roles or positions are created. Once these positions are created they must be reinterpreted by the individuals involved. This is the crux of power in human society. That is, power is inherent within all actions but it is how it is called up, manipulated, used or not used that creates increasing or decreasing inequality. Bourdieu's (1977) theory of practice shows how by daily tasks and interactions power can be consolidated, exercised, or dissipated by individuals. It is through these actions that cultural difference is created. At some times power is evidenced in the struggle between groups, at other times it constitutes public consent. Discussing power at such a general level of inquiry does not help us very much with our research questions, however. By focusing on the more specific ways power can be used within cultures we can begin to watch how it is channeled in societal change.

The modern notions of power started with the concept of conflict (Marx 1971). More recently, having power has been envisaged as including the qualities of enabling, controlling, and acting on ability (Foucault 1980; Giddens 1979; Weber 1968). It does not always have to be sinister, nor is it theoretically limited. While power is present throughout all parts of society, it does seem to be constantly restricted as different groups contest over its extent. Power grows out of tensions between people at the boundaries of common practice. In political arenas it has the capacity to create legitimated inequalities between groups of people. Power can be centralized in any domain of society (Giddens 1979). In each society some domains are more sensitive to power consolidation than others. It is in these specific parts of a culture that we will see the dynamics of both increased control or coercion in conjunction with increased responsibility: the two sides of power. The result can be either a balanced, constrained power or an aggrandizing one (Gramsci 1973).

How do we identify this power? Concepts such as contestation and negotiation represent acts of power but these are hard to identify in any setting. Power must be thought of in more concrete ways. Here, I have chosen to think of it in terms of differential control, decision making, and access to goods, labor, and activities that can be identified with certain cultural values in the Andes. By studying the internal changes seen in the data that represent these relations, we can label the cultural practices and the material constraints involved, and discuss where power seemed to be enhanced or transformed. The change will not be uniform throughout all aspects of a culture but with scrutiny of many data sets we can get a closer view. No longer do we have one locus for change within a society, since change occurs at many levels and affects people differently.

A critique of cultural evolution models as explanations for political change

The study of complexity and the rise of stratified society has been one of the most common archaeological concerns this century. Most models tend to conclude with one explanation for such a transformation. Archaeologists have continued to feel uncomfortable with these singular models, however, as a satisfying explanation eludes them. Viewing several of these traditional explanatory models in light of the information presented here, we can see how they each fall short of providing the understanding we seek. Our methodological revolution as well as our search for new approaches to the past has had an impact and should provide more information and a better sense of what might have occurred. I have not completed the quest for the explanation of the onset of inequality. But I hope the ideas presented here that focus on the active principle of power and its various enabling and constraining aspects may be an alternative for explaining political change. They allow us to see that it is insufficient to look only at one or two prime movers.

The traditional causes put forward for political hierarchy development discussed in the archaeological literature roughly fall into the following categories: (1) adaptation to ecological diversity, leading to production specialization and control of resource redistribution (Sanders 1956; Sanders and Price 1968; Service 1962); (2) innate population growth and ultimately pressure within a circumscribed area requiring organization to prevent food stress and/or warfare (Carneiro 1970; Cohen 1977); (3) warfare (Carneiro 1970; Haas 1982); (4) the need for managerial organization in agriculture or other production (Marx 1904; Wittfogel 1957; Wright 1969); and (5) specialized production and control of prestige goods (Brumfiel 1976; Earle 1978; Rowlands 1980). While there are elements of each of these participating in the Sausa sequence, none of the models adequately explains the changes seen in the data.

(1) Ecological diversity is a fact of life for the Sausa, yet the paleoethnobotanical data suggest that people did not focus on production specialization, intensification, interzone food exchange, or redistribution at the onset of change, as would be assumed by Sanders and Price (1968). What specialization did occur, first seen in the Wanka I ceramic distributions and in the spatially discrete crop preferences, was redundant in the different valleys and was never centralized at any time. This same redundancy was also found in the Hawaiian chiefdoms (Earle 1978). In addition, village populations did not expand beyond very local land-use production until their move upslope into a more restricted and isolated area and even then they were still locally oriented. The crop distributions suggest that the political boundaries dictated much of the crop choice. The botanical production evidence does not suggest a development of specialization in crops and intersite exchange.

Rather, local production evolved autonomously until the Wanka II Period, with more centralized control only over certain production technologies and only after the increased decision-making powers were evident. This is seen in the example of Tunánmarca, which required northern ally lands for subsistence but still only received what was available from their territories. Further, local cropping is demonstrated by the fact that the crop mix at Umpamalca is different from that at Tunánmarca. The details of these site differences suggest that agricultural organization was in part at the settlement level while production remained at the household level. Redistribution was not centralized, nor did it really exist except symbolically as feasting foods.

(2) A second very powerful argument for change, both for the development and for the collapse of stratified societies, is population growth (Cohen 1977). Population is most often linked to increasing lack of resources. While population growth did occur in the Andes, the socially constituted constraints on access probably had a greater impact on human/land relationships than the actual numbers of people within any region. Pressure on resources is not evident in the data except selectively, resulting from an interest in the valley lands. The move uphill does not seem to have been due to population pressure on the resources, for if it was they would have moved south into the Mantaro Valley. From the data comparisons in Chapter 11 there is little suggestion that a population density limit (carrying capacity) had been reached at the sites analyzed before the Wanka II demographic change occurred. Population size of a polity is important only in relation to broad organizational features. More likely, it seems that population and land-use pressure arose from changes in political

requirements. In this case a series of regional changes and local unrest allowed the new prominence of war leaders. Their actions included increased defense of people and agricultural or pastoral land, increased interest in valley agriculture and its products, and increased social/ritual feasting, all of which participated in the reformulation of the population and political centralization.

As opposed to Gilman's (1981) model for leadership in the Bronze Age, which stresses intensification of agriculture coming first out of population pressure and then the need for leaders to defend the agricultural systems in the landscape, the Sausa data suggest that leaders arose due to a series of political and social events, that then resulted in intensive agriculture.

Demographic change is more of an indicator of new pressures and political change, reflected here in the new political decisions that restructured the type of settlement the Sausa lived in: seen in the Wanka II settlements that maintained 15,000 or 20,000 people, rather than the earlier settlements of approximately 1000 to 5000. Without this aggregation, the region as a whole could have easily supported the Wanka II population. There were, however, increasing cultural pressures on land that accompanied the changes we see in the settlements. As the size of the political groups increased, economic and social distinctions between rulers and followers became evident (cf. Earle 1987; Trigger pers. comm.).

Scale is important in political organization. Population size can be linked to political and managerial capacities, such as increasing social sanctions to maintain order in a large community, intracommunity networking to organize settlement-wide rituals, or warrior coordination for inter-alliance battles over defense and resource-use. Yet, if the groups brought together have a history or a tradition of independence, as the Sausa seem to have had, it will be difficult to mobilize radical changes in the political structure without force. While inequalities could and did develop, they did so in the guise of maintaining balance and were probably continuously curtailed.

(3) Warfare is often considered an important component of the population growth model. Warring is a regular phenomenon in the Andes, for it has been an important social act that maintains regional relations between political different groups. This is seen in *tinku*, still practiced today in Bolivia (Arnold pers. comm.; Bastien pers. comm.; Platt 1987; Chapter 3). War is attested also in the early iconography at Formative Sechin Bajo and in the EIP human front-faced figurines at Pancán, and later in Middle Horizon Tiawanaku, and Wari trophy heads. War can be a socially regulating, equilibrating act, but it can also be expansionistic and aggressive (cf. Carneiro 1970; Haas 1982). As a locus for change and increased power, domination over others can transpire through increases in the frequency and intensity of battle (*ch'axwa*). This expansionistic war is best illustrated in the kingdom of Moche, Chimu, and the Inka, but I am sure that it occurred in other cultural settings at different times throughout the Andes (Chapter 3). Relations between competitors must break down for war to switch from being regulatory to expansionist.

When such an escalation occurs warfare requires increased leadership, group identity, and discipline. When war is expansionistic the more people (adult males and family representatives) are able to fight, the more powerful the group and its leaders.

Thus it is not surprising that war leaders, once in a stronger position, tried to perpetuate war while expanding their ranks and family ties (i.e. negotiating the situation at hand to expand their powers). They would try to keep tensions alive to keep that access to power legitimate and open. The fact that they could do so informs us about the political setting of the time.

It can be suggested in the Late Intermediate times, that the pan-Andean power vacuum and the restructuring of the local alliances triggered an escalation of local warfare. This warfare was then maintained by the war leaders until ultimately they reorganized the social groups in later Late Intermediate times. Many historic documents allude to this pattern.

For the Sausa, warfare probably was a major nexus of political change throughout their whole history. And for the Wanka II people, warfare was linked to population aggregation, political reformulation, as well as access to land for agriculture. The Wanka II war leaders aggressively tried to gain and maintain laborers and land to meet their own *ayllu*'s production needs. I conclude this from the Wanka II site agricultural production calculation discrepancies when compared to the estimated population's needs (Chapter 11). In addition, in the interviews documented by Toledo (1940) (Chapter 6) we learned how the local territories would not have supported the settlement's population and leaders were eager to conquer new lands for agriculture.

Earlier, in the EIP/MH and Wanka I phases, if warfare was involved in more than conflict resolution, there is no evidence for its use in land appropriation or settlement hierarchy, suggesting that warfare at that time was mainly linked to community maintenance, settling intercommunity disputes, and predicting the upcoming year's harvest. In other words, warfare had primarily a stabilizing managerial influence (Alencastre and Dumézil 1953; Delgado pers. comm.). In Wanka II times, warfare became a more concrete form of negotiation as people lived in a landscape of defensiveness. I propose that local warfare was then linked to land gain because of the new interests in certain lands, created by the resettlement (Chapter 5). While warfare became an important nexus for power gain, I think it was used because of its meaning and place within society, not because of population pressure.

(4) Managerial organization of agriculture leading to hierarchy is difficult to identify in the form described by Wittfogel (1957). What we can see is that agricultural technologies reflect political organization, but that does not mean the technology drives the politics. There are many places in the Andes where field organization reflects social organization. Sherbondy (1982) presents a cogent discussion of how the use and maintenance of irrigation canals near Cuzco parallels the political organization, as the canals define and separate opposing political lineages. We do have some evidence for field organization in the Sausa region. It is fair to suggest that there was some selective centralized agricultural organization in the Wanka II times seen in the intercommunity canal and stone-lined terraces associated with some settlements. The upland canals in particular were of a larger scale than the community based sectoral systems present today. But, as Chapter 11 shows, these larger-scale canals seem to have occurred after the move uphill, after a series of political changes.

Community field allocation should have operated in all periods and could have become a locus of power if a person or subgroup gained more control over the land allocation decisions or differential access to them, or gained more fields outside of the system. There is little evidence suggesting such aggrandizing occurred in the earlier phases, either in the agricultural feature evidence or in the botanical data. Pre-Wanka II agricultural intensification technologies requiring community organization could include the raised fields and, less likely, the step-slope terraces. Neither of these strategies needs to go beyond a village or *ayllu* level organization as they do not today in areas where sectoral organization is practiced. The site demographics and the paleoethnobotanical frequencies (Chapter 10) suggest that the terraces were under cultivation in EIP/MH and Wanka I times.

From what we know about the pre-Inka Sausa agricultural systems, such as the step-slope terraces, all fields were probably community owned and distributed, therefore requiring group agreement for individual access. There is not as much evidence for raised field use in the EIP/MH as there is in the Wanka I phase. These drained systems required some group coordination to keep the canals clear, as we have learned from the Lake Titicaca basin field rehabilitation projects conducted by Erickson (1985; 1988), Kolata (1986), and Rivera Sundt. In the Wanka I, therefore, we see an agricultural nexus for power consolidation in the intensive farming of the valleys.

The management of the upland canals with their multiple settlement destinations, as well as the possible need for defense of far-ranging fields, do suggest some centralized organization of agriculture in the Wanka II period, but this does not encompass much of the agricultural system, leaving most production management to small group organization.

Even in Wanka II times, therefore, agricultural strategies would not have needed a higher authority to function, while at the same time there were strategies that could have been set up by a centralized management. Leaders could have attempted to use these agricultural projects (controlling water and organizing labor) as a nexus for increasing their power by negotiating to transfer their power into other domains. Mediated through control of local agriculture as well as community well-being, local leaders could have gained more access to labor and land, mediated through the ideology of kinship and reciprocity.

As Cobo wrote about colonial-era local leaders, no leaders owned more than was needed to support their families (1956, XCII: 121). But a family may include a leader's whole *ayllu* in certain circumstances (Smith 1989). While communal land was allocated to families, if a leader could negotiate a shared identity to mean that he was the head of a larger family, the whole *ayllu* became his family. The leader thus used ideological means to gain access to a great deal for himself, even in the communal lands. Everyone in an *ayllu* exchanged labor with neighbors and kin, and leaders, requesting help (*mañay*) with their harvest, could enlist many more people, calling upon many reciprocities for these civic duties.

(5) Specialized production of valuables (Brumfiel 1976) and control of prestige goods (Rowlands 1980) is hinted at in the inventory of the Wanka II elite house compounds. Again, such evidence appears in the archaeological record after the relocation of the population. In other words it seems to be more linked to maintaining

status, or *being*, than to *becoming* hierarchical. Even then, in the case of the Sausa, the control of these valued goods is not strongly visible, although some products were made more often in the elite compounds. All excavated households seem to have had some access to all types of goods.

This is not a picture of total power over specialized production. There is no clear evidence for control of production and exchange, indentured craftsmen, or permanently inherited leadership positions. Further, evidence from the household excavations suggest that the elite also had to produce for themselves; they did not receive many goods ready-made, nor did their servants live apart, bringing finished products to their homes. The leaders too had to beg (*mañay*) female kin for help in feasts, from the *ayllu* for help in agricultural labor, from the alliance for help in battle. The documents propose that men continuously contested to gain authority by becoming *cinchekona*, thereby gaining power over decisions when to fight. These positions in turn linked them to land, labor, and goods dispersal, allowing them to expand out into other decision-making realms. The artifacts suggest that this power was checked, however, because while the richer households do have evidence for more feasts and ornaments of status, it does not seem that they monopolized these goods and in fact may have given most of them away in proper Andean reciprocal fashion.

Rather than increasing power through controlling goods, the ability to negotiate labor and reciprocity is more of an Andean path to power. Where inequality is most visible for the Sausa is in the differential access to labor in the household. Leaders' households certainly had more goods of higher value, but they also had more harder working residents, servants, and obliging kin. Heightened household production is tied to these laborers' help, which is based on the decision-making position and the social relations of the households. While control of specialized valuables might be an important nexus for power in some societies, it does not seem to have developed a critical position here (Helms 1979).

The central variables in these commonly invoked theories of hierarchical development (ecological diversity, population growth, warfare, agricultural management, specialized production of valuables, etc.) could all have participated in political development. But, given the data, each one by itself seems inadequate, and some of the causal variables do not seem to be supported.

Perhaps closer to explaining the onset of political inequality, because of their more in-depth focus on the internal dynamics of a culture undergoing change, are the newer models, such as peer polity interaction (Renfrew and Cherry 1986) and the epigenetic model (Freidman and Rowlands 1977). But these too are incomplete. While there were local peer polity relations that pressured the creation and maintenance of each Sausa alliance, I have tried to show here that this in itself would not have escalated into new political orders without the pan-Andean ruptures after the Middle Horizon. The regional archaeological data suggest that little political centralization had occurred before the Late Intermediate, as opposed to many other Andean areas where centralized polities came and went (e.g. the Moche River Valley or the Titicaca basin). The epigenetic model sees change developing out of the social structure; but this argument does not provide an active element of social action that instigates the change. While constituted and directed by the cultural principles, the action missing is the negotiation of social relations, which should be our focus in the study of change.

The onset of inequality in the Sausa region

EIP/MH

At the beginning of this temporal sequence we see evidence of production at the household level. The dispersed autonomous villages look as if they are made up of a series of households, each of which directly controls its own production, depending on a full range of local resources. In this situation, specializing in certain products or activities increases risk, since it limits control over access to one's needs. If households lose control over their access they will have to expend much more energy to meet basic needs.

In EIP/MH times the inhabitants seem to have been able to produce what they needed locally, meeting their needs by growing the most productive crops near their homes at a low labor input in an extensive system. Their location gave them a mix of warmer valley lands and hillsides, tailored to the particular conditions in the specific valleys. Estimates of population food requirements compared to the optimal potential of the land for the two sampled sites further suggest that the residents did not have to incorporate most of their land into production to meet their dietary needs. Therefore, while they were very local farmers and herders, they did not intensively farm. Neither labor nor land seem to have been scarce and no major labor projects are associated with these sites.

Politically the evidence reflects a situation of autonomous, neighbor and kin based relations, using labor exchange when necessary while maintaining social integration through familial rituals that did not seem to include elaborate or large gatherings outside the domestic area. The household-level rituals are suggested by the many animal burials and *illa* stone figurines uncovered within the excavated house compounds.

The styles of the artifacts excavated from the sites suggest that while they are Andean, they are not elaborate and therefore did not entail a great deal of labor or specialist craftsmanship. Nor do the ceramics allude to specific connotations of larger social associations as did the earlier ceramics in the Early Horizon. Some Early Horizon ceramics in the Mantaro region were very similar to the Chavín types, suggesting some sort of interregional dynamic (Hastorf et al. 1989; Matos Mendieta 1972). The EIP/MH Huacrapukio-style ceramics continued more or less unchanged for a long time, demonstrating steady local inter-household relationships before and during the Middle Horizon.

While we still do not know the extent of influence of the Wari hegemony in the northern Mantaro Valley, all data suggest that the influence was not direct. The few Wari ceramics and the lack of foreign architecture frames a picture suggesting that the Wari might have passed by regularly along the Mantaro River and up the western gorge to travel north or west from the southern Mantaro Valley. In this scenario the local Sausa might have exchanged basic foodstuffs and other items with them. I propose this because more Wari sherds and vessels were found in the Mantaro gorge to the west of the Sausa lands than within the valley lands. The local ceramics in particular do not show Wari influence nor radical stylistic change during the Middle Horizon. The other visible traits also show little effect, although there is the rebuilding of Wari Willka in the southern valley. Despite this ephemeral evidence there was enough influence to initiate a series of reactions when the Wari polity collapsed.

At the end of the Middle Horizon, even without conquest of the Sausa, the breakup of this broad sphere of interaction would have created imbalances in local relations such as trading networks, as well as in the triangulation of peer polity balance between neighboring groups. These abandoned relations could have become locations where people with new goals entered the political arena. People acted on these imbalances to readjust their community's standing, and so we see a series of changes in Late Intermediate times.

Wanka I

The broad reverberation and realignment of polities at the end of the Middle Horizon in some way altered aspects of local government in the Late Intermediate Period across the Andes. As Earles and Silverblatt (1978) point out, with the collapse of Wari in the central Andes there was a general political–economic ripple of fragmentation throughout the highlands and the coast, causing all local ethnic groups to reform into more discrete entities. Local groups became engaged in differentiating themselves from their neighbors. This "nationalism" suggests a range of internal political adjustments to the external economic breakdown.

A similar reaction to such a power vacuum is noted by historians in the early days after the Spanish arrival. Local ethnic leaders contested in the colonial courts for previously Inka controlled land. By reaffirming their ethnic differences with the Inka and their neighbors, the leaders claimed they were the rightful local leaders (Smith 1989).

While no one has yet sorted out exactly why and how Wari and Tiawanaku dissipated, the cause for their collapse could have been a combination of internal managerial overextensions as well as external pressures from unrest, war, disrupted exchange routes, and other local political shifts (Isbell and Schreiber 1978; Shady and Ruiz 1979). It does seem clear that interconnected networks disappeared as what economic stability had existed fragmented. This dissolution required realignments of each group's position, adjusting and reassessing allies and enemies.

This shake up (or what I call power vacuum) must have caused a crisis but it also formed new possibilities. Different reactions occurred throughout the highlands, as noted materially and demographically in the central Andes (Hyslop 1979; Lavallée 1973; Rostworowski 1972; Spalding 1984; Thompson 1971). The new dynamics in internal relations and the restructuring of old interregional relations set the stage for increased consolidation of local groups. In the northern Mantaro Valley there was heightened ethnic identity, selective agricultural intensification, and increased local exchange. In other words, while the instabilities led to increased political hierarchy, compared to the Late Intermediate Inka, Lupaqa, or Qolla, change for the Sausa was slight. All changes, however, culminated in the movement of towns into "higher places" associated with much fighting, as mentioned by Guaman Poma de Ayala (1944: 64). These eventualities suggest the importance of war throughout the Late Intermediate Period. Though not clearly visible in the record at this time, *tinku* probably became more common over time, increasingly becoming a locus of tension and manipulation.

The onset of increasing material and social interaction and specialization between nearby villages is also suggested in the Wanka I settlement clusters located in the tributary valleys. This trajectory is interpreted from the more restricted ceramic exchanges and the beginning of more regular color and temper in the ceramic assemblages when compared to the earlier phase. The ceramic designs became simpler, accompanying a decrease in the earlier painted Huacrapukio style. There are many more unpainted wares (52 percent of the assemblage at Pancán; Hastorf et al. 1989: 98), although functional types do not change in frequency (Hastorf and Johannessen n.d.; LeCount 1987). LeCount (in Hastorf et al. 1989) suggests that this decrease in variability and complexity coincides with fewer locations of production. This means that, unlike before, not every household or village is making pottery. The individual Wanka I households that were sampled do not show radical material differentiation amongst themselves, however.

The Wanka I botanical data suggest that farming occurred close to the settlements but required increased labor inputs. The two sampled settlements yielded crops at the same frequencies as the regional average, mixing the use of the two main production zones. The paleoethnobotanical data follow these trends, yet there are hints of valley intensification with increased maize, legumes, and quinoa production. This is especially evident at Pancán, where the mix of land-use zones is very similar to the earlier phase. It is possible that the raised fields were in use in Wanka I, if only because the wetland taxa are more common on the sites, and the settlements hover around the edge of the valleys as they cluster in larger multi-settlement, loosely affiliated groups. This raised field system would require some periodic management of the main canals in and out of the field complexes, suggesting one reason for the increased evidence of intervillage cooperation.

Further support for agricultural intensification comes from the shrinking differences between the population estimates and the optimal potential yields for the Wanka I territories. Overall, the data suggest that the populations could have managed farming on their local fields but would have invested more labor per unit area than previously. This increased cropping could have met the larger population's requirements in addition to supporting intensified social relations arising in each valley.

There is greater focus on valley agriculture. This is suggested not just because of the higher than expected maize frequencies at Ushnu, the increase in maize varieties, and many more stone hoes, but also because there are high densities of wetland wild seeds present in the structures. Some of the new maize varieties in particular can be associated with beer brewing and consuming, highly valued activities for cementing social contracts, providing reciprocal food for labor, and feasting to gain allegiance.

Feasting and food exchange for labor using maize beer is an Andean cultural principle that opens up a range of powers to the providers. Having enough maize beer and organizing a proper feast or ritual not only gains prestige and moral position for the hosts, but the latter gain access to the mountain spirits, since maize beer is a lubricant that opens communications between all things. While these activities also may have occurred earlier, the archaeological data suggest that maize beer use was called up increasingly more often through the Late Intermediate Period.

This example illustrates how subtle shifts in Sausa agriculture can become part of political transformations, and especially of the reciprocal negotiations involved in feasting. Besides developing new political relations, these agricultural shifts also promoted a more risky economic situation as people became less self-sufficient, although there was still quite a high degree of agricultural autonomy.

Whatever the extent of negotiations for increased power, there was enough resistance so that the resulting power was not consolidated in Wanka I times when compared to the later evidence. But what changes there were suggest that the communities were beginning to live in a more risky world, having to expend more effort to maintain new political and demographic relations.

Mechanisms for community regulation and balance, seen in the reciprocities of both *tinku* and maize feasting, can also be used for community expansion. By alluding to societal needs and calling upon existing nested reciprocities, larger units can be built into a hierarchy while still operating under the "same principle of equality". That is, using the concept of balanced opposition or *yanantin*, tensions can be mediated to naturalize difference while hierarchy is actually escalating.

At times, increased hierarchy does not have to be achieved by force and might even be welcomed (in a form of consensus). But an increasing threat of force, as is suggested in the Wanka I evidence with the building of new settlements on the hillsides, can also channel decisions towards certain ends, despite dissent within a community. The evidence for heightened local interaction implies increased interest in community solidarity. Perhaps this was needed in the wake of the Middle Horizon collapse. Or perhaps increased interaction between communities stimulated aggression. The evidence suggests that the domains of power were expanding and prompting the reformulation of local identities. Whatever the initial cause, group solidarity was more manifest than before. But within this community solidarity and common defence, such new boundedness required people to give up more of their autonomy than had been the case previously and live more consciously in the nested hierarchies.

Social balance may have been maintained through the reciprocity and dualism implicit in cyclical work obligations, in the exchange of work for cooked and special food, and in *tinku* fighting. But there was also the potential for negotiating new dominance and hierarchy under the guise of balanced reciprocity. The cultural and social principles legitimated hierarchy through *yanantin*. Traditional mechanisms such as *tinku* and maize beer feasting became the channels for inequalities to develop in certain domains. The political differences initiated in Wanka I times escalated and became more visible in Wanka II.

Wanka II

Evidence of increased centralized power is the hallmark of this period. The expanding social contacts seen in Wanka I did more than relocate and protect the Wanka II population. They formed new political groups, illustrated in the stunning Wanka II site hierarchies and the planned dualism of the centers. Previous settlement architecture in the region did not have such a structured form, nor were there central plazas that could hold large gatherings of people. The style of the architecture was based on balanced opposition. If these plazas were used for gatherings, the process of unifying the aggregated groups would have been facilitated. One would expect that a series of new, larger rituals would also have been created to solidify group identity with individuals promoted into broader ritual positions (Atkinson 1990).

One might propose that the leaders expanded their authority to orchestrate such a transformation by building on the previous group gatherings of ancestor, mountain, and farming rituals to unite the new social order. Thus, through the negotiation of power with the ancestors, leaders could consolidate their positions using the familiar channels of ranked deities. In this way one might expect rituals to become more prominent as they legitimated leaders, tempered contestations, and condoned larger groups across the landscape. For example, the evidence for greater planting of *malki* (cultivated trees) can be tied to an increased appeal to ancestors to legitimate access to land, as *malki* trees are associated with *malki*, ancestors (Hastorf and Johannessen 1991).

In order to integrate and socialize the large population of Tunánmarca and Hatúnmarca, the dualism of the two districts and the central plazas were created by calling upon two important cultural principles, *yanantin* and hierarchy. The hierarchy and centralization of the aggregated population was justified and masked by the balance of the two large districts. The activation of these two Andean principles embodied *power to* coordinate a group of people but also *power over* thousands of people who participated in the relocation and construction of their settlement. The use of the principles is well illustrated in the demographic and architectural changes, especially the double settlement walls. These settlement walls and entrance checkpoints were created by the increased concern for defense. While warfare was probably real it was also manipulated to increase power, as mentioned in the historical documents, where the *cinchekona* attempted to propagate skirmishes to keep the tensions high, creating a need for their services.

Instigating battles occurred within the principle of balanced opposition (*yanantin*) as *tinku* was used to resolve conflicts between groups. *Tinku* can take place without increased control by either side because of the ritualized rules of conduct. But these rules are particularly vulnerable to alteration if tensions increase or individuals try to gain new authority. Individual participation and interests may shift within this activity such that more battles occur, or more claims are made in victory. In this way, powerful war leaders have the capacity to solidify their power.

There is evidence, both in the documents and in the artifactual remains, that this path to power was occurring during the Late Intermediate Period. Power through militarism can be limited to the battle arena, or, in the case of the Sausa, these powers can be reinterpreted, allowing the war leaders to expand their powers into other domains, such as organizing villages in a plan for protection. To do this, people's opinions had to be changed and labor organized. While this managerial power for war perhaps was eagerly requested by the people, it did not necessarily always lead to increased power in other domains. But in the Wanka II phase we see the architectural result, suggesting that the war leaders did in fact expand their powers outside the original nexus of the *tinku* sphere. This is an example of individuals negotiating one position to gain power in others.

The architecture displays beautifully, therefore, how hierarchy was established and legitimated within the guise of equality for the Sausa. The populace was brought together based on the duality of *yanantin* and *tinku*, but at the same time it was hierarchical as well. As the concept of balance was used to build the site, it also incorporated the hierarchical principle.

This same negotiation of hierarchy through the principle of balance is also seen in the agriculture of the Wanka II settlements. Agriculture was intensified, but not using just any scheme. This is highlighted by the multi-site canal system ending just south of Tunánmarca (Figure 4). The tension that was inherent within this hierarchical multi-site system was mediated by the two canals which joined just below Tunánmarca in a *tinku* union (Chapter 3). With their union, these two canals could allude to the principle of balanced duality.

Evidence from the Wanka II excavated deposits allows us to suggest in what cultural domains further differences were negotiated. Not all aspects of daily life changed. Certain nexes within society were more conducive to unequal power relations. Other activities showed a resistance and retention of autonomy.

Power was fluid and negotiated, as seen in the data from the commoner and elite house compounds. The new Wanka II leaders' power is evident in their access to more high-status items, but they did not have a monopolistic control of production and accumulation of wealth. The elites' position to negotiate increased power was not solid according to the evidence of daily life activities; we see little difference between the two statuses when looking for the traditional chiefly powers: control of specialized craft production and control of long-distance exchange. While the poorer people had fewer foreign and labor-intensive goods they did possess them. The commoners had control over their own agricultural production and labor, as all basic domestic tasks are represented in their compounds. Both statuses had farming, processing, and grinding tools, a full array of wild and domesticated animals as well as all crop types. The commoners also had access to and produced metals, seen in the evidence of smelting and the ornaments in deposits and burials. Both also had useful tools like needles and tweezers. The amount of decorative copper is almost identical between the two statuses (Figure 13).

Frequency indices of lithic blades, agricultural hoes (Russell 1988b), and ceramic wasters (Costin 1986) were the same in compounds of both statuses, although different pottery types were manufactured by different people. While the elites had more high-status goods such as metal jewelry, maize, camelid meat, and spindle whorls that reflect cloth manufacturing (Costin 1984), they did not have the only access to them.

All compounds had the full array of products (Costin and Earle 1989; Earle et al. 1987; Hastorf 1990a).

In both the artifactual data and the documents there are suggestions of Wanka II leaders (*curacas/cinchekona*) having servants (*yanakona*) who lived in their households and worked for them. The servants have also been called slaves, as if they might have been captured in battle. In either case, the elites had more domestic labor. Having servants or slaves fits with the increased level of activity we see in the artifactual densities of the elite houses. This is especially evident in increased food processing (chipped stone tools, animal bones), *chicha* brewing (grinding stones and maize), wool making (spindle whorls and worked llama long bones), and many more serving dishes. The elite too produced metal objects. None of these goods were of the quality to suggest that full-time specialists were producing them in the elite compounds from where they were distributed.

Therefore we see a class of people who had access to more labor, produced more of certain items, controlled decisions about certain activities, but did not control production. This combination of activities suggests that they did not control and manage all labor. What is more, the rich gave most of what they produced away. One of the main spheres of artifact difference between the two statuses is food preparation, storing, and consumption, suggesting that the elites gave more feasts in exchange for allegiance and authority. Another illustration of this is in the elites having larger cooking bowls than previously. This particular difference is an example of how agriculture is linked directly to the derivation of power in the Andes.

In fact the botanical, stable isotope, and artifactual distributions suggest that elites may have gained the products found in their household compounds by working harder, having extra labor through larger families and servants, as well as receiving gifts. They did not have attached craft specialists, nor had they escaped from their own domestic production and community participation. The financing of centralized (elite) activities is evident but in restricted domains of society, based on the main Andean nexes for prestige manipulation, food and drink. And even then, the non-elites retained autonomy in their household decisions. The elites had to work very hard for what they had gained themselves as well as begging for help to maintain it. But the prestige and authority gained in giving feasts could be used to organize fertility rituals, launch battles, maintain the moral order of the settlements, and perhaps keep the competition between groups active.

How agriculture fits in

Agriculture provides particularly important evidence for changes in power in the Sausa record, for it shows, among other things, how much the non-elites lost as differences grew. Agricultural production is the backbone of Andean society and all segments of society exist in relation to it. It is made up of land and labor, and changes in either alter the agricultural production and its associated meanings. Land-use is determined by demographics, historic boundaries, spiritual landscapes, ancestral connections, environmental conditions, as well as by the way people have chosen to organize their production. Because of this, agriculture is a nexus for manipulation of social power as production is organized socially and the products can be converted into social relations by distribution in exchange and feasts.

The Wanka I and the Wanka II botanical data show several radical shifts that give us an additional view of the Wanka II economic and political changes. At one level there is a change in the crop frequencies from Wanka I that correlates with the move to the upland knolls. While all crops are present, maize is much less common and tubers are substantially more common than before. This reflects the move upslope and is predictable if the residents were farming just around their settlement. But further elements of agricultural pressure are seen, especially at Tunánmarca (Figure 31). There, potatoes are much more common than was required by the relocation. The inhabitants were clearly specializing in potatoes and quinoa and had little maize. Much additional production would have been necessary on the uplands as well as beyond, based on the ratio of population estimates to land productivity at the two sampled sites.

If we accept the population and harvest estimates given in Chapter 11, the Wanka II settlements studied could not support their population only using land within nearby territories. The inhabitants would have had to use all possible intensification strategies to meet their needs. In addition, they would have had to have fields some distance away, either in the deserted land to the east, or surrounding the northern settlements' territories. Access to these eastern lands, even under communal supervision, would have been very competitive and contested.

The wild seed data suggest, however, that the Wanka II crops came primarily from higher elevation zones, and so most land acquisition would probably have been throughout these higher zones. The dominant wild wetland species virtually drop out of the Wanka II assemblage, as if this microzone was not visited very much. At the same time increased quantities of local wood taxa suggest that wood was now being cultivated. This probably occurred near the sites on the hillsides and in the drainages. In fact, among many possible reasons, the production of wood could have been part of an intensification scheme to alter the microclimate of the now cooler area by shielding the fields (Hastorf and Johannessen 1992). We think that these trees were also planted to legitimate access to farming lands, as the word *malki* is a play on "*malki*," the ancestors; and we know that people received access to the use of the land through the will of the ancestors.

Accompanying the population aggregation, the per family labor costs would have increased as people had to work their nearby land more intensively in addition to paying new labor taxes. Ironically this situation could have added even more pressure on women, as farming families would have tried to expand their size to gain the extra hands. With such a labor squeeze, the servants of the elite would have been helpful to them.

In the Andes, access to land is determined by the concept of cyclical communal land-use in which households gain access to plots of land in exchange for labor. Ideally this means that households have equal access to land as long as they participate in the community labor projects. Although people theoretically gain access to land equally, having extra labor allows a family to produce more per hectare and also sometimes to get more land allocated to them. Agricultural labor is thus a nexus for equality and inequality.

In agriculture, this dynamic between responsibility (labor) and access (land) is based on *yanantin*. This duality is contradictory and contains tensions, as seen in the upper and lower *ayllus* of modern communities, halves but unequal halves that are constantly in competition with each other (B. J. Isbell 1978; Zuidema 1973). Today, in its fluid nature, one can see how the balance offers a chance for equilibrating differences, seen in the rotating land-use of the sectoral fallow system and in the rotating *varoq* (community) leadership. *Yanantin* also is invoked to bring people together in a hierarchy of ever larger communities: families, households, districts (*barrios*) within a settlement, kin groups, *ayllus*, villages, or clusters of villages. This hierarchical aspect is also found in the hierarchy of mountain deities, rising higher and higher above the villages. So, through *yanantin* the Sausa leaders were able to legitimate hierarchy within the guise of balanced opposition and most probably to gain more lands for their *ayllu*, kin, and allies as they claimed an ever larger family.

We see in the status comparisons that some households did in fact gain access to substantially higher amounts of maize. The mechanisms for doing this were many but all suggest a specific interest in having this prized social lubricant. Not surprisingly the same households that have increased evidence for metalwork, weaving, and serving of liquids have more frequent and much more dense maize. If these families did not grow the crop themselves they may have exchanged for it. The house compounds that have the greater maize also have more Base Roja and andesite jars. These two ceramic types were produced in the southern Mantaro Valley (Costin 1986). Perhaps the maize was traded in the ceramic jars.

Other types of plant exchange, present for the first time, also show status differences. Several new types of wood and coca provide evidence for stations in the eastern *ceja de montaña* that produced cultivated and wild products (Hastorf 1987; Hastorf and Johannessen 1991). Documents mention that Late Intermediate Period Sausa and Wanka communities had such outposts (LeVine 1979, 1985), as are also documented for the northern Titicaca Qolla (Goland 1988). These warm climate plants are found more commonly in the elite compounds.

The outposts imply that aggressive actions to gain such resources were initiated during Wanka II times, requiring more labor per capita. These outposts also needed management, organized defence, and transportation. Many scholars have discussed the managerial organization they must have required and, while there is no agreement about the scale of organization, all agree that some amount of centralized authority must have operated to maintain a link between the suppliers and the consumers (Dillehay 1979; Murra 1968). And so we have evidence of another aspect of management surrounding agriculture and to differential access.

It is important to learn from the diverse agricultural evidence that part of the sense of household self-sufficiency, autonomy, and access had been lost in the Tunánmarca and Umpamalca agricultural production. This change was the result of the larger societal scale but also of the new political systems in charge of land distributions and labor allocations. This loss of control crept into the daily lives of the Sausa as they tried to maintain their traditions. More labor was now required outside of the house for warring, managing the cities, transportation, and agricultural work. Increased leadership power is assumed to lie behind at least some of these new tasks, initiated first using the principle of reciprocity, illustrated in the community and household feasts as well as in the protective wars. These cultural events escalated, however still building on the concept of equality, and developed into the new inequalities that surrounded the group fusion and explosion of new labor projects.

What did the people receive for their increased "labor exchanges"? They received protection, of course, and a feast now and again. But they were restricted in their actions and access to their old lands. Gone are small-scale village decisions about where to farm, as a central multi-community authority was now responsible for dividing up and allocating the surrounding lands to achieve maximum output. These losses of autonomy could have been unintended initially, emanating from the larger regional changes, war, and tensions over the valley lands. Then people's daily lives focused on their acculturation to the new social setting and on the agricultural production needed to survive in the cooler climate.

The negotiation of inequality

As discussed in Chapter 1, increasing inequality involves the ascendancy of claims to power negotiated between people with differing goals. Claims to power in this case may be seen as, for example, *powers to* increase resource production, to gain needed goods from outside the region, and to placate the ancestors. Consensual power is enabling. Evidence of such enablement in the Sausa is manifested in, for example, the desire for increased protection with the move upslope. But at the same time there was also the basis for contestation of power. While households had to abandon their fields yet work harder to yield what they had produced before, they seemed to maintain control over their own production.

This multidimensional power also harbors the ability to obtain goods through power over people's labor and activities (Foucault 1984; Giddens 1979; Miller and Tilley 1984). All members of society act in their best interests, trying to transform parts of society while constrained to act within the accepted cultural norms. For the Sausa, "power over" increased for the Wanka II *cinchekona* as they expanded from war leaders to decision makers and goods allocators. They restructured the balance of control and responsibility in the Late Intermediate Period as battles became more common and goods were captured and distributed. They became responsible for protection and defense. Within this responsibility they expanded their domain of control as larger defensive works were constructed for protection. These social acts had an impact on people's daily lives as family activities became more restricted in the household.

Power was contested also through the wars themselves. While consolidation of power did occur, warriors probably questioned the *cinchekona* and at times withdrew their allegiance as they attempted to gain positions and goods for themselves. An example of this contested power is seen after the Inka political structures collapsed with the arrival of the Spanish. Young men in the Mantaro communities, attempting to gain access to land that was allocated by the elders, used Andean mechanisms to succeed. They escalated feasting to gain allies for *tinkus* and, through their success in gaining allies and winning intra-community battles, they gained access to lands (Mallon pers. comm.). The control of warrior allegiance in the Wanka II was probably fragile and tied to opposing goals, making it impossible to ally all Sausa young men under one *cinchekona*. The Sausa were not under one political power until the Inka arrived.

The elite, whatever their goals or powers, did not control all economic production or social views. Nor did a Sausa leader ever centralize power enough to bring all warriors together and control the whole region's populace or the region's agricultural fields. The residents contested such a power centralization through their own use of balance and reciprocity. They maintained control over their own agricultural production, they did not allow the leaders to extract much extra labor and resources, and they required reciprocity from the leaders for their efforts.

Some final thoughts

Because power is constantly in flux in all societies there will always be different material results frozen in the excavated material. The identity of power will depend on the places where power was gathered in a culture. I chose this case to illustrate that most interesting situation in which a society is in transition, with increasing inequality and power consolidation, but where the society has not yet coalesced into a permanent hierarchy through the process often described as "the rise of chiefdoms." In the Sausa example we can see how the changes are not uniform throughout society. We can see the partial and tentative nature of control and power, how it expanded but was also bounded throughout society. Though it is hard to be concrete about the exact political dimensions of the group, we can identify an escalation of energy directed towards production while at the same time a resistance to it. Production, however, cannot be isolated: it is linked to war, ritual, and social life.

The Sausa data present a picture of a polity with a tentative hereditary inequality, increasing control over labor in certain domains, changing political structures, and heightened social identity. The activities that consolidated the most power in the Sausa example include settlement protection, warfare, increased effort and organization of food production, and larger and perhaps more frequent social gatherings and feasts. While in no way a complete picture, from this example we can begin to see how power acts in a culture in transition as control increases in some parts of society and remains unchanged in others. By identifying the group's definitions and uses of power we can better track and explain increasing and decreasing inequality.

Agriculture is the fulcrum for these changes, mediated through the principles of balanced duality (*yanantin* and *tinku*), hierarchy, and the value of maize beer in social relations. One major premise of the book is that agricultural production is tailored by political and social events, not merely by the economic and the physical setting (Bartlett 1980; Bender 1978; Renfrew and Cherry 1986). Change in agricultural practices is one domain where cultural principles can be manifested. This in no way discounts the material realities of the physical world. While the environment affects people's choices it is only one constraint. It does not dictate which path is taken in agriculture or politics. People always have different ways to reach a goal.

Agriculture formed an important nexus for Sausa power and inequality, involving the social relations of labor, war, group cohesion, and food reciprocity. As changes rippled throughout society the agricultural systems reflected and shaped them, articulating with power on many levels. Individual households seemed to hold onto their own subsistence production, providing them a place in which to negotiate their position. In turn, agriculture also participated in increased inequality, seen most clearly in the differential access to maize in the Wanka II.

If the Inka had not conquered, there is no guarantee that the Sausa would have centralized their political power or inheritance of such positions any more than we see them do in the Late Intermediate period data. Under the Inka, political power aggrandizement was severely restricted for the Sausa leaders (*curacas*), who were taken to Cuzco. Local images of deities were also shifted to Cuzco and the population concentrations and upland canals were broken up and abandoned. The surplus labor was transferred to the *tambo*, or local administration center, for Inka benefit, especially for *chicha* and cloth manufacture (D'Altroy 1991; Morris 1967). This removal of power was not totally recouped with the arrival of the Spanish, despite support for the Spanish against the Inka.

Ultimately, one must ask if the Sausa lived in a hierarchical or a non-hierarchical world (Murra 1984; Schaedel 1988). Andean principles include both ideologies: hierarchy and conquest as well as regulation and balanced opposition. I conclude that neither principle gained total ascendance in the pre-Inka Sausa sequence; both were involved in the dynamic of contested and accepted political change. There is evidence of increased Wanka II political hierarchy in several realms yet we can also see it lacking in other areas. Inequality lay in the realms of public action more than in material control. The agricultural data, the artifactual material, and the documentary evidence suggest change and increased differences through time. But the Tunánmarca leaders did not gain control over the whole region. Their power was ephemeral in that they, unlike leaders at other times in the Andean sequence, did not have attached specialist producers, did not control most production, did not gain access to valley lands, and did not consolidate permanent hierarchical leadership. There is much evidence of negotiation and compromise for the richer elite. These elites perhaps had greater numbers of high-status products, but they also gave them away. The elite war leaders perhaps controlled decisions over more labor and land, but might lose them if the *tinku* battles were lost. Regulatory mechanisms within the populace were strong, realigned only by the coming of the Inka. This did not stop all would-be leaders from continuing to defend their claims to the heights.

Greater political inequality is found widely in the central Andes where there are many examples of much more complex hierarchical developments. The Sausa data is useful, however, for it provides us with an example of the constraints and actions where the negotiation of power is most fluid. Many archaeologists have written about political hierarchy. This book is only one of a group of studies on power (e.g. Earle

1978; Flannery 1972; Haas 1982; Jones and Kautz 1981; Sanders and Price 1968). Its perspective is different, however. While not formulating a simple explanation of political change, it presents a picture of active local negotiations rippling through a series of cultural dimensions that encompass the political, the economic, and the social.

Cultural domains are often left out in economically oriented discussions of hierarchy, but they can be incorporated into the explanation of political change along with the economic data. In essence, one must define the economic in terms of the cultural and political in a society. Although a productive and flexible resource base and access to it are critical at the onset of increasing complexity, and a minimal population size must exist, their roles are defined by the historical context.

While I have not put forward one mechanism as the instigator in the onset of inequality, I hope that this Andean example will demonstrate how we can include many dimensions to gain a better understanding of change in the past.

Appendix A

The northern Mantaro region sites and site sizes by phase

Early Intermediate Period/Middle Horizon

Site number	Size in ha	Site number	Size in ha
J1	1.4	J205	1.0
J47	6.0	J206	1.0
J49	2.0	J208	0.8
J51	0.4	J210	2.0
J71	1.9	J211	10.5
J73	7.1	J212	1.0
J130	10.0	J217	3.4
J131	1.7	J220	5.8
J132	17.9	J221	10.0
J133	0.6	J222	7.0
J134	3.0	J223	4.3
J135	0.9	J233	5.0
J136	2.5	J227	3.3
J140	6.3	J243	4.8
J141	5.1	J257	4.5
J142	2.8	J293	9.1
J145	1.5	J319	0.5
J200	2.2	J281	2.9
J202	2.3	J285	6.4
J203	5.5		
Number of sites 39			
Total area 164.4 ha			
Mean size of site 4.2 ha			

Wanka I

Site number	Size in ha	Site number	Size in ha
J1	1.4	J222	7.0
J2	4.9	J228	2.7
J4	4.8	J233	5.0
J38	4.2	J234	10.4
J47	6.0	J235	3.0
J49	4.3	J236	8.0
J51	0.4	J240	2.5
J53	1.4	J243	4.8
J56	2.5	J245	4.7
J136	4.3	J246	2.8
J141	4.1	J252	9.2
J142	3.1	J253	8.0
J145	2.1	J257	4.5
J200	3.2	J260	2.5
J202	2.3	J281	2.9
J203	5.5	J282	1.4
J206	1.0	J285	6.4
J207	6.0	J287	6.4
J210	3.5	J289	15.1
J211	10.1	J290	7.4
J220	8.0	J291	2.4
J221	10.0		

Number of sites	43
Total area	210.2 ha
Mean size of site	4.9 ha

Wanka II

Site number	Size in ha	Site number	Size in ha
J2	73.7	J73	5.3
J7	25.4	J84	1.8
J8	5.4	J142	2.8
J37	6.0	J228	2.7
J38	4.2	J231	2.1
J40	5.6	J246	2.8
J41	14.8	J287	6.4
J46	3.4	J289	15.1
J48	3.1	J290	7.4
J53	1.5	J291	2.4

Number of sites	20
Total area	191.9 ha
Mean size of site	9.6 ha
Mean size without the two centers	5.2 ha

Appendix B

The frequency of crops planted in six land-use zones

These results are based on the Markov chain analysis of the agricultural interview data. Each table lists a matrix of crops and the likelihood of a crop being planted the year after every other crop in the six major land-use zones. The upper number in each cell is the likelihood that the crop listed along the X axis will be followed by the crop listed along the Y axis. The lower number in every cell represents the number of fields involved from the agricultural interview data.

First bench

	Year 1								
	Fallow	Potato	Maize	Quinoa	Wheat	Barley/ oat	A. tuber	Bean/pea	Veg- etables
Fallow	0.105 1	0.020 1	—	—	0.080 2	0.300 3	—	0.120 3	—
Potato	0.632 12	0.080 4	0.077 3	0.300 3	0.240 6	0.600 6	—	0.280 7	0.200 2
Maize	0.053 1	0.420 21	0.436 17	0.200 2	0.160 4	—	—	0.120 3	0.300 3
Quinoa	—	0.140 4	0.051 2	0.100 1	—	0.100 7	—	0.080 2	—
Wheat	0.053 1	0.140 7	0.282 11	0.300 3	—	—	1.000 2	0.200 5	0.200 2
Barley/ oat	—	0.020 1	—	—	0.240 6	—	—	0.080 2	—
A. tuber	—	—	—	—	0.040 1	—	—	—	—
Bean/pea	0.158 3	0.120 6	0.103 4	0.100 1	0.200 5	—	—	0.080 2	0.100 1
Veg- etables	—	0.060 3	0.051 2	—	0.040 1	—	—	0.040 1	0.200 2

Total number of fields = 192

Valley irrigation

	Year 1								
	Fallow	Potato	Maize	Quinoa	Wheat	Barley/ oat	A. tuber	Bean/pea	Veg- etables
Fallow	0.167 1	—	—	—	0.333 2	—	—	—	—
Potato	0.833 5	0.121 4	0.244 10	0.250 1	—	0.333 1	—	0.438 7	0.615 8
Maize	—	0.545 18	0.441 15	—	0.667 4	—	1.000 1	0.438 7	0.077 1
Quinoa	—	—	—	—	—	—	—	0.063 1	—
Wheat	—	0.121 74	—	—	—	—	—	0.063	—
Barley/ oat	—	—	—	0.250 1	—	—	—	—	—
A. tuber	—	0.030 1	—	—	—	—	—	—	—
Bean/pea	—	0.091 3	0.235 8	0.250 1	—	0.667 2	—	—	—
Veg- etables	—	0.091 3	0.029 1	0.250 1	—	—	—	—	—

Total number of fields = 112

Fertile lowlands

	Year 1								
	Fallow	Potato	Maize	Quinoa	Wheat	Barley/ oat	A. tuber	Bean/pea	Veg- etables
Fallow	0.143 1	0.028 1	—	—	—	—	—	—	—
Potato	0.286 2	0.056 2	0.100 1	0.500 2	0.692 9	0.533 8	0.500 1	0.357 5	0.750 3
Maize	—	0.139 5	0.200 2	—	0.077 1	—	—	0.143 2	—
Quinoa	0.286 2	0.194 7	0.100 1	0.250 2	0.077 1	0.133 2	—	—	0.250 1
Wheat	0.143 1	0.194 7	0.100 1	—	—	0.067 1	—	0.286 4	—
Barley/ oat	0.143 1	0.111 4	0.100 1	0.125 1	0.154 2	0.133 2	—	0.214 3	—
A. tuber	—	0.028 1	0.200 2	—	—	—	0.500 1	—	—
Bean/pea	—	0.167 6	0.100 1	0.250 1	0.154 2	0.133 2	—	—	—
Veg- etables	—	0.111 1	0.100 1	—	—	—	—	—	—

Total number of fields = 107

Intensive hillsides

	Year 1									
	Fallow	Potato	Maize	Quinoa	Lupine	Wheat	Barley/ oat	A. tuber	Bean/pea	Veg- etables
Fallow	0.167 5	0.016 1	0.026 1	—	—	0.098 4	0.067 2	—	0.065 2	0.059 1
Potato	0.400 12	0.127 8	0.105 4	0.286 2	—	0.463 19	0.200 3	—	0.258 8	0.412 7
Maize	—	0.317 20	0.368 14	0.268 2	—	0.049 2	0.200 3	—	0.129 4	—
Quinoa	—	0.127 8	—	—	—	0.049 2	0.067 1	—	0.065 2	0.118 2
Lupine	—	0.032 2	—	—	0.500 1	—	—	—	—	—
Wheat	0.110 3	0.143 8	0.263 10	0.143 1	—	—	0.067 1	—	0.290 9	0.059 1
Barley/ oat	0.200 6	0.032 2	0.053 2	—	0.500 1	0.073 3	0.067 1	—	0.032 1	0.059 1
A. tuber	—	0.032 2	0.026 1	—	—	—	0.067 1	0.330 1	—	—
Bean/pea	0.133 4	0.095 6	0.132 5	0.286 2	—	0.244 10	0.267 7	0.667 2	0.129 4	0.118 2
Veg- etables	—	0.079 5	0.026 1	—	—	0.024 1	—	—	0.032 1	0.176 3

Total number of fields = 250

Extensive hillsides

	Year 1									
	Fallow	Potato	Maize	Quinoa	Lupine	Wheat	Barley/ oat	A. tuber	Bean/pea	Veg- etables
Fallow	0.230 12	0.030 2	—	—	0.060 3	0.030 1	0.170 4	0.050 1	0.030 1	—
Potato	0.510 27	0.070 4	0.180 3	0.500 3	0.200 1	0.260 10	0.330 8	0.290 6	0.180 6	0.140 1
Maize	—	0.090 5	0.180 3	0.170 1	—	0.130 5	0.040 1	0.050 1	0.060 2	0.290 2
Quinoa	—	0.030 2	0.060 1	—	—	—	—	—	—	0.140 1
Lupine	0.020 1	0.020 1	—	—	—	0.030 1	0.040 1	0.050 1	0.060 2	—
Wheat	0.050 2	0.190 11	0.290 5	—	—	0.080 3	—	0.050 1	0.470 16	0.290 2
Barley/ oat	0.090 5	0.210 12	0.060 1	—	—	0.180 7	0.040 1	0.140 3	0.060 2	—
A. tuber	0.080 4	0.120 7	—	0.170 1	—	0.030 1	0.120 3	0.190 4	0.090 3	—
Bean/pea	0.040 2	0.220 13	0.240 4	—	0.200 1	0.260 10	0.250 6	0.190 4	0.060 2	0.140 1
Veg- etables	—	0.020 1	—	0.170 1	—	0.030 1	—	—	—	—

Total number of fields = 264

First bench

	Year 1								
	Fallow	Potato	Quinoa	Lupine	Wheat	Barley/ oat	A. tuber	Bean/pea	Veg- etables
Fallow	0.306 19	0.100 4	0.556 5	0.667 2	0.143 2	0.158 3	0.380 4	0.133 2	—
Potato	0.484 30	0.300 12	0.222 1	0.333 2	0.214 3	0.526 10	0.308 4	0.200 3	—
Quinoa	—	0.150 6	—	—	0.071 1	0.115 2	0.077 1	0.067 1	1.000 1
Lupine	—	0.075 3	—	—	—	—	—	—	—
Wheat	0.032 2	0.200 8	—	—	0.071 1	0.530 1	0.154 2	0.267 4	—
Barley/ oat	0.145 9	0.100 4	0.111 1	—	—	0.053 1	—	0.200 3	—
A. tuber	0.016 1	0.050 2	—	—	0.071 1	—	0.154 2	0.067 1	—
Bean/pea	0.016 1	0.025 1	0.111 1	—	0.429 6	0.105 2	—	0.067 1	—
Veg- etables	—	—	—	—	—	—	—	—	—

Total number of fields = 174

Appendix C

Mean production yields by zone in kilograms/hectare

	Potato	Maize	Quinoa	Lupine	Wheat	Barley/ oat	Mashua	Olluco	Oca	Bean/ pea	Onions	White potato	Indig. potato	*Chuño*	*Ph. vulgaris*
First bench	1,534	139	153	119	219	173	275			190	4,500	586	613		750
Frequency	16	35	10	2	26	10	2			25	6	32	8		1
Valley irrig.	2,311	463	713		626	210			813	558		1,341	4,121		
Frequency	10	35	4		6	3			1	17		9	2		
Fertile lowland	1,022	947	191		355	1,043	13,750			575	9,090	1,605	2,134		
Frequency	17	8	10		16	14	1			14	6	16	6		
Inten. hillside	427	101	418	362	69	115	2,547	30,000	1,686	123		451	1,507		
Frequency	16	38	8	2	41	15	2	1	2	32		38	10		
Exten. hillside	368	183	205	289	42	130	1,545	1,421	776	127		433	351		
Frequency	14	17	6	5	39	21	4	13	4	34		31	16		
Hill irrig.			320		1,363	670				49		10,139	11,841		
Frequency			1		2	1				4		15	2		
High elev.	2,732		251	514	118	1,515	785	8,571	3,943	319		817	420	4,220	
Frequency	15		11	3	12	16	3	3	3	14		17	11	2	

Appendix D

Calorie and protein values of Andean crops

Crop	Calories/100 gm	Protein/100 gm
Solanum juzepczukii (bitter potato)	327	2.1
Solanum tuberosum (potato)	320	6.4
Tropaeolum tuberosum (mashua)	52	1.6
Ullucus tuberosus (olluco)	51	1.0
Oxalis tuberosa (oca)	63	1.0
Chenopodium quinoa (quinoa)	351	12.3
Chenopodium pallidicaule (cañihua)	327	14.2
Lupinus mutabilis (lupine, tarhui)	276	17.3
Zea mays (maize)	340	6.5
Phaseolus vulgaris (common bean)	150	9.8

Source: INCAP 1961

Appendix E

Botanical flotation and sorting procedures

In the water flotation system used in this project, a 55-gallon drum was filled with water and a doubled ⅛-inch screen covering the bottom of a bucket was positioned inside the drum with its top above the water line. Into this bucket a bag of soil was gently poured. Then the bucket was picked up and gently agitated within the water to loosen soil peds and release the carbonized material. These, having a lighter specific gravity than water, float to the surface. A piece of chiffon (with a mesh of 0.3–0.5 mm) attached to a hand-held sieve collected the floating material by skimming the water surface. When all of the material was collected, after several agitations of the bucket, the chiffon was removed and placed in a protected spot to allow the floated material to air-dry. Once dry, the organic remains (called the light fraction) were bagged, catalogued, and sent to the laboratory at UCLA, with permission from the Peruvian National Institute of Culture. In an attempt to control for problems of contamination, because the same water was used for more than one sample, I had a series of these 55-gallon drums, which I used in sequence, to let the fine soil and whatever was left circulating in the water settle to the bottom. After floating fifteen samples, I emptied out a drum. The heavy fraction, having sunk to the bottom of the screened bucket, was taken out and dried on a very stiff paper bag and sorted in Peru. This fraction created a systematic collection of lithics, ceramics, and animal bone, in addition to the water-logged carbonized plant remains. The plant remains from the heavy fraction are part of the flotation samples.

After weighing the whole sample, we sieved the light fraction sample of the floated remains through a 2-mm mesh geological screen, taking care not to jostle the specimens too much. This size division helped to expedite analysis, since most seeds were smaller than 2 mm and plant fragments were often not capable of being identified when smaller than this (Asch and Asch 1975: 117). Each of these two subsamples in turn were spread out across a white, rimmed tray and viewed under a microscope systematically. All carbonized seeds and fragments were extracted, separated, counted, and labeled by taxon. All specimens were counted, except when a seed fragment was very small and possibly part of a larger fragment. Most seeds were whole, while all tubers were in fragments. Categories such as tuberous remains, unknown seed fragments, or unknown botanical fragments also were included in order to maximize the information recovered from each sample. Many fragments were of the size such that I knew they had to be part of a domesticate although I could not identify the exact taxon. All analyses used counts, because the weights of these taxa subsamples were too small to register on the available scale.

The analysis of prehistoric macrobotanical specimens involves the identification of every whole and fragmentary charred plant part, based on anatomical and morphological characteristics. It was discovered during the analysis that complete seeds as small as 0.90 mm can be identified, while plant (e.g. tuber) fragments under 1.5 mm are not identifiable. Large fragments require at least two diagnostic characteristics to confirm an identification.

To determine the genera or species of seeds and domesticated crop fragments, identified modern plant and seed types were used. Besides using the pictorial seed identification texts (Delorit 1970; Martin and Barkley 1961), I gathered wild seeds and crops as a comparative type collection from the region. The wild plants were identified by Dra. Emma Cerrate de Ferreyra of the Museo Historia Natural de Javier Prado and the Universidad Nacional Mayor de San Marcos; and Dr J. Soukup of the Universidad Nacional Mayor de San Marcos, Lima. Because many crop remains in the flotation samples were incomplete fragments, they could not be identified using only the dissecting stereoscope. More detailed cellular research had to be conducted in order to identify the fragments. Thus two additional techniques were used: scanning electron microscopy (SEM) for specimens with intact cellular morphology, and stable isotopic analysis (carbon and nitrogen) for specimens so poorly preserved that only chemical analysis would suffice to identify them. Each technique required special training and the construction of type collections or identifiable signatures of the major Andean crops and likely wild plants (Buth 1982; DeNiro and Hastorf 1985; Kanai 1972; Miller 1982). The identification made from these procedures were tallied on flotation sample sheets. The results of all laboratory identifications are recorded in Appendix F.

Appendix F

Botanical data by flotation sample (sorted by site and observation number)

RAW FLOTATION DATA

OBS	FLTMCO	FLOT	BAGSIZE	SITE	FEATURE	LEVEL	LOCUS	BAGNO	CONTEXT	DATE	MZKERNAL	CUPCOBS	EMBRYOS	CHENOPOD	LUPINE	PHSPP	TUBERS	PAPAS	OCA	ULLUCO	MASHUA	LUMPS	AMARANTH	SCIRPUS	SMLEGUME	LEPIDIUM	LUCUMA	RARE	PORTULAC	VERBENA	PLANTAGO	SGRASS	LGRASS	MGRASS	MALVAST	RUBUS
1	1	790	0.8	1	.	.	.	.	0	.	.	.	.	1	.	.	.	.	.	.	.	1	.	.	.	.	.	.	.	.	.	.	.	.	.	.
2	1	619	0.9	1	4	1	1	303	9	6	.	.	.	.	.	.	.	.	.	.	.	2	.	.	1	.	.	.	.	.	.	.	.	.	.	.
3	1	422	0.9	1	4	2	1	103	9	6	.	.	.	.	.	.	.	.	.	.	.	.	6	.	.	.	.	.	.	.	.	3	.	.	.	.
4	1	572	0.9	1	4	2	1	203	9	6	.	.	.	.	.	.	.	.	.	.	.	.	.	.	.	.	.	.	.	.	.	1	.	.	.	.
5	1	426	1.0	1	4	2	1	303	9	6	.	.	.	.	.	.	.	.	.	.	.	5	.	.	.	.	.	.	.	.	.	2	.	.	.	.
6	1	613	0.8	1	4	3	1	104	1	4	.	.	.	.	.	.	.	.	.	.	.	1	.	1	.	.	.	.	.	.	.	3	.	.	.	.
7	1	584	0.9	1	4	3	1	204	1	4	.	.	.	.	.	.	.	.	.	.	.	.	1	.	.	.	.	.	.	.	.	2	.	.	.	.
8	1	585	0.8	1	4	3	1	304	1	4	.	.	.	1	.	.	.	.	.	.	.	.	2	.	.	.	.	.	.	1	.	4	.	.	.	.
9	1	428	1.0	1	4	3	1	404	1	4	.	1	2	22	.	.	.	.	.	.	.	2	1	.	1	.	.	1	.	2	.	3	.	1	.	.
10	1	569	0.6	1	4	3	3	103	8	4	.	.	.	.	.	.	.	.	.	.	.	.	.	.	.	.	.	.	.	.	.	2	.	.	1	.
11	1	425	1.0	1	4	4	1	103	8	4	.	.	.	3	.	.	.	.	.	.	.	.	1	.	.	.	.	.	1	2	.	4	.	.	.	.
12	1	620	0.9	1	4	4	1	203	8	4	.	.	.	3	.	.	.	.	.	.	.	.	1	.	.	.	.	.	.	.	.	1	.	.	.	.
13	1	581	0.8	1	4	4	1	303	8	4	.	.	.	8	.	.	.	.	.	.	.	4	.	.	.	.	.	.	.	2	.	.	.	.	.	.
14	1	480	0.3	1	4	5	1	101	8	4	1	1	.	1	15	.	.	.	.	.	.	.	2	1	.	.	.	.	.	.	.	1	.	.	1	.
15	1	627	0.9	1	4	5	1	104	8	4	1	4	.	7	1	.	1	.	.	.	.	6	.	.	.	.	.	.	.	.	.	2	3	.	.	.
16	1	605	0.9	1	4	5	1	204	8	4	.	6	.	19	.	.	.	.	.	.	.	2	1	2	1	.	.	.	.	3	1	3	1	.	1	.
17	1	513	0.9	1	4	5	1	304	8	4	.	7	.	37	6	.	.	.	.	.	.	4	5	.	.	.	.	.	.	6	.	6	.	.	.	.
18	1	477	1.0	1	4	5	1	404	8	4	27	.	1	30	13	3	2	.	.	.	.	27	.	8	.	.	.	.	.	19	3	32	.	6	.	.
19	1	489	0.4	1	4	5	3	101	8	4	4	3	2	30	8	.	3	.	.	.	.	5	24	4	6	.	.	.	.	15	1	9	.	4	6	.

OBS	BIXA	PHYSOLIS	OXALIS	AMBROSIA	NICOTIAN	SALVIA	MINT	GALIUM	OPUNTIA	CYPER	COMPOSIT	UMBELLIF	FABACEAE	UNKNWNSE	WDCT	WDWT	GRSSTKS	EUPHORB	PHORLUP	MIMOSA	VACCINIU	BERBERIS	TRITICUM	MOLLUGO	PENDFRAG	CACTUS	CALEND	CRUCIFER	SOLANUM	LGLEGUME	TLEGUME	KG	M3VOL	PHASE	STAT	LEV
1	.	.	.	.	.	.	.	.	.	.	.	.	.	.	3	.	.	.	.	.	.	.	.	.	.	.	.	.	.	.	.	4.8	0.0048		.	.
2	.	.	.	.	.	.	.	.	.	.	.	.	.	.	2	.	.	.	.	.	.	.	.	.	.	.	.	.	.	.	1	5.4	0.0054	HIII	.	1
3	.	.	.	.	.	.	.	.	.	.	.	.	.	.	.	.	1	.	.	.	.	.	.	.	.	.	.	.	.	.	.	5.4	0.0054	HIII	.	2
4	.	.	.	.	.	.	.	.	.	.	.	.	.	0	1	.	.	.	.	.	.	.	.	.	.	.	.	.	.	.	.	5.4	0.0054	HIII	.	2
5	.	.	.	.	.	.	.	.	.	.	.	.	.	.	8	.	.	.	.	.	.	.	.	.	.	.	.	.	.	.	.	6.0	0.0060	HIII	.	2
6	.	.	.	.	.	.	.	.	.	.	.	.	.	.	1	.	.	.	1	.	.	.	.	.	.	.	.	.	.	1	.	4.8	0.0048	HI	.	3
7	.	.	.	.	.	.	.	.	.	.	.	.	.	.	1	.	1	.	.	.	.	.	.	.	.	.	.	.	.	.	.	5.4	0.0054	HI	.	3
8	.	.	.	.	.	.	.	.	.	.	2	.	.	3	2	.	.	.	.	.	.	.	.	.	.	.	.	.	.	.	.	4.8	0.0048	HI	.	3
9	.	.	2	.	.	.	.	.	.	.	.	.	.	.	.	.	.	.	.	.	.	.	.	.	.	1	.	.	.	.	1	6.0	0.0060	HI	.	3
10	.	.	.	.	.	.	.	.	.	.	.	.	.	1	.	.	.	.	.	.	.	.	.	.	.	.	.	.	.	.	.	3.6	0.0036	HI	.	3
11	.	.	.	.	.	.	.	.	.	.	.	.	.	.	1	.	.	.	.	.	.	.	.	.	.	.	.	.	.	.	.	6.0	0.0060	HI	.	4
12	.	.	.	.	.	.	.	.	.	.	.	.	.	.	.	.	.	.	.	.	.	.	.	.	.	.	.	.	.	.	.	5.4	0.0054	HI	.	4
13	.	.	.	.	.	.	.	.	.	.	.	.	.	.	.	.	1	.	10	.	.	.	.	.	.	.	.	.	.	10	.	4.8	0.0048	HI	.	4
14	.	.	.	.	.	.	.	.	.	.	.	1	.	.	1	.	.	.	.	.	.	.	.	.	.	.	.	.	.	.	.	1.8	0.0018	HI	.	5
15	.	.	.	.	.	1	.	.	.	.	.	.	.	.	.	.	.	.	3	.	.	.	.	.	.	.	.	.	.	3	.	5.4	0.0054	HI	.	5
16	.	.	.	.	.	.	.	.	.	.	.	.	.	.	4	.	.	.	.	.	.	.	.	.	.	.	.	.	.	.	1	5.4	0.0054	HI	.	5
17	.	.	.	.	.	.	.	.	.	.	.	.	.	2	6	.	.	.	.	.	.	.	.	.	.	.	.	.	.	.	.	5.4	0.0054	HI	.	5
18	.	.	.	.	.	.	.	.	.	.	.	.	.	.	.	.	1	.	4	.	.	.	.	.	.	.	.	.	.	4	.	6.0	0.0060	HI	.	5
19	.	.	.	.	.	.	.	.	.	.	.	.	.	9	.	.	1	.	.	.	.	.	.	.	.	.	.	.	.	.	6	2.4	0.0024	HI	.	5

OBS	FLTMCO	FLOT	BAGSIZE	SITE	FEATURE	LEVEL	LOCUS	BAGNO	CONTEXT	DATE	MZKERNAL	CUPCOBS	EMBRYOS	CHENOPOD	LUPINE	PHSPP	TUBERS	PAPAS	OCA	ULLUCO	MASHUA	LUMPS	AMARANTH	SCIRPUS	SMLEGUME	LEPIDIUM	LUCUMA	RARE	PORTULAC	VERBENA	PLANTAGO	SGRASS	LGRASS	MGRASS	MALVAST
20	1	481	1.1	1	4	5	3	103	8	4	4	9	.	52	4	.	1	.	.	.	.	16	.	9	8	.	.	1	.	27	6	33	7	2	7
21	1	471	1.0	1	4	5	3	203	8	4	1	7	.	115	12	.	.	.	.	.	.	21	.	29	30	.	.	.	.	44	7	86	18	5	11
22	1	474	0.9	1	4	5	3	303	8	4	3	16	.	315	9	.	2	.	.	.	.	99	2	35	21	.	.	.	.	13	7	59	8	2	11
23	1	495	0.9	1	4	6	1	103	8	2	2	2	1	11	1	.	.	.	.	.	.	.	8	6	3	.	.	.	.	14	.	21	.	2	4
24	1	483	1.1	1	4	6	1	203	8	2	.	4	.	22	.	.	.	.	.	.	.	.	3	5	1	.	.	.	.	5	.	.	.	.	.
25	1	493	1.0	1	4	6	1	303	8	2	.	2	.	10	.	.	.	.	.	.	.	.	1	2	.	.	.	.	.	8	.	6	.	.	.
26	1	563	0.9	1	4	6	2	103	8	4	3	7	.	3	1	.	.	.	.	.	.	2	1	3	1	.	.	.	.	4	1	2	.	.	.
27	1	473	0.9	1	4	6	2	203	8	4	6	3	.	1	.	.	1	.	.	.	.	.	.	3	.	.	.	.	.	2	1	6	.	.	1
28	1	562	1.0	1	4	6	2	303	8	4	.	3	.	5	4	.	.	.	.	.	.	6	5	.	1	.	.	.	.	2	.	4	1	.	1
29	1	561	1.0	1	4	6	3	103	8	4	5	3	.	56	.	.	4	.	.	.	.	81	6	17	15	.	.	2	.	32	8	37	5	4	6
30	1	488	1.1	1	4	6	3	203	8	4	4	2	0	65	6	9	.	.	.	.	.	25	1	30	.	.	.	1	1	23	6	18	19	7	9
31	1	470	0.9	1	4	6	3	303	8	4	.	4	.	68	8	.	8	.	.	.	.	19	.	17	12	.	.	1	.	24	3	23	6	5	13
32	1	462	0.9	1	4	7	1	103	8	3	2	4	.	1	2	.	.	.	.	.	.	7	.	.	.	.	.	.	.	1	.	1	1	1	.
33	1	458	0.9	1	4	7	1	203	8	3	3	2	.	2	.	.	.	.	.	.	.	3	.	.	.	.	.	.	.	1	1	6	.	1	.
34	1	460	0.1	1	4	7	1	303	8	3	1	2	.	.	.	.	.	.	.	.	.	2	.	.	.	.	.	.	.	.	.	1	.	.	.
35	1	456	0.8	1	4	7	2	103	1	3	.	11	1	5	1	.	1	.	.	.	.	1	1	2	1	.	.	.	.	10	.	4	.	3	.
36	1	459	0.8	1	4	7	2	203	1	3	3	1	.	.	2	1	3	.	.	.	.	.	.	.	.	.	.	.	.	1	.	.	.	1	.
37	1	475	0.9	1	4	7	2	303	1	3	.	1	.	5	.	.	2	.	.	.	.	11	2	1	.	.	.	.	.	1	.	2	.	2	.
38	1	517	0.9	1	4	8	1	103	8	3	.	.	.	1	2	.	.	.	.	.	.	.	1	.	.	.	.	.	.	1	.	.	.	.	.

OBS	RUBUS	BIXA	PHYSOLIS	OXALIS	AMBROSIA	NICOTIAN	SALVIA	MINT	GALIUM	OPUNTIA	CYPER	COMPOSIT	UMBELLIF	FABACEAE	UNKWNSEE	WDCT	WDWT	GRSSTKS	EUPHORB	PHORLUP	MIMOSA	VACCINIU	BERBERIS	TRITICUM	MOLLUGO	PENDFRAG	CACTUS	CALEND	CRUCIFER	SOLANUM	LGLEGUME	TLEGUME	KG	M3VOL	PHASE	STAT	LEV
20	1	.	3	.	1	.	.	.	.	.	.	.	.	.	10	.	.	.	.	.	.	1	.	.	.	.	.	.	.	.	.	8	6.6	0.0066	HI	.	5
21	.	.	.	1	1	.	.	.	.	.	.	4	1	1	16	.	.	.	.	.	.	.	.	.	.	.	.	.	.	.	.	30	6.0	0.0060	HI	.	5
22	1	.	.	.	1	.	.	.	.	.	.	5	.	.	41	99	.	1	.	.	.	.	.	.	.	.	.	.	.	.	.	21	5.4	0.0054	HI	.	5
23	.	.	.	.	.	3	.	.	.	.	.	1	.	.	2	3	.	.	.	9	.	.	.	.	.	.	.	.	.	.	9	3	5.4	0.0054	MH	.	6
24	.	.	.	.	.	.	.	.	.	.	.	.	.	.	1	4	.	.	.	.	.	.	.	.	.	.	.	.	.	.	.	1	6.6	0.0066	MH	.	6
25	.	.	.	.	.	.	.	.	.	.	.	.	.	.	.	2	.	.	.	.	.	.	.	.	.	.	.	.	.	.	.	.	6.0	0.0060	MH	.	6
26	.	.	.	.	.	.	.	.	.	.	.	.	.	.	7	8	.	.	.	.	.	.	.	.	.	.	.	.	.	.	.	1	5.4	0.0054	HI	.	6
27	.	.	.	.	.	.	.	.	.	.	.	.	.	.	23	.	.	.	.	5	.	.	.	.	.	.	.	.	.	.	5	.	5.4	0.0054	HI	.	6
28	.	.	.	.	.	.	.	.	.	.	.	.	.	.	16	8	.	.	.	.	.	.	.	.	.	.	.	.	.	.	.	1	6.0	0.0060	HI	.	6
29	.	.	1	1	.	.	.	.	.	.	.	.	.	.	65	.	.	.	.	4	.	2	.	.	.	.	.	.	.	.	4	15	6.0	0.0060	HI	.	6
30	.	.	.	.	.	.	.	.	.	.	.	.	.	.	14	4	.	.	.	6	.	.	.	.	.	1	.	.	.	.	6	.	6.6	0.0066	HI	.	6
31	.	.	.	1	.	.	.	.	.	.	.	1	.	.	9	50	.	1	.	13	.	1	.	.	.	.	.	.	.	.	13	12	5.4	0.0054	HI	.	6
32	.	.	.	.	.	.	.	.	.	.	.	.	.	.	2	16	.	.	.	.	.	.	.	.	.	.	.	.	.	.	.	.	5.4	0.0054	HO	.	7
33	.	.	.	.	.	.	.	.	.	.	.	.	.	.	5	3	.	.	.	.	.	.	.	.	.	.	.	.	.	.	.	.	5.4	0.0054	HO	.	7
34	.	.	.	.	.	.	.	.	.	.	.	.	.	.	.	7	.	.	.	.	.	.	.	.	.	.	.	.	.	.	.	.	0.6	0.0006	HO	.	7
35	1	.	.	.	1	.	.	.	.	.	.	.	.	.	.	5	.	.	.	.	.	.	.	.	.	.	.	.	.	.	.	1	4.8	0.0048	HO	.	7
36	.	.	.	.	.	.	.	.	.	.	.	.	.	.	1	20	.	.	.	.	.	.	.	.	.	.	.	1	.	.	.	.	4.8	0.0048	HO	.	7
37	.	.	.	.	.	.	.	.	.	.	.	.	.	.	.	17	.	.	.	.	.	.	.	.	.	.	.	.	.	.	.	.	5.4	0.0054	HO	.	7
38	.	.	.	.	.	.	.	.	.	.	.	.	.	.	.	3	.	.	.	.	.	.	.	.	.	.	.	.	.	.	.	.	5.4	0.0054	HO	.	8

OBS	FLTMCO	FLOT	BAGSIZE	SITE	FEATURE	LEVEL	LOCUS	BAGNO	CONTEXT	DATE	MZKERNAL	CUPCOBS	EMBRYOS	CHENOPOD	LUPINE	PHSPP	TUBERS	PAPAS	OCA	ULLUCO	MASHUA	LUMPS	AMARANTH	SCIRPUS	SMLEGUME	LEPIDIUM	LUCUMA	RARE	PORTULAC	VERBENA	PLANTAGO	SGRASS	LGRASS	MGRASS	MALVAST
39	1	509	1.1	1	4	8	1	203	8	3	.	.	.	10	.	.	5	.	.	.	.	10	.	.	1	.	.	.	.	1	.	1	.	.	.
40	1	504	0.9	1	4	8	1	303	8	3	.	.	.	.	.	.	2	.	.	.	.	.	.	1	.	.	.	.	.	2	.	.	.	.	.
41	1	550	1.0	1	4	8	2	103	8	3	4	1	.	61	.	.	.	.	.	.	.	8	3	1	1	.	.	.	.	2	.	1	1	.	.
42	1	499	0.8	1	4	8	2	203	8	3	2	2	.	143	4	.	.	.	.	.	.	.	.	.	1	.	.	.	.	.	.	1	.	.	.
43	1	555	1.1	1	4	8	2	303	8	3	9	13	.	430	4	7	16	.	.	.	.	.	.	2	6	.	.	.	.	.	.	11	1	.	.
44	1	498	1.0	1	4	9	1	103	8	3	.	.	.	7	.	.	2	.	.	.	.	.	.	.	.	.	.	.	.	3	.	1	.	.	.
45	1	554	0.8	1	4	9	1	203	8	3	8	.	.	6	.	.	.	.	.	.	.	.	.	.	.	.	.	.	.	.	.	.	.	.	.
46	1	556	0.8	1	4	9	1	303	8	3	2	.	.	2	.	.	.	.	.	.	.	.	.	.	.	.	.	.	.	.	.	.	.	.	.
47	1	516	0.9	1	4	9	2	103	1	3	5	27	.	263	5	.	3	.	.	.	.	.	.	2	.	.	.	.	.	.	.	1	3	.	1
48	1	501	1.0	1	4	9	2	203	1	3	5	15	.	162	1	11	12	.	.	.	.	.	.	2	11	.	.	.	.	1	.	.	.	.	2
49	1	500	1.0	1	4	9	2	303	1	3	1	5	.	87	6	.	.	.	.	.	.	3	2	5	2	.	.	.	.	2	.	.	.	.	.
50	1	597	1.0	1	4	10	1	103	8	3	.	.	.	.	.	.	.	.	.	.	.	.	.	.	.	.	.	.	.	.	.	.	.	.	.
51	1	780	0.9	1	4	10	1	203	8	3	.	1	.	1	1	.	.	.	.	.	.	.	1	.	.	.	.	.	.	.	.	.	.	.	.
52	1	601	0.6	1	4	10	2	103	8	3	.	.	.	2	.	.	.	.	.	.	.	.	1	7	.	.	.	.	.	.	.	1	.	.	.
53	1	736	1.0	1	4	10	2	303	8	3	.	.	.	3	.	.	.	.	.	.	.	1	.	.	.	.	.	.	.	.	.	.	.	.	.
54	1	541	0.8	1	4	11	1	103	8	3	.	.	.	.	.	.	.	.	.	.	.	.	4	.	.	.	.	.	.	3	.	5	.	.	.
55	1	593	1.0	1	4	11	1	203	8	3	.	.	.	1	.	.	.	.	.	.	.	.	1	1	.	.	.	.	.	.	.	.	.	.	.
56	1	565	0.8	1	4	11	1	303	8	3	.	1	.	1	.	.	.	.	.	.	.	.	3	.	.	.	.	.	.	.	.	.	.	.	.
57	1	540	0.8	1	4	11	2	103	8	3	.	.	.	8	.	.	.	.	.	.	.	.	.	.	1	.	.	.	.	.	.	2	.	.	.

OBS	RUBUS	BIXA	PHYSOLIS	OXALIS	AMBROSIA	NICOTIAN	SALVIA	MINT	GALIUM	OPUNTIA	CYPER	COMPOSIT	UMBELLIF	FABACEAE	UNKWNSEE	WDCT	WDWT	GRSSTKS	EUPHORB	PHORLUP	MIMOSA	VACCINIU	BERBERIS	TRITICUM	MOLLUGO	PENDFRAG	CACTUS	CALEND	CRUCIFER	SOLANUM	LGLEGUME	TLEGUME	KG	M3VOL	PHASE	STAT	LEV
39	.	.	.	.	.	.	.	.	.	.	.	.	.	.	.	3	.	.	.	3	.	.	.	.	.	.	.	.	.	.	3	1	6.6	0.0066	HO	.	8
40	.	.	.	.	.	.	.	.	.	.	.	.	.	.	.	1	.	.	.	.	.	.	.	.	.	.	.	.	.	.	.	.	5.4	0.0054	HO	.	8
41	.	.	.	.	.	.	.	.	.	.	.	.	.	.	.	11	.	.	.	.	.	.	.	.	.	.	.	.	.	.	.	1	6.0	0.0060	HO	.	8
42	.	.	.	.	.	.	.	.	.	.	.	.	.	.	.	.	.	.	.	.	.	.	.	.	.	.	.	.	.	.	.	1	4.8	0.0048	HO	.	8
43	.	.	.	.	.	.	.	.	.	.	.	.	.	.	1	12	.	.	.	.	.	.	.	.	.	.	.	.	.	.	.	6	6.6	0.0066	HO	.	8
44	.	.	.	.	.	.	.	.	.	.	.	.	.	.	2	.	.	.	.	3	.	.	.	.	.	.	.	.	.	.	3	.	6.0	0.0060	HO	.	9
45	.	.	.	.	.	.	.	.	.	.	.	.	.	.	.	6	.	.	.	.	.	.	.	.	.	.	.	.	.	.	.	.	4.8	0.0048	HO	.	9
46	.	.	.	.	.	.	.	.	.	.	.	.	.	.	.	.	.	.	.	1	.	.	.	.	.	.	.	.	.	.	1	.	4.8	0.0048	HO	.	9
47	.	.	.	.	.	.	.	.	.	.	.	.	.	2	.	1	.	.	.	2	.	.	.	.	.	.	.	.	.	.	2	.	5.4	0.0054	HO	.	9
48	.	.	.	.	.	.	.	.	.	.	.	1	.	.	.	2	.	.	.	.	.	.	.	.	.	.	.	.	.	.	.	11	6.0	0.0060	HO	.	9
49	.	.	.	.	.	.	.	.	.	.	.	1	.	.	1	1	.	.	.	.	.	.	.	.	.	.	.	.	.	.	.	2	6.0	0.0060	HO	.	9
50	1	.	.	.	.	.	.	.	.	.	.	.	.	.	.	.	.	.	.	.	.	.	.	.	.	.	.	.	.	.	.	.	6.0	0.0060	HO	.	*
51	.	.	.	.	.	.	.	.	.	.	.	.	.	.	.	1	.	.	.	.	.	.	.	.	.	.	.	.	.	.	.	.	5.4	0.0054	HO	.	*
52	.	.	.	.	.	.	.	.	.	.	.	.	.	.	.	.	.	.	.	.	.	.	.	.	.	.	.	.	.	.	.	.	3.6	0.0036	HO	.	*
53	.	.	.	.	.	.	.	.	.	.	.	.	.	.	.	.	.	.	.	.	.	.	.	.	.	.	.	.	.	.	.	.	6.0	0.0060	HO	.	*
54	.	.	.	.	.	.	.	.	.	.	.	.	.	.	.	.	.	.	.	.	.	.	.	.	.	.	.	.	.	.	.	.	4.8	0.0048	HO	.	*
55	.	.	.	.	.	.	.	.	.	.	.	.	.	.	.	3	.	.	.	.	.	.	.	.	.	.	.	.	.	.	.	.	6.0	0.0060	HO	.	*
56	.	.	.	.	.	.	.	.	.	.	.	.	.	.	.	.	.	.	.	.	.	.	.	.	.	.	.	.	.	.	.	.	4.8	0.0048	HO	.	*
57	.	.	.	.	.	.	.	.	.	.	.	.	.	.	.	5	.	.	.	.	.	.	.	.	.	.	.	.	.	.	.	1	4.8	0.0048	HO	.	*

OBS	FLTMCO	FLOT	BAGSIZE	SITE	FEATURE	LEVEL	LOCUS	BAGNO	CONTEXT	DATE	MZKERNAL	CUPCOBS	EMBRYOS	CHENOPOD	LUPINE	PHSPP	TUBERS	PAPAS	OCA	ULLUCO	MASHUA	LUMPS	AMARANTH	SCIRPUS	SMLEGUME	LEPIDIUM	LUCUMA	RARE	PORTULAC	VERBENA	PLANTAGO	SGRASS	LGRASS	MGRASS	MALVAST	RUBUS	BIXA
58	1	594	0.8	1	4	11	2	203	8	3	.	.	.	.	1	.	.	.	.	.	.	.	.	.	.	.	.	.	.	1	.	.	.	.	.	.	.
59	1	542	0.8	1	4	11	2	303	8	3	.	2	.	1	.	.	.	.	.	.	.	.	.	.	.	.	.	.	.	.	.	1	.	.	.	.	.
60	1	560	0.8	1	4	12	1	104	8	3	.	1	.	7	4	.	.	.	.	.	.	.	.	1	1	.	.	.	.	1	.	8	1	.	.	.	.
61	1	533	0.8	1	4	12	1	204	8	3	.	.	.	8	.	.	.	.	.	.	.	1	.	1	.	.	.	.	.	.	.	3	.	.	.	.	.
62	1	573	0.8	1	4	12	1	304	8	3	.	5	.	14	.	.	.	.	.	.	.	1	1	.	1	.	.	.	.	.	.	3	.	.	.	.	.
63	1	590	0.8	1	4	12	1	404	8	3	.	.	.	13	1	.	.	.	.	.	.	7	3	.	.	.	.	.	.	.	.	1	.	.	.	.	.
64	1	529	0.9	1	5	1	1	104	9	6	.	.	.	.	.	.	.	.	.	.	.	4	.	.	.	.	.	1	.	.	.	.	.	.	.	.	.
65	1	610	0.8	1	5	1	1	204	9	6	.	.	.	.	.	.	.	.	.	.	.	.	.	.	.	.	.	2	.	.	.	.	.	.	.	.	.
66	1	615	0.9	1	5	1	1	304	9	6	.	.	.	.	.	.	.	.	.	.	.	.	.	.	.	.	.	.	.	.	.	.	.	.	.	.	.
67	1	616	0.8	1	5	1	1	404	9	6	.	1	.	.	.	.	.	.	.	.	.	.	.	1	.	.	.	.	.	.	.	4	.	.	.	.	.
68	1	423	0.9	1	5	2	1	203	8	6	.	.	.	.	.	.	.	.	.	.	.	3	.	.	.	.	.	.	.	.	.	2	.	.	.	.	.
69	1	576	0.8	1	5	2	1	303	8	6	.	.	.	.	.	.	.	.	.	.	.	8	.	.	.	.	.	.	.	.	.	4	.	.	.	.	.
70	1	618	0.9	1	5	3	1	103	8	6	.	.	.	.	.	.	.	.	.	.	.	.	.	.	.	.	.	.	.	.	.	3	.	.	.	.	.
71	1	420	0.9	1	5	3	1	203	8	6	.	.	.	3	.	.	.	.	.	.	.	.	.	.	.	.	.	.	.	.	.	2	.	.	.	.	.
72	1	587	0.8	1	5	3	1	303	8	6	1	1	.	.	.	.	.	.	.	.	.	.	.	.	.	.	.	.	.	.	.	.	.	.	.	.	.
73	1	514	0.9	1	5	4	1	103	1	6	.	1	.	1	.	.	.	.	.	.	.	.	.	.	.	.	.	.	.	1	.	.	.	.	.	.	.
74	1	510	0.8	1	5	4	1	203	1	6	.	.	.	.	.	.	.	.	.	.	.	.	.	1	.	.	.	.	.	1	.	1	.	.	.	.	.
75	1	512	0.9	1	5	4	1	303	1	6	.	1	.	.	.	.	.	.	.	.	.	2	.	1	.	.	.	.	.	.	.	1	.	.	.	.	.
76	1	523	0.6	1	5	4	1	404	2	6	1	7	.	.	.	2	.	.	.	.	.	1	2	1	.	.	.	.	.	3	.	.	.	1	.	.	.

OBS	PHYSOLIS	OXALIS	AMBROSIA	NICOTIAN	SALVIA	MINT	GALIUM	OPUNTIA	CYPER	COMPOSIT	UMBELLIF	FABACEAE	UNKWNSEE	WDCT	WDWT	GRSSTKS	EUPHORB	PHORLUP	MIMOSA	VACCINIU	BERBERIS	TRITICUM	MOLLUGO	PENDFRAG	CACTUS	CALEND	CRUCIFER	SOLANUM	LGLEGUME	TLEGUME	KG	M3VOL	PHASE	STAT	LEV
58	.	.	.	.	.	.	.	.	.	.	.	.	.	.	.	.	.	.	.	.	.	.	.	.	.	.	.	.	.	.	4.8	0.0048	HO	.	*
59	.	.	.	.	.	.	.	.	.	.	.	.	.	.	.	.	.	.	.	.	.	.	.	.	.	.	.	.	.	.	4.8	0.0048	HO	.	*
60	.	.	.	.	.	.	.	.	.	1	.	.	4	12	.	1	.	.	.	.	.	.	.	.	.	.	.	.	.	1	4.8	0.0048	HO	.	*
61	.	.	.	.	.	.	.	.	.	.	.	.	3	1	.	.	.	.	.	.	.	.	.	.	.	.	.	.	.	.	4.8	0.0048	HO	.	*
62	.	.	.	.	.	.	.	.	.	.	.	.	2	2	.	.	.	5	.	.	.	.	.	.	.	.	.	.	5	1	4.8	0.0048	HO	.	*
63	.	.	1	.	.	.	.	.	.	.	.	.	1	6	.	.	.	.	.	.	.	.	.	.	.	.	.	.	.	.	4.8	0.0048	HO	.	*
64	.	.	.	.	.	.	.	.	.	.	.	.	.	3	.	.	.	.	.	.	.	1	.	.	.	.	.	.	.	.	5.4	0.0054	HIII	.	1
65	.	.	.	.	.	.	.	.	.	.	.	.	.	9	.	.	.	.	.	.	.	2	.	.	.	.	.	.	.	.	4.8	0.0048	HIII	.	1
66	.	.	.	.	.	.	.	.	.	.	.	.	.	2	.	.	.	.	.	.	.	.	.	.	.	.	.	.	.	.	5.4	0.0054	HIII	.	1
67	.	.	.	.	.	.	.	.	.	.	.	.	4	8	.	1	.	.	.	.	.	.	.	.	.	.	.	.	.	.	4.8	0.0048	HIII	.	1
68	.	.	.	.	.	.	.	.	.	.	.	.	.	13	.	.	.	.	.	.	.	.	.	.	.	.	.	.	.	.	5.4	0.0054	HIII	.	2
69	.	.	.	.	.	.	.	.	.	.	.	.	.	5	.	.	.	.	.	.	.	.	.	.	.	.	.	.	.	.	4.8	0.0048	HIII	.	2
70	.	.	.	.	.	.	.	.	.	.	.	.	.	.	.	.	.	.	.	.	.	.	.	.	.	.	.	.	.	.	5.4	0.0054	HIII	.	3
71	.	.	.	.	.	.	.	.	.	.	.	.	.	5	.	1	.	.	.	.	.	.	.	.	.	.	.	.	.	.	5.4	0.0054	HIII	.	3
72	.	.	.	.	.	.	.	.	.	.	.	.	.	5	.	.	.	.	.	.	.	.	.	.	.	.	.	.	.	.	4.8	0.0048	HIII	.	3
73	.	.	.	.	.	.	.	.	.	.	.	.	.	1	.	.	.	.	.	.	.	.	.	.	.	.	.	.	.	.	5.4	0.0054	HIII	.	4
74	.	.	.	.	.	.	.	.	.	.	.	.	.	7	.	.	.	.	.	.	.	.	.	.	.	.	.	.	.	.	4.8	0.0048	HIII	.	4
75	.	.	.	.	.	.	.	.	.	.	.	.	.	1	.	.	.	1	.	.	.	.	.	.	.	.	.	.	1	.	5.4	0.0054	HIII	.	4
76	.	.	.	.	.	.	.	.	.	.	.	.	.	.	.	.	.	.	.	.	.	.	.	.	.	.	.	.	.	.	3.6	0.0036	HIII	.	4

OBS	FLTMCO	FLOT	BAGSIZE	SITE	FEATURE	LEVEL	LOCUS	BAGNO	CONTEXT	DATE	MZKERNAL	CUPCOBS	EMBRYOS	CHENOPOD	LUPINE	PHSPP	TUBERS	PAPAS	OCA	ULLUCO	MASHUA	LUMPS	AMARANTH	SCIRPUS	SMLEGUME	LEPIDIUM	LUCUMA	RARE	PORTULAC	VERBENA	PLANTAGO	SGRASS	LGRASS	MGRASS	MALVAST	RUBUS	BIXA
77	1	624	1.0	1	5	4	2	103	3	4	.	.	.	.	.	.	.	.	.	.	.	.	.	.	.	.	.	.	.	.	.	.	.	.	.	.	.
78	1	820	0.8	1	5	4	2	203	3	4	.	.	.	4	.	.	.	.	.	.	.	.	.	.	.	.	.	.	.	.	.	.	.	.	.	.	.
79	1	511	0.8	1	5	4	2	303	3	4	.	.	.	.	.	.	.	.	.	.	.	1	.	.	.	.	.	.	.	.	.	1	.	.	.	.	.
80	1	528	0.8	1	5	4	3	103	6	6	.	.	.	4	.	.	.	.	.	.	.	.	.	.	.	.	.	.	.	5	.	.	.	.	.	.	.
81	1	606	0.9	1	5	4	3	203	6	6	.	.	.	.	.	.	.	.	.	.	.	.	.	.	.	.	.	.	.	1	.	2	.	.	.	.	.
82	1	521	0.9	1	5	4	3	303	6	6	.	1	.	1	.	.	.	.	.	.	.	1	.	.	.	.	.	.	.	1	.	.	.	.	.	.	.
83	1	524	0.8	1	5	4	4	104	6	4	.	.	.	1	.	.	.	.	.	.	.	9	.	1	.	.	.	4	.	.	.	1	.	.	.	.	.
84	1	617	0.9	1	5	4	4	204	6	4	1	1	.	1	.	.	.	.	.	.	.	.	.	.	.	.	.	.	.	6	.	9	.	.	.	.	.
85	1	588	0.9	1	5	4	4	304	6	4	.	3	.	.	.	.	.	.	.	.	.	1	.	1	.	.	.	.	.	2	.	5	.	.	1	.	.
86	1	525	0.3	1	5	4	4	404	2	4	.	.	.	.	.	.	.	.	.	.	.	.	.	1	.	.	.	.	.	1	.	.	.	1	.	.	.
87	1	494	0.8	1	5	5	1	109	1	4	.	.	.	1	.	.	.	.	.	.	.	4	.	3	.	.	.	.	.	25	1	5	.	.	.	.	.
88	1	506	1.0	1	5	5	1	209	1	4	.	.	.	3	.	.	.	.	.	.	.	15	.	.	.	.	.	1	.	1	.	2	.	.	.	.	.
89	1	538	0.9	1	5	5	1	309	1	4	.	.	.	3	.	.	30	.	.	.	.	.	.	.	.	.	.	.	.	31	.	1	.	.	.	.	.
90	1	487	0.8	1	5	5	1	509	1	4	.	.	.	1	.	.	.	.	.	.	.	5	.	.	1	.	.	.	.	19	.	6	.	.	.	.	.
91	1	518	1.0	1	5	5	1	609	1	4	.	4	1	11	4	.	.	.	.	.	.	35	.	1	1	.	.	.	.	8	.	1	.	1	.	.	.
92	1	457	0.8	1	5	5	1	709	1	4	.	.	.	4	.	.	.	.	.	.	.	.	.	.	3	.	.	.	.	12	.	2	.	.	.	.	.
93	1	603	0.7	1	5	5	1	809	1	4	34	.	.	1	.	.	.	.	.	.	.	.	.	1	.	.	.	.	.	21	.	.	.	.	.	.	.
94	1	491	1.0	1	5	5	1	909	1	4	.	.	.	4	1	.	.	.	.	.	.	50	.	2	.	.	.	.	.	56	.	2	.	.	.	.	.
95	1	622	0.9	1	5	5	2	103	3	4	.	.	.	.	.	.	.	.	.	.	.	.	.	2	.	.	.	.	.	1	.	1	.	.	1	.	.

OBS	PHYSOLIS	OXALIS	AMBROSIA	NICOTIAN	SALVIA	MINT	GALIUM	OPUNTIA	CYPER	COMPOSIT	UMBELLIF	FABACEAE	UNKWNSEE	WDCT	WDWT	GRSSTKS	EUPHORB	PHORLUP	MIMOSA	VACCINIU	BERBERIS	TRITICUM	MOLLUGO	PENDFRAG	CACTUS	CALEND	CRUCIFER	SOLANUM	LGLEGUME	TLEGUME	KG	M3VOL	PHASE	STAT	LEV
77	.	.	.	.	.	.	.	.	.	.	.	.	.	2	.	.	.	.	.	.	.	.	.	.	.	.	.	.	.	.	6.0	0.0060	HI	.	4
78	.	.	.	.	.	.	.	.	.	.	.	.	.	1	.	.	.	.	.	.	.	.	.	.	.	.	.	.	.	.	4.8	0.0048	HI	.	4
79	.	.	.	.	.	.	.	.	.	.	.	.	.	.	.	.	.	.	.	.	.	.	.	.	.	.	.	.	.	.	4.8	0.0048	HI	.	4
80	.	.	.	.	.	.	.	.	.	.	.	.	.	.	.	.	.	.	.	.	.	.	.	.	.	.	.	.	.	.	4.8	0.0048	HIII	.	4
81	.	.	.	.	.	.	.	.	.	.	.	.	.	3	.	.	.	.	.	.	.	.	.	.	.	.	.	.	.	.	5.4	0.0054	HIII	.	4
82	.	.	.	.	.	.	.	.	.	1	.	.	1	1	.	.	.	.	.	.	.	.	.	.	.	.	.	.	.	.	5.4	0.0054	HIII	.	4
83	.	.	.	.	.	.	.	.	.	.	.	.	.	3	.	.	.	.	.	.	.	.	.	.	.	.	.	.	.	.	4.8	0.0048	HI	.	4
84	1	.	.	.	.	.	.	.	.	1	.	.	3	3	.	.	.	.	.	.	.	.	.	.	.	.	.	.	.	.	5.4	0.0054	HI	.	4
85	.	.	.	.	.	.	.	.	.	.	.	.	.	.	.	.	.	.	.	.	.	.	.	.	.	.	.	.	.	.	5.4	0.0054	HI	.	4
86	.	.	.	.	.	.	.	.	.	.	.	.	.	8	.	.	.	.	.	.	.	.	.	.	.	.	.	.	.	.	1.8	0.0018	HI	.	4
87	.	.	.	.	.	.	.	.	.	.	.	.	.	27	.	.	.	1	.	.	.	.	.	.	.	.	.	.	1	.	4.8	0.0048	HI	.	5
88	.	.	.	.	.	.	.	.	.	.	.	.	1	2	.	.	.	1	.	.	1	.	.	.	.	.	.	.	1	.	6.0	0.0060	HI	.	5
89	.	.	.	.	.	.	.	.	.	.	.	.	3	30	.	.	.	24	.	.	.	.	.	.	.	.	.	.	24	.	5.4	0.0054	HI	.	5
90	.	.	.	.	.	.	.	.	.	.	.	.	2	.	.	.	.	.	.	.	.	.	.	.	.	.	.	.	.	1	4.8	0.0048	HI	.	5
91	.	.	.	.	.	.	.	.	.	.	.	.	4	99	45	1	.	.	.	.	.	.	.	.	.	.	.	.	.	1	6.0	0.0060	HI	.	5
92	.	.	.	.	.	.	.	.	.	.	.	.	.	21	.	.	.	4	.	.	.	.	.	.	.	.	.	.	4	3	4.8	0.0048	HI	.	5
93	.	.	.	.	.	.	.	.	.	.	.	.	3	23	.	.	.	.	.	.	.	.	.	.	.	.	.	.	.	.	4.2	0.0042	HI	.	5
94	.	.	.	.	.	.	.	.	.	.	.	.	.	61	23	.	.	.	.	.	.	.	.	.	.	.	.	.	.	.	6.0	0.0060	HI	.	5
95	.	.	.	1	.	.	.	.	.	.	.	.	2	1	.	.	.	.	.	.	.	.	.	.	.	.	.	.	.	.	5.4	0.0054	HI	.	5

OBS	FLTMCO	FLOT	BAGSIZE	SITE	FEATURE	LEVEL	LOCUS	BAGNO	CONTEXT	DATE	MZKERNAL	CUPCOBS	EMBRYOS	CHENOPOD	LUPINE	PHSPP	TUBERS	PAPAS	OCA	ULLUCO	MASHUA	LUMPS	AMARANTH	SCIRPUS	SMLEGUME	LEPIDIUM	LUCUMA	RARE	PORTULAC	VERBENA	PLANTAGO	SGRASS	LGRASS	MGRASS	MALVAST	RUBUS
96	1	520	0.8	1	5	5	2	203	3	4	.	.	.	.	3	.	.	.	.	.	.	.	.	.	.	.	.	.	.	1	.	.	.	.	1	.
97	1	628	0.8	1	5	5	2	303	3	4	1	1	.	.	.	.	.	.	.	.	.	.	1	.	.	.	.	.	.	3	.	.	.	.	.	.
98	1	526	1.0	1	5	5	3	103	4	4	.	.	.	2	.	.	.	.	.	.	.	.	.	1	1	.	.	.	.	.	.	1	.	.	.	.
99	1	508	0.7	1	5	5	3	203	4	4	.	.	.	1	.	.	.	.	.	.	.	.	.	.	.	.	.	.	.	.	.	1	.	.	.	.
100	1	522	0.9	1	5	5	3	303	4	4	.	1	.	.	.	.	.	.	.	.	.	1	3	1	.	.	.	.	.	5	.	2	.	.	.	.
101	1	427	0.8	1	5	5	4	103	1	4	2	.	.	1	.	.	.	.	.	.	.	.	.	.	.	.	.	.	.	1	.	1	.	.	.	.
102	1	621	0.8	1	5	5	4	203	1	4	.	1	.	2	.	.	1	.	.	.	.	.	.	.	.	0	.	.	.	.	.	2	.	.	1	.
103	1	424	1.0	1	5	5	4	303	1	4	.	1	.	4	.	.	.	.	.	.	.	2	.	.	.	.	.	.	.	10	1	5	.	.	1	.
104	1	472	0.4	1	5	5	5	101	2	4	.	6	.	7	.	19	.	.	.	.	.	.	.	1	.	.	.	.	.	53	1	5	.	.	.	.
105	1	468	0.8	1	5	5	5	104	2	4	.	.	.	.	.	.	.	.	.	.	.	20	.	.	.	.	.	.	.	5	.	.	.	.	.	.
106	1	502	0.8	1	5	5	5	204	2	4	.	.	1	16	2	.	.	.	.	.	.	99	.	1	.	.	.	.	.	16	.	2	.	.	1	.
107	1	496	0.9	1	5	5	5	304	2	4	.	.	.	3	3	.	.	.	.	.	.	40	.	4	1	.	.	.	.	32	.	6	.	.	.	.
108	1	482	0.9	1	5	5	5	404	2	4	.	1	.	6	.	.	.	.	.	.	.	46	.	3	.	.	.	.	.	26	.	1	.	2	1	.
109	1	484	0.9	1	5	6	1	108	4	4	.	.	.	2	.	.	.	.	.	.	.	.	.	2	.	.	.	.	.	8	.	7	.	.	.	.
110	1	492	0.8	1	5	6	1	208	4	4	.	1	.	4	.	.	.	.	.	.	.	1	.	.	.	.	.	.	.	8	.	5	.	1	.	.
111	1	519	0.8	1	5	6	1	308	4	4	.	1	.	6	.	.	.	.	.	.	.	3	.	.	2	.	.	.	.	10	2	4	1	.	1	.
112	1	478	0.9	1	5	6	1	408	4	4	.	.	.	1	.	.	5	.	.	.	.	8	1	2	.	.	.	.	.	39	.	3	.	.	.	.
113	1	497	0.7	1	5	6	1	508	4	4	2	.	.	6	.	.	.	.	.	.	.	5	1	4	.	.	.	.	.	5	.	1	.	.	3	.
114	1	625	0.8	1	5	6	1	608	4	4	.	.	.	4	.	.	.	.	.	.	.	12	.	6	6	.	.	1	.	50	.	9	.	.	5	.

OBS	BIXA	PHYSOLIS	OXALIS	AMBROSIA	NICOTIAN	SALVIA	MINT	GALIUM	OPUNTIA	CYPER	COMPOSIT	UMBELLIF	FABACEAE	UNKWNSEE	WDCT	WDWT	GRSSTKS	EUPHORB	PHORLUP	MIMOSA	VACCINIU	BERBERIS	TRITICUM	MOLLUGO	PENDFRAG	CACTUS	CALEND	CRUCIFER	SOLANUM	LGLEGUME	TLEGUME	KG	M3VOL	PHASE	STAT	LEV
96	.	.	.	.	.	.	.	.	.	.	.	.	.	.	2	.	.	.	.	.	.	.	.	.	.	.	.	.	.	.	.	4.8	0.0048	HI	.	5
97	.	.	.	.	.	.	.	.	.	.	.	.	.	.	5	.	.	.	.	.	.	.	.	.	.	.	.	.	.	.	.	4.8	0.0048	HI	.	5
98	.	.	.	.	.	.	.	.	.	.	.	.	.	.	6	.	.	.	.	.	.	.	.	.	.	.	.	.	.	.	1	6.0	0.0060	HI	.	5
99	.	.	.	.	.	.	.	.	.	.	.	.	.	.	2	.	.	.	.	.	.	.	.	.	.	.	.	.	.	.	.	4.2	0.0042	HI	.	5
100	.	.	.	.	.	.	.	.	.	.	.	.	.	1	3	.	.	.	1	.	.	.	.	.	.	.	.	.	.	1	.	5.4	0.0054	HI	.	5
101	.	1	.	.	.	.	.	.	.	.	.	.	.	2	1	.	.	.	.	.	.	.	.	.	.	.	.	.	.	.	.	4.8	0.0048	HI	.	5
102	.	.	.	.	.	.	.	.	.	.	.	.	.	.	.	.	.	.	1	.	.	.	.	.	.	.	.	.	.	1	.	4.8	0.0048	HI	.	5
103	.	1	.	.	.	.	.	.	.	.	.	.	.	.	1	.	.	.	1	.	.	.	.	.	.	.	.	.	.	1	.	6.0	0.0060	HI	.	5
104	.	.	1	.	.	.	.	.	.	.	.	.	.	11	94	.	.	.	.	.	.	.	.	.	.	.	.	.	.	.	.	2.4	0.0024	HI	.	5
105	.	.	.	.	.	.	.	.	.	.	.	.	.	5	59	.	.	.	.	.	.	.	.	.	.	.	.	.	.	.	.	4.8	0.0048	HI	.	5
106	.	.	.	.	.	.	.	.	.	.	.	.	.	2	99	.	.	.	.	.	.	.	.	.	.	.	.	.	.	.	.	4.8	0.0048	HI	.	5
107	.	.	.	.	.	.	.	.	.	.	1	.	.	9	20	.	1	.	.	.	.	.	.	.	.	.	.	.	.	.	1	5.4	0.0054	HI	.	5
108	.	.	.	.	.	.	.	.	.	.	.	.	.	.	11	.	.	.	.	.	.	.	.	.	.	.	.	.	.	.	.	5.4	0.0054	HI	.	5
109	.	.	1	.	.	.	.	.	.	.	.	.	.	2	28	.	.	.	.	.	.	.	.	.	.	.	.	.	.	.	.	5.4	0.0054	HI	.	6
110	.	.	.	.	.	.	.	.	.	.	.	.	.	.	19	.	.	.	.	.	.	.	.	.	.	.	.	.	.	.	.	4.8	0.0048	HI	.	6
111	.	.	.	1	.	.	.	.	.	.	.	.	.	.	6	.	.	.	.	.	.	.	.	.	.	.	.	.	.	.	2	4.8	0.0048	HI	.	6
112	.	.	1	.	1	.	.	.	.	.	.	.	.	4	17	.	.	.	.	.	.	.	.	.	.	.	.	.	.	.	.	5.4	0.0054	HI	.	6
113	.	.	.	.	.	.	.	.	.	.	.	.	.	.	10	.	.	.	.	.	.	.	.	.	.	.	.	.	.	.	.	4.2	0.0042	HI	.	6
114	.	1	.	.	.	.	.	.	.	.	.	.	.	.	.	.	.	.	.	.	.	.	.	.	.	.	.	1	.	.	6	4.8	0.0048	HI	.	6

OBS	FLTMCO	FLOT	BAGSIZE	SITE	FEATURE	LEVEL	LOCUS	BAGNO	CONTEXT	DATE	MZKERNAL	CUPCOBS	EMBRYOS	CHENOPOD	LUPINE	PHSPP	TUBERS	PAPAS	OCA	ULLUCO	MASHUA	LUMPS	AMARANTH	SCIRPUS	SMLEGUME	LEPIDIUM	LUCUMA	RARE	PORTULAC	VERBENA	PLANTAGO	SGRASS	LGRASS	MGRASS	MALVAST
115	1	486	1.0	1	5	6	1	708	4	4	.	.	2	26	11	.	.	.	.	.	.	.	.	6	3	.	.	.	.	76	.	9	1	.	5
116	1	527	0.8	1	5	6	1	808	4	4	2	.	.	.	.	.	.	.	.	.	.	4	3	.	11	.	.	.	.	90	1	12	1	1	3
117	1	490	1.0	1	5	6	2	103	3	4	1	1	.	2	1	.	.	.	.	.	.	1	.	2	.	.	.	.	.	6	.	1	.	.	.
118	1	505	0.8	1	5	6	2	203	3	4	.	3	.	.	.	.	.	.	.	.	.	.	.	.	.	.	.	.	.	3	.	3	.	.	.
119	1	507	0.8	1	5	6	2	303	3	4	.	.	.	2	.	.	.	.	.	.	.	1	.	1	.	.	.	.	.	2	.	1	.	.	.
120	1	515	0.8	1	5	6	3	103	2	4	.	.	.	1	.	.	.	.	.	.	.	.	.	.	.	.	.	.	.	1	.	.	.	.	.
121	1	503	0.9	1	5	6	3	203	2	4	.	.	.	1	.	.	.	.	.	.	.	2	.	.	.	.	.	.	.	4	.	2	.	.	.
122	1	485	0.7	1	5	6	3	303	2	4	1	.	.	2	.	1	1	.	.	.	.	.	.	.	1	.	.	.	.	.	.	2	.	.	.
123	1	454	0.9	1	5	7	1	109	8	4	.	2	.	6	6	.	3	.	.	.	.	6	.	1	3	.	.	.	.	11	.	2	.	1	2
124	1	464	0.8	1	5	7	1	209	8	4	6	.	.	2	.	.	.	.	.	.	.	9	1	2	.	.	.	.	.	2	.	1	.	.	.
125	1	466	0.9	1	5	7	1	309	8	4	1	1	.	8	8	.	2	.	.	.	.	6	3	4	1	.	.	1	.	10	.	3	.	.	.
126	1	465	1.0	1	5	7	1	409	4	4	2	15	.	31	.	.	.	.	.	.	.	7	.	11	1	.	.	.	.	38	.	7	1	6	.
127	1	469	0.8	1	5	7	1	509	4	4	.	.	.	3	16	.	.	.	.	.	.	.	.	2	.	.	.	.	.	4	.	4	.	.	.
128	1	461	0.9	1	5	7	1	609	2	4	1	.	.	9	.	.	.	.	.	.	.	11	.	4	.	.	.	.	.	3	.	4	.	.	.
129	1	479	0.9	1	5	7	1	709	3	4	.	2	.	7	.	.	.	.	.	.	.	1	.	10	57	.	.	.	.	42	2	15	.	.	.
130	1	455	0.8	1	5	7	1	809	3	4	.	.	.	4	.	.	.	.	.	.	.	3	.	10	.	.	.	.	.	99	5	3	1	5	1
131	1	467	0.8	1	5	7	1	909	3	4	.	.	.	30	6	.	2	.	.	.	.	86	.	90	.	.	.	.	.	210	200	99	2	52	14
132	1	463	0.9	1	5	8	1	108	8	8	6	.	.	24	14	.	.	.	.	.	.	24	6	29	4	.	.	.	.	23	.	14	2	7	2
133	1	476	0.9	1	5	8	1	208	8	8	2	3	.	17	.	.	12	.	.	.	.	7	11	73	3	.	.	.	.	19	1	15	.	6	.

OBS	RUBUS	BIXA	PHYSOLIS	OXALIS	AMBROSIA	NICOTIAN	SALVIA	MINT	GALIUM	OPUNTIA	CYPER	COMPOSIT	UMBELLIF	FABACEAE	UNKWNSEE	WDCT	WDWT	GRSSTKS	EUPHORB	PHORLUP	MIMOSA	VACCINIU	BERBERIS	TRITICUM	MOLLUGO	PENDFRAG	CACTUS	CALEND	CRUCIFER	SOLANUM	LGLEGUME	TLEGUME	KG	M3VOL	PHASE	STAT	LEV
115	.	.	1	.	.	.	5	.	.	.	.	1	.	.	.	28	.	.	.	.	.	.	.	.	.	.	.	.	.	.	.	3	6.0	0.0060	HI	.	6
116	.	.	.	2	.	1	.	.	.	.	.	.	.	.	1	15	.	.	.	19	.	.	.	.	.	.	.	.	.	.	19	11	4.8	0.0048	HI	.	6
117	.	.	.	.	.	.	.	.	.	.	.	.	.	.	.	3	.	.	.	.	.	.	.	.	.	.	.	.	.	.	.	.	6.0	0.0060	HI	.	6
118	.	.	.	.	.	.	.	.	.	.	.	.	.	.	.	11	.	.	.	4	.	.	.	.	.	.	.	.	.	.	4	.	4.8	0.0048	HI	.	6
119	.	.	.	.	.	.	.	.	.	.	.	.	.	.	1	.	.	1	.	.	.	.	.	.	.	.	.	.	.	.	.	.	4.8	0.0048	HI	.	6
120	.	.	.	.	.	.	.	.	.	.	.	.	.	.	.	2	.	.	.	1	.	.	.	.	.	.	.	.	.	.	1	.	4.8	0.0048	HI	.	6
121	.	.	.	.	.	.	.	.	.	.	.	.	.	.	.	1	.	.	.	1	.	.	.	.	.	.	.	.	.	.	1	.	5.4	0.0054	HI	.	6
122	.	.	.	.	.	.	.	.	.	.	.	.	.	.	.	3	.	.	.	.	.	.	.	.	.	.	.	.	.	.	.	1	4.2	0.0042	HI	.	6
123	.	.	.	1	.	1	.	.	.	.	.	.	.	.	.	57	.	.	.	.	.	.	.	.	.	.	.	.	.	.	.	3	5.4	0.0054	HI	.	7
124	.	.	.	.	.	.	.	.	.	.	.	.	.	.	4	.	37	.	.	8	.	.	.	.	.	.	.	.	.	.	8	.	4.8	0.0048	HI	.	7
125	.	.	.	.	.	1	.	.	.	.	.	.	.	.	5	15	.	.	.	.	.	.	.	.	.	.	1	.	.	.	.	1	5.4	0.0054	HI	.	7
126	.	.	1	.	.	.	.	.	.	.	.	3	.	.	2	2	.	.	.	.	.	.	.	.	.	.	.	.	.	.	.	1	6.0	0.0060	HI	.	7
127	.	.	.	.	.	.	.	.	.	.	.	.	.	.	.	3	.	.	.	.	.	.	.	.	.	.	.	.	.	.	.	.	4.8	0.0048	HI	.	7
128	.	.	.	.	.	.	.	.	.	.	.	.	.	.	.	15	.	.	.	.	.	.	.	.	.	.	.	.	.	.	.	.	5.4	0.0054	HI	.	7
129	.	.	.	.	.	.	.	.	1	.	.	1	.	.	2	99	.	.	.	.	.	.	.	.	.	.	.	.	.	.	.	57	5.4	0.0054	HI	.	7
130	.	.	.	2	.	.	.	.	.	.	.	1	.	.	2	.	78	.	.	.	.	.	.	.	.	.	.	.	.	.	.	.	4.8	0.0048	HI	.	7
131	4	.	.	.	.	1	2	.	.	.	.	.	.	.	8	.	193	.	.	.	.	.	.	.	.	.	.	.	.	.	.	.	4.8	0.0048	HI	.	7
132	1	.	.	.	.	.	.	.	1	.	.	2	.	.	9	3	.	.	.	.	.	.	.	.	.	.	.	.	.	.	.	4	5.4	0.0054	HO/HI	.	8
133	.	.	.	.	.	.	.	.	.	.	.	5	.	.	.	3	.	.	.	35	.	.	.	.	.	.	.	.	.	.	35	3	5.4	0.0054	HO/HI	.	8

OBS	FLTMCO	FLOT	BAGSIZE	SITE	FEATURE	LEVEL	LOCUS	BAGNO	CONTEXT	DATE	MZKERNAL	CUPCOBS	EMBRYOS	CHENOPOD	LUPINE	PHSPP	TUBERS	PAPAS	OCA	ULLUCO	MASHUA	LUMPS	AMARANTH	SCIRPUS	SMLEGUME	LEPIDIUM	LUCUMA	RARE	PORTULAC	VERBENA	PLANTAGO	SGRASS	LGRASS	MGRASS	MALVAST
134	1	551	0.9	1	5	8	1	308	8	8	7	.	.	12	11	.	7	.	.	.	.	59	.	38	2	.	.	.	.	20	.	18	2	.	6
135	1	552	0.9	1	5	8	1	408	8	8	25	20	5	58	.	.	.	.	.	.	.	26	.	47	21	.	.	.	.	61	3	49	.	26	8
136	1	539	0.8	1	5	8	1	508	8	8	.	.	.	.	.	.	.	.	.	.	.	1	.	.	.	.	.	.	.	1	.	.	.	.	.
137	1	611	0.8	1	5	8	1	608	8	8	3	68	3	49	4	.	.	.	.	.	.	10	3	65	3	.	.	.	.	10	1	17	5	.	.
138	1	629	1.0	1	5	8	1	708	8	8	3	46	.	80	13	3	2	.	.	.	.	46	5	63	6	.	.	.	.	20	2	69	2	4	7
139	1	578	0.7	1	5	8	1	808	8	8	2	2	.	1	.	.	.	.	.	.	.	1	4	2	.	.	.	.	.	.	.	12	.	.	.
140	1	630	1.0	1	5	9	1	106	1	3	6	.	.	3	.	.	.	.	.	.	.	.	.	9	3	.	.	.	.	.	.	13	2	.	.
141	1	638	0.9	1	5	9	1	206	8	3	.	3	.	4	.	.	.	.	.	.	.	6	.	.	.	.	.	.	.	1	.	1	.	.	2
142	1	604	0.8	1	5	9	1	306	8	3	.	4	.	4	.	.	3	.	.	.	.	9	2	.	1	.	.	.	.	1	.	.	1	.	.
143	1	535	0.8	1	5	9	1	406	8	3	1	3	1	4	8	.	.	.	.	.	.	9	13	3	.	.	.	.	.	5	.	3	.	4	1
144	1	536	0.8	1	5	9	1	506	8	3	1	5	1	5	10	.	.	.	.	.	.	4	1	1	.	.	.	.	.	1	.	3	.	.	.
145	1	600	0.9	1	5	9	1	606	8	3	.	4	.	.	.	.	56	.	.	.	.	1	1	2	2	.	.	.	.	2	.	2	.	.	.
146	1	595	0.9	1	5	10	1	104	8	3	.	1	.	1	.	.	.	.	.	.	.	6	.	1	.	.	.	.	.	1	.	1	1	.	4
147	1	537	0.8	1	5	10	1	204	8	3	.	1	.	7	.	.	.	.	.	.	.	5	.	8	5	.	.	.	.	3	.	6	.	.	1
148	1	580	1.0	1	5	10	1	304	8	3	.	1	.	3	.	.	.	.	.	.	.	3	.	2	1	.	.	.	.	2	.	4	1	.	.
149	1	890	0.8	1	5	10	1	404	8	3	1	1	.	11	.	.	9	.	.	.	.	.	.	5	5	.	.	.	.	5	1	6	.	.	1
150	1	583	0.8	1	5	11	1	103	8	3	1	.	.	.	3	.	5	.	.	.	.	.	.	.	3	.	.	.	.	5	.	3	2	1	2
151	1	586	0.7	1	5	11	1	203	8	3	.	.	.	2	.	.	.	.	.	.	.	2	.	.	5	.	.	.	.	1	.	3	.	.	3
152	1	626	1.0	1	5	11	1	303	8	3	.	.	.	5	.	.	.	.	.	.	.	17	.	6	4	.	.	.	.	2	.	3	2	.	1

OBS	RUBUS	BIXA	PHYSOLIS	OXALIS	AMBROSIA	NICOTIAN	SALVIA	MINT	GALIUM	OPUNTIA	CYPER	COMPOSIT	UMBELLIF	FABACEAE	UNKNSEE	WDCT	WDWT	GRSSTKS	EUPHORB	PHORLUP	MIMOSA	VACCINIU	BERBERIS	TRITICUM	MOLLUGO	PENDFRAG	CACTUS	CALEND	CRUCIFER	SOLANUM	LGLEGUME	TLEGUME	KG	M3VOL	PHASE	STAT	LEV
134	.	.	.	.	1	.	3	.	3	.	.	.	.	.	3	.	.	1	.	.	.	.	.	.	.	.	.	.	.	.	.	2	5.4	0.0054	HO/HI	.	8
135	1	.	1	2	.	.	.	.	.	.	3	2	.	.	37	21	.	.	.	10	.	.	.	.	.	.	.	.	.	.	10	21	5.4	0.0054	HO/HI	.	8
136	.	.	.	.	.	.	.	.	.	.	.	.	.	.	.	.	.	.	.	.	.	.	.	.	.	.	.	.	.	.	.	.	4.8	0.0048	HO/HI	.	8
137	3	.	.	.	.	.	.	.	2	.	.	4	.	.	6	51	.	.	.	13	.	.	.	.	.	.	.	.	.	.	13	3	4.8	0.0048	HO/HI	.	8
138	.	.	.	1	.	.	.	.	.	.	.	2	.	.	16	64	.	1	.	5	.	.	.	.	.	.	.	.	.	.	5	6	6.0	0.0060	HO/HI	.	8
139	.	.	.	.	.	.	.	.	.	.	.	.	.	.	.	1	.	1	.	.	.	.	.	.	.	.	.	.	.	.	.	.	4.2	0.0042	HO/HI	.	8
140	.	.	.	.	.	1	.	.	.	.	.	.	.	.	5	4	.	1	.	1	.	.	.	.	.	.	.	.	.	.	1	3	6.0	0.0060	HO	.	9
141	.	.	.	.	.	.	.	.	.	.	.	.	.	.	2	.	.	.	.	4	.	.	.	.	.	.	.	.	.	.	4	.	5.4	0.0054	HO	.	9
142	.	.	.	.	.	9	.	.	.	.	.	.	.	.	3	27	.	1	.	1	.	.	.	.	.	.	.	.	.	.	1	1	4.8	0.0048	HO	.	9
143	.	.	1	,	.	4	1	.	.	.	.	.	.	.	3	4	.	.	.	.	.	.	.	.	.	.	.	.	.	.	.	.	4.8	0.0048	HO	.	9
144	.	.	.	.	.	.	.	.	.	.	.	.	.	.	1	30	.	.	.	.	.	.	.	.	.	.	.	.	.	.	.	.	4.8	0.0048	HO	.	9
145	.	.	.	.	.	.	.	.	.	.	.	.	.	.	1	13	.	.	.	.	.	.	.	.	.	.	.	.	.	.	.	2	5.4	0.0054	HO	.	9
146	.	.	.	.	.	.	.	.	.	.	1	.	.	.	1	5	.	.	.	.	.	.	.	.	.	.	.	.	.	.	.	.	5.4	0.0054	HO	.	*
147	.	.	.	.	.	.	.	.	.	.	.	.	.	.	2	29	.	.	.	1	.	.	.	.	.	.	.	.	.	.	1	5	4.8	0.0048	HO	.	*
148	.	.	.	.	.	.	.	.	.	.	.	.	.	.	2	.	.	.	.	.	.	.	.	.	.	.	.	.	.	.	.	1	6.0	0.0060	HO	.	*
149	.	.	.	.	.	.	.	.	.	.	.	.	.	.	1	39	.	.	.	.	.	.	.	.	.	.	.	.	.	.	.	5	4.8	0.0048	HO	.	*
150	.	.	.	.	.	.	.	.	.	.	.	.	.	.	3	.	.	.	.	2	.	.	.	.	.	.	.	.	.	.	2	3	4.8	0.0048	HO	.	*
151	.	.	.	.	.	.	.	.	.	.	.	.	.	.	.	.	.	.	.	1	.	.	.	.	.	.	.	.	.	.	1	5	4.2	0.0042	HO	.	*
152	.	.	.	.	.	.	.	.	.	.	.	.	1	.	3	.	.	.	.	1	.	.	.	.	.	.	.	.	.	.	1	4	6.0	0.0060	HO	.	*

OBS	FLTMCO	FLOT	BAGSIZE	SITE	FEATURE	LEVEL	LOCUS	BAGNO	CONTEXT	DATE	MZKERNAL	CUPCOBS	EMBRYOS	CHENOPOD	LUPINE	PHSPP	TUBERS	PAPAS	OCA	ULLUCO	MASHUA	LUMPS	AMARANTH	SCIRPUS	SMLEGUME	LEPIDIUM	LUCUMA	RARE	PORTULAC	VERBENA	PLANTAGO	SGRASS	LGRASS	MGRASS	MALVAST	RUBUS	BIXA
153	1	579	1.0	1	5	12	1	103	8	3	.	.	1	2	1	.	1	.	.	.	.	.	.	.	.	.	.	.	.	1	.	6	.	.	.	.	.
154	1	547	1.0	1	5	12	1	103	8	3	.	.	.	.	2	.	1	.	.	.	.	.	.	.	.	.	.	.	.	.	.	1	.	.	.	.	.
155	1	598	0.8	1	5	12	1	103	1	3	1	.	.	.	.	.	.	.	.	.	.	.	.	.	.	.	.	.	.	.	.	.	.	.	.	.	.
156	1	558	0.8	1	5	12	1	203	8	3	.	.	.	.	.	.	.	.	.	.	.	.	.	.	.	.	.	.	.	.	.	.	.	.	.	.	.
157	1	544	0.8	1	5	12	1	203	8	3	.	.	.	1	.	.	.	.	.	.	.	.	.	.	.	.	.	.	.	.	.	.	.	1	.	.	.
158	1	582	1.0	1	5	12	1	203	2	3	1	29	.	28	22	.	2	.	.	.	.	35	.	31	7	.	.	.	.	8	2	34	.	3	8	.	.
159	1	810	0.8	1	5	12	1	303	8	3	.	.	.	1	.	.	.	.	.	.	.	.	.	1	.	.	.	.	.	1	.	8	.	.	.	.	.
160	1	818	0.7	1	5	14	1	303	1	3	.	.	.	1	.	.	.	.	.	.	.	.	.	.	.	.	.	.	.	1	.	2	.	.	.	.	.
161	1	543	0.8	1	5	15	1	103	1	3	.	.	.	.	.	.	.	.	.	.	.	.	.	.	.	.	.	.	.	.	.	3	.	.	.	.	.
162	1	602	0.8	1	5	15	1	203	1	3	.	.	.	.	1	.	.	.	.	.	.	.	.	.	.	.	.	.	.	.	.	2	.	.	.	.	.
163	1	559	0.8	1	5	15	1	303	1	3	.	.	.	1	.	.	.	.	.	.	.	.	.	.	.	.	.	.	.	.	.	.	.	.	.	.	.
164	1	589	0.8	1	5	16	1	103	8	3	.	1	.	5	.	.	.	.	.	.	.	10	.	.	.	.	.	.	.	.	.	1	.	.	.	.	.
165	1	531	0.8	1	5	16	1	203	8	3	.	.	.	2	.	.	.	.	.	.	.	.	.	.	.	.	.	.	.	.	.	1	.	.	.	.	.
166	1	592	0.8	1	5	16	1	303	8	3	.	1	.	.	.	.	.	.	.	.	.	.	.	.	.	.	.	.	.	.	.	1	.	.	.	.	.
167	1	532	0.8	1	5	17	1	103	8	3	.	.	.	3	2	.	.	.	.	.	.	.	.	.	.	.	.	.	.	.	.	.	.	.	.	.	.
168	1	591	1.0	1	5	17	1	203	8	3	.	.	.	5	.	.	.	.	.	.	.	.	.	.	2	.	.	1	.	4	.	1	.	.	.	.	.
169	1	530	0.7	1	5	17	1	303	8	3	.	.	.	2	.	.	.	.	.	.	.	.	.	.	.	.	.	.	.	.	1	1	.	.	.	.	.
170	1	395	0.5	7	0	0	0	.	0	0	.	.	.	.	.	.	.	.	.	.	.	.	.	.	.	.	.	.	.	.	.	.	.	.	.	.	.
171	1	237	0.9	7	1	2	1	103	1	5	.	.	.	.	.	.	.	.	.	.	.	.	.	.	.	.	.	.	.	.	.	.	.	.	.	.	.

OBS	PHYSOLIS	OXALIS	AMBROSIA	NICOTIAN	SALVIA	MINT	GALIUM	OPUNTIA	CYPER	COMPOSIT	UMBELLIF	FABACEAE	UNKNSEE	WDCT	WDWT	GRSSTKS	EUPHORB	PHORLUP	MIMOSA	VACCINIU	BERBERIS	TRITICUM	MOLLUGO	PENDFRAG	CACTUS	CALEND	CRUCIFER	SOLANUM	LGLEGUME	TLEGUME	KG	M3VOL	PHASE	STAT	LEV
153	.	.	1	.	.	.	.	.	.	.	.	.	.	2	.	.	.	.	.	.	.	.	.	.	.	.	.	.	.	.	6.0	0.0060	HO	.	*
154	.	.	.	.	.	.	.	.	.	.	.	.	.	5	.	.	.	.	.	.	.	.	.	.	.	.	.	.	.	.	6.0	0.0060	HO	.	*
155	.	.	.	.	.	.	.	.	.	.	.	.	.	2	.	.	.	.	.	.	.	.	.	.	.	.	.	.	.	.	4.8	0.0048	HO	.	*
156	.	.	.	.	.	.	.	.	.	.	.	.	.	1	.	.	.	.	.	.	.	.	.	.	.	.	.	.	.	.	4.8	0.0048	HO	.	*
157	.	.	.	.	.	.	.	.	.	.	.	.	.	.	.	.	.	.	.	.	.	.	.	.	.	.	.	.	.	.	4.8	0.0048	HO	.	*
158	.	1	.	.	.	.	1	.	1	2	1	.	33	79	.	.	.	.	.	.	.	.	.	.	.	.	.	.	.	7	6.0	0.0060	HO	.	*
159	.	.	.	.	.	.	.	.	.	.	.	.	2	.	.	.	.	.	.	.	.	.	.	.	.	.	.	.	.	.	4.8	0.0048	HO	.	*
160	.	.	.	.	.	.	.	.	.	.	.	.	.	.	.	.	.	.	.	.	.	.	.	.	.	.	.	.	.	.	4.2	0.0042	HO	.	*
161	.	.	.	.	.	.	.	.	.	.	.	.	.	1	.	.	.	.	.	.	.	.	.	.	.	.	.	.	.	.	4.8	0.0048	HO	.	*
162	.	.	.	.	.	.	.	.	.	.	.	.	.	3	.	.	.	.	.	.	.	.	.	.	.	.	.	.	.	.	4.8	0.0048	HO	.	*
163	.	.	.	.	.	.	.	.	.	.	.	.	.	.	.	.	.	.	.	.	.	.	.	.	.	.	.	.	.	.	4.8	0.0048	HO	.	*
164	.	.	.	.	.	.	.	.	.	2	.	.	1	2	.	.	.	.	.	.	.	.	.	.	.	.	.	.	.	.	4.8	0.0048	HO	.	*
165	.	.	.	.	.	.	.	.	.	.	.	.	.	.	.	.	.	.	.	.	.	.	.	.	.	.	.	.	.	.	4.8	0.0048	HO	.	*
166	.	.	.	.	.	.	.	.	.	.	.	.	.	.	.	.	.	.	.	.	.	.	.	.	.	.	.	.	.	.	4.8	0.0048	HO	.	*
167	.	.	.	.	.	.	.	.	.	.	.	.	2	25	.	.	.	.	.	.	.	.	.	.	.	.	.	.	.	.	4.8	0.0048	HO	.	*
168	.	.	.	.	.	.	.	.	.	.	.	.	1	2	.	.	.	.	.	1	.	.	.	.	.	.	.	.	.	2	6.0	0.0060	HO	.	*
169	.	.	.	.	.	.	.	.	.	.	.	.	.	.	.	.	.	.	.	.	.	.	.	.	.	.	.	.	.	.	4.2	0.0042	HO	.	*
170	.	.	.	.	.	.	.	.	.	.	.	.	.	.	.	.	.	.	.	.	.	.	.	.	.	.	.	.	.	.	3.0	0.0030		.	0
171	.	.	.	.	.	.	.	.	.	.	.	.	.	.	.	.	.	.	.	.	.	.	.	.	.	.	.	.	.	.	5.4	0.0054	HII	.	2

OBS	FLTMCO	FLOT	BAGSIZE	SITE	FEATURE	LEVEL	LOCUS	BAGNO	CONTEXT	DATE	MZKERNAL	CUPCOBS	EMBRYOS	CHENOPOD	LUPINE	PHSPP	TUBERS	PAPAS	OCA	ULLUCO	MASHUA	LUMPS	AMARANTH	SCIRPUS	SMLEGUME	LEPIDIUM	LUCUMA	RARE	PORTULAC	VERBENA	PLANTAGO	SGRASS	LGRASS	MGRASS	MALVAST	RUBUS	BIXA
172	1	272	1.0	7	1	2	1	203	1	5	.	.	.	1	.	.	.	.	.	.	.	.	.	.	.	.	.	.	.	.	.	.	.	.	.	.	.
173	1	271	1.0	7	1	2	1	303	1	5	.	.	.	.	.	.	.	.	.	.	.	.	.	.	.	.	.	.	.	.	.	.	.	.	.	.	.
174	1	228	0.5	7	1	2	2	102	1	5	.	.	.	1	.	.	.	.	.	.	.	.	.	.	.	.	.	.	.	.	.	.	.	.	.	.	.
175	1	285	0.5	7	1	2	2	202	1	5	.	.	.	.	.	.	.	.	.	.	.	.	.	.	.	.	.	.	.	.	.	.	.	.	.	.	.
176	1	238	0.9	7	1	3	1	103	4	5	.	.	.	3	.	.	.	.	.	.	.	.	.	.	.	.	.	.	.	.	.	.	.	.	.	.	.
177	1	270	1.0	7	1	3	1	203	4	5	.	.	.	4	.	.	.	.	.	.	.	.	.	.	.	.	.	.	.	.	.	.	1	.	.	.	.
178	1	332	1.0	7	1	3	1	303	4	5	.	.	.	.	.	.	.	.	.	.	.	.	.	.	.	.	.	.	.	1	.	.	.	.	.	.	.
179	1	227	1.0	7	1	4	1	101	4	5	.	.	.	.	.	.	.	.	.	.	.	.	.	.	.	.	.	.	.	.	.	1	.	.	.	.	.
180	1	274	1.0	7	2	1	2	203	6	5	.	.	.	.	.	.	.	.	.	.	.	.	.	.	.	.	.	.	.	.	.	.	.	.	.	.	.
181	1	431	0.8	7	2	2	1	103	1	5	.	.	.	4	.	.	.	.	.	.	.	4	.	1	.	.	.	.	.	.	.	1	6	.	.	.	.
182	1	443	1.0	7	2	2	1	203	1	5	.	.	.	1	.	.	2	.	.	.	.	.	.	.	.	.	.	.	.	.	.	.	.	.	.	.	.
183	1	269	0.6	7	2	2	1	303	1	5	.	.	.	.	.	.	.	.	.	.	.	.	.	.	.	.	.	.	.	.	.	.	.	.	.	.	.
184	1	235	0.8	7	2	2	2	103	8	5	.	.	.	3	.	.	.	.	.	.	.	2	.	1	.	.	.	.	.	.	.	.	.	.	.	.	.
185	1	265	0.8	7	2	2	2	203	8	5	.	.	.	1	.	.	.	.	.	.	.	2	.	.	.	.	.	.	.	.	.	.	1	.	.	.	.
186	1	224	0.7	7	2	2	2	303	8	5	.	.	.	1	.	.	.	.	.	.	.	1	.	1	.	.	.	.	.	.	.	1	.	.	.	.	.
187	1	282	0.8	7	2	3	1	103	1	5	.	.	.	2	.	.	.	.	.	.	.	.	.	.	.	.	.	.	.	.	.	.	.	.	.	.	.
188	1	275	0.8	7	2	3	1	203	1	5	.	.	.	1	.	.	.	.	.	.	.	.	.	1	1	.	.	.	.	.	.	1	.	.	.	.	.
189	1	278	0.8	7	2	3	1	303	1	5	.	.	.	.	.	.	.	.	.	.	.	1	.	.	.	.	.	.	.	.	.	.	.	.	.	.	.
190	1	418	0.8	7	3	2	1	103	1	5	.	.	.	.	.	.	.	.	.	.	.	1	.	.	.	.	.	.	.	.	.	.	.	.	.	.	.

OBS	PHYSOLIS	OXALIS	AMBROSIA	NICOTIAN	SALVIA	MINT	GALIUM	OPUNTIA	CYPER	COMPOSIT	UMBELLIF	FABACEAE	UNKWNSEE	WDCT	WDWT	GRSSTKS	EUPHORB	PHORLUP	MIMOSA	VACCINIU	BERBERIS	TRITICUM	MOLLUGO	PENDFRAG	CACTUS	CALEND	CRUCIFER	SOLANUM	LGLEGUME	TLEGUME	KG	M3VOL	PHASE	STAT	LEV
172	.	.	.	.	.	.	.	.	.	.	.	.	.	.	.	.	.	.	.	.	.	.	.	.	.	.	.	.	.	.	6.0	0.0060	HII	.	2
173	.	.	.	.	.	.	.	.	.	.	.	.	.	.	.	.	.	.	.	.	.	.	.	.	.	.	.	.	.	.	6.0	0.0060	HII	.	2
174	.	.	.	.	.	.	.	.	.	.	.	.	.	.	.	.	.	.	.	.	.	.	.	.	.	.	.	.	.	.	3.0	0.0030	HII	.	2
175	.	.	.	.	.	.	.	.	.	.	.	.	.	.	.	.	.	.	.	.	.	.	.	.	.	.	.	.	.	.	3.0	0.0030	HII	.	2
176	.	.	.	.	.	.	.	.	.	.	.	.	.	1	.	.	.	.	.	.	.	.	.	.	.	.	.	.	.	.	5.4	0.0054	HII	.	3
177	.	.	.	.	.	.	.	.	.	.	.	.	.	.	.	.	.	.	.	.	.	.	.	.	.	.	.	.	.	.	6.0	0.0060	HII	.	3
178	.	.	.	.	.	.	.	.	.	.	.	.	.	.	.	.	.	.	.	.	.	.	.	.	.	.	.	.	.	.	6.0	0.0060	HII	.	3
179	.	.	.	.	.	.	.	.	.	.	.	.	.	.	.	.	.	.	.	.	.	.	.	.	.	.	.	.	.	.	6.0	0.0060	HII	.	4
180	.	.	.	.	.	.	.	.	.	.	.	.	.	.	.	.	.	.	.	.	.	.	.	.	.	.	.	.	.	.	6.0	0.0060	HII	.	1
181	.	.	.	.	.	.	.	.	.	.	.	.	.	1	.	1	.	.	.	.	.	.	.	.	.	.	.	.	.	.	4.8	0.0048	HII	.	2
182	.	.	.	.	.	.	.	.	.	.	.	.	.	.	.	.	.	.	.	.	.	.	.	.	.	.	.	.	.	.	6.0	0.0060	HII	.	2
183	.	.	.	.	.	.	.	.	.	.	.	.	.	.	.	.	.	.	.	.	.	.	.	.	.	.	.	.	.	.	3.6	0.0036	HII	.	2
184	.	.	.	.	.	.	.	.	.	.	.	.	.	3	.	1	.	.	.	.	.	.	.	.	.	.	.	.	.	.	4.8	0.0048	HII	.	2
185	.	.	.	.	.	.	.	.	.	.	.	.	.	6	.	.	.	.	.	.	.	.	.	.	.	.	.	.	.	.	4.8	0.0048	HII	.	2
186	.	.	.	.	.	.	.	.	.	.	.	.	.	2	.	.	.	.	.	.	.	.	.	.	.	.	.	.	.	.	4.2	0.0042	HII	.	2
187	.	.	.	.	.	.	.	.	.	.	.	.	.	2	.	.	.	.	.	.	.	.	.	.	.	.	.	.	.	.	4.8	0.0048	HII	.	3
188	.	.	.	.	.	.	.	.	.	.	.	.	.	.	.	.	.	.	.	.	.	.	.	.	.	.	.	.	.	1	4.8	0.0048	HII	.	3
189	.	.	.	.	.	.	.	.	.	.	.	.	.	.	.	.	.	.	.	.	.	.	.	.	.	.	.	.	.	.	4.8	0.0048	HII	.	3
190	.	.	.	.	.	.	.	.	.	.	.	.	.	.	.	.	.	.	.	.	.	.	.	.	.	.	.	.	.	.	4.8	0.0048	HII	.	2

OBS	FLTMCO	FLOT	BAGSIZE	SITE	FEATURE	LEVEL	LOCUS	BAGNO	CONTEXT	DATE	MZKERNAL	CUPCOBS	EMBRYOS	CHENOPOD	LUPINE	PHSPP	TUBERS	PAPAS	OCA	ULLUCO	MASHUA	LUMPS	AMARANTH	SCIRPUS	SMLEGUME	LEPIDIUM	LUCUMA	RARE	PORTULAC	VERBENA	PLANTAGO	SGRASS	LGRASS	MGRASS	MALVAST	RUBUS	BIXA
191	1	389	1.0	7	3	2	1	203	1	5	.	.	.	3	1	.	.	.	.	.	.	3	.	.	.	.	.	.	.	1	.	3	.	.	.	.	.
192	1	289	1.0	7	3	2	1	303	1	5	.	.	.	3	.	.	1	.	.	.	.	.	.	1	.	.	.	.	.	.	.	4	.	.	.	.	.
193	1	435	1.0	7	3	3	1	103	4	5	.	.	.	3	.	.	1	.	.	.	.	.	.	1	.	.	.	.	.	.	.	8	1	.	.	.	.
194	1	433	1.0	7	3	3	1	203	4	5	.	.	.	1	.	.	12	.	.	.	.	.	.	.	.	.	.	.	.	.	.	16	2	.	.	.	.
195	1	419	0.8	7	3	3	1	303	4	5	.	.	.	2	.	.	.	.	.	.	.	4	.	.	1	.	.	.	1	.	.	11	.	.	.	1	.
196	1	623	0.8	7	4	1	1	103	9	5	.	.	.	.	.	.	1	.	.	.	.	.	.	.	.	.	.	.	.	.	.	.	.	.	.	.	.
197	1	575	0.8	7	4	2	1	103	1	5	.	.	.	.	.	.	1	.	.	.	.	.	.	.	.	.	.	.	.	.	.	.	.	.	.	.	.
198	1	577	0.9	7	4	2	1	203	1	5	.	.	.	.	.	.	.	.	.	.	.	.	.	.	.	.	.	.	.	.	.	.	.	.	.	.	.
199	1	568	0.8	7	4	2	1	303	1	5	.	.	.	.	.	.	.	.	.	.	.	.	.	.	.	.	.	.	.	.	.	.	.	.	.	.	.
200	1	566	0.7	7	4	2	3	103	6	5	.	.	.	2	.	.	2	.	.	.	.	1	1	.	.	.	.	.	.	1	.	1	.	.	.	.	.
201	1	397	0.8	7	4	2	3	203	6	5	.	.	.	.	.	.	.	.	.	.	.	1	.	.	.	.	.	.	.	.	.	.	.	.	.	.	.
202	1	567	0.7	7	4	2	3	303	6	5	.	.	.	1	.	.	2	.	.	.	.	.	.	.	.	.	.	.	.	1	.	3	2	.	.	.	.
203	1	413	0.4	7	4	3	3	203	4	5	.	.	.	.	.	.	.	.	.	.	.	3	.	.	.	.	.	.	.	.	.	3	.	.	.	.	.
204	1	570	0.5	7	4	3	3	303	4	5	.	.	.	.	.	.	.	.	.	.	.	.	.	.	.	.	.	.	.	.	.	.	.	.	.	.	.
205	1	290	1.0	7	5	2	1	103	1	5	.	.	.	.	6	.	.	.	.	.	.	2	.	.	.	.	.	.	.	.	.	4	.	.	.	.	.
206	1	438	0.8	7	5	2	1	203	1	5	1	.	.	.	.	.	.	.	.	.	.	1	1	.	.	.	.	.	.	.	.	.	.	.	.	.	.
207	1	437	0.9	7	5	2	1	303	1	5	.	.	.	.	.	.	2	.	.	.	.	.	.	.	.	.	.	.	.	.	.	8	.	.	.	.	.
208	1	407	0.5	7	5	2	2	103	6	5	4	.	.	.	.	.	.	.	.	.	.	3	.	.	.	.	.	.	.	.	.	.	.	.	.	.	.
209	1	434	0.5	7	5	2	2	203	6	5	5	.	.	1	2	.	4	.	.	.	.	.	.	.	.	.	.	.	.	.	.	8	.	.	.	.	.

OBS	PHYSOLIS	OXALIS	AMBROSIA	NICOTIAN	SALVIA	MINT	GALIUM	OPUNTIA	CYPER	COMPOSIT	UMBELLIF	FABACEAE	UNKWNSEE	WDCT	WDWT	GRSSTKS	EUPHORB	PHORLUP	MIMOSA	VACCINIU	BERBERIS	TRITICUM	MOLLUGO	PENDFRAG	CACTUS	CALEND	CRUCIFER	SOLANUM	LGLEGUME	TLEGUME	KG	M3VOL	PHASE	STAT	LEV
191	.	.	.	.	.	.	.	.	.	.	.	.	.	1	.	.	.	.	.	.	.	.	.	.	.	.	.	.	.	.	6.0	0.0060	HII	.	2
192	.	.	.	.	.	.	.	.	.	.	.	.	1	.	.	.	.	.	.	.	.	.	.	.	.	.	.	.	.	.	6.0	0.0060	HII	.	2
193	.	.	.	.	.	.	.	.	.	1	.	.	1	5	.	.	.	.	.	.	.	.	.	.	.	.	.	.	.	.	6.0	0.0060	HII	.	3
194	.	.	.	.	.	.	.	.	.	.	.	.	.	.	.	.	.	.	.	.	.	.	.	.	.	.	.	.	.	.	6.0	0.0060	HII	.	3
195	.	.	.	.	.	.	.	.	.	.	.	.	.	5	.	.	.	1	.	.	.	.	.	.	.	.	.	.	1	1	4.8	0.0048	HII	.	3
196	.	.	.	.	.	.	.	.	.	.	.	.	.	11	.	.	.	.	.	.	.	.	.	.	.	.	.	.	.	.	4.8	0.0048	HII	.	1
197	.	.	.	.	.	.	.	.	.	.	.	.	.	.	.	.	.	.	.	.	.	.	.	.	.	.	.	.	.	.	4.8	0.0048	HII	.	2
198	.	.	.	.	.	.	.	.	.	.	.	.	.	.	.	.	.	.	.	.	.	.	.	.	.	.	.	.	.	.	5.4	0.0054	HII	.	2
199	.	.	.	.	.	.	.	.	.	.	.	.	.	.	.	.	.	.	.	.	.	.	.	.	.	.	.	.	.	.	4.8	0.0048	HII	.	2
200	.	.	.	.	.	.	.	.	.	.	.	.	.	7	.	.	.	.	.	.	.	.	.	.	.	.	.	.	.	.	4.2	0.0042	HII	.	2
201	.	.	.	.	.	.	.	.	.	.	.	.	.	9	.	.	.	.	.	.	.	.	.	.	.	.	.	.	.	.	4.8	0.0048	HII	.	2
202	.	.	.	.	.	.	.	.	.	.	.	.	.	2	.	.	.	.	.	.	.	.	.	.	.	.	.	.	.	.	4.2	0.0042	HII	.	2
203	.	.	.	.	.	.	.	.	.	.	.	.	.	.	.	.	.	.	.	.	.	.	.	.	.	.	.	.	.	.	2.4	0.0024	HII	.	3
204	.	.	.	.	.	.	.	.	.	.	.	.	.	1	.	.	.	.	.	.	.	.	.	.	.	.	.	.	.	.	3.0	0.0030	HII	.	3
205	.	.	.	.	.	.	.	.	.	.	.	.	.	1	.	.	.	.	.	.	.	.	.	.	.	.	.	.	.	.	6.0	0.0060	HII	.	2
206	.	.	.	.	.	.	.	.	.	.	.	.	4	11	.	.	.	.	.	.	.	.	.	.	.	.	.	.	.	.	4.8	0.0048	HII	.	2
207	.	.	.	.	.	.	.	.	.	.	.	.	.	1	.	.	.	.	.	.	.	.	.	.	.	.	.	.	.	.	5.4	0.0054	HII	.	2
208	.	.	.	.	.	.	.	.	.	.	.	.	.	9	.	.	.	.	.	.	.	.	.	.	.	.	.	.	.	.	3.0	0.0030	HII	.	2
209	.	.	.	.	.	.	.	.	.	.	.	.	1	13	.	.	.	.	.	.	.	.	.	.	.	.	.	.	.	.	3.0	0.0030	HII	.	2

OBS	FLTMCO	FLOT	BAGSIZE	SITE	FEATURE	LEVEL	LOCUS	BAGNO	CONTEXT	DATE	MZKERNAL	CUPCOBS	EMBRYOS	CHENOPOD	LUPINE	PHSP	TUBERS	PAPAS	OCA	ULLUCO	MASHUA	LUMPS	AMARANTH	SCIRPUS	SMLEGUME	LEPIDIUM	LUCUMA	RARE	PORTULACA	VERBENA	PLANTAGO	SGRASS	LGRASS	MGRASS	MALVAST	RUBUS
210	1	609	0.5	7	5	2	2	303	6	5	.	.	.	1	3	.	.	.	.	.	.	2	.	.	.	.	.	.	.	.	.	1	.	.	1	.
211	1	263	0.5	7	5	3	1	103	4	5	.	.	.	2	.	.	11	.	.	.	.	.	.	.	.	.	.	.	.	.	.	19	1	.	.	.
212	1	607	0.5	7	5	3	1	203	4	5	.	.	.	3	.	.	5	.	.	.	.	4	.	.	.	.	.	.	.	.	2	37	3	.	.	.
213	1	436	0.5	7	5	3	1	303	4	5	.	.	.	.	.	.	10	.	.	.	.	4	.	.	.	.	.	.	.	.	.	12	1	2	.	.
214	1	394	0.9	7	5	3	2	103	4	5	.	.	.	.	.	.	2	.	.	.	.	4	.	.	.	.	.	.	.	.	.	.	.	.	.	.
215	1	392	0.9	7	5	3	2	203	4	5	2	.	.	.	.	.	2	.	.	.	.	.	.	.	.	.	.	.	.	.	.	.	.	.	.	.
216	1	257	1.0	7	5	3	2	303	4	5	1	.	.	.	.	.	.	.	.	.	.	.	.	.	.	.	.	.	.	.	.	.	.	1	.	.
217	1	406	0.5	7	5	4	2	103	4	5	.	.	.	.	.	.	.	.	.	.	.	.	.	.	.	.	.	.	.	.	.	1	.	.	.	.
218	1	398	0.4	7	5	4	2	203	4	5	.	.	.	.	.	.	.	.	.	.	.	.	.	.	.	.	.	.	.	.	.	2	.	.	.	.
219	1	415	0.4	7	5	4	2	303	4	5	.	.	.	.	.	.	.	.	.	.	.	.	.	.	.	.	.	.	.	.	.	3	.	.	.	1
220	1	342	1.0	7	6	2	1	103	1	5	.	.	.	1	.	.	3	.	.	.	.	.	.	.	.	.	.	.	.	.	.	4	3	.	.	.
221	1	322	1.0	7	6	2	1	203	1	5	.	.	.	.	.	.	.	.	.	.	.	3	.	.	.	.	.	.	.	.	.	1	.	.	.	.
222	1	410	1.0	7	6	2	1	303	1	5	.	.	.	.	.	.	.	.	.	.	.	.	.	.	.	.	.	.	.	.	.	.	1	.	.	.
223	1	390	0.6	7	6	2	2	101	6	5	.	.	.	.	.	.	19	.	.	.	.	.	.	.	.	.	.	.	.	.	.	11	5	.	.	.
224	1	408	0.5	7	6	2	2	103	6	5	.	.	.	1	.	.	4	.	.	.	.	.	.	.	.	.	.	.	.	.	.	1	.	.	.	.
225	1	391	0.5	7	6	2	2	303	6	5	.	.	.	1	.	.	.	.	1	.	.	.	.	.	.	.	.	.	.	.	.	1	1	.	.	.
226	1	339	0.5	7	6	2	3	203	6	5	.	.	.	.	.	.	8	.	.	.	.	2	.	.	.	.	.	.	.	.	.	21	5	.	.	.
227	1	226	0.5	7	6	3	1	103	4	5	.	.	.	2	.	.	2	.	.	.	.	.	.	1	.	.	.	.	.	.	1	7	1	.	.	.
228	1	564	0.9	7	6	3	1	103	4	5	.	.	.	15	.	.	50	.	.	.	.	.	1	9	3	.	.	.	.	6	1	95	31	16	1	3

OBS	BIXA	PHYSALIS	OXALIS	AMBROSIA	NICOTIAN	SALVIA	MINT	GALIUM	OPUNTIA	CYPER	COMPOSIT	UMBELLIF	FABACEAE	UNKWNSEE	WDCT	WDWT	GRSSTKS	EUPHORB	PHORLUP	MIMOSA	VACCINIU	BERBERIS	TRITICUM	MOLLUGO	PENDFRAG	CACTUS	CALEND	CRUCIFER	SOLANUM	LGLEGUME	TLEGUME	KG	M3VOL	PHASE	STAT	LEV
210	.	.	.	.	.	.	.	.	.	.	.	.	.	.	20	.	.	.	.	.	.	.	.	.	.	.	.	.	.	.	.	3.0	0.0030	HII	.	2
211	.	.	.	.	.	.	.	1	.	.	.	.	.	1	.	.	.	.	.	.	.	.	.	.	.	.	.	.	.	.	.	3.0	0.0030	HII	.	3
212	.	.	.	.	.	.	.	.	.	.	.	.	.	2	.	.	.	.	.	.	.	.	.	.	.	.	.	.	.	.	.	3.0	0.0030	HII	.	3
213	.	.	.	.	.	.	.	.	.	.	.	.	.	2	.	.	.	.	.	.	.	.	.	.	.	.	.	.	.	.	.	3.0	0.0030	HII	.	3
214	.	.	.	.	.	.	.	.	.	.	.	.	.	.	1	.	.	.	.	.	.	.	.	.	.	.	.	.	.	.	.	5.4	0.0054	HII	.	3
215	.	.	.	.	.	.	.	.	.	.	.	.	.	.	7	.	.	.	.	.	.	.	.	.	.	.	.	.	.	.	.	5.4	0.0054	HII	.	3
216	.	.	.	.	.	.	.	.	.	.	.	.	.	.	1	.	.	.	.	.	.	.	.	.	.	.	.	.	.	.	.	6.0	0.0060	HII	.	3
217	.	.	.	.	.	.	.	.	.	.	.	.	.	2	.	.	.	.	.	.	.	.	.	.	.	.	.	.	.	.	.	3.0	0.0030	HII	.	4
218	.	.	.	.	.	.	.	.	.	.	.	.	.	.	.	.	.	.	.	.	.	.	.	.	.	.	.	.	.	.	.	2.4	0.0024	HII	.	4
219	.	.	.	.	.	.	.	.	.	.	.	.	.	.	.	.	.	.	.	.	.	.	.	.	.	.	.	.	.	.	.	2.4	0.0024	HII	.	4
220	.	.	.	.	.	.	.	.	.	.	.	.	.	.	.	.	.	.	.	.	.	.	.	.	.	.	.	.	.	.	.	6.0	0.0060	HII	.	2
221	.	.	.	.	.	.	.	.	.	.	.	.	.	.	.	.	.	.	.	.	.	.	.	.	.	.	.	.	.	.	.	6.0	0.0060	HII	.	2
222	.	.	.	.	.	.	.	.	.	.	.	.	.	1	.	.	.	.	.	.	.	.	.	.	.	.	.	.	.	.	.	6.0	0.0060	HII	.	2
223	.	.	.	.	.	.	.	.	.	.	.	.	.	.	.	.	.	.	.	.	.	.	.	.	.	.	.	.	.	.	.	3.6	0.0036	HII	.	2
224	.	.	.	.	.	.	.	.	.	.	.	.	.	.	1	.	1	.	.	.	.	.	.	.	.	.	.	.	.	.	.	3.0	0.0030	HII	.	2
225	.	.	.	.	.	.	.	.	.	.	.	.	.	.	.	.	.	.	.	.	.	.	.	.	.	.	.	.	.	.	.	3.0	0.0030	HII	.	2
226	.	.	.	.	.	.	.	.	.	.	.	.	.	.	.	.	.	.	.	.	.	.	.	.	.	.	.	.	.	.	.	3.0	0.0030	HII	.	2
227	.	.	.	.	.	.	.	.	.	.	.	.	.	.	1	.	.	.	.	.	.	.	.	.	.	.	.	.	.	.	.	3.0	0.0030	HII	.	3
228	.	.	.	.	.	.	.	1	.	.	.	.	.	0	6	.	.	.	.	.	.	.	.	.	.	.	.	.	.	.	3	5.4	0.0054	HII	.	3

OBS	FLTMCO	FLOT	BAGSIZE	SITE	FEATURE	LEVEL	LOCUS	BAGNO	CONTEXT	DATE	MZKERNAL	CUPCOBS	EMBRYOS	CHENOPOD	LUPINE	PHSP	TUBERS	PAPAS	OCA	ULLUCO	MASHUA	LUMPS	AMARANTH	SCIRPUS	SMLEGUME	LEPIDIUM	LUCUMA	RARE	PORTULACA	VERBENA	PLANTAGO	SGRASS	LGRASS	MGRASS	MALVAST	RUBUS
229	1	223	1.0	7	6	3	1	203	4	5	.	.	.	11	.	.	39	.	3	.	.	.	4	7	7	.	.	.	.	2	8	99	16	19	2	8
230	1	240	0.5	7	6	3	1	203	4	5	.	.	.	1	.	.	.	.	.	.	.	8	.	.	.	.	.	.	.	.	.	16	.	1	.	.
231	1	444	0.8	7	6	3	1	303	4	5	.	.	.	9	.	.	.	.	.	75	.	.	1	.	4	.	.	.	.	5	1	99	6	17	1	4
232	1	225	0.5	7	6	3	1	303	4	5	.	.	.	1	.	.	.	.	3	.	.	.	.	.	1	.	.	.	.	.	.	9	2	.	.	.
233	1	442	0.6	7	6	3	2	103	6	5	.	.	.	1	.	.	3	.	.	.	.	.	.	.	.	.	.	.	.	.	.	2	.	.	.	.
234	1	260	0.5	7	6	3	2	203	6	5	.	.	.	3	2	.	9	.	.	.	.	.	.	.	.	.	.	.	.	.	.	33	9	1	.	.
235	1	236	0.5	7	6	3	2	303	6	5	.	.	.	1	.	.	3	.	.	.	.	.	.	.	.	.	.	.	.	.	.	9	.	.	.	.
236	1	396	0.5	7	6	4	1	103	4	5	.	.	.	5	.	.	28	.	.	.	.	1	.	1	2	.	.	1	.	1	.	25	2	5	2	1
237	1	432	0.6	7	6	4	1	203	4	5	.	.	.	5	.	.	34	.	.	.	.	.	.	2	3	.	.	.	.	.	.	16	5	4	1	.
238	1	403	0.6	7	6	4	1	303	4	5	.	.	.	7	.	.	.	.	.	.	.	.	.	2	.	.	.	1	.	.	1	18	1	.	.	.
239	1	728	0.7	7	7	2	1	104	1	5	.	.	.	.	.	.	.	.	.	.	.	.	.	.	.	.	.	.	.	.	.	.	3	.	.	.
240	1	772	0.7	7	7	2	1	204	1	5	.	.	.	.	.	.	.	.	.	.	.	.	.	.	.	.	.	.	.	.	.	1	3	.	.	.
241	1	773	0.8	7	7	2	1	304	1	5	.	.	.	.	.	.	.	.	.	.	.	.	.	1	.	.	.	.	.	.	.	2	3	.	.	.
242	1	732	0.8	7	7	2	1	404	1	5	.	1	.	.	.	.	.	.	.	.	.	.	.	.	.	.	.	.	.	.	.	.	1	.	.	.
243	1	725	0.7	7	7	3	1	104	1	5	.	.	.	1	.	.	.	.	.	.	.	1	.	1	.	.	.	.	.	.	.	3	.	.	.	.
244	1	796	0.8	7	7	3	1	204	1	5	.	.	.	.	.	.	.	.	.	.	.	1	.	1	.	.	.	.	.	.	.	1	5	.	.	.
245	1	7[illegible]9	0.7	7	7	3	1	304	1	5	.	.	.	.	.	.	1	.	.	.	.	.	.	.	.	.	.	.	.	.	.	1	.	1	.	.
246	1	760	0.8	7	7	3	1	404	1	5	.	1	.	18	1	.	8	.	.	.	.	.	.	2	2	.	.	2	.	.	.	9	10	2	.	.
247	1	756	0.7	7	7	4	1	103	4	5	.	.	.	.	.	.	.	.	.	.	.	.	.	.	.	.	.	.	.	.	.	1	.	.	.	.

OBS	BIXA	PHYSALIS	OXALIS	AMBROSIA	NICOTIAN	SALVIA	MINT	GALIUM	OPUNTIA	CYPER	COMPOSIT	UMBELLIF	FABACEAE	UNKWNSEE	WDCT	WDWT	GRSSTKS	EUPHORB	PHORLUP	MIMOSA	VACCINIU	BERBERIS	TRITICUM	MOLLUGO	PENDFRAG	CACTUS	CALEND	CRUCIFER	SOLANUM	LGLEGUME	TLEGUME	KG	M3VOL	PHASE	STAT	LEV
229	.	.	.	.	.	.	.	.	.	.	10	.	.	5	2	.	.	.	.	.	.	.	.	.	.	.	.	.	.	.	7	6.0	0.0060	HII	.	3
230	.	.	.	.	.	.	.	.	.	.	.	.	.	2	.	.	.	.	.	.	.	.	.	.	.	.	.	.	.	.	.	3.0	0.0030	HII	.	3
231	.	2	.	.	.	.	.	2	.	.	2	.	.	7	.	.	.	.	.	.	.	.	.	.	.	.	.	.	.	.	4	4.8	0.0048	HII	.	3
232	.	.	.	.	.	.	.	.	.	.	.	.	.	.	.	.	.	.	.	.	.	.	.	.	.	.	.	.	.	.	1	3.0	0.0030	HII	.	3
233	.	.	.	.	.	.	.	.	.	.	.	.	.	.	.	.	.	.	.	.	.	.	.	.	.	.	.	.	.	.	.	3.6	0.0036	HII	.	3
234	.	.	.	.	.	.	.	.	.	.	.	.	.	.	.	.	.	.	.	.	.	.	.	.	.	.	.	.	.	.	.	3.0	0.0030	HII	.	3
235	.	.	.	.	.	.	.	.	.	.	.	.	.	.	.	.	.	.	.	.	.	.	.	.	.	.	.	.	.	.	.	3.0	0.0030	HII	.	3
236	.	.	.	.	.	.	.	.	.	.	4	.	.	2	1	.	.	.	.	.	.	.	.	.	1	.	.	.	.	.	2	3.0	0.0030	HII	.	4
237	.	.	.	.	.	.	.	.	.	.	1	.	.	3	.	.	.	.	.	.	.	.	.	.	.	.	.	.	.	.	3	3.6	0.0036	HII	.	4
238	.	.	.	.	.	.	.	.	.	.	1	.	.	.	1	.	.	.	.	1	.	.	.	.	.	.	.	.	.	.	.	3.6	0.0036	HII	.	4
239	.	.	.	.	.	.	.	.	.	.	.	.	.	.	.	.	.	.	.	.	.	.	.	.	.	.	.	.	.	.	.	4.2	0.0042	HII	.	2
240	.	.	.	.	.	.	.	.	.	.	1	.	.	.	.	.	.	.	.	.	.	.	.	.	.	.	.	.	.	.	.	4.2	0.0042	HII	.	2
241	.	.	.	.	.	.	.	.	.	.	.	.	.	.	2	.	.	.	.	.	.	.	.	.	.	.	.	.	.	.	.	4.8	0.0048	HII	.	2
242	.	.	.	.	.	.	.	.	.	.	.	.	.	.	6	.	.	.	.	.	.	.	.	.	.	.	.	.	.	.	.	4.8	0.0048	HII	.	2
243	.	.	.	.	.	.	.	.	.	.	.	.	.	2	1	.	1	.	.	.	.	.	.	.	.	.	.	.	.	.	.	4.2	0.0042	HII	.	3
244	.	.	.	.	.	.	.	.	.	.	.	.	.	2	6	.	.	.	.	.	.	.	.	.	.	.	.	.	.	.	.	4.8	0.0048	HII	.	3
245	.	.	.	.	.	.	.	.	.	.	.	.	.	.	3	.	.	.	.	.	.	.	.	.	.	.	.	.	.	.	.	4.2	0.0042	HII	.	3
246	.	.	.	.	.	.	.	.	.	.	.	.	.	8	4	.	.	.	.	.	.	.	.	2	.	.	.	.	.	.	2	4.8	0.0048	HII	.	3
247	.	.	.	.	.	.	.	.	.	.	.	.	.	.	.	.	.	.	.	.	.	.	.	.	.	.	.	.	.	.	.	4.2	0.0042	HII	.	4

OBS	FLTMCO	FLOT	BAGSIZE	SITE	FEATURE	LEVEL	LOCUS	BAGNO	CONTEXT	DATE	MZKERNAL	CUPCOBS	EMBRYOS	CHENOPOD	LUPINE	PHSPP	TUBERS	PAPAS	OCA	ULLUCO	MASHUA	LUMPS	AMARANTH	SCIRPUS	SMLEGUME	LEPIDIUM	LUCUMA	RARE	PORTULAC	VERBENA	PLANTAGO	SGRASS	LGRASS	MGRASS	MALVAST	RUBUS	BIXA	PHYSOLIS
248	1	731	0.8	7	7	4	1	203	4	5	.	1	.	.	.	.	.	.	.	.	.	.	.	.	.	.	.	.	.	.	.	2	1	.	.	.	.	.
249	1	795	0.8	7	7	4	1	303	4	5	2	.	.	2	.	.	4	.	.	.	.	3	.	.	.	.	.	.	.	.	.	2	2	1	.	.	.	.
250	1	76	0.6	41	0	0	0	.	.	.	.	.	.	.	.	.	.	.	.	.	.	.	.	.	.	.	.	.	.	.	.	1	.	1	.	.	.	.
251	1	18	1.0	41	1	2	1	103	1	5	.	.	.	3	2	.	.	.	.	.	.	11	.	.	.	.	.	.	.	1	.	3	.	.	.	.	.	.
252	1	11	1.0	41	1	2	1	203	1	5	.	.	.	6	.	.	.	.	.	.	.	.	.	.	1	.	.	.	.	.	.	6	2	.	.	.	.	.
253	1	22	1.0	41	1	2	1	303	1	5	.	.	.	8	.	.	.	.	.	.	.	2	.	.	1	.	.	.	.	.	.	4	.	.	.	.	.	.
254	1	15	1.0	41	1	2	2	103	6	5	.	.	.	1	.	.	1	.	.	.	.	.	.	.	.	.	.	.	.	.	1	.	.	.	.	.	.	.
255	1	14	1.0	41	1	2	2	203	6	5	.	.	.	1	.	.	.	.	.	.	.	.	.	.	.	.	.	.	.	.	.	.	2	.	.	.	.	.
256	1	8	1.0	41	1	2	2	303	6	5	.	.	.	2	.	.	.	.	.	.	.	1	.	.	.	.	.	.	.	.	.	2	2	.	.	.	.	.
257	1	12	1.0	41	1	3	1	103	4	5	.	.	.	1	.	.	.	.	.	.	.	.	.	.	.	.	.	.	.	.	.	.	.	.	.	.	.	.
258	1	13	1.0	41	1	3	1	203	4	5	.	.	.	.	.	.	.	.	.	.	.	.	.	.	.	.	.	.	.	.	.	.	.	.	.	.	.	.
259	1	19	0.9	41	1	3	1	303	4	5	.	.	.	2	.	.	.	.	.	.	.	.	.	.	1	.	.	.	.	.	.	2	.	.	.	.	.	.
260	1	7	1.0	41	1	3	2	103	4	5	.	3	.	8	.	.	.	.	.	.	.	.	.	.	.	.	.	.	.	.	.	.	1	.	.	.	.	.
261	1	10	1.0	41	1	4	1	103	1	5	.	.	.	.	.	.	.	.	.	.	.	.	.	.	.	.	.	.	.	.	.	.	.	.	.	.	.	.
262	1	9	1.0	41	1	4	1	203	1	5	.	.	.	1	.	.	.	.	.	.	.	.	.	.	.	.	.	.	.	.	.	.	.	.	.	.	.	.
263	1	23	1.0	41	1	4	1	303	1	5	.	.	.	2	.	.	.	.	.	.	.	.	.	.	.	.	.	.	.	.	.	.	.	.	.	.	.	.
264	1	798	0.8	41	1	5	1	303	4	5	.	1	.	7	.	.	.	.	.	.	.	.	.	.	.	.	.	.	.	.	.	5	.	.	.	1	.	.
265	1	59	1.0	41	2	2	1	103	1	5	.	.	.	.	.	.	.	.	.	.	.	.	.	.	.	.	.	.	.	.	.	.	.	.	.	.	.	.
266	1	51	1.0	41	2	2	1	203	1	5	.	.	.	2	.	.	.	.	.	.	.	.	.	.	.	.	.	.	.	.	.	.	.	.	.	.	.	.

OBS	OXALIS	AMBROSIA	NICOTIANA	SALVIA	MINT	GALIUM	OPUNTIA	CYPER	COMPOSIT	UMBELLIF	FABACEAE	UNKWNSEE	WDCT	WDWT	GRSSTKS	EUPHORB	PHORLUP	MIMOSA	VACCINIU	BERBERIS	TRITICUM	MOLLUGO	PENDFRAG	CACTUS	CALEND	CRUCIFER	SOLANUM	LGLEGUME	TLEGUME	KG	M3VOL	PHASE	STAT	LEV
248	.	.	.	.	.	.	.	.	.	.	.	.	.	.	.	.	.	.	.	.	.	.	.	.	.	.	.	.	.	4.8	0.0048	HII	.	4
249	.	.	.	.	.	.	.	.	.	.	.	.	.	.	.	.	.	.	.	.	.	.	.	.	.	.	.	.	.	4.8	0.0048	HII	.	4
250	.	.	.	.	.	.	.	.	.	.	.	.	.	.	.	.	.	.	.	.	.	.	.	.	.	.	.	.	.	3.6	0.0036	.	.	0
251	.	.	.	.	.	.	.	.	.	.	.	.	2	.	.	.	.	.	.	.	.	.	.	.	.	.	.	.	.	6.0	0.0060	HII	.	2
252	.	.	.	.	.	.	.	.	.	.	.	.	.	.	.	.	.	.	.	.	.	.	.	.	.	.	.	.	1	6.0	0.0060	HII	.	2
253	.	.	.	.	.	.	.	.	.	.	.	.	.	.	.	.	.	.	.	.	.	.	.	.	.	.	.	.	1	6.0	0.0060	HII	.	2
254	.	.	.	.	.	.	.	.	.	.	.	.	1	.	.	.	.	.	.	.	.	.	.	.	.	.	.	.	.	6.0	0.0060	HII	.	2
255	.	.	.	.	.	.	.	.	.	.	.	.	.	.	.	.	.	.	.	.	.	.	.	.	.	.	.	.	.	6.0	0.0060	HII	.	2
256	.	.	.	.	.	.	.	.	.	.	.	.	.	.	.	.	.	.	.	.	.	.	.	.	.	.	.	.	.	6.0	0.0060	HII	.	2
257	.	.	.	.	.	.	.	.	.	.	.	.	.	.	.	.	.	.	.	.	.	.	.	.	.	.	.	.	.	6.0	0.0060	HII	.	3
258	.	.	.	.	.	.	.	.	.	.	.	.	5	.	.	.	.	.	.	.	.	.	.	.	.	.	.	.	.	6.0	0.0060	HII	.	3
259	.	.	.	.	.	.	.	.	.	.	.	.	1	.	.	.	.	.	.	.	.	.	.	.	.	.	.	.	1	5.4	0.0054	HII	.	3
260	.	.	.	.	.	.	.	.	.	.	.	.	4	.	.	.	.	.	.	.	.	.	.	.	.	.	.	.	.	6.0	0.0060	HII	.	3
261	.	.	.	.	.	.	.	.	.	.	.	.	1	.	.	.	.	.	.	.	.	.	.	.	.	.	.	.	.	6.0	0.0060	HII	.	4
262	.	.	.	.	.	.	.	.	.	.	.	.	.	.	.	.	.	.	.	.	.	.	.	.	.	.	.	.	.	6.0	0.0060	HII	.	4
263	.	.	.	.	.	.	.	.	.	.	.	.	1	.	.	.	.	.	.	.	.	.	.	.	.	.	.	.	.	6.0	0.0060	HII	.	4
264	.	.	.	.	.	.	.	.	.	.	.	.	10	.	.	.	.	.	.	.	.	.	.	.	.	.	.	.	.	4.8	0.0048	HII	.	5
265	.	.	.	.	.	.	.	.	.	.	.	.	.	.	.	.	.	.	.	.	.	.	.	.	.	.	.	.	.	6.0	0.0060	HII	.	2
266	.	.	.	.	.	.	.	.	.	.	.	.	.	.	.	.	.	.	.	.	.	.	.	.	.	.	.	.	.	6.0	0.0060	HII	.	2

OBS	FLTMCO	FLOT	BAGSIZE	SITE	FEATURE	LEVEL	LOCUS	BAGNO	CONTEXT	DATE	MZKERNAL	CUPCOBS	EMBRYOS	CHENOPOD	LUPINE	PHSPP	TUBERS	PAPAS	OCA	ULLUCO	MASHUA	LUMPS	AMARANTH	SCIRPUS	SMLEGUME	LEPIDIUM	LUCUMA	RARE	PORTULAC	VERBENA	PLANTAGO	SGRASS	LGRASS	MGRASS	MALVAST	RUBUS
267	1	17	1.0	41	2	2	1	303	1	5	.	.	.	3	.	.	1	.	.	.	.	2	.	.	.	.	.	.	.	.	.	.	.	.	.	.
268	1	58	1.0	41	2	2	2	103	6	5	.	.	.	.	.	.	.	.	.	.	.	.	.	.	.	.	.	.	.	.	.	.	.	.	.	.
269	1	16	1.0	41	2	2	2	203	6	5	.	.	.	.	.	.	.	.	.	.	.	.	.	.	.	.	.	.	.	.	.	.	.	.	.	.
270	1	57	0.9	41	2	2	2	303	6	5	.	.	.	.	.	.	.	.	.	.	.	.	.	.	.	.	.	.	.	.	.	.	.	.	.	.
271	1	35	1.1	41	3	1	2	101	9	5	.	.	.	5	.	.	.	.	.	.	.	9	3	.	.	.	.	.	.	.	.	1	1	.	.	.
272	1	47	1.0	41	3	2	1	103	1	5	.	.	.	1	.	.	.	.	.	.	.	.	8	.	.	.	.	.	.	.	.	.	1	.	.	.
273	1	36	1.0	41	3	2	1	203	1	5	.	.	.	.	.	.	.	.	.	.	.	.	.	.	.	.	.	.	.	.	.	2	12	.	.	.
274	1	46	1.0	41	3	2	1	303	1	5	.	.	.	4	1	.	2	.	.	.	.	.	2	.	.	.	1	.	.	.	.	7	7	.	1	.
275	1	38	0.9	41	3	2	2	103	6	5	.	.	.	.	.	.	.	.	.	.	.	1	.	.	.	.	.	.	.	.	.	.	.	.	.	.
276	1	32	0.9	41	3	2	2	203	6	5	.	.	.	2	.	.	.	.	.	.	.	8	4	.	1	.	.	.	.	1	.	1	1	.	.	.
277	1	27	0.9	41	3	2	2	303	6	5	.	.	.	3	.	.	.	.	.	.	.	5	6	.	.	.	.	.	.	.	.	2	1	.	.	.
278	1	39	1.0	41	3	2	4	102	6	5	.	.	.	16	.	.	.	.	.	.	.	.	12	2	.	.	.	.	.	.	.	2	4	.	.	.
279	1	42	1.0	41	3	2	4	202	6	5	.	.	.	7	.	.	.	.	.	.	.	.	.	.	.	.	.	.	.	.	.	2	.	.	.	.
280	1	30	1.1	41	3	3	1	103	4	5	.	.	.	1	2	.	.	.	.	.	.	1	.	.	.	.	.	.	.	.	.	.	1	.	.	.
281	1	25	0.9	41	3	3	1	203	4	5	.	.	.	1	1	.	.	.	.	.	.	1	1	.	.	.	.	.	.	.	.	.	.	.	.	.
282	1	56	1.1	41	3	3	1	303	4	5	.	.	.	2	.	.	.	.	.	.	.	.	1	.	1	.	.	.	.	.	.	4	.	.	.	.
283	1	34	0.9	41	3	3	2	103	6	5	.	.	.	9	.	.	.	.	.	.	.	8	1	.	.	.	.	.	.	.	.	2	2	.	.	.
284	1	33	0.9	41	3	3	2	203	6	5	.	.	.	5	.	.	2	.	.	1	.	2	2	.	.	.	.	.	.	.	1	4	1	.	.	.
285	1	29	1.0	41	3	3	2	303	6	5	.	.	.	7	.	.	.	.	.	.	.	.	14	.	1	.	.	.	.	.	.	3	.	.	1	.

OBS	BIXA	PHYSOLIS	OXALIS	AMBROSIA	NICOTIANA	SALVIA	MINT	GALIUM	OPUNTIA	CYPER	COMPOSIT	UMBELLIF	FABACEAE	UNKWNSEE	WDCT	WDWT	GRSSTKS	EUPHORB	PHORLUP	MIMOSA	VACCINIU	BERBERIS	TRITICUM	MOLLUGO	PENDFRAG	CACTUS	CALEND	CRUCIFER	SOLANUM	LGLEGUME	TLEGUME	KG	M3VOL	PHASE	STAT	LEV
267	.	.	.	.	.	.	.	.	.	.	.	.	.	2	.	.	.	.	.	.	.	.	.	.	.	.	.	.	.	.	.	6.0	0.0060	HII	.	2
268	.	.	.	.	.	.	.	.	.	.	.	.	.	.	2	.	.	1	.	.	.	.	.	.	.	.	.	.	.	.	.	6.0	0.0060	HII	.	2
269	.	.	.	.	.	.	.	.	.	.	.	.	.	.	.	.	.	.	.	.	.	.	.	.	.	.	.	.	.	.	.	6.0	0.0060	HII	.	2
270	.	.	.	.	.	.	.	.	.	.	.	.	.	.	1	.	.	.	.	.	.	.	.	.	.	.	.	.	.	.	.	5.4	0.0054	HII	.	2
271	.	.	.	.	.	.	.	.	.	.	.	.	.	3	.	.	.	.	.	.	.	.	.	.	.	.	.	.	.	.	.	6.6	0.0066	HII	.	1
272	.	.	.	.	.	.	.	.	.	.	.	.	.	.	7	.	1	.	.	.	.	.	.	.	.	.	.	.	.	.	.	6.0	0.0060	HII	.	2
273	.	.	.	.	.	.	.	.	.	.	.	.	.	.	2	.	.	.	.	.	.	.	.	.	.	.	.	.	.	.	.	6.0	0.0060	HII	.	2
274	.	.	.	.	.	.	.	.	.	.	.	.	.	.	.	.	.	.	.	.	.	.	.	.	.	.	.	.	.	.	.	6.0	0.0060	HII	.	2
275	.	.	.	.	.	.	.	.	.	.	.	.	.	.	.	.	.	.	.	.	.	.	.	.	.	.	.	.	.	.	.	5.4	0.0054	HII	.	2
276	.	.	.	.	.	.	.	.	.	.	.	.	.	1	.	.	.	.	.	.	.	.	.	.	.	.	.	.	.	.	1	5.4	0.0054	HII	.	2
277	.	.	.	.	.	.	.	.	.	.	.	.	.	1	.	.	.	.	.	.	.	.	.	.	.	.	.	.	.	.	.	5.4	0.0054	HII	.	2
278	.	.	.	.	.	.	.	.	.	.	1	.	1	6	.	.	1	.	.	.	.	.	.	.	.	.	.	.	.	.	.	6.0	0.0060	HII	.	2
279	.	.	.	.	.	.	.	.	.	.	1	.	.	.	.	.	.	.	.	.	.	.	.	.	.	.	.	.	.	.	.	6.0	0.0060	HII	.	2
280	.	.	.	.	.	.	.	.	.	.	.	.	.	2	4	.	.	.	.	.	.	.	.	.	.	.	.	.	.	.	.	6.6	0.0066	HII	.	3
281	.	.	.	.	.	.	.	.	.	.	.	.	.	.	4	.	.	.	.	.	.	.	.	.	.	.	.	.	.	.	.	5.4	0.0054	HII	.	3
282	.	.	.	.	.	.	.	.	.	.	.	.	.	2	.	.	.	.	.	.	.	.	.	.	.	.	.	.	.	.	1	6.6	0.0066	HII	.	3
283	.	.	.	.	.	.	.	.	.	.	.	.	.	2	.	.	.	.	1	.	.	.	.	.	.	.	.	.	.	1	.	5.4	0.0054	HII	.	3
284	.	.	.	.	.	.	.	.	.	.	.	.	.	2	4	.	1	.	.	.	.	.	.	.	.	.	.	.	.	.	.	5.4	0.0054	HII	.	3
285	.	.	.	.	.	.	.	.	.	.	1	.	.	8	15	.	.	.	.	.	.	.	.	.	.	.	.	.	.	.	1	6.0	0.0060	HII	.	3

OBS	FLTMCO	FLOT	BAGSIZE	SITE	FEATUREL	LEVELS	LOCUS	BAGNO	CONTEXT	DATEL	MZKERNAL	CUPCOBS	EMBRYOS	CHENOPOD	LUPINE	PHSEP	TUBERS	PAPAS	OCA	ULLUCO	MASHUA	LUMPS	AMARANTH	SCIRPUS	SMLEGUME	LEPIDIUM	LUCUMA	RARE	PORTULAC	VERBENA	PLANTAGO	SGRASS	LGRASS	MGRASS	MALVAST	RUBUS
286	1	45	1.0	41	3	3	3	103	3	5	.	.	.	1	.	.	.	.	.	.	.	.	.	.	.	.	.	.	.	.	.	.	.	.	.	.
287	1	48	1.0	41	3	3	3	203	3	5	.	.	.	2	.	.	.	2	.	.	.	4	.	.	.	.	.	.	.	.	.	2	2	.	.	.
288	1	31	1.0	41	3	3	3	303	3	5	.	.	.	1	.	.	.	.	.	.	.	.	.	.	.	.	.	.	.	.	.	4	6	.	1	.
289	1	26	1.0	41	3	4	3	103	3	5	.	.	.	5	.	.	.	.	.	.	.	2	2	2	.	.	.	.	.	1	.	.	1	.	.	.
290	1	37	0.9	41	3	4	3	203	3	5	.	.	.	.	.	.	.	.	.	.	.	11	3	.	.	.	.	.	.	.	1	.	.	.	.	.
291	1	28	0.9	41	3	4	3	303	3	5	.	.	.	4	.	.	.	.	.	.	.	2	.	1	.	.	.	.	.	1	.	14	2	.	.	.
292	1	44	1.0	41	4	2	1	104	1	5	9	.	.	65	.	.	.	.	.	.	.	3	.	.	.	.	.	.	.	.	.	.	2	.	.	.
293	1	43	1.1	41	4	2	1	204	1	5	.	.	.	45	.	.	.	.	.	.	.	2	.	.	1	.	.	.	.	.	.	1	.	.	.	.
294	1	40	1.0	41	4	2	1	304	1	5	9	.	1	55	2	.	.	.	.	.	.	3	.	.	.	.	.	.	.	.	.	1	.	.	.	.
295	1	41	1.0	41	4	2	1	404	1	5	5	.	.	37	4	.	.	.	.	.	.	.	.	.	.	.	.	.	.	.	.	.	.	.	.	.
296	1	78	1.1	41	4	2	2	103	6	5	.	.	.	6	.	.	.	.	.	.	.	.	.	.	.	.	.	.	.	.	.	.	1	.	.	.
297	1	79	1.0	41	4	2	2	203	6	5	.	.	.	5	.	.	1	.	.	.	.	.	.	.	.	.	.	.	.	.	.	.	.	.	.	.
298	1	453	0.9	41	4	2	2	303	6	5	.	.	.	1	.	.	1	.	.	.	.	.	.	.	.	.	.	.	.	.	.	.	.	.	.	.
299	1	68	1.0	41	4	3	1	103	4	5	1	1	.	19	.	.	.	.	.	.	.	2	.	.	.	.	.	.	.	.	.	1	.	1	.	.
300	1	82	1.0	41	4	3	1	203	4	5	1	.	.	35	.	.	1	.	.	.	.	4	.	.	.	.	.	.	.	.	.	2	.	.	.	.
301	1	77	1.0	41	4	3	1	303	4	5	2	.	.	43	5	.	9	.	.	.	.	7	.	.	.	.	.	.	.	.	.	.	.	.	.	.
302	1	87	1.0	41	4	3	2	103	6	5	.	.	.	.	.	.	.	.	.	.	.	.	.	.	.	.	.	.	.	.	.	1	.	.	.	.
303	1	279	0.8	41	4	3	2	203	6	5	.	.	.	.	.	.	.	.	.	.	.	.	.	.	.	.	.	.	.	.	.	.	.	.	.	.
304	1	178	1.0	41	4	3	2	303	6	5	.	.	.	1	.	.	.	.	.	.	.	.	.	.	.	.	.	.	.	.	.	.	.	.	.	.

OBS	BIXA	PHYSALIS	OXALIS	AMBROSIA	NICOTIAN	SALVIA	MINT	GALIUM	OPUNTIA	CYPER	COMPOSIT	UMBELLIF	FABACEAE	UNKWNSEE	WDCT	WDWT	GRSSTKS	EUPHORB	PHORLUP	MIMOSA	VACCINIU	BERBERIS	TRITICUM	MOLLUGO	PENDFRAG	CACTUS	CALEND	CRUCIFER	SOLANUM	LGLEGUME	TLEGUME	KG	M3VOL	PHASE	STAT	LEV
286	.	.	.	.	.	.	.	.	.	.	.	.	.	.	2	.	.	.	1	.	.	.	.	.	.	.	.	.	.	1	.	6.0	0.0060	HII	.	3
287	.	.	.	.	.	.	.	.	.	.	.	.	.	.	.	.	.	.	.	.	.	.	.	.	.	.	.	.	2	.	.	6.0	0.0060	HII	.	3
288	.	.	.	.	.	.	.	.	.	.	.	.	.	.	.	.	.	.	.	.	.	.	.	.	.	.	.	.	.	.	.	6.0	0.0060	HII	.	3
289	.	.	.	.	.	1	.	.	.	.	.	.	.	.	20	.	1	.	.	.	.	.	.	.	.	.	.	.	.	.	.	6.0	0.0060	HII	.	4
290	.	.	.	.	.	.	.	.	0	1	.	.	.	.	1	.	.	.	2	.	.	.	.	.	.	.	.	.	.	2	.	5.4	0.0054	HII	.	4
291	.	.	.	.	.	.	.	.	.	.	.	.	.	4	22	.	1	.	.	.	.	.	.	.	.	.	.	.	.	.	.	5.4	0.0054	HII	.	4
292	.	.	.	.	.	.	.	.	.	.	.	.	.	.	12	.	.	.	1	.	.	.	.	.	.	.	.	.	.	1	.	6.0	0.0060	HII	.	2
293	.	.	.	.	.	.	.	.	.	.	.	.	.	.	1	.	.	.	9	.	.	.	.	.	.	.	.	.	.	9	1	6.6	0.0066	HII	.	2
294	.	.	.	.	.	.	.	.	.	.	.	.	.	.	2	.	.	.	1	.	.	.	.	.	.	.	.	.	.	1	.	6.0	0.0060	HII	.	2
295	.	.	.	.	.	.	.	.	.	.	.	.	.	.	1	.	.	.	.	.	.	.	.	.	.	.	.	.	.	.	.	6.0	0.0060	HII	.	2
296	.	.	.	.	.	.	.	.	.	.	1	.	.	.	.	.	.	.	.	.	.	.	.	.	.	.	.	.	.	.	.	6.6	0.0066	HII	.	2
297	.	.	.	.	.	.	.	.	.	.	.	.	.	.	.	.	.	.	.	.	.	.	.	.	.	.	.	.	.	.	.	6.0	0.0060	HII	.	2
298	.	.	.	.	.	.	.	.	.	.	.	.	.	.	.	.	.	.	.	.	.	.	.	.	.	.	.	.	.	.	.	5.4	0.0054	HII	.	2
299	.	.	.	.	.	.	.	.	.	.	.	.	.	.	10	.	.	.	2	.	.	.	.	.	.	.	.	.	.	2	.	6.0	0.0060	HII	.	3
300	.	.	.	.	.	.	.	.	.	.	.	.	.	.	7	.	1	.	4	.	.	.	.	.	.	.	.	.	.	4	.	6.0	0.0060	HII	.	3
301	.	.	.	.	.	.	.	.	.	.	.	.	.	.	5	.	.	.	.	.	.	.	.	.	.	.	.	.	.	.	.	6.0	0.0060	HII	.	3
302	.	.	.	.	.	.	.	.	.	.	.	.	.	.	.	.	.	.	.	.	.	.	.	.	.	.	.	.	.	.	.	6.0	0.0060	HII	.	3
303	.	.	.	.	.	.	.	.	.	.	.	.	.	.	.	.	.	.	.	.	.	.	.	.	.	.	.	.	.	.	.	4.8	0.0048	HII	.	3
304	.	.	.	.	.	.	.	.	.	.	.	.	.	.	.	.	.	.	.	.	.	.	.	.	.	.	.	.	.	.	.	6.0	0.0060	HII	.	3

OBS	FLTMCO	FLOT	BAGSIZE	SITE	FEATUREL	LEVELS	LOCUS	BAGNO	CONTEXT	DATEL	MZKERNAL	CUPCOBS	EMBRYOS	CHENOPOD	LUPINE	PHSEP	TUBERS	PAPAS	OCA	ULLUCO	MASHUA	LUMPS	AMARANTH	SCIRPUS	SMLEGUME	LEPIDIUM	LUCUMA	RARE	PORTULAC	VERBENA	PLANTAGO	SGRASS	LGRASS	MGRASS	MALVAST	RUBUS
305	1	450	0.9	41	4	4	1	103	4	5	.	.	.	5	.	.	.	.	.	.	.	.	.	.	.	.	.	.	.	.	.	1	.	.	.	.
306	1	73	1.2	41	4	4	1	203	4	5	.	.	.	3	.	.	.	.	.	.	.	.	.	.	.	.	.	.	.	.	.	.	.	.	.	.
307	1	183	0.9	41	4	4	1	303	4	5	.	.	.	4	.	.	.	.	.	.	.	1	2	.	.	.	.	.	.	.	.	1	.	2	.	.
308	1	92	1.0	41	4	4	2	103	6	5	.	.	.	.	.	.	.	.	.	.	.	.	.	.	.	.	.	.	.	.	.	.	.	.	.	.
309	1	168	1.0	41	4	4	2	203	6	5	.	.	.	1	.	.	.	.	.	.	.	.	.	.	.	.	.	.	.	.	.	1	.	.	.	.
310	1	102	1.0	41	4	4	2	303	6	5	.	.	.	3	.	.	.	.	.	.	.	.	1	.	.	.	.	.	.	.	.	.	.	.	.	.
311	1	69	1.0	41	4	4	3	103	3	5	.	.	.	8	.	.	2	.	.	.	.	.	.	.	.	.	.	.	.	.	.	1	.	.	.	.
312	1	106	0.9	41	4	4	3	203	3	5	.	.	.	5	1	.	.	.	.	.	.	1	.	.	.	.	.	.	.	.	.	.	.	.	.	.
313	1	67	1.0	41	4	4	3	303	3	5	.	.	.	4	.	.	.	.	.	.	.	.	.	.	.	.	.	.	.	.	.	.	.	1	.	.
314	1	281	1.0	41	4	4	4	103	6	5	.	.	.	9	.	.	.	.	.	.	.	.	.	.	.	.	.	.	.	.	.	.	.	.	.	.
315	1	81	1.0	41	4	4	4	203	6	5	.	.	.	4	.	.	.	.	.	.	.	.	.	.	.	.	.	.	.	.	.	1	.	.	.	.
316	1	80	1.0	41	4	4	4	303	6	5	.	.	.	7	.	.	1	.	.	.	.	.	1	1	.	.	.	.	.	.	.	.	.	.	.	.
317	1	447	1.0	41	5	2	1	106	2	5	.	.	.	.	.	.	5	.	.	.	.	2	.	.	.	.	.	.	.	.	.	.	.	.	.	.
318	1	557	0.8	41	5	2	1	206	2	5	.	.	.	1	.	.	.	.	.	.	.	.	.	.	.	.	.	.	.	.	.	.	.	.	.	.
319	1	75	1.0	41	5	2	1	306	2	5	.	.	.	.	.	.	1	.	.	.	.	.	.	.	.	.	.	.	.	.	.	.	1	.	.	.
320	1	548	1.0	41	5	2	1	406	1	5	.	.	.	1	.	.	.	.	.	.	.	.	.	.	.	.	.	.	.	.	.	1	.	.	.	.
321	1	70	1.0	41	5	2	1	506	1	5	.	.	.	.	.	.	.	.	.	.	.	2	.	.	.	.	.	.	.	.	.	.	.	.	.	.
322	1	181	1.0	41	5	2	1	606	1	5	.	.	.	.	.	.	.	.	.	.	.	4	.	.	.	.	.	.	.	.	.	.	.	.	.	.
323	1	287	0.8	41	5	2	2	103	6	5	.	.	.	2	.	.	.	.	.	.	.	.	.	.	.	.	.	.	.	.	.	.	.	.	.	.

OBS	BIXA	PHYSALIS	OXALIS	AMBROSIA	NICOTIAN	SALVIA	MINT	GALIUM	OPUNTIA	CYPER	COMPOSIT	UMBELLIF	FABACEAE	UNKWNSEE	WDCT	WDWT	GRSSTKS	EUPHORB	PHORLUP	MIMOSA	VACCINIU	BERBERIS	TRITICUM	MOLLUGO	PENDFRAG	CACTUS	CALEND	CRUCIFER	SOLANUM	LGLEGUME	TLEGUME	KG	M3VOL	PHASE	STAT	LEV
305	.	.	.	.	.	.	.	.	.	.	.	.	.	.	.	.	.	.	.	.	.	.	.	.	.	.	.	.	.	.	.	5.4	0.0054	HII	.	4
306	.	.	.	.	.	.	.	.	.	.	.	.	.	.	.	.	.	.	.	.	.	.	.	.	.	.	.	.	.	.	.	7.2	0.0072	HII	.	4
307	.	.	.	.	.	.	.	.	.	.	.	.	.	1	.	.	.	.	.	.	.	.	.	.	.	.	.	.	.	.	.	5.4	0.0054	HII	.	4
308	.	.	.	.	.	.	.	.	.	.	.	.	.	.	1	.	.	.	.	.	.	.	.	.	.	.	.	.	.	.	.	6.0	0.0060	HII	.	4
309	.	.	.	.	.	.	.	.	.	.	.	.	.	.	4	.	.	.	.	.	.	.	.	.	.	.	.	.	.	.	.	6.0	0.0060	HII	.	4
310	.	.	.	.	.	.	.	.	.	.	1	.	.	.	.	.	.	.	.	.	.	.	.	.	.	.	.	.	.	.	.	6.0	0.0060	HII	.	4
311	.	.	.	.	.	.	.	.	.	.	.	.	.	.	7	.	.	.	.	.	.	.	.	.	.	.	.	.	.	.	.	6.0	0.0060	HII	.	4
312	.	.	.	.	.	.	.	.	.	.	.	.	.	.	2	.	.	.	.	.	.	.	.	.	.	.	.	.	.	.	.	5.4	0.0054	HII	.	4
313	.	.	.	.	.	.	.	.	.	.	.	.	.	.	8	.	.	.	.	.	.	.	.	.	.	.	.	.	.	.	.	6.0	0.0060	HII	.	4
314	.	.	.	.	.	.	.	.	.	.	.	.	.	1	4	.	.	.	.	.	.	.	.	.	.	.	.	.	.	.	.	6.0	0.0060	HII	.	4
315	.	.	.	.	.	.	.	.	.	.	.	.	.	.	1	.	.	.	.	.	.	.	.	.	.	.	.	.	.	.	.	6.0	0.0060	HII	.	4
316	.	.	.	.	.	.	.	.	.	.	.	.	.	.	8	.	.	.	.	.	.	.	.	.	.	.	.	.	.	.	.	6.0	0.0060	HII	.	4
317	.	.	.	.	.	.	.	.	.	.	.	.	.	.	.	.	.	.	.	.	.	.	.	.	.	.	.	.	.	.	.	6.0	0.0060	HII	.	2
318	.	.	.	.	.	.	.	.	.	.	.	.	.	.	2	.	.	.	.	.	.	.	.	.	.	.	.	.	.	.	.	4.8	0.0048	HII	.	2
319	.	.	.	.	.	.	.	.	.	.	.	.	.	.	2	.	.	.	.	.	.	.	.	.	.	.	.	.	.	.	.	6.0	0.0060	HII	.	2
320	.	.	.	.	.	.	.	.	.	.	.	.	.	.	6	.	.	.	.	.	.	.	.	.	.	.	.	.	.	.	.	6.0	0.0060	HII	.	2
321	.	.	.	.	.	.	.	.	.	.	.	.	.	.	4	.	.	.	.	.	.	.	.	.	.	.	.	.	.	.	.	6.0	0.0060	HII	.	2
322	.	.	.	.	.	.	.	.	.	.	.	.	.	.	2	.	.	.	.	.	.	.	.	.	.	.	.	.	.	.	.	6.0	0.0060	HII	.	2
323	.	.	.	.	.	.	.	.	.	.	.	.	.	.	.	.	.	.	.	.	.	.	.	.	.	.	.	.	.	.	.	4.8	0.0048	HII	.	2

OBS	FLTMCO	FLOT	BAGSIZE	SITE	FEATURE	LEVEL	LOCUS	BAGNO	CONTEXT	DATE	MZKERNAL	CUPCOBS	EMBRYOS	CHENOPOD	LUPINE	PHSPP	TUBERS	PAPAS	OCA	ULLUCO	MASHUA	LUMPS	AMARANTH	SCIRPUS	SMLEGUME	LEPIDIUM	LUCUMA	RARE	PORTULAC	VERBENA	PLANTAGO	SGRASS	LGRASS	MGRASS	MALVALST
324	1	172	1.1	41	5	2	2	203	6	5	.	.	.	1	.	.	.	.	.	.	.	.	.	.	.	.	.	.	.	.	.	1	.	.	.
325	1	173	1.0	41	5	2	2	303	6	5	.	.	.	1	.	.	.	.	.	.	.	.	.	.	.	.	.	.	.	.	.	2	.	.	.
326	1	445	0.8	41	5	3	1	103	4	5	.	.	.	.	.	.	13	.	.	2	.	.	.	1	.	.	.	.	.	.	.	1	.	.	.
327	1	84	1.0	41	5	3	1	203	4	5	.	.	.	1	.	.	2	.	.	.	.	.	.	.	.	.	.	.	.	.	.	1	1	.	.
328	1	452	0.9	41	5	3	1	203	4	5	.	.	.	3	.	.	.	.	.	.	.	.	.	1	.	.	.	.	.	.	.	10	.	.	.
329	1	448	1.0	41	5	3	1	303	4	5	.	.	.	3	.	.	4	.	.	.	.	.	.	.	.	1	.	.	.	1	.	4	1	.	1
330	1	91	1.0	41	5	3	2	103	6	5	.	.	.	1	.	.	10	.	.	.	.	.	.	.	.	.	.	.	.	.	.	1	.	1	.
331	1	105	1.0	41	5	3	2	303	6	5	.	.	.	8	.	.	.	.	.	.	.	2	.	.	.	.	.	.	.	.	.	6	2	.	.
332	1	451	0.9	41	6	2	1	103	1	5	.	.	.	.	.	.	.	.	.	.	.	.	.	.	.	.	.	.	.	.	.	.	.	.	.
333	1	85	1.1	41	6	2	1	203	1	5	.	.	.	.	.	.	.	.	.	.	.	.	.	.	.	.	.	.	.	.	.	.	.	.	.
334	1	177	1.0	41	6	2	1	303	1	5	.	.	.	.	.	.	.	.	.	.	.	.	.	.	.	.	.	.	.	.	.	.	.	.	.
335	1	88	1.0	41	6	2	2	103	6	5	.	.	.	.	.	.	.	.	.	.	.	.	.	1	.	.	.	.	.	.	.	.	.	.	.
336	1	89	1.0	41	6	2	2	203	6	5	.	.	.	.	.	.	.	.	.	.	.	.	.	.	.	.	.	.	.	.	.	.	.	.	.
337	1	90	1.0	41	6	2	2	303	6	5	.	.	.	.	.	.	.	.	.	.	.	.	.	.	.	.	.	.	.	.	.	.	.	.	.
338	1	571	0.8	41	6	2	3	103	6	5	.	.	.	.	.	.	.	.	.	.	.	.	.	.	.	.	.	.	.	.	.	1	.	.	.
339	1	574	0.8	41	6	2	3	203	6	5	.	.	.	2	.	.	.	.	.	.	.	.	.	2	.	.	.	.	.	.	.	.	.	.	.
340	1	553	0.8	41	6	2	3	303	6	5	11	44	3	280	25	.	.	15	.	.	.	.	2	69	3	1	.	.	.	3	.	2	2	1	1
341	1	176	1.0	41	6	3	1	103	4	5	.	.	.	1	.	.	.	.	.	.	.	.	.	.	.	.	.	.	.	.	.	.	.	.	.
342	1	93	1.0	41	6	3	1	203	4	5	.	.	.	.	1	.	.	.	.	.	.	.	.	.	.	.	.	.	.	.	.	.	.	.	.

OBS	RUBUS	BIXA	PHYSOLIS	OXALIS	AMBROSIA	NICOTIAN	SALVIA	MINT	GALIUM	OPUNTIA	CYPER	COMPOSIT	UMBELLIF	FABACEAE	UNKWNSEE	WDCT	WDWT	GRSSTKS	EUPHORB	PHORLUP	MIMOSA	VACCINIU	BERBERIS	TRITICUM	MOLLUGO	PENDFRAG	CACTUS	CALEND	CRUCIFER	SOLANUM	LGLEGUME	TLEGUME	KG	M3VOL	PHASE	STAT	LEV
324	.	.	.	.	.	.	.	.	.	.	.	.	.	.	.	.	.	.	.	.	.	.	.	.	.	.	.	.	.	.	.	.	6.6	0.0066	HII	.	2
325	.	.	.	.	.	.	.	.	.	.	.	.	.	.	.	.	.	.	.	.	.	.	.	.	.	.	.	.	.	.	.	.	6.0	0.0060	HII	.	2
326	1	.	.	.	.	.	.	.	.	.	.	.	.	.	.	1	.	.	.	.	.	.	.	.	.	.	.	.	.	.	.	.	4.8	0.0048	HII	.	3
327	.	.	.	.	.	.	.	.	.	.	.	.	.	.	.	2	.	.	.	.	.	.	.	.	.	.	.	.	.	.	.	.	6.0	0.0060	HII	.	3
328	.	.	.	.	.	.	.	.	.	.	.	.	.	.	.	5	.	.	.	.	.	.	.	.	.	.	.	.	.	.	.	.	5.4	0.0054	HII	.	3
329	.	.	.	.	.	.	.	.	.	.	.	.	.	.	1	4	.	.	.	.	.	.	.	.	.	.	.	.	.	.	.	.	6.0	0.0060	HII	.	3
330	.	.	.	.	.	.	.	.	.	.	.	.	.	.	.	2	.	.	.	.	.	.	.	.	.	.	.	.	.	.	.	.	6.0	0.0060	HII	.	3
331	.	.	.	.	.	.	.	.	.	.	.	.	.	.	.	2	.	.	.	.	.	.	.	.	.	.	.	.	.	.	.	.	6.0	0.0060	HII	.	3
332	.	.	.	.	.	.	.	.	.	.	.	.	.	.	.	.	.	.	.	.	.	.	.	.	.	.	.	.	.	.	.	.	5.4	0.0054	HII	.	2
333	.	.	.	.	.	.	.	.	.	.	.	.	.	.	.	1	.	.	.	.	.	.	.	.	.	.	.	.	.	.	.	.	6.6	0.0066	HII	.	2
334	.	.	.	.	.	.	.	.	.	.	.	.	.	.	.	.	.	.	.	.	.	.	.	.	.	.	.	.	.	.	.	.	6.0	0.0060	HII	.	2
335	.	.	.	.	.	.	.	.	.	.	.	.	.	.	.	.	.	.	.	.	.	.	.	.	.	.	.	.	.	.	.	.	6.0	0.0060	HII	.	2
336	.	.	.	.	.	.	.	.	.	.	.	.	.	.	.	.	.	.	.	.	.	.	.	.	.	.	.	.	.	.	.	.	6.0	0.0060	HII	.	2
337	.	.	.	.	.	.	.	.	.	.	.	.	.	.	.	.	.	.	.	.	.	.	.	.	.	.	.	.	.	.	.	.	6.0	0.0060	HII	.	2
338	.	.	.	.	.	.	.	.	.	.	.	.	.	.	.	.	.	.	.	.	.	.	.	.	.	.	.	.	.	.	.	.	4.8	0.0048	HII	.	2
339	.	.	.	.	.	.	.	.	.	.	.	.	.	.	.	1	.	.	.	.	.	.	.	.	.	.	.	.	.	.	.	.	4.8	0.0048	HII	.	2
340	2	.	.	2	2	.	1	.	.	.	.	2	.	.	10	50	.	.	.	.	.	.	.	.	.	.	.	.	.	15	.	3	4.8	0.0048	HII	.	2
341	.	.	.	.	.	.	.	.	.	.	.	.	.	.	.	6	.	.	1	.	.	.	.	.	.	.	.	.	.	.	1	.	6.0	0.0060	HII	.	3
342	.	.	.	.	.	.	.	.	.	.	.	.	.	.	.	1	.	.	.	.	.	.	.	.	.	.	.	.	.	.	.	.	6.0	0.0060	HII	.	3

OBS	FLTMCO	FLOT	BAGSIZE	SITE	FEATURE	LEVEL	LOCUS	BAGNO	CONTEXT	DATE	MZKERNAL	CUPCOBS	EMBRYOS	CHENOPOD	LUPINE	PHSPP	TUBERS	PAPAS	OCA	ULLUCO	MASHUA	LUMPS	AMARANTH	SCIRPUS	SMLEGUME	LEPIDIUM	LUCUMA	RARE	PORTULAC	VERBENA	PLANTAGO	SGRASS	LGRASS	MGRASS	MALVALST
343	1	86	1.0	41	6	3	1	303	4	5	.	.	.	1	.	.	.	.	.	.	.	.	.	.	.	.	.	.	.	.	.	.	.	.	.
344	1	239	1.0	41	7	1	1	103	7	5	.	.	.	18	.	.	.	.	.	.	.	.	.	.	.	.	.	.	.	.	.	.	.	.	.
345	1	244	1.0	41	7	1	1	203	9	5	.	.	.	188	.	.	.	.	.	.	.	5	.	.	.	.	.	.	.	.	.	.	.	.	.
346	1	249	1.0	41	7	1	1	303	9	5	.	.	.	8	.	.	.	.	.	.	.	.	.	.	.	.	.	.	.	.	.	.	.	.	.
347	1	277	0.7	41	7	2	1	102	5	5	10	.	.	1200	.	.	25	.	.	.	.	.	.	.	.	.	.	.	.	.	.	.	.	.	.
348	1	231	0.8	41	7	2	1	102	1	5	.	.	.	99800	.	.	.	.	.	.	.	.	.	.	.	.	.	.	.	.	.	.	.	.	.
349	1	232	1.0	41	7	2	1	103	1	5	.	.	.	38784	.	.	.	.	.	.	.	.	.	.	.	.	.	.	.	.	.	.	.	.	.
350	1	293	0.1	41	7	2	1	202	5	5	16	.	.	940	5	.	.	21	.	.	.	20	.	.	.	.	.	.	.	.	.	.	.	.	.
351	1	230	1.0	41	7	2	1	202	1	5	.	.	.	99240	.	.	.	.	.	.	.	.	.	.	.	.	.	.	.	.	.	.	.	.	.
352	1	248	0.8	41	7	2	1	203	1	5	6	.	.	554	.	.	.	.	.	.	.	4	.	.	.	.	.	.	.	.	.	.	.	.	.
353	1	365	1.0	41	7	2	1	303	1	5	.	.	.	3000	.	.	.	.	.	.	.	5	.	.	.	.	.	.	.	.	.	.	.	.	.
354	1	242	1.1	41	7	2	1	303	1	5	12	.	.	7440	.	.	1	.	.	.	.	6	.	.	.	.	.	.	.	.	.	.	.	.	.
355	1	233	1.1	41	7	2	1	404	2	5	.	.	.	99615	4	.	10	6	.	.	.	.	.	.	.	.	.	.	.	.	.	.	.	.	.
356	1	254	1.0	41	7	2	2	103	6	5	.	.	.	15	.	.	.	.	.	.	.	.	.	.	.	.	.	.	.	.	.	.	.	.	.
357	1	250	1.0	41	7	2	2	203	6	5	.	.	.	282	1	.	.	.	.	.	.	.	.	.	.	.	.	.	.	.	.	.	.	.	.
358	1	253	0.8	41	7	2	2	303	6	5	.	.	.	69	.	.	2	.	.	.	.	.	.	.	.	.	.	.	.	.	.	.	.	.	.
359	1	234	1.0	41	7	3	1	103	4	5	1	.	.	41880	.	.	.	.	.	.	.	.	.	.	.	.	.	.	.	.	.	.	.	.	.
360	1	229	1.0	41	7	3	1	203	4	5	.	.	.	400	2	.	.	.	.	.	.	.	.	.	.	.	.	.	.	.	.	1	1	.	.
361	1	291	1.0	41	7	3	1	303	4	5	1	.	.	92	.	.	.	.	.	.	.	.	.	.	.	.	.	.	.	.	.	.	.	.	.

OBS	RUBUS	BIXA	PHYSOLIS	OXALIS	AMBROSIA	NICOTIAN	SALVIA	MINT	GALIUM	OPUNTIA	CYPER	COMPOSIT	UMBELLIF	FABACEAE	UNKWNSEE	WDCT	WDWT	GRSSTKS	EUPHORB	PHORLUP	MIMOSA	VACCINIU	BERBERIS	TRITICUM	MOLLUGO	PENDFRAG	CACTUS	CALEND	CRUCIFER	SOLANUM	LGLEGUME	TLEGUME	KG	M3VOL	PHASE	STAT	LEV
343	.	.	.	.	.	.	.	.	.	.	.	.	.	.	.	.	.	.	.	.	.	.	.	.	.	.	.	.	.	.	.	.	6.0	0.0060	HII	.	3
344	.	.	.	.	.	.	.	.	.	.	.	.	.	.	.	.	.	.	.	.	.	.	.	.	.	.	.	.	.	.	.	.	6.0	0.0060	HII	.	1
345	.	.	.	.	.	.	.	.	.	.	.	.	.	.	.	1	.	.	.	1	.	.	.	.	.	.	.	.	.	.	1	.	6.0	0.0060	HII	.	1
346	.	.	.	.	.	.	.	.	.	.	.	.	.	.	.	.	.	.	.	.	.	.	.	.	.	.	.	.	.	.	.	.	6.0	0.0060	HII	.	1
347	.	1	.	.	.	.	.	.	.	.	.	.	.	.	14	7	.	.	.	9	.	.	.	.	.	.	.	.	.	.	9	.	4.2	0.0042	HII	.	2
348	.	.	.	.	.	.	.	.	.	.	.	.	.	.	9	13	.	.	.	1	.	.	.	.	.	.	.	.	.	.	1	.	4.8	0.0048	HII	.	2
349	.	.	.	.	.	.	.	.	.	.	.	.	.	.	.	.	.	.	.	.	.	.	.	.	.	.	.	.	.	.	.	.	6.0	0.0060	HII	.	2
350	.	.	.	.	.	.	.	.	.	.	.	.	.	.	.	23	.	.	.	.	.	.	.	.	.	.	.	.	.	21	.	.	0.6	0.0006	HII	.	2
351	.	.	.	.	.	.	.	.	.	.	.	.	.	.	.	.	.	.	.	.	.	.	.	.	.	.	.	.	.	.	.	.	6.0	0.0060	HII	.	2
352	.	.	.	.	.	.	.	.	.	.	.	.	.	.	.	1	.	.	.	8	.	.	.	.	.	.	.	.	.	.	8	.	4.8	0.0048	HII	.	2
353	.	.	.	.	.	.	.	.	.	.	.	.	.	.	.	1	.	.	.	.	.	.	.	.	.	.	.	.	.	.	.	.	6.0	0.0060	HII	.	2
354	.	.	.	.	.	.	.	.	.	.	.	.	.	.	.	.	.	0	.	3	.	.	.	.	.	.	.	.	.	.	.	.	6.6	0.0066	HII	.	2
355	.	.	.	.	.	.	.	.	.	.	.	.	.	.	.	20	.	.	.	.	.	.	.	.	.	.	.	.	.	6	.	.	6.6	0.0066	HII	.	2
356	.	.	.	.	.	.	.	.	.	.	.	.	.	.	.	.	.	.	.	.	.	.	.	.	.	.	.	.	.	.	.	.	6.0	0.0060	HII	.	2
357	.	.	.	.	.	.	.	.	.	.	.	.	.	.	.	2	.	.	.	.	.	.	.	.	.	.	.	.	.	.	.	.	6.0	0.0060	HII	.	2
358	.	.	.	.	.	.	.	.	.	.	.	.	.	.	.	.	.	.	.	.	.	.	.	.	.	.	.	.	.	.	.	.	4.8	0.0048	HII	.	2
359	.	.	.	.	.	.	.	.	.	.	.	.	.	.	.	.	.	.	.	.	.	.	.	.	.	.	.	.	.	.	.	.	6.0	0.0060	HII	.	3
360	.	.	.	.	.	.	.	.	.	.	.	.	.	.	.	.	.	1	.	.	.	.	.	.	.	.	.	.	.	.	.	.	6.0	0.0060	HII	.	3
361	.	.	.	.	.	.	.	.	.	.	.	.	.	.	.	.	.	.	.	.	.	.	.	.	.	.	.	.	.	.	.	.	6.0	0.0060	HII	.	3

OBS	FLTMCO	FLOT	BAGSIZE	SITE	FEATURE	LEVEL	LOCUS	BAGNO	CONTEXT	DATE	MZKERNAL	CUPCOBS	EMBRYOS	CHENOPOD	LUPINE	PHSPP	TUBERS	PAPAS	OCA	ULLUCO	MASHUA	LUMPS	AMARANTH	SCIRPUS	SMLEGUME	LEPIDIUM	LUCUMA	RARE	PORTULACA	VERBENA	PLANTAGO	SGRASS	LGRASS	MGRASS	MALVAST	RUBUS
362	1	259	1.0	41	7	3	2	103	6	5	.	.	.	21	.	.	.	.	.	.	.	.	.	.	.	.	.	.	.	.	.	.	.	.	.	.
363	1	261	0.7	41	7	3	2	203	6	5	.	.	.	25	.	.	.	.	.	.	.	.	.	.	.	.	.	.	.	.	.	.	.	.	.	.
364	1	251	1.0	41	7	3	2	303	6	5	.	.	.	100	.	.	.	.	.	.	.	.	.	.	.	.	.	.	.	.	.	.	.	.	.	.
365	1	294	0.1	41	7	3	3	101	5	5	5	.	.	200	1	.	.	18	.	.	.	.	.	.	.	.	.	.	.	.	.	.	.	.	.	.
366	1	252	0.8	41	7	4	3	103	4	5	.	2	.	37	.	.	3	.	.	.	.	15	.	.	.	.	.	.	.	.	.	.	.	.	.	.
367	1	256	1.0	41	7	4	3	203	4	5	4	29	.	128	.	.	7	.	.	.	.	8	.	.	.	.	.	.	.	.	.	.	1	.	.	.
368	1	258	0.8	41	7	4	3	303	4	5	2	1	2	2500	8	.	3	.	.	.	.	10	.	.	.	.	.	.	.	.	.	.	.	.	.	.
369	1	363	0.8	41	7	5	2	203	4	5	.	.	.	281	.	.	.	3	.	.	.	8	.	.	.	.	.	.	1	.	.	1	.	.	.	.
370	1	255	1.0	41	7	5	3	103	4	5	.	1	.	2017	.	.	.	.	.	.	.	2	.	.	.	.	.	.	.	.	.	.	.	.	.	.
371	1	339	0.8	41	7	5	3	303	4	5	3	.	.	127	.	.	.	.	.	.	.	1	.	.	.	.	.	.	.	.	.	.	.	.	.	.
372	1	264	0.7	41	8	1	2	103	7	5	.	.	.	.	.	.	.	.	.	.	.	.	.	.	.	.	.	.	.	.	.	.	.	.	.	.
373	1	243	0.8	41	8	1	2	203	7	5	.	.	.	57	.	.	1	.	.	.	.	3	.	.	.	.	.	.	.	.	.	1	.	.	.	.
374	1	382	0.8	41	8	2	1	103	1	5	.	.	.	.	.	.	.	.	.	.	.	.	.	.	.	.	.	.	.	.	.	1	.	.	.	.
375	1	402	0.8	41	8	2	1	203	1	5	.	.	.	.	1	.	.	.	.	.	.	3	.	.	.	.	.	.	.	.	.	2	.	.	.	.
376	1	366	1.0	41	8	2	1	303	1	5	.	.	.	2	3	.	.	.	.	.	.	.	2	4	.	.	.	.	.	.	.	3	.	.	.	.
377	1	292	1.0	41	8	2	2	101	1	5	.	.	.	.	.	.	.	.	.	.	.	.	.	.	.	.	.	.	.	.	.	.	.	.	.	.
378	1	276	0.8	41	8	2	2	104	2	5	.	.	.	12	.	.	.	.	.	.	.	3	.	1	.	.	.	.	.	.	.	6	.	.	.	.
379	1	247	0.8	41	8	2	2	204	2	5	.	.	.	12	.	.	2	.	.	.	.	3	.	.	.	.	.	.	.	.	.	2	.	.	.	.
380	1	267	0.6	41	8	2	2	304	2	5	.	.	.	5	.	.	.	.	.	.	.	.	.	.	.	.	.	.	.	.	.	5	.	.	.	.

OBS	BIXA	PHYSOLIS	OXALIS	AMBROSIA	NICOTIAN	SALVIA	MINT	GALIUM	OPUNTIA	CYPER	COMPOSIT	UMBELIF	FABACEAE	UNKWNSEE	WDCT	WDWT	GRSSTKS	EUPHORB	PHORLUP	MIMOSA	VACCINIU	BERBERIS	TRITICUM	MOLLUGO	PENDFRAG	CACTUS	CALEND	CRUCIFER	SOLANUM	LGLEGUME	TLEGUME	KG	M3VOL	PHASE	STAT	LEV
362	.	.	.	.	.	.	.	.	.	.	.	.	.	.	.	.	.	.	.	.	.	.	.	.	.	.	.	.	.	.	.	6.0	0.0060	HII	.	3
363	.	.	.	.	.	.	.	.	.	.	.	.	.	.	.	.	.	.	.	.	.	.	.	.	.	.	.	.	.	.	.	4.2	0.0042	HII	.	3
364	.	.	.	.	.	.	.	.	.	.	.	.	.	.	1	.	.	.	.	.	.	.	.	.	.	.	.	.	.	.	.	6.0	0.0060	HII	.	3
365	.	.	.	.	.	.	.	.	.	.	.	.	.	.	9	.	.	.	.	.	.	.	.	.	.	.	.	.	18	.	.	0.6	0.0006	HII	.	3
366	.	.	.	.	.	.	.	.	.	.	.	.	.	8	11	.	.	.	.	.	.	.	.	.	.	.	.	.	.	.	.	4.8	0.0048	HII	.	4
367	.	.	.	.	.	.	.	.	.	.	1	.	.	.	9	.	.	.	.	.	.	.	.	.	.	.	.	.	.	.	.	6.0	0.0060	HII	.	4
368	.	.	.	.	.	.	.	.	.	.	.	.	.	.	9	.	.	.	.	.	.	.	.	.	.	.	.	.	.	.	.	4.8	0.0048	HII	.	4
369	.	.	.	.	.	.	.	.	.	.	.	.	.	.	6	.	.	.	.	.	.	.	.	.	.	.	.	.	3	.	.	4.8	0.0048	HII	.	5
370	.	.	.	.	.	.	.	.	.	.	.	.	.	.	10	.	.	.	.	.	.	.	.	.	.	.	.	.	.	.	.	6.0	0.0060	HII	.	5
371	.	.	.	.	.	.	.	.	.	.	.	.	.	.	3	.	.	.	4	.	.	.	.	.	.	.	.	.	.	4	.	4.8	0.0048	HII	.	5
372	.	.	.	.	.	.	.	.	.	.	.	.	.	.	.	.	.	.	.	.	.	.	.	.	.	.	.	.	.	.	.	4.2	0.0042	HII	.	1
373	.	.	.	.	.	.	.	.	.	.	1	.	.	.	.	.	.	.	.	.	.	.	.	.	.	.	.	.	.	.	.	4.8	0.0048	HII	.	1
374	.	.	.	.	.	.	.	.	.	.	.	.	.	.	.	.	.	.	.	.	.	.	.	.	.	.	.	.	.	.	.	4.8	0.0048	HII	.	2
375	.	.	.	.	.	.	.	.	.	.	.	.	.	.	3	.	.	.	.	.	.	.	.	.	.	.	.	.	.	.	.	4.8	0.0048	HII	.	2
376	.	.	.	.	.	.	.	.	.	.	.	.	.	5	.	.	.	.	.	.	.	.	.	.	.	.	.	.	.	.	.	6.0	0.0060	HII	.	2
377	.	.	.	.	.	.	.	.	.	.	.	.	.	.	.	.	.	.	.	.	.	.	.	.	.	.	.	.	.	.	.	6.0	0.0060	HII	.	2
378	.	.	.	.	.	.	.	.	.	.	.	.	.	.	1	.	.	.	.	.	.	.	.	.	.	.	.	.	.	.	.	4.8	0.0048	HII	.	2
379	.	.	.	.	.	.	.	.	.	.	.	.	.	.	.	.	.	.	.	.	.	.	.	.	.	.	.	.	.	.	.	4.8	0.0048	HII	.	2
380	.	.	.	.	.	.	.	.	.	.	3	.	.	8	8	.	.	.	.	.	.	.	.	.	.	.	.	.	.	.	.	3.6	0.0036	HII	.	2

OBS	FLTMCO	FLOT	BAGSIZE	SITE	FEATURE	LEVEL	LOCUS	BAGNO	CONTEXT	DATE	MZKERNAL	CUPCOBS	EMBRYOS	CHENOPOD	LUPINE	PHSPP	TUBERS	PAPAS	OCA	ULLUCO	MASHUA	LUMPS	AMARANTH	SCIRPUS	SMLEGUME	LEPIDIUM	LUCUMA	RARE	PORTULACA	VERBENA	PLANTAGO	SGRASS	LGRASS	MGRASS	MALVAST	RUBUS
381	1	283	0.8	41	8	2	2	404	1	5	.	.	.	25	.	.	.	.	.	.	.	.	.	.	.	.	.	.	.	.	.	2	1	.	.	.
382	1	368	0.8	41	8	3	1	103	4	5	.	.	.	.	.	.	.	.	.	.	.	.	.	.	.	.	.	.	.	.	.	.	.	.	.	.
383	1	262	0.8	41	8	3	1	203	4	5	.	.	.	.	.	.	.	.	.	.	.	.	.	.	.	.	.	.	.	.	.	1	.	.	.	.
384	1	246	0.8	41	8	3	1	303	4	5	.	.	.	.	.	.	.	.	.	.	.	.	.	.	.	.	.	.	.	.	.	2	.	.	.	.
385	1	288	1.0	41	8	3	2	103	4	5	.	.	.	2	.	.	.	.	.	.	.	.	.	.	.	.	.	.	.	.	.	.	.	.	.	.
386	1	280	0.8	41	8	3	2	203	4	5	.	.	.	.	.	.	.	.	.	.	.	.	.	.	.	.	.	.	.	.	.	.	.	.	.	.
387	1	286	1.0	41	8	3	2	303	4	5	.	.	.	.	.	.	.	.	.	.	.	.	.	.	.	.	.	.	.	.	.	.	.	.	.	.
388	1	766	0.8	41	9	1	2	103	7	5	.	.	.	1	.	.	.	.	.	.	.	.	.	.	.	.	.	.	.	.	1	.	.	.	.	.
389	1	733	0.9	41	9	2	1	103	1	5	.	.	.	.	.	.	.	.	.	.	.	.	.	.	.	.	.	.	.	.	.	1	.	.	.	.
390	1	726	0.8	41	9	2	1	203	1	5	.	.	.	.	.	.	.	.	.	.	.	1	.	.	.	.	.	.	.	.	.	.	.	.	.	.
391	1	757	1.0	41	9	2	1	303	1	5	.	.	.	3	.	.	1	.	.	.	.	.	.	.	.	.	.	.	.	.	.	.	.	.	.	.
392	1	771	0.8	41	9	2	2	103	1	5	.	.	.	.	.	.	.	.	.	.	.	.	.	.	.	.	.	.	.	.	.	.	.	.	.	.
393	1	734	0.8	41	9	2	2	203	1	5	.	.	.	.	.	.	.	.	.	.	.	.	.	.	.	.	.	.	.	.	.	.	.	.	.	.
394	1	767	0.8	41	9	2	2	303	1	5	.	.	.	.	.	.	.	.	.	.	.	.	.	.	.	.	.	.	.	.	.	.	.	.	.	.
395	1	776	0.8	41	9	4	2	303	4	5	.	.	.	.	.	.	.	.	.	.	.	.	.	.	.	.	.	.	.	.	1	.	.	.	.	.
396	1	759	0.7	41	10	2	1	103	1	5	.	.	.	1	.	.	.	.	.	.	.	.	.	.	.	.	.	.	.	.	.	1	.	.	.	.
397	1	722	0.8	41	10	2	1	203	1	5	.	.	.	.	.	.	.	.	.	.	.	.	.	.	.	.	.	.	.	.	.	.	.	.	.	.
398	1	774	1.0	41	10	2	1	303	1	5	.	.	.	.	.	.	.	.	.	.	.	2	.	1	.	.	.	.	.	.	.	1	.	.	.	.
399	1	808	1.0	41	10	3	1	103	4	5	.	.	.	.	.	.	.	.	.	.	.	.	.	.	.	.	.	.	.	.	.	1	.	.	.	.

OBS	BIXA	PHYSOLIS	OXALIS	AMBROSIA	NICOTIAN	SALVIA	MINT	GALIUM	OPUNTIA	CYPER	COMPOSIT	UMBELIF	FABACEAE	UNKWNSEE	WDCT	WDWT	GRSSTKS	EUPHORB	PHORLUP	MIMOSA	VACCINIU	BERBERIS	TRITICUM	MOLLUGO	PENDFRAG	CACTUS	CALEND	CRUCIFER	SOLANUM	LGLEGUME	TLEGUME	KG	M3VOL	PHASE	STAT	LEV
381	.	.	.	.	.	.	.	.	.	.	.	.	.	.	.	.	.	.	.	.	.	.	.	.	.	.	.	.	.	.	.	4.8	0.0048	HII	.	2
382	.	.	.	.	.	.	.	.	.	.	.	.	.	.	.	.	.	.	.	.	.	.	.	.	.	.	.	.	.	.	.	4.8	0.0048	HII	.	3
383	.	.	.	.	.	.	.	.	.	.	.	.	.	.	1	.	.	.	.	.	.	.	.	.	.	.	.	.	.	.	.	4.8	0.0048	HII	.	3
384	.	.	.	.	.	.	.	.	.	.	.	.	.	3	.	.	.	.	.	.	.	.	.	.	.	.	.	.	.	.	.	4.8	0.0048	HII	.	3
385	.	.	.	.	.	.	.	.	.	.	.	.	.	.	.	.	.	.	.	.	.	.	.	.	.	.	.	.	.	.	.	6.0	0.0060	HII	.	3
386	.	.	.	.	.	.	.	.	.	.	.	.	.	.	.	.	.	.	.	.	.	.	.	.	.	.	.	.	.	.	.	4.8	0.0048	HII	.	3
387	.	.	.	.	.	.	.	.	.	.	.	.	.	.	.	.	.	.	.	.	.	.	.	.	.	.	.	.	.	.	.	6.0	0.0060	HII	.	3
388	.	.	.	.	.	.	.	.	.	.	.	.	.	.	2	.	.	.	.	.	.	.	.	.	.	.	.	.	.	.	.	4.8	0.0048	HII	.	1
389	.	.	.	1	.	.	.	.	.	.	.	.	.	.	20	.	.	.	.	.	.	.	.	.	.	.	.	.	.	.	.	5.4	0.0054	HII	.	2
390	.	.	.	.	.	.	.	.	.	.	.	.	.	.	.	.	.	.	.	.	.	.	.	.	.	.	.	.	.	.	.	4.8	0.0048	HII	.	2
391	.	.	.	.	.	.	.	.	.	.	.	.	.	1	.	.	.	.	.	.	.	.	.	.	.	.	.	.	.	.	.	6.0	0.0060	HII	.	2
392	.	.	.	.	.	.	.	.	.	.	.	.	.	.	.	.	.	.	.	.	.	.	.	.	.	.	.	.	.	.	.	4.8	0.0048	HII	.	2
393	.	.	.	.	.	.	.	.	.	.	2	.	.	.	.	.	.	.	.	.	.	.	.	.	.	.	.	.	.	.	.	4.8	0.0048	HII	.	2
394	.	.	.	.	.	.	.	.	.	.	.	.	.	.	1	.	.	.	.	.	.	.	.	.	.	.	.	.	.	.	.	4.8	0.0048	HII	.	2
395	.	.	.	.	.	.	.	.	.	.	1	.	.	.	.	.	.	.	.	.	.	.	.	.	.	.	.	.	.	.	.	4.8	0.0048	HII	.	4
396	.	.	.	.	.	.	.	.	.	.	.	.	.	.	.	.	.	.	.	.	.	.	.	.	.	.	.	.	.	.	.	4.2	0.0042	HII	.	2
397	.	.	.	.	.	.	.	.	.	.	.	.	.	.	.	.	.	.	.	.	.	.	.	.	.	.	.	.	.	.	.	4.8	0.0048	HII	.	2
398	.	.	.	.	.	.	.	.	.	.	.	.	.	.	4	.	.	.	.	.	.	.	.	.	.	.	.	.	.	.	.	6.0	0.0060	HII	.	2
399	.	.	.	.	.	.	.	.	.	.	.	.	.	1	2	.	.	.	.	.	.	.	.	.	.	.	.	.	.	.	.	6.0	0.0060	HII	.	3

OBS	FLTMCO	FLOT	BAGSIZE	SITE	FEATURE	LEVEL	LOCUS	BAGNO	CONTEXT	DATE	MZKERNAL	CUPCOBS	EMBRYOS	CHENOPOD	LUPINE	PHSPP	TUBERS	PAPAS	OCA	ULLUCO	MASHUA	LUMPS	AMARANTH	SCIRPUS	SMLEGUME	LEPIDIUM	LUCUMA	RARE	PORTULACA	VERBENA	PLANTAGO	SGRASS	LGRASS	MGRASS	MALVAST
400	1	793	0.6	41	10	3	1	203	4	5	.	.	.	.	.	.	.	.	.	.	.	.	.	.	.	.	.	.	.	.	.	.	.	.	.
401	1	792	0.8	41	10	3	1	303	4	5	.	.	.	.	.	.	.	.	.	.	.	.	.	.	.	.	.	.	.	.	.	2	.	.	.
402	1	5	.	41	11	2	1	.	1	5	.	.	.	.	14	3	.	5	1	2	.	.	.	.	.	.	.	.	.	.	.	.	.	.	.
403	1	789	0.8	41	11	2	1	105	1	5	.	.	.	290	.	.	40	53	.	.	.	.	.	.	.	.	.	.	.	.	.	.	.	.	.
404	1	764	0.9	41	11	2	1	205	1	5	.	.	.	80	.	.	68	.	.	.	.	.	.	.	.	.	.	.	.	.	.	.	2	.	.
405	1	794	0.9	41	11	2	1	305	1	5	.	.	.	326	.	.	.	34	.	.	.	8	.	.	.	.	.	.	1	.	.	.	.	.	.
406	1	761	0.8	41	11	2	1	405	1	5	.	.	.	13	.	.	3	.	.	.	.	5	.	.	.	.	.	.	.	.	.	.	.	.	.
407	1	751	0.8	41	11	2	1	505	1	5	.	.	.	2523	6	.	20	.	.	.	.	.	.	.	.	.	.	.	.	.	.	.	.	.	.
408	1	749	0.8	41	11	3	1	105	1	5	.	.	.	911	.	.	99	.	.	.	.	.	4	1	.	.	.	.	.	.	.	3	5	.	.
409	1	763	0.9	41	11	3	1	205	1	5	.	.	.	13	1	.	.	.	.	.	.	1	.	3	.	.	.	.	.	.	.	.	.	.	.
410	1	758	0.8	41	11	3	1	305	1	5	.	.	.	9	.	.	4	.	.	.	.	4	.	.	.	.	.	.	.	.	.	.	.	.	.
411	1	723	0.8	41	11	3	1	405	1	5	.	.	.	659	.	.	54	88	.	.	.	.	.	1	.	.	.	.	.	.	.	1	.	.	.
412	1	727	0.7	41	11	3	1	505	1	5	.	.	.	1400	9	.	4	87	.	.	.	.	.	.	.	.	.	.	.	.	.	.	.	.	.
413	1	779	0.9	41	11	4	1	103	4	5	.	.	.	325	.	.	26	.	.	.	.	.	.	.	.	.	.	.	.	.	.	.	.	.	.
414	1	765	1.0	41	11	4	1	203	4	5	.	.	.	16	.	.	.	.	.	.	.	5	.	.	.	.	.	.	.	.	.	5	.	.	.
415	1	762	1.0	41	11	4	1	303	4	5	1	.	.	1400	1	.	81	.	.	.	.	47	.	.	.	.	.	.	.	.	.	.	.	.	.
416	1	735	0.8	41	11	5	1	103	4	5	.	.	.	1195	6	.	54	.	.	.	.	1	.	.	.	.	.	.	.	.	.	.	.	.	.
417	1	782	1.0	41	11	5	1	203	4	5	.	.	.	62	.	.	40	.	.	.	.	.	.	1	.	.	.	.	.	.	.	.	.	.	.
418	1	786	0.8	41	11	5	1	303	4	5	.	.	.	65	.	.	10	.	.	.	.	4	.	.	.	.	.	.	.	.	.	2	.	.	.

OBS	RUBUS	BIXA	PHYSOLIS	OXALIS	AMBROSIA	NICOTIAN	SALVIA	MINT	GALIUM	OPUNTIA	CYPER	COMPOSIT	CUMBELLIF	FABACEAE	UNKWNSEE	WDCT	WDWT	GRSSTKS	EUPHORB	PHORLUP	MIMOSA	VACCINIU	BERBERIS	TRITICUM	MOLLUGO	PENDFRAG	CACTUS	CALEND	CRUCIFER	SOLANUM	LGLEGUME	TLEGUME	KG	M3VOL	PHASE	STAT	LEV
400	.	.	.	.	.	.	.	.	.	.	.	.	.	.	.	.	.	.	.	.	.	.	.	.	.	.	.	.	.	.	.	.	3.6	0.0036	HII	.	3
401	.	.	.	.	.	.	.	.	.	.	.	.	.	.	2	.	.	.	.	.	.	.	.	.	.	.	.	.	.	.	.	.	4.8	0.0048	HII	.	3
402	.	.	.	.	.	.	.	.	.	.	.	.	.	.	.	3	.	.	.	.	.	.	.	.	.	.	.	.	.	5	.	.	.	.	HII	.	2
403	.	.	.	.	.	.	.	.	.	.	.	.	.	.	.	8	.	1	.	.	.	.	.	.	.	.	.	.	.	53	.	.	4.8	0.0048	HII	.	2
404	.	.	.	.	.	.	.	.	.	.	.	.	.	.	.	.	.	.	.	.	.	.	.	.	.	.	.	.	.	.	.	.	5.4	0.0054	HII	.	2
405	.	.	.	.	.	.	.	.	.	.	.	.	.	.	.	3	.	.	.	2	.	.	.	.	.	.	.	.	.	34	2	.	5.4	0.0054	HII	.	2
406	.	.	.	.	.	.	.	.	.	.	.	.	.	.	.	.	.	.	.	.	.	.	.	.	.	.	.	.	.	.	.	.	4.8	0.0048	HII	.	2
407	.	.	.	.	.	.	.	.	.	.	.	.	.	.	.	55	.	.	.	.	.	.	.	.	.	.	.	.	.	.	.	.	4.8	0.0048	HII	.	2
408	.	.	.	.	.	.	.	.	.	.	.	.	.	.	.	99	.	.	.	.	.	.	.	.	.	.	.	.	.	.	.	.	4.8	0.0048	HII	.	3
409	.	.	.	.	.	.	.	.	.	.	.	.	.	.	.	1	.	.	.	.	.	.	.	.	.	.	.	.	.	.	.	.	5.4	0.0054	HII	.	3
410	.	.	.	.	.	.	.	.	.	.	.	.	.	.	.	8	.	.	.	.	.	.	.	.	.	.	.	.	.	.	.	.	4.8	0.0048	HII	.	3
411	.	.	.	.	.	.	.	.	.	.	.	.	.	.	.	22	.	.	.	5	.	.	.	.	.	.	.	.	.	88	5	.	4.8	0.0048	HII	.	3
412	.	.	.	.	.	.	.	.	.	.	.	.	.	.	.	10	.	.	.	.	.	.	.	.	.	.	.	.	.	87	.	.	4.2	0.0042	HII	.	3
413	.	.	.	.	.	.	.	.	.	.	.	.	.	.	.	5	.	.	.	.	.	.	.	.	.	.	.	.	.	.	.	.	5.4	0.0054	HII	.	4
414	.	.	.	.	.	.	.	.	.	.	.	.	.	.	.	.	.	.	.	.	.	.	.	.	.	.	.	.	.	.	.	.	6.0	0.0060	HII	.	4
415	.	.	.	.	.	.	.	.	1	.	.	.	.	.	1	52	.	.	.	.	.	.	.	.	.	.	.	.	.	.	.	.	6.0	0.0060	HII	.	4
416	.	.	.	.	.	.	.	.	.	.	.	.	.	.	.	15	.	.	.	.	.	.	.	.	.	.	.	.	.	.	.	.	4.8	0.0048	HII	.	5
417	.	.	.	.	.	.	.	.	.	.	.	.	.	.	1	4	.	.	.	.	.	.	.	.	.	.	.	.	.	.	.	.	6.0	0.0060	HII	.	5
418	.	.	.	.	.	.	.	.	.	.	.	.	.	.	.	4	.	.	.	1	.	.	.	.	.	.	.	.	.	.	1	.	4.8	0.0048	HII	.	5

OBS	FLTMCO	FLOT	BAGSIZE	SITE	FEATURE	LEVEL	LOCUS	BAGNO	CONTEXT	DATE	MZKERNAL	CUPCOBS	EMBRYOS	CHENOPOD	LUPINE	PHSPP	TUBERS	PAPAS	OCA	ULLUCO	MASHUA	LUMPS	AMARANTH	SCIRPUS	SMLEGUME	LEPIDIUM	LUCUMA	RARE	PORTULACA	VERBENA	PLANTAGO	SGRASS	LGRASS	MGRASS	MALVAST	RUBUS	BIXA
419	1	803	1.0	49	1	2	1	103	7	6	.	.	.	1	.	.	.	.	.	.	.	.	.	.	1	.	.	.	.	.	.	1	.	.	.	.	.
420	1	819	1.0	49	1	2	1	203	7	6	.	.	.	.	.	.	.	.	.	.	.	.	.	.	.	.	.	.	.	.	.	.	.	.	.	.	.
421	1	713	0.8	49	1	2	1	303	7	6	.	.	.	.	.	.	.	.	.	.	.	1	.	.	.	.	.	.	.	.	.	.	.	.	1	.	.
422	1	717	1.0	49	1	3	1	103	1	6	1	.	.	2	.	.	.	.	.	.	.	.	.	.	.	.	.	.	.	1	.	.	.	.	.	1	.
423	1	720	0.9	49	1	3	1	203	1	6	.	.	.	1	.	.	.	.	.	.	.	.	.	1	.	.	.	.	.	.	.	2	1	.	.	.	.
424	1	802	0.8	49	1	3	1	303	1	6	.	.	.	3	.	.	1	.	.	.	.	.	.	.	.	.	.	.	.	.	.	1	1	.	.	.	.
425	1	712	1.0	49	1	3	2	103	2	4	.	.	.	3	.	.	1	.	.	.	.	.	.	.	.	.	.	.	.	.	.	1	.	.	.	.	.
426	1	817	0.8	49	1	3	2	203	2	4	.	.	.	.	.	.	.	.	.	.	.	3	.	.	.	.	.	.	.	.	.	.	.	.	.	.	.
427	1	813	0.8	49	1	3	2	303	2	4	.	.	.	2	.	.	.	.	.	.	.	.	.	.	.	.	.	.	.	.	.	.	.	.	.	.	.
428	1	804	0.9	49	1	4	1	103	4	4	.	.	.	8	.	.	2	.	.	.	.	.	.	.	.	.	.	.	.	.	.	4	.	.	.	1	.
429	1	631	1.0	49	1	4	1	203	4	4	.	.	.	7	.	.	.	.	.	.	.	.	.	.	.	.	.	.	.	.	.	.	.	.	1	1	.
430	1	797	1.0	49	1	4	1	303	4	4	.	.	.	6	.	.	.	.	.	.	.	.	.	.	.	.	.	.	.	.	.	.	1	.	1	.	.
431	1	633	1.0	49	1	5	1	103	4	3	.	.	.	3	.	.	.	.	.	.	.	1	.	.	.	.	.	.	.	.	.	2	.	.	.	.	.
432	1	637	0.8	49	1	5	1	203	4	3	.	.	.	4	.	.	.	.	.	.	.	3	.	.	.	.	.	.	.	.	.	4	.	.	.	.	.
433	1	608	0.8	49	1	5	3	103	3	4	.	.	.	8	1	.	1	.	.	.	.	1	.	1	1	.	.	.	.	1	.	3	2	.	.	.	.
434	1	639	0.7	49	1	5	3	203	3	4	.	1	.	14	.	.	3	.	.	.	.	4	.	3	.	.	.	.	.	1	.	2	1	.	.	.	.
435	1	814	0.9	49	1	5	3	303	3	4	.	1	.	16	.	.	.	.	.	.	.	3	.	1	2	.	.	.	.	.	.	6	.	.	.	.	.
436	1	636	1.0	49	1	6	1	103	4	3	.	.	.	11	1	.	1	.	.	.	.	.	.	.	.	.	.	.	.	.	.	1	.	.	.	.	.
437	1	812	0.7	49	1	6	1	203	4	3	.	3	.	2	.	.	.	.	.	.	.	.	.	.	.	.	.	.	.	.	.	.	.	.	.	.	.

OBS	PHYSOLIS	OXALIS	AMBROSIA	NICOTIAN	SALVIA	MINT	GALIUM	OPUNTIA	CYPER	COMPOSIT	CUMBELLIF	FABACEAE	UNKWNSEE	WDCT	WDWT	GRSSTKS	EUPHORB	PHORLUP	MIMOSA	VACCINIU	BERBERIS	TRITICUM	MOLLUGO	PENDFRAG	CACTUS	CALEND	CRUCIFER	SOLANUM	LGLEGUME	TLEGUME	KG	M3VOL	PHASE	STAT	LEV
419	.	.	.	.	.	.	.	.	.	.	.	.	.	2	.	.	.	.	.	.	.	.	.	.	.	.	.	.	.	1	6.0	0.0060	HIII	.	2
420	.	.	.	.	.	.	.	.	.	.	.	.	.	.	.	.	.	.	.	.	.	.	.	.	.	.	.	.	.	.	6.0	0.0060	HIII	.	2
421	.	.	.	.	.	.	.	.	.	.	.	.	.	.	.	.	.	1	.	.	.	.	.	.	.	.	.	.	1	.	4.8	0.0048	HIII	.	2
422	.	.	.	.	.	.	.	.	.	0	1	.	2	6	.	1	.	.	.	.	.	.	.	.	.	.	.	.	.	.	6.0	0.0060	HIII	.	3
423	.	.	.	.	.	.	.	.	.	.	.	.	.	5	.	.	.	.	.	.	.	.	.	.	.	.	.	.	.	.	5.4	0.0054	HIII	.	3
424	.	.	.	.	.	.	.	.	.	.	.	.	.	4	.	.	.	.	.	.	.	.	.	.	.	.	.	.	.	.	4.8	0.0048	HIII	.	3
425	.	.	.	.	.	.	.	.	.	.	.	.	.	14	.	.	.	.	.	.	.	.	.	.	.	.	.	.	.	.	6.0	0.0060	HI	.	3
426	.	.	.	.	.	.	.	.	.	.	.	.	.	7	.	.	.	.	.	.	.	.	.	.	.	.	.	.	.	.	4.8	0.0048	HI	.	3
427	.	1	.	.	.	.	.	.	.	.	.	.	.	7	.	.	.	.	.	.	.	.	.	.	.	.	.	.	.	.	4.8	0.0048	HI	.	3
428	.	.	.	.	.	.	.	.	.	.	.	.	1	43	.	.	.	.	.	.	.	.	.	.	.	.	.	.	.	.	5.4	0.0054	HI	.	4
429	.	.	.	.	.	.	.	.	.	1	.	.	.	7	.	.	.	.	.	.	.	.	.	.	.	.	.	.	.	.	6.0	0.0060	HI	.	4
430	.	.	.	.	.	.	.	.	.	.	.	.	.	12	.	.	.	1	.	.	.	.	.	.	.	.	.	.	1	.	6.0	0.0060	HI	.	4
431	.	.	.	.	.	.	.	.	.	.	.	.	.	8	.	.	.	.	.	.	.	.	.	.	.	.	.	.	.	.	6.0	0.0060	HO	.	5
432	.	.	.	.	.	.	.	.	.	.	.	.	.	14	.	.	.	.	.	.	.	.	.	.	.	.	.	.	.	.	4.8	0.0048	HO	.	5
433	.	.	.	.	.	.	.	.	.	1	.	.	.	14	.	.	.	.	.	.	.	.	.	.	.	.	.	.	.	1	4.8	0.0048	HI	.	5
434	.	.	.	.	.	.	.	.	.	.	.	.	2	11	.	.	.	.	.	.	.	.	.	.	.	.	.	.	.	.	4.2	0.0042	HI	.	5
435	.	.	.	.	.	.	.	.	.	.	.	.	.	10	.	.	.	2	.	.	.	.	.	.	.	.	.	.	2	2	5.4	0.0054	HI	.	5
436	.	.	.	.	.	.	.	.	.	.	.	.	.	50	.	.	.	.	.	.	.	.	.	.	.	.	.	.	.	.	6.0	0.0060	HO	.	6
437	.	.	.	.	1	.	.	.	.	.	.	.	.	6	.	.	.	.	.	.	.	.	.	.	.	.	.	.	.	.	4.2	0.0042	HO	.	6

OBS	FLTMCO	FLOT	BAGSIZE	SITE	FEATURE	LEVEL	LOCUS	BAGNO	CONTEXT	DATE	MZKERNAL	CUPCOBS	EMBRYOS	CHENOPOD	LUPINE	PHSPP	TUBERS	PAPAS	OCA	ULLUCO	MASHUA	LUMPS	AMARANTH	SCIRPUS	SMLEGUME	LEPIDIUM	LUCUMA	RARE	PORTULAC	VERBENA	PLANTAGO	SGRASS	LGRASS	MGRASS	MALVAST
438	1	719	0.8	49	1	6	1	303	4	3	.	.	.	2	.	.	2	.	.	.	.	1	.	2	.	.	.	.	.	1	.	3	.	.	.
439	1	644	0.8	49	1	7	1	103	4	3	.	.	.	1	.	.	.	.	.	.	.	1	.	.	.	.	.	.	.	.	.	.	.	.	.
440	1	643	0.9	49	1	7	1	203	4	3	.	.	.	2	.	.	.	.	.	.	.	.	.	.	.	.	.	.	.	.	.	.	.	.	.
441	1	654	0.9	49	1	7	1	303	4	3	.	.	.	.	.	.	.	.	.	.	.	.	.	.	1	.	.	.	.	.	.	.	.	.	.
442	1	641	0.8	49	1	8	1	103	4	3	.	.	.	.	.	.	.	.	.	.	.	.	.	.	.	.	.	.	.	.	.	1	.	.	.
443	1	646	1.0	49	1	8	1	203	4	3	.	.	.	.	.	.	.	.	.	.	.	.	.	.	.	.	.	.	.	1	.	.	.	.	.
444	1	642	0.9	49	1	8	1	303	4	3	.	.	.	.	.	.	.	.	.	.	.	.	.	.	.	.	.	.	.	.	.	1	.	.	.
445	1	807	0.9	49	2	2	1	103	7	4	.	.	.	.	.	.	.	.	.	.	.	.	.	.	.	.	.	.	.	.	.	.	.	.	.
446	1	632	0.8	49	2	2	1	203	7	4	.	.	.	.	.	.	.	.	.	.	.	.	.	.	.	.	.	.	.	.	.	.	.	.	.
447	1	716	0.8	49	2	2	1	303	7	4	.	.	.	.	.	.	.	.	.	.	.	.	.	.	.	.	.	.	.	.	.	.	.	.	.
448	1	664	0.8	49	2	3	1	103	7	4	1	.	.	1	2	.	.	.	.	.	.	.	.	.	.	.	.	1	.	1	.	1	2	.	.
449	1	801	0.8	49	2	3	1	203	7	4	1	.	.	1	.	.	.	.	.	.	.	.	.	.	.	.	.	.	.	.	2	5	4	.	.
450	1	721	0.8	49	2	3	1	303	7	4	.	.	.	1	.	.	.	.	.	.	.	.	.	1	2	.	.	.	.	1	.	7	1	.	2
451	1	718	0.8	49	2	3	2	101	4	4	.	.	.	5	.	.	.	.	.	.	.	2	.	.	1	.	.	.	.	.	.	1	4	.	.
452	1	640	0.9	49	2	4	1	103	7	4	.	.	.	25	1	.	3	.	.	.	.	4	1	5	6	.	.	.	.	6	.	80	.	.	2
453	1	806	0.9	49	2	4	1	203	7	4	.	.	.	12	.	.	.	.	.	.	.	3	.	.	.	.	.	.	.	.	.	4	.	.	.
454	1	634	0.8	49	2	4	1	303	7	4	.	1	.	12	.	.	1	.	.	.	.	.	1	.	1	.	.	.	.	.	.	1	1	.	1
455	1	815	0.8	49	2	5	1	101	3	4	.	.	.	22	.	.	9	.	.	.	.	9	.	.	.	.	.	.	.	1	.	11	.	.	.
456	1	805	0.8	49	2	5	1	102	3	4	.	.	.	11	4	.	.	.	.	.	.	21	.	4	10	.	.	.	.	8	3	26	2	.	.

OBS	RUBUS	BIXA	PHYSOLIS	OXALIS	AMBROSIA	NICOTIAN	SALVIA	MINT	GALIUM	OPUNTIA	CYPER	COMPOSIT	UMBELLIF	FABACEAE	UNKWNSEE	WDCT	WDWT	GRSSTKS	EUPHORB	PHORLUP	MIMOSA	VACCINIU	BERBERIS	TRITICUM	MOLLUGO	PENDFRAG	CACTUS	CALEND	CRUCIFER	SOLANUM	LGLEGUME	TLEGUME	KG	M3VOL	PHASE	STAT	LEV
438	.	.	.	.	.	.	.	.	.	.	.	.	.	.	.	6	.	.	.	.	.	.	.	.	.	.	.	.	.	.	.	.	4.8	0.0048	HO	.	6
439	.	.	.	.	.	.	.	.	.	.	.	.	.	.	.	2	.	.	.	.	.	.	.	.	.	.	.	.	.	.	.	.	4.8	0.0048	HO	.	7
440	.	.	.	.	.	.	.	.	.	.	.	.	.	.	.	1	.	.	.	.	.	.	.	.	.	.	.	.	.	.	.	.	5.4	0.0054	HO	.	7
441	.	.	.	.	.	.	.	.	.	.	.	.	.	.	.	1	.	.	.	.	.	.	.	.	.	.	.	.	.	.	.	1	5.4	0.0054	HO	.	7
442	.	.	.	.	.	.	.	.	.	.	.	.	.	.	.	1	.	.	.	.	.	.	.	.	.	.	.	.	.	.	.	.	4.8	0.0048	HO	.	8
443	.	.	.	1	.	.	.	.	.	.	.	.	.	.	.	.	.	.	.	.	.	.	.	.	.	.	.	.	.	.	.	.	6.0	0.0060	HO	.	8
444	.	.	1	.	.	.	.	.	.	.	.	.	.	.	.	1	.	.	.	.	.	.	.	.	.	.	.	.	.	.	.	.	5.4	0.0054	HO	.	8
445	.	.	.	.	.	.	.	.	.	.	.	.	.	.	.	.	.	.	.	.	.	.	.	.	.	.	.	.	.	.	.	.	5.4	0.0054	HI	.	2
446	.	.	.	.	.	.	.	.	.	.	.	.	.	.	.	.	.	.	.	.	.	.	.	.	.	.	.	.	.	.	.	.	4.8	0.0048	HI	.	2
447	.	.	.	.	.	.	.	.	.	.	.	.	.	.	.	.	.	.	.	.	.	.	.	.	.	.	.	.	.	.	.	.	4.8	0.0048	HI	.	2
448	.	.	.	.	.	1	.	.	.	.	.	1	.	.	3	1	.	.	.	.	.	.	.	.	1	.	.	.	.	.	.	.	4.8	0.0048	HI	.	3
449	.	.	.	.	1	.	.	.	.	.	.	.	.	.	.	4	.	.	.	.	.	.	.	.	.	.	.	.	.	.	.	.	4.8	0.0048	HI	.	3
450	.	.	.	.	.	.	.	.	.	.	.	.	.	.	.	3	.	.	.	.	.	.	.	.	.	.	.	.	.	.	.	2	4.8	0.0048	HI	.	3
451	.	.	.	.	3	.	.	.	.	.	.	.	.	1	1	16	.	.	.	.	.	.	.	.	.	.	.	.	.	.	.	1	4.8	0.0048	HI	.	3
452	5	.	.	.	.	.	.	.	.	.	.	.	.	.	3	17	.	.	.	.	.	.	.	.	.	.	.	.	.	.	.	6	5.4	0.0054	HI	.	4
453	.	.	.	.	.	.	.	.	.	.	.	.	.	.	2	6	.	.	.	.	.	.	.	.	.	.	.	.	.	.	.	.	5.4	0.0054	HI	.	4
454	1	.	.	.	.	.	.	.	.	.	.	1	.	.	3	2	.	.	.	.	.	.	.	.	.	.	.	.	.	.	.	1	4.8	0.0048	HI	.	4
455	.	.	.	.	2	.	.	.	.	.	.	.	.	.	.	11	.	.	.	3	.	.	.	.	.	.	.	.	.	.	3	.	4.8	0.0048	HI	.	5
456	2	.	.	.	.	.	.	.	.	1	1	.	.	.	13	63	.	.	.	.	.	.	.	.	.	.	.	.	.	.	.	10	4.8	0.0048	HI	.	5

OBS	FLTMCO	FLOT	BAGSIZE	SITE	FEATURE	LEVEL	LOCUS	BAGNO	CONTEXT	DATE	MZKERNAL	CUPCOBS	EMBRYOS	CHENOPOD	LUPINE	PHSPP	TUBERS	PAPAS	OCA	ULLUCO	MASHUA	LUMPS	AMARANTH	SCIRPUS	SMLEGUME	LEPIDIUM	LUCUMA	RARE	PORTULAC	VERBENA	PLANTAGO	SGRASS	LGRASS	MGRASS	MALVAST
457	1	811	0.9	49	2	5	1	202	1	4	1	.	.	17	.	.	.	.	.	.	.	.	4	4	.	.	.	.	.	3	1	6	.	.	1
458	1	791	0.4	49	2	5	1	202	3	4	.	2	.	26	.	.	2	.	.	.	.	2	.	7	13	.	.	.	.	15	1	17	2	.	3
459	1	714	0.8	49	2	6	1	103	1	4	3	1	.	23	.	.	5	.	.	.	.	.	.	1	.	.	.	.	.	3	1	4	4	.	.
460	1	657	0.8	49	2	6	1	203	1	4	6	.	.	13	.	.	1	.	.	.	.	1	.	5	2	.	.	.	.	2	.	5	.	.	.
461	1	635	0.8	49	2	6	1	303	1	4	.	.	.	14	.	.	.	5	2	.	.	2	.	8	2	.	.	.	.	11	7	22	2	.	.
462	1	651	0.8	49	2	7	1	104	4	4	5	3	.	37	.	.	3	9	.	.	.	18	.	54	15	.	.	.	.	31	14	6	4	3	6
463	1	656	0.8	49	2	7	1	204	4	4	2	.	.	51	3	.	11	.	.	.	.	18	2	41	8	.	.	.	.	24	4	20	7	2	.
464	1	647	0.8	49	2	7	1	304	4	4	.	.	.	9	1	.	.	.	.	.	.	4	.	.	2	.	.	.	.	.	.	1	1	.	.
465	1	653	0.8	49	2	7	1	404	4	4	.	.	.	16	.	.	.	.	.	.	.	1	.	2	.	.	.	.	.	4	1	10	.	1	.
466	1	648	0.8	49	2	7	2	102	4	4	.	.	.	6	2	.	.	.	.	.	.	3	1	1	2	.	.	.	.	3	.	9	7	1	2
467	1	655	0.9	49	2	7	2	202	4	4	4	1	.	58	6	.	5	.	.	.	.	3	.	21	23	.	.	.	.	14	8	60	3	2	1
468	1	658	0.8	49	2	8	1	104	4	4	.	.	.	1	.	.	.	.	.	.	.	3	.	.	.	.	.	.	.	.	.	1	.	.	.
469	1	649	1.0	49	2	8	1	203	4	4	.	.	.	.	.	.	.	.	.	.	.	.	.	.	.	.	.	.	.	1	.	4	.	1	.
470	1	645	0.8	49	2	8	1	304	4	4	.	.	.	4	.	.	.	.	.	.	.	.	.	.	1	.	.	.	.	1	.	.	.	.	.
471	1	659	0.8	49	2	8	1	404	4	4	.	2	.	14	.	.	.	.	.	.	.	12	.	2	4	.	.	.	.	.	1	1	2	.	1
472	1	688	1.0	49	3	1	1	303	9	4	.	.	.	.	.	.	.	.	.	.	.	.	.	.	.	.	.	.	.	.	.	.	.	.	.
473	1	705	0.8	49	3	2	1	103	7	4	.	.	.	1	.	.	.	.	.	.	.	1	.	.	.	.	.	.	.	.	.	3	.	.	.
474	1	.	.	49	3	2	1	203	7	4	.	.	.	4	.	.	.	.	.	.	.	6	.	.	.	.	.	.	.	.	.	3	.	.	.
475	1	663	0.8	49	3	2	1	203	7	4	.	.	.	.	.	.	.	.	.	.	.	.	.	.	.	.	.	.	.	.	.	1	.	.	.

OBS	RUBUS	BIXA	PHYSOLIS	OXALIS	AMBROSIA	NICOTIAN	SALVIA	MINT	GALIUM	OPUNTIA	CYPER	COMPOSIT	UMBELLIF	FABACEAE	UNKWNSEE	WDCT	WDWT	GRSSTKS	EUPHORB	PHORLUP	MIMOSA	VACCINIU	BERBERIS	TRITICUM	MOLLUGO	PENDFRAG	CACTUS	CALEND	CRUCIFER	SOLANUM	LGLEGUME	TLEGUME	KG	M3VOL	PHASE	STAT	LEV
457	.	.	.	.	1	.	.	.	.	.	.	.	.	.	1	45	.	.	.	.	.	.	.	.	.	.	.	.	.	.	.	.	5.4	0.0054	HI	.	5
458	.	.	.	.	1	.	.	.	.	.	.	3	.	.	5	21	.	.	.	.	.	.	.	.	.	.	.	.	.	.	.	13	2.4	0.0024	HI	.	5
459	.	.	2	.	.	.	.	.	.	.	.	.	.	.	3	15	.	.	.	.	.	.	.	.	.	.	.	.	.	.	.	.	4.8	0.0048	HI	.	6
460	.	.	.	.	.	.	.	.	.	.	.	.	.	.	.	13	.	.	.	.	.	.	.	.	.	.	.	.	.	.	.	2	4.8	0.0048	HI	.	6
461	1	.	.	.	1	.	.	.	.	.	.	6	.	.	9	15	.	.	.	.	.	.	.	.	.	.	.	.	.	5	.	2	4.8	0.0048	HI	.	6
462	6	.	1	.	1	.	3	.	.	.	.	4	.	.	6	34	.	.	.	2	.	.	.	.	.	.	.	.	.	9	2	15	4.8	0.0048	HI	.	7
463	5	.	.	.	1	.	.	.	.	.	.	13	1	.	16	73	.	.	.	.	.	.	.	.	.	.	.	.	.	.	.	8	4.8	0.0048	HI	.	7
464	1	.	.	.	.	.	.	.	.	.	.	.	.	.	.	.	.	.	.	.	.	.	.	.	.	.	.	.	.	.	.	2	4.8	0.0048	HI	.	7
465	.	.	1	.	.	.	.	.	.	.	.	2	.	.	.	14	.	1	.	.	.	.	.	.	.	.	.	.	.	.	.	.	4.8	0.0048	HI	.	7
466	.	.	.	.	.	.	.	.	1	.	.	.	.	.	6	44	.	1	.	.	.	.	.	.	.	.	.	.	.	.	.	2	4.8	0.0048	HI	.	7
467	4	.	.	.	.	.	.	.	.	.	.	.	.	.	12	31	.	.	.	.	.	.	.	.	.	.	.	.	.	.	.	23	5.4	0.0054	HI	.	7
468	.	.	.	.	.	.	.	.	.	.	.	.	.	.	.	1	.	.	.	.	.	.	.	.	.	.	.	.	.	.	.	.	4.8	0.0048	HI	.	8
469	.	.	.	.	.	.	.	.	.	.	.	.	.	.	1	3	.	.	.	.	.	.	.	.	.	.	.	.	.	.	.	.	6.0	0.0060	HI	.	8
470	.	.	.	.	.	.	.	.	.	.	.	.	.	.	.	.	.	.	.	.	.	.	.	.	.	.	.	.	.	.	.	1	4.8	0.0048	HI	.	8
471	.	.	.	1	.	.	.	.	.	.	.	2	.	.	3	3	.	.	.	.	.	.	.	.	.	.	.	.	.	.	.	4	4.8	0.0048	HI	.	8
472	.	.	.	.	.	.	.	.	.	.	.	.	.	.	.	.	.	.	.	.	.	.	.	.	.	.	.	.	.	.	.	.	6.0	0.0060	HI	.	1
473	.	.	.	.	.	.	.	.	.	.	.	.	.	.	.	.	.	.	.	.	.	.	.	.	.	.	.	.	.	.	.	.	4.8	0.0048	HI	.	2
474	.	.	.	.	.	.	.	.	.	.	.	.	.	.	.	70	.	.	.	.	.	.	.	.	.	.	.	.	.	.	.	.	.	.	HI	.	2
475	.	.	.	.	.	.	.	.	.	.	.	.	.	.	1	1	.	.	.	.	.	.	.	.	.	.	.	.	.	.	.	.	4.8	0.0048	HI	.	2

OBS	FLTMCO	FLOT	BAGSIZE	SITE	FEATURE	LEVEL	LOCUS	BAGNO	CONTEXT	DATE	MZKERNAL	CUPCOBS	EMBRYOS	CHENOPOD	LUPINE	PHSPP	TUBERS	PAPAS	OCA	ULLUCO	MASHUA	LUMPS	AMARANTH	SCIRPUS	SMLEGUME	LEPIDIUM	LUCUMA	RARE	PORTULAC	VERBENA	PLANTAGO	SGRASS	LGRASS	MGRASS	MALVAST
476	1	661	0.9	49	3	2	1	303	7	4	.	1	.	2	.	.	.	.	.	.	.	4	.	.	.	.	.	.	.	.	.	.	1	.	1
477	1	698	0.2	49	3	3	1	103	1	4	1	.	.	19	7	.	24	.	.	.	.	5	.	.	1	.	.	.	.	.	.	1	.	.	.
478	1	781	1.0	49	3	3	1	203	1	4	.	.	.	1	.	.	.	.	.	.	.	.	.	.	.	.	.	.	.	.	.	.	.	.	.
479	1	662	1.0	49	3	3	1	303	1	4	.	1	.	2	.	.	.	.	.	.	.	4	.	1	.	.	.	.	.	.	.	1	9	.	.
480	1	689	1.0	49	3	4	2	103	4	4	.	.	.	7	.	.	.	.	.	.	.	3	.	1	.	.	.	.	.	.	.	4	.	.	2
481	1	707	0.9	49	3	4	2	203	4	4	.	.	.	4	4	.	.	.	.	.	.	.	.	.	.	.	.	.	.	.	.	1	.	.	1
482	1	711	1.0	49	3	4	2	303	4	4	.	.	.	1	.	.	.	.	.	.	.	.	.	.	.	.	.	.	.	.	.	1	.	.	.
483	1	671	0.8	49	3	5	2	103	4	4	.	1	.	54	4	.	12	.	.	.	.	7	1	5	3	.	.	.	.	2	1	7	2	.	6
484	1	690	1.0	49	3	5	2	203	4	4	2	.	.	324	.	.	1	.	.	.	.	1	4	6	.	.	.	.	.	3	4	1	3	.	9
485	1	703	0.9	49	3	5	2	303	4	4	2	2	.	140	3	1	.	.	.	.	.	1	2	3	3	.	.	.	.	3	5	3	4	.	26
486	1	695	0.8	49	3	6	2	101	4	4	.	4	.	5	.	.	.	.	.	.	.	11	.	.	.	.	.	.	.	.	.	.	.	.	1
487	1	708	0.8	49	4	2	1	103	7	4	.	.	.	3	.	.	.	.	.	.	.	.	.	.	.	.	.	.	.	.	.	.	.	.	.
488	1	709	0.7	49	4	2	1	203	7	4	2	.	.	.	.	.	.	.	.	.	.	.	.	.	.	.	.	.	.	.	.	.	.	.	.
489	1	700	0.8	49	4	2	1	303	7	4	.	.	.	2	.	.	.	.	.	.	.	.	.	.	.	.	.	.	.	.	.	2	.	.	.
490	1	687	0.8	49	4	3	1	103	7	4	.	.	.	3	.	.	.	.	.	.	.	.	.	1	.	.	.	.	.	.	.	7	.	.	.
491	1	701	0.8	49	4	3	1	203	7	4	.	.	.	5	.	.	2	.	.	.	.	1	.	.	.	.	.	.	.	1	1	10	.	.	1
492	1	678	0.8	49	4	3	1	303	7	4	.	.	.	10	.	.	.	.	.	.	.	3	.	.	.	.	.	.	.	4	.	3	.	.	.
493	1	710	0.8	49	4	4	1	103	7	4	.	.	.	9	.	.	.	.	.	.	.	2	.	.	.	.	.	.	.	1	.	3	.	.	2
494	1	704	0.8	49	4	4	1	203	7	4	.	1	.	6	10	.	.	.	.	.	.	1	2	.	.	.	.	.	.	8	.	8	.	.	1

OBS	RUBUS	BIXA	PHYSOLIS	OXALIS	AMBROSIA	NICOTIAN	SALVIA	MINT	GALIUM	OPUNTIA	CYPER	COMPOSIT	UMBELLIF	FABACEAE	UNKWNSEE	WDCT	WDWT	GRSSTKS	EUPHORB	PHORLUP	MIMOSA	VACCINIU	BERBERIS	TRITICUM	MOLLUGO	PENDFRAG	CACTUS	CALENDR	CRUCIFER	SOLANUM	LGLEGUME	TLEGUME	KG	M3VOL	PHASE	STAT	LEV
476	.	.	.	.	.	.	.	.	.	.	.	.	.	.	.	1	.	.	.	.	.	.	.	.	.	.	.	.	.	.	.	.	5.4	0.0054	HI	.	2
477	.	.	.	.	.	.	.	.	.	.	.	.	.	.	.	99	.	.	.	.	.	.	.	.	.	.	.	.	.	.	.	1	1.2	0.0012	HI	.	3
478	.	.	.	.	.	.	.	.	.	.	.	.	.	.	.	4	.	.	.	.	.	.	.	.	.	.	.	.	.	.	.	.	6.0	0.0060	HI	.	3
479	1	.	.	.	1	.	.	.	.	.	.	.	.	.	.	7	.	.	.	.	.	.	.	.	.	.	.	.	.	.	.	.	6.0	0.0060	HI	.	3
480	.	.	.	.	.	.	.	.	.	.	.	.	.	.	.	14	.	.	.	.	.	.	.	.	.	.	.	.	.	.	.	.	6.0	0.0060	HI	.	4
481	.	.	.	.	.	.	.	.	.	.	.	.	.	.	.	50	.	.	.	.	.	.	.	.	.	.	.	.	.	.	.	.	5.4	0.0054	HI	.	4
482	.	.	.	.	.	.	.	.	.	.	.	1	.	.	.	5	.	.	.	.	.	.	.	.	.	.	.	.	.	.	.	.	6.0	0.0060	HI	.	4
483	.	.	.	.	.	.	.	.	.	.	.	.	.	.	9	84	.	.	.	.	.	.	.	.	.	.	.	.	.	.	.	3	4.8	0.0048	HI	.	5
484	3	.	.	.	.	.	1	.	.	.	.	1	.	.	9	30	.	.	.	.	.	.	.	.	.	.	.	.	.	.	.	.	6.0	0.0060	HI	.	5
485	.	.	.	.	.	2	3	.	.	.	.	.	2	.	6	99	.	.	.	.	.	.	.	.	.	.	.	.	.	.	.	3	5.4	0.0054	HI	.	5
486	.	.	.	.	.	.	.	.	.	.	.	.	.	.	.	99	.	.	.	1	.	.	.	.	.	.	.	.	.	.	1	.	4.8	0.0048	HI	.	6
487	.	.	.	.	.	.	.	.	.	.	.	.	.	.	.	.	.	.	.	.	.	.	.	.	.	.	.	.	.	.	.	.	4.8	0.0048	HI	.	2
488	.	.	.	.	.	.	.	.	.	.	.	.	.	.	.	7	.	.	.	1	.	.	.	.	.	.	.	.	.	.	1	.	4.2	0.0042	HI	.	2
489	.	.	.	.	.	.	.	.	.	.	.	.	.	.	.	17	.	.	.	.	.	.	.	.	.	.	.	.	.	.	.	.	4.8	0.0048	HI	.	2
490	.	.	.	.	.	.	.	.	.	.	.	.	.	.	.	4	.	.	.	.	.	.	.	.	.	.	.	.	.	.	.	.	4.8	0.0048	HI	.	3
491	1	.	.	.	.	.	1	.	.	.	.	.	.	.	.	2	.	.	.	.	.	.	.	.	.	.	.	.	.	.	.	.	4.8	0.0048	HI	.	3
492	.	.	.	.	.	.	.	.	.	.	.	.	.	.	1	3	.	.	.	4	.	.	.	.	.	.	.	.	.	.	4	.	4.8	0.0048	HI	.	3
493	1	.	.	.	.	.	.	.	.	.	.	.	.	.	1	4	.	.	.	.	.	.	.	.	.	.	.	.	.	.	.	.	4.8	0.0048	HI	.	4
494	1	.	.	1	.	.	.	.	.	.	.	.	.	.	1	6	.	.	.	.	.	.	.	.	.	.	.	.	.	.	.	.	4.8	0.0048	HI	.	4

OBS	FLTMCO	FLOT	BAGSIZE	SITE	FEATURE	LEVEL	LOCUS	BAGNO	CONTEXT	DATE	MZKERNAL	CUPCOBS	EMBRYOS	CHENOPOD	LUPINE	PHSPP	TUBERS	PAPAS	OCA	ULLUCO	MASHUA	LUMPS	AMARANTH	SCIRPUS	SMLEGUME	LEPIDIUM	LUCUMA	RARE	PORTULAC	VERBENA	PLANTAGO	SGRASS	LGRASS	MGRASS	MALVAST	RUBUS
495	1	681	0.8	49	4	4	1	303	7	4	.	.	.	13	.	.	.	.	.	.	.	.	.	.	.	.	.	.	.	1	1	2	.	.	2	.
496	1	679	0.9	49	4	5	1	103	1	4	.	.	.	8	.	.	4	.	.	.	.	1	.	3	.	.	.	.	.	1	1	2	1	.	.	.
497	1	699	0.8	49	4	5	1	203	1	4	.	.	.	27	.	.	.	.	.	.	.	2	.	.	1	.	.	.	.	.	1	7	1	.	.	.
498	1	696	0.8	49	4	5	1	303	1	4	1	1	.	15	.	.	.	.	.	.	.	12	1	.	1	.	.	.	.	.	2	4	.	.	1	.
499	1	800	0.7	49	4	6	1	103	1	4	.	1	.	16	.	.	1	.	.	.	.	6	.	.	1	.	.	.	.	4	.	5	.	.	.	.
500	1	702	0.8	49	4	6	1	203	1	4	.	.	.	26	.	.	9	.	.	.	.	.	.	.	1	.	.	.	.	2	.	5	1	.	.	.
501	1	684	0.7	49	4	6	1	303	1	4	1	.	.	22	.	.	1	.	.	.	.	1	.	1	2	.	.	.	.	4	.	16	.	.	.	.
502	1	674	0.8	49	4	7	1	104	4	4	.	.	.	5	.	.	2	.	.	.	.	.	.	.	1	.	.	.	.	.	.	3	.	.	.	.
503	1	697	0.8	49	4	7	1	204	4	4	.	.	.	4	1	.	.	.	.	.	.	5	.	.	.	.	.	.	.	.	.	2	.	.	.	.
504	1	673	0.8	49	4	7	1	304	4	4	.	1	.	4	.	.	.	.	.	.	.	2	.	.	.	.	.	.	.	.	.	3	.	.	.	.
505	1	694	0.8	49	4	7	1	404	4	4	.	.	.	1	.	.	.	.	.	.	.	.	.	.	.	.	.	.	.	1	.	.	.	.	.	.
506	1	667	1.0	49	5	2	1	103	7	6	.	.	.	.	.	.	.	.	.	.	.	.	.	.	.	.	.	.	.	.	.	.	.	.	.	.
507	1	665	0.9	49	5	2	1	203	7	6	.	.	.	.	.	.	.	.	.	.	.	.	.	.	.	.	.	.	.	.	.	.	.	.	.	.
508	1	693	0.8	49	5	2	1	303	7	6	.	.	.	.	.	.	.	.	.	.	.	.	.	.	.	.	.	.	.	.	.	.	.	.	.	.
509	1	672	1.0	49	5	3	1	103	7	6	.	.	.	.	.	.	1	.	.	.	.	.	.	.	.	.	.	.	.	.	.	.	.	.	.	.
510	1	676	0.9	49	5	3	1	203	7	6	.	.	.	1	.	.	.	.	.	.	.	.	.	.	.	.	.	.	.	.	.	.	.	.	.	.
511	1	692	0.9	49	5	3	1	303	7	6	.	.	.	1	.	.	.	.	.	.	.	.	.	.	.	.	.	.	.	.	.	1	1	.	.	.
512	1	677	1.0	49	5	4	1	103	1	4	.	.	.	.	.	.	.	.	.	.	.	1	.	.	.	.	.	.	.	.	.	1	.	.	.	.
513	1	683	1.0	49	5	4	1	203	1	4	.	.	.	.	.	.	.	.	.	.	.	.	.	.	.	.	.	.	.	.	.	.	.	.	.	.

OBS	BIXA	PHYSOLIS	OXALIS	AMBROSIA	NICOTIAN	SALVIA	MINT	GALIUM	OPUNTIA	CYPER	COMPOSIT	UMBELLIF	FABACEAE	UNKWNSEE	WDCT	WDWT	GRSSTKS	EUPHORB	PHORLUP	MIMOSA	VACCINIU	BERBERIS	TRITICUM	MOLLUGO	PENDFRAG	CACTUS	CALENDR	CRUCIFER	SOLANUM	LGLEGUME	TLEGUME	KG	M3VOL	PHASE	STAT	LEV
495	.	.	.	.	.	.	.	.	.	.	.	1	.	.	7	.	.	.	.	.	.	.	.	.	.	.	.	.	.	.	.	4.8	0.0048	HI	.	4
496	.	.	.	.	.	1	.	.	.	.	.	.	.	1	8	.	.	.	.	.	.	.	.	.	.	.	.	.	.	.	.	5.4	0.0054	HI	.	5
497	.	.	.	.	.	.	.	.	.	.	1	1	.	2	11	.	.	.	.	.	.	.	.	.	.	.	.	.	.	.	1	4.8	0.0048	HI	.	5
498	.	.	.	.	.	.	.	.	.	.	.	.	.	.	15	.	.	.	.	.	.	.	.	.	.	.	.	.	.	.	1	4.8	0.0048	HI	.	5
499	.	.	.	.	.	.	.	.	.	.	.	.	.	.	.	.	.	.	.	.	.	.	.	.	.	.	.	.	.	.	1	4.2	0.0042	HI	.	6
500	.	.	.	.	.	.	.	.	.	.	.	.	.	6	15	.	.	.	5	.	.	.	.	.	.	.	.	.	.	5	1	4.8	0.0048	HI	.	6
501	.	.	.	.	.	.	.	.	.	.	.	.	.	.	20	.	.	.	.	.	.	.	.	.	.	.	.	.	.	.	2	4.2	0.0042	HI	.	6
502	.	.	.	.	.	.	.	.	.	.	.	.	.	.	18	.	.	.	.	.	.	.	.	.	.	.	.	.	.	.	1	4.8	0.0048	HI	.	7
503	.	.	.	4	.	.	.	.	.	.	.	.	.	.	20	.	.	.	.	.	.	.	.	.	.	.	.	.	.	.	.	4.8	0.0048	HI	.	7
504	.	.	.	.	.	.	.	.	.	.	.	.	.	1	5	.	.	.	.	.	.	.	.	.	.	.	.	.	.	.	.	4.8	0.0048	HI	.	7
505	.	.	.	.	.	.	.	.	.	.	.	.	.	.	6	.	.	.	.	.	.	.	.	.	.	.	.	.	.	.	.	4.8	0.0048	HI	.	7
506	.	.	.	.	.	.	.	.	.	.	.	.	.	.	.	.	.	.	.	.	.	.	.	.	.	.	.	.	.	.	.	6.0	0.0060	HIII	.	2
507	.	.	.	.	.	.	.	.	.	.	.	.	.	.	4	.	.	.	.	.	.	.	.	.	.	.	.	.	.	.	.	5.4	0.0054	HIII	.	2
508	.	.	.	.	.	.	.	.	.	.	.	.	.	.	4	.	.	.	.	.	.	.	.	.	.	.	.	.	.	.	.	4.8	0.0048	HIII	.	2
509	.	.	.	.	.	.	.	.	.	.	.	.	.	.	1	.	.	.	.	.	.	.	.	.	.	.	.	.	.	.	.	6.0	0.0060	HIII	.	3
510	.	.	1	.	.	.	.	.	.	.	.	.	.	.	.	.	.	.	.	.	.	.	.	.	.	.	.	.	.	.	.	5.4	0.0054	HIII	.	3
511	.	.	.	.	.	.	.	.	.	.	.	.	.	2	3	.	.	.	.	.	.	.	.	.	.	.	.	.	.	.	.	5.4	0.0054	HIII	.	3
512	.	.	.	.	.	.	.	.	.	.	.	.	.	.	4	.	.	.	.	.	.	.	.	.	.	.	.	.	.	.	.	6.0	0.0060	HI	.	4
513	.	.	.	.	.	.	.	.	.	.	.	.	.	.	.	.	.	.	.	.	.	.	.	.	.	.	.	.	.	.	.	6.0	0.0060	HI	.	4

OBS	FLTMCO	FLOT	BAGSIZE	SITE	FEATURE	LEVEL	LOCUS	BAGNO	CONTEXT	DATE	MZKERNAL	CUPCOBS	EMBRYOS	CHENOPOD	LUPINE	PHSPP	TUBERS	PAPAS	OCA	ULLUCO	MASHUA	LUMPS	AMARANTH	SCIRPUS	SMLEGUME	LEPIDIUM	LUCUMA	RARE	PORTULAC	VERBENA	PLANTAGO	SGRASS	LGRASS	MGRASS	MALVAST	RUBUS	BIXA	PHYSOLIS
514	1	669	0.9	49	5	4	1	303	1	4	.	.	.	.	.	.	1	.	.	.	.	.	.	.	.	.	.	.	.	.	.	1	.	.	.	.	.	.
515	1	682	0.7	49	5	5	1	101	4	3	.	.	.	.	.	.	.	.	.	.	.	.	.	.	.	.	.	.	.	.	.	1	.	.	.	.	.	.
516	1	685	0.9	49	5	5	2	105	3	4	.	.	.	1	.	.	1	.	.	.	.	5	.	1	.	.	.	.	.	.	.	3	.	.	1	.	.	.
517	1	666	0.8	49	5	5	2	205	3	4	1	.	.	1	3	.	.	.	.	.	.	1	.	.	1	.	.	.	.	.	.	3	.	.	1	.	.	.
518	1	675	1.0	49	5	5	2	305	3	4	.	.	.	2	.	.	3	.	.	.	.	14	.	1	.	.	.	.	.	.	.	9	.	.	1	.	.	.
519	1	680	0.8	49	5	5	2	405	3	4	.	.	.	3	.	.	.	.	.	.	.	.	.	1	.	.	.	.	.	.	.	4	.	.	.	.	.	.
520	1	668	0.9	49	5	5	2	505	3	4	.	.	.	1	.	.	.	.	.	.	.	3	.	.	.	.	.	.	.	.	.	1	1	.	.	.	.	.
521	1	691	0.6	49	5	6	3	101	3	4	.	.	.	.	.	.	.	.	.	.	.	1	.	.	.	.	.	.	.	.	.	.	.	.	1	.	.	.
522	1	748	0.8	71	0	0	0	.	.	.	.	.	.	5	.	.	.	.	.	.	.	4	.	1	1	.	.	.	.	.	.	4	3	.	.	.	.	.
523	1	369	1.0	71	1	2	1	103	9	3	.	.	.	3	.	.	.	.	.	.	.	.	.	.	.	.	.	.	.	.	.	2	.	.	.	.	.	.
524	1	334	1.0	71	1	2	1	203	9	3	.	.	.	.	.	.	.	.	.	.	.	.	.	.	.	.	.	.	.	.	.	.	.	.	.	.	.	.
525	1	338	1.0	71	1	2	1	303	9	3	.	.	.	.	.	.	.	.	.	.	.	.	.	.	.	.	.	.	.	.	.	.	.	.	.	.	.	.
526	1	358	1.0	71	1	3	1	103	8	3	.	.	.	1	.	.	.	.	.	.	.	.	.	.	.	.	.	.	.	.	.	.	.	.	.	.	.	.
527	1	388	0.9	71	1	3	1	203	8	3	.	.	.	2	.	.	.	.	.	.	.	.	.	.	1	.	.	.	.	.	.	1	.	.	.	.	.	.
528	1	333	1.0	71	1	3	1	303	8	3	.	.	.	3	.	.	.	.	.	.	.	.	.	.	.	.	.	.	.	.	.	.	.	.	.	.	.	.
529	1	376	0.8	71	2	2	1	103	9	3	.	.	.	.	.	.	.	.	.	.	.	.	.	.	.	.	.	.	.	.	.	.	.	.	.	.	.	.
530	1	341	1.0	71	2	2	1	203	9	3	.	.	.	5	.	.	.	.	.	.	.	.	.	.	.	.	.	.	.	.	.	2	.	.	.	.	.	.
531	1	374	1.0	71	2	2	1	303	9	3	.	.	.	3	.	.	.	.	.	.	.	.	.	.	.	.	.	1	.	.	.	1	2	.	.	.	.	.
532	1	377	0.8	71	2	3	1	103	8	3	.	.	.	5	.	.	.	.	.	.	.	0	1	.	1	.	.	.	.	.	.	.	.	.	.	.	.	.

OBS	OXALIS	AMBROSIA	NICOTIAN	SALVIA	MINT	GALIUM	OPUNTIA	CYPER	COMPOSIT	UMBELLIF	FABACEAE	UNKWNSEE	WDCT	WDWT	GRSSTKS	EUPHORB	PHORLUP	MIMOSA	VACCINIU	BERBERIS	TRITICUM	MOLLUGO	PENDFRAG	CACTUS	CALEND	CRUCIFER	SOLANUM	LGLEGUME	TLEGUME	KG	M3VOL	PHASE	STAT	LEV
514	.	.	.	.	.	.	.	.	.	.	.	.	1	.	.	.	.	.	.	.	.	.	.	.	.	.	.	.	.	5.4	0.0054	HI	.	4
515	.	.	.	.	.	.	.	.	.	.	.	.	2	.	.	.	.	.	.	.	.	.	.	.	.	.	.	.	.	4.2	0.0042	HO	.	5
516	.	.	.	.	.	.	.	.	.	.	.	.	.	.	.	.	.	.	.	.	.	.	.	.	.	.	.	.	.	5.4	0.0054	HI	.	5
517	.	.	.	.	.	.	.	.	.	.	.	.	16	.	.	.	.	.	.	.	.	.	.	.	.	.	.	.	1	4.8	0.0048	HI	.	5
518	.	.	.	.	.	.	.	.	.	.	.	.	23	.	.	.	8	.	.	.	.	.	.	.	.	.	.	8	.	6.0	0.0060	HI	.	5
519	.	.	.	.	.	.	.	.	.	.	.	2	1	.	.	.	.	.	.	.	.	.	.	.	.	.	.	.	.	4.8	0.0048	HI	.	5
520	.	.	.	.	.	.	.	.	.	.	.	3	4	.	.	.	.	.	.	.	.	.	.	.	.	.	.	.	.	5.4	0.0054	HI	.	5
521	.	1	.	.	.	.	.	.	.	.	.	.	4	.	.	.	.	.	.	.	.	.	.	.	.	.	.	.	.	3.6	0.0036	HI	.	6
522	.	.	.	.	.	.	.	.	.	.	.	.	6	.	.	.	.	.	.	.	1	.	.	.	.	.	.	.	1	4.8	0.0048		.	0
523	.	.	.	.	.	.	.	.	.	.	.	.	5	.	.	.	.	.	.	.	.	.	.	.	.	.	.	.	.	6.0	0.0060	HO	.	2
524	.	.	.	.	.	.	.	.	.	.	.	.	3	.	.	.	.	.	.	.	.	.	.	.	.	.	.	.	.	6.0	0.0060	HO	.	2
525	.	.	.	.	.	.	.	.	.	.	.	.	.	.	.	.	.	.	.	.	.	.	.	.	.	.	.	.	.	6.0	0.0060	HO	.	2
526	.	.	.	.	.	.	.	.	.	.	.	.	1	.	.	.	.	.	.	.	.	.	.	.	.	.	.	.	.	6.0	0.0060	HO	.	3
527	.	.	.	.	.	.	.	.	.	.	.	.	.	.	.	.	.	.	.	.	.	.	.	.	.	.	.	.	1	5.4	0.0054	HO	.	3
528	.	.	.	.	.	.	.	.	.	.	.	.	.	.	.	.	.	.	.	.	.	.	.	.	.	.	.	.	.	6.0	0.0060	HO	.	3
529	.	.	.	.	.	.	.	.	.	.	.	.	1	.	.	.	.	.	.	.	.	.	.	.	.	.	.	.	.	4.8	0.0048	HO	.	2
530	.	.	.	1	.	.	.	.	.	.	.	.	.	.	.	.	.	.	.	.	.	.	.	.	.	.	.	.	.	6.0	0.0060	HO	.	2
531	.	.	.	.	.	.	.	.	.	.	.	.	.	.	.	.	.	.	.	.	1	.	.	.	.	.	.	.	.	6.0	0.0060	HO	.	2
532	.	.	.	.	.	.	.	.	.	.	.	.	0	1	.	.	.	.	.	.	.	.	.	.	.	.	.	.	1	4.8	0.0048	HO	.	3

OBS	FLTMCO	FLOT	BAGSIZE	SITE	FEATURE	LEVEL	LOCUS	BAGNO	CONTEXT	DATE	MZKERNAL	CUPCOBS	EMBRYOS	CHENOPOD	LUPINE	PHSPP	TUBERS	PAPAS	OCA	ULLUCO	MASHUA	LUMPS	AMARANTH	SCIRPUS	SMLEGUME	LEPIDIUM	LUCUMA	RARE	PORTULAC	VERBENA	PLANTAGO	SGRASS	LGRASS	MGRASS	MALVAST	RUBUS
533	1	378	1.0	71	2	3	1	203	8	3	.	.	.	7	.	.	.	.	.	.	.	.	.	.	.	.	.	.	.	.	.	2	1	.	.	.
534	1	373	0.9	71	2	3	1	303	8	3	.	.	.	2	.	.	.	.	.	.	.	0	1	.	.	.	.	.	.	.	.	4	.	.	.	.
535	1	372	0.8	71	2	4	1	103	8	3	.	.	.	1	.	.	.	.	.	.	.	.	.	.	.	.	.	.	.	.	.	1	.	.	.	.
536	1	370	0.8	71	2	4	1	203	8	3	.	.	.	4	.	.	.	.	.	.	.	.	.	.	.	.	.	.	.	.	.	.	.	.	.	.
537	1	371	0.8	71	2	4	1	303	8	3	.	1	.	.	.	.	.	.	.	.	.	.	.	.	.	.	.	.	.	1	.	.	.	.	.	.
538	1	309	0.9	71	3	2	1	103	8	3	.	.	.	.	.	.	.	.	.	.	.	.	.	.	.	.	.	.	.	.	.	.	.	.	.	.
539	1	411	1.1	71	3	2	1	203	8	3	.	.	.	.	.	.	.	.	.	.	.	.	.	.	.	.	.	.	.	.	.	.	.	.	.	.
540	1	307	1.1	71	3	2	1	303	8	3	.	.	.	.	.	.	.	.	.	.	.	.	.	.	.	.	.	.	.	.	.	1	.	.	.	.
541	1	310	0.9	71	3	3	1	102	1	3	.	.	.	.	.	.	.	.	.	.	.	3	.	.	.	.	.	.	.	.	.	.	.	.	.	.
542	1	387	1.1	71	3	3	1	202	1	3	.	.	.	3	.	.	2	.	.	.	.	1	.	.	1	.	.	.	.	.	.	.	.	.	.	.
543	1	313	1.0	71	3	4	1	102	3	3	.	.	.	2	.	.	.	.	.	.	.	.	.	1	.	.	.	.	.	.	.	.	.	.	2	.
544	1	416	1.1	71	3	4	1	202	3	3	.	.	.	1	.	.	.	.	.	.	.	.	.	.	1	.	.	.	.	.	.	5	.	.	.	.
545	1	315	0.8	71	4	2	1	106	2	3	.	.	.	6	.	.	.	.	.	.	.	.	.	.	.	.	.	.	.	.	.	1	.	.	.	.
546	1	331	0.8	71	4	2	1	206	2	3	.	.	.	1	.	.	.	.	.	.	.	.	.	.	.	.	.	.	.	.	.	1	.	.	.	.
547	1	347	0.7	71	4	2	1	306	2	3	.	.	.	.	.	.	.	.	.	.	.	.	.	.	.	.	.	.	.	.	.	.	.	.	.	.
548	1	326	1.0	71	4	2	1	406	2	3	.	.	.	3	.	.	.	.	.	.	.	3	.	2	.	.	.	.	.	.	.	.	.	.	.	.
549	1	349	0.8	71	4	2	1	506	2	3	.	.	.	1	.	.	16	.	.	.	.	.	.	1	.	.	.	.	.	.	.	1	.	.	.	.
550	1	357	0.8	71	4	2	1	606	2	3	.	.	.	1	.	.	.	.	.	.	.	.	.	.	.	.	.	.	.	.	.	2	.	.	.	.
551	1	306	0.8	71	4	3	1	106	1	3	.	.	.	2	.	.	.	.	.	.	.	.	.	.	.	.	.	.	.	.	.	.	.	.	.	.

OBS	BIXA	PHYSOLIS	OXALIS	AMBROSIA	NICOTIAN	SALVIA	MINT	GALIUM	OPUNTIA	CYPER	COMPOSIT	UMBELLIF	FABACEAE	UNKWNSEE	WDCT	WDWT	GRSSTKS	EUPHORB	PHORLUP	MIMOSA	VACCINIU	BERBERIS	TRITICUM	MOLLUGO	PENDFRAG	CACTUS	CALEND	CRUCIFER	SOLANUM	LGLEGUME	TLEGUME	KG	M3VOL	PHASE	STAT	LEV
533	.	.	.	.	.	.	.	.	.	.	.	.	.	.	.	.	.	.	.	.	.	.	.	.	.	.	.	.	.	.	.	6.0	0.0060	HO	.	3
534	.	.	.	.	.	.	.	.	.	.	.	.	.	.	.	.	.	.	.	.	.	.	.	.	.	.	.	.	.	.	.	5.4	0.0054	HO	.	3
535	.	.	.	.	.	.	.	.	.	.	.	.	.	.	0	1	.	.	.	.	.	.	.	.	.	.	.	.	.	.	.	4.8	0.0048	HO	.	4
536	.	.	.	.	.	.	.	.	.	.	.	.	.	.	.	.	.	.	.	.	.	.	.	.	.	.	.	.	.	.	.	4.8	0.0048	HO	.	4
537	.	.	.	.	.	.	.	.	.	.	.	.	.	.	1	.	.	.	.	.	.	.	.	.	.	.	.	.	.	.	.	4.8	0.0048	HO	.	4
538	.	.	.	.	.	.	.	.	.	.	.	.	.	.	1	.	.	.	.	.	.	.	.	.	.	.	.	.	.	.	.	5.4	0.0054	HO	.	2
539	.	.	.	.	.	.	.	.	.	.	.	.	.	.	.	.	.	.	.	.	.	.	.	.	.	.	.	.	.	.	.	6.6	0.0066	HO	.	2
540	.	.	.	.	.	.	.	.	.	.	.	.	.	1	.	.	.	.	.	.	.	.	.	.	.	.	.	.	.	.	.	6.6	0.0066	HO	.	2
541	.	.	.	.	.	.	.	.	.	.	.	.	.	.	22	.	.	.	.	.	.	.	.	.	.	.	.	.	.	.	.	5.4	0.0054	HO	.	3
542	.	.	.	.	.	.	.	.	.	.	.	.	.	.	49	.	.	.	.	.	.	.	.	.	.	.	.	.	.	.	1	6.6	0.0066	HO	.	3
543	.	.	.	.	.	.	.	.	.	.	.	.	.	.	39	.	.	.	.	.	.	.	.	.	.	.	.	.	.	.	.	6.0	0.0060	HO	.	4
544	.	.	.	1	.	.	.	.	.	.	.	.	.	.	16	.	.	.	.	.	.	.	.	.	.	.	.	.	.	.	1	6.6	0.0066	HO	.	4
545	.	.	.	.	.	.	.	.	.	.	.	.	.	.	.	.	.	.	.	.	.	.	.	.	.	.	.	.	.	.	.	4.8	0.0048	HO	.	2
546	.	.	.	.	.	.	.	.	.	.	.	.	.	.	1	.	.	.	.	.	.	.	.	.	.	.	.	.	.	.	.	4.8	0.0048	HO	.	2
547	.	.	.	.	.	.	.	.	.	.	.	.	.	.	1	.	.	.	.	.	.	.	.	.	.	.	.	.	.	.	.	4.2	0.0042	HO	.	2
548	.	.	.	.	.	.	.	.	.	.	.	.	.	1	2	.	.	.	.	.	.	.	.	.	.	.	.	.	.	.	.	6.0	0.0060	HO	.	2
549	.	.	.	.	.	.	.	.	.	.	.	.	.	.	.	.	.	.	.	.	.	.	.	.	.	.	.	.	.	.	.	4.8	0.0048	HO	.	2
550	.	.	.	.	.	.	.	.	.	.	.	.	.	.	1	.	.	.	.	.	.	.	.	.	.	.	.	.	.	.	.	4.8	0.0048	HO	.	2
551	.	.	.	.	.	.	.	.	.	.	.	.	.	.	2	.	.	.	.	.	.	.	.	.	.	.	.	.	.	.	.	4.8	0.0048	HO	.	3

OBS	FLTMCO	FLOT	BAGSIZE	SITE	FEATURE	LEVEL	LOCUS	BAGNO	CONTEXT	DATE	MZKERNAL	CUPCOBS	EMBRYOS	CHENOPOD	LUPINE	PHSPP	TUBERS	PAPAS	OCA	ULLUCO	MASHUA	LUMPS	AMARANTH	SCIRPUS	SMLEGUME	LEPIDIUM	LUCUMA	RARE	PORTULAC	VERBENA	PLANTAGO	SGRASS	LGRASS	MGRASS	MALVAST
552	1	311	0.9	71	4	3	1	206	2	3	.	.	.	2	.	.	.	.	.	.	.	.	.	.	.	.	.	.	.	1	.	1	.	.	1
553	1	321	1.0	71	4	3	1	306	1	3	.	.	.	3	.	.	.	.	.	.	.	.	.	.	.	.	.	.	.	.	.	1	.	.	.
554	1	343	0.8	71	4	3	1	406	2	3	.	.	.	4	.	.	17	.	.	.	.	.	.	5	1	.	.	.	.	.	.	2	.	.	.
555	1	324	1.0	71	4	3	1	506	2	3	.	.	.	2	.	.	.	.	.	.	.	.	.	.	.	.	.	.	.	.	.	2	.	.	.
556	1	323	0.8	71	4	3	1	606	2	3	.	.	.	5	.	.	3	.	.	.	.	.	.	3	1	.	.	.	.	2	.	.	.	.	.
557	1	346	0.7	71	4	4	1	103	1	3	.	.	.	6	.	.	.	.	.	.	.	.	.	.	3	.	.	.	.	.	.	2	.	.	.
558	1	404	0.8	71	4	4	1	203	1	3	.	.	.	1	.	.	.	.	.	.	.	1	.	3	.	.	.	.	.	1	.	1	.	.	.
559	1	417	1.0	71	4	4	1	303	1	3	.	.	.	4	.	.	.	.	.	.	.	.	.	.	.	.	.	.	.	.	.	3	.	.	.
560	1	384	0.8	71	4	5	3	103	3	3	.	.	.	8	.	.	.	.	.	.	.	.	.	.	.	.	.	.	.	.	.	2	.	.	.
561	1	412	0.7	71	4	5	3	203	3	3	.	.	.	3	.	.	.	.	.	.	.	.	.	2	.	.	.	.	.	.	.	.	.	.	.
562	1	330	0.7	71	4	5	3	303	3	3	.	.	.	2	.	.	.	.	.	.	.	0	1	.	.	.	.	.	.	.	.	5	.	.	.
563	1	328	1.0	71	4	5	4	103	3	3	.	1	.	11	.	.	.	.	.	.	.	4	.	.	1	.	.	.	.	.	.	23	.	.	3
564	1	354	1.0	71	4	5	4	203	3	3	.	.	.	18	.	.	.	.	.	.	.	2	.	3	6	.	.	.	.	2	3	70	.	.	29
565	1	304	0.8	71	4	5	4	303	3	3	.	.	.	2	.	.	1	.	.	.	.	.	2	.	.	.	.	.	.	2	.	9	.	.	8
566	1	296	0.6	71	4	5	5	103	3	3	.	.	.	1	.	.	.	.	.	.	.	.	.	.	.	.	.	.	1	.	.	3	.	.	.
567	1	385	0.5	71	4	5	5	203	3	3	.	.	.	1	.	.	.	.	.	.	.	.	.	.	.	.	.	.	.	.	.	.	1	.	1
568	1	351	0.5	71	4	5	5	303	3	3	.	.	.	1	.	.	.	.	.	.	.	.	.	.	.	.	.	.	.	.	.	1	.	.	.
569	1	352	1.0	71	4	6	4	103	6	3	.	.	.	3	.	.	16	.	.	.	.	.	.	.	5	.	.	.	.	.	.	7	1	.	3
570	1	335	0.8	71	4	6	4	203	6	3	.	.	.	8	.	.	.	.	.	.	.	2	.	.	1	.	.	.	.	.	.	7	3	.	1

OBS	RUBUS	BIXA	PHYSOLIS	OXALIS	AMBROSIA	NICOTIAN	SALVIA	MINT	GALIUM	OPUNTIA	CYPER	COMPOSIT	UMBELLIF	FABACEAE	UNKWNSEE	WDCT	WDWT	GRSSTKS	EUPHORB	PHORLUP	MIMOSA	VACCINIU	BERBERIS	TRITICUM	MOLLUGO	PENDFRAG	CACTUS	CALEND	CRUCIFER	SOLANUM	LGLEGUME	TLEGUME	KG	M3VOL	PHASE	STAT	LEV
552	.	.	.	.	.	.	.	.	.	.	.	.	.	.	.	.	.	.	.	.	.	.	.	.	.	.	.	.	.	.	.	.	5.4	0.0054	HO	.	3
553	.	.	.	.	.	.	.	.	.	.	.	.	.	.	.	1	.	.	.	.	.	.	.	.	.	.	.	.	.	.	.	.	6.0	0.0060	HO	.	3
554	.	.	.	.	.	.	1	.	.	.	.	.	.	.	2	1	.	.	.	.	.	.	.	.	.	.	.	.	.	.	.	1	4.8	0.0048	HO	.	3
555	.	.	.	.	.	.	.	.	.	.	.	.	.	.	.	.	.	.	.	.	.	.	.	.	.	.	.	.	.	.	.	.	6.0	0.0060	HO	.	3
556	.	.	.	.	.	.	.	.	1	.	.	.	.	.	2	.	.	.	.	.	.	.	.	.	.	.	.	.	.	.	.	1	4.8	0.0048	HO	.	3
557	.	.	.	.	.	.	.	.	.	.	.	.	.	.	.	.	.	.	.	.	.	.	.	.	.	.	.	.	.	.	.	3	4.2	0.0042	HO	.	4
558	.	.	.	.	.	.	.	.	.	.	.	.	.	.	.	.	.	.	.	.	.	.	.	.	.	.	.	.	.	.	.	.	4.8	0.0048	HO	.	4
559	.	.	.	.	.	.	.	.	.	.	.	.	.	.	.	.	.	.	.	.	.	.	.	.	.	.	.	.	.	.	.	.	6.0	0.0060	HO	.	4
560	.	.	.	.	.	.	.	.	.	.	.	.	.	.	.	1	.	.	.	.	.	.	.	.	.	.	.	.	.	.	.	.	4.8	0.0048	HO	.	5
561	.	.	.	.	.	.	.	.	.	.	.	.	.	.	.	1	.	.	.	.	.	.	.	.	.	.	.	.	.	.	.	.	4.2	0.0042	HO	.	5
562	.	.	.	.	.	.	.	.	.	.	.	.	.	.	.	.	.	.	.	.	.	.	.	.	.	.	.	.	.	.	.	.	4.2	0.0042	HO	.	5
563	.	.	.	.	.	.	.	.	.	.	.	.	.	.	2	.	.	.	.	.	.	.	.	.	.	.	.	.	.	.	.	1	6.0	0.0060	HO	.	5
564	.	.	.	.	.	.	.	.	.	.	.	8	.	.	5	1	.	.	.	.	.	.	.	.	.	.	.	.	.	.	.	6	6.0	0.0060	HO	.	5
565	.	.	.	.	.	.	.	.	1	.	.	.	.	2	3	2	.	.	.	.	.	.	.	.	.	.	.	.	.	.	.	.	4.8	0.0048	HO	.	5
566	.	.	.	.	.	.	.	.	.	.	.	.	.	.	1	2	.	.	.	.	.	.	.	.	.	.	.	.	.	.	.	.	3.6	0.0036	HO	.	5
567	.	.	.	.	.	.	.	.	.	.	.	1	.	.	.	6	.	.	.	.	.	.	.	.	.	.	.	.	.	.	.	.	3.0	0.0030	HO	.	5
568	.	.	.	.	.	.	.	.	.	.	.	.	.	.	.	5	.	.	.	.	.	.	.	.	.	.	.	.	.	.	.	.	3.0	0.0030	HO	.	5
569	.	.	.	.	.	.	.	.	.	.	.	.	.	.	2	3	.	.	.	.	.	.	.	.	.	.	.	.	.	.	.	5	6.0	0.0060	HO	.	6
570	.	.	.	.	.	.	.	.	.	.	.	1	.	.	9	7	.	.	.	.	.	.	.	.	.	.	.	.	.	.	.	1	4.8	0.0048	HO	.	6

OBS	FLTMCO	FLOT	BAGSIZE	SITE	FEATURE	LEVEL	LOCUS	BAGNO	CONTEXT	DATE	MZKERNAL	CUPCOBS	EMBRYOS	CHENOPOD	LUPINE	PHSPP	TUBERS	PAPAS	OCA	ULLUCO	MASHUA	LUMPS	AMARANTH	SCIRPUS	SMLEGUME	LEPIDIUM	LUCUMA	RARE	PORTULAC	VERBENA	PLANTAGO	SGRASS	LGRASS	MGRASS	MALVAST	RUBUS
571	1	356	0.8	71	4	6	4	303	6	3	.	.	.	8	.	.	10	.	.	.	.	1	.	.	3	.	.	.	.	.	.	16	3	.	1	.
572	1	353	0.8	71	4	6	6	103	3	3	.	.	.	.	.	.	.	.	.	.	.	.	1	.	1	.	.	.	.	.	.	1	.	.	.	.
573	1	381	1.0	71	4	6	6	203	3	3	1	.	.	12	.	.	3	.	.	.	.	.	.	1	.	.	.	.	.	.	.	5	.	.	2	.
574	1	350	0.8	71	4	6	6	303	3	3	.	.	.	10	.	.	.	.	.	.	.	.	.	2	3	.	.	.	.	1	.	8	.	.	.	.
575	1	308	1.0	71	5	1	1	203	9	3	.	.	.	.	.	.	.	.	.	.	.	0	2	.	.	.	.	.	.	.	.	.	.	.	.	.
576	1	318	1.0	71	5	2	1	103	8	3	.	.	.	.	.	.	.	.	.	.	.	.	.	.	.	.	.	.	.	.	.	.	.	.	.	.
577	1	312	0.9	71	5	2	1	203	8	3	.	.	.	.	.	.	.	.	.	.	.	.	.	1	.	.	.	.	.	.	.	.	.	.	.	.
578	1	344	1.1	71	5	2	1	303	8	3	.	.	.	.	.	.	.	.	.	.	.	.	.	.	.	.	.	.	.	.	.	.	.	.	.	.
579	1	297	1.0	71	5	2	2	101	3	3	.	.	.	.	.	.	.	.	.	.	.	.	.	.	.	.	.	.	.	.	.	3	1	.	.	.
580	1	320	0.8	71	5	3	1	103	8	3	.	.	.	.	.	.	.	.	.	.	.	.	.	.	.	.	.	.	.	.	.	.	.	.	.	.
581	1	319	1.0	71	5	3	1	203	8	3	.	.	.	1	.	.	.	.	.	.	.	3	.	.	.	.	.	.	.	.	.	.	.	.	.	.
582	1	301	1.0	71	5	3	1	303	8	3	.	.	.	.	.	.	.	.	.	.	.	.	.	.	.	.	.	.	.	.	.	.	.	.	.	.
583	1	303	1.0	71	5	3	2	103	8	3	.	.	.	3	.	.	.	.	.	.	.	4	.	.	.	.	.	.	.	.	.	2	.	.	.	.
584	1	405	0.8	71	5	3	2	203	8	3	.	.	.	3	.	.	.	.	.	.	.	.	.	.	.	.	.	.	.	.	.	1	.	1	.	.
585	1	314	0.7	71	5	3	2	303	8	3	.	.	.	5	.	.	.	.	.	.	.	.	.	.	.	.	.	.	.	.	.	.	.	.	.	.
586	1	317	1.1	71	5	4	1	102	5	3	.	.	.	.	.	.	.	.	.	.	.	1	.	.	.	.	.	.	.	.	.	1	.	.	.	.
587	1	355	1.0	71	5	4	1	202	5	3	.	.	.	.	.	.	.	.	.	.	.	.	.	.	.	.	.	.	.	.	.	.	.	.	.	.
588	1	316	1.0	71	5	4	2	103	3	3	.	.	.	744	9	.	1	.	.	.	.	3	.	1	.	.	.	.	.	.	.	4	65	.	.	.
589	1	302	1.0	71	5	4	2	203	3	3	.	.	.	24	.	.	.	.	.	.	.	.	.	1	.	.	.	.	.	.	.	2	2	.	1	.

OBS	BIXA	PHYSOLIS	OXALIS	AMBROSIA	NICOTIAN	SALVIA	MINT	GALIUM	OPUNTIA	CYPER	COMPOSIT	UMBELLIF	FABACEAE	UNKWNSEE	WDCT	WDWT	GRSSTKS	EUPHORB	PHORLUP	MIMOSA	VACCINIU	BERBERIS	TRITICUM	MOLLUGO	PENDFRAG	CACTUS	CALEND	CRUCIFER	SOLANUM	LGLEGUME	TLEGUME	KG	M3VOL	PHASE	STAT	LEV
571	.	.	.	.	.	.	.	.	.	.	2	.	.	.	1	.	.	.	.	.	.	.	.	.	.	.	.	.	.	.	3	4.8	0.0048	HO	.	6
572	.	.	.	.	.	.	.	.	.	.	.	.	.	1	3	.	.	.	.	.	.	.	.	.	.	.	.	.	.	.	1	4.8	0.0048	HO	.	6
573	.	.	.	.	.	1	.	.	.	.	1	.	.	.	3	.	.	.	.	.	.	.	.	.	.	.	.	.	.	.	.	6.0	0.0060	HO	.	6
574	.	.	.	.	.	.	.	.	.	.	.	.	.	.	.	.	.	.	.	.	.	.	.	.	.	.	.	.	.	.	3	4.8	0.0048	HO	.	6
575	.	.	.	.	.	.	.	.	.	.	.	.	.	.	.	.	.	.	.	.	.	.	.	.	.	.	.	.	.	.	.	6.0	0.0060	HO	.	1
576	.	.	.	.	.	.	.	.	.	.	.	.	.	.	.	.	.	.	.	.	.	.	.	.	.	.	.	.	.	.	.	6.0	0.0060	HO	.	2
577	.	.	1	.	.	.	.	.	.	.	.	.	.	.	.	.	.	.	.	.	.	.	.	.	.	.	.	.	.	.	.	5.4	0.0054	HO	.	2
578	.	.	.	.	.	.	.	.	.	.	.	.	.	.	10	.	.	.	.	.	.	.	.	.	.	.	.	.	.	.	.	6.6	0.0066	HO	.	2
579	.	.	.	.	.	.	.	.	.	.	.	.	.	.	10	.	.	.	.	.	.	.	.	.	.	.	.	.	.	.	.	6.0	0.0060	HO	.	2
580	.	.	.	.	.	.	.	.	.	.	.	.	.	.	.	.	.	.	.	.	.	.	.	.	.	.	.	.	.	.	.	4.8	0.0048	HO	.	3
581	.	.	.	.	.	.	.	.	.	.	.	.	.	.	.	.	.	.	.	.	.	.	.	.	.	.	.	.	.	.	.	6.0	0.0060	HO	.	3
582	.	.	2	.	.	.	.	.	.	.	.	.	.	.	2	.	.	.	.	.	.	.	.	.	.	.	.	.	.	.	.	6.0	0.0060	HO	.	3
583	.	.	.	.	.	.	.	.	.	.	.	.	.	.	10	.	.	.	1	.	.	.	.	.	.	.	.	.	.	1	.	6.0	0.0060	HO	.	3
584	.	.	1	.	.	.	.	.	.	.	.	.	.	.	4	.	.	.	.	.	.	.	.	.	.	.	.	.	.	.	.	4.8	0.0048	HO	.	3
585	.	.	.	.	.	.	.	.	.	.	.	.	.	.	6	.	.	.	.	.	.	.	.	.	.	.	.	.	.	.	.	4.2	0.0042	HO	.	3
586	.	.	.	.	.	.	.	.	.	.	.	.	.	.	.	.	.	.	.	.	.	.	.	.	.	.	.	.	.	.	.	6.6	0.0066	HO	.	4
587	.	.	.	.	.	.	.	.	.	.	.	.	.	.	.	.	.	.	.	.	.	.	.	.	.	.	.	.	.	.	.	6.0	0.0060	HO	.	4
588	.	.	.	.	.	.	.	.	.	.	.	.	.	.	16	.	.	.	.	.	.	.	.	.	.	.	.	.	.	.	.	6.0	0.0060	HO	.	4
589	.	.	.	.	.	.	.	.	.	.	.	.	.	.	16	.	.	.	.	.	.	.	.	.	.	.	.	.	.	.	.	6.0	0.0060	HO	.	4

OBS	FLTMCO	FLOT	BAGSIZE	SITE	FEATURE	LEVEL	LOCUS	BAGNO	CONTEXT	DATE	MZKERNAL	CUPCOBS	EMBRYOS	CHENOPOD	LUPINE	PHSPP	TUBERS	PAPAS	OCA	ULLUCO	MASHUA	LUMPS	AMARANTH	SCIRPUS	SMLEGUME	LEPIDIUM	LUCUMA	RARE	PORTULAC	VERBENA	PLANTAGO	SGRASS	LGRASS	MGRASS	MALVAST	RUBUS	BIXA
590	1	300	1.0	71	5	4	2	303	3	3	1	.	.	9	.	.	.	.	.	.	.	3	1	1	.	.	.	.	.	.	.	.	.	.	.	.	.
591	1	305	1.0	71	5	5	2	103	3	3	.	.	.	748	.	.	.	.	.	.	.	2	.	2	.	.	.	.	.	.	.	4	27	.	.	.	.
592	1	336	0.9	71	5	5	2	203	3	3	.	.	.	95	.	.	.	.	.	.	.	.	.	1	1	.	.	.	.	.	.	11	13	.	.	.	.
593	1	295	0.8	71	5	5	2	303	3	3	.	.	.	113	2	.	.	.	.	.	.	2	.	1	.	.	.	.	.	.	.	.	20	.	.	.	.
594	1	299	0.6	71	5	6	2	103	3	3	.	.	.	10	.	.	.	.	.	.	.	.	.	.	.	.	.	.	.	.	.	2	1	.	.	.	.
595	1	612	0.6	71	5	6	2	203	3	3	.	.	.	10	.	.	.	.	.	.	.	.	.	.	.	.	.	.	.	.	.	2	.	.	.	.	.
596	1	345	0.5	71	5	6	2	303	3	3	.	.	.	6	.	.	.	.	.	.	.	.	.	.	.	.	.	.	.	.	.	2	.	.	.	.	.
597	1	737	1.0	71	6	2	1	103	8	3	.	.	.	.	.	.	4	.	.	.	.	.	.	.	.	.	.	.	.	.	.	.	.	.	.	.	.
598	1	743	0.9	71	6	2	1	203	8	3	.	.	.	.	.	.	.	.	.	.	.	1	.	.	.	.	.	.	.	1	.	.	.	.	.	.	.
599	1	740	0.8	71	6	2	1	303	8	3	.	.	.	.	.	.	.	.	.	.	.	.	.	.	.	.	.	.	.	.	.	.	.	.	.	.	.
600	1	739	0.8	71	6	3	1	103	6	3	.	.	.	1	.	.	.	.	.	.	.	1	.	.	.	.	.	.	.	.	.	.	1	.	.	.	.
601	1	741	0.8	71	6	3	1	203	6	3	.	.	.	.	.	.	.	.	.	.	.	2	.	.	.	.	.	.	.	.	.	4	.	.	1	.	.
602	1	745	0.9	71	6	3	1	303	6	3	.	.	.	.	.	.	.	.	.	.	.	.	.	.	.	.	.	.	.	.	.	1	.	.	.	.	.
603	1	746	0.8	71	6	4	1	103	8	3	.	.	.	.	.	.	.	.	.	.	.	.	.	.	.	.	.	.	.	.	.	1	.	.	.	.	.
604	1	783	0.8	71	6	4	1	203	8	3	.	.	.	.	.	.	.	.	.	.	.	.	.	.	.	.	.	.	.	.	.	.	.	.	.	.	.
605	1	787	0.7	71	6	4	1	303	8	3	.	.	.	.	.	.	.	.	.	.	.	.	.	.	.	.	.	.	.	.	.	.	.	.	.	.	.
606	1	784	0.8	71	6	4	2	103	3	3	.	.	.	4	.	.	1	.	.	.	.	.	.	.	.	.	.	.	.	.	.	2	.	.	.	.	.
607	1	788	0.7	71	6	4	2	203	3	3	.	.	.	4	.	.	.	.	.	.	.	6	.	.	.	.	.	.	.	1	.	.	.	.	.	.	.
608	1	754	0.9	71	6	4	2	303	3	3	.	.	.	2	.	.	2	.	.	.	.	2	.	.	.	.	.	.	.	.	.	1	.	.	.	1	.

OBS	PHYSOLIS	OXALIS	AMBROSIA	NICOTIAN	SALVIA	MINT	GALIUM	OPUNTIA	CYPER	COMPOSIT	UMBELLIF	FABACEAE	UNKWNSEE	WDCT	WDWT	GRSSTKS	EUPHORB	PHORLUP	MIMOSA	VACCINIU	BERBERIS	TRITICUM	MOLLUGO	PENDFRAG	CACTUS	CALEND	CRUCIFER	SOLANUM	LGLEGUME	TLEGUME	KG	M3VOL	PHASE	STAT	LEV
590	.	.	.	.	.	.	.	.	.	.	.	.	.	12	.	.	.	.	.	.	.	.	.	.	.	.	.	.	.	.	6.0	0.0060	HO	.	4
591	.	.	.	.	.	.	.	.	.	.	.	.	.	12	.	.	.	.	.	.	.	.	.	.	.	.	.	.	.	.	6.0	0.0060	HO	.	5
592	.	.	.	13	.	.	.	.	.	.	.	.	1	2	.	.	.	.	.	.	.	.	.	.	.	.	.	.	.	1	5.4	0.0054	HO	.	5
593	.	.	.	.	.	.	.	.	.	.	.	.	2	4	.	.	.	.	.	.	.	.	.	.	.	.	.	.	.	.	4.8	0.0048	HO	.	5
594	.	.	.	4	.	.	.	.	.	.	.	.	.	.	.	.	.	.	.	.	.	.	.	.	.	.	.	.	.	.	3.6	0.0036	HO	.	6
595	.	.	.	9	.	.	.	.	.	.	.	.	.	1	.	.	.	.	.	.	.	.	.	.	.	.	.	.	.	.	3.6	0.0036	HO	.	6
596	.	.	.	4	.	.	.	.	.	.	.	.	.	.	.	.	.	.	.	.	.	.	.	.	.	.	.	.	.	.	3.0	0.0030	HO	.	6
597	.	.	.	.	.	.	.	.	.	.	.	.	.	14	.	.	.	.	.	.	.	.	.	.	.	.	.	.	.	.	6.0	0.0060	HO	.	2
598	.	.	.	.	.	.	.	.	.	.	.	.	.	15	.	.	.	.	.	.	.	.	.	.	.	.	.	.	.	.	5.4	0.0054	HO	.	2
599	.	.	.	.	.	.	.	.	.	.	.	.	.	4	.	.	.	.	.	.	.	.	.	.	.	.	.	.	.	.	4.8	0.0048	HO	.	2
600	.	.	.	.	.	.	.	.	.	.	.	.	.	1	.	.	.	.	.	.	.	.	.	.	.	.	.	.	.	.	4.8	0.0048	HO	.	3
601	.	.	.	.	.	.	.	.	.	.	.	.	1	3	.	.	.	.	.	.	.	.	.	.	.	.	.	.	.	.	4.8	0.0048	HO	.	3
602	.	.	.	.	.	.	.	.	.	.	.	.	.	1	.	.	.	.	.	.	.	.	.	.	.	.	.	.	.	.	5.4	0.0054	HO	.	3
603	.	.	.	.	.	.	.	.	.	.	.	.	.	.	.	.	.	.	.	.	.	.	.	.	.	.	.	.	.	.	4.8	0.0048	HO	.	4
604	.	.	.	.	.	.	.	.	.	.	.	.	.	1	.	.	.	.	.	.	.	.	.	.	.	.	.	.	.	.	4.8	0.0048	HO	.	4
605	.	.	.	.	.	.	.	.	.	.	.	.	.	.	.	.	.	.	.	.	.	.	.	.	.	.	.	.	.	.	4.2	0.0042	HO	.	4
606	.	.	.	.	.	.	.	.	.	1	.	.	.	.	.	.	.	.	.	.	.	.	.	.	.	.	.	.	.	.	4.8	0.0048	HO	.	4
607	.	.	.	.	.	.	.	.	.	.	.	.	.	5	.	.	.	.	.	.	.	.	.	.	.	.	.	.	.	.	4.2	0.0042	HO	.	4
608	.	.	.	.	.	.	.	.	.	.	.	.	.	10	.	.	.	.	.	.	.	.	.	.	.	.	.	.	.	.	5.4	0.0054	HO	.	4

OBS	FLTMCO	FLOT	BAGSIZE	SITE	FEATURE	LEVEL	LOCUS	BAGNO	CONTEXT	DATE	MZKERNAL	CUPCOBS	EMBRYOS	CHENOPOD	LUPINE	PHSPP	TUBERS	PAPAS	OCA	ULLUCO	MASHUA	LUMPS	AMARANTH	SCIRPUS	SMLEGUME	LEPIDIUM	LUCUMA	RARE	PORTULAC	VERBENA	PLANTAGO	SGRASS	LGRASS	MGRASS	MALVAST	RUBUS	BIXA	PHYSOLIS
609	1	747	0.9	71	6	5	2	103	3	3	2	.	.	8	.	.	.	.	.	.	.	1	.	.	.	.	.	.	.	.	.	1	1	.	.	.	.	.
610	1	777	0.8	71	6	5	2	203	3	3	.	.	.	.	.	.	.	.	.	.	.	1	.	.	.	.	.	.	.	.	.	.	.	.	.	.	.	.
611	1	753	0.8	71	6	5	2	303	3	3	1	.	.	8	.	.	.	.	.	.	.	2	.	.	.	.	.	.	.	.	.	1	.	.	1	.	.	.
612	1	327	0.5	71	7	.	.	.	.	.	.	.	.	.	.	.	.	.	.	.	.	.	.	.	.	.	.	.	.	.	.	.	.	.	.	.	.	.
613	1	329	0.7	71	8	.	.	.	.	.	.	.	.	1	.	.	.	.	.	.	.	.	.	.	.	.	.	.	.	.	.	.	.	.	.	.	.	.
614	1	348	0.6	71	9	.	.	.	.	.	.	.	.	.	.	.	.	.	.	.	.	.	.	.	.	.	.	.	.	.	.	.	.	.	.	.	.	.

OBS	OXALIS	AMBROSIA	NICOTIAN	SALVIA	MINT	GALIUM	OPUNTIA	CYPER	COMPOSIT	UMBELLIF	FABACEAE	UNKWNSEE	WDCT	WDWT	GRSSTKS	EUPHORB	PHORLUP	MIMOSA	VACCINIU	BERBERIS	TRITICUM	MOLLUGO	PENDFRAG	CACTUS	CALEND	CRUCIFER	SOLANUM	LGLEGUME	TLEGUME	KG	M3VOL	PHASE	STAT	LEV
609	.	.	.	.	.	.	.	.	.	.	.	6	1	.	.	.	.	.	.	.	.	.	.	.	.	.	.	.	.	5.4	0.0054	HO	.	5
610	.	.	.	.	.	.	.	.	.	.	.	.	8	.	.	.	.	.	.	.	.	.	.	.	.	.	.	.	.	4.8	0.0048	HO	.	5
611	.	.	.	.	.	.	.	.	.	.	.	2	6	.	.	.	.	.	.	.	.	.	.	.	.	.	.	.	.	4.8	0.0048	HO	.	5
612	.	.	.	.	.	.	.	.	.	.	.	.	.	.	.	.	.	.	.	.	.	.	.	.	.	.	.	.	.	3.0	0.0030		. .	.
613	.	.	.	.	.	.	.	.	.	.	.	.	1	.	.	.	.	.	.	.	.	.	.	.	.	.	.	.	.	4.2	0.0042		. .	.
614	.	.	.	.	.	.	.	.	.	.	.	.	1	.	.	.	.	.	.	.	.	.	.	.	.	.	.	.	.	3.6	0.0036		. .	.

```
KEY TO TITLES
OBS= Observation number
FLTMCO= Type of sample: 1= flotation sample
FLOT= Flot sample number
BAGSIZE= Size of sample prior to flotation:eg 1=6 kg.
SITE= Site number
FEATURE= Feature number
LEVEL= Level
LOCUS= Locus number
BAGNO= Number of sample within provenience:eg 103= 1st of 3
CONTEXT= Cultural context:
         1= Floor
         2= Hearth
         3= Pit
         4= Subfloor, midden fill
         5= Burial
         6= Activity area outside of structure
         7= Rooffall or wallfall
         8= Midden, probably secondary deposition
         9= Surface
DATE= Phase of occupation:
      1= Early Intermediate Period
      2= Middle Horizon
      3= Early Intermediate/Middle Horizon
      4= Wanka I
      5= Wanka II
      6= Wanka III (local)
MZKERNAL= Zea mays kernels
CUPCOBS= Zea mays cob and cupules
EMBRYOS= Zea mays embryos
CHENOPOD= Chenopodium quinoa
LUPINE= Lupinus mutabilis
PHSPP= Phaseolus spp.
TUBERS= Domesticated tubers, not identifiable to species
PAPAS= Solanum tuberosum, S. juzepczukii, and S. spp.
OCA= Oxalis tuberosa
ULLUCU= Ullucus tuberorus
MASHUA= Tropaeolum tuberosum
LUMPS= Unidentifiable plant remains
AMARANTH= Amaranthus
SCIRPUS= Scirpus
SMLEGUME= Wild Fabaceae
LEPIDIUM= Lepidium
LUCUMA= Lucuma
RARE= Unique, unidentifiable seeds
PORTULAC= Portulaca
VERBENA= Verbena
SGRASS= Small Poaceae
LGRASS= Large Poaceae (Stipa type)
MGRASS= Medium Poaceae (Panicum type)
MALVALST= Malvastrum
RUBUS= Rubus
BIXA= Bixa
PHYSOLIS= Physolis
OXALIS= Oxalis (seed)
AMBROSIA= Ambrosia
NICOTIAN= Nicotiana
SALVIA= Salvia
MINT= Lamiaceae
GALIUM= Galium
OPUNTIA= Opuntia
CYPER= Cyperaceae
COMPOSIT= Asteraceae
```

UMBELLIF= Apiaceae
FABACEAE= Fabaceae
UNKWNSEE= Unidentifiable seeds
WDCT= Wood count
WDWT= Wood weight
GRSSTKS= Poaceae stalks
EUPHORB= Euphorbiaceae
PHORLUP= Phaseolus vulgaris or Lupinus mutabilis
MIMOSA= Mimosa
VACCINIU= Vaccinium
BERBERIS= Berberis
TRITICUM= Triticum
MOLLUGO= Mollugo
PENDFRAG= Peduncle fragment
CACTUS= Cactaceae
CALENDR= Calendrinia
CRUCIFER= Brassicaceae
SOLANUM= Solanum tuberosum, S. juzepczukii, and S. spp.
LGLEGUME= Domesticated legume, unidentifiable to species
TLEGUME= Wild Fabaceae
KG= Weight of sample prior to flotation in kilograms
M3VOL= Volume of sample prior to flotation in cubic meters
PHASE= Phase of occupation
HO= Early Intermediate/Middle Horizon
MH= Middle Horizon
HI= Wanka I
HII= Wanka II
HIII= Wanka III (local)
STAT= Status of occupation
LEV= Level (*= greater than 10)

Appendix G

Botanical data by date, site, and context, summarized by percent presence (ubiquity), standardized density, and relative percentage

UBIQUITY OF TAXA PRESENT:
ALL PROVENIENCES WEIGHTED EQUALLY

CONTEXT	SITE	PHASE	_FREQ_	MAIZE	QUINOA	LEGUMES	POTATO	ANDEANT	MEDICINE	CONSTRUC	FODDER	STORAGE	WILDFOOD
	.		191	0.41	0.84	0.45	0.48	0.03	0.49	0.86	0.88	0.14	0.01
	.	EIP/MH	56	0.43	0.86	0.41	0.38	0.00	0.59	0.96	1.00	0.09	0.00
	.	WANKA1	49	0.76	0.88	0.67	0.53	0.02	0.76	0.96	0.98	0.22	0.04
	.	WANKA2	86	0.21	0.81	0.35	0.51	0.06	0.28	0.74	0.74	0.13	0.00
	1		45	0.80	0.93	0.80	0.47	0.00	0.89	0.98	1.00	0.29	0.02
	7		27	0.22	0.67	0.22	0.63	0.07	0.30	0.59	0.85	0.15	0.00
	41		59	0.20	0.88	0.41	0.46	0.05	0.27	0.81	0.69	0.12	0.00
	49		32	0.63	0.84	0.53	0.53	0.03	0.59	0.97	0.97	0.09	0.03
	71		28	0.18	0.79	0.11	0.32	0.00	0.39	0.93	1.00	0.00	0.00
	1	EIP/MH	23	0.78	1.00	0.83	0.48	0.00	0.87	1.00	1.00	0.22	0.00
	1	WANKA1	22	0.82	0.86	0.77	0.45	0.00	0.91	0.95	1.00	0.36	0.05
	7	WANKA2	27	0.22	0.67	0.22	0.63	0.07	0.30	0.59	0.85	0.15	0.00
	41	WANKA2	59	0.20	0.88	0.41	0.46	0.05	0.27	0.81	0.69	0.12	0.00
	49	EIP/MH	5	0.20	0.60	0.20	0.20	0.00	0.40	1.00	1.00	0.00	0.00
	49	WANKA1	27	0.70	0.89	0.59	0.59	0.04	0.63	0.96	0.96	0.11	0.04
	71	EIP/MH	28	0.18	0.79	0.11	0.32	0.00	0.39	0.93	1.00	0.00	0.00
BURIAL	.		3	0.67	0.67	0.67	0.67	0.00	0.00	0.67	0.33	0.00	0.00
FLOOR	.		37	0.41	0.86	0.46	0.54	0.05	0.35	0.89	0.84	0.19	0.03
HEARTH	.		11	0.36	0.91	0.36	0.73	0.00	0.64	1.00	0.91	0.18	0.00
MIDDEN	.		44	0.55	0.86	0.57	0.39	0.00	0.66	0.89	0.93	0.18	0.00
PATIO	.		29	0.17	0.83	0.24	0.52	0.07	0.45	0.69	0.76	0.10	0.00
PIT	.		22	0.45	0.86	0.50	0.45	0.00	0.55	1.00	1.00	0.14	0.05
SUBFLOOR	.		45	0.42	0.80	0.44	0.42	0.04	0.44	0.84	0.91	0.09	0.00
BURIAL	.	EIP/MH	1	0.00	0.00	0.00	0.00	0.00	0.00	0.00	1.00	0.00	0.00
BURIAL	.	WANKA2	2	1.00	1.00	1.00	1.00	0.00	0.00	1.00	0.00	0.00	0.00
FLOOR	.	EIP/MH	6	0.33	1.00	0.33	0.17	0.00	0.50	1.00	1.00	0.17	0.00
FLOOR	.	WANKA1	9	0.89	0.89	0.56	0.78	0.11	0.78	1.00	1.00	0.22	0.11
FLOOR	.	WANKA2	22	0.23	0.82	0.45	0.55	0.05	0.14	0.82	0.73	0.18	0.00
HEARTH	.	EIP/MH	3	0.33	1.00	0.33	1.00	0.00	0.67	1.00	1.00	0.33	0.00
HEARTH	.	WANKA1	5	0.60	0.80	0.40	0.40	0.00	0.80	1.00	1.00	0.20	0.00
HEARTH	.	WANKA2	3	0.00	1.00	0.33	1.00	0.00	0.33	1.00	0.67	0.00	0.00
MIDDEN	.	EIP/MH	26	0.54	0.85	0.58	0.35	0.00	0.65	0.96	1.00	0.12	0.00
MIDDEN	.	WANKA1	14	0.71	0.86	0.71	0.50	0.00	0.71	0.86	0.93	0.29	0.00
MIDDEN	.	WANKA2	4	0.00	1.00	0.00	0.25	0.00	0.50	0.50	0.50	0.25	0.00
PATIO	.	EIP/MH	4	0.50	1.00	0.50	0.75	0.00	0.75	1.00	1.00	0.00	0.00
PATIO	.	WANKA1	1	1.00	1.00	0.00	0.00	0.00	1.00	1.00	1.00	0.00	0.00
PATIO	.	WANKA2	24	0.08	0.79	0.21	0.50	0.08	0.38	0.63	0.71	0.13	0.00
PIT	.	EIP/MH	11	0.36	0.91	0.18	0.36	0.00	0.55	1.00	1.00	0.00	0.00
PIT	.	WANKA1	8	0.75	0.75	0.75	0.50	0.00	0.63	1.00	1.00	0.25	0.13
PIT	.	WANKA2	3	0.00	1.00	1.00	0.67	0.00	0.33	1.00	1.00	0.33	0.00
SUBFLOOR	.	EIP/MH	5	0.20	0.60	0.20	0.20	0.00	0.40	1.00	1.00	0.00	0.00
SUBFLOOR	.	WANKA1	12	0.75	1.00	0.83	0.50	0.00	0.83	1.00	1.00	0.17	0.00
SUBFLOOR	.	WANKA2	28	0.32	0.75	0.32	0.43	0.07	0.29	0.75	0.86	0.07	0.00
BURIAL	41		2	1.00	1.00	1.00	1.00	0.00	0.00	1.00	0.00	0.00	0.00
BURIAL	71		1	0.00	0.00	0.00	0.00	0.00	0.00	0.00	1.00	0.00	0.00
FLOOR	1		6	0.83	1.00	0.83	0.33	0.00	0.83	1.00	1.00	0.50	0.17
FLOOR	7		9	0.33	0.67	0.33	0.67	0.00	0.22	0.67	0.78	0.22	0.00
FLOOR	41		13	0.15	0.92	0.54	0.46	0.08	0.08	0.92	0.69	0.15	0.00
FLOOR	49		6	0.83	0.83	0.33	0.83	0.17	0.67	1.00	1.00	0.00	0.00
FLOOR	71		3	0.00	1.00	0.00	0.33	0.00	0.33	1.00	1.00	0.00	0.00
HEARTH	1		5	0.80	0.80	0.60	0.40	0.00	1.00	1.00	1.00	0.40	0.00
HEARTH	41		3	0.00	1.00	0.33	1.00	0.00	0.33	1.00	0.67	0.00	0.00
HEARTH	49		1	0.00	1.00	0.00	1.00	0.00	0.00	1.00	1.00	0.00	0.00
HEARTH	71		2	0.00	1.00	0.00	1.00	0.00	0.50	1.00	1.00	0.00	0.00
MIDDEN	1		24	0.75	0.96	0.83	0.54	0.00	0.88	0.96	1.00	0.29	0.00
MIDDEN	7		1	0.00	1.00	0.00	0.00	0.00	0.00	1.00	1.00	1.00	0.00
MIDDEN	41		3	0.00	1.00	0.00	0.33	0.00	0.67	0.33	0.33	0.00	0.00
MIDDEN	49		7	0.71	0.86	0.57	0.29	0.00	0.57	0.86	0.86	0.00	0.00
MIDDEN	71		9	0.11	0.56	0.11	0.11	0.00	0.22	0.89	1.00	0.00	0.00

UBIQUITY OF TAXA PRESENT
ALL PROVENIENCES WEIGHTED EQUALLY

CONTEXT	SITE	PHASE	_FREQ_	MAIZE	QUINOA	LEGUMES	POTATO	ANDEANT	MEDICINE	CONSTRUC	FODDER	STORAGE	WILDFOOD
PATIO	1		3	1.00	1.00	0.67	0.67	0.00	1.00	1.00	1.00	0.00	0.00
PATIO	7		7	0.14	0.71	0.29	0.71	0.14	0.14	0.43	0.71	0.14	0.00
PATIO	41		17	0.06	0.82	0.18	0.41	0.06	0.47	0.71	0.71	0.12	0.00
PATIO	71		2	0.00	1.00	0.00	0.50	0.00	0.50	1.00	1.00	0.00	0.00
PIT	1		4	0.75	0.75	0.75	0.25	0.00	0.75	1.00	1.00	0.25	0.00
PIT	41		3	0.00	1.00	1.00	0.67	0.00	0.33	1.00	1.00	0.33	0.00
PIT	49		4	0.75	0.75	0.75	0.75	0.00	0.50	1.00	1.00	0.25	0.25
PIT	71		11	0.36	0.91	0.18	0.36	0.00	0.55	1.00	1.00	0.00	0.00
SUBFLOOR	1		3	1.00	1.00	1.00	0.33	0.00	1.00	1.00	1.00	0.00	0.00
SUBFLOOR	7		10	0.20	0.60	0.10	0.60	0.10	0.50	0.60	1.00	0.00	0.00
SUBFLOOR	41		18	0.39	0.83	0.44	0.33	0.06	0.17	0.83	0.78	0.11	0.00
SUBFLOOR	49		14	0.50	0.86	0.57	0.43	0.00	0.64	1.00	1.00	0.14	0.00
BURIAL	41	WANKA2	2	1.00	1.00	1.00	1.00	0.00	0.00	1.00	0.00	0.00	0.00
BURIAL	71	EIP/MH	1	0.00	0.00	0.00	0.00	0.00	0.00	0.00	1.00	0.00	0.00
FLOOR	1	EIP/MH	3	0.67	1.00	0.67	0.00	0.00	0.67	1.00	1.00	0.33	0.00
FLOOR	1	WANKA1	3	1.00	1.00	1.00	0.67	0.00	1.00	1.00	1.00	0.67	0.33
FLOOR	7	WANKA2	9	0.33	0.67	0.33	0.67	0.00	0.22	0.67	0.78	0.22	0.00
FLOOR	41	WANKA2	13	0.15	0.92	0.54	0.46	0.08	0.08	0.92	0.69	0.15	0.00
FLOOR	49	WANKA1	6	0.83	0.83	0.33	0.83	0.17	0.67	1.00	1.00	0.00	0.00
FLOOR	71	EIP/MH	3	0.00	1.00	0.00	0.33	0.00	0.33	1.00	1.00	0.00	0.00
HEARTH	1	EIP/MH	1	1.00	1.00	1.00	1.00	0.00	1.00	1.00	1.00	1.00	0.00
HEARTH	1	WANKA1	4	0.75	0.75	0.50	0.25	0.00	1.00	1.00	1.00	0.25	0.00
HEARTH	41	WANKA2	3	0.00	1.00	0.33	1.00	0.00	0.33	1.00	0.67	0.00	0.00
HEARTH	49	WANKA1	1	0.00	1.00	0.00	1.00	0.00	0.00	1.00	1.00	0.00	0.00
HEARTH	71	EIP/MH	2	0.00	1.00	0.00	1.00	0.00	0.50	1.00	1.00	0.00	0.00
MIDDEN	1	EIP/MH	17	0.76	1.00	0.82	0.47	0.00	0.88	1.00	1.00	0.18	0.00
MIDDEN	1	WANKA1	7	0.71	0.86	0.86	0.71	0.00	0.86	0.86	1.00	0.57	0.00
MIDDEN	7	WANKA2	1	0.00	1.00	0.00	0.00	0.00	0.00	1.00	1.00	1.00	0.00
MIDDEN	41	WANKA2	3	0.00	1.00	0.00	0.33	0.00	0.67	0.33	0.33	0.00	0.00
MIDDEN	49	WANKA1	7	0.71	0.86	0.57	0.29	0.00	0.57	0.86	0.86	0.00	0.00
MIDDEN	71	EIP/MH	9	0.11	0.56	0.11	0.11	0.00	0.22	0.89	1.00	0.00	0.00
PATIO	1	EIP/MH	2	1.00	1.00	1.00	1.00	0.00	1.00	1.00	1.00	0.00	0.00
PATIO	1	WANKA1	1	1.00	1.00	0.00	0.00	0.00	1.00	1.00	1.00	0.00	0.00
PATIO	7	WANKA2	7	0.14	0.71	0.29	0.71	0.14	0.14	0.43	0.71	0.14	0.00
PATIO	41	WANKA2	17	0.06	0.82	0.18	0.41	0.06	0.47	0.71	0.71	0.12	0.00
PATIO	71	EIP/MH	2	0.00	1.00	0.00	0.50	0.00	0.50	1.00	1.00	0.00	0.00
PIT	1	WANKA1	4	0.75	0.75	0.75	0.25	0.00	0.75	1.00	1.00	0.25	0.00
PIT	41	WANKA2	3	0.00	1.00	1.00	0.67	0.00	0.33	1.00	1.00	0.33	0.00
PIT	49	WANKA1	4	0.75	0.75	0.75	0.75	0.00	0.50	1.00	1.00	0.25	0.25
PIT	71	EIP/MH	11	0.36	0.91	0.18	0.36	0.00	0.55	1.00	1.00	0.00	0.00
SUBFLOOR	1	WANKA1	3	1.00	1.00	1.00	0.33	0.00	1.00	1.00	1.00	0.00	0.00
SUBFLOOR	7	WANKA2	10	0.20	0.60	0.10	0.60	0.10	0.50	0.60	1.00	0.00	0.00
SUBFLOOR	41	WANKA2	18	0.39	0.83	0.44	0.33	0.06	0.17	0.83	0.78	0.11	0.00
SUBFLOOR	49	EIP/MH	5	0.20	0.60	0.20	0.20	0.00	0.40	1.00	1.00	0.00	0.00
SUBFLOOR	49	WANKA1	9	0.67	1.00	0.78	0.56	0.00	0.78	1.00	1.00	0.22	0.00

MAIZE=Zea mays kernels, embryos, cobs, and cob fragments
QUINOA=Chenopodium quinoa
LEGUMES=Phaseolus spp. and Lupinus mutabilis
POTATO=Solanum tuberosum, S. juzepczukii, and S. spp.
ANDEAN TUBERS=Tropaeolum tuberosum, Oxalis tuberosa, and Ullucus tuberosus
MEDICINE=Plantago, Verbena, Asteraceae, and Salvia
CONSTRUCTION=Cyperaceae, Scirpus, and Wood
FODDER=Wild legumes, Amaranthus, Verbena, Oxalis, Portulaca, Malvastrum, Brassicaceae, and Poaceae
STORAGE=Mint, Cyperacese, and Grass stalks

STANDARDIZED DENSITY OF TAXA PRESENT:ALL PROVENIENCES WEIGHED EQUALLY
ALL BAGS STANDARDIZED TO BAG=6KG

PHASE	SITE	CONTEXT	_FREQ_	MAIZE	QUINOA	LEGUMES	POTATO	ANDEANT	MEDICINE	CONSTRUC	FODDER	STORAGE	WILDFOOD
	.		191	2.1942	867.4	1.5552	4.483	0.102724	3.6135	12.342	10.8080	0.063757	0.0028360
EIP/MH	.		56	2.0108	21.2	1.1719	1.100	0.000000	1.0947	8.686	7.3689	0.050719	0.0000000
WANKA1	.		49	2.1129	16.9	2.7892	1.947	0.017007	12.2216	26.396	23.7441	0.087462	0.0110544
WANKA2	.		86	2.3599	1902.9	1.1017	8.130	0.218454	0.3490	6.716	5.6769	0.058739	0.0000000
	1		45	4.0647	18.2	3.5288	1.169	0.000000	11.8582	16.362	21.7838	0.128261	0.0027778
	7		27	0.3469	1.8	0.2863	4.751	0.658951	0.5656	2.844	13.4524	0.068783	0.0000000
	41		59	3.2811	2772.9	1.4748	9.676	0.016871	0.2499	8.487	2.1186	0.054143	0.0000000
	49		32	0.9578	16.1	1.2293	2.505	0.026042	3.5958	27.514	12.9724	0.042318	0.0130208
	71		28	0.0919	24.3	0.1488	0.865	0.000000	0.4099	5.824	6.4546	0.000000	0.0000000
EIP/MH	1		23	4.7219	21.5	2.6578	1.574	0.000000	2.1130	12.283	9.7033	0.123490	0.0000000
WANKA1	1		22	3.3777	14.8	4.4394	0.745	0.000000	22.0464	20.627	34.4135	0.133249	0.0056818
WANKA2	7		27	0.3469	1.8	0.2863	4.751	0.658951	0.5656	2.844	13.4524	0.068783	0.0000000
WANKA2	41		59	3.2811	2772.9	1.4748	9.676	0.016871	0.2499	8.487	2.1186	0.054143	0.0000000
EIP/MH	49		5	0.2857	2.1	0.0667	0.233	0.000000	0.2452	8.165	1.7505	0.000000	0.0000000
WANKA1	49		27	1.0823	18.7	1.4446	2.926	0.030864	4.2163	31.097	15.0505	0.050154	0.0154321
EIP/MH	71		28	0.0919	24.3	0.1488	0.865	0.000000	0.4099	5.824	6.4546	0.000000	0.0000000
	.	BURIAL	3	45.7143	2519.0	13.8095	100.952	0.000000	0.0000	70.000	0.1515	0.000000	0.0000000
	.	FLOOR	37	0.9413	1279.8	1.0288	5.488	0.022523	1.5440	12.696	5.4573	0.074592	0.0033784
	.	HEARTH	11	3.1872	8239.1	3.4151	2.707	0.000000	6.2553	27.295	12.8900	0.111111	0.0000000
	.	MIDDEN	44	2.1046	14.4	2.1132	0.937	0.000000	3.0540	7.664	11.2484	0.071517	0.0000000
	.	PATIO	29	2.0543	19.1	0.8981	2.575	0.035760	0.6391	4.771	7.1867	0.053001	0.0000000
	.	PIT	22	0.3823	33.1	0.7933	0.598	0.000000	12.2529	13.484	22.2594	0.086700	0.0189394
	.	SUBFLOOR	45	1.1437	404.7	0.9668	4.254	0.394444	3.1504	13.448	11.7137	0.035648	0.0000000
EIP/MH	.	BURIAL	1	0.0000	0.0	0.0000	0.000	0.000000	0.0000	0.000	0.4545	0.000000	0.0000000
WANKA2	.	BURIAL	2	68.5714	3778.6	20.7143	151.429	0.000000	0.0000	105.000	0.0000	0.000000	0.0000000
EIP/MH	.	FLOOR	6	1.1042	2.1	0.2361	0.152	0.000000	0.1885	8.902	4.5658	0.166667	0.0000000
WANKA1	.	FLOOR	9	2.0104	14.9	2.1863	6.191	0.092593	6.1081	35.487	12.9209	0.044753	0.0138889
WANKA2	.	FLOOR	22	0.4595	2145.8	0.7714	6.655	0.000000	0.0465	4.407	2.6471	0.061688	0.0000000
EIP/MH	.	HEARTH	3	10.0000	11.4	7.3333	3.861	0.000000	4.4051	38.447	21.7500	0.333333	0.0000000
WANKA1	.	HEARTH	5	1.0119	4.6	2.3860	0.162	0.000000	10.7852	31.988	14.0190	0.044444	0.0000000
WANKA2	.	HEARTH	3	0.0000	30190.8	1.2121	5.793	0.000000	0.5556	8.320	2.1481	0.000000	0.0000000
EIP/MH	.	MIDDEN	26	1.7246	11.2	1.0687	1.078	0.000000	1.1558	6.099	4.9481	0.032318	0.0000000
WANKA1	.	MIDDEN	14	3.4118	20.4	4.6567	0.898	0.000000	7.3180	12.182	26.0544	0.134987	0.0000000
WANKA2	.	MIDDEN	4	0.0000	14.3	0.0000	0.156	0.000000	0.4688	2.024	0.3795	0.104167	0.0000000
EIP/MH	.	PATIO	4	6.8889	48.1	2.5648	4.255	0.000000	1.9676	7.183	10.8472	0.000000	0.0000000
WANKA1	.	PATIO	1	1.8519	0.8	0.0000	0.000	0.000000	3.3333	3.148	8.9352	0.000000	0.0000000
WANKA2	.	PATIO	24	1.2569	15.1	0.6578	2.402	0.043210	0.3054	4.436	6.5038	0.064043	0.0000000
EIP/MH	.	PIT	11	0.1961	58.5	0.3485	0.264	0.000000	0.7100	8.138	12.6149	0.000000	0.0000000
WANKA1	.	PIT	8	0.7817	9.1	1.5218	1.115	0.000000	32.5433	23.017	42.0668	0.104167	0.0520833
WANKA2	.	PIT	3	0.0000	3.4	0.4815	0.444	0.000000	0.4691	7.667	4.8025	0.358025	0.0000000
EIP/MH	.	SUBFLOOR	5	0.2857	2.1	0.0667	0.233	0.000000	0.2452	8.165	1.7505	0.000000	0.0000000
WANKA1	.	SUBFLOOR	12	2.0423	26.1	2.3082	1.447	0.000000	10.3191	38.022	22.2371	0.078125	0.0000000
WANKA2	.	SUBFLOOR	28	0.9119	638.8	0.5527	6.175	0.633929	0.5969	3.859	8.9827	0.023810	0.0000000
	41	BURIAL	2	68.5714	3778.6	20.7143	151.429	0.000000	0.0000	105.000	0.0000	0.000000	0.0000000
	71	BURIAL	1	0.0000	0.0	0.0000	0.000	0.000000	0.0000	0.000	0.4545	0.000000	0.0000000
	1	FLOOR	6	2.6091	2.7	1.2240	0.764	0.000000	5.2203	9.207	10.7836	0.233796	0.0208333
	7	FLOOR	9	0.1157	1.3	0.2940	0.668	0.000000	0.0767	1.855	3.2614	0.085979	0.0000000
	41	FLOOR	13	0.6976	3630.4	1.1019	10.800	0.000000	0.0256	6.174	2.2219	0.044872	0.0000000
	49	FLOOR	6	1.5106	20.3	2.2917	8.523	0.138889	4.0608	46.676	12.3020	0.000000	0.0000000
	71	FLOOR	3	0.0000	2.9	0.0000	0.303	0.000000	0.1389	12.498	1.7229	0.000000	0.0000000
	1	HEARTH	5	7.0119	9.8	6.7860	0.495	0.000000	13.1852	52.088	26.0690	0.244444	0.0000000
	41	HEARTH	3	0.0000	30190.8	1.2121	5.793	0.000000	0.5556	8.320	2.1481	0.000000	0.0000000
	49	HEARTH	1	0.0000	1.8	0.0000	0.333	0.000000	0.0000	10.500	0.7500	0.000000	0.0000000
	71	HEARTH	2	0.0000	3.1	0.0000	4.792	0.000000	0.6076	2.171	2.1250	0.000000	0.0000000
	1	MIDDEN	24	3.7166	21.8	3.6166	1.521	0.000000	5.0223	11.090	16.9373	0.113750	0.0000000
	7	MIDDEN	1	0.0000	2.1	0.0000	0.000	0.000000	0.0000	5.595	0.8929	0.416670	0.0000000
	41	MIDDEN	3	0.0000	18.3	0.0000	0.208	0.000000	0.6250	0.833	0.2083	0.000000	0.0000000
	49	MIDDEN	7	0.4271	5.7	0.8352	0.397	0.000000	1.5972	5.374	11.0880	0.000000	0.0000000
	71	MIDDEN	9	0.0463	1.6	0.0370	0.148	0.000000	0.0874	2.817	1.0337	0.000000	0.0000000

PHASE	SITE	CONTEXT	_FREQ_	MAIZE	QUINOA	LEGUMES	POTATO	ANDEANT	MEDICINE	CONSTRUC	FODDER	STORAGE	WILDFOOD
	7	PATIO	7	0.8571	1.2	0.6667	6.209	0.09524	0.1361	5.243	15.6599	0.09524	0.000000
	41	PATIO	17	1.4216	20.8	0.6541	0.835	0.02179	0.3751	4.104	2.7336	0.05120	0.000000
	71	PATIO	2	0.0000	4.0	0.0000	4.750	0.00000	0.6250	3.185	11.3935	0.00000	0.000000
	1	PIT	4	0.8727	5.0	1.4375	0.208	0.00000	59.5509	23.454	63.9167	0.10417	0.000000
	41	PIT	3	0.0000	3.4	0.4815	0.444	0.00000	0.4691	7.667	4.8025	0.35802	0.000000
	49	PIT	4	0.6908	13.3	1.6060	2.021	0.00000	5.5357	22.580	20.2169	0.10417	0.104167
	71	PIT	11	0.1961	58.5	0.3485	0.264	0.00000	0.7100	8.138	12.6149	0.00000	0.000000
	1	SUBFLOOR	3	3.3675	8.5	4.9047	0.231	0.00000	22.5596	11.712	31.1760	0.00000	0.000000
	7	SUBFLOOR	10	0.2324	2.7	0.0417	7.880	1.71250	1.3630	1.781	22.3351	0.00000	0.000000
	41	SUBFLOOR	18	1.2894	992.2	0.8367	5.228	0.03472	0.1713	5.014	1.5647	0.03704	0.000000
	49	SUBFLOOR	14	1.1310	21.3	0.9512	1.274	0.00000	4.0983	32.997	13.0050	0.06696	0.000000
WANKA2	41	BURIAL	2	68.5714	3778.6	20.7143	151.429	0.00000	0.0000	105.000	0.0000	0.00000	0.000000
EIP/MH	71	BURIAL	1	0.0000	0.0	0.0000	0.000	0.00000	0.0000	0.000	0.4545	0.00000	0.000000
EIP/MH	1	FLOOR	3	2.2083	1.4	0.4722	0.000	0.00000	0.2381	5.306	7.4087	0.33333	0.000000
WANKA1	1	FLOOR	3	3.0099	4.1	1.9757	1.528	0.00000	10.2025	13.108	14.1586	0.13426	0.041667
WANKA2	7	FLOOR	9	0.1157	1.3	0.2940	0.668	0.00000	0.0767	1.855	3.2614	0.08598	0.000000
WANKA2	41	FLOOR	13	0.6976	3630.4	1.1019	10.800	0.00000	0.0256	6.174	2.2219	0.04487	0.000000
WANKA1	49	FLOOR	6	1.5106	20.3	2.2917	8.523	0.13889	4.0608	46.676	12.3020	0.00000	0.000000
EIP/MH	71	FLOOR	3	0.0000	2.9	0.0000	0.303	0.00000	0.1389	12.498	1.7229	0.00000	0.000000
EIP/MH	1	HEARTH	1	30.0000	28.0	22.0000	2.000	0.00000	12.0000	111.000	61.0000	1.00000	0.000000
WANKA1	1	HEARTH	4	1.2649	5.3	2.9825	0.119	0.00000	13.4815	37.359	17.3363	0.05556	0.000000
WANKA2	41	HEARTH	3	0.0000	30190.8	1.2121	5.793	0.00000	0.5556	8.320	2.1481	0.00000	0.000000
WANKA1	49	HEARTH	1	0.0000	1.8	0.0000	0.333	0.00000	0.0000	10.500	0.7500	0.00000	0.000000
EIP/MH	71	HEARTH	2	0.0000	3.1	0.0000	4.792	0.00000	0.6076	2.171	2.1250	0.00000	0.000000
EIP/MH	1	MIDDEN	17	2.6131	16.3	1.6148	1.570	0.00000	1.7214	7.837	7.0205	0.04943	0.000000
WANKA1	1	MIDDEN	7	6.3965	35.1	8.4781	1.400	0.00000	13.0387	18.991	41.0208	0.26997	0.000000
WANKA2	7	MIDDEN	1	0.0000	2.1	0.0000	0.000	0.00000	0.0000	5.595	0.8929	0.41667	0.000000
WANKA2	41	MIDDEN	3	0.0000	18.3	0.0000	0.208	0.00000	0.6250	0.833	0.2083	0.00000	0.000000
WANKA1	49	MIDDEN	7	0.4271	5.7	0.8352	0.397	0.00000	1.5972	5.374	11.0880	0.00000	0.000000
EIP/MH	71	MIDDEN	9	0.0463	1.6	0.0370	0.148	0.00000	0.0874	2.817	1.0337	0.00000	0.000000
EIP/MH	1	PATIO	2	13.7778	92.2	5.1296	3.759	0.00000	3.3102	11.181	10.3009	0.00000	0.000000
WANKA1	1	PATIO	1	1.8519	0.8	0.0000	0.000	0.00000	3.3333	3.148	8.9352	0.00000	0.000000
WANKA2	7	PATIO	7	0.8571	1.2	0.6667	6.209	0.09524	0.1361	5.243	15.6599	0.09524	0.000000
WANKA2	41	PATIO	17	1.4216	20.8	0.6541	0.835	0.02179	0.3751	4.104	2.7336	0.05120	0.000000
EIP/MH	71	PATIO	2	0.0000	4.0	0.0000	4.750	0.00000	0.6250	3.185	11.3935	0.00000	0.000000
WANKA1	1	PIT	4	0.8727	5.0	1.4375	0.208	0.00000	59.5509	23.454	63.9167	0.10417	0.000000
WANKA2	41	PIT	3	0.0000	3.4	0.4815	0.444	0.00000	0.4691	7.667	4.8025	0.35802	0.000000
WANKA1	49	PIT	4	0.6908	13.3	1.6060	2.021	0.00000	5.5357	22.580	20.2169	0.10417	0.104167
EIP/MH	71	PIT	11	0.1961	58.5	0.3485	0.264	0.00000	0.7100	8.138	12.6149	0.00000	0.000000
WANKA1	1	SUBFLOOR	3	3.3675	8.5	4.9047	0.231	0.00000	22.5596	11.712	31.1760	0.00000	0.000000
WANKA2	7	SUBFLOOR	10	0.2324	2.7	0.0417	7.880	1.71250	1.3630	1.781	22.3351	0.00000	0.000000
WANKA2	41	SUBFLOOR	18	1.2894	992.2	0.8367	5.228	0.03472	0.1713	5.014	1.5647	0.03704	0.000000
EIP/MH	49	SUBFLOOR	5	0.2857	2.1	0.0667	0.233	0.00000	0.2452	8.165	1.7505	0.00000	0.000000
WANKA1	49	SUBFLOOR	9	1.6006	32.0	1.4426	1.852	0.00000	6.2389	46.792	19.2575	0.10417	0.000000

MAIZE=Zea mays kernels, embryos, cobs, and cob fragments
QUINOA=Chenopodium quinoa
LEGUMES=Phaseolus spp. and Lupinus mutabilis
POTATO=Solanum tuberosum, S. juzepczukii, S. spp.
ANDEAN TUBERS=Tropaeolum tuberosum, Oxalis tuberosa and Ullucus tuberosus
MEDICINE=Plantago, Verbena, Asteraceae, and Salvia
CONSTRUCTION=Cyperaceae, Scirpus, and Wood
FODDER=Wild legumes, Amaranthus, Verbena, Oxalis, Portulaca, Malvastrum, Brassicaceae, and Poaceae
STORAGE=Mint, Cyperaceae, and Grass stalks
WILD FOOD=Opuntia and Berberis

RELATIVE PERCENTAGE OF MAJOR CROPS AND USEFUL PLANTS
FLOT SAMPLES ONLY:ALL PROVENIENCES WEIGHED EQUALLY

PHASE	SITE	CONTEXT	_FREQ_	MAIZE	LEGUMES	QUINOA	POTATO	ANDEANT	MEDICINE	CONSTUCT	STORAGE	FODDER	WILDFOOD
	.		191	2.8	3.4	25	5.7	.26	5.6	24	.29	23	***
	1		45	7.1	8.2	15	3	0	10	23	.44	27	.01
	7		27	2.3	1.8	15	15	1.4	2	13	.78	33	0
	41		59	1	1.9	44	4.3	.18	4.5	20	.23	15	0
	49		32	2.2	3.5	15	3.7	.07	5.2	37	.05	21	.02
	71		28	.99	.31	23	6.1	0	4.2	29	0	28	0
EIP/MH	.		56	3.6	3.2	20	4.8	0	5.3	28	.13	27	0
WANKA1	.		49	4.4	6.4	14	3.2	.04	9.2	30	.29	24	.03
WANKA2	.		86	1.4	1.8	35	7.6	.55	3.8	18	0.4	21	0
EIP/MH	1		23	7.3	7.3	18	4.2	0	6.8	24	.31	25	0
EIP/MH	49		5	1.6	.52	12	.79	0	5	46	0	27	0
EIP/MH	71		28	.99	.31	23	6.1	0	4.2	29	0	28	0
WANKA1	1		22	6.9	9.2	12	1.8	0	14	22	.58	30	.03
WANKA1	49		27	2.3	4	15	4.3	.08	5.3	36	.06	20	.03
WANKA2	7		27	2.3	1.8	15	15	1.4	2	13	.78	33	0
WANKA2	41		59	1	1.9	44	4.3	.18	4.5	20	.23	15	0
	.	BURIAL	3	1.1	.53	59	3.9	0	0	1.7	0	17	0
	.	FLOOR	37	3	2.9	26	8.1	.07	3.4	27	.45	20	.02
	.	HEARTH	11	1.9	2.9	19	14	0	6.2	29	.08	15	0
	.	MIDDEN	44	4.3	5.9	19	3	0	6.3	26	.43	25	0
	.	PATIO	29	2.3	1.2	30	7.8	.23	5.3	17	.32	26	0
	.	PIT	22	1.8	4.2	23	2.4	0	7.3	28	.37	25	.03
	.	SUBFLOOR	45	2.5	2.6	27	4.7	0.9	6.4	22	.06	24	0
	41	BURIAL	2	1.6	0.8	88	5.8	0	0	2.6	0	0	0
	71	BURIAL	1	0	0	0	0	0	0	0	0	50	0
	1	FLOOR	6	12	5	13	3.5	0	11	21	0.9	33	.09
	7	FLOOR	9	1.7	3.6	20	18	0	1.8	16	.86	25	0
	41	FLOOR	13	.87	2.5	38	3.7	.03	.31	29	.27	11	0
	49	FLOOR	6	2.6	2.3	17	11	.36	5.5	36	0	17	0
	71	FLOOR	3	0	0	28	1.5	0	2.4	45	0	22	0
	1	HEARTH	5	4.1	6.3	8.2	1.5	0	10	40	.17	21	0
	41	HEARTH	3	0	***	46	13	0	2.8	13	0	7.8	0
	49	HEARTH	1	0	0	14	5.6	0	0	52	0	11	0
	71	HEARTH	2	0	0	10	49	0	4.6	14	0	12	0
	1	MIDDEN	24	6.2	9.2	16	4	0	7.5	21	.41	26	0
	7	MIDDEN	1	0	0	15	0	0	0	52	9.1	18	0
	41	MIDDEN	3	0	0	72	.53	0	8.9	17	0	.53	0
	49	MIDDEN	7	3.3	5.2	11	1.5	0	6.9	26	0	26	0
	71	MIDDEN	9	1.9	.59	17	2.6	0	2.5	36	0	30	0
	1	PATIO	3	11	3.9	28	2.3	0	8.7	15	0	21	0
	7	PATIO	7	2.1	1.9	17	16	.63	.87	12	.63	33	0
	41	PATIO	17	1	.62	38	4.8	.13	7	20	.28	22	0
	71	PATIO	2	0	0	12	13	0	1.5	12	0	41	0
	1	PIT	4	5.8	9.3	16	0.1	0	16	27	.93	27	0
	41	PIT	3	0	5	16	7.5	0	1.8	25	1.2	30	0
	49	PIT	4	1.5	9.3	11	3.2	0	3.4	35	.17	19	.17
	71	PIT	11	1	0.3	32	1.6	0	6.9	27	0	26	0
	1	SUBFLOOR	3	8.1	14	9.4	1.2	0	26	15	0	41	0
	7	SUBFLOOR	10	3.2	.27	8.7	13	3.2	3.3	7.9	0	42	0
	41	SUBFLOOR	18	1.6	2.8	49	2.8	.45	5.8	15	.09	14	0
	49	SUBFLOOR	14	1.9	1.8	16	1.9	0	5.2	43	.07	21	0
EIP/MH	.	BURIAL	1	0	0	0	0	0	0	0	0	50	0
WANKA2	.	BURIAL	2	1.6	0.8	88	5.8	0	0	2.6	0	0	0
EIP/MH	.	FLOOR	6	4.5	2.9	20	.77	0	3.9	37	.35	31	0
WANKA1	.	FLOOR	9	6.5	3	16	9.5	.24	9.3	28	.37	21	.06
WANKA2	.	FLOOR	22	1.2	2.9	31	9.5	.02	.91	24	.51	17	0
EIP/MH	.	HEARTH	3	3	2.2	9.8	33	0	4.3	21	0.1	14	0
WANKA1	.	HEARTH	5	2.3	5	9.3	2.5	0	9.5	44	.11	20	0
WANKA2	.	HEARTH	3	0	***	46	13	0	2.8	13	0	7.8	0

PHASE	SITE	CONTEXT	_FREQ_	MAIZE	LEGUMES	QUINOA	POTATO	ANDEANT	MEDICINE	CONSTUCT	STORAGE	FODDER	WILDFOOD
WANKA1	.	MIDDEN	14	4.5	8.8	12	1.3	0	7.1	21	.37	29	0
WANKA2	.	MIDDEN	4	0	0	58	0.4	0	6.6	25	2.3	4.9	0
EIP/MH	.	PATIO	4	5.8	2.9	26	8.4	0	2.9	14	0	27	0
WANKA1	.	PATIO	1	11	0	3.6	0	0	18	14	0	36	0
WANKA2	.	PATIO	24	1.3	.99	32	8	.28	5.2	17	.38	25	0
EIP/MH	.	PIT	11	1	0.3	32	1.6	0	6.9	27	0	26	0
WANKA1	.	PIT	8	3.6	9.3	14	1.7	0	9.8	31	.55	23	.09
WANKA2	.	PIT	3	0	5	16	7.5	0	1.8	25	1.2	30	0
EIP/MH	.	SUBFLOOR	5	1.6	.52	12	.79	0	5	46	0	27	0
WANKA1	.	SUBFLOOR	12	3.6	5.2	16	2.2	0	10	35	.08	23	0
WANKA2	.	SUBFLOOR	28	2.2	1.9	34	6.4	1.4	4.9	13	.06	24	0
EIP/MH	71	BURIAL	1	0	0	0	0	0	0	0	0	50	0
WANKA2	41	BURIAL	2	1.6	0.8	88	5.8	0	0	2.6	0	0	0
EIP/MH	1	FLOOR	3	8.9	5.8	12	0	0	5.5	30	.69	40	0
EIP/MH	71	FLOOR	3	0	0	28	1.5	0	2.4	45	0	22	0
WANKA1	1	FLOOR	3	14	4.2	15	7.1	0	17	12	1.1	27	.19
WANKA1	49	FLOOR	6	2.6	2.3	17	11	.36	5.5	36	0	17	0
WANKA2	7	FLOOR	9	1.7	3.6	20	18	0	1.8	16	.86	25	0
WANKA2	41	FLOOR	13	.87	2.5	38	3.7	.03	.31	29	.27	11	0
EIP/MH	1	HEARTH	1	9.1	6.7	8.5	.61	0	3.7	34	0.3	19	0
EIP/MH	71	HEARTH	2	0	0	10	49	0	4.6	14	0	12	0
WANKA1	1	HEARTH	4	2.8	6.2	8.1	1.7	0	12	42	.13	22	0
WANKA1	49	HEARTH	1	0	0	14	5.6	0	0	52	0	11	0
WANKA2	41	HEARTH	3	0	***	46	13	0	2.8	13	0	7.8	0
EIP/MH	1	MIDDEN	17	6.4	7.8	17	5.2	0	7.5	23	.27	24	0
EIP/MH	71	MIDDEN	9	1.9	.59	17	2.6	0	2.5	36	0	30	0
WANKA1	1	MIDDEN	7	5.5	12	13	1.1	0	7.3	16	.74	32	0
WANKA1	49	MIDDEN	7	3.3	5.2	11	1.5	0	6.9	26	0	26	0
WANKA2	7	MIDDEN	1	0	0	15	0	0	0	52	9.1	18	0
WANKA2	41	MIDDEN	3	0	0	72	.53	0	8.9	17	0	.53	0
EIP/MH	1	PATIO	2	12	5.8	40	3.4	0	4.2	15	0	14	0
EIP/MH	71	PATIO	2	0	0	12	13	0	1.5	12	0	41	0
WANKA1	1	PATIO	1	11	0	3.6	0	0	18	14	0	36	0
WANKA2	7	PATIO	7	2.1	1.9	17	16	.63	.87	12	.63	33	0
WANKA2	41	PATIO	17	1	.62	38	4.8	.13	7	20	.28	22	0
EIP/MH	71	PIT	11	1	0.3	32	1.6	0	6.9	27	0	26	0
WANKA1	1	PIT	4	5.8	9.3	16	0.1	0	16	27	.93	27	0
WANKA1	49	PIT	4	1.5	9.3	11	3.2	0	3.4	35	.17	19	.17
WANKA2	41	PIT	3	0	5	16	7.5	0	1.8	25	1.2	30	0
EIP/MH	49	SUBFLOOR	5	1.6	.52	12	.79	0	5	46	0	27	0
WANKA1	1	SUBFLOOR	3	8.1	14	9.4	1.2	0	26	15	0	41	0
WANKA1	49	SUBFLOOR	9	2.1	2.4	18	2.6	0	5.3	42	.11	17	0
WANKA2	7	SUBFLOOR	10	3.2	.27	8.7	13	3.2	3.3	7.9	0	42	0
WANKA2	41	SUBFLOOR	18	1.6	2.8	49	2.8	.45	5.8	15	.09	14	0

MAIZE=Zea mays kernels, embryos, cobs, and cob fragments
QUINOA=Chenopodium quinoa
LEGUMES=Phaseolus spp. and Lupinus mutabilis
POTATO=Solanum tuberosum, S. juzepczukii, and S. spp.
ANDEAN TUBERS=Tropaeolum tuberosum, Oxalis tuberosa, and Ullucus tuberosus
MEDICINE=Plantago, Verbena, Asteraceae, and Salvia
CONSTRUCTION=Cyperaceae, Scirpus, and Wood
FODDER=Wild legumes, Amaranthus, Verbena, Oxalis, Portulaca, Malvastrum, Brassicaceae, and Poaceae
STORAGE=Mint, Cyperaceae, and Grass stalks
WILD FOOD=Opuntia and Berberis
*** = LESS THAN 0.01%

REFERENCES

Adams, Richard McC. (1966) *The Evolution of Urban Society*. Aldine, Chicago

Alberti, Giorgio, and Mayer, Enrique (eds.) (1974) *Reciprocidad e intercambio en los Andes Peruanos*. Instituto Estudios Peruanos, Lima

Alencastre Gutiérrez, Andrés and Dumézil, Georges (1953) Fêtes et usages des Indiens de Langui. *Journal de la Société des Américanistes* XLII: 21–29. Musée de l'Homme, Paris

Allen, Catherine (1988) *The Hold Life Has*. Smithsonian Institution Press, Washington, DC

Anders, Martha Biggar (1986) Dual organization and calendars inferred from the planned site of Azangaro–Wari administrative strategies. Ph.D. Dissertation, Department of Anthropology, Cornell University. University Microfilms International, Ann Arbor

Asch, David L. (1975) On sampling size problems and the uses of nonprobabilistic sampling. In *Sampling in Archaeology*, edited by J. W. Mueller, pp. 170–91. The University of Arizona Press, Tucson

Asch, N. B. and Asch, D. L. (1975) Plant remains from the Zimmerman site – Grid A: a quantitative perspective. In *The Zimmerman Site: Further Excavations at the Grand Village of Kaskakia*, edited by M. K. Brown, pp. 116–20. Illinois State Museum Reports of Investigations 32

Atkinson, Jane (1990) *The Art and Politics of Wana Shamanship*, University of California Press, Berkeley

Avila, Francisco de (1939) [1598] *Damonen und Zauber in Inkareich, aus dem Ketschua Ubersetzt und Eingeleitet*, translated by von Hermann Trimborn. Quellen und Forschungen zur Geschichte de Geographie und Volkerkunde IV, Leipzig

Bailey, Geoff (1981) Concepts, time scales and explanations in economic prehistory. In *Economic Archaeology: Towards an Integration of Ecological and Social Approaches*, edited by A. Sheridan and G. Bailey, British Archaeological Reports, International Series 96: 97–118

Bannock, G., Baxter, R. E. and Rees, R. (1978) *The Penguin Dictionary of Economics*, 2nd edn. Penguin Books, New York

Barlett, Peggy F. (ed.) (1980) *Agricultural Decision Making*. Academic Press, New York

Barthes, Roland (1973) *Mythologies*. Paladin, London

Bastien, Joseph W. (1978) *Mountain of the Condor, Metaphor and Ritual in an Andean ayllu*. American Ethnological Society, Monograph 64. Washington, DC

Begler, Elsie B. (1978) Sex, status, and authority in egalitarian society. *American Anthropologist* 80: 571–88

Bender, Barbara (1978) Gatherer-hunter to farmer: a social perspective. *World Archaeology* 10: 204–22

Bennett, Wendell (1934) *Excavation at Tiahuanaco*. Anthropological papers of the American Museum of Natural History 34 (3): 395–494

Bintliff, John (1982) Settlement patterns, land tenure, and social structure: a diachronic model. In *Ranking, Resource and Exchange: Aspects of the Archaeology of Early European Society*, edited by C. Renfrew and S. Shennan, pp. 106–11. Cambridge University Press, Cambridge

Bird, Robert McKelvy (1970) Maize and its cultural and natural environment in the sierra of

Huanuco, Peru. Ph.D. Dissertation, Department of Biology, University of California, Berkeley

Birdsell, Joseph B. (1968) Some predictions for the Pleistocene based on equilibrium systems among recent hunter-gatherers. In *Man the Hunter*, edited by R. B. Lee and I. DeVore, pp. 229–49. Aldine, Chicago

Blanton, R. E., Kowalewski, S., Feinman, G. and Appel, J. (1981) *Ancient Mesoamerica: a Comparison of Change in Three Regions*. Cambridge University Press, Cambridge

Blau, Peter M. (1977) *Inequality and Heterogeneity: a Primitive Theory of Social Structure*. The Free Press, New York

Bohrer, Vorsila (1986) Guideposts in ethnobotany. *Journal of Ethnobiology* 6 (1): 27–43

Bonavia, Duccio (1982) *Los Gavilanes, Corporación financiera de desarollo S.A.* Confide, Lima

Bonnier, E. and Rozenberg, E. (1978) L'Habitat en village a l'Epoque Prehispanique dans le Bassen Shaka-Pakamayo. *Bulletin de l'Institute Français d'Etudes Andenes* (1–2) 7, (3–4) 49–71, 59–60. Paris

Borges, Kimberly A. (1988) Political organization in the Upper Mantaro Valley during the Middle Horizon. M.A. thesis, Archaeology Program, University of California, Los Angeles

Boserup, Ester (1965) *The Conditions of Agricultural Growth*. Aldine, Chicago

Bourdieu, Pierre (1977) *Outline of a Theory of Practice*. Cambridge University Press, Cambridge

(1979) *The Disenchantment of the World. A Sense of Honor: The Kabyle House*. Cambridge University Press, Cambridge

(1984) *Distinctions. A Social Critique of the Judgement of Taste*. Harvard University Press, Cambridge, Mass.

Brady, Nyle C. (1974) *The Nature and Properties of Soils*, 8th edn. Macmillan Publishing, New York

Braun, David P. and Plog, Stephen (1982) The evolution of "tribal" social networks: theory and prehistoric North American evidence. *American Antiquity* 47 (3): 504–25

Broadbent, Sylvia M. (1963) Construcciones megaliticas en el territorio Chibcha. *Revista Colombiana de Antropologia* 12: 81–88

Brookfield, H. C. (1972) Intensification and disintensification in Pacific agriculture. *Pacific Viewpoint* 13: 30-48

Browman, David L. (1970) Early Peruvian peasants: the culture history of a central highlands valley. Ph.D. Dissertation, Department of Anthropology, Harvard University

(1975) Trade patterns in the central highlands of Peru in the first millennium BC. *World Archaeology* 6 (3): 322–29

(1987) Agro-pastoral risk management in the central Andes. *Research in Economic Anthropology* 8: 171–200

Brumfiel, Elizabeth M. S. (1976) Specialization and exchange at the Late postclassic (Aztec) community of Huexotla, Mexico. Ph.D. Dissertation, Department of Anthropology, University of Michigan

Brumfiel, Elizabeth and Earle, Tim K. (1987) *Specialization, Exchange, and Complex Societies*. Cambridge University Press, Cambridge

Brush, Stephen B. (1974) El lugar del hombre en el ecosistema andino. *Revista del Museo Nacional* 40: 277–99. Lima

(1976) Man's use of an Andean ecosystem. *Human Ecology* 4 (2): 147–66

(1977) *Mountain, Field and Family, the Economy and Human Ecology of an Andean Valley*. University of Pennsylvania Press, Philadelphia

(1990) Crop development in centers of domestication: a case study of Andean potato agriculture. In *Agro-ecology and Small Farm Development*, edited by Miguel A. Altieri and S. B. Hecht, pp. 161–70. CRC Press, Boca Raton

Brush, Stephen B. and Guillet, David (1985) Small-scale agro-pastoral production in the central Andes. *Mountain Research and Development* 5 (1): 19–30

Brush, Stephen B., Carney, Heath J. and Huaman, Zosimo (1981) Dynamics of Andean potato agriculture. *Economic Botany* 35 (1): 70–85

Bryant, V. M. (1974) The role of coprolite analysis in archaeology. *Bulletin of the Texas Archaeological Society* 45: 1–28

Burchard, Roderick E. (1972) Exogamy and patterns of interzonal exchange. Paper presented at the 71st Annual Meeting of the American Anthropological Association, Toronto

(1974) Coca y treque de alimentos. In *Reciprocidad e intercambios en los Andes Peruanos*, edited by G. Alberti and E. Mayer, pp. 209–51. Instituto Estudios Peruanos, Lima

Burger, Richard (1984) *The Prehistoric Occupation of Chavín de Huantar, Peru*. University of California Publications in Anthropology. Berkeley, Cal.

Buth, G. M. (1982) SEM study as an aid in identification of caryopses of Triticum. *Journal of Economic and Taxonomic Botany* 3: 537–40

Caballero, J. M. (1980) *Agricultura, reforma agraria y pobreze campesina*. Instituto de Estudios Peruanos, Lima

Callen, E. O. (1963) Diet as revealed by coprolites. In *Science in Archaeology*, edited by D. Brothwell and E. S. Higgs, pp. 186–94. Thames and Hudson, London

Camino, Alejandro (1982) Tiempo y espacio en la estrategia de subsistencia Andina: un caso en las vertientes orientales sud-peruanas. In *El hombre y su ambiente en los Andes centrales*, edited by L. Millones and H. Tomoeda. Museo Nacional de Etnologia, Senri Ethnological Series 10: 11–35. Japan

Camino, Alejandro, Recharte, Jorge and Bidegaray, Pedro (1981) Flexibilidad calendárica en la agricultura tradicional de la vertientes orientales de los Andes. In *La tecnologia en el mundo Andino: Runakuap kawsayninkupaq Rurasqan Kunanqa*, edited by H. Lechtman and A. Soldi, pp. 169–94. Universidad Nacional Autónoma de Mexico, Mexico

Cancian, Frank (1972) *Change and Uncertainty in a Peasant Economy: the Maya Corn Farmers of Zinacantan*. Stanford University Press, Stanford, Cal.

Carney, Heath J. (1980) *Diversity, Distribution, and Peasant Selection of Indigenous Potato Varieties in the Mantaro Valley, Peru: a Biocultural Evolutionary Process*. International Potato Center, Lima

Carneiro, Robert L. O. (1967) On the relationship between size of population and complexity of social organization. *Southwestern Journal of Anthropology* 32: 234–43

(1970) A theory of the origin of the state. *Science* 169: 733–38

(1981) The chiefdom: precursor of the state. In *The Transition to Statehood in the New World*, edited by G. D. Jones and R. R. Krantz, pp. 37–79. Cambridge University Press, Cambridge

Cashdan, Elizabeth (1985) Coping with risk: reciprocity among the Basarwa of northern Botswana. *Man* 20 (3): 454–74

Cerrón-Palomino, Rodolfo (1972) *Apuntes sobre Linguistica Wanka*. CILA, UNMSM, Doc. de Trabajo No. 5. Lima

Chayanov, A. V. (1966) *The Theory of Peasant Economy*. American Economic Association, Richard D. Irwin, Inc. Homewood, Ill.

Childe, V. Gordon (1951) [1936] *Man Makes Himself*. C. A. Watts, London

Chisholm, Michael (1962) *Rural Settlement and Land Use*. Hutchinson, London

Cieza de Leon, Pedro de (1959) [1553] *The Incas*, edited by V. W. von Hagen. University of Oklahoma Press, Norman

Clark, Colin and Haswell, Margaret (1971) [1964] *The Economics of Subsistence Agriculture*. St Martin's Press, New York

Clastres, P. (1977) *Society Against the State*. Princeton University Press, Princeton, NJ

Cobo, Bernabe (1956) [1653] *Historia del Nuevo Mundo. Obras del Padre Bernabe Cobo de la Compania de Jesus* v (1–2). Estudio Preliminar y Edición de P. Francisco Mateos de la misma compania. Biblioteca de Autores Españoles. Ediciones Atlas, Madrid

Cock, C. Guillermo (1977) Los kurakas de los Collaguas: poder politico y poder económico. *Historia y cultura* 10: 95–119. Lima

Cohen, Mark (1977) *Food Crisis in Prehistory*. Yale University Press, New Haven, Conn.

Collier, Jane and Rosaldo, Michelle (1981) Politics and gender in simple societies. In *Sexual Meanings*, edited by S. Ortner and H. Whitehead, pp. 275–329. Cambridge University Press, Cambridge

Conklin, Harold (1961) The study of shifting cultivation. *Current Anthropology* 2: 27–61

(1980) *Ethnographic Atlas of Ifuago*. Yale University Press, New Haven, Conn.

Conrad, G. and Demerest, A. (1984) *Religion and Empire: the Dynamics of Aztec and Inca Expansion*. Cambridge University Press, Cambridge

Coombs, Gary (1980) Decision theory and subsistence strategies: some theoretical considerations. In *Modeling Change in Prehistoric Subsistence Economies*, edited by T. K. Earle and A. L. Christenson , pp. 187–208. Academic Press, New York

Coser, Lewis A. (1956) *The Functions of Social Conflict*. The Free Press, New York

Costin, Cathy L. (1984) The organization and intensity of spinning and cloth production among the late prehispanic Huanca. Paper presented at the Annual Meeting of the Institute for Andean Studies, Berkeley, Cal.

(1986) From chiefdom to empire state: ceramic economy among the prehispanic Wanka of highland Peru. Ph.D. Dissertation, Department of Anthropology, University of California, Los Angeles. University Microfilms International, Ann Arbor

Costin, Cathy and Earle, T. K. (1989) Status distinction and legitimation of power as reflected in changing patterns of consumption in late prehispanic Peru. *American Antiquity* 54 (4): 691–714

Cowgill, George L. (1975) The causes and consequences of ancient and modern population change. *American Anthropologist* 77: 505–25

D'Altroy, Terence N. (1981) Empire growth and consolidation: the Xauxa region of Peru under the Incas. Ph.D. Dissertation, Department of Anthropology, University of California, Los Angeles, University Microfilms

(1987) Transitions in power: centralization of Wanka political organisation under Inka rule. *Ethnohistory* 34 (1): 78–102

(1992) *Provincial Power in the Inka Empire*. Smithsonian Institution, Washington, DC

(n.d.) Site descriptions: Wanka II and Inka. In *Prehistoric Settlement Patterns in the Jauja Region, Peru*, edited by J. Parsons and T. K. Earle. Museum of Anthropology, Monograph Series. Documentation, Ms on file, Department of Anthropology, University of California, Los Angeles

D'Altroy, T. N. and Earle, T. K. (1985) Staple finance, wealth finance, and storage in the Inka political economy. *Current Anthropology* 26 (2): 187–206

D'Altroy, Terence N. and Hastorf, Christine A. (eds.) (n.d.) *Empire and Domestic Economy: Transformation in Household Economies of Xauxa Society under the Inka*. Smithsonian Institution Press, Washington, DC (in press)

Davis, Kingsley and Moore, Wilbert E. (1945) Some principles of stratification. *American Sociological Review*, 10: 242–49

Delorit, Richard J. (1970) *An Illustrated Taxonomy Manual of Weed Seeds*. Agronomy Publications, Riverfalls, WI

DeMarrais, Elizabeth (n.d.) The architecture of Xauxa communities. In *Empire and Domestic Economy: Transformation in Household Economies of Xauxa Society under the Inka*, edited by Terence N. D'Altroy and Christine A. Hastorf. Smithsonian Institution Press, Washington, DC (in press)

Demerest, Arthur A. (1981) Viracocha, the nature and antiquity of the Andean god. Peabody Museum Monographs 6, Harvard University, Cambridge, Mass.

de Montmollin, Olivier (1987) Forced settlement and political centralization in a Classic Maya polity. *Journal of Anthropological Archaeology* 6: 220–62

Denevan, William M. (1966) The aboriginal cultural geography of the Llanos de Mojos of Bolivia. *Ibero-Americana* 48. University of California, Berkeley

DeNiro, M. J. (1987) Stable isotopy and archaeology. *American Scientist* 75 (2): 182–91

DeNiro, M. J. and Hastorf, C. A. (1985) Alteration of 13C/12C and 15N/14N ratios of plant matter during the initial stages of diagenesis: studies utilizing archaeological specimens from Peru. *Geochimica et Cosmochimica Acta* 49: 97–115

Dennell, Robin W. (1976) The economic importance of plant resources represented on archaeological sites. *Journal of Archaeological Science* 3: 229–47

Dillehay, Tom (1979) Pre-hispanic resource sharing in the central Andes. *Science* 204: 24–31

Dillon, John L. and Anderson, Jock (1971) Allocative efficiency, traditional agriculture and risk. *American Journal of Agricultural Economics* 53: 26–35

Divale, William (1971) *Warfare in Primitive Societies: a Selected Bibliography*. Bibliography Series No. 2, Center for the Study of Armament and Disarmament, California State University, Los Angeles

Dixon, W. J. (ed.) (1981) *BMDP Statistical Software*. University of California Press, Berkeley

Donham, D. L. (1981) Beyond the domestic mode of production. *Man* 16 (4): 515–41

Donkin, R. A. (1979) *Agricultural Terracing in the Aboriginal New World*. Viking Fund Publications in Anthropology 56. University of Arizona Press, Tucson

Donnan, Christopher (1978) *Moche Art of Peru*, UCLA Latin American Center Publications, Los Angeles

Douglas, Mary (1985) [1966] *Purity and Danger*. Routledge and Kegan Paul, London

Drennan, Robert D. (1984a) Long-distance transport costs in prehispanic Mesoamerica. *American Anthropologist* 88 (1): 105–14

(1984b) Long-distance movement of goods in the Mesoamerican Formative and Classic. *American Antiquity* 49 (1): 27-43

Drewes, W. U. and Drewes, A. T. (1957) *Climate and Related Phenomena of the Eastern Andean Slopes of Central Peru*. Syracuse University Research Institute. Syracuse, NY

Dumond, D. (1972) Population growth and political centralization. In *Population Growth: Anthropological Implications*, edited by B. Spooner, pp. 286–310. MIT Press, Cambridge, Mass.

Durkheim, Emile (1963) [1897] *Suicide*. Routledge and Kegan Paul, London

(1964) [1895] *The Rules of the Sociological Method*. Free Press, New York

(1965) [1893] *The Division of Labor in Society*. Free Press, New York

Duviols, Pierre (1973) Huari y llacuaz, Agricultores y pastores. Un dualismo prehispanico de oposición y complementaridad. *Revista del Museo Nacional* 39: 153–91. Lima

Earle, Timothy K. (1976) A nearest-neighbor analysis of two Formative settlement systems. In *The Early Mesoamerican Village*, edited by K. V. Flannery, pp. 196–223. Academic Press, New York

(1978) *Economic and Social Organization of a Complex Chiefdom: the Halelea District, Kaua'i, Hawaii*. University of Michigan Museum of Anthropology, Anthropological Papers 63. Ann Arbor

(1980) A model of subsistence change. In *Modeling Change in Prehistoric Subsistence Economies*, edited by T. K. Earle and A. L. Christenson, pp. 1–29. Academic Press, New York

(1987) Specialization and the production of wealth: Hawaiian chiefdoms and the Inca Empire. In *Specialization, Exchange, and Complex Societies*, edited by E. Brumfiel and T. Earle, pp. 64–75. Cambridge University Press, Cambridge

Earle, T. K. and Christenson, Andrew L. (eds.) (1980) *Modeling Change in Prehistoric Subsistence Economies*. Academic Press, New York

Earle, T. K. and Ericson, J. E. (eds.) (1977) *Exchange Systems in Prehistory*. Academic Press, New York

Earle T. K., D'Altroy, T. N. and LeBlanc, C. J. (1978) Arqueologia regional de los periodos prehispanicos tardios en el Mantaro. In *El hombre y la cultura andina: actas y trabajos del III congreso* II, edited by R. Matos M., pp. 641–72. Universidad Nacional Mayor de San Marcos, Lima

Earle, T., D'Altroy, T., Hastorf, C., Scott, C., Costin, C., Russell, G. and Sandefur, E. (1987) *Archaeological Field Research in the Upper Mantaro, Peru, 1982–1983: Investigations of Inka Expansion and Exchange*. Institute of Archaeology 28, University of California, Los Angeles

Earle, T. K., Hastorf, C. A., LeBlanc, C. J. and D'Altroy, T. N. (1980) Preliminary report of the 1979 field season of the Upper Mantaro Archaeological Research Project. Ms

Earles, J. and Silverblatt, I. (1978) Ayllus y etnías de la región Pampas-Qaracha: el impacto del estado Inca. In *El Hombre y cultura andina Actas y trabajos del III Congreso*, edited by Ramiro Matos M., Editora Lasontay, Lima

Eggan, Fred (1950) *Social Organization of the Western Pueblos*. University of Chicago Press

Ekholm, K. (1972) *Power and Prestige: the Rise and Fall of the Kongo Kingdom*. Akademisk Avhandling, Uppsala

Ellen, Roy (1982) *Environment, Subsistence and System*. Cambridge University Press, Cambridge

Engel, Frederic A. (1970) Exploration of the Chilca Canyon, Peru. *Current Anthropology* 11 (1): 55–58

Erickson, Clark L. (1977) Subsistence implications and botanical analysis at Chiripa. Paper presented at the 42nd Annual Meeting of the Society for American Archaeology. New Orleans, LA

(1985) Application of prehistoric Andean technology: experiments in raised field agriculture, Huatta, Lake Titicaca 1981–2. In *Prehistoric Intensive Agriculture in the Tropics*, edited by Ian S. Farrington. British Archaeological Reports, International Series 232: 209-32, Oxford

(1988) Raised field agriculture in the Lake Titicaca Basin, *Expedition* 30 (3): 8–16. Museum of the University of Pennsylvania, Philadelphia

Espinoza, M. F. and Mantari, C. (1954) *La mashua o isano y la experimentación*. Dirección General de Agricultura del Peru Informativo 44. Lima

Espinoza Soriano, Waldemar (1971) [1558–1561] Los Huancas, aliados de la conquista. In *Anales cientificos de la universidad del centro del Peru*, 1: 9–407, Huancayo

Fallers, Lloyd (1972) *Inequality: Social Stratification Reconsidered*. University of Chicago Press, Chicago

Farrington, Ian S. (1978) Contemporary agriculture and the vertical economy, Cusichaca project: land use and irrigation. Ms

(ed.) (1985) *Prehistoric Intensive Agriculture in the Tropics*, British Archaeological Reports, International Series 232, Oxford

Feldman, Moshe (1976) Wheats. In *Evolution of Crop Plants*, edited by N. W. Simmonds, pp. 120–28. Longman, New York

Feinberg, S. (1970) The analysis of multidimensional contingency tables. *Ecology* 51: 419–33

Feinman, Gary and Neitzel, Jill (1984) Too many types: an overview of sedentary prestate societies in the Americas. In *Advances in Archaeological Method and Theory*, edited by M. Schiffer, 7: 39–102. Academic Press, New York

Figeuroa, Adolfo (1982) Production and market exchange in peasant economies. In *Ecology and Exchange in the Andes*, edited by D. Lehmann, pp. 123–56. Cambridge University Press, Cambridge

Flannery, K. V. (1968) Archaeological systems theory and early Mesoamerica. In *Anthropological Archaeology in the Americas*, edited by B. J. Meggars, pp. 67–87. Anthropological Society of Washington, Washington, DC

(1972) The cultural evolution of civilization. *Annual Review of Ecology and Systematics* 3: 399–426

(1976) *The Early Mesoamerican Village*. Academic Press, New York

Flannery, Kent V., Marcus, Joyce and Reynolds, Robert G. (1989) *The Flocks of the Wamani*. Academic Press, San Diego

Flores Espinosa, Isabel (1959) El sitio arqueológico de Wari Willca, Huancayo. *Actas y trabajos del II Congreso Nacional de Historia del Perú: Epoca pre-hispánica* 2: 177–86. Lima

Flores Ochoa (1968) *Pastoralists of the Andes*, translated by R. Bolton. Institute for the Study of Human Issues, Philadelphia

Food and Agriculture Organization of the United Nations (FAO) (1957) *Caloric Requirements*. Second Committee on Caloric Requirements, FAO Nutrition Studies 15. Rome

Foucault, M. (1980) *Power/Knowledge*. Edited by C. Gordon. Harvester, Hassocks, Sussex

(1984) *Foucault Reader*. Edited by P. Rabinow. Pantheon Books, New York

Fonseca Martel, César (1972) La economia "vertical" y la economia de mercado en las comunidades alteñas del Peru. In *Visita de la provincia de León de Huánuco en 1562, Iñigo Ortiz de Zúñiga, visitador*, edited by J. Murra, pp. 315–38. Universidad Nacional Hermilio Valdiza, Huánuco

Ford, Richard (1972) Barter, gift, or violence: an analysis of Tewa intertribal exchange. In *Social Exchange and Interaction*, edited by E. Wilmsen. University of Michigan Museum of Anthropology, Anthropological Papers 46. Ann Arbor

Franco, E., Horton, D. and Benevides, M. (1979) *Producción y utilización de la papa en el Valle de Mantaro, Peru*. Centro Internacional de la Papa, Lima

Fried, Morton, H. (1967) *The Evolution of Political Society*. Random House, New York

Friedman, J. and Rowlands, M. (1977) Notes towards an epigenetic model of the evolution of civilization. In *The Evolution of Social Systems*, edited by J. Friedman and M. Rowlands, pp. 201–76. Duckworth, London

Fry, Robert E. (ed.) (1980) *Models and Methods in Regional Exchange*. SAA Papers, No. 1, Washington, DC

Fuji, Tatsuhiko and Tomoeda, Hiroyasu (1981) Chacra, layme y auquénidos: explotación ambiental en una comunidad Andina. In *Estudios etnográficos del Perú meridional*, edited by S. Masuda, pp. 33–64. University of Tokyo, Tokyo

Fung Pineda, Rosa (1959) Informe preliminar de las excavaciones efectuadas en el abrigo rocoso no. 1 de Tschopik. *Actas y trabajos del II Congreso Nacional de Historia del Perú: Epoca pre-hispánica* 2: 253–72. Lima

Gade, Daniel W. (1969) Vanishing crops of traditional agriculture: the case of tarwi (*Lupinus mutabilis*) in the Andes. *Proceedings of the Association of American Geographers* 1: 47–51

(1970) Ethnobiology of canihua (*Chenopodium pallidicuale*), rustic seed crop of the Altiplano. *Economic Botany* 24 (1): 55–61

(1975) Plants, man, and the land in the Vilcanota Valley of Peru. *Biographica* 16. B.V. Publishers, The Hague

Gamble, Clive (1982) Leadership and "surplus" production. In *Ranking, Resource and Exchange: Aspects of the Archaeology of Early European Society*, edited by C. Renfrew and S. Shennan, pp. 100–05. Cambridge University Press, Cambridge

Gandanillas, H. (1968) Razas de quinoa. *Boletina Experimental* 34. Ministerio de Agricultura, División de Investigaciones Agricolas. Instituto Boliviano de Cultivos Andinos

García Soto, Rubén (1987) Excavations at San Juan Pata (J223), Jauja, Peru. Ms in author's possession

Garcilaso de la Vega (El Inca) (1943) [1609] *Comentarios reales de la Incas*, edited by A. Rosenblatt. Emeci Editores, Buenos Aires

Giddens, Anthony (1979) *Central Problems in Social Theory*. Macmillan, London

Gilman, Antonio (1981) The development of social stratification in Bronze Age Europe. *Current Anthropology* 22: 1–23

Gledhill, John (1978) Formative development in the North American southwest. In *Social Organization and Settlement*, edited by D. Green, C. Haselgrove and M. Spriggs. British Archaeological Reports, International Series 47: 241–90, Oxford

Goland, Carol (1988) Prehispanic occupation of the eastern Andean escarpment: a preliminary report of the Cuyocuyo archaeological survey. Working Paper No. 1 of the Production Storage and Exchange in a Terraced Environment of the Eastern Andean Escarpment Project. Ms in author's possession

Golte, Jürgen (1980) *La racionalidad de la organización Andina*. Instituto de estudios peruanos, Lima

Goodey, Tom (1933) *Plant Parasitic Nematodes and the Diseases they Cause*. Dutton, New York

Gould, P. R. (1961) Man against environment: a game theoretic framework. *Association of American Geographers* 58: 290–97

Gramsci, Antonio (1973) *Letters from Prison*, introduction by Lynne Lawner, pp. 3–56. Quartet Books, London

Green, David, Haselgrove, Colin and Spriggs, Matthew (eds.) (1978) *Social Organization and Settlement*. British Archaeological Reports, International Series 47, Oxford

Gregory, C. A. (1980) Gifts to men and gifts to god: gift exchange and capital accumulation in contemporary Papua. *Man* 15 (4): 626–52

(1982) *Gifts and Commodities*. Cambridge University Press, Cambridge

Grobman, A., Salhuana, W. and Sevilla, R. (1961) *Races of Maize in Peru*. National Research Council Publication 915. National Academy of Sciences, Washington, DC

Guaman Poma de Ayala, Felipe (1944) [1584–1615] *Nueva coronica y buen gobierno*. Instituto "Tihuanacu" de Antropología, Etnografía, y Prehistoría, La Paz, Bolivia

Gudeman, Stephen (1978) *The Demise of a Rural Economy*. Routledge and Kegan Paul, London

Guillet, David (1978) The supra-household sphere of production in the Andean peasant economy. *Actes du XII Congrès International de Américanistes* 4: 89–105. Musée de l'Homme, Paris

(1981) Surplus extraction, risk management and economic change among Peruvian peasants. *Journal of Development Studies* 18 (1): 3–24

(1987a) Terracing and irrigation in the Peruvian highlands. *Current Anthropology* 28 (4): 409–30

(1987b) Agricultural intensification and deintensification in Lari, Colca Valley, southern Peru. *Journal of Economic Anthropology* 8: 201–24

Gursky, M. (1970) Diet and physical characteristics of Quechua Indians from three Peruvian highland communities (abstract). *American Journal of Physical Anthropology* 33: 131

Guttierez Noriega, Carlos (1937) Ciudadelas chullparias de los Wankas. *Revista del Museo Nacional* 6 (1): 43–51. Lima

Haas, Jonathan (1982) *The Evolution of the Prehistoric State*. Columbia University Press, New York

Hack, John T. (1942) *The Changing Physical Environment of the Hopi Indians of Arizona*. Peabody Museum, Harvard University, Reports of the Awatobi Expedition 35 (1)

Haggett, Peter (1965) *Locational Analysis in Human Geography*. Edward Arnold, London

Hagstrum, Melissa B. (1989) Technological continuity and change: ceramic ethnoarchaeology in the Peruvian Andes. Ph.D. Dissertation, Institute of Archaeology, University of California, Los Angeles. University Microfilms International, Ann Arbor

Hally, David (1981) Plant preservation and the content of paleobotanical samples: a case study. *American Antiquity* 46 (4): 732–42

Halstead, Paul and O'Shea, John (1982) A friend in need is a friend indeed: social storage and the origins of social ranking. In *Ranking, Resource and Exchange: Aspects of the Archaeology of Early European Society*, edited by C. Renfrew and S. Shennan, pp. 92–99. Cambridge University Press, Cambridge

(eds.) (1989) *Bad Year Economics: Cultural Responses to Risk and Uncertainty*. Cambridge University Press, Cambridge

Hansen, Barbara C. S., Wright, H. E. Jr and Bradbury, J. P. (1984) Pollen studies in the Junín area, central Peruvian Andes. *Geological Society of America Bulletin* 95: 1454–65

Harlan, J. R. (1976) Barley. In *Evolution of Crop Plants*, edited by N. W. Simmonds, pp. 93–98. Longman, New York

Harlan, J. R. and Zohary, D. (1966) Distribution of wild wheats and barley. *Science* 153: 1074–80

Harms, Herman von (1922) *Ubersicht der Bisheren altperuanishen Grabern gefundenen Pflanzenreste*. Festschrift Edvard Seler, pp. 157–86. Stuttgart

Harris, David R. (1969) Agricultural systems, ecosystems and the origins of agriculture. In *Domestication and Exploitation of Plants and Animals*, edited by P. J. Ucko and G. W. Dimbleby, pp. 3–15. Duckworth, London

Harris, David R. and Hillman, Gordon C. (eds.) (1989) *Foraging and Farming: the Evolution of Plant Exploitation*. Unwin and Hyman, London

Harris, Olivia (1978) Complementarity and conflict: an Andean view of woman and men. In *Sex and Age as Principles of Social Differentiation*, edited by J. S. LaFontaine, pp. 21–40. Academic Press, New York

(1982) Labour and produce in an ethnic economy, Northern Potosi, Bolivia. In *Ecology and Exchange in the Andes*, edited by D. Lehmann, pp. 70–96. Cambridge University Press, Cambridge

(1985) Ecological duality and the role of the center: northern Potosi. In *Andean Ecology and Civilization*, edited by S. Masuda, I. Shimada and C. Morris, pp. 331–36. University of Tokyo Press, Tokyo

Harrison, John V. (1943) The geology of the Central Andes in part of the Province of Junín, Peru. *Boletín de la Sociedad Geologica del Peru* 16: 55–97

(1956) *La geologia del valle del Rio Mantaro*. Instituto Nacional de Investigaciones y Fomento Minero Boletin 15. Lima

Haselgrove, C. (1982) Wealth, prestige and power: the dynamics of late Iron Age political centralization in S.E. England. In *Ranking, Resource and Exchange: Aspects of Early European Society*, edited by C. Renfrew and S. Shennan, pp. 79–88. Cambridge University Press, Cambridge

Hastings, Charles M. (1981) Prehistoric vertical economy in the eastern Andes: a preliminary report of the 1979–1980 field season. Ms

(1986) The eastern frontier: settlement and subsistence in the Andean margins of central Peru. Ph.D. Dissertation, Department of Anthropology, University of Michigan. University Microfilms International, Ann Arbor

(1987) Implications of Andean verticality in the evolution of political complexity: a view from the margins. In *The Origins and Development of the Andean State*, edited by J. Haas, S. Pozorski and T. Pozorski, pp. 145–57. Cambridge University Press, Cambridge

Hastorf, Christine A. (1981) Preliminary report on land and plant use from the flotation recovered remains in the Jauja– Mantaro region, Peru. Ms in author's possession

(1983) Prehistoric agricultural intensification and political development in the Jauja region of central Peru. Ph.D. Dissertation, Department of Anthropology, University of California, Los Angeles. University Microfilms International, Ann Arbor

(1987) Archaeological evidence of coca (*Erythroxylum coca*) in the Upper Mantaro Valley, Peru. *Economic Botany* 41 (2): 292–301

(1990a) The effect of the Inka state on Sausa agricultural production and crop consumption. *American Antiquity* 55 (2): 262–90

(1990b) Prehistoric agricultural production in the central Andes: lost strategies. In *Food and Farm*, edited by K. Gladwin and C. Truman, pp. 117–33. University Press of America, New York

(1991) Food, space, and gender in prehistory. In *Engendering Archaeology: Women in Prehistory*, edited by J. Gero and M. Conkey, pp. 132–59. Basil Blackwell, Oxford

(n.d.) Traditional storage of food in the central Andes. Ms. in the author's possession

Hastorf, C. A. and DeNiro, M. J. (1985) Reconstruction of prehistoric plant production and cooking practices by a new isotopic method. *Nature* 315: 489–91

Hastorf, C. A. and Earle, T. K. (1985) Intensive agriculture and the geography of political change in the Upper Mantaro region of Central Peru. In *Prehistoric Intensive Agriculture in the Tropics*, edited by I. Farrington. British Archaeological Reports, International Series 232: 569–95, Oxford

Hastorf, C. A., Earle, T. K., Wright, H. E., Russell, G. S., LeCount, L. J. and Sandefur, E. (1989) Settlement archaeology in the Jauja region of Peru: evidence from the Early Intermediate Period through the Late Intermediate Period: a report on the 1986 field season. *Andean Past* 2: 81–129

Hastorf, C. A. and Johannessen, Sissel (1991) Understanding changing people/plant relationships in the prehispanic Andes. In *Processual and Postprocessual Archaeologies: Multiple Ways of Knowing the Past*, edited by R. W. Pruecel. Center for Archaeological Investigations, Occ. ppr 10, pp. 140–55, Southern Illinois University Press, Carbondale

(1992) Pre-Hispanic political change and the role of maize in the central Andes of Peru. *American Anthropologist*, in press

Hastorf, C. A. and Popper, V. (eds.) (1988) *Current Paleoethnobotany: Analytical Methods and Cultural Interpretations of Archaeological Plant Remains*. University of Chicago Press

Hather, John (1988) The morphological and anatomical interpretation and identification of charred parenchymatous plant remains. Ph.D. Dissertation, Institute of Archaeology, University College, London

Hawkes, J. G. (1963) A revision of the tuber bearing Solanum. *Records of the Scottish Plant Breeding Station*, pp. 76–181

(1990) *The Potato: Evolution, Biodiversity, and Genetic Resources*. Smithsonian Institution Press, Washington, DC

Hayden, Brian (1990) Nimrods, piscators, pluckers, and planters: the emergence of food production. *Journal of Anthropological Archaeology* 9 (1): 31–69

Hegmon, Michelle (1986) Sharing as social integration and risk reduction: a computer simulation involving the Hopi. Ms. on file at the University of Michigan

(1987) To share and share alike: food sharing and agricultural risk. Paper presented at the 1987 American Anthropological Society, Chicago, Il.

Helms, Mary (1979) *Ancient Panama: Chiefs in Search of Power*. University of Texas, Austin

Helwig, J. T. and Council, K. A. (1979) *SAS User's Guide*. SAS Institute, Cary, NC

Hemming, John, (1970) *The Conquest of the Incas*. Harcourt, Brace Jovanovich, New York

Hillman, Gordon C. (1973) Crop husbandry and food production: Modern basis for the interpretation of plant remains. *Anatolian Studies* 23: 241–44

(1984) Interpretation of archaeological plant remains: the application of ethnographic models from Turkey. In *Plants and Ancient Man*, edited by W. van Zeist and W. A. Casparie, pp. 1–41. A. A. Balkema, Rotterdam

Hipsley, E. H. and Kirk, N. E. (1965) *Studies of Dietary Intake and the Expenditure of Energy by New Guineans*. South Pacific Commission, Technical Paper 147. Noumea, New Caledonia

Hodder, Ian (1982) *Symbols in Action*. Cambridge University Press, Cambridge

(1986) The meaning of discard: ash and domestic space in Baringo. In *Method and Theory for Activity Area Research*, edited by S. Kent, pp. 424–48. Columbia University Press

(1990) Style as historical quality. In *The Uses of Style in Archaeology*, edited by M. Conkey and C. A. Hastorf, pp. 44–51. Cambridge University Press, Cambridge

Hodder, Ian and Orton, Clive (1976) *Spatial Analysis in Archaeology*. Cambridge University Press, Cambridge

Holdridge, L. R. (1947) *Life Zone Ecology*. Tropical Science Center, San Jose, Costa Rica

Holguin, Diego Goncales (1952) *Legua QQuichua*. Edición del Instituto de Historia, Universidad Nacional Mayor de San Marcos, Lima

Hubbard, R. N. L. B. (1975) Assessing the botanical component of human paleoeconomies. *Bulletin of the Institute of Archaeology* 12: 197–205

(1976) On the strength of the evidence for prehistoric crop processing activities. *Journal of Archaeological Science* 3: 257–65

Hurwicz, Leonid (1951) Optimal criteria for decision-making under ignorance. Cowles Commission Discussion Paper, Statistics 370

Hyslop, John (1976) An archaeological investigation of the Lupaca Kingdom and its origins. Ph.D. Dissertation, Anthropology Department, Columbia University. University Microfilms International, Ann Arbor

(1979) El area Lupaqa bajo de domino inciaco, un reconocimiento arqueológico. *Histórica* 3 (1): 53–81, Lima

INCAP (1961) *Tabla de composición de alimentos para uso en america latina*. Instituto de Nutrición de Centro America y Panama. Guatemala

Isbell, Billie Jean (1978) *To Defend Ourselves, Ecology and Ritual in an Andean Village*. Institute of Latin American Studies, University of Texas, Austin

Isbell, William (1978) Cosmological order expressed in prehistoric ceremonial centers. *Actes du XII Congrès International des Américanistes* 4: 269–99. Musée de l'Homme, Paris

(1987) State origins in the Ayacucho Valley, central highlands, Peru. In *The Origins and Development of the Andean State*, edited by J. Haas, S. Pozorski and T. Pozorski, pp. 83–90. Cambridge University Press, Cambridge

Isbell, William H. and Schreiber, Katarina (1978) Was Huari a state? *American Antiquity* 43: 372–89

Izumi, Seiichi (1971) Development of the Formative culture in the Ceja de Montaña of the central Andes. In *Dumbarton Oaks Conference on Chavin*, edited by E. P. Benson, pp. 49–72. Dumbarton Oaks, Washington DC

Jackman, Mary R. (1987) Paternalism and conflict in intergroup relations. Ms. in author's possession

Jarman, H. N., Legge, A. J. and Charles, J. A. (1972) Retrieval of plant remains for archaeological sites by froth flotation. In *Papers in Economic Prehistory*, edited by E. S. Higgs, pp. 39–48. Cambridge University Press, Cambridge

Jochim, Michael A. (1976) *Hunter-gatherer Subsistence and Settlement, a Predictive Model*. Academic Press, New York

Johannessen, S. and Hastorf, C. A. (1989) Corn and culture in central Andean prehistory. *Science* 244: 690–92

(1990) A history of Andean fuel use (AD 500 to the present) in the Mantaro Valley, Peru. *Journal of Ethnobiology* 10 (1): 61–90

Johns, Timothy and Towers, G. H. N. (1981) Isothiocyanates and thioureas of *Tropaeolum tuberosum* from Andean South America. *Phytochemistry* 20 (12): 2687–89

Johnson, A. M. (1966) The climate of Peru, Bolivia, and Ecuador. In *Climates of Central and South America*, pp. 147–202. Elsevier Scientific Publishing Company, New York

Johnson, Alan and Earle, Timothy (1987) *The Evolution of Human Society*. Stanford University Press, Stanford

Johnson, Gregory (1973) *Local Exchange and Early State Development in Southwestern Iran*. University of Michigan Museum of Anthropology, Anthropological Papers 51. Ann Arbor

(1982) Organizational structure and scalar stress. In *Theory and Explanation in Archaeology*, edited by C. Renfrew, M. J. Rowlands and B. A. Segraves, pp. 389-421. Academic Press, New York

Johnsson, Mick (1986) Food and culture among Bolivian Aymara. *Acta Universitatis Upsaliensis*. Uppsala

Jones, Glynis E. M. (1984) Interpretation of archaeological plant remains: ethnographic models from Greece. In *Plants and Ancient Man*, edited by W. van Zeist and W. A. Casparie, pp. 43–62. A. A. Balkema, Rotterdam

Jones, Glynis E. M., Wardle, Kenneth, Halstead, Paul and Wardle, Diana (1986) Crop storage at Assiros. *Scientific American* 254 (3): 96–103

Jones, Grant D. and Kautz, Robert R. (eds.) (1981) *The Transition to Statehood in the New World*. Cambridge University Press, Cambridge

Josephides, Lisette (1985) *The Production of Inequality*. Tavistock Publications, London

Julien, Catherine J. (1978) Inca administration in the Titicaca basin as reflected at the provincial capital of Hatunqolla. Ph.D. Dissertation, University of California, Berkeley. University Microfilms International, Ann Arbor

(1982) Inca decimal administration in the Lake Titicaca region. In *The Inca and Aztec States: 1400–1800*, edited by G. Collier, R. Rosaldo and J. Wirth, pp. 119–51. Academic Press, New York

Kadane, J. and Hastorf, C. (1988) Bayesian paleoethnobotany. In *Bayesian Statistics III*, edited by J. Bernardo, M. H. DeGroot, D. V. Lindley and A. M. F. Smith, pp. 243–60. Oxford University Press, London

Kanai, Hiroo (1972) A carbonized timber artifact. In *Excavations at Kotosh, Peru, 1963 and 1966*, edited by S. Izumi and K. Terada, pp. 317–18. University of Tokyo Press, Tokyo

Keene, Arthur S. (1981) *Prehistoric Foraging in a Temperate Forest*. Academic Press, New York

Kemeny, J. G. and Snell, J. L. (1960) *Finite Markov Chains*. Van Nostrand, Princeton, NJ

Kidder, Alfred II (1967) Digging in the Titicaca Basin. In *Peruvian Archaeology: Selected Readings*, edited by J. Rowe and D. Menzel, pp. 132–45. Peek Publications, Palo Alto, Cal.

Kimura, Hideo (1985) Andean exchange: a view from Amazonia. In *Andean Ecology and Civilization*, edited by S. Masuda, I. Shimada and C. Morris, pp. 491–504. University of Tokyo Press, Tokyo

Kirkby, Anne V. T. (1973) *The Use of Land and Water Resources in the Past and Present Valley of Oaxaca, Mexico*. University of Michigan Museum of Anthropology, Memoirs 5. Ann Arbor

Knapp, Gregory W. (1984) Soil, slope, and water in the equatorial Andes: a study of prehistoric agricultural adaptation. Ph.D. Dissertation, Department of Geography, University of Wisconsin. University Microfilms International, Ann Arbor

Kolata, Alan L. (1982) Tiwanaku, portrait of an Andean civilization. *Field Museum of Natural History Bulletin* 53 (6): 13–28

(1983) The South Andes. In *Ancient South Americans*, edited by J. D. Jennings, pp. 241–85. W. H. Freeman, San Francisco

(1986) The agricultural foundations of the Tiwanaku state: a view from the heartland. *American Antiquity* 51 (4): 748–62

Kroeber, A. L. (1944) *Peruvian Archaeology in 1942*. Viking Fund Publications in Anthropology 4. Wenner-Gren Foundation, New York

Krzanowski, Andrzej (1977) Yuramarca, the settlement complex in the Alto Chicama region (northern Peru). In *Polish Contributions in New World Archaeology*, edited by J. Krzysztof Kozolowski, pp. 29–58. Zaklad Narodowy im Ossolinkich, Karkow

LaFontaine, J. S. (1978) *Sex and Age as Principles of Social Differentiation*. Academic Press, London

LaLone, Mary (1985) Indian Land Tenure in southern Cuzco, Peru: from Inka to colonial patterns. Ph.D. dissertation, University of California, Los Angeles, University Microfilms International, Ann Arbor

Lanning, Edward P. (1967) *Peru Before the Incas*. Prentice-Hall, Englewood Cliffs, NJ

Lathrap, Donald W. (1971) The tropical forest and the cultural context of Chavin. In *Dumbarton Oaks Conference on Chavin*, edited by E. P. Benson, pp. 73–100. Dumbarton Oaks, Washington DC

(1977) Our father the cayman, our mother the gourd: Spinden revisited, or a unitary model for the emergence of agriculture in the New World. In *Origins of Agriculture*, edited by C. Reed, pp. 713–51. Aldine, Chicago

Lavallée, Daniele (1967) Types céramiques des Andes Centrales du Pérou. *Journale de la Société des Américanistes* 56: 411–47

(1973) Estructura y organización del habitat en los Andes centrales durante el Periodo Intermedio Tardio. *Revista del Museo Nacional* 39: 91–116. Lima

Lavallée, Daniele and Julien, M. (1973) *Les etablissementes asto a l'époque prehispanique*. Travaux de l'Institut français d'études Andines, xv. Lima

Leach, Edmund (1965) *Political Systems of Highland Burma*. Beacon Press, Boston

Leacock, Eleanor (1978) Women's status in egalitarian society: implications for social evolution. *Current Anthropology* 19 (2): 247–55

LeBlanc, Catherine J. (1981) Late prehispanic Huanca settlement patterns in the Yanamarca Valley, Peru. Ph.D. dissertation, Department of Anthropology, University of California, Los Angeles. University Microfilms International, Ann Arbor

LeCount, Lisa J. (1987) Towards defining and explaining functional variation in Sausa ceramics from the upper Mantaro Valley, Peru. M.A. thesis, Department of Anthropology, University of California, Los Angeles

Lee, Richard B. (1969) !Kung bushman subsistence: an input–output analysis. In *Contributions to Anthropology: Ecological Essays*, edited by D. Damus. National Museums of Canada Bulletin 3-94, 230, Anthropological Series 86. Queen's Printers for Canada, Ottowa

Lee, Ronald D. (1986) Malthus and Boserup: a dynamic synthesis. In *The State of Population Theory*, edited by D. Coleman and R. Schofield. Basil Blackwell, Oxford

Lees, Susan (1983) Environmental hazards and decision making: another perspective from human ecology. In *Economic Anthropology*, edited by S. Ortiz. Monograph 1: 183–94. University Press of America, New York

Lehmann, David (ed.) (1982) *Ecology and Exchange in the Andes*. Cambridge University Press, Cambridge

Lennon, Tom (1982) Raised fields of lake Titicaca, Peru: a pre-hispanic water management system. Ph.D. Dissertation, Department of Anthropology, University of Colorado. University Microfilms International, Ann Arbor

Lennstrom, Heidi A. (1992) Intrasite spatial variability and resource utilization in the prehispanic Peruvian highlands: an exploration of method and theory in paleoethnobotany. Ph.D. Dissertation, Center for Ancient Studies, University of Minnesota. University Microfilms International, Ann Arbor

(1992) Old wives' tales, in paleoethnobotany: A comparison of bulk and scatter sampling schemes from Pancán Peru. *Journal of Archaeological Science* 19: 205–29

Leon, Jorge (1964) *Plantas alimenticas andinas*. Instituto Interamericano de Ciencias Agricolas, Zona Andina, Boletin Técnico 6. Lima

LeVine, Terry Y. (1979) Prehistoric economic and political change in highland Peru: an ethnohistorical study of the Mantaro valley. M.A. thesis, Archaeology Program, UCLA

(1985) Inka administration in the central highlands: a comparative study. Ph.D. dissertation, University of California, Los Angeles. University Microfilms International, Ann Arbor

Lévi-Strauss, Claude (1963) *Structural Anthropology*. Basic Books, New York

Long, Norman and Roberts, Bryan (1984) *Miners, Peasants, and Entrepreneurs: Regional*

Development in the Central Highlands of Peru. Cambridge Latin American Studies Series 48, Cambridge University Press, Cambridge

Lumbreras, Luis G. (1957) La cultura Wanka. *Ondas Isabelinas Organo de la gran unidad escolar Santa Isabel de Huancayo* 223: 15–18

(1959) Esquema arqueologico de la sierra central del Peru. *Revista del Museo Nacional* 28: 64–117. Lima

(1974) *The People and Cultures of Ancient Perú*, translated by B. Meggers. Smithsonian Institution Press, Washington, DC

Lumbreras, Luis G. and Amat, Hernán (1965–66) Informe preliminar sobre las galerías interiores de Chavín. *Revista del Museo Nacional* 34: 143–97. Lima

Lynch, Thomas (1980) *Guitarrero Cave: Early Man in the Andes*. Academic Press, New York

Lynch, Thomas, et al. (1985) Chronology of Guitarrero Cave, Peru. *Science* 229: 864–67

MacBride, J. F. (1949) *Flora of Peru*. Field Museum of Natural History Botanical Series. Chicago

McEwen, Gordon F. (1982) Pikillacta and the Wari state storage facility hypothesis. Ms. in author's possession

(1990) Some formal correspondences between the imperial architecture of the Wari and Chimu cultures of ancient Peru. *Latin American Antiquity* 1 (2): 97–116

McFarland, David D. (1981) Spectoral decomposition as a tool in comparative mobility research. In *Sociological Methodology*, edited by S. Leinhardt, pp. 338–58. Jossey-Bass, San Francisco

(1982) Markov chains in APL computing. Ms. in author's possession

McGuire, Randall (1983) Breaking down cultural complexity and heterogeneity. In *Advances in Archaeological Methods and Theory*, edited by M. Schiffer, 6: 91–142. Academic Press, New York

MacNeish, R. S. (1981) Synthesis and conclusions. In *Prehistory of the Ayacucho Basin, Peru* II: *Excavations and Chronology*, edited by R. MacNeish, A. Garcia-Cook, L. G. Lumbreras, R. K. Vierra and A. Nelken-Turner, pp. 199–257. University of Michigan Press, Ann Arbor

MacNeish, R. S., Nelken-Terner, A. and Garcia-Cook, A. (1970) *Second Annual Report of the Ayacucho Archaeological–Botanical Project*. Peabody Foundation of Archaeology. Andover, Mass.

Mallon, Florencia E. (1983) *The Defense of Community in Peru's Central Highlands: Peasant Struggle and Capitalist Transition 1860–1940*. Princeton University Press, Princeton, NJ

Marcus, Joyce (1989) From centralized systems to city-states: possible models for the epiclassic. In *Mesoamerica after the Decline of Teotihuacan A.D. 700–900*, edited by R. A. Diehl and J. C. Berlo, pp. 201–08. Dumbarton Oaks, Washington DC

Martin, A. and Barkley, W. (1961) *Seed Identification Manual*. University of California Press, Berkeley

Martins-Farias, R. (1976) New archaeological techniques for the study of cereal and root crops in Peru. Ph.D. Dissertation,. Department of Botany, University of Birmingham

Marx, Karl (1904) [1859] *Capital: a Critique of Political Economy*. Modern Library, New York

(1971) [1867] *Capital* 1: *A Critical Analysis of Capitalist Production*. Progress Publishers, Moscow

Masuda, Shozo, Shimada, Izumi and Morris, Craig (eds.) (1985) *Andean Ecology and Civilization*. University of Tokyo Press, Tokyo

Matos Mar, José (1964) La propiedad en la isla de Taquile (Lago Titicaca). In *Estudios sobre la cultura actual del Perú*, edited by L. Valcárcel, pp. 64–142. Universidad Nacional Mayor de San Marcos, Lima

Matos Mendieta, Ramiro (1959) Los Wanka, datos históricos y arqueológicos. *Actas y trabajos del II Congreso Nacional de Historia del Perú: Epoca pre-hispánica* 2: 187–210. Lima

(1966) La economia durante el periodo de reinas y confederaciones en Mantaro, Perú. *Actas y Memorias del 36 Congreso Internacional de Americanistas* 2: 95–99

(1968) Wari-Willka, santuario Wanka en el mantaro. *Cantuta* 2: 116–27. Lima

(1971) El periodo formativo en el Valle del Mantaro. *Revista del Museo Nacional* 37: 41–51. Lima

(1972) Ataura: un centro Chavín en el Valle del Mantaro. *Revista del Museo Nacional* 38: 93–108. Lima

(1975) Prehistoria y ecologia humana en la punas de Junín. *Revista del Museo Nacional* 41: 37–80. Lima

(1978) Cultural and ecological context of the Mantaro Valley during the Formative Period. In *Advances in Andean Archaeology*, edited by D. L. Browman, pp. 307–25. Mouton, The Hague

Mayer, Enrique (1972) Censos insensatos: evaluación de los censos campesinos en la historia de Tangór. In *Visita de la Provincia de Leon de Huánuco* II, edited by J. Murra, pp. 339–66. Universidad Hermilio Valdizan, Huanuco, Peru

(1979) *Land Use in the Andes: Ecology and Agriculture in the Mantaro Valley of Peru with Special Reference to Potatoes.* Centro Internacional de la Papa, Lima

(1985) Production zones. In *Andean Ecology and Civilization*, edited by S. Masuda, I. Shimada and C. Morris, pp. 45–84. University of Tokyo Press, Tokyo

Megard, François (1968) *Geologia del cuadrangulo de Huancayo.* Dirección General de Mineria, Servicio de Geologia y Mineria Boletin 18. Lima

Merriam, Charles E. (1934) *Political Power.* McGraw Hill, New York

Miller, Daniel (1985) *Artefacts as Categories: a Study of Ceramic Variability in Central India.* Cambridge University Press, Cambridge

Miller, Daniel and Tilley, Christopher (1984) Theoretical perspectives. In *Ideology, Power and Prehistory*, edited by D. Miller and C. Tilley, pp. 1–15. Cambridge University Press, Cambridge

Miller, Naomi (1982) Economy and environment of Malyan, a third millennium BC urban center in southern Iran. Ph.D. dissertation, Department of Anthropology, University of Michigan. University Microfilms International, Ann Arbor

(1988) Ratios in paleoethnobotanical analysis. In *Current Paleoethnobotany*, edited by C. Hastorf and V. Popper, pp. 72–85. University of Chicago Press, Chicago

Minnis, Paul E. (1978) Paleoethnobotanical indicators of prehistoric environmental disturbance: a case study. In *The Nature and Status of Ethnobotany*, edited by R. I. Ford, pp. 347–66. University of Michigan Museum of Anthropology, Anthropological Papers 60. Ann Arbor

Minnis, Paul and LeBlanc, Steven (1976) An efficient, inexpensive arid lands flotation system. *American Antiquity* 41 (4): 491–93

Mintzer, M. J. (1933) Las quinoas su cultivo en la Argentina, su importancia como planta alimenticia. *Ministerio de Agricultura Boletin Mensual* 34: 59–77

Mishkin, Bernard (1946) The contemporary Quechua. In *The Handbook of South American Indians* 2: 441–70. Smithsonian Institution, Washington DC

Mitchell, William P. (1976) Irrigation and community in the central highlands. *American Anthropologist* 78 (1): 25–44

Mohr Chavez, Karen (1988) The significance of Chiripa in Lake Titicaca Basin developments. *Expedition* 30 (3): 17–26

Monk, M. A. and Fasham, P. J. (1980) Carbonized plant remains from two Iron Age sites in central Hampshire. *Proceedings of the Prehistoric Society* 46: 321–44

Montaldo, A. (1977) *Cultivo de raices y tuberculos tropicales.* Instituto Interamericano de Ciencias Agricolas de la OEA. San Jose, Costa Rica

Moore, Henrietta (1986) *Space, Text, and Gender.* Cambridge University Press, Cambridge

(1988) *Feminism and Anthropology*, Polity Press, Oxford

Moran, Emilio (ed.) (1990) *The Ecosystem Approach in Anthropology*. University of Michigan Press, Ann Arbor

Morgan, L. H. (1964) *Ancient Society*. Harvard University Press, Cambridge, Mass.

Morris, Craig (1967) Storage in Tawantinsuyu. Ph.D. Dissertation, Department of Anthropology, University of Chicago

Moseley, Michael E. (1975) *The Maritime Foundations of Andean Civilization*. Cummings Publications, Palo Alto, Cal.

Moseley, Michael E. and Watanabe, Luis (1974) The adobe sculpture of Huaca de los Reyes. *Archaeology* 27: 154–61

Mujica, Elias (1978) Nueva hipotesis sobre el desarrollo temprano del altiplano, del Titicaca y de sus areas de interacción. *Arte y Arqueologia* (La Paz) 5 and 6: 285–308

Munson, P. J., Parmalee, P. W. and Yarnell, R. A. (1971) Subsistence ecology of Scovill, a terminal Middle Woodland village. *American Antiquity* 36: 401–31

Murphy, Robert (1971) *The Dialectics of Social Life*. Basic Books, New York

Murra, John V. (1960) Rite and crop of the Inka state. In *Culture in History*, edited by S. Diamond, pp. 393–407. Columbia University Press, New York

(1964) Una apreciación etnologica de la visita. In *Visita hecha en la provincia de Chucuito en el ano 1567 por Garcia Diez de San Miguel*, edited by J. Murra, pp. 421–44. Casa de la Cultura del Peru, Lima

(1968) An Aymara kingdom in 1567. *Ethnohistory* 15 (2): 115–51

(1970) Current research and prospects in Andean ethnohistory. *Latin American Research Review* 5: 3–36

(1972) El control vertical de un maximo de pisos ecologicos en la economia de las sociedades andinas. In *Visita de la Provincia de Leon de Huánuco* II, edited by J. Murra, pp. 429–76. Universidad Hermilio Valdizan, Huánuco, Peru

(1980) [1956] *The Economic Organization of the Inka State*. JAI Press, Greenwich, Conn.

(1984) Andean societies before 1543. In *The Cambridge History of Latin America*, edited by L. Bethell, I: 59–90. Cambridge University Press, Cambridge

Muyskens, Deborah (1989) A study of activity areas within prehispanic Wanka households in the Yanamarca Valley, Peru. M.Phil. Dissertation, Department of Archaeology, Cambridge University, Cambridge

Nash, Daphne (1978) Territory and state formation in central Gaul. In *Social Organization and Settlement*, edited by D. Green, C. Haselgrove, and M. Spriggs. British Archaeological Reports S47: 455–75

Netting, Robert McC. (1968) *Hill Farmers of Nigeria: Cultural Ecology of the Kofyar of the Jos Plateau*. University of Washington Press, Seattle

(1990) Population, permanent agriculture, and polities: unpacking the evolutionary portmanteau. In *The Evolution of Political Systems*, edited by S. Upham, pp. 21–61. Cambridge University Press, Cambridge

Netting, Robert McC., Wilk, R. and Arnould, E. (1984) *Households: Comparative and Historical Studies of the Domestic Group*. University of California Press, Berkeley, Cal.

Nordstrom, Carol (1990) Evidence for the domestication of *Chenopodium* in the Andes. A report submitted to the National Science Foundation, Archaeology Program, Department of Anthropology, University of Minnesota, Minneapolis.

Nuñez, A. Lautaro and Dillehay, Thomas D. (1978) *Movilidad giratorio, armonia social y desarrollo en los Andes meridionales: patrones de tráfico e interacción económica*. Universidad del Norte (Chile), Antofagasto

Oberg, Kalervo (1955) Types of social structure among the lowland tribes of South and Central America. *American Anthropologist* 57 (3): 472–7

Ochoa, Carlos (1975) Potato collecting expeditions in Chile, Bolivia, and Peru, and the genetic erosion of indigenous cultivars. In *Crop Genetic Resources for Today and Tomorrow*, edited by O. H. Frankel and J. G. Hawkes, pp. 167–74. Cambridge University Press, Cambridge

(1976) Review of progress in explorations. 1973–1975, cultivated potatoes. In *Planning Conference: Exploration and Maintenance of Germplasm Resources*, pp. 19–26. International Potato Center, Lima

Oficina Nacional de Evaluación de Recursos Naturales (ONERN) (1976) *Inventario y evaluación de los recursos naturales de la SAIS "Tupac Amaru"*. Lima

Orlove, Benjamin S. and Godoy, Ricardo (1986) Sectoral fallowing systems in the central Andes. *Journal of Ethnobiology* 6 (1): 169–204

Owen, Bruce (1986) The role of common metal objects in the Inka state. M.A. Thesis, Department of Anthropology, University of California, Los Angeles

(n.d.) Analysis of prehistoric metals from the Upper Mantaro Valley region of Peru. Report as of 1986, ms. on file at the Department of Anthropology, UCLA

Pachacuti Yamqui Salcamaygua, Joan de Santacruz (1950) [± 1613] Relación de antiguedades deste Reyno del Piru. In *Tres relaciones de antiguedades peruanos*, pp. 207–81. Reproduction of edition of Marcos Jiminez de la Espada. Editorial Guarani, Asunción

Palomino Flores, Salvador (1971) Duality in the socio-cultural organization of severl Andean populations. *Folk* 13: 65–88. Copenhagen

Papadakis, J. (1961) *Climatic Tables for the World*. Buenos Aires

Parsons, J. J. and Bowen, W. A. (1966) Ancient ridged fields of the San Jorge River flood plain, Colombia. *Geographical Review* 56: 317–43

Parsons, J. J. and Denevan, W. M. (1967) Pre-columbian ridged fields. *Scientific American* 217: 93–100

Parsons, Jeffrey R. (1976) Prehistoric settlement patterns in the Upper Mantaro, Peru: preliminary report of the 1975 field season. Ms.

(1978) El complejo hidraulico de Tunanmarca: canales, acueductos y reservorios. In *El hombre y la cultura andina: actas y trabajos del III Congreso* II, edited by R. Matos M., pp. 556–66. Universidad Nacional Mayor de San Marcos, Lima

Parsons, J. R. and Hastings, C. M. (1977) Prehispanic settlement patterns in the Upper Mantaro, Peru: a progress report for the 1976 field season. Ms.

Parsons, J. R. and Matos M., R. (1978) Asentamientos pre-hispanicos en el Mantaro Peru: informe preliminar. In *El hombre y la cultura andina: actas y trabajos del III Congreso* II, edited by R. Matos M., pp. 539–55. Universidad Nacional Mayor de San Marcos, Lima

Patterson, Thomas C. (1986) Ideology, class formation, and resistance in the Inca state. *Critique of Anthropology* 6 (1): 75–85

Patterson, Thomas C. and Gailey, Christine W. (1987) *Power Relations and State Formation*. American Anthropological Association, Washington DC

Paynter, Robert (1989) The archaeology of equality and inequality. *Annual Review of Anthropology* 18: 369–99

Pearsall, Deborah M. (1978) Phytolith analysis of archaeological soils: evidence for maize cultivation in formative Ecuador. *Science* 199 (4325): 177–78

(1980) Pachamachay ethnobotanical report: plant utilization at a hunting base camp. In *Prehistoric Hunters of the High Andes*, edited by J. Rick, pp. 191–231. Academic Press, New York

(1983) Evaluating the stability of subsistence strategies by use of paleoethnobotanical data. *Journal of Ethnobiology* 3 (2): 121–37

(1988) Interpreting the meaning of macroremain abundance: the impact of source and context. In *Current Paleoethnobotany*, edited by C. Hastorf and V. Popper, pp. 97–118. University of Chicago Press, Chicago

(1989) *Paleoethnobotany*. Academic Press, San Diego

Pickersgill, Barbara (1969) The archaeological record of chili peppers (*Capsicum* spp.) and the sequence of plant domestication in Peru. *American Antiquity* 34 (1): 54–61

Pimentel, D. and Pimentel, M. (1979) *Food, Energy and Society*. Edward Arnold, London

Platt, Tristan (1986) Mirrors and maize. In *Anthropological History of Andean Politics*, edited by J. V. Murra, N. Wachtel, and J. Revel, pp. 228–59. Cambridge University Press, Cambridge

(1987) Entre ch'axwa y mixsa. Para una historia del pensamiento politico Aymara. In *Tres reflexiones sobre el pensameinto Andino*, pp. 61–132. Hisbol, La Paz, Bolivia

Polgar, Steven (1972) Population history and population policies from an anthropological perspective. *Current Anthropology* 13: 203–11

Ponce Sangines, Carlos (1977) *Tiwanaku, tiempo, y cultura ensayo de sintesis arqueologia*. 2nd edn. Editorial los amigos del libro, La Paz, Bolivia

Poole, Deborah (1984) Ritual-economic calendars in Paruro: the structure of representation in Andean ethnography. Ph.D. Dissertation, Department of Anthropology, University of Illinois, Urbana. University Microfilms International, Ann Arbor

Popper, V. (1988) Selecting quantitative measurements in paleoethnobotany. In *Current Paleoethnobotany: Analytical Methods and Cultural Interpretations of Archaeological Plant Remains*, edited by C. Hastorf and V. Popper, pp. 53–71. University of Chicago Press, Chicago

Popper, V. and Hastorf, C. (1988) Introduction. In *Current Paleoethnobotany: Analytical Methods and Cultural Interpretations of Archaeological Plant Remains*, edited by C. Hastorf and V. Popper, pp. 1–16. University of Chicago Press, Chicago

Posnansky, Arthur (1945) *Tiahuanacu: la cuna del hombre americano.* (*Tihuanaku: the Cradle of American Man*) I and II. J. J. Augustin, New York

(1958) *Tihuanacu: la cuna del hombre americano.* (*Tihuanaku: the Cradle of American Man*) III and IV. Ministerio de Educación, La Paz, Bolivia

Pozorski, Shelia (1987) Theocracy vs. militarism: the significance of the Casma Valley in understanding early state formation. In *The Origins and Development of the Andean State*, edited by J. Haas, S. Pozorski and T. Pozorski, pp. 15–30. Cambridge University Press, Cambridge

Pozorski, Shelia, and Pozorski, Thomas (1987) Chronology. In *The Origins and Development of the Andean State*, edited by J. Haas, S. Pozorski and T. Pozorski, pp. 5–8. Cambridge University Press, Cambridge

Pozorski, Thomas (1975) El complejo de Caballo Muerto: los Frisos de barro de la Huaca de los Reyes. *Revista del Museo Nacional* 41: 211–51

(1982) Early social stratification and subsistence systems: the Caballo Muerto complex. In *Chan Chan: Andean Desert City*, edited by M. E. Moseley and K. Day, pp. 225–53. University of New Mexico Press, Albuquerque

Pozorski, Thomas and Pozorski, Shelia (1987) Chavin, the Early Horizon and the Initial Period. In *The Origins and Development of the Andean State*, edited by J. Haas, S. Pozorski and T. Pozorski, pp. 36–46. Cambridge University Press, Cambridge

Pryor, F. L. (1986) The adoption of agriculture: some theoretical and empirical evidence. *American Anthropologist* 88: 879–97

Pulgar Vidal, Javier (1967) *Geografia del Perú: las ocho regiones naturales del Peru*. Editorial Universo, Lima

Quinn, Naomi, R. (1971) Mfantse fishing crew composition: a decision making analysis. Ph.D. Dissertation, Department of Anthropology, Stanford University. University Microfilms International, Ann Arbor

Radcliffe-Browne, A. R. (1941) The study of kinship systems. *Journal of the Royal Anthropological Institute* 71

Rappaport, R. A. (1968) *Pigs for the Ancestors: Ritual in the Ecology of a New Guinea People*. Yale University Press, New Haven

Rathje, William (1972) Priase the lord and pass the metates: a hypothesis of the development of lowland rainforest civilizations in Mesoamerica. In *Contemporary Archaeology*, edited by M. Leone. Southern Illinois University Press, Carbondale

Ravines, Rogger and Isbell, William H. (1975) Garagay: sitio ceremonial temprano en el Valle de Lima. *Revista del Museo Nacional* 41: 253–81

Read, Dwight W. (1974) Some comments on typologies in archaeology and an outline of a methodology. *American Antiquity* 39 (2): 216–42

Reinhard, Johann (1990) Tiahuanaco, sacred center of the Andes. In *The Cultural Guide of Bolivia*, edited by P. McFarren. Fundación Quipus, La Paz

Renfrew, C. (1986) Introduction. In *Peer Polity, Interaction and Socio-political Change*, edited by C. Renfrew and J. Cherry, pp. 1–18. Cambridge University Press, Cambridge

Renfrew, Colin and Cherry, John (eds.) (1986) *Peer Polity, Interaction and Socio-political Change*. Cambridge University Press, Cambridge

Renfrew, Colin and Shennan, Stephen (eds.) (1982) *Ranking, Resource and Exchange: Aspects of the Archaeology of Early European Society*. Cambridge University Press, Cambridge

Renfrew, Jane M. (1973) *Paleoethnobotany*. Columbia University Press, New York

Rhoades, Robert E. and Thompson, Stephen I. (1975) Adaptive strategies in alpine environments: beyond cultural particularism. *American Ethnologist* 2: 535–51

Rick, John W. (1980) *Prehistoric Hunters of the High Andes*. Academic Press, New York

Riley, T. J. and Freimuth, G. (1977) Prehistoric agriculture in the Upper Midwest. *Field Museum of Natural History Bulletin* 48 (6): 4–8. Chicago

Roper, Donna (1979) The method and theory of site catchment analysis: a review. In *Advances in Archaeological Method and Theory*, II, edited by M. Schiffer, pp. 119–40. Academic Press, New York

Rosas, Hermilio and Shady, Ruth (1970) Pacopampa: un complejo temprano del Periódo Formativo Peruano. *Arqueologia y Sociedad* 3: 1–16

Rostworowski de Diez Canseco, Maria (1960) Pesos y medidas en el Perú pre-hispanicao. *Actas y trabajos del II Congreso Nacional de Historia del Perú*, Lima

(1972) Las etnias de valle de Chillón. *Revista del Museo Nacional* 38

(1977a) *Etnia y sociedad: costa peruana prehispánica*. Historia Andina 4. Instituto de Estudios Peruanos, Lima

(1977b) La estratificación social y el Hatún curaca en el mundo Andina. *Histório* 1 (2): 249–85, Lima

(1987) Voz mochica en el quechua cusqueno. *Boletin de Lima* 50 (9): 5–6

Roumasset, James A., Boussard, Jean-Marie and Singh, Indinjit (1979) *Risk, Uncertainty, and Development*. Agricultural Development Council, New York

Rowe, John (1944) *An Introduction to the Archaeology of Cuzco*. Papers of the Peabody Museum of American Archaeology and Ethnology 27 (2). Cambridge, Mass.

(1946) Inca culture at the time of Spanish conquest. In *The Handbook of South American Indians* 24, edited by J. H. Steward, pp. 183–330. Smithsonian Institution, Washington, DC

(1960) Cultural unity and diversification in Peruvian archaeology. In *Men and Cultures, Selected Papers*, edited by A. F. C. Wallace, pp. 627–31. Proceedings of the 5th International Congress of Anthropological and Ethnological Sciences, University of Pennsylvania Press, Philadelphia

(1962a) Stages and periods in archaeological interpretation. *Southwestern Journal of Anthropology* 18: 40–54

(1962b) *Chavin Art: an Inquiry into its Form and Meaning*. Museum of Primitive Art, New York

Rowlands, Michael J. (1980) Kinship, alliance, and exchange in the European Bronze Age. In *Settlement and Society in the British Later Bronze Age*, edited by J. Barrett and R. Bradley. British Archaeological Reports, British Series 83: 15–55

Russell, Glenn S. (1985) Lithic evidence for Wanka household response to the imposed Inka state economy. In symposium, Transformation of the domestic economy within Inka conquest of the Mantaro Valley, 50th Annual Meeting of the Society for American Archaeology. Denver, Colo.

(1988a) Long term subsistence change among the Sausa of Peru: the lithic evidence. In symposium, Long term change and continuity in the Sausa culture: results from recent research on central Andes adaptation and social mediation, 53rd Annual Meeting of the Society for American Archaeology. Phoenix, Arizona

(1988b) The impact of Inka policy on the domestic economy of the Wanka, Peru: stone tool production and use. Ph.D. Dissertation, Department of Anthropology, UCLA. University Microfilms International, Ann Arbor

Sahlins, Marshall D. (1958) *Social Stratification in Polynesia*. University of Washington, Seattle

(1972) *Stone Age Economics*. Aldine, Chicago

(1985) *Islands of History*. Chicago University Press, Chicago

Salera, B., Lewis, A. B., Wells, L. T. and Preston, H. J. (1954) *The Agricultural and Economic Development of the Mantaro Region of Peru*. 2 vols. International Development Services, New York

Salomon, Frank (1986) *Native Lords of Quito in the Age of the Incas*. Cambridge University Press, Cambridge

Sandefur, Elsie (1988a) Domestic animal use in the central Andes: Early Intermediate Period to the Late Horizon. In symposium, Long-term change and continuity in the Sausa culture: results from recent research on central Andean adaptation and social mediation, 53rd Annual Meeting of the Society for American Archaeology. Phoenix, Arizona

(1988b) Andean zooarchaeology: animal use and the Inka conquest of the Upper Mantaro Valley. Ph.D. Dissertation, Archaeology Program, UCLA. University Microfilms International, Ann Arbor

Sanders, William T. (1956) The central Mexican symbiotic region: a study in prehistoric settlement patterns. In *Prehistoric Settlement Patterns in the New World*, edited by G. R. Willey, pp. 115–27. Wenner-Gren Foundation, New York

Sanders, W. T. and Price, Barbara J. (1968) *Mesoamerica, the Evolution of a Civilization*. Random House, New York

Sanders, William T. and Webster, D. (1978) Unilinealism, multilinealism, and the evolution of complex society. In *Social Archaeology: Beyond Subsistence and Dating*, edited by C. Redman et al., pp. 249-302. Academic Press, New York

Sarmiento de Gamboa, Pedro (1947) [1572] *Historia de los Incas*. 3rd edn. Biblioteca Emecé, Buenos Aires

Scarry, Clara Margaret (1986) Change in plant procurement and production during the emergence of the Moundville chiefdom. Ph.D. Dissertation, Department of Anthropology, University of Michigan. University Microfilms International, Ann Arbor

Schaedel, Richard P. (1988) Andean world view: hierarchy or reciprocity, regulation, and control? *Current Anthropology* 29 (5): 768–75

Schreiber, Katarina (1978) Planned architecture of Middle Horizon Peru: implications for social and political organization. Ph.D. Dissertation, Department of Anthropology, SUNY Binghamton. University Microfilms International, Ann Arbor

(1987) Conquest and consolidation. A comparison of the Wari and Inka occupations of a highland Peruvian valley. *American Antiquity* 52 (2): 266–84

Schwerdtfeger, Werner (ed.) (1976) *Climates of Central and South America*. World Survey of Climates, vol. 12. Elsevier Scientific Publishing Co., Amsterdam

SCIPA (1956) *Mapa de suelos del Valle del Mantaro y mapa de capacidad de uso del Valle del Mantaro*. Washington DC

Scott, Gregory (1985) *Markets, Myths, and Middlemen: a Study of Potato Marketing in Central Peru*. International Potato Center, Lima, Peru

Seltzer, Geoffrey O. (1987) Glacial history and climatic change in the central Peruvian Andes. M.A. Thesis, University of Minnesota, Minneapolis

(1991) Glacial history and climate change in the Peruvian-Bolivian Andes. Ph.D. Dissertation, Department of Geology, University of Minnesota, Minneapolis

Seltzer, Geoffrey O. and Hastorf, Christine A. (1990) Climatic change and its effect on prehistoric agriculture in the Peruvian Andes. *Journal of Field Archaeology* 17: 397–417

Service, Elman R. (1962) *Primitive Social Organization: an Evolutionary Perspective*. Random House, New York

(1975) *Origins of the State and Civilization: the Process of Cultural Evolution*. W. W. Norton, New York

Shady, Ruth and Ruiz, Arturo (1979) Evidence for interregional relationships during the Middle Horizon on the north central coast of Peru. *American Antiquity* 44: 676–84

Sherbondy, Jenette (1982) The canal systems of Hanan Cuzco. Ph.D. Dissertation, Department of Anthropology, University of Illinois, Urbana. University Microfilms International, Ann Arbor

(1986) *Mallki: ancestros y cultivos de arboles en los Andes*. Document de trabajo No. 5, Proyecto FAO-Holanda/Infor GCP/PER/207/NET, Lima

Sheridan, Alison and Bailey, Geoff (eds.) (1981) *Economic Archaeology: Towards an Integration of Ecological and Social Approaches*. British Archaeological Reports, International Series 96, Oxford

Sherratt, Andrew (1981) Plow and pastoralism: aspects of the second products revolution. In *Studies in Honor of David Clarke*, edited by I. Hodder, G. Isaac and N. Hammond, pp. 261–305. Cambridge University Press, Cambridge

Shimada, Izumi (1978) Economy of a prehistoric urban context commodity and labor flow at Moche V Pampa Grande, Peru. *American Antiquity* 43 (4): 569–92

Shows, E. W. and Burton, R. H. (1972) *Microeconomics*. Heath, Lexington, Mass.

Sikkink, Lynn L. (1988) Traditional crop processing in central Andean households: an ethnoarchaeological perspective. In *Multidisciplinary Studies in Andean Anthropology*, edited by V. Vitzhum. Michigan Discussions in Anthropology 18. University of Michigan, Ann Arbor

Silverblatt, Irene M. (1981) Moon, sun, and devil: Inca and colonial transformations of Andean gender relations. Ph.D. Dissertation, Department of Anthropology, University of Michigan. University Microfilms International, Ann Arbor

(1987) *Moon, Sun, and Witches*. Princeton University Press, Princeton, NJ

Silverman, Helaine (1988) Cahuachi: non-urban cultural complexity on the south coast of Peru. *Journal of Field Archaeology* 15 (4): 403–30

Simmonds, N. W. (1965) The grain chenopods of the tropical American highlands. *Economic Botany* 19: 223–35

Skar, Harold O. (1982) *The Warm Valley People: Duality and Land Reform among the Quechua Indians of Highland Peru*. Universitetsforlaget, Oslo and New York

Skar, Sarah L. (1979) The use of the public/private framework in the analysis of egalitarian societies: the case of a quechua community in highland Peru. *Women's Studies International Quarterly* 2: 449–60

(1981) Andean women and the concept of space/time. In *Woman and Space*, edited by S. Ardener, pp. 35–49. Croom Helm, London

Smith, C. Earle, Jr. (1980) Ancient Peruvian highland maize. In *Guitarerro Cave: Early Man in the Andes*, edited by T. Lynch, pp. 121–44. Academic Press, New York

Smith, C. T., Denevan, W. M. and Hamilton, P. (1968) Ancient ridged fields in the region of Lake Titicaca. *Geographical Journal* 131: 353–67

Smith, Gavin (1989) *Livelihood and Resistance: Peasants and the Politics of Land in Peru.* University of California Press, Berkeley

Soldi, Ana Maria (1981) *La agricultura traditional en hoyas.* Pontificia Universidad Catolica del Peru, Lima

Soukup, S. B. D. Jaroslav (1970) *Vocabulario de los nombres vulgares de la flora Peruana.* Colegio Salesiano, Lima

Spalding, Karen (1984) *Huarochiri, an Andean Society under Inca and Spanish Rule.* Stanford University Press, Stanford, Cal.

Spencer, Paul (1965) *The Samburu.* Routledge and Kegan Paul, London

Spriggs, Matthew (1981) Vegetable kingdoms: taro irrigation and Pacific prehistory. Ph.D. Thesis, University of Australia, Canberra

Spooner, Brian (ed.) (1972) *Population Growth: Anthropological Implications.* MIT Press, Cambridge, Mass.

Stanish, Charles (1989) Household archaeology: testing models of zonal complementarity in the south central Andes. *American Anthropologist* 91 (1): 7–24

Steponaitis, Vincas P. (1981) Settlement hierarchies and political complexity in non-market societies: the formative period of the Valley of Mexico. *American Anthropologist* 83 (2): 320–63

Steward, Julian H. (1955) *Theory of Culture Change.* University of Illinois Press, Urbana, Ill.

Steward, J. and Faron, L. C. (1959) *The Native Peoples of South America.* McGraw Hill, New York

Strathern, Andrew (1971) *The Rope of Moka: Big-men and Ceremonial Exchange in Mount Hagen, New Guinea.* Cambridge University Press, Cambridge

(1982) *Inequality in New Guinea Highland Societies.* Cambridge University Press, Cambridge

Struever, Stuart (1968) Flotation techniques for the recovery of small-scale archaeological remains. *American Antiquity* 33: 353–62

Stuiver, M. and Reimer, P. J. (1986) A complete program for radiocarbon age calibration. *Radiocarbon* 28: 1022–30

Sumner, William M. (1979) Estimating population by analogy: an example. In *Ethnoarchaeology: Implications of Ethnography for Archaeology,* edited by C. Kramer, pp. 167–74. Columbia University Press, New York

Tainter, Joseph (1977) Modeling change in prehistoric social systems. In *For Theory Building in Archaeology,* edited by L. Binford, pp. 327–52. Academic Press, New York

Tapia Vargas, Gualberto (1976) *La quinoa: un cultivo de los Andes altos.* Academia Nacional de Ciencias de Bolivia, La Paz

Tello, Julio C. (1942) Origen y desarrollo de las civilizaciones prehistóricas Andinas. *Actas y trabajos cientificos, 23 Congreso Internacional de Americanistas,* pp. 589–720. Lima

(1943) Discovery of the Chavin culture in Peru. *American Antiquity* 9: 135–60

(1960) *Chavin, cultura matrix de la civilización andina.* Universidad Nacional Mayor de San Marcos, Lima

Tello, J. C. and Mejia, Xesspe T. (1979) *Paracas* II. Universidad Nacional Mayor de San Marcos, Lima and Institute of Andean Research, New York

Thomas, Julian (1988) Neolithic expansions revisited: the mesolithic-neolithic transition in Britain and southern Scandinavia. *Proceedings of the Prehistoric Society* 54: 59–66

Thomas, R. Brooke (1973) *Human Adaptation to a High Andean Energy Flow System.* Occasional Papers in Anthropology 7. Pennsylvania State University, University Park, Penn.

Thompson, Donald (1971) Late Prehispanic occupation in the eastern Peruvian Andes. *Revista del Museo Nacional* 37: 116–23. Lima

Tiffany, Joseph A. (1974) An application of eigenvector techniques to the seed analysis of the Bigley Rockshelter (47-GT-156). *Wisconsin Archaeologist* 55 (1): 1–41

Toledo, Francisco de (1940) [1570] Información hecha por orden de Don Francisco de Toledo en su visita de las provincias del Peru, en la que declaran indios ancianos sobre el derecho de los caciques y sobre el gobierno que tenian aquellos pueblos antes que los Incas los conquistasen. In *Don Francisco de Toldeo, supremo organizador del Perú, su vida, su obra 1515–1582* II, edited by R. Levillier, pp. 14–37. Espasa-Calpe, Buenos Aires

Topic, John R. (1982) Lower-class social and economic organization at Chan Chan. In *Chan Chan: Andean Desert City*, edited by M. Moseley and K. Day, pp. 145–75. University of New Mexico, Albuquerque

Topic, John R. and Topic, Teresa L. (1983) Coast–highland relations in northern Peru: some observations on routes, networks, and scales of interaction. In *Civilization in the Ancient Americas*, edited by R. M. Leventhal and A. L. Kolata, pp. 237–59. University of New Mexico Press, Albuquerque

Torrero F. de Cordova, Alfredo (1974) Linguistica e historia de la sociedad Andina. *Anales Cientificos* 8 (3–4): 231–63

Tosi, Joseph A., Jr. (1960) *Zonas de vida natural en el Perú: memoria explicativa sobre el mapa ecologico del Perú*. Instituto Interamericano de Ciencias Agricolas de la OEA, Zona Andina, Boletin Technico 5

Towle, Margaret A. (1961) *The Ethnobotany of pre-Columbian Peru*. Viking Fund Publications in Anthropology 30. Aldine, Chicago

Trigger, Bruce (1963) Order and freedom in Huron Society. *Anthropologica* 5: 151–69

(1990) Maintaining economic equality in opposition to complexity: an Iroquoian case study. In *The Evolution of Political Systems*, edited by S. Upham, pp. 119-45. Cambridge University Press, Cambridge

Troll, Carl (1935) Los fundamentos geográficos de las civilaciones Andinas y del imperio Inciaco. *Revista de la Universidad de Arequipa* 9: 129–82

(1968) The cordilleras of the tropical Americas. In *Geo-ecology of the Mountainous Regions of the Tropical Americas*, edited by C. Troll. Proceedings of the UNESCO Mexico Symposium, 1966. Ferd. Dummlers, Bonn

Tschopik, Harry (1946) Some notes on rock shelter sites near Huancayo. *American Antiquity* 12: 73–80

Tufte, E. R. (1983) *The Visual Display of Quantitative Information*. Graphics Press, Cheshire, Conn.

Tukey, John W. (1977) *Exploratory Data Analysis*. Addison-Wesley Publishing, Reading, Mass.

Turner, B. L. II and Doolittle, W. E. (1978) The concept and measure of agricultural intensity. *Professional Geographer* 30 (3): 297–301

Turner, B. L. II and Harrison, P. D. (1983) *Pulltrouser Swamp: Ancient Maya Habitat, Agriculture, and Settlement in Northern Belize*. University of Texas Press, Austin

Ugent, D. (1968) The potato in Mexico: geography and primitive culture. *Economic Botany* 22: 108–23

Ugent, D., Pozorski, S. and Pozorski, T. (1982) Archaeological potato and tuber remains from the Casma Valley of Peru. *Economic Botany* 36 (2): 182–92

United States Department of Commerce (1966) *World Weather Records, 1951–1960* 3. United States Government Printing Office, Washington DC

Upham, Steadman (1982) *Politics and Power, an Economic and Political History*. Academic Press, New York

(ed.) (1990) *The Evolution of Political Systems*. Cambridge University Press, Cambridge

van der Merwe, N. J. and Vogel, J. C. (1979) C-13 content of human collagen as a measure of prehistoric diet in Woodland North America. *Nature* 276: 815–16 van Zeist, Willem, Behre, Karl-Ernst, and Wasylikowa, Krystyna (eds.) (1991) *Progress in Old World Paleoethnobotany*. Balkema Press, Rotterdam

Vayda, A. P. and McCay, B. J. (1975) New directions in ecology and ecological anthropology. In *Annual Review of Anthropology*, edited by B. J. Siegal, A. R. Beals and S. A. Tylor. Annual Reviews Inc., Palo Alto

Vazqúez de Espinoza, P. Antonio (1969) [1617] *Compendio y descripción de la Indias occidentales biblioteca de autores Españoles* 231. Ediciones Atlas, Madrid

Vega, Andres de (1965) [1582] La descripción que se hizo en la provincia de Xauxa por la instrucción de su majestad que a la dicha provincia se invio de molde. In *Relaciones geograficas de Indias: Peru* 1, edited by Don Marcos Jimenez de la Espada, pp. 166–75. Biblioteca de autores Espanoles, Madrid

Vellman, Paul F. and Hoaglin, David C. (1981) *Applications, Basics, and Computing of Exploratory Data Analysis*. Duxbury Press, Boston

Vita-Finzi, C. and Higgs, E. S. (1970) Prehistoric economy in the Mt. Carmel area of Palestine: site catchment analysis. *Proceedings of the Prehistoric Society* 36: 1–37. London

von Neumann and Morgenstern, Oskar (1944) *Theory of Games and Economic Behavior*. Princeton University Press, Princeton

Wachtel, Nathan (1973) *Sociedad e ideologia: ensayos de historia y antropologia andinas*. Institut de Estudios Peruanos, Lima

(1977) *The Vision of the Vanquished*. Harvester Press, Hassocks, Sussex

Waddell, Eric (1973) Raipu Enga adaptive strategies. In *The Pacific in Transition*, edited by H. Brookfield. Edward Arnold, London

Wagner, Gail E. (1981) Uses of plants by the Fort Ancient Indians. Paper presented at the 4th Ethnobiology Conference. Columbia, Mo.

(1982) Testing flotation recovery rates. *American Antiquity* 47 (1): 127–32

(1988) Compariability among recovery techniques. In *Current Paleoethnobotany: Analytical Methods and Cultural Interpretations of Archaeological Plant remains*, edited by C. Hastorf and V. Popper, pp. 17–35. University of Chicago Press, Chicago

Wallerstein, Immanuel (1974) *The Modern World System* 1. Academic Press, New York

Watson, Patty Jo (1976) In pursuit of prehistoric subsistence: a comparative account of some contemporary flotation techniques. *Midcontinental Journal of Archaeology* 1: 77–100

Weber, Max (1968) [1947] *Economy and Society, an Outline of Interpretive Sociology*, edited by G. Roth and C. Wittich. Bedminster Press, New York

Weberbauer, Augusto (1945) *El mundo vegetal de los Andes peruanos*. Estudio Fitogeografico. Estación Experimental Agricola, La Molina, Lima

Webster, S. (1973) Native pastoralism in the Andes. *Ethnology* 12: 115–33

Werge, Robert (1977) *Sistemas de almacenamiento de la papa en la región del Valley del Mantaro (Perú)*. International Potato Center, Lima

(1979) *The Agricultural Strategy of Rural Households in Three Ecological Zones of the Central Andes*. International Potato Center, Lima

Whalen, Michael (1976) Zoning within an early formative community in the Valley of Oaxaca. In *The Early Mesoamerican Village*, edited by K. Flannery, pp. 75–79. Academic Press, New York

White, Leslie A. (1959) *The Evolution of culture*. McGraw-Hill, New York

Wiessner, Polly (1977) Hxaro: a regional system of reciprocity for reducing risk among the !Kung San. Ph.D. Dissertation, Department of Anthropology, University of Michigan. University Microfilms International, Ann Arbor

(1982) Risk, reciprocity and social influences on !Kung San economics. In *Politics and History in Band Societies*, edited by E. Leacock and R. Lee, pp. 61–84. Cambridge University Press, Cambridge

Wilk, Richard R. (1989) *The Household Economy*. Westview Press, Boulder, Colo.

Willcox, G. H. (1974) A history of deforestation as indicated by charcoal analysis of four sites in eastern Anatolia. *Anatolian Studies* 24: 117–33

Wilson, David (1988) *Warfare in the Santa Valley*. Smithsonian Press, Washington DC

Wilson, H. D., Heizer, B. and Charles, J. F. (1979) The origin and evolutionary relationships of "huazontle" (*Chenopodium nuttalliae* Safford), domesticated chenopod of Mexico. *American Journal of Botany* 66 (2): 198–206

Winter, Marcus, and Pires-Ferreira, Jane W. (1976) Distribution of obsidian among households in two Oaxacan villages. In *The Early Mesoamerican Village*, edited by K. Flannery, pp. 306–11. Academic Press, New York

Winterhalder, Bruce (1986) Diet choice, risk, and food sharing in a stochastic environment. *Journal of Anthropological Archaeology* 5: 369–92

Winterhalder, Bruce and Smith, Eric Alden (1981) *Hunter-gatherer Foraging Strategies*. University of Chicago Press, Chicago

Winterhalder, Bruce P. and Thomas, R. Brooke (1978) *Geo-ecology of Southern Highland Peru: a Human Adaptation Perspective*. Institute of Arctic and Alpine Research Occasional Paper 27, University of Colorado

Wittfogel, Karl A. (1957) *Oriental Despotism*. Yale University Press, New Haven, Conn.

Woodburn, Marcus A. (1987) Architecture at Pancán. Archaeobotany Laboratory Report 4, on file at the Department of Anthropology, University of Minnesota, Minneapolis

Wright, Henry T. (1969) *The Administration of Rural Production in an Early Mesopotamian Town*. Anthropological Papers 38, Museum of Anthropology, University of Michigan, Ann Arbor

(1978) Towards an explanation of the origins of the state. In *Origins of the State*, edited by E. R. Service and R. Cohen, pp. 49–68. Institute for the Study of Human Issues, Philadelphia

Wright, Henry T. and Johnson, Gregory A. (1975) Population, exchange, and early state formation in southwestern Iran. *American Anthropologist* 77: 267–89

Wright, H. T. and Zeder, M. (1977) The simulation of a linear exchange system under equilibrium conditions. In *Exchange Systems in Prehistory*, edited by T. K. Earle and J. Ericson, pp. 233–53. Academic Press, New York

Wright, Herbert E., Jr. (1980) Environmental history of the Junin plain and the nearby mountains. In *Prehistoric Hunters of the High Andes*, edited by J. Rick, pp. 253–56. Academic Press, New York

(1984) Local glacial and Late Holocene moraines in the Cerros Cuchpanga, Central Peru. *Quaternary Research* 21: 275–85

(1988) Recent glacier recession and environmental change in the Peruvian Andes. Final Report to the National Geographical Society, Washington DC

Xesspe, Toribio Mejoa (1978) Kausay. Alimentación de los Indios. In *Tecnologia Andina*, edited by R. Ravines, pp. 205–26. Instituto de Estudios Peruanos, Lima

Yacovleff, E. and Herrera, F. L. (1934) El mundo vegetal de los antiguos peruanos. *Revista del Museo Nacional* 3: 241–322. Lima

(1935) El mundo vegetal de los antiguos peruanos. *Revista del Museo Nacional* 4: 29–102. Lima

Yamamoto, Norio (1981) Investigación preliminar sobre las actividades agro-pastoriles en el districto de Marcapata, Departmento del Cuzco, Perú. In *Estudios entográficos del Perú meridional*, edited by S. Masuda, pp. 85–137. University of Tokyo, Tokyo

(1985) The ecological complementary of agro-pastoralism: some comments. In *Andean Ecology and Civilization*, edited by S. Masuda, I. Shimada and C. Morris, pp. 85–100. University of Tokyo Press, Tokyo

(1986) *La técnica tradicional del procesamiento de la Papa en los Andes y la posibilidad de su aplicación a las otras regiones*. Social Science Report, International Potato Center, Lima

Yen, D. E. (1974) The sweet potato in Oceania. *Bishop Museum Bulletin* 236. Honolulu, Hawaii

Zeitlin, Robert N. (1978) Long distance exchange and the growth of a regional center on the Southern Isthmus of Tehauntepec Mexico. In *Prehistoric Coastal Adaptations: the Economy and Ecology of Maritime Middle America*, edited by B. Stark and B. Voorhies, pp. 183–210. Academic Press, New York

Zohary, D. (1969) The progenitors of wheat and barley in relation to domestication and agricultural dispersal in the Old World. In *The Domestication and Exploitation of Plants and Animals*, edited by G. W. Dimbleby and P. Ucko. Duckworth, London

Zuidema, R. Tom (1964) *The Ceque System of Cuzco, the Social Organization of the Capital of the Inca*. E. J. Brill, Leiden

(1967) Decendencia paralela en una familia indigena noble del Cuzco. *Fenix* 17: 29–62. Lima

(1973) Kinship and ancestor cult in three Peruvian communities, Hernández Principes account in 1627. *Boletin del IFEA* 2 (10): 16–33

(1978) Shaft tombs and the Inca empire. *Journal of the Steward Anthropological Society* 9 (1–2): 133–79. Urbana, Il

(1986) Inka dynasty and irrigation: another look at Andean concepts of history. In *Anthropological History of Andean Polities*, edited by J. V. Murra, N. Wachtel, and J. Revel, pp. 177–200. Cambridge University Press, Cambridge

INDEX